HEARING AND SPEAKING THE WORD

Scholars Press
Homage Series

HEARING AND SPEAKING THE WORD

Selections from the Works of James Muilenburg

edited by

Thomas F. Best

Scholars Press
Chico, California

HEARING AND SPEAKING THE WORD

Selections from the Works of James Muilenburg

edited by

Thomas F. Best

©1984
Scholars Press

Library of Congress Cataloging in Publication Data

Muilenburg, James.
  Hearing and speaking the Word.

  (Scholars Press homage series ; no. 7)
  Bibliography: p.
  1. Bible. O.T.—Criticism, interpretation, etc.—
Addresses, essays, lectures. 2. Bible. O.T.—Antiquities —
Addresses, essays, lectures. 3. Muilenburg, James—
Bibliography. I. Best, Thomas F. II. Title. III. Series.
BS1192.M84 1984   220.6   83–20147
ISBN 0–89130–665–X

Printed in the United States of America
on acid-free paper

Dr. James Muilenburg

Photo credit: John H. Popper, N.Y.

To the Memory
of
James and Mary Muilenburg

CONTENTS

Part Four: Scholarship and Interpretation

Part Five: Archaeology

Part Six: Homiletics and Meditations

Part Seven: Early Writings and Reportage

Part Eight: Bibliography

Contributors

ALLEN LOVEJOY

PAUL & ELIZABETH ACHTEMEIER
JAMES ACKERMAN
RICHARD ARTHUR
WILLIAM BEARDSLEE
WALTER BRUEGGEMANN
FREDERICK BUECHNER
DUANE CHRISTENSEN
TONI CRAVEN
DAVID FREEDMAN
RONALD GRAHAM
JONAS GREENFIELD
JOHN HAMLIN
DOROTHEA HARVEY
ROBERT JACKSON
MARK JUERGENSMEYER
DOUGLAS KNIGHT
KENNETH KUNTZ

GEORGE LANDES
CHARLES McCOY
MARJORIE McCOY
IAN McCRAE
ROSALIE MALONE
EUGUNE MARCH
JOHN MARSH
PAUL MINEAR
RONALD OSBORN
ALBERT OUTLER
ELIZABETH OVER
J. A. SANDERS
PHYLLIS TRIBLE
JAMES WARD
AMOS WILDER
BARBARA ZIKMUND

PACIFIC SCHOOL OF RELIGION
UNION THEOLOGICAL SEMINARY

Acknowledgments

"James Muilenburg as Man and Scholar" by Frederick Buechner, from *Now and Then* by Frederick Buechner, pp. 15–19. Copyright 1983 by Frederick Buechner. Reprinted by permission of Harper & Row, Publishers, Inc.

"The New Frontier of Rhetorical Criticism: A Tribute to James Muilenburg" by Bernhard W. Anderson, from *Rhetorical Criticism: Essays in Honor of James Muilenburg*, pp. ix–xviii, edited by Jared J. Jackson and Martin Kessler (Pittsburgh, Penn.: Pickwick Press, 1974). By permission of Pickwick Press.

"Form Criticism and Beyond" by James Muilenburg, from *Journal of Biblical Literature* 88 (1969), 1–18. By permission of the Society of Biblical Literature.

"Literary Form in the Fourth Gospel" by James Muilenburg, from *Journal of Biblical Literature* 51 (1932), 40–53. By permission of the Society of Biblical Literature.

"The Literary Character of Isaiah 34" by James Muilenburg, from *Journal of Biblical Literature* 59 (1940), 339–65. By permission of the Society of Biblical Literature.

"Psalms 47" by James Muilenburg, from *Journal of Biblical Literature* 63 (1944), 235–56. By permission of the Society of Biblical Literature.

"The Form and Structure of the Covenantal Formulation" by James Muilenburg, from *Vetus Testamentum* 9 (1959), 347–65. By permission of E. J. Brill.

"The 'Office' of the Prophet in Ancient Israel" by James Muilenburg, from *The Bible in Modern Scholarship*, pp. 74–97, edited by J. Philip Hyatt (Nashville, Tenn.: Abingdon Press, 1965). By permission of the Society of Biblical Literature.

"A Liturgy on the Triumphs of Yahweh" by James Muilenburg, from *Studia Biblica et Semitica*, pp. 233–51, edited by W. C. van Unnik and A. S. van der Woude (Wageningen, Netherlands: H. Veenman en Zonen, 1966). By permission of Drukkerij Veenman.

"The Intercession of the Covenant Mediator (Exodus 33:1a, 12–17)" by James Muilenburg, from *Words and Meanings*, pp. 159–81, edited by Peter R. Ackroyd and Barnabas Lindars (Cambridge: Cambridge University Press, 1968). By permission of Cambridge University Press.

"The Linguist and Rhetorical Usages of the Particle ki in the Old Testament" by James Muilenburg, from *HUCA* 32 (1961), 135–60. By permission of Hebrew Union College–Jewish Institute of Religion.

"A Study in Hebrew Rhetoric" by James Muilenburg, from *Vetus Testamentum*, Supplement 1 (1953), 97–111. By permission of E. J. Brill.

"The Terminology of Adversity in Jeremiah" by James Muilenburg, from *Translating and Understanding the Old Testament*, pp. 42–63, edited by Harry Thomas Frank and William L. Reed. Copyright 1970 by Abingdon Press. Used by permission.

"Baruch the Scribe" by James Muilenburg, from *Proclamation and Presence*, pp. 215–38, edited by John I. Durham and J. R. Porter (Richmond, Virg.: John Knox Press, 1970). By permission of John Knox Press and SCM Press Ltd.

"Father and Son" by James Muilenburg, from *Theology and Life* 3 (1960), 177–87. By permission of Lancaster Theological Seminary.

"The Beginning of the Gospels and the Qumran Manual of Discipline" by James Muilenburg, from *Union Seminary Quarterly Review* 10 (1955), 23–29. By permission of Lawrence E. Muilenburg for the James Muilenburg Estate.

"Introduction" by James Muilenburg, from *The Psalms: A Form Critical Introduction* by Hermann Gunkel, pp. iii–ix. Copyright 1967 by Fortress Press. Used by permission.

"Prolegomenon" by James Muilenburg, from *Lectures on the Religion of the Semites: The Fundamental Institutions* by W. Robertson Smith, pp. 1–27 (New York: Ktav, 1969 [orig. publ. 1927]). Used by permission of Ktav Publishing House.

"Buber as an Interpreter of the Bible" by James Muilenburg, and "Replies to My Critics" by Martin Buber, from *The Philosophy of Martin Buber*, pp. 381–402 and pp. 726–28, respectively, edited by Paul Arthur Schilpp and Maurice Friedman (La Salle, Ill.: Open Court, 1967). By permission of Open Court Publishing Company.

"Report of the Director of the School in Jerusalem" by James Muilenburg, from *Bulletin of the American Schools of Oriental Research* 136 (1954), 4–7. By permission of the American Schools of Oriental Research, 4243 Spruce Street, Philadelphia, PA 19104.

"A Letter from Palestine" by James Muilenburg, from *Union Seminary Quarterly Review* 9 (1954), 22–25. By permission of Lawrence E. Muilenburg for the James Muilenburg Estate.

"A Hyksos Scarab Jar Handle from Bethel" by James Muilenburg, from *Bulletin of the American Schools of Oriental Research* 136 (1954), 20–21. By permission of the American Schools of Oriental Research, 4243 Spruce Street, Philadelphia, PA 19104.

"A Qoheleth Scroll from Qumran" by James Muilenburg, from *Bulletin of the American Schools of Oriental Research* 135 (1954), 20–28. By permission of the American Schools of Oriental Research, 4243 Spruce Street, Philadelphia, PA 19104.

"Fragments of Another Qumran Isaiah Scroll" by James Muilenburg, from *Bulletin of the American Schools of Oriental Research* 135 (1954), 28–32. By permission of the American Schools of Oriental Research, 4243 Spruce Street, Philadelphia, PA 19104.

"The Site of Ancient Gilgal" by James Muilenburg, from *Bulletin of the American Schools of Oriental Research* 140 (1955), 11–27. By permission of the American Schools of Oriental Research, 4243 Spruce Street, Philadelphia, PA 19104.

"A Confession of Jeremiah" by James Muilenburg, from *Union Seminary Quarterly Review* 4 (1949), 15–18. By permission of Lawrence E. Muilenburg for the James Muilenburg Estate.

"A Meditation on Divine Fatherhood" by James Muilenburg, from *Union Seminary Quarterly Review* 6 (1950), 3–5. By permission of Lawrence E. Muilenburg for the James Muilenburg Estate.

"Introduction: History of the Problem" by James Muilenburg, from *The Literary Relations of the Epistle of Barnabas and the Teaching of the Twelve Apostles* (dissertation, Yale University, 1926; Marburg, 1929), pp. 1–9. By permission of Lawrence E. Muilenburg for the James Muilenburg Estate.

"Luther and Zwingli Quartercentenary" by James Muilenburg, from *Congregationalist*, December 26, 1929, pp. 854–56. By permission of the National Association of Congregational Christian Churches.

"A Bibliography of James Muilenburg's Writings" by R. Lansing Hicks, from *Israel's Prophetic Heritage*, pp. 233–42, edited by Bernhard W. Anderson and Walter Harrelson. Copyright 1962 by Bernhard W. Anderson and Walter Harrelson. By permission of Harper & Row, Publishers, Inc.

"Additions to a Bibliography of James Muilenburg's Writings" by Ivan Jay Ball, Jr., from *Rhetorical Criticism: Essays in Honor of James Muilenburg*, pp. 285–87, edited by Jared J. Jackson and Martin Kessler (Pittsburgh, Penn.: Pickwick Press, 1974). By permission of Pickwick Press.

Part One

JAMES MUILENBURG

James Muilenburg as Man and Scholar:

A Personal Appreciation and Editor's Introduction

In the middle 1960s—now, astonishingly, twenty years ago—I sat in the chief lecture hall of Union Theological Seminary, New York City, waiting to hear a lecture on the Old Testament. Or, rather, to hear the lecturer: James Muilenburg at the height of his powers, long the holder of the senior Old Testament chair at what was then arguably the most prestigious graduate seminary in America; member of the Revised Standard Version translation team; author of the *Peake's Commentary* general article on prophecy, and its commentary on Ezekiel; author of an anchor article for Volume I of the *Interpreter's Bible*, on the history and religion of ancient Israel, and of its commentary on what was for many the core of the Old Testament, II Isaiah; already at work on the article on that other central figure, Jeremiah, for what was to be the next major production of American biblical scholarship, the *Interpreter's Dictionary of the Bible*; and, in that era perhaps most impressive of all, awaited eagerly by a packed classroom of theological students.

The Scholar appeared precisely at the appointed hour. His whole bearing, but particularly his face, created an immediate and vivid impression, a unique compound of intelligence, old age, and raw energy which he seemed to project tangibly, almost physically, upon each one of us. He began to speak about T. S. Eliot.

He spoke with extraordinary insight and passion ("not as the scribes" kept running through my mind: I had just completed a degree in English Literature at Harvard). What mattered to Muilenburg was not the technical details of Old Testament scholarship (those would be introduced later), but that his students grasp the fundamental reality of the scriptures, for him an interaction between God and humanity which he spoke about in many ways but most centrally as Israel "hearing" the Word, grappling with its meaning, and then "doing" that Word. He felt that this primal communication was best captured today not by theologians but by the poets, and that is where, uncompromisingly, he began.

When next I encountered James Muilenburg, in 1969, both of us were in vastly different circumstances. He had retired as a scholar-in-residence at the Graduate Theological Union, Berkeley, attached directly to San Francisco Theological Seminary in San Rafael. Meanwhile I had become a beginning Ph.D. student, anticipating, with equal measures of hope and dread, the chance to sit at The Master's feet.

These few years in the natural beauty of Marin County formed for Muilenburg a kind of lovely professional Indian Summer. To be sure, the term "retirement" in its conventional sense had no meaning for him whatsoever. His last act each day was to type out a list of the tasks he had appointed for himself for the morrow; this he left in the typewriter, to greet him when he arrived in the office at 9:00 the next morning. He remained very active professionally, devoting himself to extensive reading, intensive thinking, and graduate seminars in a few areas especially close to his heart. He worked with special pleasure on the Inaugural Lecture ("Form Criticism and Beyond") for what he regarded as the crowning honor of his career, his term as President of the Society of Biblical Literature. He received distinguished visitors (D. T. Niles comes at once to mind) from his many contacts in the ecumenical movement. And, above all, he continued teaching.

For those of us in these final seminars Muilenburg was a living link to the grand tradition of graduate study, where the student apprenticed him- or herself to a master scholar to absorb not only the mechanics, but also the style and ethos of academic work. And of course he knew Everyone—not only the leading American Old Testament figures, several of whom had been his own students, but the German giants of an earlier era such as Gunkel and Bultmann.

At this time Muilenburg turned in particular to two areas of study. The first was Jeremiah, that most "personal" and "inward" of prophets. He was working on what he hoped would be—though with his characteristic realism he could not see how he would have time to finish it—the crowning achievement of his career, a definitive commentary on Jeremiah. The subject of each seminar, then, was an especially significant or problematic text. We always proceeded according to the same rigid pattern: to one student had been assigned the text-critical problems of the passage, to another its literary structure, to a third its rhetorical features, and so on. Each had to report both extensively and intensively upon his or her area of responsibility. And the whole thing began, of course, with reading the text aloud in Hebrew; we passed around the table, each reading a verse in turn and translating it at sight. After the student contributions were finished, Muilenburg would deliver himself of his own considered opinions about the passage and its problems. Everything was done with the highest degree of seriousness and professionalism, and no one was ever excused from anything, especially the reading aloud of the Hebrew text.

The other subject which engaged his attention was, surprisingly, the early church Fathers. He showed an astonishing command of this literature in its original Greek. Actually this was surprising only if one did not know the course of Muilenburg's career and understand its inner coherence and logic. For here he was only returning to his earliest theological interests; his dissertation at Yale had been written not in the Old Testament field at all, but on the literary relationship between *Barnabas* and the *Didache*. I saw gradually that this fell into a larger pattern of Muilenburg returning to his roots ("Urzeit gleicht Endzeit," he was fond of quoting from Gunkel), which he was expressing even geographically in returning to the San Francisco Bay area, for his first major seminary teaching position had been at Pacific School of Religion in Berkeley.

The Grand Manner of his classes was all the more remarkable in that this was not the present era of conservative student reaction, but precisely the time which produced the reaction, the heyday of student activism and educational experimentation of the late 1960s and early 1970s. And Muilenburg could be incredibly obstinate in matters of principle. When the proposal was floated that, since traditional term papers were of no educational value (!), they should be abolished, his immediate reaction was to assign each of us a colossal term paper. It was not that he was unsympathetic to the need for educational reform, or for the serious political concerns which motivated some of us. But to Muilenburg being a doctoral student was, first of all, a moral category; there were Obligations, transcending political questions and uniting us as scholars in a common search for truth. We accepted this because it appeared neither meaningless nor arbitrary, but sprung from Muilenburg's inmost convictions and appealed to the best within us. And while he could be harshly, almost brutally critical of his students, one knew that this was a mark of his confidence in our abilities and that, in any case, he reserved his severest criticism for himself.

Eventually Muilenburg left San Anselmo and took up residence at Pilgrim Place, a retirement community in the Claremont area. He was increasingly troubled by Parkinson's Disease but maintained a steady and lively correspondence—touching, among many other subjects, the possibility of an anthology of his works, a matter about which he had very strong opinions.

This brings me to the principles which have guided the selection of works for this anthology. Muilenburg was prolific; the bibliographies in his two *Festschrifts* run to many pages. The negative principles of selection can be simply put. In accordance with Dr. Muilenburg's own wishes, expressed repeatedly and with great force, I have included only works which already have been published. He had a horror of losing control of his own production, fearing, more than the neglect of later generations, the misguided zeal of "admirers" who might search out his unpublished notes, discussion papers, drafts, and the like, and rush them into print. Such material—however fascinating and valuable some of it undoubtedly is—has been rigidly excluded. The major, perhaps even tragic, omission is his unfinished work on the Jeremiah commentary. What he had done has been lodged at Princeton under the care of Bernhard Anderson; hopefully it will eventually see the light of day. Of the published work, one or two larger pieces have been omitted which Muilenburg himself regarded as significant more because of where they had appeared than for their content. And I have not taken space to reprint the works most widely available, his major articles in *Peake's Commentary*, the *Interpreter's Bible*, or the *Interpreter's Dictionary of the Bible*, as well as material from his book *The Way of Israel*.

Thus this is not a "best of Muilenburg." Indeed his own such list was almost absurdly short, consisting exclusively of highly technical articles and showing only one side of his abilities. Rather I have been guided by two positive principles. The first is to show the almost incredible diversity of Muilenburg's interests, talents, and competence. There are few analogies in our age of specialization; one thinks rather of those transcendent European musicians of the 1930s, 1940s, and 1950s such as Artur Schnabel or Dinu Lipatti, who, though their primary career was in concert performance, considered themselves to be complete and authentic musicians only if they also composed original music, prepared new editions of the classics, and taught. While today the selective memory of the scholarly enterprise associates Muilenburg with "rhetorical criticism," he also produced excellent contributions in fields as diverse as historical theology, exegesis, the history of Old Testament scholarship, and archaeology. And in his early career he published in the fields of English Literature and History, including an interesting and original contribution to the political history of his own Dutch heritage.

The second principle has been to show the penetration of Muilenburg's work by his special literary qualities of eloquence and lucidity. This appears particularly in the homilies and meditations, and most beautifully in his sudden poetic outburst describing the light playing over the desert in "A Letter from Palestine."

My final task is to thank those who over the years have contributed to the creation of this anthology. One special quality of James Muilenburg can scarcely be shown in a work such as this, but has made its production a positive pleasure. This is his capacity for forming intense and enduring relationships with his family and friends, and for evoking an intense respect and loyalty from his students. He remained close to his children, for whom he had great respect, and idolized his beloved wife Mary. To those in his family I extend sincere thanks for their ready and generous help. The same is true of many of Dr. Muilenburg's students over several generations, in particular Bernhard Anderson, Walter Harrelson, and Jack Lundbom, as well as the individuals and publishers who have extended permission to reprint Dr. Muilenburg's (or in a few cases their own) works.

Since Muilenburg served as President of the Society of Biblical Literature it is uniquely appropriate that this anthology should appear with Scholars Press. Its preparation has seen the regimes of no less than three editors, and I should like to offer sincere thanks to Charles Bowman—himself a Muilenburg student—for catching the vision; to Davis Perkins, for continuing support, professional competence, and, not least of all, patience; and to John Crowell, for bringing the project to its final fruition. A special thanks is due to our supporters, whose contributions reflect far more than a merely financial gift. Their response and enthusiasm has been my primary support over the long and complicated course of the project. One in particular, who shall remain nameless, has been of decisive importance.

I close with quiet thanks to a friend, perhaps the greatest student Muilenburg ever had, certainly the one who best captured his unique spirit, and to me a continuing source of inspiration and hope.

Thomas F. Best
Executive Secretariat, Faith and Order Commission
World Council of Churches
Geneva, Switzerland

Summer, 1984

James Muilenburg as Man and Scholar

Frederick Buechner

But for me, as for most of us studying there in those days, there was no one on the faculty who left so powerful and lasting an impression as James Muilenburg. He was an angular man with thinning white hair, staring eyes, and a nose and chin which at times seemed so close to touching that they gave him the face of a good witch. In his introductory Old Testament course, the largest lecture hall that Union had was always packed to hear him. Students brought friends. Friends brought friends. People stood in the back when the chairs ran out. Up and down the whole length of the aisle he would stride as he chanted the war songs, the taunt songs, the dirges of ancient Israel. With his body stiff, his knees bent, his arms scarecrowed far to either side, he never merely taught the Old Testament but *was* the Old Testament. He would be Adam, wide-eyed and halting as he named the beasts—"You are . . . an elephant . . . a butterfly . . . an ostrich!"—or Eve, trembling and afraid in the garden of her lost innocence, would be David sobbing his great lament at the death of Saul and Jonathan, would be Moses coming down from Sinai. His face uptilted and his eyes aghast, he would be Yahweh himself, creating the heavens and the earth, and when he called out, "Let there be *light!*" there is no way of putting it other than to say that there would *be* light, great floods of it reflected in the hundreds of faces watching him in that enormous room. In more or less these words, I described him in a novel later, and when I showed him the typescript for his approval, he was appalled because it seemed to confirm his terrible fear that he was making a fool of himself. And, of course, if it hadn't been for his genius, for the staggering sincerity of his performance, he might almost have been right. It was a measure of folly as well as of strength and courage, I suppose, to let himself come so perilously close to disaster.

"Every morning when you wake up," he used to say, "before you reaffirm your faith in the majesty of a loving God, before you say *I believe* for another day, read the *Daily News* with its record of the latest crimes and trage-dies of mankind and then see if you can honestly say it again." He was a fool in the sense that he didn't or couldn't or wouldn't resolve, intellectualize, evade, the tensions of his faith but lived those tensions out, torn almost in two by them at times. His faith was not a seamless garment but a ragged garment with the seams showing, the tears showing, a garment that he clutched about him like a man in a storm. In teaching the prophets, he wrenched into juxtaposition faith, on the one hand, as passion, as risk, as shuddering trust even in the face of despair and darkness, and, on the other, as mere piety, sentimentality, busyness. He held up Jeremiah in his cis-tern over against the Every Member Canvass, committee-manship, the mimeograph machine, and would prance down the aisle parodying the cozy old Jesus hymns — "He walks with me, and he talks with me, and he tells me I am his own." The cluck of his laugh was always in part a cluck at himself. The flush of his smile, with his eyes delicately lowered like a girl's and his chin tucked in, was a smile both of deprecation and self-deprecation. His prayers, he once told me, were mostly blubbering, and you felt that he prayed endlessly.

He was a fool, I suppose, in the sense that he was an intimate of the dark, yet held fast to the light as if it were something you could hold fast to; in the sense that he wore his heart on his sleeve even though it was in some ways a broken heart; in the sense that he was as absurdly himself before the packed lecture hall as he was alone in his office; a fool in the sense that he was a child in his terrible candor. A fool, in other words, for Christ. Though I was no longer at Union when he gave his final lecture there, I am told that a number of students from the Jewish seminary across the street attended it and, before entering the great room, left their shoes in the corridor outside to indicate that the ground on which they stood with him was holy ground.

In her book *Holy the Firm,* Annie Dillard writes, "The higher Christian churches . . . come at God with an unwarranted air of professionalism, with authority and pomp, as though they knew what they were doing, as though people in themselves were an appropriate set of creatures to have dealings with God. . . . If God were to blast such a congregation to bits, the congregation would be, I believe, genuinely shocked. But in the low churches you expect it any minute."[3] In that sense, I think, Muilenburg never knew what he was doing, was never a pro. But, as a scholar, he knew plenty and demanded plenty from his students. He was uncompromising in his insistence, especially, upon the necessity of exposing the Bible to all the modern instruments of literary and historical criticism and refused ever to sacrifice, or to let any of us sacrifice, scholarly integrity to the demands and presuppositions of conventional religiosity. In order to impress upon his students what he felt to be the crucial importance of this approach, he assigned us the task of writing what was known to fame as the Pentateuch Paper. In it we were to expound and support by close textual analysis the hypothesis that the first five books of the Old Testament could not be a single work written by Moses, as traditionally supposed, but were a composite work consisting of some four or more documents, each of which had its own style, theological outlook, and polemical purpose. The paper came as the climax of Muilenburg's introductory course, but the shadow it cast was a long one, and from the earliest weeks it loomed less as a paper than as a rite of passage. It had to be very long. It had to be very good. It had to hold water. And I remember still the acute apprehension with which I launched into it, the first paper I had written for anybody about anything since college. It turned out to be the opening of a door.

I had read here and there in the Bible before, the way people do — dutifully, haphazardly, far from sure either what I was looking for or what I was supposed to find. I was aware that there was said to be great treasure buried somewhere among all those unpromising, double-columned pages, but I had never had anybody point me very adequately to a place to start digging. I must have already been through a fair sampling of the Gospels, some of the psalms, some of Genesis, of Job; and though I have no specific memories of it, I remember having been moved and having sensed that there was something deeper down than I had ever gone to move me more deeply still. But it all seemed very hazy and elusive. Then, suddenly, with the monumental Pentateuch Paper to contend with, and the no-less-monumental Muilenburg to show the way, I was forced to look at it in a different light altogether. Muilenburg never expressed any doubt as to its being a holy book—a book not only rooted deep in the memories of Israel and rich with hope that the ancient promises would be fulfilled, but a book through which God himself speaks to his people—yet he maintained always that in another sense it was a book like any other book. It was no less a product of the times and of the peoples who had produced it. It presented the same kinds of difficulties, contradictions, ambiguities as any ancient document. On the one hand, it was to be read with the eye of faith and to the heart's uplifting; on the other hand, it was to be read as critically and searchingly as anything else.

It was from the Jacob narratives in Genesis that we were asked to glean evidence to support the documentary hypothesis, and in the process of doing that, I saw, I think for the first time, that holiness is not something hazy and elusive that we know apart from the earth but something we can know only as it wells up out of the earth, out of people even as clay-footed as Jacob, the trickster and crook, out of places as elemental as the river Jabbok, where he wrestled in darkness with a Stranger who was no stranger, out of events as seamy as the time he gulled his half-blind father out of Esau's blessing. "See, the smell of my son is as the smell of a field which the Lord has blessed,"[4] old Isaac says as he lays his hands upon Jacob, and there it is all in a moment: Jacob betrays his brother, dupes his father, all but chokes on his own mendacity, yet the smell of him is the smell of blessing because God, no less than Isaac, has chosen to bless him in spite of everything. Jacob reeks of holiness. His life is as dark, fertile, and holy as the earth itself. He is himself a bush that burns with everything, both fair and foul, that a man burns with. Yet he is not consumed because God out of his grace will not consume him.

What I began to see was that the Bible is not essentially, as I had always more or less supposed, a book of ethical principles, of moral exhortations, of cautionary tales about exemplary people, of uplifting thoughts—in fact, not really a religious book at all in the sense that most of the books you would be apt to find in a minister's study or reviewed in a special religion issue of the *New York Times* book section are religious. I saw it instead as a great, tattered compendium of writings, the underlying and unifying purpose of all of which is to show how God works through the Jacobs and Jabboks of history to make himself known to the world and to draw the world back to himself.

For all its vast diversity and unevenness, it is a book with a plot and a plot that can be readily stated. God makes the world in love. For one reason or another the world chooses to reject God. God will not reject the world but continues his mysterious and relentless pursuit of it to the end of time. That is what he is doing by choosing Israel to be his special people. That is what he is doing through all the passion and poetry and invective of the prophets. That is why history plays such a crucial part in the Old Testament—all those kings and renegades and battles and invasions and apostasies—because it was precisely through people like that and events like those that God was at work, as, later, in the New Testament, he was supremely at work in the person and event of

Jesus Christ. Only *"is* at work" would be the more accurate way of putting it because if there is a God who works at all, his work goes on still, of course, and at one and the same time the Biblical past not only illumines the present but becomes itself part of that present, part of our own individual pasts. Until you can read the story of Adam and Eve, of Abraham and Sarah, of David and Bath-sheba, as your own story, Muilenburg said, you have not really understood it. The Bible, as he presented it, is a book finally about ourselves, our own apostasies, our own battles and blessings; and it was the discovery of that more than of the differences between the Jahwist, Elohist, Deuteronomic, and Priestly sources of the Pentateuch that constituted the real reward of writing that apocalyptic paper.

INTRODUCTION

The New Frontier of Rhetorical Criticism

A Tribute to James Muilenburg

Bernhard W. Anderson

Princeton Theological Seminary

The invitation to write the introduction to this volume provides a welcome opportunity to join with other students of James Muilenburg in offering a tribute to our teacher, whom we honor as a creative and dynamic interpreter of Israel's faith and one of the greatest Old Testament teachers and scholars of the past generation. This is actually the second Muilenburg Festschrift. The first, Israel's Prophetic Heritage,[1] was presented to him in 1962, just prior to his retirement from Union Theological Seminary in New York City. The present Festschrift differs from the former in two respects: without exception the essays have been written by his students (other than those who contributed to the first volume); and the contributions reflect the impact of the "rhetorical criticism" which he advocated in his presidential address to the Society of Biblical Literature in 1968.[2] In this monumental address, which represented the crowning climax of his career, he pressed the frontier of biblical studies into new regions which will be explored further in years to come.

It is fitting that this volume is published under the aegis of Pittsburgh Theological Seminary, where the bulk of his personal library is now deposited in Barbour Library with his name on the bookplates of each book. On May 10, 1966 Dr. Muilenburg gave the commencement address to the graduating class of the seminary. His text, according to his own translation and arrangement, was taken from the prophecy of Second Isaiah which he knows and loves so well:

> Behold, the former things have already come to pass,
>   now I tell you of new things.
>
> From now on I am causing you to listen to new things,
>   hidden things which you have not known.
> They are created now, not long ago;
>   before today you have never heard them.
>
> Remember not the former things,
>   nor consider the days of old.
> Behold, I am doing a new thing;
>   it is springing forth, don't you realize it?
>
> Sing to the Lord a new song,
>   his praise from the ends of the earth.
>   (Isa. 42:9-10; 43:18-19)

---

[1] Israel's Prophetic Heritage: Essays in Honor of James Muilenburg (eds. Bernhard W. Anderson and Walter Harrelson; New York: Harper, 1962).

[2] "Form Criticism and Beyond," JBL 88 (1969) 1-18.

X

The theme of the sermon, relevant not only to his immediate audience but
to all who are sensitive to the interior meaning of Israel's scriptures,
was that "Our God is the innovating God," who leads into new paths and
new frontiers. "The man who is free," he said, "knows that life is always
open, open to new possibilities, open to the unprecedented, open to God
and history. He will not stay put in any status quo ante, indeed in any
status at all, for time and history do not allow it."[3]

Dr. Muilenburg's scholarly writings also are animated by the inability
to "stay put in any status quo ante," and this is eminently true of his
presidential address in which he advocated "Form Criticism and Beyond,"
the "beyond" being rhetorical criticism of Israel's scriptures. It should
be realized, however, that his advocacy of rhetorical criticism, while
representing a creative thrust into a new frontier, was actually a sharpen-
ing of concerns that had been present from the very beginning of his scholarly career. Indeed, in this time when biblical critics   ersing with
literary critics in the field of the humanities, it i.   embering
that he began his teaching career at the University of ..eoraska (1920-1923)
as an instructor in English composition, where he wrote a book dealing with
specimens of biblical literature. His encounter with Hermann Gunkel, however, transformed his literary interest in the Bible. He was deeply influenced, as he has told me in correspondence, by the volume on The
Oriental Literatures in the Kultur der Gegenwart series, in which Gunkel
presented a sketch of what he considered to be a proper literary history of
Israel. And while teaching at Mount Holyoke he was granted a sabbatical
for study at Marburg, Germany (1929-1930), which provided him with the
opportunity to visit several universities, especially the University of
Halle where Gunkel was teaching. He attended Gunkel's seminar, visited him
in his home, and read many of his works, including The Legends of Genesis.
In his presidential address Dr. Muilenburg paid a very high tribute to
Gunkel. "It is not too much to say," he stated, "that Gunkel has never
been excelled in his ability to portray the spirit which animated the biblical writers, and he did not hesitate either in his lectures or in his seminars to draw upon the events of contemporary history or the experiences of
the common man to explicate the interior meaning of a pericope."[4] Muilenburg's
students undoubtedly would testify that this is an overstatement, for
Gunkel's grasp of the meaning of Israel's scriptures was too much under
the influence of the presuppositions of the Religionsgeschichtlicheschule.
When it comes to grasping the interior, theological dimensions of Israel's
faith, James Muilenburg is unexcelled, as those who have experienced his
demanding and sensitive scholarship and the charismatic power of his teaching know.

His emphasis upon rhetorical criticism could easily be misunderstood
if it is not seen in the context of his whole scholarly career. Since it
was my privilege to be his first student to go into graduate study, and
since I have kept in close touch with him through the subsequent years, it
may be helpful for me to review the three phases of his career: his years
at Pacific School of Religion (1936-1945), his period at Union Theological
Seminary (1945-1963), and his very active "retirement" at San Anselmo

---

[3] Sermon, "The Innovating God," May 10, 1966. I am grateful to Dr.
Muilenburg for providing me with a copy.

[4] "Form Criticism and Beyond," 2.

xi

Theological Seminary (1963-1969). In retrospect each of these phases was
characterized by different accents, each of which represents an important dimension of his presidential address. His continuous concern through
his whole career, however, has been to give an exposition of Israel's
historical faith which belongs essentially to the witness of the Christian
community. As a scholar he has always been a churchman.

    James Muilenburg began his career in theological education at Pacific
School of Religion when new theological winds, emanating from Europe, were
sweeping across the United States, though their intensity had diminished
considerably by the time they reached the West. In those days Old Testament scholarship was still under the domination of the Wellhausen school
which, supported by an analysis of the "sources" of the Pentateuch, advocated
a unilinear, evolutionary interpretation of Israel's history. This view had
been popularized by the writings of Harry Emerson Fosdick, minister of River-
side Church in New York City, whose radio sermons were heard nationally.
Fosdick's books, such as The Modern Use of the Bible (1924) and A Guide to
Understanding the Bible (1938), had a liberating effect upon many college
students who were dissatisfied with a naive view of Scripture. This was the
prevailing atmosphere when I entered Pacific School of Religion in 1936, the
first year of Dr. Muilenburg's career in theological education. I remember
that right away we were plunged into the problem of the Pentateuch in his
course on Introduction to the Old Testament. One of our assignments was to
go through the Pentateuch and mark with colored pencils the four sources
(J,E,D,P) according to the diagrammatic analysis given in S.R. Driver's
Introduction to the Literature of the Old Testament. The other assignment
was to write a paper on "The Composition of the Pentateuch," an assignment--
as I came to learn--that was given annually to generations of students at
Pacific School of Religion and, later, at Union Theological Seminary.
Muilenburg's teaching, however, exploded the constricting framework of the
Wellhausen view. This occurred, first of all, because of his intuitive
penetration into the dimensions of Israel's experience of the reality of
God in her history and his ability to dramatize the scriptural story so that
students were drawn into it personally. And, secondly, he was profoundly influenced by Gunkel's Gattungsforschung--a word that is emblazoned on my memory
from those days. In a course on Jeremiah, I became aware of the principles
of interpretation which later were articulated as "rhetorical criticism:" the
isolation of a discrete literary unit, the analysis of its structure and balance, and the attention to key words and motifs. Yet what stands out most in
my memory from those years is his profound exposition of Yahweh's revelation
in historical events and the eschatological import of that revelation. Students
found themselves caught in the creative tension between James Muilenburg, an
Old Testament teacher who was sympathetic with some aspects of "neo-orthodoxy,"
and C. C. McCown, a New Testament teacher who fervently advocated a "natural-
istic" interpretation of Scripture.[5]

    When Dr. Muilenburg moved to Union Theological Seminary in 1945, he found
himself on the crest of the so-called Biblical Theology Movement. He approved

_____

    [5] See Harland E. Hogue, Christian Seed in Western Soil: Pacific School
of Religion through a Century (Berkeley, California: Pacific School of
Religion, 1965), chap. 8, "World War II and its Aftermath."

of the church's demand for a biblical theology and made his own contribution
to the movement, although expressing his qualifications. "The task of the
biblical theologian," he said during this period, "is a precarious one;"
for Israel's scriptures, having come out of life, resist any simple sche-
matization. In this respect, he confessed that he was a "liberal," profoundly indebted to historical criticism. One of the primary characteristics
of biblical faith, he never wearied of saying, is "the historical character of revelation"--"Israel's sense of the eventfulness of life and of
God's activity in history;" and it is to liberalism, he said, that we owe
this insight. It is essential, therefore, for the biblical critic to understand the historical setting in which words were spoken and to appreciate
how those words were shaped in concrete social situations.[6]

Consistent with these historical concerns, he championed even more
vigorously the method of form criticism, as evidenced by some of his writings from this period.[7] Like Gunkel, Muilenburg never repudiated in
principle the method of source criticism, but he shifted the emphasis
to a method which he believed to be more fruitful in understanding the
relation of scripture to the life of the people. He spoke appreciatively
of "the gains of form criticism." The task of the form critic, he said,
is not only to identify the Gattungen but "to restore them to their original spokenness (Gesprochenheit), for they must be heard in order to be
understood or made contemporary."[8] Yet even when he wrote those words in
1960, he was not unaware of the excesses and exaggerations of the method,
evident in the reduction of literary units to "mere snippets" or the
unduly heavy emphasis upon cultic provenance or Near Eastern parallels.
His reservations about the omnicompetence of the form-critical method
were surely nourished by his work on Second Isaiah for the Interpreter's
Bible (1956). His masterful commentary, which was severely reduced from
notes that could have extended it several times in length, displays
disagreement with form critics who divide the material into small units,
thereby confusing strophes with independent poems, and it evinces a fine
sensitivity to rhetorical and structural features of the poetry. It was
from Gunkel that he gained an appreciation of the forms and patterns in
Hebrew literary composition; and this interest, always evident in his
teaching and writing from the first, became more prominent,[9] though not
excluding other interests ranging from archaeology to biblical theology.

---

[6] See his essay, "Is There a Biblical Theology?" USQR XII, 4 (1957)
29-37, especially p. 35.

[7] For instance, "The Birth of Benjamin," JBL 75 (1956) 194-201;
"The Form and Structure of the Covenantal Formulations," VT 9 (1959)
347-65.

[8] See "The Gains of Form Criticism in Old Testament Studies," ExpT 71;
No. 8 (1960) 229-33, especially p. 231.

[9] See "A Study in Hebrew Rhetoric: Repetition and Style," VTSup I (1953)
97-111; "The Linguistic and Rhetorical Usages of the Particle כי in the Old
Testament," HUCA 32 (1961) 135-60.

xiii

Dr. Muilenburg's later years at San Anselmo Theological Seminary brought
to fulfillment what was seminally present from the beginning of his career
in theological education. In his essay on "Form Criticism and Beyond," he
says clearly that he does not intend to repudiate form criticism, any more
than he repudiated completely the older method of source criticism. There
are some instances in which form criticism works well. But when carried
to an extreme, it has certain inherent weaknesses. For one thing, form-
critical analysis of a literary genre tends "to lay such stress upon the
typical and representative that the individual, personal, and unique features
of the particular pericope are all but lost to view." Often, he points out,
we do not find a Gattung in pure form but rather imitations of it, detached
from its original Sitz im Leben and refashioned with such superb literary
artistry that we are enabled "to think the thoughts of the biblical writer
after him." A second criticism is that form criticism, when strictly
applied, resists all efforts to gain a psychological understanding of an
author or to sense the concrete historical situation in which he spoke.[10]

The immediate context of Dr. Muilenburg's sensitivity to the extremes
of form criticism was his work on the prophecy of Jeremiah, which has been
one of his major interests throughout his career. At San Anselmo he was
engaged in writing a commentary on Jeremiah, using the method of rhetorical
criticism. The unfinished manuscript, which I have been privileged to read,
seeks to demonstrate that the literature, although making use of traditional
literary genres,provides access to the mind of the prophet and the concrete
situations in which his words were spoken. "The call of Jeremiah," he
observes in his presidential address, "is something more than the recitation
of a conventional and inherited liturgy within the precincts of the temple
[contra H. G. Reventlow, Liturgie und prophetisches Ich bei Jeremia], and
the so-called confessions of the prophet are more than the repetition and reproduction of fixed stereotypes, despite all the parallels that one may
adduce from the Old Testament and the Near Eastern texts for such a position."[11] What the critic finds in the case of Jeremiah is also evident
elsewhere in the Old Testament. Very often, he emphasizes, the literary
genres do not appear in pure form but are imitated, that is, they are
used creatively by a writer who draws them into the context of his own
thought. Thus the conventional is stamped with individuality, the old
wine is poured into new wineskins. For this reason it behooves the scholar
to hold fast to the assured gains of form criticism but to go beyond. The
sensitive literary critic, he says, "will not be completely bound by the
traditional elements and motifs of literary genre; his task will not be
completed until he has taken full account of the features which lie beyond
the spectrum of the genre."

———————

In his presidential address Dr. Muilenburg suggested that rhetorical
criticism is applicable to all of Israel's scriptures, but he concentrated on the poetic, and especially the prophetic, sections of the Old
Testament. He did not face directly the implications of rhetorical criticism for the Pentateuch which traditionally has been the testing-ground

———————————————————————————————

[10] "Form Criticism and Beyond," 4-6.

[11] Ibid., 6.

[12] Ibid., 7.

for critical method. It was in this area, of course, that Gunkel, whom Muilenburg acclaims as "the pioneer and progenitor" of Gattungsforschung, carried out his investigation with fruitful results. It is my conviction that Muilenburg in his own way has raised some important questions concerning "The Composition of the Pentateuch," to hark back to the paper that his students were required to write. The following brief remarks are intended only to indicate the new frontier which demands exploration.

Let us begin with Muilenburg's observation that genres are often transformed when appropriated for new literary contexts. Gunkel, of course, maintained that the proper starting-point in form-critical investigation is the isolation of discrete genres, such as the Sagen of Genesis. Moreover, it was alleged that the genres of oral tradition are usually brief pericopes which can be detached from their present narrative context and studied from within, in their own Sitz im Leben. Indeed, one of the guidelines in traditio-historical investigation of the Pentateuch, as I have formulated it with reference to Martin Noth's work, is: "Earliest traditions are formulated in small units and in concise style in contrast to later material which tends to appear in large units composed in discursive (ausgeführt) style."[13] Now, it is undoubtedly true that the Pentateuchal tradition does contain hints of units that were closely related to folk life, and often the critic can isolate them and study them by themselves (e.g. Gen. 6:1-4; 32:22-32). The problem is that in many cases Gunkel's small unit is beyond recovery and, in any case, is so closely integrated into the narrative complex (Gunkel's Sagenkranz) that its meaning cannot be understood from within. The unit, whatever its original setting, now functions in a new context which has transformed its original meaning.[14]

This hermeneutical problem is illustrated in a perceptive essay on Genesis 22 by George Coats, one of the leading younger form critics.[15] The point of departure for his form-critical study, he states, is "the received text [including the somewhat "anticlimactic" verses 15-18], not a hypothetical reconstruction of earlier levels," and this demands that the passage must be understood in relation to the larger context in which it now functions, that is, "the scope of theology about Abraham and his promise." This is an important statement, one that suggests "form criticism and beyond." No longer does the genre have a vague setting in

---

[13] See the introductory essay to my translation of Martin Noth, A History of Pentateuchal Traditions (Englewood Cliffs, N.J.: Prentice-Hall, 1972), xxiii-xxiv. This essay was presented to, and discussed by, a group of form critics, including James Muilenburg, at the 1968 meeting of the Society of Biblical Literature.

[14] Here I acknowledge my indebtedness to a paper on "Saga" by Robert Neff at a form-critical seminar held during the 1973 meeting of the Society of Biblical Literature.

[15] George W. Coats, "Abraham's Sacrifice of Faith: A Form-Critical Study of Genesis 22," Int 27 (1973) 389-400.

XV

folk life, as Gunkel would have maintained, but has a narrative setting or _Sitz im Text_, whether that setting was provided by oral prose composition or by a literary author/redactor.[16] If this is the case, the situation in the book of Genesis is analogous to that of the poetry of Second Isaiah where, as Muilenburg points out, traditional genres like the covenant lawsuit (_rîb_) or the _Heilsorakel_ are creatively appropriated by a literary artist and made to function in a new context.[17]

Let us turn to another matter, which is related to the foregoing discussion. At the conclusion of his presidential address, Dr. Muilenburg raises the question of the source of Hebrew rhetoric. "Persistent and painstaking attention to the modes of Hebrew literary composition," he states, "will reveal that the pericopes exhibit linguistic patterns, word formations ordered or arranged in particular ways, verbal sequences which move in fixed structures from beginning to end." These phenomena, he insists, "cannot be explained by spontaneity." Even though the writers creatively produced their own literary style, "it is also apparent that they have been influenced by conventional rhetorical practices." And on the heels of this question comes another: "How are we to explain the numerous and extraordinary literary affinities of the _Gattungen_ or genres and other stylistic formulations of Israel's literature with the literatures of the other people of the Near East?"[18]

These questions are particularly puzzling when we turn to the literature of the Pentateuch, whose history moves from oral composition to written fixation. In contrast to Wellhausen, who placed excessive emphasis upon the "sources" of the Pentateuch which were dated in the period of the monarchy, Gunkel maintained that the oral (pre-state) period was the creative time, when the experiences of the people found expression in genres related to folk life. Undoubtedly Gunkel was inspired by a sound insight. For the prose narratives of the Pentateuch not only rest upon ancient oral tradition, as form critics emphasize, but bear "the formal and rhetorical stigmata" of oral composition.

As Dr. Muilenburg admits, here we are moving into a misty area in which it is difficult to find our way. Since we have no immediate access to the prehistory of the Pentateuchal narratives, the problem is to find some analogy in a preliterate society, still open to investigation, which may help us to understand the rhetoric of oral composition. This problem becomes peculiarly difficult when we contemplate the possibility that no analogy can do full justice to ancient Israelite society which may have been unique in its understanding of the spoken and written word. Perhaps some light may be cast on the problem by Albert Lord's reconsideration of

---

[16] Coats seems to abandon the search for a _Sitz im Leben_ in Gunkel's sense. In his brief section on "Setting" (p. 199), he states that the legend "reflects a folk tradition, a style of storytelling that cannot easily be tied to one particular institution," and that the story in its present form has been consciously adapted to fit it into a "literary construct."

[17] See the Princeton Theological Seminary doctoral dissertation by Edgar W. Conrad, _Patriarchal Traditions in Second Isaiah_ (1974), where the implications of Muilenburg's approach are further, and fruitfully, explored.

[18] "Form Criticism and Beyond," 18.

Homeric literature in his work, The Singer of Tales, even though it must
be admitted that no exact parallel can be drawn between non-literate folk
communities of Yugoslavia and ancient societies, especially Israel. He
challenges the notion that poets "did something to a fixed text or fixed
group of texts"[19] and maintains that stylistic features, which seem to
suggest a writer "with pen in hand," actually arose in oral narration in
which the singer creatively utilized formulaic patterns and various stereotyped devices in his improvisations.[20] This study, it seems to me, may have
a heuristic value in that it helps us to perceive aspects of Israelite
composition and particularly to consider the relation between the spoken
and the written word. Dr. Muilenburg has observed that "the difficulty
with historical criticism," meaning the kind of criticism practiced pre-
eminently by the Wellhausen school, "is that it always tended to view the
literary material too much as written products;" and he sides with Gunkel
who "sought to liberate the literary forms from the written page and to
place them. . . into the immediacy and concreteness of speaking."[21] It
should be added, however, that even when the narratives of Genesis were
written, say, by the Yahwist, they were intended for oral reading--not
for silent reading in some library! This was also true of the oracles
of the prophets, at least in the first stage: when they were dictated to
a disciple, as in the case of Jeremiah's scroll, they were intended to
be read publicly or perhaps they were preserved for reading in years to
come when the people might listen and understand. It is very likely that
when the Old Epic tradition of the Pentateuch was reduced to writing, it
reflected the rhetoric of oral performance, so that even today we are able
to listen to "the speaking of Israel," as Muilenburg used to tell his students.

In any event, we now have the traditions in written form and it is with
the final text that the literary critic must deal. Albert Lord stresses
that a decisive act occurred when the Singer of Tales allowed his oral
composition to be written down finally and to become, as it were, a canonical text. Something similar must have occurred when the Old Epic tradition
was written down and, above all, when it was incorporated into the Priestly
Writing. For the Pentateuchal materials to which scholars have assigned
the siglum P does not represent the work of a mere editor who harmonized
the Old Epic (JE) tradition with an independent priestly "source;" rather,
as Frank Cross has rightly observed, P was an author (or "tradent") who
creatively "shaped and supplemented the received Epic tradition of Israel"[22]
and, in so doing, gave the tradition a definitive and final written form.

---

[19] Albert B. Lord, The Singer of Tales (Harvard University Press, 1960),
11.

[20] Ibid., 57.

[21] "The Gains of Form Criticism. . . ." 231.

[22] Frank Moore Cross, Canaanite Myth and Hebrew Epic: Essays in the
History of the Religion of Israel (Harvard University Press, 1973),
chap. 11, "The Priestly Work," especially 301-21.

xvii

Rhetorical criticism is a new impulse which may well shift the emphasis in Pentateuchal studies. Under the influence of Gunkel, the investigation of the literary "sources" of the Pentateuch ceased to have ascendency and scholars turned their attention to the preliterary period, the stage of oral transmission. This is supremely evident in the monumental commentary on Genesis by Claus Westermann, who in his own way is profoundly indebted to Gunkel.[23] The question that many are raising these days, however, is: What is the relative value of going behind the final text into previous levels of tradition that can be reconstructed only hypothetically? How much light does the prehistory of the text throw upon the final text-- the one that has functioned in Judaism and Christianity and the one that we read today?[24]

This kind of question has been raised by literary critics in other fields. Roland Frye, for instance, has pointed out that in the field of the humanities literary critics have found explorations behind the text to be unfruitful,and he has issued a challenge to biblical critics to show "a primary exegetical respect for the final literary work itself."[25] Speaking of the Gospels, he writes: "To dissect them, put each segment under a microscope, and then reassemble the parts in some hypothetical form hopefully representing an earlier form of the tradition can be a fascinating endeavor, but again it will divert our attention and energies from a more productive kind of study. To attempt to dissect the Gospels as historical dramas and force the fragments back into earlier forms and stages is like putting Ariel back in the pine cleft."[26] Frye's remarks about the Gospels as dramatic history could apply mutatis mutandis to the Pentateuchal story. This kind of literary criticism, however, could lead to the dubious conclusion that all attempts to go behind the text and inquire into authorship, provenance, life situation, are in vain and have no bearing upon exegesis. I am sure that Dr. Muilenburg, who has a profound appreciation of both English literature and biblical literature, would be the first to rise to his feet and protest the extremes of the new literary criticism. Nevertheless, in a period when the scholarly habit has been to engage in excursions behind the text, there is much to be said in favor of "a primary exegetical respect for the final literary work itself"--its rhetorical features and its dramatic quality. For the final text is not just the result of adding together various units of tradition, each of which can be studied by itself and whose meaning is contained within itself, but is a whole which is more than the sum of its parts. What Nahum Sarna says about documentary analysis is eminently true: "things in combination possess properties and produce

---

23 See Claus Westermann, Erträge der Forschung: Genesis 1-11 (Darmstadt: Wissenschaftliche Buchgesellschaft, 1972) 1-2. This little book summarizes the history of research presupposed in his Genesiskommentar.

24 See my review of the first five fascicles of Westermann's commentary on Genesis, JBL 91 (1972) 243-245.

25 Roland M. Frye, "A Literary Perspective for the Criticism of the Gospels," Jesus and Man's Hope (eds. Donald G. Miller and Dikran Y. Hadidian, Vol II; Pittsburgh Theological Seminary, 1971) 193-221; quotation from p. 215.

26 Ibid, 212.

xviii

qualities neither carried by, nor inherent in, any of the components in isolation."[27]

    In his presidential address Dr. Muilenburg makes it clear that he does not intend for a moment to forfeit the substantial accomplishments of the scholarly tradition in which he stands. He has been a debtor to Wellhausen, despite reservations about his historical criticism, and to Gunkel, from whom he learned most. This is especially clear to me as I consider his thesis "form criticism and beyond" in the context of his whole career. His essay opens up a new frontier for exploration, not least of all in the field of Pentateuchal studies. He concludes the essay by saying: "We affirm the necessity of form criticism"-- and that demands appropriate exploration of the prehistory of the text; "but we also lay claim to the legitimacy of what we have called rhetorical criticism"-- and that requires attention to the text itself: its own integrity, its dramatic structure, and its stylistic features.

[27] Nahum M. Sarna, Understanding Genesis (New York: McGraw-Hill, 1966 xxv.

Part Two

CRITICISM AND EXEGESIS

FORM CRITICISM AND BEYOND*

JAMES MUILENBURG
SAN FRANCISCO THEOLOGICAL SEMINARY

THE impact of form criticism upon biblical studies has been profound, comparable only to the subsequent influence of historical criticism as it was classically formulated by Julius Wellhausen about a century ago. Its pioneer and spiritual progenitor was Hermann Gunkel, for many years professor of Old Testament at the University of Halle. The magnitude of his contribution to biblical scholarship is to be explained in part by the fact that historical criticism had come to an impasse, chiefly because of the excesses of source analysis; in part, too, by Gunkel's extraordinary literary insight and sensitivity, and, not least of all, by the influence which diverse academic disciplines exerted upon him.[1] At an early age he had read Johann Gottfried Herder's work, *Vom Geist der Ebräischen Poesie* (1782–83), with ever-growing excitement, and it kindled within him an appreciation not only of the quality of the ancient Oriental mentality, so characteristic of Herder's work, but also and more particularly of the manifold and varying ways in which it came to expression throughout the sacred records of the Old and New Testaments. Then there were his great contemporaries: Eduard Meyer and Leopold von Ranke, the historians; Heinrich Zimmern, the Assyriologist; Adolf Erman, the Egyptologist; and perhaps most important of all Eduard Norden, whose *Antike Kunstprosa* (1898) and *Agnostos Theos* (1913) anticipated Gunkel's own work in its recognition of the categories of style and their application to the NT records. Mention must also be made of his intimate friend and associate, Hugo Gressmann, who in his detailed studies of the Mosaic traditions pursued much the same methods as Gunkel,[2] and, more significantly, produced two monumental volumes on *Altorientalische Texte und Bilder* (1909[1], 1927[2]), surpassed today only by the companion volumes of James B. Pritchard (1950; 1954). Gunkel possessed for his time an extraordinary knowledge of the other literatures of the ancient Near East, and availed himself of their forms and types, their modes of discourse, and their rhetorical features in his delineation and elucidation of the biblical

---

* The Presidential Address delivered at the annual meeting of the Society of Biblical Literature on December 18, 1968, at the University of California, Berkeley, California.

[1] W. Baumgartner, "Zum 100 Geburtstag von Hermann Gunkel," *Supplements to VetT*, 1962, pp. 1–18.

[2] *Mose und seine Zeit* (1913).

---

texts. What is more — and this is a matter of some consequence — he had profound psychological insight, influenced to a considerable degree by W. Wundt's *Völkerpsychologie*, which stood him in good stead as he sought to portray the cast and temper of the minds of the biblical narrators and poets, but also of the ordinary Israelite to whom their words were addressed. It is not too much to say that Gunkel has never been excelled in his ability to portray the spirit which animated the biblical writers, and he did not hesitate either in his lectures or in his seminars to draw upon the events of contemporary history or the experiences of the common man to explicate the interior meaning of a pericope.

One need not labor the benefits and merits of form-critical methodology. It is well to be reminded, however, not only of its distinctive features, but also of the many important contributions in monograph, commentary, and theology, in order that we may the better assess its rôle in contemporary biblical research. Professor Albright, writing in 1940, remarked that "the student of the ancient Near East finds that the methods of Norden and Gunkel are not only applicable, but are the only ones that can be applied."[3] The first and most obvious achievement of *Gattungsforschung* is that it supplied a much-needed corrective to literary and historical criticism. In the light of recent developments, it is important to recall that Gunkel never repudiated this method, as his commentary on the Book of Genesis demonstrates, but rather averred that it was insufficient for answering the most pressing and natural queries of the reader. It was unable, for one thing, to compose a literary history of Israel because the data requisite for such a task were either wanting or, at best, meager. Again, it isolated Israel too sharply from its ethnic and cultural environment as it was reflected in the literary monuments of the peoples of the Near East. Further, the delineation of Israel's faith which emerged from the regnant historico-critical methodology was too simply construed and too unilinearly conceived. Not least of all, its exegesis and hermeneutics failed to penetrate deeply into the relevant texts. The second advantage of the form-critical methodology was that it addressed itself to the question of the literary genre represented by a pericope. In his programmatic essay on the literature of Israel in the second volume of Paul Hinneberg's *Die Kultur der Gegenwart* Gunkel provided an admirable sketch of the numerous literary types represented in the OT, and many of the contributions to the first and second editions of *Die Religion in die Geschichte und Gegenwart* bore the stamp and impress of his critical methodology. It is here where his influence has been greatest and most salutary because the student must know what kind of literature it is that he is reading, to what literary category it belongs, and what its characteristic features are. The third merit of the method is its concern to discover

---

[3] *From the Stone Age to Christianity*, p. 44.

the function that the literary genre was designed to serve in the life of the community or of the individual, to learn how it was employed and on what occasions, and to implement it, so far as possible, into its precise social or cultural milieu. Of special importance, especially in the light of later developments in OT scholarship, was its stress upon the oral provenance of the original genres in Israel, and beyond Israel, among the other peoples of the Near East. Finally, related to our foregoing discussion, is the comparison of the literary types with other exemplars within the OT and then, significantly, with representatives of the same type in the cognate literatures. Such an enterprise in comparison releases the Scriptures from the bondage to parochialism.

The reflections of form-critical methodology are to be discerned all along the horizons of OT studies since the turn of the century, although it must be added that it has also been consistently ignored by substantial segments of OT scholarship. Thus R. H. Pfeiffer in his *magnum opus* on the *Introduction to the Old Testament* (1941) scarcely gives it a passing nod, in sharp contrast to the introductions of Otto Eissfeldt (1934[1]; Engl. transl. 1965), George Fohrer (1965; Engl. transl. 1968), Aage Bentzen (1948), and Artur Weiser (1948; Engl. transl. 1961), all of whom devote a large part of their works to the subject. In many commentaries, too, the literary types and forms are seldom mentioned. On the other hand, there have been many commentaries, such as those in the *Biblischer Kommentar* series, where they are discussed at some length. Equally significant is the important rôle that form criticism has played in hermeneutics. In theology, too, it has influenced not only the form and structure of the exposition, but also the understanding of the nature of biblical theology, as in the work of Gerhard von Rad, which is based upon form-critical presuppositions. Many works have been devoted to detailed studies of the particular literary genres, such as Israelite law,[4] the lament and dirge,[5] historical narrative,[6] the various types of Hebrew prophecy,[7] and wisdom.[8] In quite a different fashion, the method is

---

[4] G. von Rad, *Deuteronomium-Studien* (1948; Engl. transl. 1953); A. Alt, *Die Ursprünge des israelitischen Rechts* in *Kleine Schriften zur Geschichte des Volkes Israel*, I (1959), pp. 278–332; Engl. transl. in *Essays on Old Testament History and Religion* (1966), pp. 79–132; Karlheinz Rabast, *Das apodiktische Recht im Deuteronomium und im Heiligkeitsgesetz* (1949).

[5] Hedwig Jahnow, *Das hebräische Leichenlied im Rahmen der Völkerdichtung*, BZAW, 36 (1923).

[6] R. A. Carlson, *David, the Chosen King* (1964).

[7] J. Lindblom, *Die literarische Gattung der prophetischen Literatur* (1924); and *Prophecy in Ancient Israel* (1962); C. Westermann, *Grundformen prophetischer Rede* (1960), Engl. transl., *Basic Forms of Prophetic Speech* (1967).

[8] W. Baumgartner, *Israelitische und altorientalische Weisheit* (1933); J. Fichtner, "Die altorientalische Weisheit in ihrer israelitisch-jüdischen Ausprägung," BZAW, 62 (1933); J. Hempel, *Die althebräische Literatur und ihr hellenistisch-jüdisches Nachleben* (1930).

reflected in recent studies of the covenant formulations,[9] the covenantal lawsuits,[10] and the covenant curses.[11]

Now, having attempted to do justice to the substantial gains made by the study of literary types, I should like to point to what seem to me to be some of its inadequacies, its occasional exaggerations, and especially its tendency to be too exclusive in its application of the method. In these reservations I do not stand alone, for signs are not wanting, both here and abroad, of discontent with the prevailing state of affairs, of a sense that the method has outrun its course. Thus its most thoroughgoing exponent, H. G. Reventlow, in a recent study of Psalm 8, comments: "One gets the impression that a definite method, precisely because it has demonstrated itself to be so uncommonly fruitful, has arrived at its limits."[12] It would be unfortunate if this were taken to mean that we have done with form criticism or that we should forfeit its manifest contributions to an understanding of the Scriptures. To be sure there are clamant voices being raised today against the methodology, and we are told that it is founded on an illusion, that it is too much influenced by classical and Germanic philology and therefore alien to the Semitic literary consciousness, and that it must be regarded as an aberration in the history of biblical scholarship.[13] If we are faced with such a stark either-or, my allegiance is completely on the side of the form critics, among whom, in any case, I should wish to be counted. Such criticisms as I now propose to make do not imply a rejection so much as an appeal to venture beyond the confines of form criticism into an inquiry into other literary features which are all too frequently ignored today. The first of these is the one that is most frequently launched against the method. The basic contention of Gunkel is that the ancient men of Israel, like their Near Eastern neighbors, were influenced in their speech and their literary compositions by convention and custom. We therefore encounter in a particular genre or *Gattung* the same structural forms, the same terminology and style, and the same *Sitz im Leben*.

---

[9] V. Kurošec, *Hethitische Staatsverträge* in *Leipziger rechtswissenschaftliche Studien* (1931); G. E. Mendenhall, *Law and Covenant in Israel and the Ancient Near East* (1955); K. Baltzer, *Das Bundesformular. Wissenschaftliche Monographien zum alten Testament* (1960); Dennis J. McCarthy, *Treaty and Covenant, Analecta Biblica*, 21 (1963).

[10] H. B. Huffmon, "The Covenant Lawsuit in the Prophets," *JBL*, 78 (1959), pp. 285–95; G. E. Wright, "The Lawsuit of God: a Form-Critical Study of Deuteronomy 32," in *Israel's Prophetic Heritage* (1962), pp. 26–67); Julien Harvey, S.J., "Le 'Ribpattern,' requisitoire prophetique sur le rupture de l'alliance," *Biblica*, 45 (1962), pp. 172–96.

[11] Delbert R. Hillers, Treaty Curses and the Old Testament Prophets, in *Biblica et Orientalia*, 16 (1964); H. J. Franken, "The vassal-treaties of Esarhaddon and the dating of Deuteronomy," *Oudtestamentische Studiën*, 14 (1965), pp. 122–54.

[12] H. G. Reventlow, "Der Psalm 8" in *Poetica: Zeitschrift für Sprach- und Literatur-Wissenschaft*, I, 1967, pp. 304–32.

[13] Meir Weiss, "Wege der neuen Dichtungswissenschaft in ihrer Anwendung auf die Psalmenforschung," *Biblica*, 42 (1961), pp. 255–302.

Surely this cannot be gainsaid. But there has been a proclivity among scholars in recent years to lay such stress upon the typical and representative that the individual, personal, and unique features of the particular pericope are all but lost to view. It is true, as Klaus Koch says in his book, *Was ist Formgeschichte?* (1964), that the criticism has force more for the prophetic books than for the laws and wisdom utterances; and I should add for the hymns and laments of the Psalter too, as a study of *Die Einleitung in die Psalmen* by Gunkel-Begrich will plainly show, although the formulations exhibit diversity and versatility here too. Let me attempt to illustrate my point. In the first major section of the Book of Jeremiah (2 1–4 4*) we have an impressive sequence of literary units of essentially the same *Gattung*, i. e., the *rib* or lawsuit or legal proceeding, and the *Sitz im Leben* is the court of law. Yet the literary formulation of these pericopes shows great variety, and very few of them are in any way a complete reproduction of the lawsuit as it was actually carried on at the gate of the city.[14] What we have here, for the most part, are excerpts or extracts, each complete in itself, to be sure, but refashioned into the conventional structures of metrical verse and animated by profuse images. Only the first (2 1–13) and final pericopes (3 1–4 4*) are preserved with any degree of completeness. But what is more, precisely because the forms and styles are so diverse and are composed with such consummate skill, it is clear that we are dealing with imitations of a *Gattung*. Even when we compare such well-known exemplars of the type as Deut 32 and Mic 6 1–8, the stylistic and rhetorical differences outweigh the similarities. The conventional elements of the lawsuit genre are certainly present, and their recognition is basic to an understanding of the passage; but this is only the beginning of the story. To state our criticism in another way, form criticism by its very nature is bound to generalize because it is concerned with what is common to all the representatives of a genre, and therefore applies an external measure to the individual pericopes.[15] It does not focus sufficient attention upon what is unique and unrepeatable, upon the particularity of the formulation. Moreover, form and content are inextricably related. They form an integral whole. The two are one. Exclusive attention to the *Gattung* may actually obscure the thought and intention of the writer or speaker. The passage must be read and heard precisely as it is spoken. It is the creative synthesis of the particular formulation of the pericope with the content that makes it the distinctive composition that it is.

Another objection that has often been made of the criticism of literary types is its aversion to biographical or psychological interpretations and its resistance to historical commentary. This is to be explained

[14] Ludwig Köhler, "Justice in the Gate," in *Hebrew Man* (1956), pp. 148–75.
[15] H. G. Reventlow, *op. cit.*, p. 304.

only in part as a natural, even inevitable, consequence of its disregard of literary criticism. One has only to recall the rather extreme stress upon the nature of the prophetic experience of former times. The question is whether the specific text or passage gives any warrant for such ventures. There are cases, to be sure, as with Jeremiah and Ezekiel, where it is difficult to see how one can cavalierly omit psychological commentary of some kind. The call of Jeremiah, for example, is something more than the recitation of a conventional and inherited liturgy within the precincts of the temple,[16] and the so-called confessions of the prophet are more than the repetition and reproduction of fixed stereotypes, despite all the parallels that one may adduce from the OT and the Near Eastern texts for such a position. Perhaps more serious is the skepticism of all attempts to read a pericope in its historical context. The truth is that in a vast number of instances we are indeed left completely in the dark as to the occasion in which the words were spoken, and it is reasonable to assume that it was not of primary interest to the compilers of the traditions. This is notably the case with numerous passages in the prophetic writings. In Jeremiah, for example, more often than not, we are simply left to conjecture. Nevertheless, we have every reason to assume that there were situations which elicited particular utterances, and we are sufficiently informed about the history of the times to make conjecture perfectly legitimate. The prophets do not speak *in abstracto*, but concretely. Their formulations may reflect a cultic provenance as on the occasion of celebration of a national festival, although one must be on his guard against exaggeration here, especially against subsuming too many texts under the rubric of the covenant renewal festival, as in the case of Artur Weiser in his commentaries on Jeremiah and the Book of Psalms, or of the festival of the New Year, as in the case of Sigmund Mowinckel in his *Psalmenstudien*.

The foregoing observations have been designed to call attention to the perils involved in a too exclusive employment of form-critical methods, to warn against extremes in their application, and particularly to stress that there are other features in the literary compositions which lie beyond the province of the *Gattungsforscher*. It is important to emphasize that many scholars have used the method with great skill, sound judgment and proper restraint, and, what is more, have taken account of literary features other than those revealed by the *Gattung*, such as H. W. Wolff's commentary on Hosea in the *Biblischer Kommentar* series. Further, we should recognize that there are numerous texts where the literary genre appears in pure form, and here the exclusive application of form-critical techniques has its justification, although one must be quick to add that even here there are differences in formulation. But there are many other passages where the literary genres are being

---

[16] H. G. Reventlow, *Liturgie und prophetisches Ich bei Jeremia* (1963), pp. 24–77.

imitated, not only among the prophets, but among the historians and lawgivers. Witness, for example, the radical transformation of the early Elohistic laws by the deuteronomists, or, perhaps equally impressively, the appropriation by the prophets of the curse formulae, not only within the OT, but also in the vassal treaties of the Near Eastern peoples.[17] Let me repeat: in numerous contexts old literary types and forms are imitated, and, precisely because they are imitated, they are employed with considerable fluidity, versatility, and, if one may venture the term, artistry. The upshot of this circumstance is that the circumspect scholar will not fail to supplement his form-critical analysis with a careful inspection of the literary unit in its precise and unique formulation. He will not be completely bound by the traditional elements and motifs of the literary genre; his task will not be completed until he has taken full account of the features which lie beyond the spectrum of the genre. If the exemplars of the *Gattung* were all identical in their formulations, the OT would be quite a different corpus from what it actually is.

It is often said that the Hebrew writers were not motivated by distinctively literary considerations, that aesthetics lay beyond the domain of their interests, and that a preoccupation with what has come to be described as stylistics only turns the exegete along bypaths unrelated to his central task. It may well be true that aesthetic concerns were never primary with them and that the conception of *belles lettres*, current in ancient Hellas, was alien to the men of Israel. But surely this must not be taken to mean that the OT does not offer us literature of a very high quality. For the more deeply one penetrates the formulations as they have been transmitted to us, the more sensitive he is to the rôles which words and motifs play in a composition; the more he concentrates on the ways in which thought has been woven into linguistic patterns, the better able he is to think the thoughts of the biblical writer after him. And this leads me to formulate a canon which should be obvious to us all: a responsible and proper articulation of the words in their linguistic patterns and in their precise formulations will reveal to us the texture and fabric of the writer's thought, not only what it is that he thinks, but as he thinks it.

The field of stylistics or aesthetic criticism is flourishing today, and the literature that has gathered about it is impressive. Perhaps its foremost representative is Alonzo Schökel, whose work, *Estudios de Poetica Hebraea* (1963), offers us not only an ample bibliography of the important works in the field, but also a detailed discussion of the stylistic phenomenology of the literature of the OT. In this respect it is a better work than Ed. König's *Stilistik, Rhetorik, und Poetik* (1900), an encyclopedic compendium of linguistic and rhetorical phenomena, which nevertheless has the merit of providing many illuminating parallels

[17] See n. 11.

8   JOURNAL OF BIBLICAL LITERATURE

drawn from classical literature and of availing itself of the many stylistic
studies from the earliest times and throughout the nineteenth century.
It would be an error, therefore, to regard the modern school in isolation
from the history of OT scholarship because from the time of Jerome and
before and continuing on with the rabbis and until modern times there
have been those who have occupied themselves with matters of style.
One thinks of Bishop Lowth's influential work, *De sacra poesi Hebraeorum
praelectiones academicae* (1753), and of Herder's work on Hebrew poetry
(1772–83), but also of the many metrical studies, most notably Ed.
Sievers' *Metrische Studien* (I, 1901; II, 1904–05; III, 1907).[18] Noteworthy,
too, are the contributions of Heinrich Ewald, Karl Budde, and Bernhard
Duhm, and more recently and above all of Umberto Cassuto. W. F.
Albright has devoted himself to subjects which are to all intents and
purposes stylistic, as *inter alia* his studies on the Song of Deborah and
his most recent work on *Yahweh and the Gods of Canaan* (1968). His
students too have occupied themselves with stylistic matters, notably
Frank M. Cross and D. N. Freedman in their doctoral dissertation on
Studies in Yahwistic Poetry (1950) and in their studies of biblical poems.[19]
Among the many others who have applied stylistic criteria to their
examination of OT passages are Gerlis Gerleman in his study on the
Song of Deborah,[20] L. Krinetski in his work on the Song of Songs,[21]
Edwin Good in his analysis of the composition of the Book of Hosea,[22]
R. A. Carlson in his scrutiny of the historical narratives of II Samuel
in *David, the Chosen King* (1964), and William L. Holladay in his studies
on Jeremiah.[23] The aspect of all these works which seems to me most
fruitful and rewarding I should prefer to designate by a term other than
stylistics. What I am interested in, above all, is in understanding the
nature of Hebrew literary composition, in exhibiting the structural
patterns that are employed for the fashioning of a literary unit, whether
in poetry or in prose, and in discerning the many and various devices
by which the predications are formulated and ordered into a unified
whole. Such an enterprise I should describe as rhetoric and the methodology as rhetorical criticism.

The first concern of the rhetorical critic, it goes without saying, is to

---

[18] For literature on the subject see Otto Eissfeldt, *The Old Testament: an Introduction* (1967), p. 57.

[19] "A Royal Song of Thanksgiving — II Samuel 22=Psalm 18," *JBL*, 62 (1953),
pp. 15–34; "The Song of Miriam," *JNES*, 14 (1955), pp. 237–50; "The Blessing of
Moses," *JBL*, 67 (1948), pp. 191–210. See also Freedman's "Archaic Forms in Early
Hebrew Poetry," *ZAW*, 72 (1960), pp. 101–07.

[20] "The Song of Deborah in the Light of Stylistics," *VetT*, I (1951), pp. 168–80.

[21] *Das Hohelied* (1964).

[22] "The Composition of Hosea," *Svensk Exegetist Årsbok*, 31 (1966), pp. 211–63.

[23] "Prototype and Copies, a New Approach to the Poetry-Prose Problem in the
Book of Jeremiah," *JBL*, 79 (1960), 351–67; "The Recovery of Poetic Passages of
Jeremiah," *JBL*, 85 (1966), pp. 401–35.

define the limits or scope of the literary unit, to recognize precisely where and how it begins and where and how it ends. He will be quick to observe the formal rhetorical devices that are employed, but more important, the substance or content of these most strategic loci. An examination of the commentaries will reveal that there is great disagreement on this matter, and, what is more, more often than not, no defence is offered for the isolation of the pericope. It has even been averred that it does not really matter. On the contrary, it seems to me to be of considerable consequence, not only for an understanding of how the *Gattung* is being fashioned and designed, but also and more especially for a grasp of the writer's intent and meaning. The literary unit is in any event an indissoluble whole, an artistic and creative unity, a unique formulation. The delimitation of the passage is essential if we are to learn how its major motif, usually stated at the beginning, is resolved. The latter point is of special importance because no rhetorical feature is more conspicuous and frequent among the poets and narrators of ancient Israel than the proclivity to bring the successive predications to their culmination. One must admit that the problem is not always simple because within a single literary unit we may have and often do have several points of climax. But to construe each of these as a conclusion to the poem is to disregard its structure, to resolve it into fragments, and to obscure the relation of the successive strophes to each other. This mistaken procedure has been followed by many scholars, and with unfortunate consequences.

Now the objection that has been most frequently raised to our contention is that too much subjectivity is involved in determining where the accents of the composition really lie. The objection has some force, to be sure, but in matters of this sort there is no substitute for literary sensitivity. Moreover, we need constantly to be reminded that we are dealing with an ancient Semitic literature and that we have at our disposal today abundant parallel materials from the peoples of the ancient Near East for comparison. But we need not dispose of our problem so, for there are many marks of composition which indicate where the finale has been reached. To the first of these I have already alluded, the presence of climactic or ballast lines, which may indeed appear at several junctures within a pericope, but at the close have an emphasis which bears the burden of the entire unit. A second clue for determining the scope of a pericope is to discern the relation of beginning and end, where the opening words are repeated or paraphrased at the close, what is known as ring composition, or, to employ the term already used by Ed. König many years ago and frequently employed by Dahood in his commentary on the Psalter, the *inclusio*. There are scores of illustrations of this phenomenon in all parts of the OT, beginning with the opening literary unit of the Book of Genesis. An impressive illustration is the literary complex of Jer 3 1—4 4, with deletion of the generally recognized prose insertions. While most scholars see more than one unit here, what we actually have before us is a superbly composed and beautifully ordered poem of three series of strophes of three strophes each. The major motif of turning or repentance is sounded in the opening casuistic legal formulation and is followed at once by the indictment:

> If a man sends his wife away,
>   and she goes from him,
> and becomes another man's wife,
>   will she return to him [with the corrected text]?
> Would not that land
>   be utterly polluted?
> But you have played the harlot with many lovers,
>   and would you return to me? (Jer 3 1).

The word שׁוּב appears in diverse syntactical constructions and in diverse stylistic contexts, and always in strategic collocations.[24] The poem has of course been influenced by the lawsuit, but it also contains a confessional lament and comes to a dramatic climax in the final strophe and in the form of the covenant conditional:

> If you do return, O Israel, Yahweh's Word!
>   to me you should return (Jer 4 1a).

The whole poem is an Exhibit A of ancient Hebrew rhetoric, but it could easily be paralleled by numerous other exemplars quite as impressive.

The second major concern of the rhetorical critic is to recognize the structure of a composition and to discern the configuration of its component parts, to delineate the warp and woof out of which the literary fabric is woven, and to note the various rhetorical devices that are employed for marking, on the one hand, the sequence and movement of the pericope, and on the other, the shifts or breaks in the development of the writer's thought. It is our contention that the narrators and poets of ancient Israel and her Near Eastern neighbors were dominated not only by the formal and traditional modes of speech of the literary genres or types, but also by the techniques of narrative and poetic composition. Now the basic and most elemental of the structural features of the poetry of Israel, as of that of the other peoples of the ancient Near East, is the parallelism of its successive cola or stichoi. Our concern here is not with the different types of parallelism — synonymous, complementary, antithetic, or stairlike, etc.— but rather with the diversities of sequence of the several units within the successive cola, or within the successive and related bicola or tricola. It is precisely these diversities which give the poetry its distinctive and artistic character. It is always tantalizing to the translator that so often they cannot be reproduced into English or, for that matter, into the other Western tongues. In recent years much attention has been given to

---

[24] William L. Holladay, *The Root ŠÛBH in the Old Testament* (1958).

the repetitive tricola, which is amply illustrated in Ugaritic poetry.[25] But this repetitive style appears in numerous other types of formulation, and, what is more, is profusely illustrated in our earliest poetic precipitates:

> The kings came, they fought;
>   then fought the kings of Canaan,
> at Taanach, by the waters of Megiddo;
>   they got no spoils of silver.
> From heaven fought the stars,
>   from their courses they fought against Sisera.
> The torrent Kishon swept them away,
>   the onrushing torrent, the torrent Kishon.
> March on, my soul with might (Judg 5 19–21).

Within so small a compass we have two instances of chiasmus, the fourfold repetition of the verb נִלְחָמוּ, the threefold repetition of נַחַל, and a concluding climactic shout. There are numerous cases of anaphora, the repetition of key words or lines at the beginning of successive predications, as in the series of curses in Deut 27 15–26 or of blessings in the following chapter (Deut 28 3–6), or the prophetic oracles of woe (Isa 5 8–22), or the repeated summons to praise (Ps 150), or the lamenting "How long" of Psalm 3. Jeremiah's vision of the return to primeval chaos is a classic instance of anaphora (Jer 4 23–26). In the oracle on the sword against Babylon as Yahweh's hammer and weapon, the line "with you I shatter in pieces" is repeated nine times (Jer 50 35–38). Examples of a different kind are Job's oaths of clearance (Job 31) and Wisdom's autobiography (Prov 8 22–31). These iterative features are much more profuse and elaborate in the ancient Near Eastern texts, but also more stereotyped.[26]

The second structural feature of Israel's poetic compositions is closely related to our foregoing observations concerning parallel structures and is particularly germane to responsible hermeneutical inquiry and exegetical exposition. The bicola or tricola appear in well-defined clusters or groups, which possess their own identity, integrity, and structure. They are most easily recognized in those instances where they close with a refrain, as in the prophetic castigations of Amos 4 6–11 or in Isaiah's stirring poem on the divine fury (9 7–20, 5 25–30) or the personal lament of Pss 42–43 or the song of trust of Psalm 46 in its original form, or, most impressively in the liturgy of thanksgiving of Psalm 107. They

[25] H. L. Ginsberg, "The Rebellion and Death of Ba'lu," *Orientalia*, 5 (1936), pp. 161–98; W. F. Albright, "The Psalm of Habakkuk," *Studies in Old Testament Prophecy*, ed. by H. H. Rowley (1950), pp. 1–18; *idem, Yahweh and the God of Canaan* (1968), pp. 4–27; J. H. Patton, *Canaanite Parallels in the Book of Psalms* (1944), pp. 5–11.
[26] S. N. Kramer, *The Sumerians* (1963), pp. 174 ff., 254, 256, 263; A. Falkenstein and W. von Soden, *Sumerische und Akkadische Hymnen und Gebete*, pp. 59 f., 67 f.; J. B. Pritchard, *ANET*, pp. 385b–86a, 390, 391b–92.

are readily identified, too, in the alphabetic acrostics of Psalms 9–10, 25, and 119 and in the first three chapters of Lamentations. But, as we shall have occasion to observe, there are many other ways to define their limits. In the literatures of the other peoples of the ancient Near East the same structural phenomena are present.[27] But how shall we name such clusters? The most common designation is the *strophe*, but some scholars have raised objections to it because they aver that it is drawn from the models of Greek lyrical verse and that they cannot apply to Semitic poetic forms. It is true that in an earlier period of rhetorical study scholars were too much dominated by Greek prototypes and sought to relate the strophes to each other in a fashion for which there was little warrant in the biblical text. If we must confine our understanding to the Greek conception of a strophe, then it is better not to employ it, and to use the word *stanza* instead. The second objection to the term is that a strophe is to be understood as a metrical unit, i. e., by a consistent metrical scheme. There is also some force in this objection. Many poems do indeed have metrical uniformity, but often this is not the case. Indeed, I should contend that the Hebrew poet frequently avoids metrical consistency. It is precisely the break in the meter that gives the colon or bicolon its designed stress and importance. But we can say with some confidence that strophes have prevailingly consistent meters. My chief defense for employing the word *strophe* is that it has become acclimated to current terminology, not only by biblical scholars, but also by those whose province is Near Eastern literature. By a strophe we mean a series of bicola or tricola with a beginning and ending, possessing unity of thought and structure. The prosody group must coincide with the sense. But there is still another observation to be made which is of the first importance for our understanding of Hebrew poetry. While very many poems have the same number of lines in each strophe, it is by no means necessary that they be of the same length, although in the majority of cases they are indeed so. Where we have variety in the number of lines in successive strophes, a pattern is usually discernible. In any event, the time has not yet passed when scholars resort to the precarious practice of emendation in order to produce regularity. Just as we have outlived the practice of deleting words *metri causa* for the sake of consistency, so it is to be hoped that we refuse to produce strophic uniformity by excision of lines unless there is textual support for the alteration.

Perhaps there is no enterprise more revealing for our understanding of the nature of biblical rhetoric than an intensive scrutiny of the composition of the strophes, the manifold technical devices employed for

---

[27] See A. Falkenstein and W. von Soden, *op. cit.*, for full discussion, especially pp. 37 ff.

their construction, and the stylistic phenomena which give them their unity. Such a study is obviously beyond the province of our present investigation. We may call attention, however, to a number of features which occur with such frequency and in such widely diverse contexts that they may be said to characterize Hebrew and to a considerable extent ancient Near Eastern modes of literary composition. We have already mentioned the refrains which appear at the close of the strophes. There are not a few examples of where they open in the same fashion. Thus the succession of oracles against the nations in Amos 1 3–2 16 are all wrought in essentially the same mold, and the stylistically related sequence of oracles in Ezek 25 3–17 follows precisely the same pattern. Psalm 29 is, of course, a familiar example with its iteration of קוֹל יהוה in five of the seven strophes. In the opening poem of Second Isaiah (40 1–11) the proem comes to a climax in the cry, קְרָאוּ אֵלֶיהָ. This now serves as a key to the structure of the lines that follow: קוֹל קוֹרֵא (3a), קוֹל אֹמֵר קְרָא (6a), and הָרִימִי בַּכֹּחַ קוֹלֵךְ (9b). The poem which follows is a superb specimen of Hebrew literary craft and exhibits the same sense of form by the repetition of key words at the beginning of each strophe, and the succession of interrogatives couched in almost identical fashion reach their climax in the awesome וּרְאוּ מִי־בָרָא אֵלֶּה, which is answered in the final strophe by the words to which all the lines have been pointing:

> Yahweh is an everlasting God,
>   Creator of the ends of the earth (40 28 b).

Perhaps the most convincing argument for the existence of strophes in Hebrew poetry as in the poetry of the other ancient Near Eastern peoples is the presence within a composition of turning points or breaks or shifts, whether of the speaker or the one addressed or of motif and theme. While this feature is common to a number of literary genres, they are especially striking in the personal and communal laments. Psalm 22, which fairly teems with illuminating rhetorical features, will illustrate. We cite the opening lines of each strophe:

> My God, my God, why hast thou abandoned me? (1–2)
> But Thou art holy (3–5)
> But I am a worm and no man (6–8)
> Yet thou art he who took me from my mother's womb (9–11)
> I am poured out like water (14–15)
> Yea, dogs are round about me (16–18)
> But thou, O Yahweh, be not far off (19–21)
> I will tell of thy name to my brethren (22–24)
> From thee comes my praise in the great congregation (25–28)
> Yea to him shall all the proud of the earth bow down (29–31)
>   (emended text. See B. H. *ad loc.*).

Particles play a major rôle in all Hebrew poetry and reveal the rhetorical cast of Semitic literary mentality in a striking way. Chief

among them is the deictic and emphatic particle כִּי, which performs a
vast variety of functions and is susceptible of many different renderings,
above all, perhaps, the function of motivation where it is understood
causally.[28] It is not surprising, therefore, that it should appear in strategic
collocations, such as the beginnings and endings of the strophes. For
the former we may cite Isaiah 34:

> For Yahweh is enraged against all the nations (32 2a)
> For my sword has drunk its fill in the heavens (34 5a)
> For Yahweh has a sacrifice in Bozrah (34 6c)
> For Yahweh has a day of vengeance (34 8a).

The particle appears frequently in the hymns of the Psalter immediately
following the invocation to praise, as in Psalm 95:

> For Yahweh is a great God,
>   and a great King above all gods (95 3),

or later in the same hymn:

> For he is our God,
>   and we are the people of his pasture (95 7).

The motivations also conclude a strophe or poem:

> For Yahweh knows the way of the righteous,
>   but the way of the wicked shall perish (Ps 1 6);

or, as frequently in Jeremiah:

> For I bring evil from the north,
>   and great destruction (Jer. 4 6b);

> For the fierce anger of Yahweh
>   has not turned away from us (Jer 4 8b);

> For their transgressions are many,
>   their apostasies great (Jer 5 6c).

Significantly, in the closing poem of Second Isaiah's eschatological
"drama" (Isa 55) the particle is employed with extraordinary force,
both at the opening and closing bicola of the strophes, and goes far to
explain the impact that the poem has upon the reader. As the poems
open with the threefold use of the particle in the opening strophe, so
they close with a fivefold repetition of the word.

A second particle, frequently associated with כִּי is הִנֵּה or הֵן, the word
which calls for our attention. Characteristically it appears in striking
contexts, either by introducing a poem or strophe or by bringing it to
its culmination. Thus the third and climatic strophe of the long and
well-structured poem of Isa 40 12–31 begins dramatically after the long
series of interrogatives:

> Behold (הֵן), the nations are like a drop from a bucket,
>   and are accounted as dust on the scales;
> Behold, he takes up the isles like fine dust (40 15).

[28] James Muilenburg, "The Linguistic and Rhetorical Usages of the Particle in the
Old Testament," *HUCA*, 32 (1961), pp. 135–60.

The poem which follows is composed of three series of three strophes each, and the climax falls in each case upon the third strophe. The "behold" always appears in crucial or climactic contexts. The judgment of the nations appears at the close of two strophes:

> Behold, you are nothing,
>> and your work is nought;
>> an abomination is he who chooses you (Isa 41 24);
>
> Behold, they are all a delusion
>> their works are nothing;
>> their molten images are empty wind (Isa 41 29).

It is at this point that the Servant of Yahweh is now introduced:

> Behold my servant, whom I uphold,
>> my chosen, in whom I delight;
> I have put my spirit upon him,
>> he will bring forth justice to the nations (42 1).

The last of the so-called Servant poems begins in the same way:

> Behold, my servant yet shall prosper,
>> he shall be exalted and lifted up,
>> and shall be very high (Isa 52 13).

The particle may appear in series, as in Isa 65 13–14:

> Therefore thus says Yahweh God:
> "Behold, my servants shall eat,
>> but you shall be hungry;
> behold, my servants shall drink,
>> but you shall be thirsty;
> behold, my servants shall rejoice,
>> but you shall be put to shame;
> behold, my servants shall sing for gladness of heart,
>> but you shall cry out for pain of heart,
>> and shall wail for anguish of spirit.

Frequently it brings the strophe or poem to a climax:

> Behold your God!
> Behold, the Lord Yahweh comes with might,
>> and his arm rules for him;
> behold, his reward is with him,
>> and his recompense before him (Isa 40 9–10).

The particle appears in many other modes and guises in the OT, as, for example, in introducing oracles of judgment where הִנְנִי is followed by the active participle.[29]

There are other particles which would reward our study, among which we may mention לָכֵן, which characteristically introduces the threat or verdict in the oracles of judgment, or לָמָה, with which the laments so frequently open, or וְעַתָּה, so central to the covenant formulations, but perpetuated in the prophets and singers of Israel.

---

[29] Paul Humbert, *Opuscules d'un Hebräisant* (1958), pp. 54–59.

Numerous other stylistic features delineate the form and structure of the strophes. Most frequent are the vocatives addressed to God in the invocations. Take the opening cola of the successive strophes in Psalm 7:

> O Yahweh, my God, in thee do I take refuge. 7 1a (Heb. 2a);
> O Yahweh, my God, if I have done this 7 3a (Heb. 4a);
> Arise, O Yahweh, in thy anger 7 6a (Heb. 7a).

Or the inclusio of Psalm 8:

> O Yahweh, my Lord,
> how spacious is thy name in all the earth (8 1, 9 [Heb. 2, 10]);

or the entrance liturgy:

> O Yahweh, who shall sojourn in thy tent?
> Who shall dwell on thy holy hill? (15 1).[30]

Rhetorical questions of different kinds and in different literary types appear in strategic collocations. As we should expect, they are quite characteristic in the legal encounters:

> What wrong was it then that your fathers found in me
> that they went far from me? (Jer 2 5);
>
> Why do you bring a suit against me? (Jer 2 29).[31]

The questions often provide the climatic line of the strophe:

> How long must I see the standard,
> and hear the sound of the trumpet? (Jer 4 21),

or in the moving outcry of the prophet:

> Is there no balm in Gilead?
> Is there no physician there?
> Why then has the health of the daughter, my people, not been restored? (Jer 8 22).

Especially striking is the threefold repetition of a keyword within a single strophe. This phenomenon is so frequent and the words are so strategically placed that it cannot be said to be fortuitous. We have observed it in connection with our study of the particles. We select an example almost at random, though it is lost in translation:

> קוּמִי אוֹרִי כִּי בָא אוֹרֵךְ   וּכְבוֹד יְהוָה עָלַיִךְ זָרָח:
> כִּי־הִנֵּה הַחֹשֶׁךְ יְכַסֶּה־אֶרֶץ וַעֲרָפֶל לְאֻמִּים
> וְעָלַיִךְ יִזְרַח יְהוָה   וּכְבוֹדוֹ עָלַיִךְ יֵרָאֶה:
> וְהָלְכוּ גוֹיִם לְאוֹרֵךְ   וּמְלָכִים לְנֹגַהּ זַרְחֵךְ:   (Isa 60 1–3).

---

[30] Cf. also Pss 3 1 (Heb. 2), 6 1 (Heb. 2), 22 1 (Heb. 2), 25 1, 26 1, 28 1, 31 1 (Heb. 2), 43 1, 51 1 (Heb. 2).

[31] Cf. also Pss 2 1, 10 1, 15 1, 35 17, 49 5 (Heb. 6), 52 1 (Heb. 2), 58 1 (Heb. 2), 60 9 (Heb. 11), 62 3 (Heb. 4); Jer 5 7a, also Isa 10 11, 14 32, 42 1–4; Jer 5 21d, 9 9.

Amos' oracle on the Day of Yahweh is another good example (Amos 5 18–20). If we may accept the present masoretic text of Isa 55 1, it is not without significance that the prophet's final poem opens with the urgent invitations, which is all the more impressive because of its assonance:

> Ho, every one who thirsts,
>   come (לְכוּ) to the waters;
> and he who has no money
>   come (לְכוּ) buy and eat!
> Come (לְכוּ), buy wine and milk
>   without money and without price (Isa 55 1).[32]

Repetition serves many and diverse functions in the literary compositions of ancient Israel, whether in the construction of parallel cola or parallel bicola, or in the structure of the strophes, or in the fashioning and ordering of the complete literary units. The repeated words or lines do not appear haphazardly or fortuitously, but rather in rhetorically significant collocations. This phenomenon is to be explained perhaps in many instances by the originally spoken provenance of the passage, or by its employment in cultic celebrations, or, indeed, by the speaking mentality of the ancient Israelite. It served as an effective mnemonic device. It is the key word which may often guide us in our isolation of a literary unit, which gives to it its unity and focus, which helps us to articulate the structure of the composition, and to discern the pattern or texture into which the words are woven. It is noteworthy that repetitions are most abundant in crucial contexts. Perhaps the most familiar of these is the call of Abram (Gen 12 1–3) which opens the Yahwist patriarchal narratives. As Ephraim Speiser has seen, it is a well-constructed poem of three diminutive strophes of three lines each. But what is notable here is the fivefold repetition of the word *bless* in differing syntactical forms, which underscores the power of the blessing that is to attend not only Abram, but all the nations of the earth. It is not surprising, therefore, that the motif should recur again and again and always in decisive places. An example of another kind is the much controverted verse at the beginning of the book of Hosea:

> לֵךְ קַח־לְךָ אֵשֶׁת זְנוּנִים   וְיַלְדֵי זְנוּנִים
>
> כִּי־זָנֹה תִזְנֶה הָאָרֶץ   מֵאַחֲרֵי יהוה   (1 2).

In the following chapter the motif of the new covenant reaches its climax in another repetitive text:

> And I will betroth you to me for ever; I will betroth you to me in righteousness and in justice, in steadfast love, and in compassion. I will betroth you to me in faithfulness; and you shall know that I am Yahweh (Hos 2 19–20 [Heb 21–22]).

[32] Cf. Judg 5 19–21; Pss 25 1–3, 34 1–3 (Heb. 2–4), 7–10 (Heb. 8–11), 121 7–8, 139 11–12 (Heb. 12–13), 145 1–3; Isa 55 6–9; Jer 5 15c–17.

18   JOURNAL OF BIBLICAL LITERATURE

The structure of the first chapter of Ezekiel is determined by the recurring motif of the *demuth* at the beginning of each of its major divisions, and in the finale reaches its climax by the dramatic threefold repetition:

> And above the firmament over their heads was the likeness of a throne, in appearance like sapphire; and seated above the likeness of a throne was a likeness as it were in human form (Ezek 1 26).

Persistent and painstaking attention to the modes of Hebrew literary composition will reveal that the pericopes exhibit linguistic patterns, word formations ordered or arranged in particular ways, verbal sequences which move in fixed structures from beginning to end. It is clear that they have been skillfully wrought in many different ways, often with consummate skill and artistry. It is also apparent that they have been influenced by conventional rhetorical practices. This inevitably poses a question for which I have no answer. From whom did the poets and prophets of Israel acquire their styles and literary habits? Surely they cannot be explained by spontaneity. They must have been learned and mastered from some source, but what this source was is a perplexing problem. Are we to look to the schools of wisdom for an explanation? It is difficult to say. But there is another question into which we have not gone. How are we to explain the numerous and extraordinary literary affinities of the *Gattungen* or genres and other stylistic formulations of Israel's literature with the literatures of the other peoples of the Near East? Were the prophets and poets familiar with these records? If not, how are we to explain them? If so, in what ways?

But there are other latitudes which we have not undertaken to explore. T. S. Eliot once described a poem as a raid on the inarticulate. In the Scriptures we have a literary deposit of those who were confronted by the ultimate questions of life and human destiny, of God and man, of the past out of which the historical people has come and of the future into which it is moving, a speech which seeks to be commensurate with man's ultimate concerns, a raid on the ultimate, if you will.

Finally, it has not been our intent to offer an alternative to form criticism or a substitute for it, but rather to call attention to an approach of eminent lineage which may supplement our form-critical studies. For after all has been said and done about the forms and types of biblical speech, there still remains the task of discerning the actuality of the particular text, and it is with this, we aver, that we must reckon, as best we can, for it is this concreteness which marks the material with which we are dealing. In a word, then, we affirm the necessity of form criticism, but we also lay claim to the legitimacy of what we have called rhetorical criticism. Form criticism and beyond.

LITERARY FORM IN THE FOURTH GOSPEL

JAMES MUILENBURG
MOUNT HOLYOKE COLLEGE

IT is over fifty years ago now since Matthew Arnold wrote about the Fourth Gospel in these words: "It may be said with certainty that a literary artist capable of inventing the most striking sayings of Jesus to Nicodemus or to the woman of Samaria would have made his composition as a whole more flawless, more artistically perfect than the Fourth Gospel actually is. Judged from an artist's point of view, it has blots and awkwardnesses which a master of imaginative invention would never have suffered his work to exhibit."[1] And elsewhere he observes that the narrative of the gospel "might well be thought but a matter of infinitely little care and attention ..., a mere slight framework, in which to set the doctrine and discourses of Jesus."[2] Much water has flowed under the bridge since Arnold's day; yet it cannot be said that the difficulties of the literary composition of the Fourth Gospel have been resolved. J. Estlin Carpenter[3] confesses that he has no solution of the mystery of its composition, and Percy Gardner[4] ends his chapter on the gospel as biography by declaring the gospel a tangled skein. On the other hand, F. R. Montgomery Hitchcock devotes one chapter in his book, *A Fresh Study of the Fourth Gospel* (1911) to the

[1] Quoted by James Moffatt, *Introduction to the Literature of the New Testament*, 1923, p. 563, Note.

[2] *God and the Bible*, Macmillan, 1883, p. 231.

[3] *The Johannine Writings*, 1927, p. 192. See p. 225f. where he proposes his theory of communal authorship.

[4] *The Ephesian Gospel*, 1916, p. 122.

dramatic development of the gospel and another to its artistic structure.[5] The climax of the drama is approached by scenes of rising interest; there is development of plot, character, and purpose.[6] E. F. Scott is also impressed by the numerous marks of a deliberate artistic plan; the gospel unfolds itself, he says, "with something of the ordered majesty of a Greek tragedy."[7] And Lord Charnwood can even go so far as to declare the gospel "in a very high degree a compact and well-ordered whole, of which every part falls in with a design thought out beforehand"[8] while Kenneth Saunders compares the structure of the gospel to that of the early Christian basilica.[9]

But the formal literary manner of the writer of the Fourth Gospel is even more apparent in his lesser units. Rendel Harris,[10] Loisy,[11] Burney,[12] Bacon,[13] and a score of others have commented upon the structure of the Prologue. Both as a unit in itself and as a preface to the gospel as a whole, it illustrates the literary quality and form of the gospel. Many passages easily resolve themselves into the acts and scenes of a drama with astonishingly little change of text.[14] The stereotyped form of Fourth Gospel controversy has been frequently observed. Lothar Schmid has demonstrated the feeling for form in the conversation with the Samaritan woman.[15] Hans Win-

[5] Chapters V and VI, pp. 102—142.

[6] Hitchcock, *A Fresh Study of the Fourth Gospel*, p. 102.

[7] *The Fourth Gospel*, 2. ed., 1908, p. 16. Compare with this the remarks of F. R. Montgomery Hitchcock, "The Dramatic Development of the Fourth Gospel," *Expositor*, Series 7, vol. IV, 1907, pp. 266—279.

[8] *According to Saint John*, 1926, p. 62.

[9] *The Gospel for Asia*, 1928, p. 101f.

[10] *The Origin of the Prologue to St. John's Gospel*, 1917.

[11] *Le quatrième évangile*, 1921. The original form of the Prologue was "une sorte d'ode au Verbe incarné, logiquement construite, exactement rythmée" p. 46.

[12] *The Aramaic Origin of the Fourth Gospel*, 1922.

[13] "Punctuation, Translation, Interpretation," *Journal of Religion*, 1924, pp. 243—260.

[14] See, e. g., F. R. Montgomery Hitchcock, *A Fresh Study of the Fourth Gospel*, Chap. VI; J. M. Thompson, "An Experiment in Translation," *Expositor*, Series 8, vol. XVI, 1918, pp. 117—122.

[15] "Die Komposition der Samaria-Szene," *ZNTW*, 1929, vol. 28, pp. 148 to 158.

disch, in his contribution to the Gunkel *Festschrift*,[16] discerns a
literary plan in the gospel, but the plan embodies a great variety
of literary materials. Yet the same definite structure is to be observed within each pericope or witness discourse or detailed dramatic narrative as the case may be. He presents the dramatic interest of the writer by dialogue, stage directions, and division into acts
and scenes.

There are few characteristics that are so apparent as the literary,
yet it is important to know which characteristics are significant.
The value of any literary undertaking will depend largely upon
whether the right questions are raised or not. How does the writer
begin and end his literary units? How does he develop his theme?
How does he articulate his materials? Is there unusual word order?
What is the relation of words, phrases, and clauses to each other,
and to the whole? We shall naturally be sensitive to those essentials
of composition which we were taught to observe in our preparatory
school days: unity, coherence, emphasis, and proportion. It is a
primary canon of ours that form and content are intimately inter-
related. And in the case of the Fourth Gospel, where the dramatic
element obtrudes itself so obviously, one will analyze his materials
according to setting, inciting impulse, antagonistic forces, presence
of obstacles, and the resolution of obstacles and conflicts. Analysis
there must be, minute and painstaking, but the chief end should
be the perception of the literary unity in which one gains a sense
of form, a central purpose, and, if possible, the occasion which inspired the narrative. The more obvious are the signs of literary
composition and art, the more important do such criteria become.

The passage selected for our study is the group of Baptist narratives immediately following the Prologue: first, because they begin
the gospel proper, and secondly, because attention is usually directed to the longer narratives where the mode of composition is more
apparent. The following analysis helps to visualize the structure:

John 1 19–28

A. (19) And *this is the witness of John* (καὶ αὕτη ἐστὶν ἡ μαρτυρία τοῦ
Ἰωάννου) when the Jews *sent* (ἀπέστειλαν) unto him from Jerusalem priests
and Levites *to ask him, Who art thou?* (σὺ τίς εἶ;)

---

[16] Der johanneische Erzählungsstil, *Eucharisterion*, Part II, pp. 174—213.

a. (20) And he confessed and denied not, and he confessed: "*I am not the Christ.*"

(21) And they asked him, "What then? Art thou Elijah?"
And he said, "*I am not.*"
                "Art thou the prophet?"
And he answered: "*No.*"

b. (22) They said therefore unto him "*Who art thou* (τίς εἶ) that we may give answer to them that sent us. What sayest thou of thyself?"

Conclusion: (23) "I am the voice of one crying in the wilderness,
                Make straight the way of the Lord,
                as said Isaiah the prophet."

(24) And they had been sent (ἀπεσταλμένοι) of the Pharisees (cf. 19).

B. (25) And *they asked him* (cf. 19), and said unto him, "Why then baptizest thou, if thou art not the Christ, neither Elijah, neither the prophet?"

Conclusion: (26) "I baptize in water. In the midst of you standeth *one whom ye know not* (ὃν ὑμεῖς οὐκ οἴδατε), (27) even he that cometh after me, the latchet of whose shoe I am not worthy to unloosen."

(28) These things were done in Bethany beyond the Jordan where John was baptizing.

The gospel proper begins with a demonstrative formula: "And this is the witness of John."[17] It serves as a title for the four following narratives, for it is John's witness that dominates the whole. Such formulae abound throughout the gospel.[18] John's is pre-eminently a demonstrative gospel. It seeks to prove and convince (cf. 20 30—31). It is centered about the conception of μαρτυρία. The controversies embody contemporary polemic and deal much with testimony. There are seven great self-asseverations of Jesus, all of them with the emphasis upon ἐγώ. The almost invariable result of Jesus' work is to inspire belief. There are frequent side-comments by the writer in order to indicate the true sense and correct interpretation of a word or statement.

The key to the narrative lies in the words addressed to John, "Who art thou?" This must be answered before the more central

---

[17] Observe the relation of these words to vv. 6—8, 15 of the Prologue.

[18] Note, for example, 1 15, 30, 33, 34; 2 11; 3 8d, 16, 19; 4 19, 29, 42, 54; 6 39, 40, 50, 58; 7 40, 41, 46; 14 25; 15 11, 12, 17; 16 1, 4a, 4b, 25, 33; 17 1, 3, 13; 18 1; *etc.*

question "Who is Jesus?" can be faced.[19] The figure of the Baptist forms an obstacle which it is the purpose of this section to remove. After the threefold denial, the question is raised again, this time more urgently and emphatically. The question is repeated, it is paraphrased, and the reason for the request is given. Such repetitions are numerous, but they are usually motivated.[20] The effect is dramatic: "Who is he *then*, this leader with a tremendous following, if he is not the Messiah so many think him to be?" The answer is an accommodation to Synoptic tradition, but the notable difference illustrates the literary quality of John. In the Synoptic gospels the quotation is given as such from Isaiah. In John it is put into the mouth of the Baptist himself and in the first person. The Synoptists give the quotation as part of a straightforward account. The emphasis in Mark and Luke is upon the coming of John; in Matthew, to be sure, the Baptist is directly equated with the voice. In the Fourth Gospel not only the setting and form are dramatic; the emphasis seems to have shifted from "making the paths straight to "the voice crying in the wilderness."[21] **B** (vv. 22—23) also states its question directly, "Why do you baptize then?" That this was another question in contemporary polemic we need have no doubt. And the answer to the question, evasive as it may seem, is "I baptize in water" without any reference to the greater baptism that is to follow.

The analysis has made clear the form of the pericope. It is set in a very clearly-marked framework with an introductory demonstrative formula as a possible title for all four sections, an introduction to each division, and a conclusion. There are two primary divisions, **A** (19—24) and **B** (25—28). Each has its own important question stated at the beginning, trebly important when read in the light of its historical context, and each its significant answer. Within each division we observe the same sense for form. In **A** (19—24)

[19] This is the question which the Fourth Gospel seeks to answer. Cf. e. g. 4 10a; 8 25, *etc.*

[20] The explanation of Johannine repetitions is both literary and psychological. For opposite view, see Stange, *Die Eigenart der johanneischen Produktion*, Dresden, 1915.

[21] Thus enshrouding John in mystery and indefiniteness, which are gradually dispelled in the succeeding sentences not by emergence of a clear figure but by his complete disappearance.

there is the threefold denial, each time with telling and increasing
brevity[22] and the repetition of the question "Who art thou" just
before the dramatic answer. The concluding sentence in the section
serves more to separate the two sections than to unite them. That
the author conceives them as part of the same section, however, is
clear from the contents of **B** (25—28), from the chronological phrases
at the beginning of the following section, and from the similar character of many Johannine literary units.[23] The question in **B** (25—28)
recapitulates the substance of **A** (19—24) but presses the question
further. The answer is most dramatic, and gains in significance when
one compares it with the Synoptic parallels. There the statement
"I baptize in water" is everywhere paralleled by "he shall baptize
you in the Holy Spirit." Here the expected contrast is left incomplete, and in disagreement with the Synoptists John refers to the
one whom ye know not who is soon to come and is even now stand-
ing in their midst ($\mu\acute{\epsilon}\sigma os$ $\acute{v}\mu\hat{\omega}\nu$ $\sigma\tau\acute{\eta}\kappa\epsilon\iota$). This device of dramatic
anticipation is not uncommon in the Fourth Gospel. The reply
creates an atmosphere of suspense and thus prepares the way for
what is to follow. Its vagueness lends a feeling of mystery. We are
now face to face with the gospel's one question: WHO IS HE?
Like the theme of a symphony, it recurs again and again with infinite variations: now quiet and pastoral, now mystic and passionate, now grand and sublime, now warm and intimate. After the
reply the second episode is closed, but the writer completes his
framework by adding a characteristic stereotyped comment.

Two or three further stylistic elements may be noted. First of
all, the solemnity of v. 20. This solemn pronouncement "he confessed and denied not, but confessed"[24] at the beginning of the
gospel attempts to express the writer's conviction of the significance

[22] Cf. the similar style of 9 8—9.

[23] Windisch makes **B** (vv. 25—28) a separate *Gesprächsfolge*.

[24] This type of repetition is included in Stange's list of 'negierte Anti-
thesen' or 'doppelte Umkehrungen' ("eine Aussage wird unmittelbar her-
nach dadurch wiederholt, daß der zum Hauptbegriff kontradiktorische Be-
griff negiert wird"). N.B. 1 3; 2 24—25a; 3 16b, 17, 16—17; 4 14; 5 19, 24;
7 18; 8 12b and c; 10 18; 12 47b, 49; 14 10; 15 4 and 5b, 15, 16, 19b; 16 13,
25—29; 17 9b; 18 20. Cf. also 1 33a—31; 6 51a—48; 7 8b—6a; 10 9—7; 13 3b—1a;
15 5—1; 16 18—17. Numerous other similar examples might be cited. Cf. e. g.
Stange's list (II) of 'repetitions for clearness.'

of what he is about to testify. Again the section is for the most part in direct discourse. Indeed, so dramatic is the whole that one should have no difficulty in dramatizing it.[25] The plot begins *in medias res*. We ask in vain concerning the history preceding the coming of the embassy, and the response of the Jews to the outspoken "confession." Finally, it may be observed that every characteristic of the pericope finds frequent parallels throughout the entire gospel.

The analysis of the second pericope of the Baptist's witness may be represented as follows:[26]

John 1 29—34

A. (29) *On the morrow* he *seeth* ($\beta\lambda\epsilon\pi\epsilon\iota$) Jesus *coming* (cf. v. 27) unto him, and saith: "*Behold* ($\mathring{\iota}\delta\epsilon$) the Lamb of God, that taketh away the sin of the world."
(30) "This is he of whom ($o\mathring{v}\tau\acute{o}s$ $\mathring{\epsilon}\sigma\tau\iota\nu$ $\mathring{v}\pi\grave{\epsilon}\rho$ $o\mathring{v}$) I said, 'After me *cometh* a man who is become before me: for he was before me.' (31) *And I knew him not*; but that he should be made manifest to Israel;
Conclusion: "for this cause ($\delta\iota\grave{a}$ $\tauo\mathring{v}\tauo$) *came* I baptizing in water."

B. (32) And John *bare witness* ($\mathring{\epsilon}\mu\alpha\rho\tau\acute{v}\rho\eta\sigma\epsilon\nu$) saying, "*I have beheld* ($\tau\epsilon\theta\acute{\epsilon}\alpha\mu\alpha\iota$) the Spirit descending as a dove out of heaven; and it abode upon him. (33) *And I knew him not*; but he that sent me to baptize in water, he said unto me, 'Upon whomsoever thou shalt see the Spirit descending, and abiding upon him, the same is he that baptizeth in the Holy Spirit'."
Conclusion: (34) "And *I have seen* ($\mathring{\epsilon}\acute{\omega}\rho\alpha\kappa\alpha$) and have borne witness ($\mu\epsilon\mu\alpha\rho\tau\acute{v}\rho\eta\kappa\alpha$) that this is the Son of God" ($\mathring{o}\tau\iota$ $o\mathring{v}\tau\acute{o}s$ $\mathring{\epsilon}\sigma\tau\iota\nu$ $\mathring{o}$ $\upsilon\mathring{\iota}\grave{o}s$ $\tauo\mathring{v}$ $\theta\epsilono\mathring{v}$).

Again the evidences of form are most striking. The section is divided into two parts. Each has its introduction, and each its conclusion. Each contains a striking pronouncement from the Witness, and in each the pronouncement is followed by "and I knew him not, but" (cf. the $\mathring{o}\nu$ $\mathring{v}\mu\epsilon\mathring{\iota}s$ $o\mathring{v}\kappa$ $o\mathring{\iota}\delta\alpha\tau\epsilon$ of the preceding pericope). This, in turn, is followed by the "witness" exactly as in the preceding pericope after "who art thou." The "on the morrow" binds the pericope with what precedes and what follows. It is a purely

---

[25] Cf. J. M. Thompson in the *Expositor*, 1918, "An Experiment in Translation," pp. 117—125.

[26] Windisch makes this Scene 3 of Act I. but refuses to call it a separate pericope. It must be admitted that it does stand in intimate connection with the foregoing section. But its kinship with the following section, which Windisch makes a separate Act, is almost as intimate. The uniform structure of each pericope, according to my own division and quite evidently the author's, seems rather to argue for the above classification.

literary device, nothing more. The solemn words "he seeth Jesus *coming* unto him" are designed to furnish the setting, give emphasis to the momentous claim that is to follow, but above all to relate him with the Unknown Coming One of v. 27. The sentence "Behold the Lamb of God ..." is the culmination of the Baptist's witness. It stands out boldly at the moment when Jesus first appears. It is as inadequately motivated as the embassy of the Jews. It has nothing to do with the section as a unit. It stands in the way of the otherwise noticeable unfolding of testimony. It is not elaborated in what follows. On the contrary, the following words, *"this is he" etc.* are the real center of the witness. It equates Jesus specifically with the *Unknown One*, the ἐρχόμενος of the preceding section. The new figure is coming to the foreground of the Johannine stage, but the Baptist is still there. The question "Why do you baptize, then?" of the preceding pericope must still receive an answer. Here it is plainly given: "in order that he might be manifested to Israel," even though this was an inadequate witness (κἀγὼ οὐκ ᾔδειν αὐτόν).

The unfolding of revelation progresses more strikingly in **B** (vv. 32—34). This is the Johannine counterpart to the baptism. But in John we have the account given as the direct testimony of the Baptist himself. The emphasis is upon "beheld." But even yet the full significance of his experience does not dawn upon him. It is only when the heavenly token is interpreted directly from God (which acts as corroborative evidence) that he realizes WHO it is that has come to him (v. 29). Here, finally, the incomplete contrast of the preceding section is completed: I baptize in water, he shall baptize in the Holy Spirit. The witness ends most solemnly and climactically: and I have seen and borne witness that this is the Son of God. This is the true literary climax of the section and in a sense the dramatic climax of the whole chapter. A milestone has been reached in the development of the central purpose (20 30f.).

"He must increase, but I must decrease." We have seen this process going on. The third section carries us farther along until the Baptist disappears completely from the scene.

John 1 35—42
A. a. (35) Again *on the morrow* (cf. 29 43) *John* was standing, and two of his disciples; (36) and he *looked* (ἐμβλέψας) *upon Jesus as he walked*, and saith, "Behold the Lamb of God!"

(37) And the two disciples heard him speak and followed Jesus.

b. (38) And Jesus turned, and *beheld* them following, and saith unto them, "*What seek ye?*" (τί ζητεῖτε.)

And they said unto him, "Rabbi" (which is to say, being interpreted, Teacher), "where abidest thou?"

(39) He saith unto them, "*Come and ye shall see.*"

Conclusion: *They came therefore and saw* where he abode; and they abode with him that day.

It was about the tenth hour.

B. (40) One of the two that heard John speak, and followed him, was Andrew, Simon Peter's brother. (41) He first findeth his own brother Simon, and saith unto him, *We have found the Messiah* (which is, being interpreted, Christ).

(42) He brought him unto Jesus.

Conclusion: Jesus looked upon (ἐμβλέψας) him, and said, "Thou art Simon, the son of John: thou shalt be called Cephas (which is by interpretation, Peter)."

The literary features of the passage are at once observable. Its structure is the same as that of the two preceding sections. Again we have the two divisions each with introduction and conclusion. There is a striking dramatic setting, the two figures stand alone in their grandeur, and John's representation of the scene is not without an element of augustness: John is *standing*, and he *looks upon* Jesus. His repetition of "Behold the Lamb of God" may seem at first to be at variance with our explanation above. But closer examination of the entire passage as well as of the gospel as a whole substantiates our view. In the first place, this repetition at the beginning of a section of something in a preceding section frequently acts as a transition. So we find the Baptist sections linked to the Prologue and with each other. In the second place, the repetition here gives an effect of solemnity and emphasis. Again, it acts as a summary statement of the Witness. And finally, there is a more specifically literary argument. From one point of view, literary technique would seem to demand "Behold the *Son* of God;" from another, however, there is good reason for placing a colossal assertion such as John's at the beginning of his witness for its dramatic effect. It is one of many foreshadowings of the Cross which occur

throughout the gospel. Such evidences of what might appear to be
a confusion in literary technique are encountered elsewhere in the
Fourth Gospel, but usually the writer's reason for the confusion is
not difficult to trace.

The narrative bears, throughout, the marks of literary structure.
The central question of **A** (vv. 35—39) is "What seek ye?" ($\tau\iota$
$\zeta\eta\tau\epsilon\hat{\iota}\tau\epsilon$). The answer is not an indirect but a direct question.
"Rabbi" is motivated by theological interest, and the parenthesis
accentuates this. Jesus utters the pregnant words: *"Come and see."*
In Johannine style it is added, "They came and saw where he
abode," and the conclusion is "And they abode with him that
day." The next sentence, "It was about the tenth hour" has the
same purpose as 1 24, 2 12, and numerous other similar sentences.
These serve as much to separate units as to enclose them in a framework. The same vagueness and obscurity that we have previously
observed in the first pericope is seen here. As there we still ask,
"Why does John baptize then?" and "Who is the Unknown One?",
so here we ask, "What is it that they were really seeking?" or
"What did they see?" But whereas in the first pericope we have
to wait for a further narrative for a full explanation, here we get
out answer in **B** (vv. 40—42).

The introductory clause of the second division (v. 40a) summarizes the introductory sentences of **A** (35—36).[27] The prominence of
Andrew is one of the many peculiar features of the gospel, and the
position that Peter holds here in the center of the stage may be
variously explained as a reflection of the contemporary situation
or as a Synoptic tradition in Johannine literary setting.[28] A comparison with the Synoptic account of Peter's call again reveals the
strongly literary character of John. There is a degree of freshness,
vividness, and color in the former that is completely lacking here.
On the contrary, we feel that behind the Fourth Gospel account
there lies a long period of reflection. The writer seems to move in
literary *grooves*. Whereas at the beginning of the narrative John

---

[27] Is there any such relationship, perhaps, between **A** and **B** of the preceding sections ?

[28] Peter is second in importance only to the 'beloved disciple.' Cf. Wrede,
Charakter und Tendenz des Johannesevangeliums, pp. 35—37.

looks upon (ἐμβλέψας) Jesus and is impelled to utter his lofty testimony, here Jesus looks upon (ἐμβλέψας) a disciple and confers upon him distinction. Whoever is familiar with Johannine literary method will recognize that such phenomena are not accidental. *We have found the Messiah*: here is the complete answer to section **A** (35—39). The disciples were asking the gospel's pervasive question, WHO IS HE? They come to see, and they find *the Messiah* (cf. 20 31). It is a parallel to the vocative "Rabbi" in **A** as is also the parenthetical explanation. The answer to **A** is the inciting impulse to **B** (40—42). Andrew finds Peter, and the Christian mission continues until Samaritans and Greeks also come seeking Jesus.[29]

Our final pericope is still a part of the Baptist narratives. To be sure, the Baptist is now completely off the stage, but it is his influence and witness that conditions the narrative here.

John 1 43—51

A. (43) *On the morrow* he was minded to go forth into Galilee, and *he findeth* Philip, and Jesus saith unto him, "Follow me." (44) (Now Philip was from Bethsaida of the city of Andrew and Peter.)

(45) Philip *findeth* Nathanael, and saith unto him, "We *have found* him of whom Moses in the Law, and the prophets, wrote, Jesus the son of Joseph, of *Nazareth*" (cf. v. 41).

(46) And Nathanael said unto him, "Can any good come out of Nazareth?" (ἐκ Ναζαρὲτ δύναταί τι ἀγαθὸν εἶναι.)

Conclusion: Philip saith unto him, "Come and see."

B. (47) Jesus *saw* Nathanael *coming* to him, and saith of him, "*Behold* an Israelite indeed in whom is no guile!"

(48) Nathanael saith unto him, "Whence knowest thou me?"

Jesus answered and said unto him, "Before Philip called thee, when thou wast under the fig tree, *I saw* thee."

Conclusion: (49) Nathanael answered him, "Rabbi, thou art the Son of God; thou art King of Israel."

(50) Jesus answered and said unto him: "Because I said unto thee, *I saw* thee underneath a fig tree, believest thou? *Thou shalt see* greater things than these."

(51) And he saith unto him: "Verily, verily, I say unto you, *Ye shall see* the heaven opened, and the angels of God descending upon the Son of man."

[29] 4 30, 36?; 12 20—21.

The introductory τῇ ἐπαύριον indicates not only a transition but
also identity of literary grouping. "He was minded to go forth into
Galilee" is literary framework. This is the explanation of the constant shifting between Judea and Galilee in the Fourth Gospel.
The idea of *finding* has been a thread running through the narrative
ever since the dramatic pronouncement of the discovery in v. 41.
This is but one example of what is a most striking Johannine literary characteristic; namely, whenever a significant statement has
been made, the author goes back again and again and plays upon
and repeats the central words of significance. There are numerous
such words in the gospel as a whole, and also in the individual sections. For our purpose here, it is well to see that the repeated references to "finding" enshrine the initial sentence with greater solemnity. The command of Jesus is characteristically brief. The parenthetical comment is also typical. Philip bears the lighted torch
farther by *finding* Nathanael and telling him that he has *found* him
whom Moses and the prophets foretold. So Andrew had *found* Peter
and had said, "We have *found* the Messiah." Thus another step is
made in the advance of the witness. The cue is *Nazareth*, which in
the Greek appears last in Philip's words. This serves both polemical
and literary interests, for Nathanael can ask in amazement, "From
Nazareth can any good be" (literally), and Philip can answer quite
effectively, "Come and see" (cf. v. 39), thus reaching back to the
previous pericope and anticipating his discovery of Jesus in the
next. And the question implies in the answer *what* (or *who*) is it
that can come from Nazareth ?

The second division begins in a fashion we have hitherto become
familiar with (cf. 29, 35—36, 38). The greeting of Jesus is in the
manner of all Johannine utterances which attempt to point out
some great fact or introduce a new theme. So John greets Jesus,
and so Jesus greets Peter. The short declaration, revealing unexpected insight and hence an unusual personality, is the inciting
moment for the dialogue. On this basis most of the following narratives and controversial scenes are also constructed. To Jesus'
manifestation of a secret and higher knowledge and of divine insight, Nathanael can but burst forth in adoring wonder, "Rabbi,
thou art the Son of God; thou art King of Israel!", which serves
the purpose of all Johannine narratives and especially of this group

of pericopes. This declaration of Nathanael is, of course, the climax
to the section. The last two verses form the completion of the framework into which the four little pericopes have been set. They were
introduced by "Now this is the witness of John," and the "apoc-
alyptical conclusion" is its fitting and, in the quality of its contents, majestic close. The words fit easily and admirably, it must
be confessed, into the content and character of the fourth pericope,
but their relationship must also be seen as a conclusion suitable to
the whole chapter (after the prologue). The twofold introduction
to Jesus' words reflects the fervency of the writer and the solemnity and majesty of his words. This is accentuated by the "Verily,
verily (only in John) I say unto you." The "things greater than
these" is another Johannine theme, and the lofty prophecy at
the close together with this phrase is the final and the most
dramatic of the anticipations which we have met with in the
chapter.

We may, then, conclude our examination of the Baptist narratives as follows:

1) The four little sections all exhibit a formal literary manner
with a very definite method of literary composition.

2) The writer has a powerful dramatic sense. He loves to draw
his narrative to a dramatic close. Climactic arrangement is evident
everywhere: frequently he *begins* with some striking pronouncement, but more frequently he ends with the real "witness" of the
narrative, and always the conclusion is of the revealing sort. His
use of dialogue and his device of focussing the real point in some
pithily phrased question accentuate the dramatic character of the
whole. Similarly striking is the presence of dramatic anticipations.
The element of suspense is well-centered about the major interest
of the gospel. It serves the purpose of drawing the pericopes into a
unity and of giving progress to the whole.

3) A large question, and a difficult one, for the interpretation of
the gospel concerns the degree to which one is to allegorize the contents. There are those who discover profound meaning in every
sentence. Words and expressions are always being used cryptically.
The truth is that this element is undoubtedly present. But to what
extent? Commentators are sometimes Alexandrian Philos, only
they use the Fourth Gospel instead of the Pentateuch as the ob-

ject of their elucidations. How inward and spiritual a meaning are we to attribute to such words as *come, find, abide,* and *see* ?

4) Repetitions and paraphrases abound everywhere. Erich Stange[30] has made a study of many of these in an effort to understand the workings of the Johannine mind. The above analysis of the Baptist narratives agrees with Stange's conclusion that the older partition theories do not furnish an adequate explanation of the literary phenomena of the gospel.

5) In general the order of the testimony is cumulative. At first it is only John that wins our attention, but John's mission is a self-effacing one. There is the Unknown One who stands over against him. Then the Unknown One appears, a momentous claim is uttered, but this falls out of the cumulative order. It is the Coming One, the One whom John knew not, that appears. The heavenly token reveals One who baptizes not in water, but in the Holy Spirit. And John bears witness that this is the Son of God. Then the mission begins. The disciples seek, and find the Messiah, the one foretold by Moses and the prophets. Nathanael's experience culminates in the witness of "Son of God" and "King of Israel."

6) John is the "one who baptizes in water." It is a title designed to remind one of his inferior position. John is disposed of without a single word. After he has served his purpose, the author is no longer concerned with him. No exit is announced. So, too, the delegation in the first pericope is disposed of; so, too, Nicodemus; and so, too, are the Greeks.

7) Finally, one raises the question of the historicity of the narratives. The literary argument seems to tell against them. One may contend, perhaps, that historical material might very well be set in such a framework and dramatic form as have been revealed above. But if likelihood is to be a criterion, then the narratives must be viewed not primarily as historical accounts but as literary moulds embodying a theological theory.

[30] *Op. cit.*

THE LITERARY CHARACTER OF ISAIAH 34

JAMES MUILENBURG

PACIFIC SCHOOL OF RELIGION

THE literary features of the eschatological poem of Isaiah 34 are so clear and striking, so numerous and varied in character, that they afford a good insight into the methods of Hebrew literary composition and Hebrew literary taste. The poem opens with a clearly-defined, well-organized, and finely-conceived introduction. Each word has its place, each serves its special function. Parallelism and principles of euphony are carefully worked out. The introduction is in the manner of many Biblical poems. It is a dramatic appeal to the world of man and nature to hear the proclamation of Yahweh's imminent judgment. Certain literary patterns are followed in introductions of this sort, but always with a diversity of style, so that the lines seldom become a stereotyped formula.[1] A study of the prophetic imperatives in these introductions shows that they are employed with a high degree of conscious literary art.[2] This is particularly true of our eschatological poem where the appeal is given great emphasis: in each case the verb has a different form (the *qal* imperative, the *hiphil* imperative, and the jussive); in each case it appears in a most important position (the beginning of the first stichos, the end of the second, and the beginning of the third); its three-fold iteration is especially important, for the presence of triads of one sort or

---

[1] Gunkel has listed the opening imperatives of the hymn and other literary types as they appear in the Book of Psalms. See his *Einleitung in die Psalmen*, 33 f.

[2] For literary form and diction compare such representative passages as Isa 1 2, 10, 41 1, 49 1, 51 4; Mic 1 2, 6 2; Deut 32 1; Ps 49 2–3. Cf. also Gen 49 2; Isa 28 14, 32 9, 42 23, 43 8, 9, 48 16, 51 1; Jer 7 2.

another is a constant characteristic of the poem from beginning
to end. While every word and phrase has its close parallel in
other introductions of prophetic poetry, nowhere do we have
precisely this literary structure. The stichoi fall into the familiar
moulds of Hebrew parallelism, yet they show at the same time
the greatest possible variety in order and grammatical construction. The form of the introduction is somewhat more elaborate
than elsewhere, with the possible exception of Isa 41 1, where
the exhortation or appeal is expressed by five verbs.

After the imperatives, the most significant literary element
in the introduction is the six-fold address: nations and peoples,
the earth and its fulness (cf. Mi 1 2), the world and all its offspring. It is against this vast and panoramic background that
the stage of the entire poem is set.[3] The poet's perspective is
colossal in its range; one may expect him to employ categories
commensurate with the purport of his message. Mythological
reminiscence, imagery of cosmic scope, ancient conceptions rich
in cultural associations, the flotsam and jetsam of demono-
logical lore, indeed, all that emerges suggestively from the
hinterland of Hebrew racial tradition, may here find congenial
setting.

Intimately connected with the literary form of the introduction is the close identification of sound stress and thought.
As we shall have occasion to observe repeatedly, extraordinary
sensitiveness to euphony and to the relationship of assonance
and thought characterizes the method and manner of the
entire poem. Thus the first word of the first stichos is parallel
in construction, and partly in sound, to the last of the second
(הַקְשִׁיבוּ, קִרְבוּ), while the final word of the first stichos becomes
the first of the third (תִּשְׁמַע, לִשְׁמֹעַ), and the characteristic
sound of the first word of the second stichos is reproduced in
the last of the third (וּמְלֹאָה, וּלְאָמִים). The first three stichoi
read, then, as follows:

קִרְבוּ גוֹיִם לִשְׁמֹעַ וּלְאָמִים הַקְשִׁיבוּ
תִּשְׁמַע הָאָרֶץ וּמְלֹאָה

---

[3] This should suggest at the outset the necessity of caution in identifying
the object of Yahweh's judgment with the historic people of Edom.

The fourth stichos, without any word of appeal or exhortation, illustrates a constantly recurring feature of Hebrew poetry, and especially of Isaiah 34.   While retaining its parallelism, and maintaining a close relationship with the rest of the introduction, it nevertheless represents the addition of a new element of sound, form, and movement, which has the effect of thrusting the line forward, giving it climatic emphasis, bringing the introduction to an impressive close, yet preparing the way for its expansion in the body of the poem by the phrase *all its offspring*.   Two varieties of assonance appear in the introduction: 1. the similarity sounds of certain key-words placed in strategic position at the beginning or the end of stichoi, 2. the predominance of one tone throughout a single line (here it is the long *i* of the first two stichoi).   To these might be added a third, viz., the slow movement and sound of the fourth stichos תֵּבֵל וְכָל־צֶאֱצָאֶיהָ.

The body of the poem opens with the familiar particle כִּי.[4] To the reader of the English Bible this word is obscured by its occasional omission in translation, by the variety of ways in which it is rendered, and by its apparent insignificance.   But from the point of view of Hebrew literary form and usage the word is important.   Frequently it introduces the main section of a poem, not only of the hymn but of other literary types as well.[5]   Just as often it marks the conclusion of strophes and poems.[6]   In not a few instances it sets off both introduction and conclusion.[7]   Again, it is sometimes used to designate the subdivisions or the general structure of a poem.[8]   A fourth usage of the term is its introduction to some weighty or impres-

[4] Cf. Hermann Gunkel, *Einleitung in die Psalmen*, 42 f.

[5] Isa 1 2c, 2 6, 3 1, 3 16, 8 6, 11, 23, 14 29c, 16 9, 23 1, 30 9, 31 7, 43 2, 44 3a, 47 1c, 51 2c, 3b; Mic 1 3 and many other passages.

[6] Amos 4 5cd; Isa 1 20, 2 3f, 4 6, 5 7, 10, 24, 6 5e, 7 16, 8 4, 10e, 10 23, 11 9c, 14 32, 15 5–6, 8–9, 16 8, 12, 17 10, 18 5, 40 2e, 5c, 7b, 60 20c, 61 11, 66 23c; Jer 4 6c, 8c, 22a, etc.

[7] Isa 14 29b and 32c, 21 16a and 21 17b, 23 1 and 14, 30 9 and 15, 30 18 and 33, 30 10 and 30 13, 14.   Compare Ps 109 2 and 31, 47 3, 10, 96 4, 13.

[8] Isa 9 3, 4, 5, 15; Ps 5 3c, 5a, 10a.   Note also the three-fold use of כִּי in the following passages: Isa 26 3–5, 28 15, 40 2, 43 2–3, 55 8–10; Ps 49 17–19. Cf. the five-fold כִּי in 28 18–22.

342   JOURNAL OF BIBLICAL LITERATURE

sive statement,[9] as in the concluding lines of Isaiah's Song of
the Vineyard:

> For (כִּי) the vineyard of Yahweh of hosts is the house of Israel,
> And the men of Judah are his cherished planting.   (5 7)

Three of the foregoing usages are illustrated in our poem:
1. as an introduction to the poem as a whole, 2. as the initial
word of the strophe, and 3. as a preface to some climax or
important statement.[10]   At four points in the passage Isa 34 2–9
a line opens with כִּי, in three out of the four cases (2a, 5a, 6e, 8a)
it introduces a phrase of fixed pattern. Thus, the poem opens
with the words כִּי קֶצֶף לַיהוה; somewhat farther on (6e) we
have כִּי זֶבַח לַיהוה, and toward the close of the first half of the
poem (8a) כִּי יוֹם נָקָם לַיהוה. The only exception in form is the
second case (5a) where we should naturally expect כִּי חֶרֶב לַיהוה.
As a matter of fact, we find in the immediate context (6a) precisely this expression, yet without the כִּי (6a). But the line
introduced by כִּי and corresponding to the phrase "sword of
Yahweh" (5a) constitutes one of the most generally recognized
difficulties of Isa 34. At the present time, it reads כִּי רִוְּתָה
בַשָּׁמַיִם חַרְבִּי, so we may leave the text exactly as it is, so far as
the structure of the poem is concerned. With the clues provided by the connective כִּי and the formal phrases which it
introduces, we arrive at our major conclusion regarding literary
form and structure. The four expressions introduced by כִּי
give us the four main themes of the first great section of the
eschatological poem, which are plainly *the wrath of Yahweh*
(2–4), *the sword of Yahweh* (5–6d), *the sacrifice of Yahweh* (6e–7),
and *the Day of Yahweh* (8–9). Each division represents a separate
strophe with pronounced literary characteristics. Each possesses
a perfect unity and is controlled by a single dominant thought,
reaching deep into the mythology and religious world view of

---

[9] Amos 3 7, 5 5cd, 5 3ab, 5 4ab, 6 14; Isa 2 12, 3 1, 5 7, 7 8, 8 10, 10 7, 13, 22, 23,
11 9, 13 6, 41 13; Jer 2 13, 4 6c, 27.

[10] At first one is tempted to see in 16d an example of כִּי marking the conclusion of the poem. The pronouncement is solemn and very similar to many
prophetic conclusions. But its relationship is rather to the strophe, as both
its usage and position clearly show.

the ancient Hebrews. Each has its impressive beginning, and each its impressive close. Yet each contributes directly to the main theme of the poem, God's impending act of judgment upon the world, and carries it on to its powerful and inevitable climax.

The opening words of the first strophe are immediately rooted in the opening words of the introduction. The call to *the nations* is motivated by the imminence of Yahweh's judgment against *all the nations*. Thus the *first* word of address in the introduction (1a) finds its place as the first object of the divine anger (2a) in the first strophe, but the form of the phrase "*all* the nations" (2a) is influenced by the concluding member of the six-fold address (1d), with which the introduction closes. This combination of the first and last elements of a literary unit in some phrase or sentence is a common feature of Hebrew literary style. The long, slow sound and movement of the second stichos וְחֵמָה עַל־כָּל־צְבָאָם is in sharp contrast to the short, crisp syllables of the opening words of the strophe. This expression gives us our second literary triad: *all its offspring, all the nations, all their host*. The phrases are consciously arranged with the emphasis upon כָּל־צְבָאָם, precisely where it belongs from the point of view of climax, possible literary allusion, sound sequence, and literary structure. In this manner, the transition from the introduction to the body of the poem is effected, while the two remaining members of the triad outline the structure of the first strophe. The last stichos (2b) echoes quiveringly through the whole next line. The words are meant to be read slowly, each sound receiving maximum stress, צְבָאָם הֶחֱרִימָם נְתָנָם לַטָּבַח. Nowhere is the great care with which the poem is composed more convincingly shown than here, for it is these emphatic expressions that guide its further movement. The first strophe, by far the longest in the poem, develops the first complete line, *Yahweh's wrath against the nations and his fury against all their host*; the second describes the *herem* wrought by *Yahweh's sword*; the third, the *slaughter of Yahweh's sacrifice*. The words of the third stichos, like the last line of the introduction, are at once independent and separate, forming a tristich, yet intimately bound with the first two stichoi to lend them strong emphasis and a moving,

dramatic quality. They stand, moreover, in clear and direct
parallelism with the impressive first line of the next two
strophes, and in both cases these words are employed to produce striking paranomasia with the key-words of the strophes.
The exception of the fourth strophe from this scheme, as in the
case of the fourth stichos of the introduction, is explained, as we
shall see, by the author's conscious literary method and purpose.
In fact, it is this very separation of the fourth strophe from
the foregoing lines which places it in the most central and
strategic position of the whole poem.

The foregoing remarks give us sufficient justification for
retaining the present text exactly as it is, though many scholars
seek to improve upon it by the addition of a word.[11] In every
case which I have examined, the poem is definitely harmed by
the proposed change. The expression *for slaughter*, with which
the tristich ends, forms a climax to the first four stichoi of the
strophe קֶצֶף, חֵמָה, חָרֶם, טֶבַח and strikes the chord of a motif
which resounds through four great strophes. It gives us the
frame for the horrible picture of the next two stichoi, where
the initial words balance each other impressively וְהַלְלֵיהֶם,
וּפִגְרֵיהֶם, and the line ends with the revolting reference to the
stench of rotting corpses. The utter horror of the scene is
enhanced by the striking order of the words themselves, and by
its position as conclusion and climax to God's judgment of the
nations.

But this is not the close either of the general eschatological
picture or of the strophe. The scope of the divine judgment
includes the heavens, the earth, and all their host. The description, cosmic in its sweep and perspective, is one of the most
realistic, as it is one of the most appalling, in all Hebrew literature. As a literary achievement it is a superb example of
Hebrew literary manner and taste. Each of the following
three stichoi (3c, 4a, b) begins with a word of about the same

[11] For example, Bernhard Duhm, *Das Buch Jesaja*, Third edition, 1914,
223, adds the infinitive absolute הַחֲרֵם as does Karl Marti, (*Das Buch Jesaja*,
1900, 242) following Duhm in his earliest edition, 1892. Duhm also suggests
the possible addition כֻּלָּם cf. Deut 3 6.

form and sound, the first two an obvious paranomasia: וְנָמַסּוּ,
וְנָגֹלּוּ, וְנָמַקּוּ. The three verbs follow in climactic order, thus
producing a triad of eschatological proportion and power.

> The mountains *shall melt* with their blood,
> All the host of heaven *shall dissolve*,
> And the heavens *be rolled* like a scroll.

Here we have God's undoing of the work of creation; indeed,
the whole description seems a probable reminiscence of Genesis
2 1 וַיְכֻלּוּ הַשָּׁמַיִם וְהָאָרֶץ וְכָל־צְבָאָם. If this is the case, and, indeed
in any event, we have a magnificent illustration of the favorite
eschatological motif of the reversion in the end of time to what
was before the creation. *Urzeit gleicht Endzeit*. One needs to
recall Hebrew conceptions of cosmogony, certain descriptions of
the Psalms[12] and the Book of Job,[13] and not least of all that
greatest of eschatological poems, Jeremiah 4 23–27, to enter
the sphere of the poet's thought. The three areas of creation
especially marked for destruction are the mountains, the host
of heaven,[14] and the heavens themselves, all of them significant
in Semitic cosmogony. But the next stichos, וְכָל־צְבָאָם יִבּוֹל,
while belonging to the parallelism of the passage, is obviously
separated from the preceding three stichoi by being outside the
verb-triad, by its repetition of the main word of the whole context, כָּל־צָבָא, and by the introduction of a new figure. We
have encountered precisely this kind of situation before (1d, 2c,
3bc), and we need not be in doubt as to the purpose of the poet.[15]

[12] E. g., Pss 8, 19, 24, 33, 74, 89, 104, 136. See Gunkel, *Einleitung in die
Psalmen*, sec. 48, 50 for further references, especially examples from Babylonian, Assyrian, and Egyptian literature.

[13] Especially chs. 38–39.

[14] Most commentators delete כָּל־צְבָא הַשָּׁמַיִם and insert גְּבָעֹות in its place.
So Duhm, Marti, Guthe in Kautzsch's *Die Heilige Schrift des Alten Testa-
ments*, I, 603, T. K. Cheyne in Haupt's *SBOT*, 116. Cf. Kent, *Student's
Old Testament, The Sermons, Epistles and Apocalypses of Israel's Prophets*,
in loc.; Alex. R. Gordon in *The Bible: an American Translation*; William
Popper, *The Prophetic Poetry of Isaiah*, emends to "valleys."

[15] Duhm's misunderstanding of the literary character of the poem is
illustrated by the following comment on the text here: "34 4 ist nicht in
Ordnung. Zweimal צבא und zweimal שָׁמַיִם ist zu viel und die ganze Bilder-
reihe konfus: die Sterne zerfliessen, die Himmel rollen sich zusammen, die

From the foregoing triad, and indeed from the first line of the strophe, he selects the key-word כָּל־צְבָאָם and describes the destruction of the host in one of the most moving figures of the poem: *and all their host shall wither* (יִבּוֹל). The stichos gives an admirable conclusion to the poem, brings it to a powerful climax, repeating at the end what was announced at the beginning, yet introducing a new element to fire the imagination. The poet was fully aware of the power of the figure of the stars falling from heaven as leaves from trees, for two final stichoi, constituting a metrically perfect line (3' 2'), take up the figure to end the strophe, employing it most effectively, from the points of view of sound, form, and structure. We have here another of the great triads of the poem: כְּנָבָלָת, כִּנְבֹל, יִבּוֹל. But what is more revealing is the stirring, almost healing effect of the closing comparison:

> As foliage wilts from the vine,
> As leaves which fall from the fig tree. (Torrey's translation)

The care with which the strophe is constructed has become ·apparent. The poet's subject is *the wrath of God* against the nations (2cd, 3ab) and against all their host (3cdef). The strophe is connected with the introduction both by the introductory כִּי and by the two impressive phrases. It is knit together into firm unity and carried forward by at least seven series of parallel relationships, most of them in the form of triads in climactic arrangement. Throughout, the effect of sound is noticeable, and in every instance the important sounds are identical with the stress of thought.

The subject of the second strophe is the sword of Yahweh. It is a theme encountered frequently in the OT[16] and is rich in

Sterne zerfallen. צבא השמים wird von Bickell mit Recht als eine Glosse zu צבאם angesehen die einem Leser nötig schien, weil v. 2 צבאם einen anderen Sinn hat" (p. 223).

[16] Deut 32 41–43 (a chapter closely related to Isa 34); Isa 27 1, 66 16; Jer 12 12, 46 10, 47 6f; Ezek 21 9ff. Cf. Josh 5 13; Ju 7 20; Job 6 4; Isa 31 8; Jer 50 35–38; Zech 13 7.

its mythological associations. Although the opening כִּי is absent from the Greek, there is no reason to doubt that the masoretic text represents the original here. Yet the opening stichos is full of difficulties. 1. There is a sudden change to the first person for no apparent reason whatever. The immediate context contradicts this change. 2. The form of the verb רִוְּתָה is difficult, and the great majority of scholars prefer another reading such as רָוְתָה[17]. 3. If we have a full line here, there is obviously something missing. It is not surprising therefore that many scholars add מֵעַם after the verb and change the חרב׳ to חָרֶב יהוה and חַרְמִי to חַרְמוֹ[18]. The alternative here is to recognize verse 5, with Professor Torrey, as an instance of a triple line.[19] As to the verb, we shall do well to maintain the masoretic reading and interpret it as a *pi'el* intensive. An alternative possibility proposed by Professor Torrey (but rejected by him) is that the verb be read as the *pu'al* form of רָאָה, giving us *my sword appears in the heavens*. This is an exceedingly attractive proposal, which tempts one greatly. My rejection of it is only tentative.

With the two words in the first person, the case is somewhat different. Considering the striking and apparently unmeaning shift in person, it is certainly not rash to see here an abbreviation of חָרֶב יהוה. The Greek, to be sure, witnesses here to the masoretic reading, but in the second instance חרמ׳ it is without the first person, reading simply τῆς ἀπωλείας. I should not wish to attach too great authority to the Greek text of Isaiah 34, but it seems here to have preserved a more original reading, for the idea of a *herem Yahweh* would be infelicitous in the context and would violate the meter, but the words *hereb Yahweh* (assuming that originally the manuscript read חרב י״) would improve matters greatly. I should therefore feel that the balance of the evidence would favor reading "sword of Yahweh" and "ban." Other proposals, which have been made by Duhm,

[17] Duhm, Marti, Cheyne, Kent, Box. Ehrlich, *Randglossen zur Hebräischen Bibel*, reads the opening words כָּרוֹת.
[18] Duhm, Marti, Cheyne, Box, Kent, and others.
[19] *The Second Isaiah*, 284: "We have here an irreproachable line."

Cheyne, Marti, and others, seem less satisfactory. The opening
line would then read as follows:

כִּי רִוְּתָה בַשָּׁמַיִם חָרֶב יהוה

The activity of Yahweh's sword *in the heavens* should not come
as a surprise, for the last strophe has prepared us for it. Twice
in the last verse reference has been made to the heavens, so
that when the third strophe reads "For anointed *in the heavens*
is Yahweh's sword," the words sound natural and unforced.
The practice of employing the dominant word or sound of an
immediately preceding context to introduce a new literary unit
is in the manner of the poet elsewhere.

The graphic picture of the third and fourth stichoi, where the
sword descends from heaven *upon Edom* and *upon the people of
the ḥerem*, have their parallels in the first strophe, where
Yahweh's wrath falls *upon the nations* and *upon their host*. The
ghastly and revolting representation in vs. 6 of Yahweh's sword
bathed in blood and anointed with fat must be read in the light
of its derivation from the scene of sacrifice. At the same time
the ancestry of the whole representation is obviously mythological. The present picture is a combination of both backgrounds.
It is to be observed again that the third member of the first
stichos of vs. 6 (דָם) becomes the first member of the third
stichos (מִדָּם) while the last member of the second stichos
(מֵחֵלֶב) becomes the first of the fourth (מֵחֵלֶב). The last two
stichoi of the second strophe have the same general construction
as the last line of the preceding strophe, are attached in much
the same way to the foregoing description, and serve as an
addition to fill out the strophe and bring it to a close, and yet
to prepare the way for the succeeding strophe.

The third strophe describes Yahweh's sacrifice. First, Yahweh's
wrath, then his sword in the heavens descending to earth for
the great *ḥerem*, and now the sacrifice with its great slaughter.
The words immediately following the opening phrase, "in
Bozrah" and "in the land of Edom," are paralleled in the
opening lines of both of the preceding strophes. The first words
of the two stichoi contain one of the striking instances of paranomasia in the poem, זֶבַח and טֶבַח, another indication of the

poet's feeling for sound and his interest in assonance. The reference to the "great slaughter" is, as we have seen, a development of the phrase at the beginning of the first strophe (2d); it is suggested, as a matter of fact, by all that has preceded. The development of the poet's thought is clear. In the first strophe, the description of divine judgment is general, against all nations and against all the host; in the second, we are given a picture of the sword in the heavens descending to earth; here, in the third strophe, the description is entirely on earth, and the imagery is no longer mythological but wholly sacrificial. The repetition in the last line of the strophe of the reference to the land (of Edom) which appears in the first line is in accordance with Hebrew literary method. The remaining lines of the strophe yield further instances of the poet's feeling for sound. The second line is dominated throughout by the sound of *īm* and gives us another characteristic sound triad in the words וּפָרִים עִם־אַבִּירִים, while the third and last line is dominated by the sound *ām* and contains another sound triad אַרְצָם מִדָּם וַעֲפָרָם. Again, we observe how the lines are forged together, for the last members of the third and the fifth stichoi of the strophe harmonize in sound, עִמָּם and מִדָּם, as do also the first members of the fourth and sixth, וַעֲפָרָם and וּפָרִים. In the former case, the word עִמָּם has perplexed a number of scholars. Ehrlich[20] deletes the word completely, but Duhm, Marti, Popper, Gordon, and Kittel[21] emend to read עִם מְרִיאִם "with fatlings." But if assonance is to constitute any guide at all, the change must be rejected, for it would make of an otherwise pleasing line a bad exhibition of cacophony. Two instances of a common stylistic feature appear in the last line of the strophe. The first word רֻוְּתָה gives us a notable example of a word previously employed in another context in a somewhat different way (5a). The last two words of the line מֵחֵלֶב יְדֻשָּׁן also reach back to a preceding strophe (6ab) הֻדַּשְׁנָה מֵחֵלֶב and employ them in a new

---

[20] *Randglossen zur Hebräischen Bibel*, IV, 123: "Streiche das beziehungslose עמם das durch Dittographie aus dem Vorherg entstanden ist. Das erste Glied wird dann allerdings etwas kurz, aber es geschieht auch sonst nicht selten, dass ein Versglied kürzer ausfällt."

[21] Critical apparatus of the third edition of his *Biblia Hebraica, in loc.*

context: in the first case they refer to Yahweh's sword, in the second to the very *soil* itself. We meet in this line the third instance (7cd) of the parallelism of the words for blood and fat (6ab, cd). It is to be observed that the strong hyperbole of *the land drenched in blood* and *the dust anointed with fat* gives us not only the final line of the third strophe, but *the climax of all three strophes*. It is a vivid illustration of the perspective of the poet's conception. Another indication of the conscious literary method that is employed in our poem from beginning to end is shown by a further remarkable fact: the two-fold reference to blood and fat which *ends* the stichoi of the last line of this strophe is parallel to a similar two-fold reference which *introduces* the concluding stichoi of the preceding strophe. Similarly, the dust and land, which are the key-words of the closing stichoi of the third strophe, are in turn the key-words of the closing stichoi of the fourth strophe. Whoever has familiarized himself with Hebrew literary methods of composition will not be surprised at this, but the example here is important and illuminating.

The fourth strophe constitutes the culmination of the entire poem. Its theme is the Day of Yahweh. From the first words of the introduction with its call to men and nations to approach and hear, through each single line of each strophe, the poem has moved steadily on to this great dramatic moment. Yet it does not fall into the pattern of the impressive triad in the first lines of the first strophe. We have just observed that the first three strophes have a unity of their own and reach their culmination in the final line of the third strophe. The fourth strophe is very much a part of the poem, but there is a sense in which it is separated too. But this separation is clearly for the purpose of giving great emphasis, and the theme of the Day of Yahweh is supremely suited for such a position. We have seen this characteristic of the poet's literary method everywhere. The additional element gives new force and impressiveness both by its separation and by its intimate connection with the growth of the poem. The theme is stated without any elaboration whatsoever: *Yahweh has a day of vengeance*. Each syllable is large and full; there is neither need nor space for more. Similarly, the parallel stichos merely balances the great announcement term for term, without the addition of any new motif or element: *Zion's Champion has a year of requital*. The description of the great Day is brief, but effective. The three-fold destruction is doubtless meant to be read climatically:

> Her streams shall be turned to pitch,
> Her soil to brimstone,
> Her land shall become
> Burning pitch.

The preceding strophe took up that part of the central subject which was concerned with the destruction of the earth (cf. 1c); it began with a reference to *the land of Edom*; it ended with the *land drenched with blood*. The last strophe develops this description to its conclusion in the third term of its own three-fold impressive climax. The picture of the land ablaze — all burning pitch — is lurid and deeply moving. If we have here a genuine reminiscence of the overthrow and destruction of the Cities of the Plain, as the vocabulary seems to suggest, the effect is overwhelming — at least to Hebrew imagination. Only silence can follow such a picture.

But a word must be added about the assonance of this strophe. Considering the tendency of the poet to introduce in new literary units the dominant sound of the immediately preceding context, it is possible that the נָקָם of the first stichos is meant to echo the *am* of the foregoing stichoi. The last line is to be read not with emphasis on what seems to be rhyme, though this is not impossible, but with recognition of the long *a* throughout: וְהָיְתָה אַרְצָה לְזֶפֶת בֹּעֵרָה. The last member of the first strophe לְזֶפֶת becomes the first of the fourth. As we have seen, the reference to the *dust* and the *land* is paralleled in the last line of the preceding strophe. Both strophes end with this emphatic reference, giving force to our suggestion that the introduction to the poem envisages the complete structure of the work. The last two words I am considering very tentatively as a separate stichos, 1. because the addition of a new phrase at such an important point would be quite in the manner of the author elsewhere, 2. because it is the poet's practice to

give special emphasis and position to important expressions, and
3. because it prepares us more effectively for the next lines.

The two lines immediately following the description of the
burning land raise one of the chief questions of the poem:

> Night and day it shall not be quenched,
> Its smoke shall ascend forever.
> From age to age her land shall be waste,
> For ever and ever.

There can be no question that these lines occupy an extremely
important position. Indeed, they appear as the fulcrum which
holds the entire poem in perfect balance, both as to form and
content. In a sense, they may be said to hold the secret to the
artistry and literary method of the writer. One possibility is
that they are the conclusion of the fourth strophe since they
certainly continue the description of the burning land. But this
is strictly true only of the first line and not of the second. Yet
it is difficult to see how we may separate the lines since the
parallelism is so obvious and intimate. Moreover, the antecedent in the mind of the poet is the same in both lines, although
at first it seems to present great difficulty. It is *the burning land*
which will never be extinguished, whose smoke will rise up,
which will lie waste from generation to generation. Consequently, the two lines must be read together. Another suggestion might be that these lines form the conclusion to the entire
poem thus far. That there is a break in the structure of the
poem at this point cannot be doubted; the only question is
how this verse is related to the break. The profound impressiveness of the lines would argue for such a solution. It is
possible, however, that we have a case here of the lyric interlude, which is related both to the foregoing and to the following
lines. That the lines are actually so related becomes obvious in
reading the immediate context. This is in all likelihood the
best answer to our question, though it is not without its difficulties. One needs only to inquire whether the burning land of
verses 9–10 is really the scene of the succeeding strophes. The
haunting description of the birds and wild animals and demons
seems hardly consistent with this. On the other hand, the
feminine pronominal suffixes in verses 11f. can only refer to the

land. It could be argued, of course, that in eschatological
poetry considerations of this sort should not be pushed too far,
that the second half of the poem is only another picture of the
desolation after destruction (N. B. תֶּחֱרָב). But we shall have
more to say on this matter at a later point.

The stress on the long duration of the blazing earth at the
beginning of each of the four stichoi has no parallel elsewhere
in the poem. Nowhere is emphasis so dramatically and power-
fully placed as here. Nowhere is the language so distinctive.
Again, with the exception of the last three words of the second
line, the two lines are perfect in their structure. The sound
effects, too, are especially strong:

לַיְלָה וְיוֹמָם לֹא תִכְבֶּה   לְעוֹלָם יַעֲלֶה עֲשָׁנָהּ
מִדּוֹר לָדוֹר תֶּחֱרָב   לְנֵצַח נְצָחִים

The stirring effect of its smoke עֲשָׁנָהּ as an additional element in
the sound scheme deserves attention. So, too, the two pairs
מִדּוֹר לָדוֹר and נֵצַח נְצָחִים illustrate the independence of the
poet. The language here is our poet's alone, and is of a sort to
dispel the not uncommon contention that the poet is in reality
a second-rate imitator. The poem as we have it in our hands
today may not be without its difficulties, but of one thing we
may be sure, and that is the originality and genius of its author.

There remains but one small piece, the three tantalizing
words אֵין עֹבֵר בָּהּ which conclude the lines. One is tempted
to dismiss them as a gloss, especially as they are absent from
the Greek of B and other manuscripts. Moreover, they seem to
overload the line heavily. No natural reading could contain
them within one stress; on the contrary, they seem to demand
a slow reading. One might argue, however, that such additions
are not out of keeping with the poet's procedure elsewhere. But
the reply to this is that everywhere else the additional element
falls within the normal rhythm and parallelism, and thus serves
a distinctive, artistic purpose. This can hardly be said of these
three words. Yet, it is conceivable that the poet meant these
words to be read with deliberation after the close of the stichos,
giving them great emphasis. One might support this view by
suggesting that the closing בָּהּ is meant to be in assonance with

the same word at the end of the next line. Such links we have
seen repeatedly before, connecting the introduction and the
main part of the poem, and indeed all of the foregoing strophes.
Probably the poet felt that it would serve as an effective transition to the second part of the poem where the antecedent is
far from clear.[22]

The evidences of structure are not so externally apparent in
Part II of our poem as in Part I. From the point of view of
form, the conspicuous characteristic is the three-fold אַף־שָׁם or
שָׁמָּה which introduces the three successive lines in vss. 14 and 15.
When the poem is carefully read, one sees that these lines do,
as a matter of fact, possess a unity in themselves; that the
succeeding verses, for example, represent a definite break in
continuity. One also recognizes a distinct change after vs. 12, as
we shall soon see. Difficult as are the problems connected with
the meaning of some of the words, these general indications
show that what we have here is in reality four strophes of
approximately six stichoi each. The last line in verse 17 is
obviously separated from the rest of the poem and is, in fact,
the conclusion to the whole poem.

One of the most marked features of the second part of the
poem is the repressed reference to the land, or the desert, or
whatever the place that is described may be. It is referred to
again and again by a pronoun or adverb. The consequent
vagueness and mysteriousness of the picture is thus greatly
heightened. That this was the design of the poet will become
increasingly clear as the poem is read. In the first strophe, we
are to envisage the birds flying about the ruins. The line of
תֹהוּ and the plummet of בֹהוּ are stretched over the land and its
rulers. Finally, the name of the region is disclosed: it is *No
Kingdom There*, and the rulers of the region are *Nothing*. The
assonance of the strophe is interesting. There is, first of all,
the paranomasia contained within the two phrases קֹרְאֻתָהוּ

---

[22] It would not be difficult to adduce parallels to this phenomenon. A
conspicuous instance, if the text is preserved correctly, is to be discovered
in Isa 40 7 אָכֵן חָצִיר הָעָם. It is to be observed, however, that these words
are absent from the Greek text of Lucian.

וְאַבְנֵי־בֹהוּ, but these are included within a larger sound frame-work which reading aloud at once makes clear:

וְנָטָה עָלֶיהָ קַו־תֹהוּ וְאַבְנֵי־בֹהוּ חֹרֶיהָ

The first two words are doubtless to be connected with the last word of the preceding line, giving us another of the numerous sound trilogies of the poem (cf. 2bcd, 4cde, 7b, 7cd, 14ac, 15b). The first and last words are to be compared with vss. 1 and 4bc. The total picture is one of utter desolation; the vacuous names of the kingdom and its rulers are a suitable finale and climax.

In the second strophe we get a more intimate glimpse of the realm. Thorns cover her citadels, briers and brambles her fortresses. Jackals and ostriches stalk through the ruined halls. The picture grows in the intensity of its stark drearness; and now to this is added an eerie, spectral atmosphere as the demons of the desert gather with the goblins, and the satyr cries for his mate. A haunting sense of loneliness pervades the entire scene. Another paranomasia of great suggestiveness is the gathering of the צִיִּים with the אִיִּים. The first words of the first and third stichoi were probably meant to be in assonance with each other, as also the first words of the second and fourth (cf. 7ac and bd above, and somewhat differently 6ab and cd).

The third strophe underlines the suggestion made above concerning the repressed reference to the eschatological land of *No Kingdom There*, without princes and nobles; its only population birds and jackals and demons. The three-fold introductory expression given in emphatic form שָׁם, אַךְ־שָׁם, שָׁמָּה tells us that *there*, in that region, Lilith has her home and finds rest for herself, *there* the owl nests aud lays, hatches and broods, *there* the kites gather together, each one seeking its mate. Next to the effect of the emphasis produced by the opening words of the three lines is the sound triad of 15b, וּבָקְעָה וְדָגְרָה בְצִלָּה, which surely echoes the שָׁמָּה at the beginning of the line, and may possibly echo the *a* sound of the second stichos (14b).

The fourth and last strophe of the poem is difficult; the text has surely not been preserved in its purity. No one of the suggested changes seems completely satisfactory. If the אִשָּׁה רְעוּתָה of the second line is original (and the character of the

356   JOURNAL OF BIBLICAL LITERATURE

poem would suggest that it is), then it seems very possible that words have fallen out, probably through homoioteleuton. Despite the confusion, certain things are nevertheless clear. The strophe is concerned with Yahweh's book, in which the names of all the creatures are listed. In other words, the land that has been described is Yahweh's creation and work; it is he who has gathered the animals together; he has given the command. The first and last words of the first stichos (like 1ab) are parallel וְקָרָאוּ, דְּרְשׁוּ; the expression אִשָּׁה רְעוּתָהּ recalls the same words in the last words of the previous strophe; the dominant sound of this line is surely the *shureq*, and, as so frequently in our poem, it is the same sound that begins the next line וְהוּא. Finally, the first and last words of the last stichos are so closely in assonance that one suspects that they were meant as another paranomasia וְיָדוֹ בַּקֵּו, . The poem began with the theme of Yahweh's imminent act of divine wrath; it ends with a re-assertion of Yahweh's purpose in all that has happened. The total picture is not one of horror and vengeance; rather, the effect of the description of judgment is a kind of sublimity. The closing lines produce a marvelously healing effect, and one is able to read the poem again with renewed appreciation and understanding.

The conclusion is a model of the poet's literary method and manner. The introductory phrases לְדוֹר וָדוֹר, עַד עוֹלָם are drawn from the lyric interlude, while the remaining words are derived from the opening of the second part of the poem. In this way, the poet weaves the poem into a unity, gathers up its central emphasis, and witnesses to a literary method which is to be found in every part of the OT, where the concluding lines repeat the opening words and thus tie the literary unit together.

The general structure of the eschatological poem is now before us complete. It opens with an introduction. This is followed by four strophes, each with carefully conceived composition; the first of 12 lines, the second of 8, the last two of 6. Then comes the interlude, binding the two parts of the poem together. The second part of the poem is composed of four strophes of 6 lines each. The conclusion appropriately strikes the note of an eschatological finale, both in its form and in its content.

Literary Characteristics

One of the results which have emerged from our discussion thus far is the unusual sensitiveness of the poet of Isaiah 34 to considerations of euphony. It is easy to carry this emphasis to absurd extremes, and the student will be careful to guard against that danger. On the other hand, we should expect an intimate connection between thought rhythm and sound rhythm. The following lists of various kinds of assonance illustrated in the poem give an insight into one of its major features. It is especially important to observe that this sensitiveness to sound is discerned in the most important literary situations: e. g. at the logical divisions of the poem, at the beginning and end of each strophe, of each line, and of each stichos. It is even more important that the poem be read aloud again and again until sound and thought emerge clearly:

1. *Paranomasia*

    3b and 4a וְנָמַסּוּ ,וְנָמַקּוּ;   5b and d חָרָב, or חַרְמִי, חַרְבִּי, חָרָם;

    6e and f זָבַח, טָבָח;   11c and d בֹּהוּ, תֹּהוּ;

    14a אִיִּים, צִיִּים;

    Torrey (p. 283) also refers to קִפּוֹד, קָאַת in 11a. Other words approximating paranomasia are מַחֲלָב, חָרָב (6a and b).

2. *Succession of words ending in the same dominant sound*

    2bcd צְבָאָם הֶחֱרִימָם נְתָנָם;   7b (cf. also 7a); (רְאֵמִים) וּפָרִים עִם אַבִּירִים;

    7cd אַרְצָם מִדָּם וַעֲפָרָם;   9bc וַעֲפָרָה לְנָפְרִית הָיְתָה אַרְצָה לְזֶפֶת בֹּעֵרָה

    11bc יִשְׁכְּנוּ־בָה וְנָטָה עָלֶיהָ;

    15b וּבָקְעָה וְדָגְרָה בְצִלָּה; cf. also 14d.

3. *Lines characterized by a dominant sound*

    1ab, 4de, 6cd, 6ef, 7ab, 7cd, 9cd, 11b^c cd, 15ab, 16cde.

4. *Words and phrases appearing in pairs*

8b שְׁנַת שִׁלּוּמִים ;   10c מָדוֹר לָדוֹר ;

10d נֶצַח נְצָחִים ;   11 קָאַת וְקִפּוֹד ;

11cd קְרָאתִהוּ וְאַבְנֵי־בֹהוּ ;   14a צִיִּים אֶת־אִיִּים ;

17d לְדוֹר וָדוֹר .

5. *Phrases in intimate relation in some kind of assonance with each other*

1a מִדַּם כָּרִים וְעַתּוּדִים מֵחֵלֶב ;   6cd קִרְבוּ גוֹיִם לִשְׁמֹעַ וּלְאֻמִּים

כְּלָיוֹת אֵילִים ;

10aba לַיְלָה וְיוֹמָם תִּכְבֶּה לְעוֹלָם יַעֲלֶה :

7a and c וַיֵּרְדוּ רְאֵמִים עִמָּם . . . וְרִוְּתָה אַרְצָם מִדָּם ;

11cd קְרָאתִהוּ וְאַבְנֵי־בֹהוּ ;   11ca and 12aa וְנָטָה עָלֶיהָ . . . חֹרֶיהָ ;

17b וְיָדוֹ . . . בַּקָּו .

6. *Instances in which successive stichoi or lines begin with words of similar form or sound:*

3c, 4a, 4b כִּי זֶבַח . . . וְטָבַח ;   6e and f וְנָמַסּוּ, וְנָמַקּוּ, וְנָגֹלּוּ ;

7c and d וּפָרִים . . . וַעֲפָרָם ;

13a and c וְעָלְתָה . . . וְהָיְתָה ;   13b and d קִמּוֹשׁ . . . לִבְנוֹת

14c, 15a and c אַךְ־שָׁם, שָׁמָּה, אַךְ־שָׁם   cf. also 3a and b, 4d and e.

7. *Instances in which successive stichoi or lines end with words of similar form or sound:*

2a and b הַשָּׁמַיִם, עַל־כָּל־צְבָאָם, עַל־כָּל־הַגּוֹיִם ;   4a and b

6c and d אֵילִים, וְעַתּוּדִים ;   7a, c, and d עִמָּם, מִדָּם, יְדֻשָּׁן ;

9c and d בֶעָרָה, אַרְצָה ;   10b and d בָּהּ, עֲשָׂנָהּ .

cf. with 10b and d; also 11b and 12aa.

13a, c, and 14a אִיִּים, תַנִּים, סִירִים

13b and d יִקְרָא, יַעֲנָה, בְּמִבְצָרֶיהָ

cf. also the opening words of the stichoi, 13a and c, b and d.
For a very similar situation, cf. vs. 7. This line is peculiarly
instructive because of the comparative word order of the
two stichoi.

cf. also 1c and d, 2b and c, 3b and c, 9a and b, 15b and d.

8. *Instances in which similar sound or construction begins and ends a stichos or line:*
   1a and b הַקְשִׁיבוּ, קִרְבוּ;   6a and b מֵחֲלָב, חֶרֶב;
   8a and b צִיּוֹן; כִּי יוֹם   16a וּקְרָאוּ, דְּרְשׁוּ
   cf. also 7b, 7d, 9cd, 11a and b, 11c and 12aa, 13a and b, c and d, 15a and b, 15b.

9. *Parallel phrases*
   The opening rubrics of vss. 2, 6a, 6e (cf. 5a), and 8.
   2a and b: cf. 7 above.
   4d and e כְּנֹבֵל . . . מִגֶּפֶן וּכְנֹבֶלֶת מִתְּאֵנָה
   5c and d מִדָּם, מֵחֲלָב   6c and d עַל־אֱדוֹם וְעַל־עַם חֶרְמִי
   6e and f בְּבָצְרָה בְּאֶרֶץ אֱדוֹם   10a and b לַיְלָה, וְיוֹמָם לְעוֹלָם
   10c and d מִדּוֹר לָדוֹר . . . נֵצַח נְצָחִים
   11c and d, cf. 4 above. Cf. also 6a and b and 7c and d; 14c, 15a and c.

10. *Trilogies*
    a. *Of phrases and words in immediate context*
       1d, 2a, and b עַל־כָּל־צְבָאָם, עַל־כָּל־הַגּוֹיִם, וְכָל־צֶאֱצָאֶיהָ
       3c, 4a, and b כְּנֹבֶלֶת, כְּנֹבֵל, יְבוֹל; וְנָגֹלּוּ, וְנָמַקּוּ, וְנָמַסּוּ 4cde
       14c, 15a and c אַף־שָׁם, שָׁמָּה, אַף־שָׁם
    b. *Of phrases and words in larger context*
       2b, 4a, and c וְכָל־צְבָאָם, כָּל־צְבָא, עַל־כָּל־צְבָאָם
       4a, b, and 5a הַשָּׁמַיִם (bis)
       6a, c, and 7c מִדָּם, מִדָּם, דָּם
       6b, d, and 7d מֵחֲלָב (ter)
       6f, 7c, and 9c (cf. 1a)
    c. *Of sound*
       (See 2. above "Succession of words ending in the same dominant sound.") Cf. also the two references to חֶרֶב and the one to חָרַם in immediate context (5b, d, and 6a) on the basis of restoration of text.

11. *Instances in which the beginning of a line repeats the final or dominant sound of the preceding line or stichos:*
    2c and 2b הַחֲרִימָם, צְבָאָם, 4d and 4c כְּנֹבֵל, יְבוֹל, 10a and 9cd בְּעֶרָה, לַיְלָה, 17a and 16c-e וְהוּא, וְרוּחוֹ הוּא cf. 11c and 11b.

12. *Different forms of the same word in immediate context* (a kind of epanalepsis, in which words or phrases are repeated after other words have intervened, for the purpose of giving emphasis.)[23]

1a and c עַל־כָּל־הַגּוֹיִם, לִשְׁמֹעַ; תִּשְׁמַע; 1a and 2a גּוֹיִם

4a and c כְּנֹבְלַת, כִּנְבֹל יְבוּל, כָּל־צְבָאָם, וְכָל־צְבָא 4c, d, and e

5b and 6a מְדַּם, דָּם, חָרֶב יהוה, חַרְבִּי 6a and c

6b and d מֵחָלָב (*bis*) 9a and d לְזָפָת (*bis*)

15c and 16d קִבְצָן, נִקְבְּצוּ cf. the phrases in 10c and d.

It is possible, of course, that many of the foregoing sound combinations are to be explained by the character of Hebrew grammar, but it is likely that the poet, sensitive to the possibilities for creating euphony in the nature of the Hebrew language, used them to maximum advantage. A most important evidence of this is the order of the words and the nature of the parallelism.

Other stylistic elements may be summarized as follows:

13. *Addition of a new element to the literary unit, usually within the structure of the parallelism.*

2d כִּנְבֹל עָלֶה מִנֶּפֶן וּכְנֹבֶלֶת מִתְּאֵנָה; 3b בְּאֵשָׁם; 4de לַטֶּבַח; 5d

לְמִשְׁפָּט; 9d בְּעָרָה; 10b עָשְׂנָה;

10d אֵין עֹבֵר בָּהּ; 10 (whole verse);

12aa חָרְיָה; 15b בְּצֵלָהּ; cf. also the two closing terms of stichoi 1c and d, and especially stichos 1d.

The two most important examples, however, are the last strophes of each major part of the poem, the strophe on the Day of Yahweh (8–9) and the strophe on the Book of Yahweh (16–17ab).

14. *Instances of repetition in which some important word or phrase is employed in another context*:
    (See 10 b above "Triads of phrases and words in larger context.")

---

[23] Essentially the same literary habit is illustrated in many of the examples in 4 and 10 above.

2c and 5d וְטָבַח לַטָבַח‎, חַרְמִי הַחֲרִימָם‎; 2d and 6f ;

5a and 7c רֻוְּתָה (bis); 10b and 17c לְעוֹלָם (bis); 10c and 17d לְדוֹר וָדוֹר‎, מִדּוֹר לָדוֹר‎;

11a and 17c יִי‎, וִירֵשׁוּהָ‎; 11b and 17d יִשְׁכָּנוּ־בָהּ (bis);

11c and 17b בָּקּוּ‎, קָרְתֵהוּ‎; 15c and 16d קִבְּצָן‎, נִקְבָּצוּ‎;

15d and 16c אִשָּׁה רְעוּתָהּ (bis).

15. *Words, phrases, and other literary units in climactic order:*

Most important here is the order of the strophes in the first half of the poem with their respective themes of the wrath of Yahweh, the sword of Yahweh, the sacrifice of Yahweh, the Day of Yahweh. There is definite movement in the four strophes of the second half of the poem, too, but it is more difficult to discern the design of the poet's working here.

Vs. 1. The six-fold address to nations, peoples, the earth and its fulness, the world and all its offspring seems at least to move toward greater emphasis and probably something more.

Vs. 2. The wrath of Yahweh, his fury, his ban, his slaughter,

Vss. 3c, 4ab. Both subjects and verbs appear to be in some kind of climactic order.

Vs. 5. The sword in the heavens (5a) descends to earth (5c) for the purpose of judgment (5d).

Vs. 6e and f seem to be phrased so that the emphasis falls on the great slaughter.

Vs. 7cd. The description here goes much farther than the parallel in 6c and d.

Vs. 9a, b, and c(d). Each succeeding stichos heightens the description of the range and awfulness of destruction.

Vs. 10. Whether the four-fold reference to the everlasting duration of the burning is meant to be climactic is not certain. Surely, 10b goes beyond the expression of 10a, and 10d beyond 10c.

Vs. 11. The three lines are climactically arranged, each line giving a more vivid and impressive picture of desolation than the former.

Vss. 13–14ab. The lines follow each other in increasing power and unearthliness: first only the thistles and thorns over the ruins, then the jackals and the ostriches, and finally the demons of the desert crying to each other.

Vss. 14cd–15. The former strophe showed indications of increasing movement and life. This strophe confirms this impression. Lilith finds her home, the owls nest, and lay, and hatch their brood; the kites gather together, each one seeking its mate.

Vss. 16–17ab. There is certainly progress in the thought here. In the translation of Professor Torrey the whole meaning of this part of the poem becomes clear, as the activity of Yahweh is described with more definiteness and concreteness in each succeeding stichos.

16. *Vocabulary and language*

    a. The following words and expressions are peculiar to Isaiah 34:

      מָדוֹר לָדוֹר (10) (cf. לָדוֹר וָדוֹר vs. 17); נֶצַח נְצָחִים (10);
      לִילִית (14); קִפּוֹז (15).

    b. Other words of interest are as follows: vs. 1 צֶאֱצָא (11 times in OT, 4 in Job, 5 in Isaiah 40–66, 2 in Isaiah 1–39); vs. 3 בָּאַשׁ (6 times in OT, 3 in Isaiah 1–39, once each in Amos, Joel, Job); vs. 4 מָקַק (9 times in OT, 3 each in Ezek and Zech, once each in Ps and Lev); vs. 4 נָבֵל (18 times, 3 in Isa 34 (כְּנֹבֶלֶת, כִּנְבֹל, יִבּוֹל), twice in Isa 40–66); vs. 6 דֶּשֶׁן (9 times, twice in Isa 34); vs. 7 רְאֵם (10 times); vs. 7 אַבִּיר (17 times, 5 in Ps, 4 in Jer, 1 in Isa 40–66); vs. 8 נָקָם (17 times, 1 in Isa 35, 4 in Isa 40–66); vs. 9 זֶפֶת (twice, Ex 2 3; in connection with ark of bulrushes); vs. 9 גָּפְרִית (7 times, in at least 3 of which the reference is to Sodom and Gomorrah); vs. 11 קָאַת (5 times, this particular form paralleled only by Zeph 2 14); vs. 11 קִפּוֹד. (The only occurrences outside of vs. 11 are in passages in close literary relationship with Isa 34; Isa 14 23; Zech 2 14); vs. 11 יַנְשׁוֹף (3 times, Lev 11 17, Deut 14 16); vs. 11 תֹהוּ . . . בֹהוּ (the combined expression only here, Gen 1 2, and Jer 4 23; תֹהוּ occurs 20 times in OT; 8 in Isa 40–66, 3 in Job); vs. 13 סִיר (6 times with this meaning); vs. 13 קִמּוֹשׂ (3 times); vs. 14 צִי (6 times, in two cases of which there is obvious literary connection with Isa 34); vs. 14 (3 times, twice in same passages of literary relation as above, Isa 13 21 and

Jer 50 29); vs. 14 שָׂעִיר (3–5 times, esp. Isa 13 21); vs.
14 רָגַע (7 times as verb); vs. 14 מָנוֹחַ (7 times); vs. 15
קָנַן (4 times as verb); vs. 15 דָּגַר (twice, Jer 17 11 and
here); vs. 15 דַּיָּה (the only other instance is Deut 14 13).

17. *Significant allusions and reminiscences*

a. As has been suggested, it seems very likely that we
   have in the first strophe a recollection of the representation of Genesis 2 1 referring to the completion of
   creation, the heavens, the earth, and all their host.
   The discussion has made clear how large a part their
   destruction plays in the thought of the poet. See p. 345.

b. Duhm, Torrey, and others see in the expression חֶרֶב
   לַיהוה a possible reference to the Gideon narrative (Ju
   7 20). If this is indeed the case, it is worth calling
   attention to the Messianic hymn of Isaiah 9 where
   reference is made to the same passage.

c. The description of the destruction in 34 9 has recalled
   to many commentators the account of the destruction
   of Sodom and Gomorrah (cf. Jer 49 18) in Gen 19.

d. Few expressions in the entire poem are as interesting
   as the קַרְתֹהוּ וְאַבְנֵי־בֹהוּ of 34 11. Only twice in the OT
   do we meet a like expression. Many writers refer to
   Gen 1 as the source; if there is any borrowing at all
   here, I am more inclined to see an influence from
   Jeremiah's poem (4 23–26).

18. *Mythological and similar allusions*

a. The mythological heavenly tree[24]

b. The sword of Yahweh[25]

---

[24] For interesting discussions, see Hugo Gressmann, *Der Ursprung der
israelitisch-jüdischen Eschatologie*, 19 ff., esp. 28. ("Infolge der gewaltigen
Hitze wird auch der Himmelsbaum verdorren, sodass die Sterne abwelken,
die wie goldene Früchte oder Blätter an ihm hängen."); Hermann Gunkel,
Das Märchen im Alten Testament, 21; Wilhelm Bousset, *Die Religion des
Judentums im späthellenistischen Zeitalter*, Third edition edited by Gressmann, 489.

[25] Gressmann, *Ursprung*, 71 ff., esp. 83 f.; Gunkel, *Märchen*, 56; *Genesis*,
Third edition, 25; Bousset, *Religion*, 218 ff., esp. 221; Johannes Hempel,
Gott und Mensch im Alten Testament 15, 33 ff., etc..

c. The sacrifice of Yahweh[26]

d. ‏²⁷תֹהוּ וָבֹהוּ‎

e. The demonology of the poem[28]

19. *Variation in the parallelism*

One of the most distinctive features of Isaiah 34 is the great flexibility of the author's use of parallelism. He exhibits the same characteristic here as elsewhere, viz., control of his material, mastery of form, aversion to harsh sounds, remarkable ability in the composition of all literary units (stichoi, lines, or strophes). In the poet's employment of parallelism he combines sensitiveness to literary form with unusual freedom in his use of form. The following scheme will suggest something of his manner:

Vs. 1.	a	b	c	
		b′	a′	
	a	b(2)		
		b′(2)		
Vs. 6.	a	b	c	
		b′	c′	
			c	d(2)
			c′	d′(2)
Vs. 9.	a	b	c	
		b′	c′	
	a	b		
			c	d
Vs. 10.	a(2)	b		
	a′	b′	c′	
	a(2)	b		
		b′(2)		
				d(3)
Vs. 11.	a	b(2)		
		b′(2)	a	
	a	b	c	
	c′	b′		

[26] Gressmann, 136 ff.

[27] Gunkel, *Schöpfung und Chaos*, 138 f. and *passim*; *Genesis*, 103.

[28] Gressmann, 86 ff.; W. Robertson Smith, *The Religion of the Semites*, Third Edition, 138 and note, 441; Gunkel, *Märchen*, 89; *Schöpfung*, 132;

20. The subject of the metre of Isaiah 34 deserves more extended discussion than can be given to it here. The majority of critics are quite certain that the metre in this chapter, as well as in chapter 35, is 3'3' throughout.[29] Everyone must recognize that we are far from being in a position to be dogmatic on matters of metre. If we were only sure how the poem was read, there would be little difficulty. Yet, in this paper we have sought to draw attention to the importance of the relationship between sound and thought. One will be accused of subjectivity in literary judgments such as those with which we have been concerned. Still I find it difficult to believe that the poem is throughout in the 3'3' metre. Nor have I been able to follow the metrical analysis of Oesterley and Robinson: Qinah in vss. 1–5a, 3'3' in 5b–8, Qinah in 9, 3'3' in 10–17.[30] The longer I have dwelt with the poem, the more I have become convinced that the prevailing metre of 34 1–10 is Qinah, while 11–17 is certainly 3'3'. The only exceptions are 3ab and 6bc, and 10ab. I am uncertain about 2cd (one of Torrey's triple lines), 3cd, 5cd, 6ef, 8ab, but there is good reason in every case except the first for reading 3'2'. The only support I have found for this judgment is the criticism of Duhm's views by Professor G. B. Gray (*The Forms of Hebrew Poetry*, 227 f.) in which he finds the Qinah metre throughout 1–10, and 3'3' throughout 11–17. This is important and gratifying confirmation not only of my own view but of the literary structure and style of the poem as a whole

Torrey, 289, where references to other literature will be found. On Lilith, see now Emil Kraeling, *Bulletin of the American Schools of Oriental Research*, No. 67, 17 f.

[29] Duhm, Marti, Kittel, Cheyne (?), Torrey. In the case of Duhm and Marti, this conclusion is reached only through a radical alteration of the text.

[30] *Introduction to the Books of the Old Testament*, 257.

PSALM 47

JAMES MUILENBURG

PACIFIC SCHOOL OF RELIGION

THE forty-seventh psalm has a many-sided interest. More than any other poem that has been transmitted to us in the pages of the Old Testament, it has a claim to be an authentic enthronement hymn. It is intimately related in length, style, composition, and content to the other poems which have become generally known, since the publication of Mowinckel's influential monograph, as *Thronbesteigungslieder*.[1] Like the other members of this group (93, 96–99), it bears intimate affinities with the wide range of ancient literature of the Near East. One of the chief reasons which led Mowinckel to propound his famous theory is the apparent connection of these poems with the cultic celebrations of the Babylonian New Year. Unfortunately, Mowinckel never entered into a detailed comparison of the actual liturgical materials, but the similarities between the Babylonian rituals and the Hebrew poems must be apparent to anyone who will examine even cursorily the relevant pages in Gressmann's *Altorientalische Texte und Bilder*[2] or Thureau-Dangin's *Rituels accadiens*.[3] Egyptian affinities have been

---

[1] Sigmund Mowinckel, Psalmenstudien, II. *Das Thronbesteigungsfest Jahwäs und der Ursprung der Eschatologie*, Kristiania [Oslo], 1922.

[2] Hugo Gressmann (Editor), *Altorientalische Texte und Bilder zum alten Testament*. Zweite Auflage. Berlin and Leipzig, 1926. The similarities are rather in the dominant themes than in literary style or form. With respect to style the similarities to the poems of Second Isaiah are striking; cf. especially the ritual for the New Year's festival in Babylon on pp. 295–303.

[3] F. Thureau-Dangin, *Rituels accadiens*. Paris, 1921, pp. 129–146. See also Heinrich Zimmern's "Das babylonische Neujahrsfest" in *Der Alte Orient*, Band 25, Heft 3, for excellent examples with striking parallels both in form and content.

pointed out by Ratschow, above all with the Ramesseum papyrus.[4] So far as the writer is aware, nothing has yet been done to show the affinities of the enthronement hymns with the Ugaritic materials, but even surface exploration leads one to suspect kinship.[4a] That Psalm 47 played an important role, together with Psalm 81, in the New Year's celebrations in the synagogue gives support to Mowinckel's view. In the Christian community the psalm has been associated with the ascension of Christ.

Recent years have done greater justice to the place of the cult in ancient Israel.[5] As a result, many passages have achieved fresh significance and meaning.[6] Psalm 47 is unquestionably a product of the living cult. It has, moreover, often been given

[4] Karl Heinz Ratschow, "Epikrise zum Psalm 47" (*ZAW* 53 [1935] 176 ff.). In form and style the Egyptian rituals are widely separated from the Hebrew. They are in the form of expansive cult dramas with scenic directions and notes. The Hebrew hymn is above all a short poem composed according to rather severe and definite standards of Hebrew form. Ratschow fails to recognize this fundamental difference.

[4a] Cf. e. g. the couplet in Virolleaud, *La Déesse 'Anat*, p. 80:

> Aleyan Baal is our King,
> Our Judge, no one higher than he!

This is as perfect a statement of the central theme of the enthronement hymns as one could wish to find. No attempt is made to cite other relevant passages, or the literature bearing upon them.

[5] J. P. Peters, *The Psalms as Liturgies* (Macmillan's 1922) appeared in the same year as the great monograph of Mowinckel. Since then the cultic interpretation has grown steadily. Cf., e. g., the work of Hans Schmidt, Balla, Paul Humbert, and others of the school of literary types.

[6] This applies not merely to many psalms, but to numerous other Old Testament passages as well. Cf. the recent discussions, *inter alia*, of Gunkel on Isaiah 33 in *ZAW* 42 (1924) 177–208, and on the close of Micah in *Zeitschrift für Semistik* 2 (1924) 145–178 (later published in *What Remains of the Old Testament*, pp. 115–149); of Paul Humbert on the Book of Nahum in *RHPR* 12 (1932) 1–15, and on the first chapter of Genesis in *RHPR* 15 (1935) 1–27; of Ernst Sellin on the Book of Habakkuk in his commentary *Das Zwölfprophetenbuch* II, 1929–1930 (cf. Balla in *RGG* II, pp. 1556 f., and Elmer A. Leslie, *The Prophets Tell their Own Story*, pp. 204–226); and of Otto Eissfeldt in *Record and Revelation*, p. 93 (cf. also his *Einleitung in das alte Testament*, pp. 437 f.).

messianic or eschatological interpretation. Mowinckel's theory, which discovers the roots of Hebrew eschatology in the annual celebrations of Yahweh's enthronement as King in the festival of the New Year, gave wider and more modern currency to this interpretation. Both the general theme and the language of the poem, as of all the enthronement hymns, make an eschatological interpretation permissible, if not plausible. Further, if we are permitted to take Psalm 47 in its present textual form, translating it as it stands before us, there is no passage of more genuine universalism in the whole of the Old Testament, not even Mal 1 11.

As striking in its own way as any of the foregoing features is the literary character of the hymn. It is one of many ancient Hebrew lyrics which give us a vivid insight into Hebrew literary method and style. The literary features lie so much on the surface to the reader of the Hebrew text that for that very reason they somehow elude his recognition. One must, for example, learn to be sensitive to words and sounds, and to observe the articulation of individual words and sentences into a larger structure.[7]

Finally, the text of Psalm 47 has an exceptional interest. In recent years it has received extensive though varied treatment. The purpose of the present paper is to examine briefly some of the textual changes that have been proposed, with a view to arriving as nearly as possible to the original form. When the text has been determined, an attempt will be made to analyse the literary form and character of the poem as a basis for determining its primary meaning and major emphases. It cannot be repeated too often that this determination of form is an essential prerequisite for the determination of meaning. The more we learn of Hebrew literary manner and habit, the more apparent and important does this become. From literary analysis we shall turn to the elements which connect the poem with the coronation of the king, with the living worship of the cult, and with eschatology.

[7] The *elemental* character of Hebraic literary practice is seldom or never lost in the Old Testament.

I

The problem raised by Psalm 47 and the consequent clue to its proper understanding is the presence within it of divine names. In the course of this little hymn of 71 words the ancient and distinctive *Elyon* appears once, *Yahweh* twice, *Elohim* eight times, and *Melek* as an ascription of God thrice. In the *International Critical Commentary* Briggs sought to show that the two references to Yahweh (3a, 6b) were suspicious in the present form of the psalm.[8] They were present he contended, however, in the original Korahite psalter; in fact this original edition was without any reference to Elohim, and had Yahweh wherever Elohim now appears.[9] Charles Foster Kent followed Briggs entirely in this.[10] Briggs made another interesting suggestion, however, *viz.*, the insertion of Elyon in the concluding stichos of the poem: *Greatly exalted is Elyon.*[11] In this latter suggestion he was guided by a sure intuition, though he attempted to satisfy it, as so frequently in his commentary, by operations that are textually precarious. J. P. Peters was also troubled by the two-fold appearance of Yahweh.[12] The first in 3a he removed as a later substitution of an original Elohim, but the second in 6b he thought might be original. Bernhard Duhm changes the Elohim in vss. 6–10 to Yahweh, though he does not undertake

[8] *A Critical and Exegetical Commentary on the Book of Psalms*, 2 vols. The International Critical Commentary (New York, 1906), Vol I, p. 400.

[9] Except of course in the phrase *'Elohe Abraham* in 10b.

[10] The Student's Old Testament. *The Songs, Hymns and Prayers of the Old Testament*, p. 116.

[11] The value of Briggs' suggestion is his implied recognition of the importance of the divine name Elyon for an interpretation of the poem. The repetition of the name which appeared at the focal position at the beginning of the poem would be according to Hebrew practice. That the Greek, Aquila, and the Latin version of Jerome translate the verb as plural, with "shields of the earth" as subject, is no argument for Briggs' proposed change. On the contrary, the brevity of the closing stichos is in keeping with the dramatic tone of the poem, and the paronomasia which Briggs' suggestion would produce would not be felicitous for a poet of the subtlety of the author of Psalm 47.

[12] *Ibid.*, p. 289.

to explain or defend the procedure.[13] In 1926 appeared Hermann
Gunkel's great commentary on the Psalms.[14] Although critical
of Mowinckel's views concerning the enthronement hymns,
believing that the latter greatly exaggerated the number of
psalms he included in this class, Gunkel nevertheless saw in
Pss 47, 93, 96, 97, 98, and 99 genuine enthronement hymns
which were to be interpreted eschatologically.[15] In the case of
Psalm 47, Gunkel believed that the poem was originally the
creation of the living Yahweh cult and that it had been transformed in no less than six places by the substitution of Elohim
for Yahweh (2a, 6b, 8a, 9a, 9b, 10c). By a characteristically shrewd
emendation he read for the difficult *maginne-erets* in 10c *negide-
erets*,[16] the line then reading *Denn 'Jahve' gehören die 'Fürsten'
der Welt.*

In an interesting and stimulating article K. H. Ratschow
undertook to test Gunkel's theory.[17] He was prompted to this
step by his own researches into the King cult. Like Mowinckel
and many others both before and after him, he became completely convinced of the presence of the cult of the divine king
in ancient Israel. He found in Psalm 47 a perfect specimen in
which the references to the King (3b, 7b, 8a, cf. 9a) were clear,
emphatic, and highly suggestive. Yet the present form of the
text did not admit of their provenance in the King cult. The
obvious explanation was that it represented a later redaction.
This is not to imply that Ratschow was necessarily motivated
by any preconceived theory. Like Gunkel, he was sure that the
psalm did not appear in its original form, but Gunkel's solution
did not seem to him to correspond to the natural inference of

[13] *Die Psalmen*, Kurzer Hand-commentar zum alten Testament. (Freiburg
i. B., 1899), pp. 133 f.

[14] *Die Psalmen*. Göttinger Handkommentar zum alten Testament. Göttingen, 1926.

[15] See his exhaustive and extremely detailed *Einleitung in die Psalmen*,
which was brought to completion by his pupil Joachim Begrich in 1933. The
relevant pages are 94–116.

[16] *Die Psalmen, ad loc.*

[17] *Supra*, n. 4.

the psalm as we have it. Adopting F. Buhl's suggestion for
10c[18] he read *mugan* for *maginne*, rendering the verse as follows:

> *Denn dem Gotte ist die Welt geschenckt.*
> *Er ist sehr erhoben.*

The reference he believed to be to the divine king (cf. Ps 45 7).
He next turned to the parallelism of *Elohim* and *Melek* in vss. 7
and 8. Here he felt that the emphasis fell upon *melek*, an observation which form and style clearly admit. But in the crucial
vs. 6 the parallelism with *melek* falls out, and Yahweh appears
instead. On the basis of the inference of 10c and the plain meaning
of vss. 7–8 Ratschow felt justified in reading *melek* for *Yahweh*,
a change which would be almost decisive for his interpretation.

With 5b Ratschow deals somewhat more venturesomely. In
the present text "the pride of Jacob" is parallel to "our inheritance," and the meaning of the former has generally been understood since the time of Theodore of Mopsuestia to be "the
beautiful land of Canaan."[19] This does not satisfy Ratschow,
who is impressed by the form of the phrase *ge'on Ya'akob* and
sees in it a reference to one of the early nomadic deities discussed
in Albrecht Alt's *Der Gott der Väter*.[20] This suggestion came to
the writer independently before he had seen Ratschow's article,
especially because of the parallel reference to *the God of Abraham*
in 10b and the mention of "the shields of the earth" which may
have been somehow suggested by the phrase "Shield of Abraham" (cf. Gen 15 1). The theory naturally presents itself, and
it is possible that something of the sort was in the mind of the
original poet. The present text does not easily permit this
interpretaton however.

In 3a Ratschow deletes *Yahweh* and substitutes the pronoun
hu' in its stead. This has no legitimate support whatsoever and
must be rejected. Stylistic analogies and form-critical considera-

---

[18] In the second edition of Kittel's *Biblia Hebraica*. The third edition omits
it and suggests another emendation of the text.

[19] Hans Lietzmann, *Der Psalmenkommentar Theodor von Mopsuestia.*
Sitzungsberichten der Berkiner Akademie. 1902, p. 344. I am indebted to
König's commentary for this reference.

[20] Pp. 49 ff.

tions are against it.[21] The attempt to get a consistent 3:3 meter prompts the excision of *kol* from 2b and of *qodsho* from 9b. Neither change is necessary or helpful. Other considerations outweigh the metrical argument. Finally, Ratschow is troubled by the introductory *ki*, which appears at the beginning of three lines, which he rightly recognizes as crucial and central (3a, 8a, 10c): he decides to delete each *ki* there. Commenting upon Ratschow's treatment of Psalm 47, Millar Burrows made the interesting suggestion that the letters of the conjunction were abbreviations for *koh°ne Yahweh* or *koh°nim*.[21a] The objection to Ratschow's excision is that the words belong to the characteristic form of the Hebrew hymn.[22] To excise them is to do violence to form and style. Burrow's explanation, ingenious as it is, similarly fails to take account of this characteristic stylistic usage and the natural position of the word.[23]

Into Ratschow's theory that the hymn has its provenance in the King cult we cannot enter here. It is certainly an attractive proposal. His textual operations are comparatively conservative. The crucial line in his theory is vs. 6 If *melek* is to be read for *Yahweh*, Ratschow's case is strong. The want of textual support for the change must not be too strongly pressed. The revision of the psalm may easily have been made at a relatively early date. But if the intent was to remove the odium of a hymn to the divine King, why did not the redactor proceed further? Other lines like vs. 7 would probably have offended him quite as much. Moreover, there is still the first consideration of all: is it possible to defend the text as it is? Do the divine names give us any clear and constructive clue to the meaning of the poem as a whole?

---

[21] Psalm 24 2 seems at first to contradict this, but I do not believe it to be a true literary parallel.

[21a] *ZAW* N. F. 14 (1937) 176.

[22] Cf., e. g., Ex 15 21, which Gressmann has called the most ancient Hebrew hymn (*Mose und seine Zeit, ad loc.*). Gunkel, *Einleitung*, 42 f., counts almost a hundred instances of this usage. To be sure, it is not indispensable to the hymn, nor does it always occur after the introductory call or appeal. Psalm 47 may be said to represent an unusually perfect form of the hymn.

[23] One might question also whether Ratschow's disposition of materials, e. g. his allocation of these three lines to the priest, is correct.

Other textual alterations have been proposed. We cite only the more important of these. The majority of scholars accept Stade's emendation of *yivḥar* to *yarḥev*, thus reading *he expanded for us our inheritance.*[24] It is hazardous, however, to make the change without any textual support for it, since the word "choose" cannot be said to be harsh or meaningless. In 7a the Greek reads *Elohenu* for *Elohim*, and this change has also commended itself to many. The parallel to *malkenu* in the succeeding stichos and euphony support it, but the constant repetition of Elohim in this part of the poem may have been intentional as we shall point out later. In 8a many manuscripts insert *'al* before *kol-ha-'arets*, thus giving: *For a king over all the earth is Elohim.* There is no real objection to this; in many ways it is an improvement, and it has a stylistic parallel with 3b. These lines bear the main meaning of the poem. The change would support Hebrew style elsewhere. The suggestion to read *mlk* as a verb is also possible, and has the approval of Gunkel and Oesterley among others. This would give us the regular coronation cry (with the proposed change in divine name) *Yahweh has become King over all the earth*, at an exceedingly strategic point in the poem. One is tempted to accept it. Yet there are arguments against it: (1) the stichos is too closely parallel to the important stichos of 3b, to warrant the change, (2) the change would rob the next line (9a) of its effectiveness, for this is precisely the great disclosure there, and (3) there is no textual support for it. The second stichos of vs. 9 seems over-full, and the repetition of Elohim awkward. Naturally many scholars delete the divine name from 9b. If there were no larger considerations out-weighing the metrical argument, it should certainly be deleted. But such larger considerations do exist.

More important than the foregoing changes, however, is the text of 10b Our masoretic text reads *people of the God of Abraham* whereas the Greek and the Syriac have *with the God of Abraham*, that is, the Greek read *'im* where *M* has *'am*. The vast majority of scholars therefore combine the two readings, giving *'im 'am*,

[24] *ZAW* 23 (1903) 169.

together with the people of the God of Abraham.[25] The change in
meaning is great, as will be readily recognized. The unpointed
text easily explains the difficulty. The reduplication of the
letters seems to the writer gratuitous. There are not a few
scholars of the first rank who have consistently refused to yield
to the change.[26] One might adduce stylistic objections to *'im-'am*.
Delitzsch contends that it is inadmissible "since one does not
say *ne''saph 'im* but *l'* or *el*. Eusebius also commends Symmachus
and Theodotion because they translate the λαὸς τοῦ Θεοῦ
Ἀβραάμ. So, according to Delitzsch, the passage is understood
by the Targum, Jerome, Luther, and most of the Jewish expositors, and among modern expositors Crusius, Hupfeld, and
Hitzig.[27] There is the most powerful argument of all, however,
and that is that the logic of the entire poem from the beginning
leads directly to this amazing statement, that the princes of the
peoples are gathered as the people of the God of Abraham. To
alter the text in a way that is stylistically awkward, without
strong manuscript support, since the Greek translator had
precisely the same text as the Masoretes before him, and in a
way that is contrary to the movement of the poem as a whole,
is to distort the obvious purport of the poem.

We may render Psalm 47 somewhat literally as follows:

> All ye peoples, clap (your) hands,
> Shout to Elohim with jubilant cry (*b'qol rinnah*),
> For Yahweh Elyon is terrible,
> A great King over all the earth.
> He subdued peoples beneath us,
> And nations (*ul'umin*) beneath our feet.
> He chose for us our inheritance
> The pride of Jacob whom he loved.
> Elohim is gone up with a shout,
> Yahweh with the blast of the shophar (*b'qol shophar*).

[25] So, e. g., Olshausen, Lagarde, Ewald, Duhm, Gunkel, Briggs, Oesterley
and Buttenwieser.

[26] Kittel, Baethgen, Staerk, Bertholet. Franz Delitzsch, a scholar of unusual literary sensitivity and insight, although excessively conservative in
critical matters, clearly understands the meaning and significance of the line.
Cf. his *Biblical Commentary on the Psalms* (Edinburgh, 1871), II, p. 100. So
also Eduard König, *Die Psalmen* (Gütersloh, 1927), p. 224.

[27] Franz Delitzsch. *Ibid.*, p. 100.

> Sing ye to Elohim, O sing ye,
> Sing ye to our King, O sing ye,
> For a King 'over' all the earth is Elohim,
> Sing ye with a maskil.
> Elohim has become King over the nations,
> Elohim is seated on his holy throne,
> The princes of the peoples are gathered together,
> A people of the God of Abraham,
> For the shields of the earth belong to Elohim.
> He is greatly exalted.

Several stylistic features may be observed at once. The openings of the two strophic hymns are unmistakeable. The strophes are of equal length, five full lines or ten stichoi. This is not essential in Hebrew poetry, but it is not infrequent. The more characteristically Oriental form is a series of stanzas nearly all of the same length but with an occasional divergence. Observe the similar phrases at the close of the first and last full lines of the first strophe. Observe, too, that the striking phrases *pride of Jacob* and *God of Abraham* occupy the same relative position in the strophes. Again, the place of the *ki* line, following the opening exordium of each strophe, is exactly the same. Finally, and most significant of all, are the key words and the positions of *Elyon* (עֶלְיוֹן), *is gone up*, (עָלָה) and *He is exalted* (נַעֲלָה). It is not too much to say that this furnishes us with a major clue to the interpretation of the poem.

II

The poem opens with the characteristic exordium of the Hebrew hymn. An imperative appeal is addressed to *all peoples*. The view of A. B. Ehrlich,[28] Hans Schmidt,[29] and others that "all peoples" refers to the peoples of Palestine is plainly contradicted by the poem as a whole. All the peoples of the earth are clearly meant: three different words [*goyyim* (9a), *le'umim* (4b), *'ammim* (2a, 4a, 10a)] are used to give emphasis to this ad-

---

[28] *Die Psalmen* (Berlin, 1905), pp. 105 f.
[29] *Die Psalmen* (Tübingen, 1934), p. 91.

dress,[30] and the writer says in the three pivotal points of the poem
that the whole earth is the range of his vision (3b, 8a, 10c). The
first half-line calls upon *all the peoples* to applaud, in the primitive
fashion of early peoples, by clapping their hands; the second calls
upon them to *shout* in the characteristic manner of Israel's
jubilant cultic celebrations. The object of the rejoicing and
excitement is Elohim. The spirit and mood of the poem breathes
through each word of this opening line.

The second line of the strophe opens in the fashion typical
of many Hebrew poems. The transitional word from the formal
exordium to the poem proper is the small and unpretentious
word *ki*.[31] In the numerous instances of such lines introduced
by *ki* which I have examined, the burden and the stress of the
poem seems frequently to be placed after it.[32] Note that here
it is not the general term Elohim but the covenant name Yahweh
about whom the central affirmation is made. The reference to
Yahweh is followed by the ancient and venerable appellation
Elyon, *Most High* or *Exalted One*. Each of the divine names
figures in the pattern of the poem's composition. The first

[30] Note the opening appeal to the nations and peoples in Isa. 34. This
motif, it need scarcely be observed, is dominant in the poems of Second Isaiah
throughout.

[31] The *formal* function of this word is not confined to the Hebrew hymn.
It is apparent in numerous other literary types both within and without the
Book of Psalms. A study of this word in Hosea, a book where the formal
characteristics have frequently been effaced, is as revealing for the textual
critic as for the *Gattungkritiker*. Its usage in Second Isaiah is also highly
illuminating. It may be pointed out here, however, that *ki* is but one of many
such words which perform special formal functions. Cf., e. g. *hinneh*, *laken*,
the interrogatives *mi*, *mah*, etc., the personal pronouns, etc. Whoever has
actually sought to discern Hebraic literary style and method will not consider
such phenomena accidental collocations. On the contrary, they frequently
furnish the clue for discerning the unity, emphasis, and articulation of the
poem. The strophic critic will recognize the justice of these claims at once.

[32] The following examples drawn from the Book of Psalms are taken at
random from the Hebrew text: 1 6; 5 3, 5, 13; 11 6, 7; 13 6; 21 4, 7, 8, 14; 26 3,
cf. vs. 11; 36 10; 37 2, 39; 57 11; 63 3, 12; 75 3, 9; 96 13; 98 9; 99 9; 100 5. The
meaning of *ki* is not always to be understood causally. Cf. the remarks on the
word in Johannes Pedersen, *Israel, its Life and Culture* (London, 1926) pp.
117 ff.

stichos in this crucial passage reads *Yahweh Elyon is terrible*.
But it is the second stichos that receives the major stress of the
line and gives us the clue for the emphasis of the poem as a whole.
The meaning is that Yahweh Elyon is now King over all the
earth. The poem is athrill with the excitement of this affirmation.
It is monotheism in an exultant mood, conflate of the prophetic
rhapsodies of Second Isaiah and the fervent liturgies of the cult.
The first stichos (3b) constitues the theme of the succeeding
lines (vss. 4–5), while the second (3b) provides the theme for the
second half of the poem (vss. 7–10), which describes the actual
enthronement of Yahweh as King and Elohim.[33]

The lines immediately following (vss. 4–5) are an account of
the conquest of the nations and of the apportionment of an
inheritance to Israel. The theme is eschatological, and the
portrait is of God as Conqueror and Judge, as Subduer of nations
and Vindicator of Israel. With restraint and conscious literary
art the divine names are conspicuously absent. It is Israel's
witness to the righting of the wrongs and injustices of history:

> He subdued peoples beneath us,
> And nations beneath our feet;
> He chose for us our inheritance,
> The pride of Jacob whom he loved.

The lines are articulated into a well-knit unity not only by the
single thought which pervades them, but also by the assonance
of the stichoi, the meter, and the structure of the lines. The
first three stichoi end with the same sound (4a, 4b, 5a, cf. also
lanu in 5a), the meter is clearly the regular 3:3, the parallelism
is complementary in both verses, and the verb takes the initiative
in both (note the *beneath* and the sign of the direct and definite
object *eth*). *The pride of Jacob* is the obvious climax (in meaning,
in mood, and in form) to which the lines lead. The stichos in
which it appears contains an additional element, which sets it
apart, gives it emphasis, and serves as a kind of echo of the
preceding. The liturgical direction *selah* appears after it. It is
possible that the strophe was meant to end here and that the

---

[33] A practically unnoticed feature of Hebrew style which can be illustrated
by impressive examples.

succeeding verse was a kind of extra or over-hanging line. This suggestion is enforced by the circumstance that the second main strophe can be similarly construed.

Here we are at the center of the poem (vs. 6). It appears immediately after the *selah*, which may have been a signal for raising the cultic shout of victory. The lines which follow this crucial verse are obviously a new hymn. This sets off our verse in peculiar fashion and calls attention to the significance of its contents:

> Elohim has gone up with a shout,
> Yahweh with the blast of the trumpet.

Here Yahweh and Elohim are clearly equated. The Yahweh who ascends with the blast of the New Year's trumpet is Elohim. The word describing the ascent (*'ala*) is obviously related to the Elyon of the opening of the strophe. He who ascends with a shout is the Elohim of the exordium. This is none other than Israel's covenant God Yahweh, who after His judgment over the nations assumes His kingship with a ringing blast of the ram's horn (note 1b). It is significant that all three divine names of the first strophe receive illumination in this solemn and impressive act of Yahweh's ascension, which doubtless includes the festal pilgrimage referred to elsewhere in the Old Testament. In this respect again it reaches back to the beginning of the hymn.

The response to Yahweh's ascent is tumultuous. The Temple choirs are bidden strike up their music in words which only the Hebrew can reproduce adequately:

> *zamm^eru Elohim zammēru*
> *zamm^eru l^emalkenu zammēru*
> *ki melek 'al kol ha-'arets Elohim*
> *zamm^eru maskil.*

The lines are a hymanl introduction of the same kind as the exordium of the first strophe. A jubilant five-fold imperative "to make melody" binds them into a firm unity. The exordium of praise and jubilation introducing this second hymn is followed by the not infrequent *ki*, and the first stichos of the impressive and revealing sentence corroborates eloquently our claim that it is the theme already announced in the similar line at the beginning of the first strophe (3b). In the first strophe the exalted Yahweh is King over all the earth. Here in the second hymn it is Elohim about whom precisely the same words are used. Yahweh disappears completely in the poet's exultation at the thought of the covenant God being exalted as Elohim, the sovereign King of all the earth (cf. 3b and 8a).

> Sing ye to Elohim, sing ye,
> Sing ye to *our King*, sing ye,
> For a King of all the earth is Elohim,
> Sing ye a maskil.

The coronation cry sounds out: *Elohim has become King over the nations.* The procession has arrived at its destination. Elohim is now seated upon His holy throne (9b). Without question this is the culmination of the poem. To it every line has led, and what follows is the inevitable interpretation of what has taken place. Whatever may have been the actual *Sitz im Leben* of the poem, whatever its use in the cult of the Jewish community, or whatever the nature of its eschatological associations, the conception of Elohim's coronation as King was one to stir the imagination profoundly. The small compass of the poem must not deceive one. Its true significance is reflected both by its striking relationship to Second Isaiah and the other enthronement hymns and by its employment in the Jewish festival of the New Year.

The princes and representatives of the nations gather about to pay Elohim his homage. Here we encounter the crowning achievement of the poet's vision. It is so striking as to seem incredible. But as we have seen, the text of 10b does not in reality present us with the difficulties that many scholars have found here, and the Greek text cannot be called as a witness for the modern interpretation which sees the princes gathered together with the people of Abraham's God. If we are not to tamper with the text, we have to choose between *the gathering of the princes with the God of Abraham*, which is awkward and not too illuminating, and *the gathering of the princes as a people of the God of Abraham*. This latter interpretation is consistent with the tenor of the psalm as a whole, and certainly the whole psalm points in its direction from the very beginning. As many commentators have seen, the thought here is consistent with such passages as Gen 12 3. Even more, however, the poem as a whole and this insight in particular are thoroughly in the mood and temper of Second Isaiah. The reference to Abraham belongs to a comparatively late stratum of prophetic thought and may conceivably belong also to that tendency in eschatology which weaves primitive legends and traditions into the fabric of contemporary insights.

But one line remains, and if we know anything about Hebrew literary manner or rightly discern the movement of our, little hymn, we shall expect something momentous. The conclusion is introduced, as often, with *ki*:

> For to Elohim belong the shields of the earth,
> He is highly exalted.

The rulers of the earth are under the rule of the one God of all the earth. Yahweh Elyon has gone up amidst the cultic cries of his devotees to become crowned King of all the nations with their princes and kings. *He is highly exalted.*

We are now prepared to understand something of the significance of the divine names in our little hymn. If the foregoing argument on the basis of literary form has been followed, it will be seen that the divine names supply us with the key to the solution of the poem's meaning. Moreover, the names must stand as they are found at the present time in our masoretic text. At the beginning and at the end of the first strophe all names are represented. In both something important is said concerning Yahweh. He ascends to become King over all the earth. At the termination of the ascent, the second hymn leaves the covenant name behind. The poet is intoxicated with the vision he sees of a universal God as Sovereign of the nations. We must, therefore, reject the proposed emendations of Briggs and Gunkel and their followers. Ratschow's view is textually less radical than Gunkel's and it is difficult to resist its attractiveness. One may admit fairly close affinities of the enthronement poems with the Semitic New Year celebration of the divine enthronement. Yet these affinities can be variously explained;

they do not necessarily mean that this hymn was at one time a liturgy of the cult of the divine king. The explanation offered seems to the writer, everything considered, to be a safer alternative. The present pattern is too internal and intrinsic to the poem, the divine names too carefully studied, the movement of the thought too inevitable for it to be the result of textual manipulation. But more than this, the universal sweep and lofty grandeur of the poet's conception of God are not likely to have been the work of a post-exilic redactor.

III

From an examination of the literary form and character of the hymn, we now turn to the elements in it which associate it with the coronation of the King. Most noticeable is the mention of the King in the poem's most strategic places, above all 3b and 8a. *Yahweh is King over all the earth.* The coronation praises are to be addressed to Elohim as *our King,* and the characteristic coronation cry is echoed in the line *Elohim has become King over the nations.* In general, the prophets, especially those of the pre-exilic period, betray an almost studied avoidance of the ascription of royalty to Yahweh. There are notable exceptions like Isaiah 6, but they are few in number. This doubtless reflects a protest against the prevailing Semitic cult of the divine king. But in our coronation hymns we find a precisely opposite tendency. It is this prominence of God as King that encourages such a thesis as Ratschow's. Yet it should be remarked, too, that unless we greatly alter the poem, what is proclaimed is that Elohim is king, not that the King is Elohim.

In the second place, the terminology and subject matter of the hymn is clearly drawn from the coronation ceremonies of the earthly king. The clapping of hands,[34] the shout,[35] and the sounding of the trumpets[36] are fully attested by the accounts

[34] Cf. II Kings 11 12; cf. also Ps 98 8.

[35] Cf. the *tᵉruaḥ melek* of Num 23 21; also I Sam 10 24; II Sam 16 16 and the references given in note 37 below. Cf. Ps 98 4, 6; Zeph 3 14 f.; Zech 9 9.

[36] Cf. II Sam 15 10; I Kings 1 34, 39, 41; II Kings 9 13; 11 14.

of coronation which appear in the historical literature. The coronation cry appears repeatedly both in the historical references and in the other enthronement hymns.[37] The gathering of the people from far and near on the occasion of the choice of a new king or the royal festival is clearly corroborated.[38] The coming together of the sheiks of the clans or the leaders of the people was characteristic.[39] The ascent of the King to the holy hill is described more than once, though it is not too clear from the references whether this was meant to be customary.[40] The instance of Solomon certainly must not be pressed, as has been constantly done by those who support the theory of Yahweh's enthronement. But the actual appearance of the King before the throne and his being seated thereon is the very culmination of the enthronement festival. The roots of this poem in the coronation of the earthly King cannot be denied. Hans Schmidt is so impressed by this that he writes: "Auch diese Gleichartigkeit eines Vorgangs im profanen Leben bestätigt, dass wir hier an eine Feier in Raum und Zeit, an ein Tempelfest und nicht an den Himmel oder an den jüngsten Tag zu denken haben."[41] This does not take any account of whether the language is after all the language of imagery drawn from the earthly cult and transferred to the heavenly. No one would deny — least of all the proponents of the eschatological interpretation — that the origin of the imagery is the celebration of the temporal king. *Cela va sans dire.* Nevertheless, a complete appreciation of the poem demands a constant recognition that language and imagery and form all serve the single purpose of proclaiming that Elohim is King over all the peoples of the world.

Closely associated with the derivation of the hymn in some sense or other from the coronation, is the intimate connection of the hymn with the living cult. Its interest is obviously strongly liturgical. The *Gattung* is unquestionably that of a

---

[37] Cf. I Sam 10 24, II Sam 15 10; 16 16; I Kings 1 25, 34, 39; II Kings 9 13; 11 12; Pss 93 1; 96 10; 97 1; 99 1; cf. also 98 6.

[38] Cf. I Sam 10 17 ff.; 11 15; II Sam 2 4; 3 21; 5 1, 3; I Kings 12 1, 20.

[39] Cf. II Sam 5 3; Deut 33 5.

[40] Cf. II Sam 6 1–15; I Kings 1 40, 45; II Kings 11 19 (?).

[41] *Die Psalmen,* p. 90.

hymn.[42] The clapping of hands probably reaches back in its origins to the cultic dance. The joyful and somewhat hilarious shouting in praise of God is in keeping with the ancient Oriental temperament and practice; very impressive, too, is the blowing of the *shophar* on cultic occasions, supremely perhaps on New Year's day.[43] Yahweh's ascent at the blast of the shophar is as we have seen the very center of the poem. The poem rests on this line. And the poem reflects, doubtless, something of the actual course of the cultic celebration. After the blowing of the ram's horn proclaiming the ascent of God, the temple choirs (the inference seems legitimate) are called upon with a five-fold appeal to sing their praises. The joyous, even ecstatic mood of the gathering could not be better revealed. Yet these elements are all relatively minor in comparison with the two great cultic acts of the poem: first, *the procession to the sanctuary:*

> Elohim ascends with a shout (*teru'ah*)
> Yahweh with the blast of the shophar.

and second, the *enthronement of Yahweh as King* of all the nations:

> Elohim has become King over the nations,
> Elohim is seated upon His holy throne.

The cultic style of the poem is clear. Liturgy from remote antiquity to our own day has relied upon the effectiveness of repetition. First to be observed is the repetition of the divine names, and the place of their appearance. Elohim appears in the first and last lines of the first strophe, which was stylistically characteristic of our poet and especially intentional on his part. Incidentally it provides us with the accent of the poem. In the coronation hymn Elohim (in the absolute form) appears five times, each time with carefully studied attention to emphasis. The effect of this constant repetition is greatly enhanced by being read aloud. The ear can hear what the eye fails to see. Similarly Yahweh is repeated but twice, yet, as we have had

[42] See Gunkel, *op. cit.*, 201, especially Gunkel and Begrich's *Einleitung*, pp. 94–116.

[43] Note the place of the shophar in the celebrations of the *rosh ha-shanah*. The whole ceremonial has interesting connections with our psalm.

occasion to see, only at those points where the meaning demands it: Yahweh is exalted as Elohim and King. Again, we are twice reminded in the two most crucial stichoi that He is *King of all the earth*. The praises are directed to *our King*, and the cultic cry tells of his becoming King. The seven-fold repetition in the poem of Elohim, and the three fold ascription of *melek* are not likely to be accidental.[44] Similarly, the admonition to sing praises is repeated five times, the extension of God's power to the whole earth is emphasized three times, the reference to the peoples is three-fold. Here we may be reminded once more of the position and function of Elyon (3a) at whose ascent (cf. *'ala* in 6a) he is greatly exalted (10d). This latter example also emphasizes the *dramatic* character of the hymn. This dramatic style is also reflected elsewhere: in the urgent and exultant calls at the opening of the strophes, the climactic conclusions, the order of words, and indeed in the articulation of all the stichoi. The rhythm is unusually smooth and clear, making the poem especially easy to read. The meter is prevailingly 3:3, the striking exception being the last line, which is clearly 3:2.

The cultic terminology is implied in what we have written. It is so rich and abundant, however, that it is well to list the most significant of the expressions which clearly emanate from the worship of the community. Almost all the commentators call attention to the word *'ala*, to *go up* or *ascend*, and with few exceptions they recognize its provenance from the cult. Duhm's comment of many years ago would be controverted by few scholars since his day: *wahrscheinlich liegt ein Terminus der alten Kultsprache vor*. Mowinckel naturally made a great deal of the word and its noun form *ma'alah* for his *Thronbesteigung* theory in which he related all the psalms of ascent (120–134) to the enthronement festival. Criticism has for the most part recognized the cultic significance of these latter psalms, and though we may not agree that they are *always* "Termini für das Hinaufsteigen zum Heiligtum in kultischen Absicht," the frequent use of the word *'ala* in a cultic sense cannot be contro-

---

[44] The excessive appeal to number by the pseudo-aesthetic criticism of a generation ago must not blind one to the very real importance of certain numbers in Hebrew literary form. Most common are 3, 5, 7, 10 and 12.

verted. The *teru'ah* (*hārî'û*) of vs. 2 and the *teru'ah shophar* of
vs. 6 are drawn from worship practices. The much controverted
selah is doubtless a cultic direction for the execution of the hymn;
it is possibly meant to indicate a pause.[45] The reference to the
maskil in 47 8 is apparently to a cult song.[46] Finally, we may
point to the five-fold *zamar* (cf. *mizmor*). We shall refrain from
comment on the superscription because it is not likely that it is
original. Yet it witnesses to the association with the cult. So
far as the writer is aware a thorough study has never been made
of the relations of the superscriptions of the Psalter to the
abundant materials with which they seem to be related in the
Books of Chronicles. Such a study should be exceptionally
fruitful.

The cult lives on its reverent memories of the past. Venerable
names, ancient events, terms hallowed by historic usage, all
these it feeds upon. In our little poem the reference to Elyon
would be especially rich in ancient suggestion.[47] Its connotations probably transcend the horizons even of those who have
discovered the place of this deity in the cults of ancient Canaan.
The references to the patriarchs in the phrases *pride of Jacob*
and *God of Abraham* would surely stimulate the devotion and
memory of the pious worshiper. The recollection of Yahweh's
ancient conquests, his subjection of peoples, his choice of an
inheritance in Israel's behalf, all these would fire the imagination of the ancient Israelite. Indeed, it is this combination of
national feeling and sentiment, and the universal perspectives
in the poem that make it so striking.

The psalm has been interpreted messianically and eschatologically. But the eschatological interpretation has also been
vigorously denied. In arriving at a decision it is always well to
remind ourselves that we are reading neither a theological

[45] Cf. R. H. Pfeiffer, *Introduction to the Old Testament*, pp. 642 f.

[46] See Mowinckel's discussion in Psalmenstudien. IV. *Die technischen
termini in den Psalmenüberlieferungen*. Kristiania: Kommission bei Jacob
Dybwald, 1923.

[47] Note again the lines from the Ras Shamra poem in Virolleaud's *La Déesse
'Anat*, p. 80. On Elyon see "El 'Elyon in Gen 14 18–20" by G. Levi Della Vida
in *JBL* 43 (1944) 1–9.

treatise nor an apocalypse but an Oriental hymn drawn from the worship of the people. We shall not expect ideas to appear systematically fórmulated. What we can say with assurance is that the imagery and ideas that we have here later became associated with eschatology. The portrait of God as Judge and His universal sovereignty are characteristic eschatological ideas. His coming to rule the world belongs to the heart of eschatology. Psalm 47 is closely related to the poems of Second Isaiah, and with the latter the eschatological message is central and determinative. It is possible that we are moving in the world of eschatological thoughts, but that these are not yet expressed in the language of prophecy or apocalypse but of religious lyric. We cannot be sure that the poem is consciously eschatologically oriented, but neither can we deny this. At any rate, it is not difficult to understand how Gunkel and his followers and even Mowinckel with his striking theory of the origins of eschatology in the enthronement of Yahweh could discern much that is eschatological in the poem.

IV

Psalm 47 raises many interesting questions. To many of these we have not succeeded in discovering a clear or convincing answer. But a study of the text, of literary form and style, and of its cultic character has led us to the following conclusions.

1. The text of the psalm is remarkably well preserved. The history of investigation took a sharp turn for the worse through modern attempts to remedy what was considered a corrupt text. It is highly significant that these attempts were focused for the most part precisely upon that area of the psalm which yields maximum light for its interpretation. Briggs, Gunkel, Ratschow, and others have correctly observed that the divine names were peculiar in this psalm, though they did not understand either the scope of the problem (i. e., the various divine names employed), the peculiar collocation of these names, or the relation of the divine names to each other. Our examination has shown that in the four divine appellations (Yahweh, Elyon, Elohim, and *melek*) the psalm achieves an intelligible interpretation, an

interpretation, it is not too much to say, which not only contradicts other modern interpretations but also gives the poem a significance and value which is consistent with its literary associations, notably the enthronement hymns and the poems of the Second Isaiah.

2. The psalm is constructed according to characteristic principles of Hebrew form and style. Such principles are seen in word order; the relationships of words, stichoi, and lines; sense of symmetry and balance combined with a distinctive aversion to stereotype; fondness for euphony, concrete imagery, and love of the scenic; portrayal of incident and event as over against rational exposition; sense of the dramatic and climactic which does not necessarily become rhetorical.

In Psalm 47 clause follows clause with inevitability. There are two strophes equal in length, each centering about a profoundly significant cultic event: the procession of Yahweh to the sanctuary and His coronation as King and Elohim. Each strophe opens with an enthusiastic, lyrical exordium and each closes with a breath-taking climax. The opening appeals with their urgent imperatives are followed by well-known transitional devices which communicate the reasons for the call to praise and worship.

3. The association of the hymn with the King and the pervasive cultic language and imagery support the view that the poem had some connection with what may without exaggeration be called the enthronement and coronation of Yahweh. The employment of the psalm in the celebration of the New Year in the synagogue gives ground for the supposition that it had its provenance in something like a divine enthronement on New Year's day. It is unfortunate that no direct reference has been preserved in our Old Testament records of an enthronement festival, but this psalm as well as others suggests the strong probability that the New Year's celebration did include a ceremony, akin to the Babylonian, in which Yahweh was highly exalted as King of all the earth.

THE FORM AND STRUCTURE OF THE COVENANTAL FORMULATIONS

BY

JAMES MUILENBURG
New York

In no area of biblical study has the application of the critical methodologies employed in recent decades proved more fruitful than in our investigations of the Deuteronomic literature. Thanks to the criticism of literary types and to the analysis of the history of traditions we have come to a truer estimate of the range and character of this literature and of the creative forces which went to its making. It has become increasingly clear that behind the promulgation of the Deuteronomic Code of 621 B.C. lies a long history of literary and cultic activity and that this history extends through the rest of the Old Testament, notably in the great prophetic corpuses of Jeremiah and Ezekiel, the hymns and liturgies of the Psalter, and the work of the Chronicler, and beyond these into the Dead Sea Scrolls and the New Testament. [1]) It should be possible now to trace the course of this development from its beginnings to its culmination in the Qumran texts and early Christian literature with some degree of clarity and to discern the contexts in which they most characteristically appear. Even though Deuteronomic style and theology come to classical expression in the Book of Deuteronomy, it is questionable whether the term "Deuteronomic" is altogether satisfactory since it tends to call too exclusive attention to the Book and to the Josianic Reformation and does less than justice to the whole stream of develop-

---

[1]) The extent of Deuteronomic influence in the literary compositions and the cultic rituals of the Qumran community is now quite generally recognized. We see it most clearly in the liturgical section at the beginning of the *Manual of Discipline* (i. 1-iii. 15), in the anticipation of the coming of the prophet, in the legalistic prescriptions, and the covenant contexts throughout. In the New Testament its influence is to be discerned in the frequent use made of the book (see G. Ernest WRIGHT, *Interpreter's Bible* 2 (1953), p. 311), especially in the Synoptic Gospels. Cf. C. F. EVANS, "The Central Section of Luke's Gospel" in *Studies in the Gospels*: Essays in Memory of R. H. Lightfoot (edited by D. E. NINEHAM), 1957, pp. 37-54.

ment which precedes and follows it. [1]) It is to the researches of Martin
NOTH that we are indebted for a clearer comprehension of the character of the great Deuteronomic work extending from Deuteronomy
through Second Kings and for an analysis of the history of the
traditions which are there present. [2]) Gerhard VON RAD has isolated
and described many of the *Gattungen* of Deuteronomy, has stressed
the place and function of the cult in the formulation of the traditions,
and has sought to trace the origins of Deuteronomic religion and
practice. More particularly, he has succeeded in exposing the central
motifs which determine the form and structure both of the Book
and of the "theology of history" in 1-2 Kings. [3]). Many other scholars
have subjected this literature to their scrutiny with the result that
there is now a greater unanimity on the major issues than a generation
ago and we are in a better position than before to do justice to its
range and history. Yet, despite these many contributions, much still
remains to be done: the large and varied terminology associated
with covenantal formulations requires closer attention, the composition and rhetoric and structural forms need to be studied more carefully, and the *Sitz im Leben* of many contexts must be examined more
closely. On a different level, the place of the northern kingdom in the
history of Israel's literature and religion demands greater recognition.

The following conclusions commend themselves to a large number
of scholars: (1) The present book of Deuteronomy is composed of
various strata of tradition, but at its base there is a *Grundschrift* emanating from a much earlier period than the time of Josiah. (2) The
origin of this *Urdeuteronomium* is variously defined. Albrecht ALT
locates it in the period immediately following the fall of the northern
kingdom. [4]) GALLING, [5]) ROST, [6]) and OESTERLEY and ROBINSON [7])

---

[1]) The Book of Deuteronomy itself witnesses to a long history, being composed
of a variety of traditions.

[2]) Martin NOTH, *Überlieferungsgeschichtliche Studien* I. Die sammelnden und be-
arbeitenden Geschichtswerke im Alten Testament (1943), pp. 3-100.

[3]) Gerhard VON RAD, *Deuteronomiumstudien.* FRLANT, N.F. 40 (1947), Zweite
Ausgabe. English Translation, *Studies in Deuteronomy* in Studies in Biblical Theology, No. 9 (1953). Cf. also *Das Gottesvolk im Deuteronomium*, BWANT, 3 (1929);
Das Geschichtsbild des chronistischen Werkes, BWANT, 4, 3 (1930); *Das formgeschichtliche Problem des Hexateuchs*, BWANT, 4, 26 (1938). Taken together, these
works are an impressive testimony to the vast scope of the Deuteronomic tradition in the O.T. writings.

[4]) Albrecht ALT, „Die Heimat des Deuteronomiums", *Kleine Schriften zur
Geschichte des Volkes Israel II* (1953), pp. 250-275. Note ALT's observations on
p. 73 concerning the relationship of the Elohist, Hosea, and the Elijah-Elisha
narratives to *Urdeuteronomium*, "die vor allem auf das doch wohl ebenfalls aus

adopt a very similar view. W. F. Albright apparently traces the nucleus of the Book to the ninth century. [1]) The complex of traditions associated with the Sinaitic covenant have their locus in the old Shechemite amphictyony according to von Rad and Noth, and this view has found wide support. [2]) It is now generally held that the Reformation of 621 was a movement of restoration, and that its ultimate origin is to be discovered in the amphictyony of Shechem. [3]) (3) The provenance of Deuteronomy is the northern kingdom, and the covenantal traditions which it preserves are northern. [4]) (4) More important is the generally accepted view of the relationship of Deuteronomic covenantal traditions to the Elohist, and in this connection the close affinities of both the Elohist and Deuteronomy with Hosea and Jeremiah. [5]) (5) Of considerable consequence, too, is the cultic

dem Reiche Israel stammende elohistische Erzählungswerk im Hexateuch und auf die Erzählungen von Elia, und Elisa zu erstrecken wäre."

[5]) Kurt Galling, "Das Gemeindegesetz im Deuteronomium", *Festschrift für Alfred Bertholet* (1950), pp. 176-191; „Das Königgesetz im Deuteronomium", *TLZ* 76, 3 (1951), p. 138. Galling dates *Urdeuteronomium* in the last period of northern Israel.

[6]) Leonard Rost, „Sinaibund und Davidsbund", *ThLZ* 72 (1947), pp. 130-34. Rost also believes that the original book was brought to Judah by fugitives from the northern kingdom (p. 132). Cf. also Sellin-Rost, *Einleitung in das alte Testament*, Eighth edition (1949), pp. 61 f.; „Es dürfte etwa um 700 entstanden sein."

[7]) W. O. E. Oesterley and T. H. Robinson, *An Introduction to the Books of the Old Testament* (1934), p. 58. Like von Rad, Alt, and others, the writers stress the close affinities to the Elohist and Hosea.

[1]) W. F. Albright, *The Archaeology of Palestine and the Bible* (1932), p. 155: "The most natural explanation is that Deuteronomy represents a selection from the religious and family legislation of the region of Shechem, in so far as it was believed in the ninth century B.C. to go back to Moses." Cf. *From the Stone Age to Christianity* (1940), pp. 241, 244.

[2]) Noth, *Das System der zwölf Stämme Israels* (1930), pp. 140-51: *Die Gesetze im Pentateuch* (1940), re-printed in *Gesammelte Aufsätze* (1957), pp. 53-58. Von Rad, *Das formgeschichtliche Problem des Hexateuchs*, pp. 30-37; *Studies in Deuteronomy*, p. 45: „Deuteronomy renews the cultic tradition of the old Shechemite amphictyony." The supposition that it was in „the Holy War even more than the Covenant Festival at Shechem that ancient Israel really first entered into her grand form" seems less probable. But see p. 359, n. 1.

[3]) So Alt, von Rad, Noth, Albright, Wright. Cf. also H. J. Kraus, *Gottesdienst in Israel* (1954), pp. 43-66 and F. Dummermuth, „Zur deuteronomischen Kulttheologie und ihren Voraussetzungen", *ZAW* 70 (1958), p. 60.

[4]) H. Gressmann, „Josia und das Deuteronomium", *ZAW* 42 (1924), pp. 313 46; A. C. Welch, *The Code of Deuteronomy* (1924); *Deuteronomy: the Framework to the Code* (1932). So also Albright, Alt, Galling, Rost, Oesterley and Robinson, G. E. Wright, von Rad.

[5]) J. Hempel, *Die Schichten des Deuteronomiums* (1914), p. 268 and *passim*. So Alt, Albright, Dummermuth, von Rad, Welch, Wright, Sellin, Rost

setting of the traditions, more particularly of course those associated with the Sinaitic revelation in Exod. xix-xxiv [1]). (6) Many scholars believe that the Elohistic covenantal traditions, preserve to some degree an authentic memory of Mosaic religion and that these traditions lie behind the work of the prophets. [2])

The problem of the dates of the Elohist and of *Urdeuteronomium* needs review. [3]) The arguments which led to the eighth century date of E have little force today in view of modern reconstructions of the early history of Israel and Israel's early literary history. If the origins of Deuteronomic language, style, and literary structure are to be traced to the latter part of the eighth century and before that period to the Shechemite amphictyony in the period of the settlement, then it is clear that the history of Israel's religious faith requires restatement. This applies *a fortiori* to the covenant formulations of the Elohist and the Deuteronomists, the royal covenant pericopes, and the covenant contexts in the prophets, above all Hosea and Jeremiah.

The Book of Deuteronomy is the covenant book κατ' ἐξοχήν. But it comes to us as a "second law" and is based in its prevailing terminology upon the formulation of the covenant in Exod. xix-xxiv. G. VON RAD has shown convincingly that the general structure of the two correspond. [4]) What is more, not only Deuteronomy but many of the other covenant contexts of the Old Testament as well as the theophanies show the influence in representation, language, and structure of the Sinaitic revelation. [5]) The source analysis of this section has been much controverted from the days of WELLHAUSEN, but it is

---

and others. Cf. OESTERLEY and ROBINSON, *Introduction*, p. 58: "It would, in fact, not be unfair to describe D as E modified by the teaching of Hosea."

[1]) S. MOWINCKEL, *Le décalogue* (1927), pp. 121 f., 132-138. See above all VON RAD, *Das formgeschichtliche Problem*, pp. 23-37. Cf. also NOTH, KRAUS, and WRIGHT.

[2]) So WELCH, ALBRIGHT, WRIGHT. Cf. KRAUS, *op. cit.*, p. 35: „Alle Hinweise, die Alt und v. Rad geben, führen uns in die erste Zeit der Existenz Israels züruck".

[3]) Modern study of the history of traditions confirms in many ways the judgment pronounced by Otto PROCKSCH, *Das nordhebräische Sagenbuch: Die Elohimquelle* pp. 307 f., in which he argued for the very early date of the Elohist. Appeal to historical background is notoriously tenuous here, and the contention that E represents a more developed theology can be readily explained if the origins of the election-covenant faith are to be traced to the northern tribes, especially Ephraim and Manasseh. See also NOTH, *Überlieferungsgeschichte des Pentateuch*, pp. 248-9.

[4]) G. VON RAD, *Das formgeschichtliche Problem des Hexateuchs*, pp. 24 f.; H. J. KRAUS, *Gottesdienst in Israel*, pp. 51-53.

[5]) This has been emphasized particularly by Arthur WEISER, especially in his commentaries on the Psalms (*Die Psalmen*, ATD, 1955[4]) and Jeremiah (*Das Buch des Propheten Jeremia*, ATD, 1956[2]).

generally agreed that by far the greater part of it belongs to the
Elohist.

Exodus xix 3-6: the Covenant at Sinai

Of crucial importance for our purposes is the little pericope of
Exod. xix 3-6 which KÖNIG characterized long ago as „die durch-
herrschende Dominante aller alttestamentlichen Weissagungen" [1]).
and KRAETZSCHMAR as „die ausführlichste Darlegung der am Horeb
festgesetzten Bundesbedingungen in D". [2]) The WELLHAUSEN school
tended in general to ascribe the passage to D, and this view is still
supported by NOTH. [3]) But in general the tendency today is to assign
it to the Elohist in whole or in part. [4]) It is doubtful whether the
hand of the Deuteronomist is to be found anywhere in the Tetrateuch; [5]) the line which separates the literary style of the Elohist
from the Deuteronomist is often hard to define. Further, since the
whole section of Exod. xix-xxiv is so prevailingly Elohist exceptions
require demonstration. Again, other sections of the Pentateuch which
betray a very similar style have often been given to the Elohist (cf.
Exod. xv 18). As we shall see, the composition of Exod. xix 3-6 is
so closely woven and the structure so apparent that the excision
of any line of verse actually mars its unity and destroys its literary
character. [6]) Finally, when the words and phrases of the passage are
compared with their Deuteronomic contexts, in every instance the
priority belongs to the Elohist; i.e. it becomes clear that it is the
Deuteronomist who is borrowing in his characteristic manner elsewhere and making such transformations as suit his more expansive

---

[1]) Ed. KÖNIG, *Das alttestamentliche Prophetentum und die moderne Geschichts-
forschung* (1910), pp. 63 f.

[2]) *Die Bundesvorstellung im Alten Testament in ihrer geschichtlichen Entwicklung*
(1896), p. 130.

[3]) *Überlieferungsgeschichte des Pentateuch*, p. 33.

[4]) O. EISSFELDT, *Hexateuch-Synopse* (1922), p. 47, 146 attributes it to E; G.
BEER, *Exodus* (HAT) (1939), pp. 96 f. to E[1]; STEUERNAGEL, *Einleitung in das
Alte Testament*, (1912), pp. 150 f. accepts an Elohist *Grundlage* as do OESTERLEY
and ROBINSON. BENTZEN, SELLIN-ROST, DUMMERMUTH, and apparently VON RAD
all assign it to the Elohist. While S. R. DRIVER gives it to J, his subsequent discussion supports the Elohistic provenance (*Introduction to the Old Testament* (1916),
p. 32).

[5]) Cf. G. E. WRIGHT, *Interpreter's Bible* 2, p. 320.

[6]) Martin BUBER, *Moses* (1946), p. 101, maintains that the protasis of Exod. xix 5
is out of place and renders it "when ye hearken, hearken unto my voice and keep
my Covenant:"! Such a deletion not merely destroys the pattern of the structure
but robs the passage of its force.

homiletic and parenetic style. What we have in Exod. xix 3-6 is a
special covenantal *Gattung*, [1]) and it is scarcely too much to say that
it is *in nuce* the *fons et origo* of the many covenantal pericopes which
appear throughout the Old Testament.

The literary type is the *message* or proclamation, and belongs to the
fixed forms of ancient Near Eastern utterance. Its provenance is
probably to be seen in the royal message, whether in the manner of
the suzerainty treaties which have been illuminated by Korošec [2])
and Mendenhall [3]) or in the epilogues to the great legal corpuses
of the Near East. [4]) It is the language of direct address, of proclamation and urgent call to hearing, of stress upon the first and second
persons, the *I* and the *Thou*, and above all of the covenant contigency
with its protasis and apodosis, which lies at the heart of the message.

The structure of the message may be represented as follows:

> Thus shall you say to the house of Jacob,
>> and speak to *the sons of Israel*:
>
> You אתם have seen what I did to the Egyptians,
>> how I bore you on eagles' wings,
>> and brought you to me.
>
> And now עתה if you will listen to my voice,
>> and keep my covenant
>>> then you will become my own possession among all
>>> peoples
>
> For all the earth is mine
>
> You אתם shall become to me a kingdom of priests
> and a holy nation.

These are the words you shall speak to *the sons of Israel*.

The compass of the unit is indicated by the opening and closing
lines with the accent falling upon *sons of Israel*. Similarly the first
and last lines of the message are introduced by the emphatic second

---

[1]) A part, to be sure, of the larger covenant complex, which von Rad has
described in *Das formgeschichtliche Problem des Hexateuchs*, p. 19.

[2]) *Hethitische Staatsverträge: ein Beitrag zu ihrer juristischen Wertung*, Leipziger
rechtswissenschaftliche Studien, Heft 60 (1931), especially pp. 88f.

[3]) *Law and Covenant in Israel and the Ancient Near East* (1955), pp. 24-50.

[4]) Note the extended conditional formulations (not to be confused with the
casuistic laws) in the epilogue to the Code of Hammurabi in Pritchard *ANET*,
pp. 178 f. Cf. the close of the treaty between Suppiluliumas and Mattizawa
(*ANET*, p. 206). Observe how the style here conforms to some of the Deuteronomic contexts.

person pronoun אתם. The tricola in the first division is paralleled
by the tricola of the second, which opens with the emphatic ועתה.
The first division culminated appropriately in the climactic "and
brought you to me" (ואבא אתכם אלי) whereas the concluding
colon of the second opens with "and you will become to me"
(והייתם לי). More striking is the pronounced *I-Thou* style which
pervades the whole unit: note the effect of the two-fold אתכם in
the first division and the three-fold לי in the second, thus producing
a remarkable climactic effect in the *I-Thou* relation, which is enhanced
by the assonance of the whole unit. The nature of the parallelism
is clear from the text given above, but there is one feature that deserves
special notice, for it reveals clearly how the burden of the message is
represented in the literary form. It is apparent from the foregoing
analysis that the final colon of the second division requires a parallel
to match the bicola of the protasis, that is, the clause *you will become
to me* needs the corresponding line of the final climactic colon, and
you will become to me. And it is precisely this final line which contains
the burden of the whole message as is shown by the introductory
pronoun אתם, the preceding *for all the earth is mine*, which serves to
set it apart and yet to relate it to the whole, and by placing the גוי קדוש
in the crucial position it requires. Indeed the whole message culminates
in these words. The first division stresses the mighty acts which
brought Israel into the presence of Yahweh on the mountain, the
second places Israel before the choice between obedience or disobe-
dience in the great conditional sentence introduced by ועתה אם and
culminating in the two-fold "you shall be to me" with the stress
falling first on סגלה of the final colon of the second division and then
more emphatically still on the ממלכת כהנים and גוי קדוש. Whoever
has undertaken a study of Hebrew literary composition and rhetoric
will be quick to see that such phenomena are by no means fortuitous
and that they may be illustrated by scores of examples, not least of
all in the contexts of the covenant message. Here we have an example
of Hebrew prose style in a very elemental form; one need only read
it aloud to catch its nuances and stresses, its keywords and assonance,
its proclaiming or preaching style. It is the form which gives us the
pattern of the thought. The relationship between Yahweh and Israel
is set forth in the very structure of the passage, a conspicuous feature
of numerous literary compositions. [1]) Israel is witness to what

---

[1]) Note, e.g., the literary structure of the Song of Deborah in Judg. v, the
Song of the Sea in Exod. xv 1-18 in its original form, and many of the psalms.

Yahweh has done for her, that is the message of the first division; now she must confront the call to obedience, and upon her decision rest the fateful promises which bring the unit to a climax: סגלה, ‏גוי קדוש ,ממלכת כהנים‎.

We are now prepared to examine the covenant message more closely:

Oracular opening (xix 3b). This style is familiar to us from the similar phraseology of the Mari royal texts and the Hittite treaties. [1]) It is the characteristic speech of the messenger, the rôle which Moses is to assume here. [2]) As we have seen, it is probable that the style and form of the whole unit have their origin in royal discourse. The same manner was employed by the prophets in their proclamations, and it was greatly elaborated in the parenetic, homiletic discourses of the Deuteronomists.

Proclamation of the mighty acts (xix 4). Israel is *witness* to the mighty acts of Yahweh. For the phraseology ‏אתם ראיתם‎, cf. Exod. xx 22 (E); Deut. xxix 1 (Heb. 2); Josh. xxiii 3 *etc*. This motif of the witness has its ancient Near Eastern parallels, [3]) and in the Old Testament plays of course a significant rôle, particularly in the covenant contexts (Gen. xxxi 44, 48 (E); Deut. xxx 19, xxxi 28; Josh. xxii 27 f.; xxiv 22-27; 1 Sam. xii 5 (cf. emended text of vs. 6); cf. Isa. xliii 10, 12). For the figure of the eagles' wings Deut. xxxii 11 is to be compared. [4])

The covenant condition (Exod. xix 5-6). Despite the external similarity to the casuistically formulated laws, the affinities of style and terminology are rather with the apodictic constructions, [5]) as is confirmed by the history of the *Gattung* in the Old Testament. The introductory word ‏ועתה‎ is encountered in many similar contexts and is perpetuated in the later oracles of salvation. The use of the infinitive absolute

---

[1]) NOTH, "History and the Word of God in the Old Testament" *BJRL* 32 (1950), pp. 194-206. Compare KOROŠEC, *Hethitische Staatsverträge*; MENDENHALL, *Law and Covenant in Israel and the Ancient Near East*; J. B. PRITCHARD, *ANET*, pp. 202-3.

[2]) For the probable royal provenance of the form and terminology see G. E. WRIGHT "The Terminology of Old Testament Religion and Its Significance" *JNES* I (1942), pp. 404-14; Ludwig KÖHLER, *Deuterojesaja stilkritisch untersucht*, pp. 103 ff. Martin BUBER, *Moses*. Cf. also BUBER and ROZENZWEIG, *Die Schrift und ihre Verdeutschung*, pp. 55-75 („Die Sprache der Botschaft").

[3]) MENDENHALL, *Law and Covenant in Israel and the Ancient Near East*, p. 35. See p. 356, n. 1.

[4]) Cf. BUBER, *Moses*, pp. 101-9

[5]) A. ALT, *Die Ursprünge des israelitischen Rechts*, re-printed in *Kleine Schriften*, pp. 278-332. See the section on „Das apodiktisch formulierte Recht", pp. 302 ff.

in the call to hearing is noteworthy (Exod. xv 26; Deut. xi 13 f.;
xv 5; xxviii 1; Jer. vii 5-7; Zech. vi 15. cf. also Deut. viii 19; Josh.
xxii 12; Jer. xii 6). The verb *to hear* at the opening of the prophetic
oracles is in all probability derived from the same style. The demand
for obedience lies at the center of the covenant relation, though the
freely given mighty acts of grace precede it. The first promise of the
apodosis is that Israel become Yahweh's *segullah*, his treasured possession. [1]) The Deuteronomists are aware of the covenant associations
of the word (Deut. vii 6-8; xiv 2; xxvi 18 f. Cf. also Mal. iii 17),
and elaborate it in various ways, especially by the idea of the נחלה.
The second promise that Israel will become a kingdom of priests
has no close parallel and is absent from Deuteronomy. It is probably
derived from royal speech. The climactic promise is the גוי קדוש,
which the Deuteronomists naturally alter to עם קדוש, as in vii 6; xiv 2,
21; xxvi 19; xxviii 9.

A scrutiny of other covenant contexts in the Old Testament confirms the view that the little *Gattung* with which we have been occupied
in the foregoing discussion exercised an influence upon their terminology, formulation, and structure. [2]) There is diversity, to be sure,
for covenant speech comes to include a more varied and richer
terminology, the formulation is often influenced by its particular
setting, and the structure of the protasis-apodosis is elaborated both
positively and negatively (i.e. *if .. if not*). But the essential features
persist. The presence of the covenant mediator, the motif of the
witness ("you have seen for yourselves"), the pronounced *I-Thou*
style, the recital of the mighty acts, the emphatic call to obedience,
the inclusion of apodictic requirements, the conditional sentence, and
the transitional *and now* appear in many covenant contexts. It is
noteworthy too that the deliverance from Egypt continues to be the

---

[1]) Mosche GREENBERG, "Hebrew sᵉgulla: Akkadian sikiltu", *JAOS* 71 (1951),
pp. 172-74.

[2]) Gen. xxvi 26-30 (J?); xxxi 44-50 (E); Exod. xv 22-26 (E); xxiii 22 (E); Lev.
xxvi 2-45 (H); Num. xxxii 20-27 (J?); Deut. viii 11-20; xi 13-15, 22-25, 26-28;
xxviii 1-6; xxviii 15-19; xxviii 58-60; xxx 15-20; Josh. xxiv (E); Judg. ix 15,
16-20; 1 Sam. vii 3-4 (E?); 12; 1 Kings vi 12-13; ix 1-9 (note vss. 4-9); xi 38-39;
1 Chron. xxviii 2-10; 2 Chron. vii 11-22; Neh. i 8-10; Ps. lxxxi; lxxxix 30-37;
cxxxii 11-19 (cf. Ps. l, but without the conditional); Jer. iv 1-2; vii 1-15; xii 16-17;
xvii 24-27; xviii 7-11; xxii 4-5; xxvi 4-6 (cf. vii 5-7); xxxi 36-37; xxxiii 19-26;
Mal. ii 1-5. The same style appears in the vows, as we should expect: cf. Judg. xi
29-30; Ezek. xvii 16, 19. For similar formulations compare Josh. ii 14; 1 Sam.
xxvi 17-20; 2 Sam. xv (vss. 8, 25-26); 2 Chron. x 6-8; xv 1-2; xxx 9; Ezek. xviii
3-15. The list is by no means complete, but may be said to be representative.

decisive redemptive event (Josh. xxiv; Lev. xxvi 45; Deut. viii 11-20; xi 3-4; 1 Sam. xii *etc. etc.* Cf. Neh. i 8-10). It is significant also that the covenant formulation appears at the conclusion of the codes of law (Exod. xxiii 22; Deut. xxviii; Lev. xxvi) in the manner of the Hittite treaties noted above and the Code of Hammurabi. [1]) It is clear that we are following a stream of tradition here, as is shown by the preponderance of passages ascribed to the Elohist. In most of the passages the cultic provenance is plain to see. While several of the most impressive references have their setting at Shechem (Josh. xxiv; Judg. ix 15, 16-20. cf. Gen. xxxv 1-8), it seems clear that the covenant *Gattung* was also employed in the royal cult of the House of David at Jerusalem. A cursory inspection of such psalms as l, lxxxi, lxxxix, and cxxxii will reveal the degree to which the covenant terminology and form was adapted for use in worship. [2]) In this connection it is worth observing that they also appear in the context of prayers. [3]) The prophets also employed covenant words

---

[1]) The Hittite treaties given in PRITCHARD, *ANET*, pp. 201-5 contain a number of interesting features many of which are recognized by KOROŠEC and MENDENHALL. It is noteworthy that in the treaty between Mursilis and Duppi-Tessub of Amurru the appeal to the witnesses (cf. Exod. xix 3b-4) is followed at once by the conditional (cf. Exod. xix 5-6) (p. 205). The situation in the treaty between Suppiluliumas and Mattizawa is even more striking. Here we have the same succession of witness and treaty condition, but the latter is greatly expanded and contains several interesting similarities to the Deuteronomic formulations, such as the reference to the succession of wives, children, children's children. Note the following: " . . . at the conclusion of the words of this treaty let them be present, let them listen and let them serve as witnesses. If you, Mattizawa, the prince and (you) the sons of the Hurri country do not fulfil the words of this treaty, may the gods, lords of the oath, blot you out . . . If (on the other hand) you, Mattizawa, the prince, and (you), the Hurrians, fulfill this treaty and (this oath), may these gods protect you . . . ". Translation by Albrecht GOETZE.

[2]) The association of Pss. l and lxxxi with the Sinaitic theophany and covenant have been frequently noted, especially by VON RAD. In Ps. lxxxix the covenant terminology, structure, ideology, and major motifs have been appropriated by the royal theology of the House of David and is therefore focussed upon the king (cf. also 2 Sam. vii; also the discussion *infra* of 1 Sam. xii). The central section (20-37) preserves the two major divisions of the proclamation of saving deeds (20-30) and the exhortation with the conditional protasis and apodosis (31-38). Similarly, in Ps. cxxxii the "oath" sworn to David (11, cf. lxxxix 34-35) preserves the same forms of proclamation (11) and covenantal contingency (12). Cf. S. MOWINCKEL, *He That Cometh* (1954), pp. 73 f.; Aubrey R. JOHNSON, *Sacral Kingship* (1955), pp. 23-27 and *passim*; Hans-Joachim KRAUS, *Die Königherrschaft Gottes im Alten Testament* (1951), pp. 73-78.

[3]) Israel responds to Yahweh's election-covenant acts in the same language and indeed in the same rhetorical forms as were addressed to her in the proclamation and exhortation of the covenant revelations. In Solomon's prayer of dedication

and forms, most notably Hosea and Jeremiah, though the conditional, strangely, is nowhere present in the former.

Joshua xxiv: the Covenant at Shechem

It is not our purpose here to enter into the textual and historical problems associated with this account nor to attempt any source analysis. Several comments are in order, however. In the first place, the LXX must be used only with great reserve. It is particularly precarious to read *Shiloh* in vss. 1, 25 for M. T. *Shechem*; both textually and historically the latter reading is to be preferred. Secondly, before historical questions can be answered, it is essential to determine the literary character and form of the material, as it has been transmitted. Historical problems often arise because the literary forms are ignored. In this connection it is important to stress the cultic setting in which the event is reported and unfolded and the fact that we are dealing with cultic speech and cultic forms. Finally, source analysis in and of itself often goes astray in failing to view the unit as a whole, to discern its structure and rhetoric, to do justice to the kind of style represented here. The presence of doublets is particularly questionable. One need only examine similar contexts in the ancient Near Eastern texts where repetitions are much more profuse than in their biblical counterparts to appreciate the manner of ancient Semitic style. Our task, then, is primarily to come to a better understanding of this admittedly difficult text.

The Elohistic provenance of the *Grundlage* is generally accepted, and the hand of the Deuteronomic redactor widely recognized. It is possible that the original form has been altered, but we must always reckon with the possibility of omission as well as addition. Be that as it may, an analysis of the rhetoric and structure of the chapter helps us to see something of what was in all probability the original form. Since it is always our first task to discover the limits of the composition, we may observe that the basic narrative is com-

---

(1 Kings viii 22-53) we have an elaborate composition. The king stands "before the altar in the presence of all the assembly of Israel" and there invokes the covenant with David, constantly calls upon Yahweh to hear, and then articulates the basic protasis-apodosis formulation of the covenant in concrete situations. Interestingly he pleads more than once that Yahweh's eyes may be open (29, 52). The motif of the holy people appears in a climactic context (51), and of course the basic appeal to the deliverance from Egypt receives the emphasis characteristic of the classical covenant contexts (51, 53).

prised in xxiv 1-25, as the opening and concluding verses make clear:

> Then Joshua gathered all the tribes of Israel *to Shechem*.
> So Joshua made a covenant with the people that day, and
> made statutes and ordinances for them *at Shechem*.
> cf. Exod. xix 3b, 6b.

The report of the covenant event shows the same sense for form, the expression *Yahweh, the God of Israel* appearing in Joshua's first and last words (vss. 2b, 23b). Compare Exod. xix 4a, 6a. It is not denied that vss. 26-28 belong to the tradition, but they are not within the literary unit.

The following outline will suggest what may well have been the original structure:

I. Introduction: the cultic setting: ויתיצבו לפני האלהים xxiv 1.
II. The Covenant Event at Shechem: xxiv 2-24

    A. Joshua's proclamation of Yahweh's saving deeds: vss. 2-13.
       1. From the call of Abraham to the Exodus: vss. 2-7.
          a. The gracious deeds to Abraham (vss. 2-4), concluding *but Jacob went down to Egypt*.
          b. The mighty acts in Egypt (vss. 5-6a), concluding *then I brought your fathers out of Egypt*.
          c. The deliverance at the Exodus (vss. 6b-7), concluding *and your eyes saw what I did to Egypt*.
       2. From the entrance into the land to the settlement (cf. 8a and 13a): vss. 8-13.
          a. The conquest of the Amorites (vs. 8), concluding *I gave them into your hand . . . and destroyed them before you*.
          b. The defeat of Balak, king of Moab (vss. 9-10), concluding *so I delivered you out of his hand*.
          c. The victory at Jericho (vs. 11), concluding *and I gave them into your hand* (vs. 12 is difficult: note the antecedent to *them* and the reference to the Amorites, then the generalized conclusion of 12b-13, where the style is certainly Deuteronomic).

    B. Joshua's exhortation and Israel's response: xxiv 14-24.
       1. The choice between the foreign gods and Yahweh (vss. 14-15), concluding *but as for me and my house, we will serve Yahweh*.

2. The decision against the foreign gods for Yahweh (vss. 16-18), concluding *therefore we also will serve Yahweh, for he is our God.*

3. The fateful consequences of the decision and Israel's renewed affirmation (vss. 19-21), concluding *no, but Yahweh we will serve.*

C. Covenant witnesses and commitment (vss. 22-24), concluding *Yahweh our God we will serve, and his voice we will obey.*

III. Conclusion: vs. 25.

It is clear from the foregoing presentation not only that we are dealing with a formal literary unit but also that it is articulated according to a definite pattern and one which can be paralleled by numerous examples from the prose and poetry of ancient Israel. Yet it is just as clear that an original report has been altered. It is apparent, for example, that while vss. 2-7 and vss. 14-25 contain numerous terminological and structural features associated with covenantal formulations, vss. 8-13 are of quite a different order although a form is easy to recognize here also. To be sure ancient Israel was no slave to literary form, but compositions such as this certainly were originally more coherently and elaborately fashioned. It seems likely, then, that what we have here is a precis or abridgement of what was once a much more elaborate account. If so, it is all the more striking that the original form has been preserved so well.

Only a few general observations are permitted here. In the first place, the affinities with the covenant message of Exod. xix 3b-6 are numerous. The two major divisions are introduced similarly: כה אמר יהוה (2b. cf. Exod. xix 3b) and ועתה (14a. cf. Exod. xix 5a). In both, the first section is a proclamation of the mighty acts of Yahweh and the second an exhortation or parenesis. Throughout both the *I-Thou* style is pronounced. Both begin with the gathering together of the assembly (cf. also Josh. xxiv 1 and Exod. xix 6). In both we are in a definitely cultic situation (1a: "they presented themselves before God"; cf. Exod. xix 3a). [1] The appeal to witness in Exod. xix 4

---

[1] See the study of Walter HARRELSON in *Biblical Researches* III (1958), pp. 1-14, in which he offers an illuminating discussion of the verb *hithyaṣebh* and suggests that it belongs to the terminology of the Holy War. "To take one's stand before Yahweh would thus refer, in its original setting, to the gathering of the able-bodied men before Yahweh . . . Then as the annual gathering of the tribes at the central sanctuary for covenant renewal became a fixed part of the life and worship of Israel, the term was employed to indicate the act of standing at the disposal

("you have seen for yourselves what I did to the Egyptians") is
preserved in the climatic line of 7d ("and your eyes saw what I did
to Egypt" cf. also 5c). The contrast between Yahweh's acts of grace
in the kerygma of xxiv 2-13 and the covenant obligation to serve
him in vss. 14-23 is more extended than in the crisp, succinct words
of Exod. xix 3b-6 and is greatly accentuated by the choice between
the foreign gods, the motif of which is struck at the opening (2d)
and then sounded again and again in the parenesis of vss. 14-24, and
Yahweh, whose name appears in all the climactic contexts (see the
outline), above all at the beginning and end: *Yahweh, the God of
Israel* (2b, 23b). This is the choice which the twelve tribes gathered
at Shechem are called upon to make, and their decision is the basis
for the amphictyony. Again we have the conditional (15, 20), but it is
not given in so solemn and well-fashioned a structure as in Exodus.
The urgent call to obedience with which the protasis of Exod. xix
5-6a opens אם שמוע תשמעו בקולי is superbly preserved in the final
words of the assembled tribes ובקלו נשמע. A comparison of the
relationship between the two passages favors the priority of Exod.
xxiv 3b-6. As so often in the Old Testament, the earlier exemplars
of a literary type reveal the strictest form, as, for example, in their
parallelism. Moreover, the manner in which the various motifs
appear in Josh. xxiv suggest that they are borrowed from a literary
type, and this we find in a perfect form in Exod. xix. That we are
standing within the same tradition is obvious, but the tradition was
transmitted according to fixed forms, and an examination of the
covenant formulations cited above (p. 355, n. 2) strongly confirms our
view that the covenant structure was preserved in the memories
of the cult, in its festival celebrations, in its rituals and liturgies, in
the oracles of the prophets, and in the royal psalms.

1 Samuel xii: the Covenant at Gilgal(?)

We come now to the third great event of Israel's history under Yahweh, Lord of the covenant. It is the hour of the kingdom. The old
order is passing away, a new order is about to dawn. The days of
the amphictyony associated with Gilgal, Shechem, and Shiloh have
come to a close. Again we have the gathering of "all Israel", presumably at Gilgal. Samuel pronounces his great valedictory to the people,

---

of the covenant God, ready to join in the rehearsal of his saving deeds and to
affirm loyalty to him and him alone" (p. 5).

but he does so in language which belongs to a long history of cove
nant tradition. He appears to us in a three-fold guise, as covenant
representative, covenant mediator, and covenant intercessor. That
the stream of tradition with which we have to do here is the same
as that in Exod. xix-xxiv (especially xix 3-6) and Joshua xxiv is certain.

The Elohist provenance of the chapter is quite generally recognized;
the so-called Deuteronomic phraseology which is present here and
there is not surprising, for, as we have seen, Elohist and Deuteronomist not infrequently merge with each other, i.e. the Elohist stream
of tradition flows into the Deuteronomic and the latter in turn, has its
sources in the former. It is often said that the report has been fashioned
after the model of Joshua xxiv, but it is more likely that both accounts
go back to the literary genre which receives its classical form in the
Sinaitic pericope and was perpetuated in the active cult at the amphictyonic centers. Here we have the same terminology, the same style,
the same major motifs, key words, historical memories, and other
characteristic features of the covenant *Gattung*. The conservatism
shown in the preservation of identical structural features is especially
noteworthy, and this is often apparent in the preservation not only
of names and events in the same form-critical contexts but also of
the rich terminology of covenant speech in the same literary types.

The contents of the chapter may be ordered as follows:

I. The Passing of the Old Order: Samuel's faithfulness to the covenant: vss. 1-6.

   A. Introduction: the situation: *"I have made a king over you"*: vs. 1.

   B. Israel's witness to Samuel's obedience as Yahweh's covenantal
      mediator.

      Introduction: *And now, behold the king walks before you* vs. 2.

      1. Samuel's obedience to the apodictic laws vss. 3-5.

      2. Conclusion: *Yahweh has brought your fathers out of the land of
         Egypt* vs. 6

II. The Covenantal Order of the Kingdom introduced by ועתה
    התיצבו vss. 7-15.

   A. Samuel's proclamation of the saving acts of Yahweh (צדקות
      יהוה) vss. 7-12.

      Introduction: the witness vs. 7.

      1. The Exodus from Egypt: Yahweh sent Moses and Aaron
         vs. 8.

2. The period of the Conquest: Yahweh sent deliverers vss. 9-11.

3. The Ammonite war and the request for a king: ... *you said to me, "No, but a king shall reign over us," when Yahweh your God was your king.*

B. Samuel's exhortation or parenesis, introduced by ועתה הנה.

1. The presentation of the king: *And now behold the king whom you have chosen ...; behold, Yahweh has set a king over you.* vs. 13.

2. The covenantal contingency vss. 14-15.

III. Yahweh's Act: *"this great event which Yahweh will do before you eyes"*, introduced by גם עתה התיצבו.

A. The sending of thunder and rain, concluding *And all the people greatly feared Yahweh and Samuel* vss. 16-18.

B. Samuel's intercession for Israel vss. 19-25.

1. The people's request vs. 19.

2. Samuel's response vss. 20-25.

In the first division the motif of the "witness" is dominant. Now that Israel has been given a king, Samuel calls upon them to testify to his covenantal obedience to a pentad laws, which are here transformed into questions: [1]

את שור מי לקחתי

וחמור מי לקחתי

ואת מי עשקתי

את מי רצותי

ומיד מי לקחתי כפר

The solemn engagement takes place before Yahweh and his anointed (3b, 5b), probably in the sanctuary of ancient Gilgal. The dialogical style here is similar to Joshua xxiv and is doubtless to be understood as cultic affirmation and cultic response (cf. vss. 5-6; cf. Exod. xix 7-8), culminating in the climactic covenant words: "and brought your fathers out of the land of Egypt" (6b). With this final pronouncement Samuel is prepared to meet the radically new situation which

---

[1] On the nature of the *Gattung* preserved here see K. GALLING, "Der Beichtspiegel: Eine gattungsgeschichtliche Studie" *ZAW* 47 (1929), pp. 125-130 and especially G. VON RAD. "Die Vorgeschichte der Gattung von 1 Kor. xiii, 4-7", originally published in the Festschrift for ALT in *Geschichte und Altes Testament* (Beiträge zur historischen Theologie), 1953, pp. 153-168 and now in his *Gesammelte Studien zum Alten Testament*, pp. 281-296. See pp. 292 f.

has arisen by the presence of the king. What makes the event here described so impressive is that the ancient covenant speech and literary forms are now placed in the service of the new order of the kingdom. The proclamation of the "saving events" is introduced in precisely the same manner as in Joshua xxiv: "They presented themselves before Yahweh" (7). The recital of Yahweh's deliverance from Egypt reaches its climax in the words: "and made them dwell in this place", corresponding to the "and brought you to myself" of Exod. xix 4. The deeds of the Conquest are given much in the style of Josh. xxiv, but, as there, they do not have the richness of covenantal terminology, suggesting that this again is an addition to the original proclamation at Sinai, where every line is essential to the structure. The recital comes to a close in the account of the Ammonite war and its upshot in the demand for a king; here the contrast between covenant and kingship is tightly drawn and thus presents the new situation in which Israel finds itself: "You said to me, 'No, but a king shall reign over us,' when Yahweh your God was your king."

The exhortation or parenesis opens again with the characteristic "And now" (cf. Exod. xix 5; Josh. xxiv 14), but it is given in the context of the new situation: "behold the king whom you have chosen, for whom you have asked; behold Yahweh has set a king over you", thus opening characteristically with the same motif with which the whole episode began (vs. 2). Then follows the covenant conditional, closer to Exod. xix than to Josh. xxiv but more expanded, yet preserving the very heart of the Mosaic formulation: ושמעתם בקולו . . ואם לא תשמעו בקול יהוה (14-15), and again the new situation is accentuated in the final words of the apodosis, "Then the hand of Yahweh will be against you and your king". This concludes the proclamation and exhortation, and it conforms throughout to the covenant types of Exodus and Joshua.

The report of the new event which follows is still in the covenant style: not only the solemn introductory words, "And now present yourselves", but also the call to witness, "See this great event, which Yahweh will perform before your eyes" (cf. Exod. xix 4a; Josh. xxiv 7d), which, again characteristically, is repeated at the close: כי ראו את אשר הגדל עמכם . The people ask Samuel to intercede with Yahweh on their behalf because they have been faithless to their covenant Lord in asking for a king to rule over them. As Yahweh's covenant mediator and intercessor he accedes to their request, reminding them of the great evil they have done, but calling them back to covenant obedience and service, for Yahweh has not rejected Israel but 'has taken it upon himself' to make Israel a people for himself כי הואיל יהוה לעשות אתכם לו לעם (cf. Exod. xix 5-6) He assures them that he will continue to intercede for them, but again calls them back to their vocation as witness to Yahweh's saving deeds (cf. vs. 24 and 7b!), ending climactically with the covenantal conditional with which we have become familiar (25).

The fundamental stylistic features of the chapter are those of the Sinaitic and Shechemite covenant accounts. We are dealing with the same literary form with its division into proclamation and exhortation, covenant witness and covenant requirement, recital of saving events and call to obedience. It is clear, too, that the terminology is basically the same, although there is a development and an enrichment in Josh. xxiv and 1 Sam. xii. In all three the covenant mediator plays a distinctive role. It has often been said that Joshua is a second Moses, and indeed the Deuteronomic editor of Joshua is at great pains to make this clear throughout the book; Samuel, too, is a second Moses, for he plays the same role as Moses at the decisive moment of the institution of the kingdom. Both Moses and Samuel play the part of intercessor for Israel; a motif perpetuated in the prayers of the King and in the petitions of the prophets in behalf of the people.

In all three instances we are placed in a cultic situation "before Yahweh", and it is apparent that the sanctuary is the locus of all three, as is most apparent in Josh. xxiv and 1 Sam. xii. It has not been our concern here to identify the precise occasion; it is likely, however, that the events at Shechem and Gilgal(?) are thought of in some sense as covenant renewals. The central event in all three is the deliverance from Egypt, as the literary analysis makes indisputably clear, but to the covenant recital at Shechem the events of the conquest are added, as in the covenant recital at Gilgal(?) also. The new event on the occasion of defection to the kingdom (1 Sam. xii 16 ff) comes outside the covenant recital and parenesis, but it belongs to the same basic ideology and literary form and style. In the cult the ancient memories are preserved and transmitted, but each occasion has its own concrete setting: the original covenant at Sinai (the representation of all Israel is of course later accomodation), the covenant of the twelve tribes at Shechem, and the meeting of kingdom and covenant at the end of the old amphictyony at Gilgal (?). In all three covenant events the place of the covenant condition is noteworthy. Inspection of other covenant contexts cited above shows that this feature was

COVENANTAL FORMULATIONS   365

persistently retained; indeed it formed the background against which the prophets (especially from the north) launched their invectives and threats and made their promises for a felicitous future. This basis is classically formulated in Exod. xix, but more fully elaborated in 1 Sam. xii. It is not without significance that the Hittite suzerainty treaties have the same conditional forms, much in the style of 1 Sam. xii and later formulations and that they appear in the epilogues or closing words.

Our examination of the three covenant contexts suggests that we are dealing with an ancient literary form, that terminology and structure may be derived from royal compacts or treaties, and that the covenant mediator and intercessor plays a definite role in all of them. When we turn to the prophetic literature, we see that the covenant types are employed in new settings, especially in the Book of Jeremiah, and that here the protasis-apodosis constructions are given new emphasis in contexts of proclamation and exhortation. It is significant that it is in the Temple that Jeremiah makes his great address (vii 1-15) and that the language he employs is drawn throughout from covenant speech. More than that, the Temple speech is appropriately followed by the motif of the prophet as intercessor (vii 16 ff.). Finally, the question may be raised whether the two basic forms of covenant proclamation ($\varkappa\acute{\eta}\rho\nu\gamma\mu\alpha$) and exhortation ($\delta\iota\delta\alpha\chi\grave{\eta}$) may not be perpetuated in the general structure of the letters of Paul and other early Christian literature.

3
Prophecy
And Apocalyptic

JAMES MUILENBURG

The "Office" of the
Prophet in Ancient Israel

When one ventures to survey the course of scholarly inquiry into the OT records throughout the course of the period beginning with the organization of our Society in 1881 and to assess the present situation in OT studies in relation to that period, it soon becomes apparent that the most profound changes have taken place in two major areas. The first of these is clearly the book which bears the altogether infelicitous and certainly mistaken title of Deuteronomy, a work which has long been recognized as occupying a peculiarly strategic position not only in the history of Israel's literary compositions, but also in the history of her faith.[1] The second area where the transformation is most clear covers the extensive range of Israelite prophecy and of our understanding of the prophets.[2] The rigid separation between the law and the prophets, so characteristic of the time of Julius Wellhausen and his successors, is today universally regarded as mistaken, for we now see, as never before, how deeply prophecy has penetrated the so-called legal formulations, above all the sacral tra-

[1] Gerhard von Rad, *Deuteronomiumstudien*, *FRLANT*. N. F. XL (1947), Zweite Ausgabe. English tr., *Studies in Deuteronomy* in *SBT*, IX (1953), 37: "Deuteronomy is the beginning of a completely new epoch in Israel. In every respect, therefore, Deuteronomy is to be designated as the middle point of the Old Testament. The question of its derivation is possibly the most difficult in the history of the Old Testament traditions." See Muilenburg, "The Form and Structure of the Covenant Formulations," *VT* IX (1959), 347 f.

[2] Georg Fohrer, "Neuere Literatur zur alttestamentlichen Prophetie," *Theol. Rundschau* N.F., XIX (1951), 277-345; XX (1952), 193-271. See also his critical evaluation of recent trends in "Remarks on Modern Interpretation of the Prophets," *JBL*, LXXX (1961), 309-19.

74

ditions embodied in the book of Deuteronomy, and how much the prophets were indebted to Israel's legal traditions both for the form and for
the substance of their proclamations.[3] We have gone a long way from
the time of Bernhard Duhm [4] and Carl Cornill [5] and Gustav Hölscher,[6]
or indeed from the days of John Skinner [7] and George Adam Smith [8]—
to mention but a few of those who have contributed to our understanding
of the prophets of Israel. One has only to compare the commentaries in
the *Biblischer Kommentar* or the *Kommentar zum Alten Testament* or
the *Handbuch zum Alten Testament* series with those of the *Handkommentar zum Alten Testament,* edited by W. Nowack (1892 ff.) or the
Kurzer Handcommentar, edited by Karl Marti (1897 ff.) or the *International Critical Commentary,* edited by C. A. Briggs, S. R. Driver, and
Alfred Plummer (1895 ff.) to appreciate something of the revolutionary
change that has taken place.

The reasons for this striking change in our understanding of both
Deuteronomy and the prophets are not far to seek. For one thing, we have
come to see that the methodology of historical criticism, taken by itself,
was unable to offer satisfactory answers to many of our most insistent

[3] Otto Procksch, *Theologie des alten Testaments,* pp. 561-63; Ernst Sellin, *Mose und seine Bedeutung für die israelitisch-jüdische Religionsgeschichte* (1922), pp. 6 f.: "Die weitere Untersuchung hat mir dann ergeben, dass gerade diese Mosetradition der rote Faden ist der durch die nachmosaischen Jahrhunderte bei den meisten Propheten sich findet und sie miteinander verbindet . . . dass für den göttlichen Willen, wie ihn nach jener Tradition Mose formuliert hat." Paul Volz, *Mose und seine Werk,* 1932, pp. 229 ff.; *idem, Prophetengestalten des alten Testaments,* 1938, pp. 74, 123 f. G. von Rad, *Old Testament Theology,* I (1962), 99: ". . . what stands unmistakably in the forefront of Deuteronomy is an interest in prophecy and the problems which it set." Compare, however, von Rad's observations in *Studies in Deuteronomy,* p. 69. For the prophetic employment of the legal traditions, cf. von Rad, *Theologie des alten Testa-ments,* II, 416: "Schärfer und bedrohlicher als durch die Propheten ist in Israel nicht mehr 'gesetz gepredigt' worden . . . Beim Deuteronomium und Deuteronomisten liegt unter allen Umständen eine Beeinflussung vor." See also Walther Eichrodt, *Theology of the Old Testament,* I, 293 f.; Yehezkel Kaufmann, *The Religion of Israel* (tr. and abridg. from Hebrew), 1960, pp. 224-29, esp. p. 228. Abraham J. Heschel, *The Prophets,* p. 472.

[4] *Das Buch Jesaia* (1892, 4th ed., 1923); *Das Buch Jeremia. Kurzer Handcom-mentar zum alten Testament* (1901); *Israels Propheten* (1916).

[5] *Das Buch Jeremia* (1905); *Das Buch des Propheten Ezechiel* (1886).

[6] *Die Propheten* (1914).

[7] *The Book of Ezekiel* in the Expositor's Bible (1895); *The Book of the Prophet Isaiah* in The Cambridge Bible for Schools and Colleges (1905); *Prophecy and Re-ligion* (1922).

[8] *The Book of the Twelve Prophets,* 2 vols., in the Expositor's Bible (1896-98 and subsequent eds.); *The Book of Isaiah* in the Expositor's Bible (1889-90 and later eds.).

questions concerning the composition, function, and exegesis of the biblical texts. It was this impasse that gave rise to *Gattungsforschung,* associated above all with the name of Hermann Gunkel and his students.[9]
Gunkel undertook to identify and describe the types and forms represented in our biblical material, to call our attention to the oral provenance of many of the traditions, to delineate, at least to a degree, something of the structure and rhetoric of a particular *Gattung,* and to point,
so far as it is possible, to the concrete social or cultural milieu in which
the *Gattung* was spoken, i.e. its *Sitz im Leben,* whether in the court of
law or on the various occasions of celebration and festival. More recently we have advanced our form-critical investigations into an examination of the history of the traditions, and it is precisely in the manifold
traditions preserved in the book of Deuteronomy and the prophetic
literature where we have made our most notable and, as I believe, our
most salutary advance. Intimately related to the foregoing ways of working with the biblical texts has been a stress upon the place of the cult in
ancient Israel, best illustrated by the many contributions of Sigmund
Mowinckel,[10] but also by perhaps the majority of OT scholars today.
Scores of passages both in the historical and prophetic books, as well as
in the book of Psalms, have been assigned to cultic forms and celebrations. *Pari passu* with the application of these newer methodologies to
the biblical texts has been the recovery of the records from the peoples of
the ancient Near East, records of many different forms and styles, which
have cast a welcome light upon Israel's literary compositions as well as
upon the motifs and modes of thought that they embody. To be sure,

[9] *Genesis übersetzt und erklärt* (1901); the introduction to Hans Schmidt's *Die
grossen Propheten übersetzt und erklärt* in Die Schriften des alten Testaments, pp.
ix-lxx (1905); "Die israelitische Literatur" in *Kultur Der Gegenwart,* ed. Paul Hinneberg I, 7, *"Die orientalischen Literaturen"* (1906), pp. 53-112; *Reden und Aufsätze*
(1913), esp. "Die Grundprobleme der israelitischen Literaturgeschichte," pp. 29-38;
Einleitung in die Psalmen; Die Gattungen der religiösen Lyrik Israels, zu Ende geführt
von Joachim Begrich. See also Gunkel's various contributions to the first edition of *RGG,*
esp. "Propheten seit Amos," IV, 1875 ff.

[10] Psalmenstudien II. *Das Thronbesteigungsfest Jahwäs und der Ursprung der
Eschatologie* (1922); III. *Kultusprophetie und prophetische Psalmen* (1923); *Le
Décalogue* (1927); *Religion og Kultus* (1950). German tr., *Religion und Kultus* (1953).
Aubrey R. Johnson, *The Cultic Prophet in Ancient Israel,* 2nd ed., 1962. For a thorough
and detailed treatment of the cult in the book of Deuteronomy, see Walter Brueggemann, *A Form-Critical Study of the Cultic Material in Deuteronomy: an Analysis of
the Nature of Cultic Encounter in the Mosaic Tradition,* Dissertation, Union Theologi-
çal Seminary (1961).

Gunkel availed himself of the extrabiblical texts and made exemplary use of them in his study of the forms and types of Israel's speech,[11] but many of the most important collections were discovered or translated after he had done his major work. It is noteworthy that these more recent materials have served to illuminate in a special way the traditions preserved in Deuteronomy and the prophets. One thinks of the compilations of laws, the international and other suzerainty treaties, the Mari letters, and other inscriptional materials.

Unhappily, there has been a proclivity to press our inquiries too far in all the areas to which I have referred. We are all aware, for example, of the excesses of source analysis in the early decades of our Society's existence, or of the reduction of literary compositions to mere snippets, or of the common confusion of strophes with independent poems, or of the dissection of traditio-historical criticism to such a degree that the original work all but vanishes or disintegrates beneath the deftness of our analytical skill. Or we have witnessed the invocation of the cult in every possible situation, with the upshot that psychological and historical understanding is somewhat cavalierly dismissed by the pejorative words liberalism and historicism. Yet these excesses by no means invalidate the methods themselves. Finally, let it be said that the results we achieve in our study will in large part be conditioned by the techniques we employ. The exclusive use of historical criticism will often yield one set of results; form criticism and traditio-historical criticism without reference to historical and literary criticism will often yield quite another.

We have proceeded in our investigations, then, from the identification of the *Gattung* and the comparison of various specimens of a particular *Gattung* to the determination of the *Sitz im Leben,* and today we are engaged in still another inquiry, one that was inevitable so long as we subjected a pericope to patient and careful scrutiny. I refer to the speakers who address us in the literary forms or to the "office" which they may represent or to the role they assume. A substantial literature has gathered about this legitimate concern.[12] Here I wish to emphasize what

[11] Above all, of course, Hugo Gressmann's *Altorientalische Texte und Bilder zum Alten Testament,* 2 vols. (1909, 2nd expanded ed., 1926-27), but also many other inscriptional materials (see, e.g., his *Reden und Aufsätze* and his commentaries on Genesis and the Psalms).

[12] Albrecht Alt, *Die Ursprünge des israelitischen Rechts* in *Kleine Schriften zur Geschichte des Volkes Israel,* I (1959), 278-332, esp. pp. 300-302; Martin Noth, "Das

has now become fairly common knowledge among us, that many of the
materials, i.e. many of the forms which we seek to understand, have an
oral provenance, and this holds particularly for the sacral traditions of
the book of Deuteronomy and the prophetic traditions. As Klostermann
saw long ago [13] and as G. von Rad has stressed recently,[14] the diverse
materials assembled in Deuteronomy were originally designed for public proclamation. They were meant to be spoken to the gathered community of Israel. Now nowhere in the whole range of Scripture is the
speaking style more in evidence than here. This is illustrated by the
stirring and eloquent rhetoric of the book, by the character of its different
literary genres, such as the sermon or the lawsuit or the treaty (or covenant), by the repeated summons to hearing and the numerous vocatives,
by the ever-recurring appeals to contemporaneity and to Israel's own
historic past, and by the passionate mood of the speakers. But if this is
true, and I do not see how it can well be gainsaid, then we are confronted
in an acute way with the problem of the speaker, i.e. the one who is

---

Amt des 'Richters Israels,' " *Bertholet Festschrift* (1950) pp. 404-17; *idem, Amt und
Berufung im Alten Testament*, Bonner Akademische Reden 19 (1958) ; Ernst Würtwein,
"Der Ursprung der prophetischen Gerichtrede," *ZAW*, XLIX (1952) , 1-15; W. Zimmerli,
"Ich bin Jahwe," in *Geschichte und das Altes Testament, Beiträge zur historischen
Theologie, Alt Festschrift* (1953), pp. 179-210, esp. pp. 186-92; Hans-Joachim Kraus,
Gottesdienst in Israel, 2nd enlarged ed.; *idem, Die prophetische Verkündigung des
Rechts in Israel.* Theol. Studien 51 (1957) ; J. J. Stamm, *Der Dekalog im Lichte der
neueren Forschung* (1958) ; Henning Graf Reventlow, "Das Amt des Mazkir," *Theol.
Zeitschrift XV* (1959) , 161-75; *idem,* "Prophetamt und Mittleramt," *ZTK* LVIII
(1961) , 269-84; *Das Amt des Propheten bei Amos, FRLANT* LXXX (1962) ; *idem,
Wächter über Israel* (1962) (Das prophetische Amt Ezechiels) ; *idem, Liturgie und
prophetisches Ich bei Jeremia* (1963) ; Eberhard von Waldow, *Der traditions-
geschichtliche Hintergrund der prophetischen Reden, BZAW,* LXXXV (1963) ; Hans
Wildberger, *Jahwes Eigentumsvolk*, Abhandlungen zur Theologie des Alten und
Neuen Testaments 37 (1960) ; H. J. Boecker, "Erwägungen zum Amt des Mazkir,"
Theol. Zeitschrift, XVII (1961) , 212-16.

[13] *Der Pentateuch, Beiträge zu seinem Verständnis und seiner Entstehungsgeschichte,*
Zweite Auflage (1907) , pp. 344 f.; "Aus dieser Untersuchung des Abschnittes Dt. 12-28
ergibt sich Erstens: dass auch er seiner literarischen Art nach kein für sich bestehendes
und für sich zu verstehendes Gesetzbuch ist, sondern vielmehr eine Sammlung von
Materielien für den öffentlichen Gesetzvortrag. Zweitens: der öffentliche Gesetzvortrag
geschah bei den solennen Zusammenkünften am Heiligtum, wohin man ging 'um die
Furcht Jahwes zu lernen' . . . Viertens: von anderen und älteren Gesetzsammlungen,
welche die Form der Gottesrede hatten, unterschied diese Gesetzschrift charakterisch
dadurch, dass sie ihren Inhalt als Rede eines autoritativen menschlichen Ichs, als
Weisung eines anerkannten Dolmetschers des göttlichen Willens gab." See further,
pp. 345-47.

[14] *Studies in Deuteronomy*, p. 15; *Das formgeschichtliche Problem des Hexateuchs,*
=*Gesammelte Studien zum Alten Testament* (1958) , pp. 37-41.

playing the role or taking the place of Moses. Who, then, is Moses or *mutatis mutandis* who is the Mosaic figure who addresses us in the sacral traditions of Deuteronomy, or, if we may anticipate ourselves, how are we to understand the figure of the prophet like Moses (Deut. 18:15 ff.)? [15] What is the relation of the prophetic speech of Deuteronomy to the speech of the prophets,[16] or what is the relation of the laws of Deuteronomy, notably the apodictic laws, and other legal formulations of the OT in their various forms and guises to the legal formulations of the prophets? [17]

Before we are able to render a decision on these matters, it is essential that we scrutinize the sacral traditions preserved in Deuteronomy in order to determine their character and to see what light they may shed upon the Mosaic figure and the various traditions associated with him. First a word about the provenance of the book. It is now generally recognized that the work as we have it before us represents a long period of development and growth. We clearly have to do with strata of tradition, the earliest of which were doubtless oral, but these are supplemented by accretions from later periods. Literary forms and types are transformed and expanded, often parenetically; at times they are reordered and refashioned in such a way as to revise or alter the original traditions.[18] The homiletical interests of the traditionists have left their stamp upon a large part of the book; both the historical narratives and the legal formulations come to us in the guise of preaching.

The affinities of the Deuteronomic traditions with those of the Elohist

[15] Ernst Sellin, *Mose und seine Bedeutung für die israelitisch-jüdische Religionsgeschichte*, p. 1: "Die letzte und wichtigste Frage aller israelitisch-jüdischen Religionsforschung wird immer die bleiben: Wer war Mose?"; Ludwig Köhler, *Der hebräische Mensch* (1953), p. 164; English tr., *Hebrew Man*, p. 144.

[16] Karl Budde, "Das Deuteronomium und die Reform König Josias," *ZAW*, XLIV (1926), 177-224. Cf. p. 220: "Somit nimmt das Prophetentum hier offen und unbestritten die Verfasserschaft des Deuteronomium für sich in Anspruch, und wir brauchen niemand weiter danach zu fragen. Eine schöne Bestätigung für diese abschliessende Stelle des Prophetentums in der Reihe der theokratischen Autoritäten erwächst uns in der Geschichte des Deuteronomium, oder besser der Vorlage der josianischen Reform, noch aus der Tatsache, dass das letzte Wort dabei dem Prophetentum zufällt." See also n. 3.

[17] See *infra*, pp. 83-84.

[18] Otto Eissfeldt, *Einleitung in das Alte Testament*, 3., neubearbeitete Auflage (1964), pp. 292-97; Artur Weiser, *The Old Testament: its Formation and Development* (tr. from the 4th German ed., 1957) (1961), pp. 131-32.

have long been observed.[19] Now in order to evaluate the relation of the two bodies of tradition it is essential to reconsider the date of the Eliohist.[20] The arguments supporting an eighth-century date are increasingly difficult to uphold, and it seems probable that we should assign it to a much earlier period. The writer has long maintained that the Yahwist depends upon the oral traditions of the northern Elohist, above all in the sections in Exodus which recount the conclusion of the covenant and the giving of the Torah. This, as we shall see, brings the origins of the sacral traditions of Deuteronomy and those of the Elohist into close temporal connection. In the opening sermons it is clear that Deuteronomy leans heavily upon the Elohist narrative traditions of the Tetrateuch.[21] The Elohist decalogue of Exod. 20:1-17 is repeated, albeit with characteristic alterations and additions. The Covenant Code of Exod. 20:23—23:33 is elaborated and reinterpreted within the contexts of later times and situations.[22] Indeed, von Rad has shown that the structure of Deuteronomy conforms completely with that of the Sinai pericope of Exod. 19—24, by far the greater part of which belongs to the Elohist.[23] The city of Shechem occupies a strategic place in the Deuteronomic sacral traditions, as is suggested by the not infrequent references to Gerizim

[19] See the introductions to the OT of C. Steuernagel, S. R. Driver, O. Eissfeldt, R. H. Pfeiffer, A. Weiser, W. O. E. Oesterley, and T. H. Robinson, the commentaries of Alfred Bertholet, Steuernagel, and S. R. Driver, and Johannes Hempel, *Die althebräische Literatur und ihr hellenistisch-jüdisches Nachleben* (1934), p. 139; Karl Budde, *op. cit.*, pp. 177-224; Adam C. Welch, *Deuteronomy: the Framework to the Code* (1932), *passim*; R. Brinker, *The Influence of Sanctuaries in Early Israel* (1945), pp. 196 f., p. 211: "*Deuteronomy* is almost entirely based on a document which is generally called E." Perhaps the most eloquent witness to the close affinities of the Elohist and Deuteronomic writers is the way in which the same passages have been assigned by some scholars to the Elohist, by others to the Deuteronomists. Many of the passages which were heretofore ascribed to the Elohist are now assigned to the Deuteronomist by Martin Noth and others.

[20] Note especially the work of Otto Procksch, *Das nordhebräische Sagenbuch: Die Elohimquelle*, pp. 307 f.; Martin Noth, *Überlieferungsgeschichte des Pentateuch*, pp. 248-49; Ephraim Speiser, *Genesis* (Anchor Bible, 1964), p. XXX, n. 5.

[21] This is recognized by the majority of scholars; for succinct statements, see especially A. C. Welch, *op. cit.*, p. 7; Brinker, *op. cit.*, pp. 197 f.

[22] S. R. Driver, *An Introduction to the Old Testament*, 9th ed. (1913), pp. 73-76. Note, however, the contention of Eissfeldt and Weiser that the intent of the Deuteronomist is to replace the Covenant Code. Be that as it may, the basis of Deuteronomic laws is the Covenant Code. The work of the Deuteronomic traditionists represents an illuminating illustration of Israelite hermeneutics.

[23] *Das formgeschichtliche Problem des Hexateuchs*, pp. 33-35; *Studies in Deuteronomy*, pp. 14 f.

and Ebal, and this obviously connects with the crucial report of Josh. 24, another prevailingly Elohist deposit, where the twelve tribes of Israel enter together into the covenant federation.[24]

The connection of the traditions associated with the Shechemite amphictyony with those in Deuteronomy is supported by many scholars, and it is agreed by most of these that they were originally employed in the celebrations of a festival of covenant renewal (Deut. 11:26-32; 27:1-26; Josh. 8:30-36).[25] A number of attempts have been made to articulate the structure of the covenant liturgies, and it is noteworthy that the Elohist and the *Urdeuteronomium* stand in the closest possible relation with one another here.[26] Since Shechem occupies so central a place in both traditions, it is not improbable that we should look to it for the *mise en scène* of both; i.e. we may assume that the various traditions in their

[24] A. Alt, *Die Ursprünge des israelitischen Rechts*, pp. 324 ff.; M. Noth, *Das System der zwölf Stämme Israels* (1930), pp. 140-51; *Die Gesetze im Pentateuch* (1940), pp. 29-33, =Gesammelte Aufsätze (1957), pp. 53-58; G. von Rad, *Das formgeschichtliche Problem des Hexateuchs*, pp. 41-48; *Studies in Deuteronomy*, p. 40; G. Ernest Wright, *IB*, II (1953), 326; *Shechem: the Biography of a Biblical City* (1964), pp. 20 f.; H. J. Kraus, *Die prophetische Verkündigung des Rechts in Israel*, p. 5; Murray Lee Newman, *The People of the Covenant*, pp. 108 ff. and *passim;* Eduard Nielsen, *Shechem* (1955), ch. IX; Bernhard Anderson, *Biblical Archaeologist Reader*, II (1964), 265-74=*BA*, XX (Feb., 1957); Norman W. Porteous, "Actualization and the Prophetic Criticism of the Cult" in *Tradition und Situation (Weiser Festschrift)* (1963), p. 100. Note also the unpublished dissertation of Walter J. Harrelson, Union Theological Seminary, *The City of Shechem: Its History and Importance* (1953).

[25] So Alt, Noth, von Rad, G. E. Wright, Kraus, Brinker, B. Anderson, Harrelson, Murray Newman, Porteous. See also Otto Procksch, *Theologie des alten Testaments* (1950), pp. 250 f.; G. E. Mendenhall, *Law and Covenant in Israel and the Ancient Near East* (1955), p. 47; E. Neilsen, *Shechem*, pp. 35 f.; pp. 347-57, esp. p. 352; H. Graf Reventlow, "Kultisches Recht im Alten Testament," *ZTK*, LX (1963), 269 f.; W. Beyerlin, *Herkunft und Geschichte der ältesten Sinaitraditionen* (1961), pp. 136 f. and *passim;* J. J. Stamm, *Der Dekalog im Lichte der neueren Forschung;* H. Ringgren, *Israelitische Religion* (1964), p. 46. This view was anticipated as long ago as 1924 by Ernst Sellin in *Geschichte des israelitisch-jüdisches Volkes*, I, 98 ff.; also in *Oriental Studies Dedicated to Paul Haupt*, "Seit welcher Zeit verehrten die israelitischen Stämme Jahwe?" pp. 124-34. Also to be observed is Mowinckel's identification of the *Sitz im Leben* of the decalog with the autumnal festival (*Le décalogue* (1927), pp. 120 ff.).

[26] Von Rad understands the Sinaitic traditions of Exod. 19—24 as representing the content of the ancient Shechemite covenant festival and discerns the same general structure in Deuteronomy (*Das formgeschichtliche Problem des Hexateuchs*, pp. 34 f., 47). For a more detailed and impressive analysis of the *Festlegende* of Exod. 19—24, both in its Yahwistic and Elohist forms, see Murray Newman, *The People of the Covenant*, ch. 2, pp. 39-71, though Newman adheres to the Sinaitic provenance of the passage. For other attempts to reconstruct the Shechemite liturgies, see Harrelson, *Shechem*, ch. XII, pp. 545-65; E. Nielsen, ch. I, pp. 39-85. Compare Muilenburg, "The Form and Structure of the Covenantal Formulations," *VT*, IX (1959), 347-65.

different forms not only reflect a Shechemite provenance, but also the cultic ceremonies and celebrations that took place at Shechem and later at Shiloh, Gilgal, and Jerusalem.[27] Be that as it may, an early date of the Deuteronomic sacral traditions is widely held.[28] The upshot of our discussion is to bring the Elohist and the early traditions of *Urdeuteronomium* close together. When one undertakes to examine the Elohist source as a whole, fragmentary though it may be, and then turn to the Deuteronomic traditions, he can scarcely resist the impression that we are dealing with one and the same stream of sacral traditions, traditions which by and large center in the covenant and the complex of traditions associated with it. But there is more. The prevailingly prophetic character of the Deuteronomic traditions is directly related to the prophetic traditions of the Elohist.[29] Differences there are to be sure, but

[27] M. Noth, "Das Amt des Richters Israels" in *Festschrift für A. Bertholet;* H. J. Kraus, *Die prophetische Verkündigung des Rechts in Israel,* Heft 51 (1957); Artur Weiser, *Die Psalmen,* 3rd ed. (1959), English tr., 1962; Norman W. Porteous, "Actualization and the Prophetic Criticism of the Cult," in *Tradition und Situation (Weiser Festschrift)*, pp. 96 ff.

[28] Edward Robertson, *The Old Testament Problem: a Re-Investigation* (1950), pp. 44 ff., 52 (=*BJRL,* XXVI (1941-42), pp. 183-205); R. Brinker, *The Influence of Sanctuaries in Early Israel,* pp. 205 ff.; Lester Kuyper, "The Book of Deuteronomy," *Interpretation,* VI (1952), 321-40, esp. p. 324 date the book in the time of Samuel; Eissfeldt, W. F. Albright, and Beyerlin place Deut. 32 in the same period (see *infra,* p. 84). T. Oestreicher, "Das deuteronomische Grundgesetz," (1923) and A. C. Welch, *The Code of Deuteronomy* (1924), and *Deuteronomy: the Framework to the Code* (1932), assign the book in its original form to a slightly later period. W. F. Albright at one time suggested the ninth century as the appropriate date and derived it from the region of Shechem, *The Archaeology of Palestine and the Bible* (1932), p. 155; more recently he seems to support an even earlier date in The Goldenson Lecture for 1961, "Samuel and the Beginnings of the Prophetic Movement," p. 10. Albrecht Alt, "Die Heimat des Deuteronomiums," *Kleine Schriften,* II (1953), 250-75 locates it in the period immediately following the fall of the northern kingdom in 722/1; K. Galling, "Das Gemeindegesetz im Deuteronomium," *Festschrift für A. Bertholet* (1950), pp. 176-91 places it during the last period of northern Israel; W. O. E. Oesterley and T. H. Robinson, *An Introduction to the Books of the Old Testament* (1934), p. 58 apparently take a similar view as does Leonard Rost, "Sinaibund und Davidsbund," *TLZ,* LXXII (1947), 130-34. S. W. Yeivin, "Jerusalem under the Davidic Dynasty," *VT,* III (1953), 153 upholds a time towards the end of the reign of Solomon. See also his article in Hebrew in the Dinaburg Jubilee volume (inaccessible to me).

[29] J. Estlin Carpenter, *The Composition of the Hexateuch* (1902), p. 217; J. A. Bewer, *The Literature of the Old Testament* (1938), 6th ed., p. 74; K. Budde, *op. cit.,* pp. 220 ff.; J. Hempel, *Die althebräische Literatur und ihr hellenistisch-jüdisches Nachleben,* p. 139; W. O. E. Oesterley and T. H. Robinson, *op. cit.,* p. 58; O. Procksch, *Die Theologie des alten Testaments,* pp. 225 ff.; 561 ff.; G. Mendenhall, *op. cit.,* pp. 46 f.; G. von Rad, *Old Testament Theology,* I, 293 f.; T. Vriezen, *de literatur van oud-Israel,* 2nd ed. (1961), p. 127; A. Weiser, *The Old Testament: its Formation and De-*

no greater, perhaps, than one would expect during the course of the history of transmission.[30] Contemporary criticism of the Gospels offers, perhaps, a relevant parallel. But the point where the two streams of tradition
reach their culmination is in the representation of Moses as the covenant
mediator and prophet.[31] Here again, and most impressively, the Deuteronomic traditions attach themselves directly with those of the Elohist.

The book of Deuteronomy is the covenant book *kat' exochēn*. The
three pillars of Mosaic faith undergird and support the entire work: the
exodus from Egypt, referred to no fewer than fifty times; the covenant at
Horeb about thirty times; and the giving of the Law at least twenty-two
times. The motifs of the Sinaitic theophany are recalled again and again,
and are elaborated at considerable length: the terror of the divine appearing,[32] the summons to self-witness ("your eyes have seen"),[33] the
'am qadosh [34] and the 'am segullah,[35] the call to obedience, and the
mediation of Moses.[36] An inspection of the *Gattungen* will reveal how intimately they are related to covenant types: the casuistic and especially
the various types of apodictic law, which have been fruitfully studied by
von Rad [37] and more especially by Karlheinz Rabast [38]; the covenant

---

velopment, p. 135; Dennis J. McCarthy, *Treaty and Covenant*, Analecta Biblica 21
(1963), pp. 118 f. See also nn. 3 and 19.

[30] See n. 18.

[31] H. H. Rowley, "The Nature of Old Testament Prophecy in the Light of Recent
Study," in *The Servant of the Lord and Other Essays on the Old Testament* (1952),
p. 113. The article was first published in *HTR*, XXVIII (1948), 1-38. O. Procksch,
op. cit., pp. 78-81, 225 ff.; W. Eichrodt, *Theology of the Old Testament*, I, 289 ff.; W.
Beyerlin, *Herkunft und Geschichte der ältesten Sinaitraditionen*, pp. 119, 169 f., 187;
Y. Kaufmann, *Religion of Israel* (1960), pp. 222 ff.; H. Graf Reventlow, "Kultisches
Recht im alten Testament," *ZTK*, LX (1963), 300: J. Scharbert, *Heilsmittler im alten
Testament und im alten Orient* (1964), pp. 91-95. Cf. also von Rad, *Old Testament
Theology*, pp. 293 f. where the contrast between the Elohistic and Deuteronomic repre-
sentations of Moses as prophet is stressed. Note again the contrast drawn by Eissfeldt
between the Covenant Code (Exod. 20:23—23:33) and the Deuteronomic Code of
laws.

[32] Deut. 4:11-12, 32-36; 5:4-5, 22-26; 9:10; 10:4; 18:18.

[33] Deut. 4:3, 9, 34 ff.; 7:18-19; 10:21; 11:7; 29:2; 34:12. See Muilenburg, "The Form
and Structure of the Covenantal Formulations," p. 354; also H. Wildberger, *Jahwes
Eigentumsvolk*, p. 11 and pp. 55 ff.

[34] Deut. 7:6; 14:2, 21; 26:19. Cf. 28:9.

[35] Deut. 7:6; 14:2; 26:18.

[36] The mediatorial work of Moses is stressed by many scholars, *inter alios*, W. Beyerlin, W. Eichrodt, Y. Kaufmann, H. J. Kraus, M. Newman, O. Procksch, von Rad,
H. Graf Reventlow, J. Scharbert, H. Wildberger.

[37] *Studies in Deuteronomy*.

[38] *Das apodiktische Recht im Deuteronomium und im Heiligkeitsgesetz* (1949).

sermons which have been influenced by the "royal speech" of Exod. 19:3*b*-6 [39]; the covenantal *rib* or lawsuit of Deut. 32, which has been examined in one way or another by many scholars.[40] Of the first importance, however, is the presence of the many conditionals, above all those which appear at the conclusion of the code in Deut. 28.[41] It is these conditionals which in reality dominate the work, a consideration which would seem to qualify to a degree at least von Rad's contention that Deuteronomy is to be understood as the composition of the so-called "false prophets." [42] It is the conditionals which lie behind many of the later formulations: the oracles of judgment as well as the lawsuits.[43] Fortunately, our understanding of the covenantal character of Deuteronomy has now been greatly enhanced by the recovery of the ancient treaties from the Near East. The contributions of almost a score of scholars have helped us to see ever more clearly the degree to which the treaty

[39] H. Wildberger, *Jahwes Eigentumsvolk*, also Muilenburg, "The Form and Structure of the Covenantal Formulations."

[40] U. Cassuto in *Atti del XIX Congresso Internationale degli Orientalisti Roma 23-29, Settembre, 1935* (1938), pp. 480-84. I have not seen this article; the reference is G. E. Wright's. O. Eissfeldt, *Das Lied Moses Deut. 32:1-43 und das Lehrgedicht Asaphs Psalm 78 samt einer Analyse der Umgebung des Mose-Liedes* in *Berichte über die Verhandlungen der sächsischen Akademie der Wissenschaften zu Leipzig*. Philologisch-historische Klasse, Bd. 104, Heft 5 (1959); W. F. Albright, "Some Remarks on the Song of Moses in Deuteronomy XXXII," *VT* IX (1959), 339-46; Patrick W. Skehan, "The Structure of the Song of Moses in Deuteronomy," *CBQ*, XIII (1951), 153-63; G. E. Wright, "The Lawsuit of God: a Form-Critical Study of Deuteronomy 32," in *Israel's Prophetic Heritage* (1962), pp. 26-67; Julien Harvey, S.J., "Le 'Ribpattern,' réquisitoire prophétique sur le rupture de l'alliance," *Biblica*, XLV (1962), 172-96; W. Beyerlin, "Gattung und Herkunft des Rahmens im Richterbuch," *Weiser Festschrift*, pp. 17-27. Cf. also H. B. Huffmon, "The Covenant Lawsuit in the Prophets," *JBL*, LXXVIII (1959), 285-95.

[41] See "Form and Structure of the Covenantal Formulations," pp. 354-57 for details; note especially the parallels to the treaties of the ancient Near East. To these should now be added the Sefire treaty. See M. Andre Dupont-Sommer, *Les Inscriptions Araméennes de Sifré (Stèles I et II)* (1958); J. A. Fitzmyer, S.J., "The Aramaic Suzerainty Treaty from Sefire in the Museum of Beirut," *CBQ* XX (1958), 444-76; idem, "The Aramaic Inscriptions of Sefire I and II," *JAOS*, LXXXI (1961), 178-221. Delbert R. Hillers, *Treaty Curses and the Old Testament Prophets* in *Biblica et Orientalia*, XVI (1964) does ample justice to the curse forms in Deut. 28 but fails to recognize that they are placed in a context of conditionals and thus conform to what we have both in the OT and the treaties. Note esp. the characteristic openings in 28:1 and 15.

[42] "Die falschen Propheten," *ZAW*, LI (1933), 109-20.

[43] Observe the characteristic *because . . . therefore* style of the indictments, for example, in such contexts as Deut. 28:47 ff. Observe too that the imagery of the conditionals with their blessings and curses is perpetuated in some of the prophets.

formulations have left their impress not only upon the structure, formulation, and terminology of the covenant, but also, to some degree, upon the substance or thought.[44] *Yahweh is the suzerain, Israel the vassal.* But Yahweh is no earthly monarch, and so the presence of the mediator is surely required. It has been contended that the Hittite treaties also have a mediator, but of this I am not sure.[45] At any rate, the mediator is the messenger, the one sent with a word from the divine suzerain.[46] The Mari archives provide striking parallels in terminology and phraseology to the announcements and proclamations of the prophets, who also have been sent with a commission to speak in behalf of the sovereign.[47]

Finally, throughout the book of Deuteronomy it is the design of the transmitter of the traditions to bring the age of Moses and the figure of Moses into the context of contemporaneity. I do not refer solely to the frequent repetition of the urgent *today,* or the emphatic use of the second person pronoun (whether singular or plural), or the recurring $w^{e\cdot}att\hat{a}$.

[44] V. Kurosec, *Hethitische Staatsverträge* in *Leipziger rechtswissenschaftliche Studien,* 1931; G. E. Mendenhall, *op. cit.;* D. J. Wiseman, *The Vassal-Treaties of Esarhaddon* (1958) ; Klaus Baltzar, *Das Bundesformular. Wissenschaftliche Monographien zum alten Testament* (1960) ; Julien Harvey, *op. cit.;* Meredith G. Kline, *Treaty of the Great King* (1963) ; Dennis J. McCarthy, *op. cit.;* William L. Moran, "The Ancient Near Eastern Background of the Love of God in Deuteronomy," *CBQ,* XXV (1963) ; W. Beyerlin, *Herkunft und Geschichte der ältesten Sinaitraditionen,* pp. 60 ff.; idem, "Gattung und Herkunft des Rahmens im Richterbuch" in *Weiser Festschrift,* pp. 1-28; H. Graf Reventlow, "Kultisches Recht im Alten Testament"; Murray Newman, *People of the Covenant, passim.* For a full bibliography on the treaties, see McCarthy, *op. cit.,* pp. xiii-xxiv.

[45] I have not been able to see the work of Morstad who defends this view.

[46] Ludwig Köhler, *Deuterojesaja stilkritisch untersucht* (1923), pp. 102-9; idem, *Kleine Lichter* (1945), pp. 11-17; Johannes Lindblom, *Die literarische Gattung der prophetischen Literatur* (1924), pp. 97 ff.; H. Wildberger, *Jahwewort und prophetische Rede* (1942), pp. 42-77; M. Noth, "History and Word of God in the Old Testament," *BJRL,* XXXII (1950) ; Y. Kaufmann, *The Religion of Israel,* pp. 212-16; Claus Westermann, *Grundformen prophetischer Rede,* pp. 66-91; James Ross, "The Prophet as Yahweh's Messenger," in *Israel's Prophetic Heritage,* pp. 98-107. See also the critical comments of Rolf Rendtorff, "Botenformel und Botenspruch," *ZAW* LXXIV (1962), 165-77 and C. Westermann, *Forschung am alten Testament* in *Neudrucke und Berichte aus dem 20. Jahrhundert,* XXIV (1964), 171 ff.

[47] W. von Soden, "Verkündung des Gotteswillens durch prophetisches Wort in den altbabylonischen Briefen aus Mari," *Die Welt des Orients* (1950), 397-403; A. Lods, "Une tablette inédite de Mari," in *Studies in Old Testament Prophecy, Festschrift for T. H. Robinson,* ed. H. H. Rowley (1956), pp. 103-10; F. M. Th. de Liagre Böhl, "Profetisme en plaatsvervangend Lijden in Assyrie en Israel," *Nederlands Theologisch Tijdschrift* (1949), pp. 81-91; M. Noth (see foregoing note) ; C. Westermann, *Grundformen prophetischer Rede,* pp. 82-91; idem, "Die Mari-Briefe und die Prophetie in Israel," in *Forschung zum alten Testament,* pp. 171-88.

Rather it is the collocation, the strategic position, in which these words are used and the urgency they have in their contexts. The concern to make the Mosaic figure and the Mosaic age immediate and contemporary is consistent with our understanding of the original oral character of the traditions which lie at the base of the book. So the question of the speaker again becomes pressing. Who is this Moses of whom the traditionists speak? How are we to understand the role of Moses who is preaching to us here? For an answer to this question we turn to the *locus classicus* of the covenant mediator, the aetiology of the prophet like Moses (Deut. 18:15 ff.).

The literary complex to which our pericope belongs has as its common subject the office-bearers of ancient Israel: judge, king, priest, and prophet (Deut. 17:8–18:22).[48] That the "office" of the prophet is designed by the collector of the sacral traditions to be climactic is apparent not only from the context in which our pericope (Deut. 18:15-22) appears, but also from the important transition between the other offices and that of the prophet (Deut. 18:9-14). Here we have to all intents and purposes a Deuteronomic rendering of two apodictic commands (9b-10, 13) followed by two impressive motivations, each introduced by the characteristic climactic particle *ki* (12, 14). Israel is not to learn to follow the *tôʻēbôt* of the nations, the various modes and techniques of evoking revelation, or to resort to diviners, soothsayers, augurs, sorcerers, charmers, necromancers *etc.*, because these are all an abomination to Yahweh. Israel is to be blameless (*tāmîm*) before Yahweh her God: "For these nations which you are about to dispossess, listen to soothsayers and to diviners; but as for you, Yahweh your God has not permitted you to do so" (Deut. 18:14). It is precisely in this strategic context that the impressive words about the prophet appear. Prophecy stands over against all these alien practices, and the revelation which the prophet receives in Israel is of a radically different order from that of the nations. It is the Word of Yahweh which surpasses all other ways of revealing. But I think we may go farther to suggest that the passage about the prophet occupies a crucial place in the structure of the whole book, for here the office of the Mosaic speaker is described with a succinctness and compression, a formality of style and a profusion of prophetic and covenantal

---

[48] M. Noth, *Amt und Berufung im Alten Testament*, pp. 23-26; H. J. Kraus, *Die prophetische Verkündigung des Rechts in Israel*, pp. 12-20.

motifs and terms unmatched elsewhere. The three divisions of the composition are dominated by the word *nabiʾ*:

15a נביא מקרבך מאחיך כמני יקים לך יהוה אלהיך

18a נביא אקים להם מקרב: אחיהם כמוך

20a אך הנביא אשר יזיד לדבר דבר בשמי . . .

The first is Moses' defense or legitimation of his office, a kind of *apologia pro officio suo;* the second a sacramental ordination in the divine first person,[49] the third a pronouncement and interdict against the speaker who speaks falsely. Controlling all three parts is the centrality of the *dabar* and the command to hear and obey, the very heart of covenantal allegiance.[50]

Moses is surely speaking here as mediator of the covenant, and, what is more, he is identifying the office of the mediator with that of the prophet (15-16). That the word *nabiʾ* is meant collectively and not individually is generally admitted. Certainly there is no eschatological allusion here. It is precisely at the point of the *apologia* that the *locus classicus* of the covenant mediator in the event at Sinai-Horeb is remembered and quoted, the place where the people implore Moses to mediate between them and Yahweh: "Let me not again hear the voice of Yahweh my God or see this great fire any more, lest I die" (cf. Exod. 20:18-20, and Deut. 5:2-5, 22 ff.). This is the prophet of the Elohist traditions, whom Yahweh knew face to face, *pānim ʾel pānim* (Deut. 34: 10), with whom he spoke mouth to mouth, *peh ʾel peh* (Num. 12:8). Moses is here understood as the supreme prophet, the archetypal prophet, the first of the prophetic order, and it is he who is here passing on his office to speak and proclaim the Word of Yahweh. But is the succession handed down from prophet to succeeding prophet in an *unbroken* chain, the one following the other in lineal order? This is frequently assumed in much of the literature on the subject today. But the text surely

[49] Compare above all Jer. 1:9, but see also Num. 22:38; 23:5, 12; Isa. 6:7; 51:16; 59:21. For detailed discussion, see H. G. Reventlow, *Liturgie und prophetisches Ich bei Jeremia* (1963), pp. 64 ff. To be observed, too, is the motif of the mouth in the Elohist traditions of Moses.

[50] The noun appears some six times, the corresponding verb form eight times, the verb "to hear" three times. On the nature of the word spoken here, cf. Kraus, *ibid.,* p. 15, n. 16. See also E. Jacob, *Theology of the Old Testament* (1958), pp. 129 ff.

does not make this at all clear. It is just as possible and perhaps probable that the meaning is that Yahweh will raise up prophets "from time to time" or "as occasion may demand" [51] or "as need arises" (G. Ernest Wright). If this is the true meaning, then the whole vexing problem of the tensions between charisma and office is somewhat relieved. If the meaning should be an unbroken chain of prophets, as many hold, then we would have, to be sure, another instance of the Deuteronomic proclivity to structuralize the sequences of history by accompanying it with prophetic messengers, as in the Deuteronomic history of the kings.[52] What is clear, however, is that Deut. 18:15 ff. is giving an account of the prophetic office, a characterization, too, perhaps of the institution of prophecy, and an assurance that Yahweh will ever and again raise up prophets like Moses for the proclamation of his Word. The Yahwist account of the covenant mediator provides a good parallel: "Lo, I am coming to you in a thick cloud, that the people may hear when I speak with you, and may also believe you for ever" (Exod. 19:9). In a striking passage in his *Studies in Deuteronomy*, von Rad denies that the prophetic element in Deuteronomy represents a stream of tradition, that there is any prophetic tradition behind it. The prophetic, he says, is merely a form, and is not to be taken seriously (p. 69). On the contrary, I should contend that our pericope is in reality bringing to a culmination the prophetic motifs of the old traditions, especially those of the Elohist. Similarly, Noth greatly minimizes the importance of the pericope, contending that the prophet does not represent an office at all, that in the very nature of the case the charismatic speaker called to Yahweh's service could not fulfill an office.[53] But this is to ignore the context of our passage, and, as will become apparent, the whole of the subsequent stream of prophetic traditions which have their source in the traditions associated with Moses. This is not meant to argue for the historicity of the latter—though I do think there is a nucleus of material which has a legitimate claim to historicity. Rather, I believe that already at a fairly early period, say at the time of the early amphictyonies (Shechem, Shiloh, Gilgal), we already

[51] S. R. Driver, *Deuteronomy, International Critical Commentary* (1895), p. 227. Driver aptly refers to Judg. 6:16, 18 as a parallel.

[52] Von Rad, *Studies in Deuteronomy*, pp. 74-91. The numerous striking parallels between Moses and Joshua in the book of Joshua are probably to be explained by the same Deuteronomic propensity. Joshua serves as the Mosaic figure throughout the book.

[53] *Amt und Berufung im alten Testament*, p. 25.

have a substantial quantity of traditions centering in the Mosaic figure.

In passing from a consideration of Moses, the prophet and covenant mediator, to the succession of prophets who follow him, we are confronted at once with the old problem of continuity and discontinuity in the history of Israel's faith. The Wellhausen school tended to view the prophets as isolated, solitary figures, monolithic men rising precipitately into their times, breaking into history as sudden mutations. The situation is, of course, quite otherwise today. We recognize clearly how the prophets rise out of the past, how the traditions of the Mosaic age or associated with it condition much of what they have to say. What was once viewed as unique and unprecedented is now seen as typical and representative. Form criticism and traditio-historical criticism as well as the recovery of the texts from the ancient Near East tend to a considerable degree to confirm such a position. But in certain quarters the stress upon the typical has become so great that the historical contexts in which the prophets speak and the individuality of the particular prophet are dismissed almost completely. While it is certainly true that the prophets employ conventional types and forms of speaking, *the forms and types are never mere stereotypes.* One has only to compare the accounts of the prophetic calls or the various *Gattungen* which they employ to observe the *distinctive* elements and, indeed, the distinctive styles too. Failure to recognize what is distinctive in the context of the conventional characterizes the work of many of our younger scholars today, notably the work of such a stimulating and often discerning scholar as H. G. Reventlow.[54] Thus the prophets, we are told, have nothing at all new to say, that they do not reflect or speak out of their own times, but merely repeat traditional words, familiar clichés drawn from the cult. Now it is just as precarious to minimize the importance of the cult in the life of ancient Israel and to ignore its profound influence upon many of the prophetic formulations as it is to find a liturgy lurking in every prophetic corner. If there is continuity and indeed the degree of continuity which the prophetic records plainly reveal, then it is essential that we face the question of the matrix or structure which will best explain it. To this question the most plausible answer is cult or worship, but it must not be permitted to

[54] *Das Amt des Propheten Amos; Wächter über Israel; Liturgie und Prophetisches Ich bei Jeremia.* See also Gerstenberger, "The Woe-Oracles of the Prophets," *JBL,* LXXXI (1962), 249-63.

subsume everything within its sphere. Conventionality is certainly not to be restricted to the cultic sphere alone.

To speak more concretely, in dealing with the motif of Moses and the prophet like Moses, we must take into account the early traditions associated with the amphictyonic centers, such as Shechem, Shiloh, Gilgal, Bethel, and other sanctuaries. What is more, we must scrutinize these traditions very closely in order to discern their nature and form, the terminology and the keywords, the rhetoric or the way thought is articulated into speech, and not least of all their interior structures. I refer, for example, to one type of such investigation in the studies of many contemporary scholars of the Hittite and other suzerainty treaties and their striking affinities to the covenant formulations.[55] Or one could mention almost a score of works dealing with the influence of the legal *Gattungen* upon the prophetic proclamations.[56] Or one could refer to the detailed analysis of such crucial covenantal expressions as the divine first-person self-asseveration, "I am Yahweh," [57] or the classical covenant formula, "You shall be my people, and I will be your God,[58] or to the messenger's speech.[59] The conclusions to which all of these and many other similar studies point are incontestable: far from drawing a firm line of demarcation between the law and the prophets, we are now compelled by the evidence to recognize a prevailing continuity.

Now it is essential to recognize that the issue of continuity must not be too simply stated. One could argue plausibly and perhaps convincingly that continuity is by no means unilinear or that our contention by no means holds for all the prophets or, as we have already noted, that there

[55] Mendenhall, Huffmon, Baltzar, Newman, Harvey, McCarthy, Kline, Beyerlin, Hillers. See n. 44.

[56] Note, for example, E. Würtwein, "Amos-Studien," *ZAW* (1949-50), pp. 10-52; H. G. Reventlow, *Das Amt des Propheten bei Amos;* Robert Bach, "Gottesrecht und weltliches Recht in der Verkündigung des Propheten Amos," in *Festschrift für Gunther Dehn* (1957), pp. 23-54 on the affinities of the Covenant Code and other laws with the prophet Amos. Note also the studies of the *rib* Gattung by Huffmon, G. E. Wright, Beyerlin, Harvey, and others. Also Reventlow on the connections of the Holiness Code with the prophecies of Ezekiel, in *Wächter über Israel;* Claus Westermann *Grundformen prophetischer Rede* (1962) on the *Gerichtsrede,* and especially Julien Harvey on the breach of covenant. Cf. the discussion of the covenant conditionals in the writer's "Covenantal Formulations."

[57] Walther Zimmerli, "Ich bin Jahwe," in the *Alt-Festschrift, Geschichte und Altes Testament* (1953), pp. 179-210.

[58] Rudolph Smend, *Die Bundesformel.*

[59] See n. 46.

is diversity in the way that traditional types are appropriated. This is surely true. But I think we may say with some degree of confidence that we can clearly discern a continuous stream of tradition in those records which come to us from the northern kingdom of Israel, notably in the Elohist, Samuel, the Deuteronomic speakers, Elijah, Hosea, Jeremiah, and, to a degree, Second Isaiah. If we were to press our inquiry, we should be compelled to turn to the rituals and thanksgiving hymns of the covenant community at Qumran and to assess the influence of the age of Moses upon the eschatological community of the Essenes or the role played by Moses in the figure of the Teacher of Righteousness. But let us confine our attention to only two of the prophets: Samuel and Hosea.

The traditions which gather about Samuel are of a varied kind and in all probability reflect varying provenances and points of view. He is portrayed in ways which seem contradictory, and it is clear that each stratum of tradition betrays its own *Tendenz.* It is nevertheless questionable that the Deuteronomist has greatly altered the traditions concerning him. The affinities with the Elohist seem much clearer, as has been well argued and documented by Joseph Bourke, S. J., in an illuminating article.[60] Like Joshua, Samuel comes from the tribe of Ephraim, and if we could trust the striking reference of Josh. 18:1, then his association with the sanctuary at Shiloh would connect him with Joshua. Be that as it may, Samuel receives his call in the presence of the ark of the covenant, "the tangible symbol of the Sinai covenant." The imperious summons, "Samuel, Samuel" and the response reminds one of the call of Moses (cf. I Sam. 3:4, 8, 10 and Exod. 3:4), and the strong stress upon hearing is very characteristic both of the Elohist and the Deuteronomist. Similarly, the manner in which the *dabar* of Yahweh determines the structure and dominates the accounts is characteristic of the northern traditions of the Elohist, Elijah, Deuteronomy, and Jeremiah (cf., for example, I Sam. 3:1*b*, 7, 20 and I Kings 17:2, 8, 24). Samuel delivers a covenant speech (I Sam. 12), much in the manner and style of the royal covenant speech to Moses (Exod. 19:3*b*-6) and the speech of Joshua on the occasion of the establishment of the twelve-tribe federation at Shechem (Josh. 24). We listen again to the great asseveration of the divine deliverance, this time with the messenger's formula, "Thus says

[60] Joseph Bourke, S. J., "Samuel and the Ark, A Study in Contrasts," *Dominican Studies,* VII (1954), 73-103.

Yahweh, the God of Israel," to the breach of covenant motif (I Sam. 10:
18-19), and especially to the climactic conditionals of the treaties and
covenants (12:14-15, cf. 7:3). Samuel is endowed like Moses with the
charisma, and he stands at the head of the group of ecstatic prophets at
Naioth. We have, too, what appear to be the remnants of the covenant
lawsuit (I Sam. 8:7-9, 19-22), reminiscent of the lawsuits which Beyerlin
has uncovered in the frameworks to the book of Judges. Surprisingly, in
a laconic observation Samuel is said to have told the people the *mishpat*
of the kingdom, "and he wrote it in a book and placed it before Yahweh,"
a passage which bears the marks of an early provenance (I Sam. 10:25).
In an illuminating essay, Murray Newman contends that the call of
Samuel is the aetiology of the office of the prophet; if this is right, then
the connection with Deut. 18:15 ff. becomes very interesting.[61] At any
rate, the man who was the maker of a king can have been no mean
figure. Eissfeldt and Albright assign the lawsuit of Deut. 32 to the time
of Samuel, and Beyerlin supports their position.[62] While it is difficult
to think of the present composition as emanating from so early a period,
the role of Samuel in the traditions associated with his name is apparently
that of the mediator of the covenant as is the figure of Moses in the lawsuit of Deut. 32. Moreover, Samuel is perpetuating the theology of the
Shechem federation. He is both prophet and covenant mediator,[63] Yah-

---

[61] "The Prophetic Call of Samuel," *Israel's Prophetic Heritage*, pp. 86-97.

[62] See especially Albright's stimulating discussion in "Samuel and the Beginnings of
the Prophetic Movement," pp. 21-26. Note p. 26: "We can, at all events, use *Ha'azinū*
to illustrate the great religious reform which Samuel brought about and without which
Elijah and Jeremiah could not have fulfilled their place in history." Beyerlin relates
his discussion of Deut. 32 to the *rib* patterns which he finds in the frameworks of
Judges.

[63] Among the many scholars who would support this position, see most recently
J. Scharbert, *Heilsmittler im Alten Testament und im Alten Orient:* "Samuel ist der
letzte der grossen Gottesmänner aus Israels Vorzeit, der *alle Bundesmittler-
funktionen in einer Person vereint.* Die Tradition, die der Deuteronomist im wesent-
lichen unverändert wiedergibt, schildert ihn geradezu als einen zweiten Mose," p. 116.
"Als Prophet ist er *Übermittler des Gottesworts und Gotteswillens,*" p. 117. "Aber
Samuel ist wie Moses und Josue nicht nur Übermittler des Wünsche des Volkes an
Gott, sondern aus Liebe und inniger Verbundenheit mit Israel auch *Fürbitter* und
Sühnemittler," p. 118. The italics are the author's. See also H. Wildberger, "Samuel
und die Errichtung des israelitischen Königtums," *Theol. Zeitschrift,* XIII (1957),
442-69: A. Weiser, *Samuel, FRLANT,* LXXXI (1962), 82-93; Rudolph Smend, *Jah-
wekrieg und Stämmebund, FRLANT,* LXXXIV (1962); J. Kraus, *Die prophetische
Verkündigung des Rechts in Israel,* pp. 23 ff.; M. Noth, "Das Amt des 'Richters
Israels,'" pp. 404-17.

weh's messenger in a time of transition and change, "the faithful guardian of the Mosaic heritage" as Volz puts it, "the first great religious reformer after Moses," as Albright says. Again and again from the time of Wellhausen on scholars have called him the second Moses.

The prophet Hosea ben Beeri, probably from the tribe of Ephraim, stands midway in the history of the covenant traditions of ancient Israel as they were preserved by the northern traditionists. He is intimately acquainted, for example, with the Elohist narratives and legal formulations;[64] and his prophecy teems with parallels, both linguistic and theological, to the sacral traditions in Deuteronomy.[65] The major motifs of the age of Moses are so closely woven into the texture of his thought and the forms of his speaking, often drawn from the amphictyonic celebrations, come so congenially and naturally to him that it cannot be doubted that he conceived his prophetic office in relation to them. This is all the more significant because the coventional *Botenformel* is often wanting where we should most expect it. Again we discern the echoes from the ancient Near Eastern treaties, above all that of the breach of treaty. While the covenant conditionals are all but absent, the indictments and sentences have their source in these formulations. It is not too much to say that the time of Moses was normative for Hosea. Israel must return to the desert again, there to recover her ancient election-covenant

[64] On Hosea's familiarity with the Elohist, there is, so far as I am aware, universal agreement. So Steuernagel, Budde, Procksch, Sellin, von Rad, H. W. Wolff, and many others.

[65] See above all the commentary of H. W. Wolff in the *Biblischer Kommentar* series. Note his words in the introduction to his commentary, p. xxvi: "Alle drei Überlieferungskomplexe des Hoseabuches stellen insofern Parallelen dar, als jeder von ihnen den Weg von der Anklage und Strafdrohung bis zur Heilsverkündigung durchschreitet. Sie mögen auf verschiedene Hände zurückgehen, gehören aber doch alle in den gleichen Kreis zeitgenössischer Freunde des Propheten (s. S. XIV), der identisch ist mit den Vorläufern der deuteronomischen Bewegung.

"Darauf weisen die im Kommentar auf Schritt und Tritt aufzudeckenden Beziehungen der Hosea-Überlieferung zu Sprache und Theologie des Deuteronomiums hin. Ganze Denkbewegungen, die für die deuteronomische Paränese kennzeichnend sind, finden wir erstmals bei Hosea, so die Kombination der Erinnerung an den Auszug aus Ägypten, an die Leitung durch die Wüste und die Hineinführung ins Kulturland mit den Folgen: Sattwerden, Überheblichwerden, Jahwe vergessen (s. S. 48, 294); ferner den Kampf gegen Bündnispolitik (s. S. 273), die Art, von *tôrâ* zu sprechen (s. S. 176 f.), von Jahwe als 'Erzieher' (s. S. 125), von 'Liebe' Jahwes (s. S. 255), von 'Erlösung' (s. S. 162), vom Leben des rechten Propheten 'mit Gott' (s. S. 203), von Bruderschaft (s. S. 33), von Mazzeben der Kanaanäer (s. S. 225), von 'Korn, Most und Olivensaft' (s. S. 44)."

heritage.[66] Hosea recalls Yahweh's great theophanic words of self-revelation, "I am Yahweh from the land of Egypt" (12:9; 13:4); more than once he repeats the formal pronouncement by which the covenant was concluded, "You shall be my people, and I will be your God" (1:9; 2:23); like the Elohist before him he speaks of Israel as Yahweh's son (11:1 ff.; cf. Exod. 4:22-23). Israel's flouting of the first of all the commands in the Elohistic decalog sounds again and again throughout his prophecy; it is the breach of treaty *kat' exochēn.* Hosea knows the apodictic laws, both in his direct citation of them and in his indirect allusions to them. He employs the characteristic imperatives calling upon Israel to hear and the vocatives associated with them. He has apparently listened to the legal encounters of the litigants before the elders at the gates. Hans Walter Wolff suggests plausibly that most of his utterances have their *Sitz im Leben* in this context.[67] The prophet Moses stands at the head of the succession of prophets, the messengers called to speak for Yahweh to the people, and there can be no question that Hosea considered himself to belong to that succession (6:5; 9:7; 12:11, 14). His attitude toward the establishment of the kingdom is close to that of the law for the king in Deuteronomy and to the traditions associated with Samuel.[68] Hosea perpetuates the forms of speech and not infrequently the terminology of the old amphictyonic traditions; one thinks of the apodictic laws, the covenant lawsuits, the historical confessions of the Credos, the indictments and sentences, the exhortations and the speeches of the messengers. He is the proclaimer of the law, the announcer of judgment, the watchman of Ephraim, the prophet whose memories are rooted in the *magnalia Dei,* the mediator of the covenant in inchoate times. He summons his people to *da'ath elohim,* and in this he is again close to the Deuteronomic traditionists (Hos. 4:1, 6; 5:4; 6:6; 14:10. Cf. Deut. 4:39; 7:9 ff.; 8:5; 9:3).[69] Like them he appeals to the love of God

[66] Note, for example, O. Procksch, *Theologie des Alten Testaments,* p. 588: "Schon Hosea sieht die Mosezeit als ein Vorspiel der Zukunft an; wie zu Moses Zeit soll Israel auch in Zukunft noch einmal durch die Wüste wandern (Hos. 12:10) wie ehedem, als Mose es hütete (v. 14), der ausdrücklich hier als Prophet bezeichnet ist."

[67] *Hosea* in Biblischer Kommentar series, pp. xv, 83, and *passim.*

[68] Albrecht Alt, "Die Heimat des Deuteronomiums," *Kleine Schriften,* II (1953), 267 f.

[69] H. W. Wolff, "'Wissen um Gott' bei Hosea als Urform von Theologie," *EvT,* XII (1952/53), 533-54. See also Porteous' judicious criticism in *Tradition und Situation (Weiser Festschrift),* p. 97.

with intimate nuances, and here again we recognize a parallel with the treaties. In this connection it is well to note his polemic against the treaty politics of Israel, another Deuteronomic motif (5:13; 7:11; 8:9; 10:4; 12:2; 14:4. Cf. Deut. 7:2; 17:16; 20:16). In the prophecies of Hosea we listen to echoes from the great covenant lawsuit of Deut. 32.[70]

How are we to explain this extraordinary familiarity of the prophet Hosea with the traditions and the formal and covenantal patterns of speech? Wolff sees the prophet as a member of Levitical circles, and this may well be, but it must always be remembered that according to an important tradition it was Moses who transmitted the law to the Levites (Deut. 33:10).[71] And this may account for his reference to Moses and for the relation of his prophecy to the Mosaic traditions.

We may now attempt to state some of the conclusions which would seem to follow from our discussion. It has been apparent that we have had to deal with many issues in a rather sketchy fashion. This is perhaps unfortunate since the force of the argument depends in no small part upon the detailed scrutiny of numerous literary contexts in the light of form and traditio-historical criticism.

1. There were many prophets in ancient Israel, and it is probable that the canon has preserved the memory of only a relatively small number of them. But there were also different kinds of prophets too, and it is precarious to undertake to understand them in the light of a single background or cultural provenance.[72] While it has been our intention to speak of those who preserve the northern traditions, it must be remembered that the southern prophets not infrequently avail themselves of the same traditions, notably Amos and Micah.[73]

2. The traditions which we have examined have as their common matrix the covenant of Yahweh with Israel at Sinai-Horeb. Not only the literary forms and types but also the treaties from the ancient Near

---

[70] E. Baumann, "Das Lied Mose's (Dt. xxxii. 1-43)," *VT*, VI (1956), 421 f.

[71] H. W. Wolff, "Hoseas geistige Heimat," *TLZ*, LXXXI (1956), 83-94.

[72] H. H. Rowley, "The Nature of Old Testament Prophecy in the Light of Recent Study," in *The Servant of the Lord and Other Essays on the Old Testament* (1952), pp. 91-128; A. Jepsen, *Nabi. Soziologische Studien zur alttestamentlichen Literatur und Religionsgeschichte*, 1934.

[73] E. Würtwein, "Amos-Studien," *ZAW*, LXII (1949), 10-52; W. Beyerlin, *Die Kulttraditionen Israels in der Verkündigung des Propheten Micha. FRLANT*, LXXII (1959).

East now show how the prophets from the north were speaking within a covenantal framework.

3. That there were prophets who understood themselves as having participated in the decisions and announcements of the divine council is certainly true, but it is doubtful if we can say this of all of them, especially those from the north. As Huffmon has demonstrated, there were at least two major types of lawsuit, one of them centering in the Sinaitic covenant.

4. In early traditions Moses is viewed as the mediator of the covenant and as prophet. Among the types of traditions associated with his name are the messenger's speech, the royal covenant speech, the apodictic and casuistic laws with their striking motivations, the lawsuit, and the great conditionals, which we understand to be the basis of the indictments and sentences, on the one hand, and the assurances of felicity, on the other. What is important to observe here is that the prophets avail themselves of the same types of material and thus are continuous with Moses or the Mosaic figure.

5. The question of the *Sitz im Leben* of the *Gattungen* is difficult, but there is a substantial number of contexts which suggest the existence of an annual festival in which the covenant memories of Israel were reactivated into the present, perhaps the autumnal festival. But it is unnecessary to hold that all the kinds of speaking we have mentioned were associated exclusively with that celebration. Inevitably one raises the question of how our "literary" materials were employed in the life of the people. They certainly were not designed to be read as literature.

6. This raises the vexing question of the relationship of the prophets to the cult. On the one hand, they seem to stand over against it in their bitter criticisms of it, but on the other hand there are not a few contexts which more than suggest that they bore some relation to it. One thinks of Amos at Bethel or of Jeremiah in the Temple, or in an earlier period, of Samuel at Gilgal. Moreover, one cannot well ignore the presence of cultic formulations in the prophets. One thinks, for example, of the liturgy (Isa. 33; Mic. 7:9-20; Jer. 14:1—15:3, and others).

7. Who, then, is Moses and who are the prophetic figures who follow him? First of all they are *messengers*. This understanding of the prophetic function has long been recognized by scholars (Ludwig Köhler, Johannes Lindblom, Claus Westermann, H. W. Wolff, M. Noth, Reventlow, and

others) .[74] In the second place, they are *speakers for Yahweh, proclaimers of the law, apostles sent to particular times to speak particular words.* They do more than repeat inherited and traditional cliches; they seek to make the Word of God immediate and relevant and contemporary. They are politicians, to use the word G. Mendenhall and G. E. Wright have taught us—Yahweh's politicians proclaiming covenantal proclamations. But more, they are charismatically endowed by Yahweh to perform their fateful missions. The succession of prophets is a succession of charismatic persons, and we must remind ourselves once more that there were many more such persons in Israel than those of whom the OT tells us. Yehezkel Kaufmann does not go too far in maintaining that there was a long succession of apostles in Israel.

What then shall we say of the prophets of whom we have been speaking? In the light of our general survey of one major strand of tradition in the OT it does not seem to me to be out-running the evidence to say that they were indeed prophets like Moses, Yahweh's messengers, his covenant mediators, intercessors for the people, speakers for God. They are sent from the divine King, the suzerain of the treaties, to reprove and to pronounce judgment upon Israel for breach of covenant. The work of Mendenhall, Baltzar, G. E. Wright, Julien Harvey, S. J., Kline, and others have made this very clear.

But, more than all else, Moses comes and the prophets come to speak the Word of Yahweh, and it is the power of his Word which lies behind their various pronouncements. This stress upon the Word of Yahweh in the northern traditions is not the same as that of the prophets from the south. From beginning to end in the north the Word assumes a central role.

So today we no longer speak of Moses *or* the prophets, or of the law *or* prophecy, but rather of Moses *and* the prophets.

---

[74] Note especially James F. Ross, "The Prophet as Yahweh's Messenger," in *Israel's Prophetic Heritage,* pp. 98-107, but also the criticisms of R. Rendtorff and C. Westermann. See n. 46.

A LITURGY ON THE TRIUMPHS OF YAHWEH

Among the early poetic compositions of ancient Israel few, if any, have exercised such fascination for scholarly inquiry as the so-called 'Song of the Sea' (Ex 15:1–18).[1] Its theme is central not only for the formative period of Israel's history, but also for the religious faith of Israel throughout the centuries and in the history of Christian liturgy.[2,3] No event was longer remembered or better remembered.[4] It is the most primitive of the affirmations of the old credos (Dt 26:8; 6:21–23; Josh 24:6–7; 1 Sam 12:6),[5] and from early times

[1] The following are among the most important for the present study: A. Bender, *Das Lied Exodus 15*, ZAW XXIII (1903), pp. 1–48; Paul Haupt, *Moses' Song of Triumph*, AJSL XX (1904), pp. 149–72; S. Mowinckel, *Psalmenstudien II: Das Thronbesteigungsfest Jahwäs und der Ursprung der Eschatologie* (Videnskapsselkaptes Skrifter II, Hist.-Filos. Klasse, 1921, No. 6), 1922, *passim*; idem, *The Psalms in Israel's Worship*, translated by D. R. Ap-Thomas, 2 vols., 1962 (*passim* in vol. I); Hans Schmidt, *Das Meerlied, Ex 15:2–19*, ZAW XLIX, N.F. 8 (1931), pp. 59–66; Martin Buber, *Königtum Gottes. Das Kommende: Untersuchungen zur Entstehungsgeschichte des messianischen Glaubens*, 1932, pp. 129–30; idem, *Moses*, 1946, pp. 74–79; Joh. Pedersen, *Passahfest und Passahlegende*, ZAW LII (1934), pp. 161–75; *Israel: its Life and Culture III–IV*, Eng. edition, 1947, pp. 384–415; 728–37; Georg Beer, *Exodus*, mit einem Beitrag von K. Galling in Handbuch zum Alten Testament series, Erste Reihe, No. 3, 1939, pp. 79–84; M. Rozelaar, *The Song of the Sea*, V.T. II (1952), pp. 221–28; U. Cassuto, *A Commentary on the Book of Exodus* (Hebrew), Second edition, 1953; F. M. Cross and D. N. Freedman, *The Song of Miriam*, JNES XIV (1955), pp. 237–250; John D. Watts, *The Son of the Sea – Ex. XV*, V.T. VII (1957), pp. 371–80; Georg Fohrer, *Überlieferung und Geschichte des Exodus: eine Analyse von Ex 1–15*, Berlin 1964, pp. 112–16.

[2] Martin Noth, *Überlieferungsgeschichte des Pentateuch*, 2. Auflage, Stuttgart 1948, pp. 50–4; G. von Rad, *Das formgeschichtliche Problem des Hexateuchs*, 4. Folge, Heft 26, Stuttgart 1938 = *Gesammelte Studien zum Alten Testament*, 1958, pp. 9–86; K. Galling, *Die Erwählungstraditionen Israels*, BZAW 48, 1928, pp. 5ff; A. Weiser, *Glaube und Geschichte im Alten Testament und andere ausgewählte Schriften*, Göttingen, 1961, pp. 99–181 (originally published in BZAW, 4. Folge, Heft 4, 1931); C. Westermann, *Forschung am Alten Testament*, Neudrücke und Berichte aus dem 20. Jahrhundert 24, Munich 1964, p. 193: 'Der Pentateuch ist von der Mitte Ex 1–15 her entstanden oder um die Mitte herum gewachsen... Das dem Alten Testament oder der Religion Israels Eigene, Eigentümliche ist nun eindeutig in der Mitte, im Kern dieses weit ausgebauten Ganzen zu finden, während die Anbauten oder Anfügungen auf den ersten Blick die stärkere Berührung mit der oder den stärkeren Einfluß der Umwelt erkennen lassen'; G. E. Wright, *The Old Testament Against Its Environment* in Studies in Biblical Theology series, No. 4, 1950, pp. 49f: 'The Exodus or deliverance from Egypt, therefore, is the central point in Israelite history and faith.'

[3] *La Sainte Bible, traduite en français sous la direction de l'École Biblique de Jérusalem*, Paris 1956, p. 76 (nt): 'le premier et le plus célèbre des "cantiques" que la liturgie chrétienne emprunte à l'A.T.'

[4] John Bright, *A History of Israel*, Philadelphia 1959, p. 111: 'Israel remembered the exodus for all time to come as the constitutive event that had called her into being as a people... A belief so ancient and so entrenched will admit of no explanation save that Israel actually escaped from Egypt to the accompaniment of events so stupendous that they were impressed forever on her memory.'

[5] G. von Rad, *Das formgeschichtliche Problem des Hexateuch*.

to late was celebrated and contemporanized in song and ritual.[1] However variously one may construe the source analysis of Ex 1–15, the literary materials as they are ordered at present reach their culmination and finale in the Song.[2] Its affinities with Ex 14 are numerous and close, and the final verse (14:31) serves not only as a climax to all that has gone before, but also as a superb introduction to the words of exultant singing and epic recounting that follow: 'And Israel saw the great work which Yahweh had done against the Egyptians, and the people feared Yahweh, and they believed in Yahweh and in his servant Moses'. It is clear, then, that the Song occupies a strategic position in the composition of the Book of Exodus, or, for that matter, in the composition of the entire Pentateuch. What is more, it has had its career in the life of the worshipping community, for we listen to echoes and reminiscences again and again in the hymns, prayers, and liturgies of Israel.[3] *Habent libelli fata sua.*

The Song belongs, too, to the extensive literature relating to the Sea in the Old Testament[4] and in the literatures of the other peoples of the ancient Near East.[5] That the motif is designed to be of central

[1] Ps 66:1–7; 74:12–17; 77:11–20; 80:1–3; 89:8–10 (Heb 9–11); 114; 135:8–9; 136:10ff. Cf. also Ps 105:23–45; 106:8–12; Is 63:7–14. C. Westermann, *op.cit.*, p.201: 'Zur Struktur des die Geschichte Israels begründenden Geschehens gehört das Gotteslob. Das Wirken Gottes in der ganzen Bibel ist dialogisches Geschehen; mit dem Handeln und Reden Gottes gehört von Anfang an bis zum Ende die Antwort, die Reaktion im Sagen und im Tun hinzu. Wo Gott handelt, da wacht das Lob auf; das zeigt exemplarisch für die ganze Bibel der Aufbau des Buches Exodus: dem Bericht von der Rettungstat (1–14) folgt das Lob der Erretteten im Kap. 15.' Cf. also p.208. See the full and detailed references in M. Noth, *Überlieferungsgeschichte des Pentateuch*, pp.50–54.

[2] It is now commonly held that Exodus 15:1–18 cannot be assigned to any of the sources J.E.D.P. So Eißfeldt, Noth, S.R.Driver, Cross and Freedman, and others. When and by whom the poem came to assume its present position we are not able to say, but it may well have been composed in relation to the Yahwist and Elohist traditions. That it was consciously inserted in its present context and was designed to perform a special function in relation to it seems probable. This is the element of validity in Pedersen's thesis (see *infra*). The source analysis of Ex 14 is complicated and much controverted. Compare, *inter alios*, the analyses of S.R.Driver, *An Introduction to the Literature of the Old Testament*, New edition revised in 1913, New York 1916, p.29; M. Noth, *Überlieferungsgeschichte des Pentateuch*, 2. Auflage, 1948, pp.32 and *passim*; O. Eißfeldt, *Hexateuch-Synopse*, Leipzig 1922, pp.134–7. It is noteworthy that Eißfeldt assigns the materials to L, J, and E. See also his *Einleitung in das Alte Testament*, 3. neubearbeitete Auflage, Tübingen 1964, pp.258, 265, 266. E.T. *The Old Testament: an Introduction*, translated by Peter R. Ackroyd, New York 1965, pp.195, 199, 201.

[3] Besides Noth's references *(supra)* see S.R.Driver, *The Book of Exodus* in Cambridge Bible for Schools and Colleges, Cambridge 1929, p.131 for a list of reminiscences to the Song.

[4] Note *inter alia* Ps 66:6; 74:12–15; 77:16–20; 78:13; 53; 89:9–10 (Heb 10–12); 93:3–4; 95:5; 96:11; 98:7–9; 106:7–12; 114:3–5; 136:13–15.

[5] Hermann Gunkel, *Schöpfung und Chaos in Urzeit und Endzeit. Eine religionsgeschichtliche Untersuchung über Gen 1 und Ap Joh 12*, Göttingen 1921; Otto Eißfeldt, *Baal Zaphon, Zeus Kasios und der Durchzug der Israeliten durchs Meer*, BRA 1, Halle 1932; Philippe Reymond,

importance for the author is demonstrated by the immediate framework in which it is enclosed. The word *Sea* appears no fewer than sixteen times in the preceding chapter,[1] and in the verses immediately following it appears five times (Ex 15:19 *(ter)*, 21, 22). Within the poem itself the terminology of the Sea is employed with great versatility, and the words appear almost invariably in strategic rhetorical collocations or climatic contexts: ים (1*d*, 4*b*, 10*b*), ים סוף (4*d*), תהמת (5*a*, 8*d*), מצולת (5*b*) מים (8*a*), מים אדירים (10*b*). A comparative study of the motif in the Song with related materials in the Accadian and Ugaritic epics and poems will reveal numerous stylistic, rhetorical, and linguistic affinities, but it will also show that Israel is going its own way here, that it is faithful to its historical heritage and narrative life, and that the uniqueness of Yahweh's historical deed is not lost or dissipated in the wonder of cosmic miracle or the imagery of the cosmogonic chaos dragon myth. This becomes especially clear when one observes the movement of the composition from past to future, from memories to expectations, from the turbulence of the flood waters to the period of the progress through the desert and, beyond that, to the security and peace of the sanctuary (cf. Ps 29; 93; 99).

The Song contains another primary motif. It is the celebration of Yahweh's victory and belongs to the substantial literature gathered about the wars of Yahweh.[2] Yahweh triumphs over the recalcitrant forces which resist and impede his people's advance and is indeed making a way in the Sea for the redeemed to pass over (cf. Is 43:16). *Yahweh is a man of war!* His power shatters the armies of Pharaoh and stirs the waters into raging turbulence against them. The poem is so composed that its very structure reveals the role of Yahweh, on the one hand, and of the enemy, on the other. So Yahweh comes to Israel at the beginning as Leader in holy engagement, as Conqueror and Victor, as One whose majesty overcomes the hostile

---

L'Eau, sa Vie, et sa Signification dans l'ancien Testament, Supplements to V.T. VI, Leiden 1958; Otto Kaiser, *Die mythische Bedeutung des Meeres in Ägypten, Ugarit und Israel,* zweite überarbeitete und um einen Nachtrag vermehrte Auflage, BZAW 78, Berlin 1962. Kaiser gives a full bibliography.

[1] Ex 14:2(bis), 9, 16(bis), 21(ter), 22, 23, 26, 27(ter), 28, 29. Cf. also *waters* or *water* (14:22, 26, 28, 29).

[2] W. Caspari, *Was stand im Buche der Kriege Jahwes?,* Zeitschrift für wissenschaftliche Theologie 54 (1912), pp. 110–154; H. Fredriksson, *Jahwe als Krieger,* Lund 1945; O. Eißfeldt, *Jahwe Zebaoth,* in Miscellanea Academica Berolinensis, Berlin 1950, pp. 128–50; G. von Rad, *Der Heilige Krieg im alten Israel,* Zürich 1951; Roland de Vaux, O.P., *Ancient Israel: its Life and Institutions,* translated from the French by John McHugh, New York, London, and Toronto 1961, pp. 258–67.

powers of history and nature. It is not surprising, then, that the composition has often been described as a song of victory.[1] Some scholars have thought of it, rather, as a hymn,[2] still others as a liturgy or litany.[3] Sigmund Mowinckel classifies it among the hymns of the divine enthronement (cf., for example, Ps 47; 93; 96–99).[4] There is much to be said for this view because the affinities of the latter with our passage are striking, not only in the final line of the poem with its acclamation of Yahweh's kingship, but also in the motif of conflict, the supremacy of Yahweh over the other gods, and the presence of the same key words. But it is to be observed that in our poem the conflict is not with the Sea, but with the divinely-procreated Pharaoh and his armies. Aage Bentzen speaks similarly of the Song of Miriam (Ex 15:21) and the Song of the Sea as 'hymns to the accession festival of Yahweh' which were celebrated in the Temple in Jerusalem.[5] Johannes Pedersen thinks of the whole of Ex 1–15 as 'the cult legend of the Passover reflecting the annual re-living of historical events, as it took shape throughout the ages.'[6] G. Beer also associates the Song with the Passover celebrations and views the composition as a Passover cantata, but rejects Pedersen's understanding of Exod 1–15 as a literary or cultic unit, as do most scholars because of the presence of different literary strata or sources in the composition.[7] If our understanding of the passage is correct, then we are to view it much in the manner of Beer as a liturgy or litany. It was in all probability employed in the celebrations of the autumnal festival within the precincts of the sanctuary, and the participants are in actuality 'Moses' (i.e. the one playing the role of Moses in the cult) and 'all the people' and perhaps the Temple choirs.[8]

[1] Haupt, Cassuto, Fredriksson, Cross and Freedman, and others.
[2] Galling, Kaiser, Rozelaar, Watts, Fohrer.
[3] H. Schmidt, G. Beer, G. von Rad.
[4] *Psalmenstudien II, passim; The Psalms in Israel's Worship*, II, p. 247 and *passim*.
[5] *Op. cit.*, I, p. 163. Similarly H. Schmidt, A. Weiser, *Einleitung in das Alte Testament*, Göttingen 1957[4], pp. 90–1. See the critical discussion of K. G. Rendtorff, *Sejrhymnen i Exodus 15 og dens forhold til tronbestigelsessalmerne*, Dansk Teologisk Tidsskrift 22 (1959), pp. 65–81, 156–71; also G. Fohrer, *op. cit.*, p. 112, nt. 5.
[6] *Israël: its Life and Culture III–IV*, p. 726. See also Additional Note I, pp. 728–37, and *Passahfest und Passahlegende*, ZAW LII (1934), pp. 161–75.
[7] *Op. cit.*, p. 84: 'So möchte Ex 15 die Passahkantate sein, die für die Osterfeier in Jerusalem, wie sie sich seit der Kultreform Josias eingebührt hat – bzw. für die große Ostfeier in Jahr 621 2 R 23:21ff selbst – gedichtet worden ist und schließlich die mit Ex 15 anhebenden und als Festliturgie für Passah dienenden Texte abschließt und krönt.' For telling arguments against this view, see Fohrer, *op. cit.*, p. 112 nt.
[8] The association of the Song with the cult is today widely recognized among scholars. Though many of them associate it with the Passover celebrations, it is more probable

We should expect that a composition that was designed for use in the cult should reveal its particular character in its form and structure, in its different styles and rhetorical features, in the various ways in which its content is articulated into varying types of speech, and in the kinds of language employed by the several participants. We shall observe, for example, that the liturgy has a particular beginning and a particular ending, each standing separate and independent, and that the two stand in relation with each other, a feature, one need not add, typical of many of Israel's cultic compositions. The major divisions are of approximately the same length and are clearly marked by the presence of hymnic refrains which appear at strategic points (15:6, 11, 16cd). Each division is in turn divided into two strophes, each with its own particular content and literary form and style. Key words appear in striking collocations and serve to guide in discerning the progress or movement of the lines. While the 2′2′ meter prevails throughout, there are exceptions, but there is always a reason for such shifts. The parallelism of the lines shows considerable diversity, but it is not employed indiscriminately, as is illustrated not only by the refrains, but also by the different ways in which the key words are ordered into changing parallelistic patterns. The figures or images appear in climactic contexts and interestingly confirm the structural analysis derived from the refrains (note, for example, *like a stone* (5b), *like lead* (10b), *like a stone* (16b). A further confirmation of this analysis is seen in the repetition of the same or similar cola in the same literary contexts, as, for example, in 5a, *the floods cover them* and in 10b, *the sea covered them*. Of special importance is the alternation between the confessional speech of praise, on the one hand, and the narrative concerning the enemy, on the other (2–3 and 4–5, 7–8 and 9–10, 12–13 and 14–16).[1] As has been observed by many scholars, the third division (15:12ff) is somewhat more irregular in its composition than the two preceding sections.[2] This suggests that it may possibly have

that it belongs to the complex of liturgical materials belonging to the autumnal festival. For a recent proponent of this view see R. E. Clements, *Prophecy and Covenant* in Studies in Biblical Theology series, No. 43, Naperville, Ill., p. 74.

[1] For similar combinations of hymnic and narrative style see Ps 68, 118 and 135. Compare Beer, p. 80: 'Das Besondere des Liedes liegt darin, daß hymnische Klänge (2.3.6.7.11. 12) durch balladartige (4.5.8–10.13–17) erläutert werden und mit ihnen zu einem Ganzen verschmelzen.' Rylaarsdam, *Interpreter's Bible* I, Nashville 1952, p. 942, also recognizes the alternation of hymn (vss. 2–3, 6–7, 11–12) and 'historical ballad' (vss. 4–5, 8–10, 13–17), but comments that the latter are 'possibly not from one source'.

[2] John D. W. Watts, *op. cit.*, p. 376: 'The formation of verses 13–17 is much looser, and the meter not nearly so compact, yet the general form is patterned after that in verses

passed through a long period of transmission, 15:1–12 (13?) being earlier than the rest. Yet it cannot be denied that the third division has features which belong with the other two, as in its use of key words and the closing refrain.

Hymnic introit (15:1*b*)

I will sing to Yahweh
  for he is highly exalted,
Horse and chariotry
  he has cast into the Sea.

The two bicola are in 2'2' meter (*contra* Cassuto, Mowinckel, Noth who read 4'4'). Such hymnic invocations usually appear in the imperative (cf. Miriam's Song in 21), but the first person formulations are by no means infrequent (Judg 5:3; Pss 89:1 [Heb 2]; 101:1; 108:1 [Heb 2]. Cf. also Ps 14:6*b*; 57:7, 9 [Heb 8, 10]; 59:17 [Heb 18].[1] The stress of the opening colon falls emphatically upon *Yahweh*, and the lines that follow elaborate upon the divine name (15:2–3). Among other peoples of the Near East such ascriptions opening with 'I will sing' or 'I will praise' are offered to the king (so Cassuto).[2] Compare the Nikkal poem from Ugarit: *'ašr nkl w'eb ... ḫrḫb mlk qẓ.* As is characteristic of the hymn, the opening ascription of praise is followed by the motivation, introduced by the characteristic deictic *ki*, and provides the basis for the cultic celebrations: כי גאה גאה[3]. The LXX renders ἐνδόξως γὰρ δεδόξασται and the Vulgate *ex gloriose enim magnificus est.* The Hebrew is fond of such collocations, in part for reasons of assonance and emphasis, in part to accentuate and to call attention to the major theme. The colon is then developed into a bicolon and states concretely the nature of Yahweh's triumph: *horse and chariotry/he has cast into the Sea.*[4] The self-summons to singing is inspired by the wonder of this historical event.

8–10.' Also p. 377: 'The very loose, even poor, poetic form makes one wonder what has happened to the verses.' Note the attempt at reconstruction on p. 378.
[1] Hermann Gunkel, *Einleitung in die Psalmen: Die Gattungen der religiösen Lyrik Israels*, zu Ende geführt von Joachim Begrich in the Göttinger Handkommentar zum Alten Testament, Göttingen 1933, p. 38.
[2] See, for example, A. Falkenstein and W. von Soden, *Sumerische und Akkadische Hymnen und Gebete*, Zürich/Stuttgart 1953, p. 61: 'Nusku, oberster Kämmerer Enlils, dich wil lich preisen / mein König, ein Lied will ich dir singen;' '(Hoch) erheben (will ich) den groß-mächtigen Anschar, / den Herrscher der Götter, den Herrn der Länder.' See also p. 93.
[3] Gunkel-Begrich, *op.cit.*, p. 42f. It will be observed that many of the motivations are pregnantly and tersely phrased and that, further, they frequently strike the key note for the entire hymn. See the writer's *The Linguistic and Rhetorical Usages of the Particle ki in the Old Testament*, in HUCA, XXXII, pp. 135–60.
[4] See the excellent discussion of C. Westermann in *The Praise of God in the Psalms*, translated from the German by Keith R. Crim, Richmond 1965, pp. 89f, 106–8.

238

Hymnic confession (15:2–3), *epic narrative* (15:4–5)

My strength and my Protector is Yah,
  he has become my salvation.
This is my God, and I will extol him,
  my father's God will I exalt.
Yahweh is a man of war,
  Yahweh his Name!

Chariots of Pharaoh[1]
  he has cast into the Sea.
The chosen of his officers
  are drowned in the Reed Sea.
The floods cover them,
  they go down to the depth like a stone.

Hymnic response (15:6):

Thy right arm, O Yahweh,
  awesome in power,
Thy right arm, O Yahweh,
  shatters the enemy.

The two strophes contain three bicola each (15:2–3, 4–5). The first centers completely upon the divine name, and is clearly an elaboration of the first bicolon of the introit (15:1*b*).[2] It is a hymn of praise describing and praising the attributes of Yahweh, but moves inevitably into the hymnic confession of the second bicolon: *This is my God,*[3] *God of my father.*[4] The third bicolon (3) is probably a cultic shout or battle cry.[5] The first two bicola are in the first person singular in which the singer is the subject; the third, appropriately, in the third person and Yahweh is the subject. The second strophe (4–5) has a style different from the first, and the style conforms to a change in motif. Here the concern is all with the enemy. While in the first strophe (2–3) the poet elaborates upon the first bicolon of

[1] With Albright and Cross and Freedman we take 'chariots of Pharaoh' and 'Pharaoh and his chariots' as ancient variants. The former is to be preferred.
[2] Hans-Joachim Kraus, *Psalmen* in Biblischer Kommentar series, Neukirchen 1960, p.xlii: 'Im Zentrum des Lobpreises steht der Name Jahwes, auf den sich alle Prädikationen beziehen. Jahwe kann in der 2 pers. angesprochen oder in der 3 pers. verherrlicht werden. Auch Mischungen sind hier möglich. Die Aussagen kreisen dann um Jahwes Macht und Güte, um sein Wort und um sein Wirken in Schöpfung und Geschichte.'
[3] This form of confessional style is typical of other contexts too. Cf. Ps 18:2 (Heb 3); 22:2; 48:15; 118:28. See Otto Eißfeldt, *'Mein Gott' im Alten Testament*, ZAW (1945/48), pp.3–16, reprinted in The Evangelical Quarterly, XIX (1947), pp.7–20.
[4] J. Philip Hyatt, *Yahweh as 'the God of my father'*, V.T. V (1955), pp.130–6. Hyatt argues for a Mosaic date for the original form of the liturgy.
[5] Such cultic outcries are frequent in the Psalter. See Fredriksson's discussion of 'battle words' addressed to Yahweh or referring to him, on pp.81–3.

239

the introit, in the second strophe (4–5) he elaborates upon the second in the manner of the epic or declarative narrative. This feature is not at all unusual in Hebrew poetic compositions. In the first strophe the divine names are given in a climactic progression:[1] *Yah, my God, God of my father, Yahweh, Yahweh!* Parallel to these divine names are the possessive ascriptions: *my strength, my Protector,*[2] *my salvation, my God, my father's God.* Similarly, the verbs are synonymous with the *I will sing* of the introit: *I will extol, I will exalt.* In the second strophe we witness the same feature. Here the key word is *sea,* and each bicolon contributes to the motif in its own way: *sea, Sea of Reeds, floods, deeps.* Again the verbs are synonymous with the colon *he has cast* (רמה) *into the sea* of the introit: *he has cast* (ירה) *into the sea, are drowned, the floods cover them, they go down into the deeps.* The meter is 2′2′, except in vs. 2, which is 3′3′. The latter should not for that reason be excised, as is sometimes proposed, because it performs the function for which it is designed in the strophe and the liturgy as a whole, and is essential, moreover, to the structure of the strophe. It is noteworthy that Is 12:2 and Ps 118:14 contain the same wording, and there is every reason to believe that they derive it from our text. The terminology of the bicolon is military throughout, as is confirmed *inter alia* by the parallels in related literature (1 Sam 2:1–2, 10; Ps 18:1–3 [Heb 2–4]; 49–50 [Heb 50–51]; 20; 21; 68:4 [Heb. 5], 32–34 [Heb. 33–35]), but naturally came to be employed in other contexts (Ps 28:7–9; 59:9, 17 [Heb. 10, 18]; Is 25:1; 26:1. Cf. also Ps 96:2; 98:2–3; 140:7 [Heb. 8]. The confession of the second bicolon (2cd) also has its stylistic and contentual parallels (Ps 48:14 [Heb 15]; 105:7; 118:28. Cf. also Ps 18:2 [Heb 3]; 28:7; 59:9 [Heb 10]; Jer 16:19). The third bicolon brings the strophe to its climax impressively: *Yahweh is a man of war* (Is 42:13; Ps 24:8. Cf. Judg 5:23; Hab 3:9ff), *Yahweh his name* (Am 4:13; 5:8; 9:6;

---

[1] Cross and Freedman prefer to read *Yahweh* here on the basis of their restoration of the text in its original orthography. This is, of course, very possible, but stylistic reasons favor the M.T. It is doubtful that Yah was originally an ecstatic shout, although by no means impossible. See G. R. Driver, *The Original Form of the Name Yahweh. Evidence and Conclusions*, ZAW XLVI (1928), pp. 7–25; Martin Buber, *Moses*, Oxford 1946, p. 50, where the suggestion is offered that Yahweh may be derived from an original dervish cry, Ya-hu, which was interpreted to mean 'O-He'. See also Raymond Abba, *The Divine Name Yahweh*, J.B.L. LXXX (1961), pp. 320–28, esp. pp. 321f. The monosyllable is effective in its present context, and makes the repeated Yahweh at the close all the more impressive.

[2] D. Winton Thomas, E.T. xlviii (1937), p. 478; T. H. Gaster, E.T. xlviii (1936), p. 45; Cross and Freedman, *op. cit.*, p. 243, nt.

Is 42:8; 47:4 (so LXX); 48:2; 51:13).[1] The dramatic power and intensity of the bicolon is to be grasped by the way in which it brings to a culmination the succession of cola which precede it, by the stylistic difference in formulation, by the two-fold repetition of *Yahweh*, by the brevity of the lines, and by the momentous role that such an asseveration must have played in the earliest theology of ancient Israel. It is Israel's earliest theology *in nuce*.[2]

The second strophe (4–5) deserves further attention. As we have seen, it is governed throughout by the motif of the Sea, just as the first strophe is dominated by the triumphant Yahweh. Four different terms are employed to designate the Sea: תהמת, ים סוף, ים, מצולת‎ לת; each time the word is given a special position: in the first two bicola at the close, in the third at the beginning, and in the fourth in the middle. The situation may be represented as follows:

a b / c d
a′ b′ / c′ d′
d″ c″ / c″ d″ e

The final three-beat line brings the strophe to its climax, and is the more striking because of the emphasis upon the closing figure: *they go down into the deeps like a stone*. It is noteworthy that whereas the preceding strophe repeats the divine name in many forms, here it is completely absent.

The hymnic response follows. It is characteristic of the poets of Israel to break forth into such hymnic refrains after dramatic and climactic contexts. In view of the intent of the poet to 'sing to Yahweh' concerning his triumphs, such a predication as we have here is only to be expected. The meter is 2′2′, and the parallelism conforms to many exemplars both within the Old Testament and in the Ugaritic epics, as has been demonstrated by W. F. Albright and Cross and Freedman.[3] The central psycho-physical symbol and anthropomorphism of the right arm, also paralleled in many ancient

---

[1] Oskar Grether, *Name und Wort Gottes im Alten Testament*, Gießen 1934, p. 55. The writer's judgment that the passages are almost entirely post-Deuteronomic can hardly be sustained today, however.

[2] Note the frequently quoted words of J. Wellhausen, *Israelitische und jüdische Geschichte*³, p. 26: 'Das Kriegslager, die Wiege der Nation, war das älteste Heiligtum. Da war Israel, und da war Jahwe.' Cf. von Rad, *Der Heilige Krieg*, p. 14.

[3] W. F. Albright, *The Psalm of Habbakuk* in *Studies in Old Testament Prophecy*, T. H. Robinson Festschrift, Edited by H. H. Rowley, Edinburgh 1950, pp. 1–18; Cross and Freedman, *op. cit*. See also H. L. Ginsberg, *The Ugaritic Texts and Textual Criticism*, J.B.L. LXII (1913), pp. 109–118.

Near Eastern texts and pictorial representations, here receives a
most impressive formulation, as the parallelism shows:

    a b / c d
    a b / e f

The image is, of course, profusely employed in the Old Testament
(Ps 20:6 [Heb 7]; 21:8 [Heb 9]; 44:3 [Heb 4]; 45:4 [Heb 5]; 48:10
[Heb 11]; 60:5 [Heb 7]; 77:10 [Heb 11]; 89:13 [Heb 14]; 42 [Heb
43]; 98:1; 108:6 [Heb 7]; 118:15–16; Is 51:9 etc.). Now the divine
name appears twice in the repeated apostrophe, and is surely meant
to conform to the same repetition at the close of the first strophe (3).
The word נאדרי has its Ugaritic and Accadian cognates.[1] The
bicolon of the refrain comes to a close with a reference to the enemy
(אויב) and thus prepares the way for the strophes which follow.

Hymnic confession (15:7–8), *epic narrative* (15:9–10).
In the greatness of thy majesty
  thou overthrowest thy adversaries;
Thou sendest forth thy fury,
  it consumes them like stubble.
At the blast of thy nostrils
  the waters are heaped up;
The streams stood like a wall,
  the deeps churned in the heart of the sea.

The enemy said:
  'I will pursue, I will overtake,
I will divide the spoil,
  my desire will be sated.
I will bare my sword
  my hand will drive them off.'
Thou didst blow with thy wind,
  the sea covered them,
They sank like lead
  in the fearful waters.

Hymnic response (15:11)
Who is like thee
  among the gods, O Yahweh?
Who is like thee,
  feared among the holy ones?
Terrible in praiseworthy deeds,
  doing wonders?

[1] Cross and Freedman, pp. 245–6; W. Moran, *The Use of the Canaanite Infinitive Absolute as
a Finite Verb in the Amarna Letters*, Journal of Cuneiform Studies IV (1950), pp. 169–72.

The structure is the same as that of the first division. It is again composed of two strophes, with four bicola in the first and five in the second, and is followed by a refrain with the same style and parallelism as before. The meter is 2'2' throughout. The two final bicola of each strophe (8, 10) are completely parallel in style, content, and imagery (note that the figure (8c, 10c) appears in precisely the same position in both quatrains!). The first line in both significantly employs the same key word *at the blast* (רוח) *of thy nostrils* (8a) *and thou didst blow with thy wind* (רוח) (10a), and each strophe ends with an emphatic expression of our major motif: *in the heart of the sea* (8d), *in the fearful waters* (10d). The אדירים of the final colon of the division (10d) picks up in characteristic manner the נאדרי of the first refrain (6b). To be observed also is that the last three cola of each strophe employ the motif of the sea in much the same manner and with the same diversity of terminology.

The first strophe opens with a reminiscence of the major motif of the introit and gives it exceptional stress (ברב גאון cf. גאה גאה 1b), just as the opening bicolon of the second strophe of the first division similarly recalls the second bicolon of the introit. In the opening and closing bicola of this division (7b, c, 10a), the liturgy employs the same declarative style of narrative confession. On the face of it, this would seem to mar the structure we are defending, but such mixed elements are not all infrequent in Old Testament literary forms. Moreover, the motif of the enemy persists throughout the strophe. It is precarious to subject the *Gattungen* to too strict consistency. As we have had occasion to observe, shifts between the second and third person, especially in relation to the divine name, are characteristic of hymnic style (so Gunkel-Begrich and Westermann). It is again noteworthy that the divine name is absent throughout the second strophe (cf. also 4–5), but appears twice in the refrain that follows (cf. 6). To revert to our previous analysis *supra*, the opening lines of the quatrains of each strophe (7a, 8a) are designed to stand in parallelism with each other ברוח אפיך, ברב גאונך. It is quite characteristic of Hebrew literary craftsmanship for strophes to fall into two parts. Interestingly, the beginning of the second strophe (9) repeats the motif of the enemy from the beginning of the second strophe of the first division (chariots of Pharaoh) and from the closing colon of the first refrain (אויב 6d), but now, in the manner of Israel's poets, cites the words of the foe. Such style is also to be encountered in the Ugaritic texts (so Cross and Freedman and

243

Albright) and has its parallels in the Old Testament also in the boasts and braggadocio of the enemy. The climax of the enemy's words repeats the motif of the hand (or arm). The two words are often used interchangeably.

The lines of the refrain or hymnic response (15:11) fall into three bicola in the 2'2' meter. They bring to a stirring climax the motif of Yahweh's victory, which is demonstrated not only by his supremacy above all gods (Ps 35:10; 71:19; 77:13; 86:8; 89:6, 9 [Heb 7, 10]; 85:3; 96:4; 99:9; 113:5), but also by his mighty acts to which the impressive cola refer: *terrible in praiseworthy deeds, doing wonders.* The meter and parallelism are the same as those of the first refrain (6). Significantly the word נאדרי of the first refrain (6*b*) is repeated in the second (reading נאדרי with the Sam) and is of course echoed in the last and climatic colon of the immediately preceding strophe (10*d*). The poets of Israel are fond of employing rhetorical questions, especially in their contemplation of the incomparability of Yahweh (Ps 18:31 [Heb 32]; 35:10; 71:19; 89:6, 8 [Heb 7, 9]; 113:5–6; Is 40:18, 25; Mic 7:18). In 11*d* we should either emend קדש to the plural with the LXX and Syro-Hexaplar or more probably take the word as a collective, and thus restore the original parallelism: *among the gods, among the holy ones.*[1] Behind such formulations lies the ancient Near Eastern ideology of the heavenly council (Ps 58:1; 82:1 [Heb 2]; 86:8; Is 40:1–11; Job 1:6ff. Cf. also Ps 103:19ff; 135:5). Again, as before (6), the divine name is spoken in the vocative, and surely in a superlative way: there is no god like Yahweh who performs such wonders as the preceding lines have so vividly described.

Hymnic confession (15:12–14), *epic narrative* (15:15–16*b*)

Thou didst stretch out thy right hand,
   earth swallowed them.
Thou didst lead in thy steadfast love
   the people thou hast redeemed.
Thou didst guide them in thy strength
   to thy holy abode.
The peoples heard and trembled,
   pangs seized the inhabitants of Philistia.

Now are dismayed
   the chieftains of Edom.

---

[1] Patrick D. Miller, Jr., *Two Critical Notes on Psalm 68 and Deuteronomy 33*, Harvard Theological Review 57 (1964), p. 241, nt. 6.

244

The nobles of Moab
  trembling seizes.
Then melted away all
  the inhabitants (enthroned?) of Canaan
Thou didst descend upon them
  terror and dread.
By the greatness of thy arm
  they are still like a stone.

Hymnic response (15:16cd)

Until thy people pass over, O Yahweh,
  until thy people pass over whom thou hast created.

As we have already observed, the composition of this division is beset with stylistic and structural difficulties. It is significant that these difficulties appear at the point where the liturgy passes from Yahweh's victory to his leading of his people to their destination in the land of Canaan. While it has sometimes been suggested by scholars that the third division represents a later addition or expansion of a poem which originally dealt exclusively with the conquest of the enemy, which in itself would be very possible and even plausible, one would then have to explain the numerous affinities which certainly exist between the final division and the foregoing divisions. One might contend, indeed, that the later traditionists appropriated to themselves the form and style of the original composition. On the other hand, a good case could be made out for the contention that different traditional forms are actually associated with the Exodus or Sea motif, on the one hand, and with the desert sojourn and occupation of the land, on the other. More important, perhaps, would be a careful scrutiny of parallel contexts either in the Psalms or in other books of the Old Testament where we encounter a literary, structural, and thematic situation not unlike that which we meet here (see *infra*). While one cannot categorically deny that the poem may have gone through a history of transmission, it is best to take the liturgy as we have it before us at the present time and to attempt to follow the course of its thought and the sequence of the bicola as they advance to their goal.

First, then, let us consider the stylistic problems and difficulties. Vs. 12 seems to belong to the motif of the Sea, while vs. 13 obviously belongs to the motif of the wilderness wandering and the progress of Israel to Canaan. Cross and Freedman think of the former as a kind of coda to the foregoing division. This has much to be said for it, since such coda' do in reality exist in many biblical poems and in contexts similar to ours, both in the Psalms and in the prophetic books. A second difficulty is that the motif of the enemy, which appears in the other divisions in the second strophe, is here to be found already in the concluding bicolon of the first. The reference to the peoples in general and to the Philistines in particular in vs. 14 seems premature, especially because the beginning of vs. 15 has the introductory particle אָז. Again, one might argue plausibly that vs. 13 would be an excellent opening for a new strophe since it strikes the important motif of the people, which is hymnically celebrated in the refrain of 16*ef*.

Full weight must be given to these difficulties, but there are considerations which may well be adduced on the other side. First, the second singular pronominal address referring to Yahweh of vss. 12–13 corresponds to the use of the same style after the two other refrains (7, 17). Moreover, it is to be observed that vss. 12–13 form a sequence in the same hymnic confessional style as we have elsewhere, three bicola, each with its distinctive theme: the victory of Yahweh at the Sea, the wilderness wandering, and the destination.[1] The introductory verbs of the relevant cola confirm our judgment here, and the assonance, which is so striking a feature of the liturgy throughout, reenforces our understanding: נָטִיתָ (12*a*), נָחִיתָ (13*a*), נֵהַלְתָּ (13*c*). If one may press the point, it may be suggested that the final phrase, *to thy holy abode*, gains its force precisely because of the succession of cola that have preceded it. Again the motif of Yahweh's right arm or hand assumes an important place in the composition since it appears in the opening and closing cola (12*a*, 16*c*). Perhaps more persuasive is the consideration that the structure of vss. 12–13 and 15–16 is much the same. After the first three bicola in each strophe we meet the same response; that is, vss. 14 and 16 are completely parallel in content. It is well to be reminded that we have encountered similar correspondences before.

Despite what may appear to us to be irregularities and infelicities, the preponderance of evidence seems to us to favor the foregoing analysis. If this view can be maintained, then we have the same literary situation in the third division as in the other two preceding divisions. It should be remarked, incidentally, that while the poets

[1] See Martin Noth, *Exodus* in the Old Testament Library series, Eng. trans., Philadelphia, 1962, p. 1962: 'With brief reference to the three themes of the saving act of the sea, the guidance through the wilderness and the conquest, vv. 12f make a transition to the second main theme of the "Hymn of the Reed Sea", the Entry into the Promised Land.'

of Israel are influenced by form and convention in their compositions, they are seldom completely bound to them. It is the merit of
the work of Gunkel and Greßmann that they recognized this.
Especially when we encounter a change in theme as clear as in our
liturgy, we should not be surprised by a change of style and terminology.

The hymnic confession of the first strophe (12–14) contains four
bicola, all but the last in 2′2′ meter. The final bicolon is 3′3′, and
thus conforms, as we have seen, to stylistic practice elsewhere in the
Old Testament. The parallelism of vss. 12–14 is as follows:

    a b / c d
    a' b' / e f
    a" b" / g h
    a b c / d e f

Taking the cola as units in vss. 15–16, the form is as follows:

    a b / b' a' / a" b"

We have pointed out that the divine second personal pronouns in
the three bicola of the hymnic confession (12–13) are followed by
third person in the fourth (14); similarly in the hymnic confession
of the first division (2–3) we move from the first person (2) to the
third (3), and in the hymnic confession of the second division (7–8)
we move from the second (7) to the third person (8). A comparison
of such contexts as Pss 77:11f and 78:50ff with our pericope will
reveal numerous stylistic and formal affinities, not least of all in the
sequence of events or in the succession of themes. Thus after a long
literary sequence describing the deeds and wonders of Yahweh
(Ps 74:11–15 [Heb 12–16]. Cf. Ex 15:11*ef*) the poet turns to the
wonder of the Sea (74:16–19 [Heb 17–20]) and forthwith adds,
'Thou didst lead thy people like a flock by the hand of Moses and
Aaron' (cf. 13). Compare also Ps 78:51–53.

Each of the three bicola of the first half of the second strophe (15)
is devoted to a particular enemy, and thus form a characteristic
progression: *the chieftains of Edom, the nobles of Moab, the enthroned of
Canaan*. The verbs similarly form a progression: *are dismayed*, (trembling) *seizes, melted away*.[1] The composition of these bicola exhibits

[1] The motif of the fear, terror, and trembling of the enemy is characteristic of the Holy
War formulations throughout the Old Testament. Cf. Fredricksson, *Jahwe als Krieger*,

extraordinary versatility in the parallelism of the lines. The bicolon which follows (16) turns to the confessional style of the divine second personal pronoun (cf. the same context in vs. 10), and thus recasts and summarizes the three preceding bicola. The final bicolon reverts to the motif of Yahweh's conquering arm (cf. vss. 6, 12. cf. vs. 9) and comes to a close in the same manner as the other major divisions by the use of the same or similar simile: *like a stone* (cf. 5*b*, 10*c*).

The final refrain (16*cd*) is in every way an excellent work of craftsmanship. Every word and phrase performs its special function and contributes to the finale. The repetition of the colon, *until thy people pass over*, not only accentuates the temporal movement from the progress through the lands of Trans-Jordan to the land of Canaan (cf. vs. 15) but also brings to a focus what lies behind all the words, the uniqueness of the people of Israel: *thy people*. That this is uppermost in the mind of the writer is demonstrated by the parallel lines: עם זו גאלת (13*b*) and עם זו קנית (16*f*). The parallelism of the lines conforms again to that of the other refrains:

a b c / a b d

Here the meter, however, is appropriately 3′3′. Again the divine name which has been absent from the foregoing strophes is addressed in the vocative (so too in vss. 6 and 11).

A hymnic celebration of Yahweh's occupation of the land and his enthronement in the sanctuary[1]

Thou wilt bring them in, wilt plant them
   in the mount of thy heritage,
the place for thy dwelling
   thou hast made, O Yahweh,
the sanctuary, O Yahweh (with Sam. and 86 Mss.)
   thy hands have established.

The strophe is placed outside the structural pattern of the three

p. 115, esp. nt. 4: 'Durch das ganze AT hindurch aber findet man ihn (den Schrecken) im Zusammenhang mit Jahwes Auftreten als Krieger, vgl. 2.19f; 19.16; 30.31.' See also von Rad, *Der Heilige Krieg*, pp. 10–11. It is apparent from numerous contexts that we are dealing with the same conventional terminology. Note, for example, besides references given above Ex23:27f; Dt2:25; 11:25; Josh2:9, 24; 5:1; 10:2; 24:12; 1 Sam4:7-8 (von Rad).

[1] For an illuminating comparison with Ps2:5, see M. Dahood, *Psalms* (The Anchor Bible, vol. 16; New York 1966), p. 9. Note, too, his discussion of the frequent use of animals in a metaphorical sense both in the Old Testament and among the Canaanites.

divisions because it is designed to bring the worshipping congregation to the present. From the perspective of the writer they point of course to the future and are given as an assurance, which has now been long since fulfilled. The strophe contains three bicola in 2'2' meter. Once more we observe the divine second person declarative following the refrain. The lines are carefully wrought, as a scrutiny of the parallelism will show. The great verbs and the impressive cola referring to land and sanctuary are superbly interwoven; the accents fall in every case at precisely the right points. Thus the opening colon (17a) contains the two climactic verbs, and in striking assonance: תְּבִאֵמוֹ וְתִטָּעֵמוֹ (2 Sam 7:10; Ps 44:2 [Heb 3]; Jer 32:41; Am 9:15). These are followed in turn by the words towards which the whole liturgy has been moving: *the mount of thy heritage* (Dt 3:25; Is 11:9; Ps 78:54), *the place for thy dwelling* (cf. 14b, 15e; 1 Kings 8:13), *thy sanctuary, O Yahweh*.[1] The first obviously refers to the land of Canaan and naturally comes first in the series. The second is a word for word repetition of the ancient words embedded in the prayer of Solomon (1 Kings 8:13), derived from the Book of Jashar (so LXX). If we should accept the rendering of W.F. Albright and Cross and Freedman, *the dais of thy throne*, then the reference would surely be to the enthronement of Yahweh in his sanctuary, conceivably Shiloh, but more likely the Temple in Jerusalem or Mount Zion. The striking Ugaritic affinities to which Albright and Cross and Freedman refer do not argue to the contrary; we should expect precisely such connections with the Jerusalem Temple or Mount Zion with its Canaanite associations.[2] Notable in the strophe

[1] My colleague, David Noel Freedman, reminds me that in Ugaritic and Hebrew poetry, the suffix of the first noun carries over to the second also. See G.R. Driver, JRAS, 1948, 165ff; M. Dahood, *Ugaritic Studies and the Bible*, Gregorianum Ann. XLIII (1962), Vol. XLIII, 1, p. 68.

[2] I am indebted to Professor Freedman for the following comment: 'The statement that Yahweh has made a sanctuary or dais for his throne tends, in my opinion, to eliminate a specific reference to any earthly structure, since, so far as I am aware, it is never argued in the Bible that God made the tabernacle or temple. These rather are replicas or imitations of the *tabnith* which Moses beheld; in other words, the temple which God made is his own in heaven. So I regard the language here as mythological or cosmological rather than terrestrial and historical. There is, of course, an historical application, in the sense that the temple at Shiloh and Jerusalem, and the tabernacle before them reflected the temple or tabernacle in heaven. But they are not the same thing. The mount of inheritance likewise is a heavenly place, but its counterpart is the holy hill or precinct in Canaan, ultimately Zion.' With much of this the writer is in hearty agreement; the Ugaritic affinities cannot be ignored. But the present context with all its historical references and the movement of the poem from the Exodus to the occupation of the land and the mount of Yahweh's inheritance would seem to point to Mount Zion and the Temple. For a thorough and careful discussion of the matter, see R.E. Clements, *God and Temple* (Oxford 1965), pp. 51ff.

are the words expressing stability, a wonderful and impressive contrast to the first division and a fine consummation of the movement
expressed in the second (note esp. vs. 13): *thou wilt plant, the place
thou hast made for thy dwelling (or dais of thy throne?), the sanctuary thy
hands have established* (כוננו). *Coda* (15:18): Yahweh will reign for
ever and ever.

The closing acclamation (cf. 3) celebrates the kingship of Yahweh.
The motif is not necessarily late; it may well have been the central
affirmation in the credo of the early tribal federations (Num 23:31;
Judg 8:23; 1 Sam 8:7; 12:12). It is present also in relatively early
poems (Ps 24:7–10; 29:10; 68:24 [Heb 25]. cf. Dt 33:5). Such terse
concluding bicola are not infrequent in Israel's poetry (Ps 47:10*b*
[Heb 11*b*]; 48:14*c* [Heb 15*c*]; 111:10*c*; 146:10, etc.). The formulation
יהוה ימלך corresponds to that of the enthronement hymns (Ps 93:1;
96:10; 97:1; 99:1). The triumphs of Yahweh reach their culmination
in the cry of the worshipping congregation.[1] The pregnant line of
the opening bicolon of the introit כי גאה גאה, has achieved its
purpose. Yahweh is now indeed highly exalted, victorious and
triumphant as Israel's Leader and King,[2] and he will rule for ever.
Psalm 47 provides an interesting parallel.[3] The succession of references to Yahweh in the concluding lines (16*e*, 17*d*, *e*) comes to a
climax here (cf. 1*b*–3).

The foregoing study represents an attempt to subject a biblical
passage to rhetorical analysis. It would be a mistake to regard it
merely as an aesthetic exercise. On the contrary, it is designed to be
an exegetical tool. It seeks to examine the ways in which the writer's
Semitic ways of thinking are articulated into Semitic ways of speech.
The test of the validity of such an approach is both auditory and
visual. If one will undertake to read the liturgy aloud in Hebrew,
he will be quick to sense not only the large role that assonance of
different kinds plays in the composition, but also the effect of repeated sounds in particular contexts. Or if one will transcribe the
liturgy into its several parts and underline the key words, he will
recognize that their collocations are by no means fortuitous or
accidental. Such an approach does not question the importance of

[1] Cf. Beer, p. 83: 'Die mit la beginnende via triumphalis Jahwes wird mit seinem Ein-
zug in Jerusalem und seinem Heiligtum, dem Zentrum seines ewigen Weltkönigtums,
gekrönt.
[2] Werner Schmidt, *Königtum Gottes in Ugarit und Israel*, in BZAW 80 (1961), pp. 64ff.
[3] See the writer's analysis of Psalm 47 in J.B.L. LXIII (1944), pp. 235–256.

historical or literary criticism, of *Gattungkritik*, or of traditio-historical criticism, but attempts, rather, to understand the composition of the passage in its present form. Numerous parallels might be adduced to this type of poetic construction. Examination of other Old Testament literary units will show that we are dealing with a characteristic literary method and practice.

It is a pleasure to the writer to make this small offering to a good friend and to a scholar whose work throughout the years has been marked not only by competence and control of the requisite disciplines, but also by wisdom, insight, and appreciation.

San Anselmo (Calif.)   JAMES MUILENBURG

12

THE INTERCESSION OF THE COVENANT MEDIATOR (EXODUS 33: 1*a*, 12–17)

by James Muilenburg

Among the many contributions Professor Winton Thomas has made to lexical studies, not a few have been devoted to the Hebrew verb ידע, especially in those contexts where its true meaning had hitherto been uncertain or obscure.[1] It goes without saying that the verb with its congeners is one of the most important in the Old Testament. It is susceptible of many different renderings, due in part to its appearance in no fewer than eight stems, in part to its numerous syntactical constructions, and in part, also, to the variety of usages in the major classifications of Hebrew literature.[2] In several books, such as Hosea and Ezekiel, it holds a status approximating centrality.[3] It is rich in denotations and richer still in its connotations, a many-faceted word with numerous nuances and accents. Not infrequently it plays a decisive role in the composition of the *Gattungen* or literary genres, both in connection with the terminology characteristic of the particular genre in question and as a keyword in climactic or strategic collocations. One thinks, for example, of its usages in the hymns and royal hymns or

---

[1] For references see the Bibliography.

[2] Such as the legal, cultic, historical, prophetic, and sapiential literatures. There is much semantic overlapping, to be sure, but there is also much that is characteristic of the general type of speech within each classification.

[3] H. W. Wolff, '"Wissen um Gott" bei Hosea als Urform von Theologie', *Evangelische Theologie*, XII (Munich, 1952/53), 533–52 = *Gesammelte Studien zum Alten Testament, Theologische Bücherei*, XXII (Munich, 1964), 182–205; W. Zimmerli, *Erkenntnis Gottes nach dem Buche Ezechiel. Eine theologische Studie (Abhandlungen zur Theologie des alten und neuen Testaments*, XXVII, Zürich, 1954) = *Gottes Offenbarung. Gesam. Aufsätze (Theologische Bücherei*, XIX, Munich, 1963), pp. 41–119; James M. Ward, *Hosea: a Theological Commentary* (New York, 1966), pp. 83–9 and *passim*.

JAMES MUILENBURG

liturgies, in confessions and laments, in the divine self-disclosures and, for want of a better term, the *confessiones fidei*, in prophetic calls and in the several types of covenant formulations. It is our wont to render the verb by *to know*. But knowing is of many kinds and dispositions, depending not only upon the particular context in which it appears, but also upon the particular attitude or frame of mind that is intended in the context. So if we are to attempt to define the precise meaning of the word, we may find ourselves at times at a loss to discover *le mot juste* for the English equivalent, but, what is more, we shall be compelled by the very nature of the case to resort to well over a score of words in order to do justice to the wide range of meaning that the word covers in the original Hebrew.

It was our original design, therefore, to scrutinize a number of representative *Gattungen* or literary types in order to call attention to the precise meaning that the verb bears in its linguistic and literary settings and in relation to the *Sitz im Leben* of the genre, and then to describe, as well as one is able, the function that the verb performs in the pericope under inspection. Such an undertaking is of course too wide-ranging and spacious for an essay of the present length. We shall content ourselves, therefore, with examining a passage of very limited scope, the impassioned and fateful dialogical encounter between Moses and Yahweh on Mount Sinai, as it is reported to us in Exod. 33: 12–17, with a view first of all to pointing out the features which mark its composition and then to determining the different meanings of the verb ידע, which appears no fewer than six times within a literary unit of fewer than one hundred words, and always in striking collocations.

If we are to assess with any degree of confidence the particular function and intention of our pericope, then it is essential, first of all, to establish its setting within the complex of traditions in which it finds its place. We observe at once that it appears in a *covenant* context, indeed within the *locus classicus* of the Sinaitic covenant (Exod. 19–24, 32–4). The two major blocs of tradition define the limits of the section. While they are separated by a substantial insertion from the Priestly source (Exod. 25–31), there can be no question that at some stage in

Intercession of the Covenant Mediator

the history of transmission they were continuous, although not
in the present ordering of materials in chapters 32–4. The old
Pentateuchal sources, the Yahwist and the Elohist, are present
in both, albeit with accretions and elaborations in chapters 32–
4, and in somewhat different guise and certainly in different
types of formulation. The first complex (Exod. 19–24) is quite
generally recognized today as a unified and coherent whole and
as representing a particular *Gattung*, whether one thinks of it
as reflecting the structure and component parts of the suzerainty
treaties such as we find among other peoples of the Near East,
notably the Hittites, Accadians, and Assyrians,[1] or as the *Festlegende* or liturgy employed in connection with the annual celebrations of the covenant renewal festival.[2] The traditions in our
second complex (Exod. 32–4) have clear affinities with the first
(Exod. 19–24). They are, in the first place, *covenant* traditions
and presuppose the conclusion of the covenant between Yahweh
and Israel. The *mise en scène* is still Sinai, the mountain of God.
Moses continues to serve as mediator of the covenant (cf. Exod.
20: 18–20). The motif of the liberation from Egyptian slavery
which forms the historical preamble to the covenant in Exod.
19–24 appears again and again as a major motif and always in
the same rhetorical and stylistic form (32: 1, 4, 8, 11, 23; 33: 1;
34: 18), and the giving of the law recounted in the first section
may be said to constitute the framework of the whole complex
of tradition preserved in the second (Exod. 32–4), since it opens
with the breaking of the tablets in chapter 32 and concludes

[1] V. Kurošec, *Hethitische Staatsverträge* (*Leipziger Rechtswissenschaftliche
Studien*, IX, 1931); G. E. Mendenhall, *Law and Covenant in Israel and the
Ancient Near East* (Pittsburgh, 1955); Julien Harvey, S.J., 'Le "Rîb-
pattern" réquisitoire prophétique sur la rupture de l'alliance', *Biblica*,
XIV (1962), 172–96; R. Frankena, 'The vassal-treaties of Esarhaddon and
the dating of Deuteronomy', *Oudtestamentische Studiën*, XIV (1965), 122–54.
For a full bibliography on the treaties, see Dennis J. McCarthy, S.J.,
Treaty and Covenant (*Analecta Biblica*, XXI, Rome, 1963), pp. xiii–xxiv.

[2] G. von Rad, *The Problem of the Hexateuch and Other Essays*, trans. by E. W.
Truman Dicken (Edinburgh and London, 1966), pp. 27 ff.; *Old Testament
Theology*, I, trans. by D. M. G. Stalker (Edinburgh and London, 1962),
pp. 188 f.; Murray Newman, *The People of the Covenant: a Study of Israel
from Moses to the Monarchy* (New York and Nashville, 1962); Walter
Beyerlin, *Origins and History of the Oldest Sinaitic Traditions*, trans. by S. Rudman (Oxford, 1965).

JAMES MUILENBURG

with their renewal and the restoration of the covenant bond in chapter 34.

But such similarities as we have pointed to must not obscure the striking differences between the two sections, for, whereas the first is a recognizable unity, the second has every appearance of being a catena of originally separate pieces which originally had little or nothing to do with each other. They are more perhaps than a *disiecta membra*, but the several parts do not cohere well with each other. This impression of disunity is confirmed when one undertakes the difficult task of source analysis.[1] Chapter 33 is a case in point.[2] To begin with, it interrupts the

[1] The most important discussions are the following: S. R. Driver, *An Introduction to the Literature of the Old Testament* (Edinburgh, twelfth edition, 1906); A. H. McNeile, *The Book of Exodus* (*WC*, London, 1908); Gustav Westphal, *Jahwes Wohnstätten nach den Anschauungen der Alten Hebräer* (*BZAW*, xv, 1908); Hugo Gressmann, *Mose und seine Zeit. Ein Kommentar zu den Mose-Sagen* (Göttingen, 1913); Otto Eissfeldt, *Hexateuch-Synopse* (Leipzig, 1922); W. Rudolph, 'Der Aufbau von Exodus 19–34', *Werden und Wesen des Alten Testaments*, edited by Paul Volz, Friedrich Stummer, and Johannes Hempel (*BZAW*, LXVI, 1936); Gerhard von Rad, *The Problem of the Hexateuch and Other Essays*, especially 'The Form-critical Problem of the Hexateuch', pp. 1–78 (English translation, 1966. Original German edition published in *BWANT*, xxvi, 1938); Walter Beyerlin, *Origins and History of the Oldest Sinaitic Traditions*, trans. by S. Rudman (Oxford, 1965. Original German edition published in 1961); Martin Noth, *Überlieferungsgeschichte des Pentateuch* (Stuttgart, 1948) and *Exodus: a Commentary* (English translation, London, 1962).
While the area of disagreement is considerable, perhaps the following conclusions would commend themselves to at least the majority of the foregoing scholars: (1) While chapter 32 belongs with the complex of materials in chapters 32–4, it nevertheless represents a later insertion designed to form the introduction or background for chapter 34. Driver and Beyerlin assign most of the chapter to E; others like Rudolph and Noth argue for J. (2) Chapter 33 is composed of several independent pieces; the opening section (verses 1–6) is certainly composite and contains a substratum of J, which joins well with verses 12–17. Verses 7–11 are an intrusion into the context and may well have originally displaced a pericope on the ark. The remainder of the chapter (verses 12–17 and 18–23) represents a later redaction of J. (3) Our pericope (verses 12–17) connects well with Exod. 24: 3–11, which was very likely its original locus (see Rudolph, *BZAW*, LXVI, 46 and Eissfeldt, *Hexateuch-Synopse*, pp. 53 ff.).
[2] Cf. Noth, *Überlieferungsgeschichte des Pentateuch*, p. 33 n. 113: 'Auf eine literarkritische Analyse von Ex. 33 muss man wohl verzichten. Es handelt sich hier anscheinend um ein Konglomerat von sekundären Wucherungen

Intercession of the Covenant Mediator

natural sequence of chapters 32 and 34, despite the excellent
transition provided by 32:34a. On the face of it, we have before
us here four separate literary units (33:1–6, 7–11, 12–17, 18–
23), but upon closer examination it becomes apparent that
verses 1–6 are composite. Verses 3b–6 contradict what is said
in their immediate context. It is generally recognized that verses
7–11 constitute a unit by itself, and have nothing to do with what
precedes or follows, although the editor or compiler may have
considered verse 11 as a fitting context for verses 12–17: 'Thus
Yahweh used to speak to Moses face to face, as a man speaks
to his friend.' Perhaps the majority of scholars hold verses 12–
17 to be composite also,[1] but their unity is supported by more
recent studies.[2] Nor is there any agreement as to the precise
scope of the literary unit since verse 17 is assigned by many to
the following pericope (33:18–23), a view that fails to do justice
to the form and structure of the passage. It is in contexts such
as these that stylistic and rhetorical criticism proves a great
boon, for it helps us to see what the methodologies of literary
and historical criticism taken by themselves cannot disclose.

With Rudolph and Beyerlin and others we hold 33:12–17
to be a self-contained unity. But it is without a satisfactory introduction. This, by itself, need not be taken too seriously for it is
the manner of many of Israel's literary compositions to begin
quite *in medias res*, but the situation here requires some sort of
preliminary statement in view of the opening words of Moses,
'Consider! you say to me, "Lead forward this people!"' Now

in Anschluss an Ex. 32, 34a², das vielleicht schon innerhalb der noch
gesonderte J-Erzählung entstand (in vv. 1 ff. begegnen wir sogleich wieder
deuteronomische Stil). Für E spricht nichts in diesem Kapitel; als Gottes-
name kommt — und zwar sehr häufig — nur יהוה vor.' On the other
hand, Noth recognizes the motivation that lies behind all the literary
units: 'The varied pieces of Ex. 33 are held together by the theme of the
presence of God in the midst of his people, which plays some part in all of
them. This common theme was evidently also the reason for the collection
of all the passages.' See his commentary on *Exodus*, p. 253. See also
von Rad, *The Problem of the Hexateuch*, pp. 17 ff.

[1] S. R. Driver, A. H. McNeile, A. Westphal, H. Gressmann, and Curt
Rylaarsdam in *IB*, 1 (1952).

[2] W. Rudolph, M. Beyerlin, and Noth. Eissfeldt apparently takes the
whole of verses 12–23 as a unit. See *Hexateuch-Synopse*, p. 157.

JAMES MUILENBURG

it is only in the opening verse of the chapter that we have such a word from Yahweh: 'Yahweh said to Moses "Depart, lead forward this people".' Rudolph contends rightly that this must form the beginning of our pericope. Beyerlin would add verse 3 to 1*a* and Westphal would include 3*b*–4 also. But this runs counter to the style of the words which follow in verses 12–17, and, moreover, it is doubtful whether the words belong to the same source. It is to be observed that the keyword עלה is strategically placed not only in Yahweh's command to Moses, but in Moses' immediate reply (12*a*) and then, later, in the climactic and concentrated plea preceding the long motivation of verse 16: 'if your Presence will not go, do not cause us to press forward (תַּעֲלֵנוּ) from this (place).' The qal imperative of the verb in verse 1*a* is followed appropriately by the twofold hiph'il imperative at the beginning (12) and close (15*c*) of the discourse proper. Though we shall return to the point again, it is well to notice that the ambulatory terminology, so frequent and so revealing in other Old Testament contexts, is stressed by the close relation between leading forward (עלה) and going (הלך, note especially the moving contexts of verses 14*a* and 15*a*). There are other connections between verse 1*a* and verses 12–17. The phrase 'from here' (מִזֶּה, 1*a*) is repeated in connection with the same verb עלה in the same dramatic climax of verse 15*c*. Even more significant is the phrase 'you and the people' (1*c*) which is taken up and stressed by Moses twice in the final words of his impassioned plea: 'I and your people' (16*c* and 16*e*). The opening directive of Yahweh in 33: 1*a* is certainly very brief, but this comports well with the compressed style of the words that follow. On the other hand, one must always reckon with the possibility that in contexts such as these the tradition may well have been telescoped. Subtractions are fully as important as additions in the history of transmission.

In the translation which follows I have attempted to articulate the wording and forms of the successive predications, but without strict adherence to their possible poetic structure[1]

---

[1] Compare J. Arvid Bruno, *Die Bücher Genesis–Exodus. Eine rhythmische Untersuchung* (Stockholm, 1953). While most scholars will have their reservations concerning the poetic guise of these books, Bruno's rendering

Intercession of the Covenant Mediator

and have retained the usage of the verb *to know* for the time being.[1]

33: 1 *a.*
    And Yahweh said to Moses:
      'Go, depart from here,
        you and the people.'

12. And Moses said to Yahweh:
      'Consider! you (אתה) say to me,
        "Lead forth this people!"
    Yet you (אתה) have not let me know[a]
      whom you will send with me,
    But you (אתה) have said:
      "I know you by name[b]
        and you have indeed (וגם) found favour in my eyes."[c]

13. And now (ועתה)[d] if I have truly (אם־נא) found favour in your eyes,[e]
      Pray (נא) make me to know your ways[f] that I may know you[g]
        in order that (למען) I may find favour in your eyes.
    Consider! that (כי) this nation is your people.'[h]

14. And he said:
    'My Presence will go (פני ילכו)[i]
      and I will give you rest.'[j]

15. And he said to him:
    'If (אם־אין) your Presence will not go[k]
      do not lead us forth from here!

16. For in what way (וכמה) will it ever (אפוא) be known that
      (כי) I have found favour in your eyes,
      I and your people?

does call attention to the rhythms that may well lie behind our present text; moreover it has the advantage of revealing the way in which the predications are articulated and related to each other. Compare Martin Buber, *Die Fünf Bücher der Weisung*. Verdeutscht in Gemeinschaft mit Franz Rosenzweig (Cologne, 1954). For the rendering of our pericope, see pp. 246 f.

[1] The merit of preserving the English word 'know' is that it calls attention to the presence of the same word. As we shall see, the word bears different connotations in different contexts.

JAMES MUILENBURG

Is it not (הלוא) in your going with us
    that we may be distinct,[1] I and your people,
    from every people on the face of the earth?'
17. And Yahweh said to Moses:
    'This very word (גם את הדבר הזה) that you have spoken
    I will do,
        for you have found favour in my eyes,
        and I know you by name.'

TEXTUAL COMMENTARY

[a] The Greek renders MT the second person singular hiph'il of ידע by ἐδήλωσας, 'revealed, made manifest or visible'. Vulg. *et non indicas mihi*.

[b] MT 'by name'. Greek παρὰ πάντας, 'above all'. So also in verse 17. Vulg. *novi te ex nomine*.

[c] Greek παρ' ἐμοί.

[d] MT 'and now if'. Greek εἰ οὖν. Vulg. *si ergo*.

[e] MT 'in your eyes'. Greek ἐναντίον σου. Vulg. *in conspectu tuo*.

[f] Greek ἐμφάνισόν μοι σεαυτόν 'reveal yourself to me'.

[g] Greek has γνωστῶς ἴδω σε 'that I may see Thee clearly'.

[h] The Greek seeks to overcome the awkwardness of MT by 'in order that I may know that this great nation is your people'.

[i] Greek Αὐτὸς προπορεύσομαι.

[j] Arnold B. Ehrlich, *Randglossen zur Hebräischen Bibel*, I (Leipzig, 1908), p. 405, finds the Hebrew here 'impossible', and proposes the emendation והנחיתיך 'and I will lead you'. Cf. W. Eichrodt, *Theology of the Old Testament*, II (English translation, London, 1967), p. 38 n. 1.

[k] Greek Εἰ μὴ αὐτὸς σὺ πορεύῃ. Vulg. *si non tu ipse praecedes*.

[l] For MT 'be distinct' or 'be distinguished' Greek has ἐνδοξασθήσομαι. So too Vulg. *glorificemur*.

It is of the first importance for our understanding of the passage to recognize the *kind* of speaking that is going on and to delineate as well as one may where the major accents lie. Such an endeavour is the more important because of the presence of several leading motifs. We may begin by stressing that the participants in the encounter are Moses and Yahweh: Moses, the covenant mediator, and Yahweh, the Lord of the covenant. Hugo Gressman subsumes the pericope under the

Intercession of the Covenant Mediator

theophanic rubric of the פני יהוה (פנים) (Exod. 23: 20–33; 33: 1–6, 12–23; 34: 5 *b*–9; Num. 10: 29–36).[1] There can be no doubt that the פנים (lit. 'face') does indeed play a central role in all of these texts, but, surprisingly, Gressman draws no inference from this circumstance as to the nature of the literary genre. Nils Johansson classifies the passage among the intercessions of Moses (Exod. 8: 8–14 (Heb. 4–10); 8: 28–32 (Heb. 8: 24–8); 9: 27–9; 10: 16–19; 32: 11–14, 30–6; 33: 12–17; 34: 8 f.; Num. 12: 9–16; 14: 13–19 (especially verses 17–19); 21: 4–7).[2] P. A. H. de Boer in his thorough study recognizes the affinities of our text with the intercessions, but does not devote any separate treatment to it.[3] H. H. Rowley counts the following among the intercessory prayers of Moses: Exod. 32: 11 ff., 31 f.; 33: 12 ff.; 34: 9; Num. 11: 11 ff.; 14: 13 ff.; 21: 7; Deut. 9: 18 ff.; 10: 10.[4] Martin Buber characterizes the pericope simply as one of the conversations of Moses with Yahweh (Exod. 32: 7–14, 31–4; 33: 1–5, 12–23; 34: 1–10).[5] They are reminiscent of the dialogical engagements at the Burning Bush (J; 3: 1–4*a*, 5, 7–8, 16–22; 4: 1–9 with additions. E: 3: 4*b*, 6, 9–15; 4: 17. Cf. Noth, *Überlieferungsgeschichte des Pentateuch*), although the formulation and style are quite different.

If we take into account the history of tradition and raise the question as to the place and function of this intercession in

---

[1] *Mose und seine Zeit*, p. 218. Gressmann's comment on the difficulties of source analysis is quite revealing here. 'Die Bezeichnung der Varianten mit J und E ist hier, wie gleich zu Anfang betont sei, völlig willkürlich; dennoch ist sie aus praktischen Gründen beibehalten worden, besonders des bequemeren Zitierens wegen.' He recognizes that verses 12–17 form a single complex, but views it as highly composite.

[2] *PARAKLETOI: Vorstellungen von Fürsprechern für die Menschen vor Gott in der alttestamentlichen Religion, im Spätjudentum und Urchristentum* (Lund, 1940), pp. 5 ff., 181 f.

[3] *De Voorbede in het Oude Testament* (Leiden, 1943), pp. 42–121. De Boer does not include our text among the intercessions strictly speaking, but he clearly recognizes the primary relationship between Moses and Yahweh: 'Zijn verzoeningsdaad geschiedt niet, doordat hij in zulk een nauwe relatie met zijn volk staat, maar doordat hij in biezonderen dienst van Jhwh staat' (p. 57).

[4] *Worship in Ancient Israel* (London, 1967), p. 163 n. 6.

[5] Martin Buber and Franz Rosenzweig, 'Das Leitwort und der Formtypus der Rede', in *Die Schrift und ihre Verdeutschung* (Berlin, 1936), pp. 262 ff.

JAMES MUILENBURG

Israel's life, then it seems to the writer that we must conclude that it is cultic in intent and design. Its original position immediately following the covenant liturgy of Exod. 19–24, its dialogical character, and, above all, the significance of the פנים for Israel's worship and faith would suggest as much. We may think of our passage at least tentatively as a liturgy. It is much more than a legendary memory; more, too, than a 'historical' episode or a scrap of ancient tradition. It is the plea or intercession of the mediator of the covenant, the representative of Yahweh, Israel's Lord and Suzerain, on behalf of the people and Yahweh's answering assurance. In the encounter a momentous issue is at stake. The style is correspondingly elevated and solemn, without any historical or geographical or descriptive reference or concrete detail. It is the kind of speech that is congenial to and suited for the worship of the covenant community. It is shrouded in holy awe, freighted with urgency and passion, and burdened with the sense of destiny.

The most striking feature of the passage is its extraordinary concentration into the very minimum of speech. The composition is superbly fashioned. The keywords and key-sentences and dominant motifs (and there are several) are interwoven into the linguistic and literary fabric with consummate skill; the architectonics of rhetoric, the interior structure of the succeeding lines, and their movement towards their consummation is the work of someone more than a diligent craftsman; in actuality it is the product of extraordinary literary sensitivity.[1] Yet there is nothing contrived or aesthetic here, no striving after effect, no description or self-conscious rhetoric. It has the stamp of authenticity marked upon it.

Observe, first of all, the speaking quality (*Sprachlichkeit*) of

---

[1] Cf. *ibid.* p. 262: 'Das immer wieder aufgenommene Zwiegespräch Gottes mit Moses nach der Sünde des Volkes, 2M. 32: 7–14, 31–34; 33: 1–5, 12–23; 34: 1–10, ist, im Zusammenhang gefasst, von unerhörter Gebautheit, unerhörter tektonischer Dichtigkeit. Ich kenne kein andres Werk rednerischen Charakters, in dem die Beredtheit, in deren Wesen es zu liegen scheint dem Geheimnis abzusagen, so geheimnistreu bleibt, aber auch keins, wo so wie hier immer wieder die festen Wortbrücken, Leitwortbrücken geschlagen werden, um den zitternden Fuss über die Abgründe zu tragen.'

Intercession of the Covenant Mediator

the pericope. The *formulae citandi* are well contrived and in chiastic form: 'Moses said to Yahweh' (12*a*), 'and he said' (14*a*), 'and he said to him' (15*a*), 'and Yahweh said to Moses' (17*a*; cf. 33:1*a*!). But the *verba dicendi* penetrate into the citations themselves: 'Consider! you say to me' (12*b*), 'you have not informed me' (12*d*), 'but you have said' (12*f*). These rhetorical phenomena are accented by the way in which Moses quotes Yahweh's own words (12*c* and 12*gh*) and by the way he enters into engagement with them (12*de* and 13). Yahweh's concluding words, 'you have found favour in my eyes', is immediately taken up on the lips of Moses, 'And now, if I have really found favour in your eyes' (13*a*). Similarly, Yahweh's momentous assurance, 'My Presence will go' is forthwith taken up in Moses' rejoinder, 'If your Presence will not go', which is immediately followed by harking back to the opening crucial line (12*c*): 'do not lead us forth from here' (15*c*). Repeatedly, throughout the little liturgy, we listen again and again to the motif, 'find favour in…eyes' (12*h*, 13*a*, 13*c* and then again in 16*b* and finally in the climactic close, 17*c*).[1] This literary device is frequent in the Ugaritic texts as well as within the Old Testament, most notably in Jeremiah and the Psalter. It is, of course, particularly characteristic of cultic contexts.

But we turn to another illustration of the oral or spoken character of our passage. It fairly teems with particles of many different sorts, each performing its own particular function in its particular context, as our translation has attempted to indicate. No translation can reproduce the nuances and effects of these particles in the original Hebrew. It is unfortunate that it should be so, for it is precisely these vocables and sounds that serve to articulate the interior sequences of the successive lines and to reveal the texture of the linguistic fabric. Observe, for example, the function that is served by the deictic and climactic particle *ki* in 13*d*, 16*b*, and 17*c* and the related word of motivation

---

[1] For the favourable disposition of the suzerain to his vassal and the vassal's love of his suzerain, see William L. Moran, S.J., 'The Ancient Near Eastern Background of the Love of God in Deuteronomy', *CBQ*, xxv (1963), 77–87. While the stress upon the mutuality of love is pronounced in Deuteronomy, it would seem to be implied here in the gracious gift of 'finding favour in his eyes'. See below, p. 177, n. 1.

JAMES MUILENBURG

למען in 13c; also the function played by גם in the opening and closing speeches (12h and 17b) and by the conditions אם נא and אם אין in 13a and 15b. A closely related feature of the first consequence is the presence of assonance; what the eye may often fail to discern, the ear can grasp at once. If the passage is to be 'understood', it must be heard. The repetitions of key-words and key-sentences produce their own euphony or sonorous effect, but, more than that, they reveal where the stresses lie. Finally, it is the pervasive stress upon the speaking that is going on line after line which gives special force to the final assurance of Yahweh to his mediator: 'This very word that you have spoken I will perform.'

We turn now to a somewhat closer scrutiny of our text. It is surely a continuing and unbroken dialogue from beginning to end. Yet, despite this continuity and brevity, it falls into two divisions with two subdivisions each. In each the plea of the mediator is followed by a divine assurance or promise (12–13 and 14, 15–16 and 17). The pleas are of about the same length and also contain two parts, as is clear in the first plea from the striking and significant ועתה (13a) and in the second by the direct and climactic question introduced by הלוא (16d), which should not be emended. The divine responses are very short as we should expect from such cultic and oracular formulations. We may articulate the structure, then, somewhat as follows:

Introduction: Depart from here!   33: 1a
1. The mediator's plea and the divine response: 33: 12–14
   a. The mediator's plea: 12–13
      (1) 'You have not let me know the one who will lead us.'   12
      (2) 'Let me know your ways.'   13
   b. The divine response: My Presence will go.   14
2. The mediator's plea and the divine response: 33: 15–17
   a. The mediator's plea: 15–16
      (1) 'How will it ever be known?'   15
      (2) 'Is it not in your going with us?'   16
   b. The divine response: the Word fulfilled.   17

The opening plea of verses 12–13 begins and ends impressively. The initiating call to attention expressed by the imperative of

Intercession of the Covenant Mediator

the verb ראה[1] is followed dramatically by the motif which lies within and behind all the words of the pericope: 'Consider! [or Realize!] you say to me, "Bring forth this people"' (12 bc). The concluding line (13 c) returns superbly to the opening motif and is fashioned in much the same way: by the repetition of the imperative, by bringing its focus to bear again upon the people, thus echoing the central affirmation of the old covenant credos and confessions: 'Consider that this nation is your own people.' It should occasion no surprise that the major motif of the people is repeated three times in the second plea and in a singularly effective manner (16 c, e, f).

Particularly revealing is the threefold use of the second person singular pronoun in addressing Yahweh: אתה אתה אתה. Then follows at once at the turning point of the plea the adverbial ועתה. The assonance is striking, both because of the threefold repetition of the personal pronoun, and more especially because of the assonant ועתה at the opening of the second part of the plea (13 a).[2] It is in this manner that the crucial issue is brought home and with remarkable effect. Further, the function of the conditional formulations in each division, i.e. within the pleas, deserves special notice. The first appears immediately after the ועתה, אם נא (13 a), the second at the very beginning אם אין (15 b). These conditional formulations are noteworthy because they

---

[1] Compare Gen. 27: 27; 41: 41; Exod. 7: 1; 31: 2; 33: 12; and especially Deut. 1: 8, 21; 2: 24; 3: 27; 11: 26; 30: 15 and often.

[2] See André Laurentin, 'Weʿattah-Kai nun. Formule caractéristique des textes juridiques et liturgiques (à propos de Jean 17, 5)', Biblica, XLV (1964), 168–97. Note the observation on p. 174: 'Kai nun est une formule presque technique dans la langue d'Israël; or cela apparaît très tôt, peut-être même avant l'écriture.' While I am somewhat dubious about the connection between 33: 7–11 and 12–17, which Laurentin stresses, I am in accord with his understanding of the nature of the speech as liturgical (p. 184). Note his concluding comment concerning the importance of the word 'and now': 'c'est une expression très forte, avec des résonnances émotives qui la porte aux extrêmes, enthousiasme ou détresse, acceptation ou refus, autorité ou indignation' (p. 194). See also the valuable treatment by H. A. Brongers in VT, xv (1965), 289–99. Both Laurentin and Brongers recognize the strategic role the word plays in biblical compositions: 'Innerhalb der Rede bildet es den Wendepunkt' (Brongers, p. 298). See too the writer's discussion in 'The Form and Structure of the Covenantal Formulations', VT, IX (1959), 347–65 and Klaus Baltzer's Das Bundesformular (Neukirchen, 1960).

JAMES MUILENBURG

appear in profusion not only in the Old Testament legal and covenant texts, but also in the treaties and laws of the peoples of the ancient Near East.[1] One may query, further, whether the apodoses of the two conditionals are not meant to bear some connection with each other since Moses' request to know Yahweh's ways that he may know him (13 b) may possibly refer specifically to the question uppermost in his mind, the leading forth from Mount Sinai (15 c).

The response of Yahweh to the earnest plea of Moses (14) is in the manner of early oracular and theophanic utterance:[2]

פני ילכו

והנחתי לך

'My Presence will go,[3] and I will give you rest.'[4] Despite the

[1] See the writer's discussion in the essay referred to above. The importance of the conditionals in treaty or covenant formulations has received much attention since then, most notably in R. Frankena, 'The vassal-treaties of Esarhaddon and the dating of Deuteronomy', *Oudtestamentische Studiën*, XIV (Leiden, 1965), 189–200.

[2] Hermann Gunkel, *Die Kultur der Gegenwart*, Teil I, Abteilung VII. *Die orientalischen Literaturen*, 'Die israelitische Literatur', pp. 83 f. See also Claus Westermann, *Basic Forms of Prophetic Speech*, trans. by Hugh Clayton White (Philadelphia, 1967), pp. 24 f.: 'Prophetic speech begins chiefly with short utterances.' 'The basic unit of prophetic speech is the short saying, the short single saying which is in itself independent.' This would apply *mutatis mutandis* to all early oracular utterances.

[3] The nuance of פנים as literally 'face' or 'countenance' should not be lost. It indeed signifies Yahweh himself and is thus employed as synecdoche. See A. R. Johnson, 'Aspects of the use of the term פנים in the Old Testament', *Festschrift Otto Eissfeldt* (Halle, 1947), pp. 155–60. See *Textual Comments* above for LXX and Vulgate. Luther retains the anthropomorphism 'Angesicht' as does Martin Buber 'Antlitz'. But see his *Moses* (London, 1946), p. 155: 'That God's "face" goes with means...that Yhvh goes ahead of the people in order to overthrow foes who meet them on the way; for which reason Moses also talks in this connection of the impression on the world.' AV and RSV both render פנים by 'presence', which seems to the writer the best way to preserve the original denotation of the word and its use in the theophanic or covenant cult.

[4] The promise of 'rest' does not refer so much to 'resting places' (*contra* KBL, p. 602 and Beyerlin, *Origins and History of the Oldest Sinaitic Traditions*, p. 109) as protection from annihilation. Cf. von Rad, *Old Testament Theology*, I, 288: 'Jahweh himself protects his people from this annihilating encounter, and takes precautions in order that his design to "give Israel rest" (Exod. 30: 14) may achieve its end.'

Intercession of the Covenant Mediator

admitted awkwardness, it is doubtful whether we should resort to emendation or addition. The words are meant as oracular (note 2′2′ metre! cf. 33:1). Moses replies:

אם אין פניך הלכים
אל תעלנו מזה

'If your Presence will not go, do not make us go forth from here.' The repetition of Yahweh's words is characteristic of dialogical cultic style and argues for the retention of the Massoretic Text in both instances. Be that as it may, the words of Yahweh and the reply of Moses, the one at the close of the first division, the other at the beginning of the second, appear in the middle of the pericope and strike its dominant keynote. The issue at stake here, as we have been at pains to point out, is of supreme moment. This accounts for the passionate urgency of the mediator's plea.[1] Will Yahweh indeed leave his holy habitation on Mount Sinai and accompany his people to Canaan and remain with them there as their God? That would seem on the face of it to be utterly impossible and unprecedented according to the prevailingly spatial mentality of the peoples of the ancient Near East for whom the gods have their own provinces and holy places and for whom land and people are psychically related.[2]

[1] Noth in his commentary on *Exodus* says, 'The demanding and forceful tone in which Moses speaks to Yahweh is striking' (p. 256). That it is forceful and striking is certainly true, but it is hardly demanding. It is rather urgent and passionate. On the other hand Noth is one of the few scholars to recognize the true force of Yahweh's words in verse 14, which is quite generally understood as a question (cf. *GK*, §150a). Cf. Noth, *ad loc.*: 'The present wording does not favour this conception. The text rather means that the first, brief promise of Yahweh, which is to give Moses "rest" (verse 14b should be understood in this simple way) is still not a sufficient reply to Moses' urgent request and that he requires a specific confirmation over and above this.'

[2] Beyerlin, *Origins and History of the Oldest Sinaitic Traditions*, pp. 101 f.: 'The passion with which the argument is conducted and with which the narrative of the Midianite Ḥobab ben Reʿuel is abruptly set aside is only intelligible against the background of a burning, existing problem. Obviously this consisted in establishing and getting recognition for the conviction that the God who once revealed himself fully and for the first time on *Sinai* was now present with his people in *Canaan* also.' Cf. also pp. 161 f.: 'Accordingly, the tradition of Exod. 33:12b–17, the nucleus

JAMES MUILENBURG

It was precisely Yahweh's deed of deliverance in the alien land of Egypt that had evoked Jethro's great confession: 'Now I know that Yahweh is greater than all gods because he delivered the people from under the power of the Egyptians' (Exod. 18: 11). But for him to leave Sinai to accompany them to Canaan and to establish his residence there was quite another matter (cf. Judg. 5: 4; Hab. 3: 3 ff.). It is indeed probable that for a long time throughout the pre-exilic period pilgrimages were made to Sinai, as we see most clearly in the case of Elijah (1 Kings 19: 3 ff.).[1] The momentousness of Yahweh's words to Moses, 'My Presence will go', is clearly reflected in Deut. 4: 32–40 (especially verse 37; cf. Isa. 63: 9). It is no wonder that Moses as the mediator of the covenant should press the issue 'If your Presence will not go, do not make us go forth from here' (15).

The pulsebeat of destiny throbs through the words. The future of Israel lies in the balances of the divine decision. That this is by no means an overstatement is conclusively demonstrated by the powerful lines that follow. The solemnity and portentousness of the conditional are to be discerned in the extraordinary

of which certainly goes back to the early history of Israel and which strives to establish that the God of Sinai did, in fact, go up in person with his people to Canaan (pp. 99–112), remained alive right up to the period of the monarchy, and indeed it was first given literary expression in the later Yahwistic source (pp. 100 f.). In connection with Exod. 33: 12 b–17, and 33: 3 b–4, 5–6, the Jehovistic redaction has been at pains to establish that Yahweh did not only then appear at Sinai (34: 5 f.) but thanks to Moses' prayer of intercession (pp. 92 f.), appears even now in the midst of a stiff-necked people in Canaan and shows himself as Israel's living God' (pp. 90–8, 110 f.). For the wider implications of the פנים or Face of God in the history of religions, see especially Mircea Eliade, *Cosmos and History: the Myth of the Eternal Return* (New York, 1924), pp. 102 ff. on 'History Regarded as Theophany'.

[1] Martin Noth, 'Der Wallfahrtsweg zum Sinai (Num. 33)', *PJB*, xxxvi (1940), 5–28. Cf. R. E. Clements, *God and Temple: the Idea of the Divine Presence in Israel* (Oxford, 1965), p. 27: 'Perhaps there were some in Israel who had thought of Yahweh as bound in some way to Sinai, so that the migration to Canaan was a departing from him. Consequently, it was out of a certain religious tension and struggle that the belief gained firm hold that Yahweh had given his word to Moses that his presence (Heb. *panim*) would be with his people. The way in which this word was fulfilled was given outward expression in the cult and worship of Israel.'

Intercession of the Covenant Mediator

terseness of the protasis and apodosis. The crucial significance of the words is further confirmed by the immediately following extended motivation in two parts of three cola each (16*abc* and 16*def*). Even more important, each part contains an urgent question directed to Yahweh. The first is formulated in an unusual, though by no means unprecedented fashion: 'in what way will it ever be known?' Then follows the election motif, the choosing of Moses as mediator and of the people as the people of the covenant. It is precisely the interrogative form spoken in this way to Yahweh that gives the line its weight. But the second question is even more direct. Moses is reminding Yahweh of the supreme meaning of this holy hour: 'Is it not in your going with us (here explicitly for the first time and surely intentionally so!) that we shall be distinguished from every people on the face of the earth.' We have encountered this same boldness of the mediator before in Moses' reply to Yahweh's demand in 33: 12. The ambulatory motif, so pregnantly stated in Yahweh's two words in 14*b*, so urgently repeated in Moses' laconic response (15*b*), here turns into a breathless climax. Israel here emerges upon the stage of world history as the people whose God is Yahweh, the One who will go to the Land of Promise. The same motif is in all probability present in Abram's migration (Gen. 12: 1–3) and on the occasion when David the King wishes to build a temple to Yahweh (2 Sam. 7: 4 ff.).

But surely this is not our finale. The intercession demands an answer. Yahweh will set his seal on the fateful words that have been spoken by his mediator, his imprimatur on his words, his confirmation of his assurance. Again, as in verse 14, he takes to himself Moses' perplexity and bafflement and transmutes them into decision and promise. The opening *formula citandi* is particularly impressive here: 'And Yahweh said to Moses' (cf. 33: 1*a* and 12*a*). But, what is more, Yahweh has been entering into the encounter of spoken speech from the very beginning, and now brings it to its culmination: 'This very word you have spoken will I perform.' That would seem to be sufficient for Moses and for the people, but, again, as so frequently in many different types of divine pronouncements in the Old Testament,

JAMES MUILENBURG

the words are followed by a weighty motivation, all the more moving because we have listened to the mediator's long motivations immediately preceding, and the words are fashioned out of the citations in the first plea (12–13).

In the foregoing discussion we have attempted to demonstrate that the composition of Exod. 33: 1*a*, 12–17 has been meticulously wrought, that the major motifs and keywords have been so carefully woven into the literary fabric that it is difficult to believe that it represents anything less than a unified and coherent whole. Moreover, we need have no doubt that the stress upon the divine presence accompanying Israel was responsible for its inclusion within the complex of materials centring in the covenant at Sinai. But, more than that, it was preserved because its content focused upon the motif that is central to all worship, namely, the presence of God, for worship is only possible when and where God is believed to be present. It was not a motif that could be cavalierly taken for granted because Yahweh belonged to Sinai, it was there that he surely was present, there that he had revealed himself to his people, there that Moses had served as mediator, there that the covenant had been concluded and its stipulations set forth.

Nevertheless, if we are to penetrate more deeply into our pericope, discern the interior nature of its dialectic, gain a synoptic view of its contents, we shall see that there is a word which holds a position of pre-eminence throughout, a word to which we have heretofore done less than justice. We referred at the beginning of our discussion to the importance of the verb ידע in the Old Testament and more particularly in our present passage. In the Book of Exodus it appears frequently and often in crucial contexts, but, so far as I am aware, we shall look in vain for any passage to rival this. Within the compass of five verses, it appears six times and always, let it be remembered, in significant collocations.

How are we to explain this terminology? It is surely more than fortuitous that it should appear so profusely in so small a literary unit and always in striking contexts. We have already stressed the centrality of the covenant relationship in the large

Intercession of the Covenant Mediator

literary complexes of which our passage forms a part. The
covenant associations of the word have long been recognized,
not only here but frequently elsewhere in the Old Testament.
In recent years, however, we have come to see more clearly
than before the function that the word plays in the treaty formulations of the peoples of the ancient Near East and the close
relationships they reveal to the biblical formulations. To the
divine command to go forth from Sinai Moses replies, 'You
have not let me know the one you will send with me'. That
knowledge is necessary, but it remains undisclosed. Unless
Moses knows who the leader will be, the future remains dark
and ominous. But Moses presses on to another kind of knowing
of which Yahweh has already given him assurance, 'I know you
by name'. Here we arrive at an important juncture. Nothing
is more clear than that here again, as so often in the Old
Testament, knowing implies a personal relationship, indeed a
very personal inward relation.[1] It is a freely-offered gift of grace
on the part of the divine Suzerain to his representative and
mediator. So we may render the verb best perhaps by the verb

---

[1] Eberhard Baumann, 'ידע und seine Derivate im Hebräischen', ZAW,
xxviii (1908), 22–41, 110–43. See especially, p. 30: 'Danach bezeichnet
ידע hier im Grunde eine persönliche Verbindung, auf Grund deren ein
enger Verkehr stattfindet, ein Austausch nicht nur von Wissen, sondern
mehr noch von Achtung, Liebe, Fürsorge, Wohltaten, Diensten u.s.f., wes-
halb der ידוע eigentlich der jemand Zugehörige, danach nicht nur der
Vertraute, sondern ebenso sehr der Geachtete, Geliebte, Ersehnte, Ge-
pflegte etc. sein kann.' See further, p. 33: 'Der Sinn wäre demnach: Jahwe
hat Mose mit Namen genannt und damit dokumentiert, dass Mose zu
seiner Verfügung wie unter seinem Schutze steht, dass Mose von ihm
erwählt und berufen sei zu ganz bestimmten Beruf. Genaueres lässt sich
nicht ausmachen.' This interior understanding of the verb is supported
in an illuminating way by the call of Jeremiah where the verb stands in
close relation to the verb יצר, on the one hand, and to the verb הקדשתיך,
on the other. We have an excellent parallel from Egypt from the stele of
king Pianchi (25th dynasty, c. 751–730 B.C.), in the speech of Amun to the
king: 'It was in the belly of your mother that I said concerning you that
you were to be ruler of Egypt; it was as seed and while you were in the
egg, that I knew you, that I knew you were to be Lord.' (M. Gilula,
VT, xvii (1967), 114.) E. A. Speiser suggests that ידע in such contexts as
ours means 'to single out', and this is surely involved in the meaning here.
See his commentary on *Genesis* (Anchor Bible series, New York, 1962),
p. 133 and note on Gen. 18: 19.

JAMES MUILENBURG

'to choose'.[1] Moses is to know who he is in relation to Yahweh and his people by being given the word of grace and of responsibility implied in the appointment. While we do not have exact parallels to this particular formulation, 'I know you by name', the meaning is clear. He has been singled out as a person, given his identity, released from bondage to his own knowing by the prior divine knowing. The roots of such knowing by name doubtless lie in the field of magic where the name plays a crucial role. But to be known of God is to be liberated from the coercions of magical techniques. For Yahweh to know Moses is a demonstration to him that he has found favour with him. That should be sufficient to dispel all doubt and anxiety. But Moses asks for more, and he presses his intercession on the frontiers of the divine knowing in order that he may himself live in the reciprocity and mutuality of knowing. So immediately following the decisive ועתה he seeks to clarify his situation in relationship to the momentous demand upon his life: 'And now, if I have truly found favour in your eyes, please let me know your ways that I may know you.' The human-divine dialectic is very striking. The relevant predications of the first major section of the pericope are so closely linked, indeed so closely interwoven and interlaced, that they form a remarkable sequence. But what is more, the verb appears twice in each subsection, and each pair is related to the other:

You have not let me know the one you will send with me (12 de)
But you have said, 'I know you by name' (12 fg)
Please let me know your ways (13 b)
that I may know you (13 b)

The second and fourth predications are connected with the first and third, and it is the relation of the second and fourth (where

---

[1] So perhaps the great majority of scholars. Compare Gen. 18: 19 (RSV): 'No, for I have chosen him (Hebrew ידע), that he may charge his children and his household after him to keep the way of the Lord by doing righteousness and justice; so that the Lord may bring to Abraham what he has promised him (Hebrew אשר דבר עליו).' Cf. also Amos 3: 2. For the expression, 'I have called you by name', cf. especially Isa. 43: 1; 45: 3–4; 49: 1 and their contexts. In this connection, see also the important discussion by William L. Moran, 'The Ancient Near Eastern Background of the Love of God in Deuteronomy', CBQ, xxv (1963), 77–87.

Intercession of the Covenant Mediator

the accents surely lie) which is crucial for our interpretation. What is involved is the mutuality of the knowing relationship between Yahweh and Moses. It is a *covenantal* knowing, a knowing between Lord and servant, between King and subject, between Suzerain and vassal.[1] It is clear that Moses is the mediator here, for the climax of verse 13 *d* brings this out in a most impressive way: 'Consider that this nation is your people.'

In the second division of the pericope the word 'to know' likewise plays a central role. This is apparent again from the *precise* context of the word. After receiving the divine assurance of his accompanying Presence, Moses repeats the crucial words and makes an issue of them. First the conditional in the manner of the covenant and treaty formulations with the decisive apodosis, 'do not lead us forth from here' (cf. 33: 1 *a*ᵇ, 12 *c*) which is followed by the moving and climactic motivation: ובמה יודע אפוא: 'For in what way will it ever be known?' (cf. Gen. 15: 8). How will it ever be 'realized' or 'recognized' that Moses is indeed Yahweh's chosen instrument, that he is indeed Yahweh's mediator? This meaning of the verb ידע is of course frequent in the Old Testament, notably in Second Isaiah and the Psalms. It may be observed in passing that it is very close to the verb ראה (cf. 12 *b* and 13 *d*) and is not infrequently used in conjunction with ראה to form a hendiadys. The following question is rather awkward, but should not for that reason be simply connected with the preceding words by such a conjunction as 'unless', for this is to dissipate the force of the interrogation. No, what we have here is a word of the deepest import and consequence. It must, therefore, retain its own independence. 'Is it not in your going with us that we will be distinguished from all other peoples on the face of the earth?' Nothing is said about a human guide, about the ark or tent of meeting, of the pillar of cloud by day and pillar of fire by night. It is in this

---

[1] As often in Hosea. H. W. Wolff, '"Wissen um Gott" bei Hosea als Urform von Theologie', *Evangelische Theologie*, xⅡ (Munich, 1952–3), 116–68= *Gesam. Stud. zum A.T.* (*Theologische Bücherei*, 1964), pp. 182–205, esp. pp. 193–9. On p. 197 Wolff writes of the knowledge of God as 'a summa summarum of the covenant relation'. For Baumann's criticism, see *Evangelische Theologie*, xv (Munich, 1955), 416–25 and Wolff's reply, *ibid.* 426–31.

JAMES MUILENBURG

event of the Leader going on before, the theophanic פנים present, Yahweh in his self-manifestation, that Israel will recognize her distinction from all other peoples and confess it in her holy rituals and celebrations.[1]

We have confined our study thus far to a single Old Testament passage, although we have had occasion from time to time to point to the affinities between the covenant formulations in the Old Testament, notably Exod. 19–24 (cf. also the Book of Deuteronomy), and the suzerainty treaties of the peoples of the ancient Near East. It has long been recognized by scholars that the terminology of knowing finds its parallels in not a few of the royal texts from these peoples.[2] More recently, however, H. B. Huffmon of Johns Hopkins University has demonstrated that the nature of the relationship between suzerain and vassal in the treaties is described in terms of the mutuality of knowing much as we encounter it in a substantial number of Old Testament contexts.[3] 'The most obvious technical usage of "know" is that

[1] This is not to deny that the presence of Yahweh is related to the ark. Some scholars believe that our pericope was at one time preceded by one of the ark, and it is also contended that our text was at one time followed immediately by the ark songs in Num. 10: 29 ff. This may well be right, but it is significant that no such reference is suggested in the pericope itself. This is, of course, what we should expect in a cultic formulation of this kind. Yahweh is *invisibly* present. See the excellent comment by Buber, *The Prophetic Faith*, p. 49: 'The paradox on which the sanctity of the ark is based (every "holy" thing is founded on a paradox) is this, that an invisible deity becomes perceptible as One Who comes and goes.'

[2] A. Zimmern in E. Schrader's *Keilinschriften und das Alte Testament* (Berlin, 1903), p. 403, and S. Mowinckel, 'Motiver og stilformer i profeten Jeremias diktning', *Nordisk Tidsskrift for Litteraturforskning* (Oslo, 1926), 257.

[3] 'The Treaty Background of Hebrew YĀDA'', *BASOR*, CLXXXI (1966), 31–7. Note, for example, his citation of the treaty between the Hittite king, Suppiluliumas and Haqqanas from eastern Asia Minor: 'And you, Huqqanas, know only the Sun regarding lordship; also my son (of) whom I, the Sun, say, "This one everyone should know (*sakdu*)...you, Huqqanas know him (*apun sa[k]*)! Moreover (those) who are my sons, his brothers (or) my brothers...know (*sak*) as brother and associate. Moreover, another lord...do not...know".' In the Amarna letter from Abdi-Asirta, king of Amurri, to his suzerain Amenophis III, we have the same usage: 'may the king, my lord, know me and put me under the charge of Paha(m)nate, my (royal) governor' (p. 32). See also H. B. Huffmon and Simon D. Parker, 'A Further Note on the Treaty Background of Hebrew YĀDA'', *BASOR*, CLXXXIV (1966), 36–8.

Intercession of the Covenant Mediator

with reference to mutual legal recognition on the part of suzerain and vassal' (*op. cit.*, p. 180, n. 3 above). We have the requests of the vassal and the promises and assurances of the suzerain, just as we have with Moses on behalf of Israel. Father Moran has also called attention to the motif of the mutuality of love in the treaties and the Book of Deuteronomy (*CBQ*, xxv (1963), 77–87), and it is apparent that the knowing relationship both in our text and in other biblical passages[1] carries with it the same connotation (see p. 177, n. 1 above). It is only to be expected that we should encounter the verb in the lawsuits for breach of treaty (Isa. 1: 3; Jer. 2: 8; Hos. 4: 1 ff.) and in the prophet's call (Jer. 1: 5). It may not be without significance that some of the most illuminating parallels are associated with Abraham (Gen. 18: 19), Moses (Deut. 34: 10), and David (2 Sam. 7: 20).

In the light of the intimate associations of our text with the covenant and more especially with the mediator of the covenant, and in the light, too, of the many striking parallels from the Near Eastern treaties with their emphasis upon the relations between suzerain and vassal, it was only natural that our little liturgy should be preserved. It was not confined to the archives of Israel as among the other Near Eastern peoples, nor yet to her treasured memorabilia in the manner of antiquarians, nor to the fickle winds of time. Rather it was probably employed in the ancient sanctuaries, such as the amphictyonic centres at Gilgal, Shiloh, and Shechem, and each time the words were heard Israel could rejoice that Yahweh had indeed come from Sinai, his Presence had accompanied them on their way to Canaan, the Land of Promise, and had made his abode at some point in the history of the tradition upon Zion's holy hill. But more than that, they made contemporary the awesome event in which Yahweh had spoken the formula of ordination and induction, 'I know you by name' and the mediator had come as no other to know him and his ways.

[1] Amos 3: 2; Hos. 2: 20 (Heb. 22); 6: 3, 6; 8: 2; 13: 4, cf. 4: 1, 6; Jer. 1: 5; 15: 15 (?), etc.

A STUDY IN HEBREW RHETORIC: REPETITION AND STYLE

BY

JAMES MUILENBURG
New York

In 1741, at the age of thirty, RICHARD LOWTH was appointed Professor of Poetry at Oxford University, and it was in that capacity that he delivered his famous lectures on the poetry of ancient Israel. In 1753 these lectures were published under the title *de sacra poesi Hebraeorum praelectiones academicae*. The importance and value of this work transcends any of the specific theories or literary judgments which are expressed in it. For LOWTH was something of a poet, and he read biblical poetry with the mind of a poet. For one thing he recognized the wide range of poetic utterance in the Old Testament, and drew the consequences of this literary form for the interpretation of the sacred records. He was aware, too, that poetry has its special techniques: thus he sought to discern its cadences and rhythms, its lineaments and configurations. But he was more than a technician or craftsman. He had an acute sensitivity to the connotations which words possess beyond all the precision of their denotations, and he perceived the ever-changing nuances which words achieve in fresh contexts. His description of the sententious quality of Hebrew speech has never been surpassed; his feelings for imagery and the effects that imagery produces upon the reader gives his work an aesthetic authenticity rivalled in our day only by the work of HERMANN GUNKEL; his openness to the spontaneity, immediacy, concreteness, and primitive vitality of the Hebrew mind classes him among the peers of Old Testament study.

That LOWTH was in many respects a representative of his own age goes without saying. It would be easy to mark the defects of his work or to show the many ways in which his work has been superseded. Not least of all the theory by which he is best known has required restatement and reformulation. For it is now obvious to most students that the theory of *parallelismus membrorum* is far more complicated and involved than LOWTH supposed although he did

seek to guard himself on this matter, especially in his preliminary
dissertation in the commentary on Isaiah [1]). The first major type of
parallelism to which Lowth called attention was the synonymous.
But if one inspects his examples either in the lectures or in the Isaiah
commentary, it will be seen that the parallelism is in reality very
seldom precisely synonymous. The parallel line does not simply
repeat what has been said, but enriches it, deepens it, transforms
it by adding fresh nuances and bringing in new elements, renders it
more concrete and vivid and telling. One example must suffice [2]):

> Arise, shine, for thy light has come,
>   and the glory of Yahweh has dawned upon thee;
> For, behold, darkness shall cover the earth,
>   and deep gloom the peoples;
> But upon thee Yahweh dawns forth,
>   on thee his glory appears,
> And nations shall come to thy light,
>   and kings to the brightness of thy dawning. (Isa. lx 1-3)

It is clear that there is repetition in the parallel lines. But almost
invariably something is added, and it is precisely the combination
of what is repeated and what is added that makes of parallelism the
artistic form that it is. This intimate relation between old and new
elements is an important feature of Hebrew composition and Hebrew
thought. On the one hand we observe form and pattern; on the other
form and pattern are radically altered. Here, as elsewhere, there is a
native resistance to stereotype or fixity, and yet form is clearly present
and registers its effect upon the mind. In our modern study of Old
Testament poetry synonymous speech has been recognized in the
criticism of literary types (*Gattungkritik*), above all, of course, in
the studies of Hermann Gunkel, and especially in his commentary
on the Psalms. In the hymn, the lament, the song of thanksgiving,

---

[1]) *Isaiah: a New Translation with Preliminary Dissertation* (Cambridge, 1834),
p. xx: "Sometimes the parallelism is more, sometimes less exact; sometimes
hardly at all apparent. It requires indeed particular attention, much study of the
genius of the language, much habitude in the analysis of the construction, to be
able in all cases to see and to distinguish the nice rests and pauses which ought
to be made, in order to give the period or the sentence its intended turn and
cadence and to each part its due proportion." The influence of Lowth's classical
studies in Greek and Latin is apparent here as elsewhere in his work and is one
of the features which the discovery of the other literatures of the ancient Near
East has in large measure corrected. See also Lowth, *Lectures on the Sacred Poetry
of the Hebrews* (Andover, 1829), p. 35 for a cautious statement of parallelism.

[2]) Compare also Ps. cxiv; Is. liii 1-5; Nah. i 2; Ps. xciii 3 f.; Dt. xxxii 42.

and other literary types synonymous speech plays a major role; indeed, it is not too much to say that the dominant impression that these poetic compositions make upon us is to be explained by the profuse employment of synonymous words, phrases, and lines. The studies of GUNKEL are yet to be extended into a more detailed consideration of literary structure, but even a cursory examination of biblical poetry will show that the appearance of synonymity is seldom fortuitous or capricious. In the present discussion we shall endeavour to survey in a very general fashion the phenomenon of repetition in ancient Hebrew literature as a major feature of Hebrew rhetoric and style. For the most part we shall confine ourselves to actual repetition, i.e., where the same words and sentences are repeated.

Repetition plays a diverse role in the Old Testament. It serves, for one thing, to center the thought, to rescue it from disparateness and diffuseness, to focus the richness of varied predication upon the poet's controlling concern. The synthetic character of biblical mentality, its sense for totality, is as apparent in Israel's rhetoric as in her psychology. Repetition serves, too, to give continuity to the writer's thought; the repeated word or phrase is often strategically located, thus providing a clue to the movement and stress of the poem. Sometimes the repeated word or line indicates the structure of the poem, pointing to the separate divisions; at other times it may guide us in determining the extent of the literary unit. Our commentaries contain numerous instances where words and phrases have been deleted as mere repetition. It is a highly precarious procedure, one which violates the character of biblical writing, both prose and poetry, and is refuted quite decisively by the other extant literatures of the Near East, above all, perhaps, by the Ugaritic epics, which cast a strong light on the method and mentality of ancient Semitic thinking and literary composition. Finally, repetition provides us with an open avenue to the character of biblical thinking [1]).

---

[1]) See especially JOHANNES PEDERSEN, *Israel: its Life and Culture*, Vol. I-II (London, 1926), p. 123: "The very language shows how Israelite thought is dominated by two things: *striving after totality* and *movement*. Properly speaking it only expresses that the whole soul takes part in the thinking and creates out of its own essence. The thought is charged with the feeling of the soul and the striving of its will after action. This characterizes the Hebrew manner of argumentation. We try to persuade by means of abstract reasoning, the Hebrew by directly influencing the will. In expressing a thought he makes the souls of his listeners receive his mind-image, and thus the matter itself; but at the same time

100   J. MUILENBURG

This iterative propensity of ancient Israel extends beyond its
expression in poetry. In narrative, the literary genre most characteristic of her life and thought, repetition appears as a major stylistic
feature. In such accounts, for example, as the wooing of Rebecca [1]),
or the Elijah stories [2]), it is used with a high degree of artistic skill,
both because of its great variety and because of its power to relate
speaker and hearer in the immediacy and concreteness of dialog or to
bring them into participation with common words. It is an eloquent
witness to the literary genius of ancient Israel that this constant
resort to iterative discourse so seldom palls or wearies the reader.
In the cult, too, repetition rendered a special service. In the annual
festivals commemorating the unique historical events of the sacred
past, Israel recited year after year her memorabilia: the theophanic
accounts of the holy places, the stories of the Fathers, the epic events
associated with the Exodus and with the covenant at Sinai, and the
toroth that were incumbent upon her. The various rituals and liturgies
were themselves filled with numerous repetitions as we can see most
readily in such books as Deuteronomy and Ezekiel, some of the
Psalms, and the Priestly Code and history. In the instruction of the
young, too, iteration proved an effective device for stamping the
mind with the things that must be remembered [3]). Psalm cxxxvi,
where every alternate line reads, "For his steadfast love endures
forever", is reminiscent of the endless repetitions in the Near Eastern
liturgies, but there is evidence that it was not only one of the best
loved but also one of the most familiar of all of Israel's liturgies [4]).

---

he produces an effect by the feeling and will which he puts into the words. His
argumentation therefore consists in assurance and repetition. The *"parallelismus
membrorum"* has become his natural manner of expression; he expresses his
thought twice in a different manner, the result of which is a totality with a double
accent: "Therefore the wicked shall not stand in the judgment, nor sinners
in the congregation of the righteous" (Ps. i 5). When the Preacher wants the
reader to see that "to everything there is a season" then he proves it by constantly
repeating first one thing, then another (Eccles. iii). Upon the whole the book
of the Preacher is characteristic of Israelite argumentation. He repeats and repeats,
and it seems to us that he practically ends where he began." Also J. G. HERDER,
The Spirit of Hebrew Poetry (Burlington, 1833), pp. 39 ff.; S. A. COOK, "The
Semites", *Cambridge Ancient History*, Vol. I, pp. 195-197; AUBREY R. JOHNSON,
The Vitality of the Individual in the Thought of Ancient Israel (Cardiff, 1949).
   [1]) Gen. xxiv.
   [2]) I Kings xvii-xix, xxi; II Kings i-ii.
   [3]) Deut. iv 9 ff.; xi 18 ff.; Exod. xii 14; xiii 9-10, 16.
   [4]) It is significant that the Chronicler quotes this line in connection with the
establishment of the ark in Jerusalem (I Chron. xvi 41), with the response of the

The fact that the refrain appears in other liturgies is not surprising; we encounter the same circumstance again and again in the Ugaritic poems.

The roots of repetition lie deeply embedded in the language and literature of Israel [1]). An examination of the various modes of reduplication in Hebrew syntax or of the repetition of single words in elemental contexts of unreflected speech will reveal very clearly how the primitive spirit of the language continues to be preserved and lends to it an intensity, a spontaneity and freshness, a directness and immediacy which would be difficult to achieve in any other fashion [2]). Thus in such stems as the *Pᵉʿalʿal*, *Pilpel*, and *Hithpalpel* the verb is given a special energy or movement. The verb פחר, e.g., in the *pᵉʿalʿal* may describe the palpitation of the heart or "to go about quickly" or the *Pilpel* גלגל from the root גלל meaning "to roll". This repetition of the root to denote rapidity of movement is also characteristic of other languages, modern as well as ancient [3]). It is only to be expected that this same primitive survival should express the superlative: *ṣedeq ṣedeq tirdoph*, "justice, only justice you shall pursue" (Deut. xvi 20), or *ʿamok ʿamok*, "deep, very deep" (Eccles. vii 24), or *rᵃa rᵃa*, "it is bad, bad" (Prov. xx 14), or *mᵉʾod mᵉʾod*, "exceedingly great" (Ezek. ix 9; xvi 13), or *qadosh, qadosh, qadosh* — "utterly" or "supremely holy" (Isa. vi 3). The same intensity is implied in such expressions as *ʿebed ʿebadim*, "servant of servants" (Gen. ix 25), *qodesh ha-qᵒdashim*, "holy of holies" (Exod. xxvi 23), or "God of gods" (Deut. x 17; Josh. xxii 22; Dan. ii 47) or "Lord of lords" (Deut. x 17; Ps. cxxxvi 3). Similarly a word is frequently

---

people upon the descent of the holy fire after Solomon's dedicatory prayer (II Chron. vii 3), and with the preparation for battle against Moab and Ammon in Jehoshaphat's reign (II Chron. xx 21). It is probable that in all three of these cases the line is simply an incipit for the entire psalm. The view of H. WHEELER ROBINSON (*Inspiration and Revelation in the Old Testament*, p. 115, nt. 17) that the repetition of the refrain is accidental has nothing to commend it.

[1]) See ISRAEL EITAN, "La Repetition de la Racine en Hebreu", *Journal of the Palestine Oriental Society*, 1921, pp. 171-186.

[2]) Cf. EITAN, *ibid.*, p. 172: "Se différenciant en plusieurs procédés grammaticaux ou syntaxiques, ou en séries-types d'expressions idiomatiques, la *répétition de la racine* a fourni à la langue hébraïque, par voie de formation *spontanée*, souvent même *populaire* et sous l'influence de l'action *analogique*, des ressources précieuses pour rendre d'une façon plus vive et intense, surtout plus *concrète et intuitive*, certaines nuances d'expression sur lesquelles on tient à insister sans les affaiblir par un langage abstrait."

[3]) GESENIUS-KAUTZSCH-COWLEY, *Hebrew Grammar*, Sec. 55 d-g and 84ᵇ k-p.

102   J. MUILENBURG

repeated to express urgency as in the Song of Deborah, the great
classic of the iterative style, 'uri 'uri:

> Awake, awake, Deborah!
>> Awake, awake, utter a song!   (Ju v 12)

To this is to be compared the similarly passionate outcry in Second
Isaiah:

> Awake, awake, put on thy strength,
>> O arm of Yahweh;
> Awake as in primeval days,
>> the generations long ago.   (Isa. li 9. cf. lii 1)

Other examples of almost equal interest are *naphᵉlah naphᵉlah Babel*,
"fallen, fallen is Babylon" (Isa. xxi 9) or "I pine away, I pine away"
(Isa. xxiv 16), "comfort, O comfort" (Isa. xl 1) or "for my sake,
for my sake" (Isa. xlviii 11) or *shalom shalom* (Jer. vi 4; viii 11) or
'amen 'amen (Pss. lxxii 19; lxxxix 53). Emphatic vocatives are expressed in the same manner, thus "Abraham, Abraham" in the
crisis of the story of Isaac's sacrifice (Gen. xxii 11) or "Moses, Moses"
as he is about to violate the divine holiness (Exod. iii 4) or David's
heartbroken apostrophe, *bᵉni Abshalom bᵉni bᵉni* (II Sam. xviii 33;
Heb. xix 1) or *'abi 'abi*, Elisha's cry at the ascent of Elijah in a
chariot of fire (II Kings ii 12) or the forlorn words *'eli 'eli* of Ps. xxii.
Interjections are repeated as in Amos' *ho ho*, "alas, alas!" (v 16), or
Ezekiel's *'oi 'oi*, "woe, woe!" (xvi 23), or the psalmist's *heᵃh heᵃh*,
"aha, aha!" (lxx 4). Not unrelated to the foregoing discussion is the
vast area of assonance in its many varied forms, of euphony and
cacophony, of alliteration and the prevalence of single sounds
throughout a context to express the mood and temper of the passage [1]).
An outstanding example is the confessional lament of Isa. liii 1-9,
another classic of iterative composition.

The foregoing discussion has dealt with what we may call elemental or primitive iteration, the kind of language which is used
spontaneously in moments of excitement or urgency. Many other
types might be adduced, but we shall now turn to an aspect of
repetition which has so far received less than sufficient observation.
We refer to the relation of repetition to the literary forms of the Old

---

[1] IGNAZ GABOR, *Der Hebräische Urrhythmus*, BZAW 52 (1929). GABOR believes
that the masoretic accentuation has obscured the original stresses, that originally
the tone fell not on the last but the first syllable. For an assessment of this view,
see O. S. RANKIN, "*Alliteration in Hebrew Poetry*", JTS 31 (1930), pp. 285-291.

Testament. If we were to include within our inquiry words, phrases, and sentences which are synonymous, the evidence for the relationship would be very impressive indeed. But we restrict ourselves almost exclusively to repetition in the narrower sense. A good example, though not necessarily the most felicitous, is the acrostic poem as it is found in the Book of Lamentations. The alphabetic arrangement of the successive verses would naturally encourage repetition, but the phenomenon penetrates much more deeply. And here we are confronted with a characteristic of Hebrew literature in general: wherever the writer shows any inclination to employ the iterative style he does so in a variety of ways, i.e., he uses repetition as a creative literary device. This is especially true of *Lamentations* where the repetitions are abundant and varied. Condamin suggested some years ago that the first two acrostic poems form a kind of concentric setting in such a manner that the same key-words appear in the first and last strophe, in the second and the second from the last, in the third and the third from the last, and so on. He encountered several exceptions to this form, but, interestingly enough, scholars had detected textual confusion in precisely those instances which did not conform to the rule [1]). What is notable about this ancient poetry is that such an artificial contrivance does not stand in the way of producing literature of a high order, in which the emotions find full expression and the language bodies forth the intensity and passion of the poet.

The Old Testament provides a number of instances where the verbal structure of a poem is completely conditioned by repetition. Most notable, of course, are Jotham's fable [2]) and Amos' oracles against the foreign nations [3]), but Job's great apologia [4]), and many of the passages in Ezekiel [5]), illustrate the same phenomenon. Jotham's fable has an interesting parallel in *Baal and Anath* where the general context appears to have many elements in common with the setting of *Judges* (e.g. Lebanon with its trees, the fire, food and drink for men and gods, etc.) [6]). It is worth observing that the pattern of

---

[1]) ALBERT CONDAMIN, "Symmetrical Repetitions in *Lamentations* Chapters I and II", JTS 7 (1906), pp. 137-140.

[2]) Judges ix 8-15.   [3]) Amos i-ii.   [4]) Job xxxi.

[5]) For example, Ezek. xiv 12-30; xviii 5 ff.; 25. Note also the elaborate "because ... therefore" constructions.

[6]) H. L. GINSBERG (JAMES B. PRITCHARD, *Ancient Near Eastern Texts Relating to the Old Testament*, p. 140a) renders the inscription, unfortunately only partially preserved, as follows:

the Ugaritic poem is similarly determined by repetition, as, to be
sure, are many other contexts in the Ugaritic literature. Jotham's
fable is the most perfect and detailed of all biblical iterative poems.

The presence of refrains sometimes serves to articulate the structure of a poem, most notably in such instances as Pss. xlii-xliii,
xlvi, cvii, cxxxvi, Isa. ix 8-x 4, v 25-30; Amos iv 6-11 [1]). Sometimes
the last line of the poem repeats the opening as in the eighth psalm.
Similarly the last line of the Nikkal poem from Ugarit practically
repeats the beginning [2]). In many instances the key-word of the
opening line or introduction is repeated at the close [3]). More important is the repetition of central key-words throughout a poem.
There are many examples of this phenomenon. A noteworthy example
is the poem contained in Jer. iii 1-iv 4. After the prose additions,

> "Hark, Lady A(sherah of the S)ea
>   Give one of thy s(ons I'll make king."
> Quoth Lady Asherah of the Sea:
>   "Why, let's make Yadi' Yalhan king."
> Answered kindly One EL Benign:
> "Too weakly, He can't race with Baal,
>   Throw jav'lin with Dagon's Son Glory-Crown!"
>
> Replied Lady Asherah of the Sea:
>   "Well, let's make it Ashtar the Tyrant;
>   Let Ashtar the Tyrant be king."
> Straightway Ashtar the Tyrant
>   Goes up to the *Fastness* of Zaphon
>   (And) sits on Baal Puissant's throne.
> (But) his feet reach not down to the footstool,
>   Nor his head reaches up to the top.
> So Ashtar the Tyrant declares:
>   "I'll not reign in Zaphon's *Fastness!*"
> Down goes Ashtar the Tyrant,
>   Down from the throne of Baal Puissant,
> And reigns in El's Earth, all of it.

[1]) Note also the use of refrains in Pss. xxxix 5d and 11c (Heb. 6 and 12);
xlix 12 and 20 (Heb. 13 and 21); lvii 5 and 11 (Heb. 6 and 12); lxvii 3 and 5
(Heb. 4 and 6).

[2]) ALBRECHT GOETZE, "The Nikkal Poem from Ras Shamra", *JBL* LX,
pp. 353-373. Observe the characteristic hymnic opening, common both in ancient
Near Eastern and Western poetry:

> "Let me praise and exalt Hirihbi."

For other discussions of the poem, see C. H. GORDON in *BASOR*, 65 (1937),
pp. 29-33; H. L. GINSBERG in *Orientalia*, N. F. viii (1939), pp. 317-327.

[3]) Compare Pss. i 1bc and 6b; xx 1a and 10b; lxvii 1a and 7a; xcvii 1 and 12;
ciii 1-2 and 20-22; cvi 1a and 48d; cxi 1a and 9c (cf. cvi supra and also cxvii;
cxlvi-cl); cxviii 1 and 29; cxxxv 1-2 and 19-21; cxxxvi 1 and 26; cxxxix 1-3 and
23-24; cxlv 1 and 26.

generally recognized as secondary, have been excised, we have ten strophes, three series of three strophes each (iii 1, 2-3b, 3c-5; 12b-13, 19-20, 21-22; 23-24, 25-26, iv 1-2) followed by a most impressive climax to the whole (iv 3-4). The strophic construction here is especially well marked by the characteristic opening and concluding formules. But what gives the poem its unity and determines its progress is the verb שׁוּב and the noun מְשֻׁבָה. Thus the first three strophes open with a dual reference: *shall return to her again* (ld) *and would you return to me* ? (lh), the second three open with the appeal, *Return, apostate Israel* (12b) שׁוּבָה מְשֻׁבָה and end, *Return, apostate sons, I will heal your apostasies* (22a) שׁוּבוּ בָנִים שׁוֹבָבִים אֶרְפָּה מְשׁוּבֹתֵיכֶם, while the third strophe of the third series reads, *If thou return, O Israel, oracle of Yahweh, return to me* (iv 1ab). The poem is fused into a whole by the repetition of other words also, above all perhaps by the iteration of Yahweh, Yahweh our God, Yahweh thy God, but others also. Psalm cxxxix is another excellent example where the verb ידע dominates the opening and closing lines. Psalm lxxxix is rich in many key-words: *steadfast love* (lxxxix 1a, 2a, 14b, 24a, 28a, 33a, 49a), *faithfulness* (1b, 2b, 5b, 8c, 33b, 49b. cf. 28b), *the throne of David* (4b, 14a, 29, 36, 44), *David my servant* (3b, 20a. cf. 35b, 49b and 50a), *anoint* (20a, 38b, 51b), *covenant* (3a, 28b, 34a, 39a), the reference to the primeval sea (9-10, 25).

Perhaps no poem in the whole Old Testament more rewards examination from the point of view of the art of repetition than the Song of Deborah [1]). Here the primitive characteristics of repetition, which arise from the depths of the soul deeply aroused and completely liberated in an outburst of uninhibited emotion, come to superb expression; yet it must be recognized that, despite its exultancy and passion, it is nevertheless a masterpiece of literary form and structure [2]). Other Hebrew poems achieve great elevation and

---

[1]) The literature on the subject is vast. See *inter alia* JULIAN MORGENSTERN, *JQR*, IX (1919), pp. 359-369; C. F. BURNEY, *The Book of Judges* (London, 1920), pp. 78 ff.; W. F. ALBRIGHT, *JPOS* I (1922), pp. 68-83; *BASOR.* No 62, pp. 26-31, esp. 30-31; DUNCAN BLACK MACDONALD, *The Hebrew Literary Genius* (Princeton, 1933), pp. 16-19; ERNST SELLIN, "Das Deboralied", *Festschrift Otto Procksch* (Leipzig, 1934), pp. 148-166; MARTIN BUBER, *The Prophetic Faith* (New York, 1949), pp. 8-12; GILLIS GERLEMAN, "The Song of Deborah in the Light of Stylistics", *Vetus Testamentum*, I, No. 3 (July, 1951), pp. 168-180.

[2]) Cf. DUNCAN BLACK MACDONALD, *ibid.*, p. 18: "This song may seem to us disjointed, but it was not, is not so in reality." In the light of the many Canaanite parallels in Ugaritic literature, however, the structure is now susceptible of

power through the art of repetition. The twenty-ninth psalm is all repetition, the seven-fold *qol Yahweh* as well as the impressive opening with its three-fold *habu la-Yahweh*, and its moving finale raising it to the level of sublimity. Equally impressive, though in quite a different manner, is Jeremiah's vision of chaos in iv 23-26.

The one word used above all others in biblical poetry is the divine name. As we should expect it appears most frequently at the beginning and end of poems, but in other cases it is repeated frequently throughout the whole of the composition. In such a short psalm as the sixth, Yahweh appears eight times; in the seventh the divine name occurs thirteen times but in a variety of usages: my God, thou righteous God, Yahweh Elyon, Yahweh my God (*bis*), Yahweh (four times), God (four times). This diversity of usage is characteristic of scores of Old Testament poems, especially of those literary types like the hymn and lament where the mood is impassioned and intense. The poet exhausts every resource of speech to address his God. As a true Israelite, he lives in a name relation to his God. Yahweh has communicated his name to his people, and he has given Israel her name. The interior psychic reality of dialog in which the egocentric boundaries are overcome are concretized in the name relationship [1]). So it is not surprising that in many poems *Yahweh* and *Israel* become not only the central key-words but also determine the structural patterns of the poem, as, for example, in the Song of Deborah [2]) and Ps. cxxxv [3]). This psychic rapport embodied in names is illustrated in Ps. cxxxii by the proper names, Yahweh and David.

In recent years we have come to recognize the place of repetitive parallelism. Attention has been drawn particularly to its presence in the tristich or tricola [4]). But this repetitive parallelism is much

---

better understanding. Note also MACDONALD, p. 19: "Hebrew poetry was all under impulse and the Hebrew poet could not rule and control his form." On the contrary, it is the genius of much biblical poetry that with all the spontaneity and excitement of mood which characterizes it the presence of form is perceptible. See especially ALBRIGHT's rendering in *JPOS* I, pp. 68-83, where the structural features of the poem are clearly evident.

[1]) JOHANNES PEDERSEN, *Israel, its Life and Culture*, I-II, pp. 244-259.
[2]) MARTIN BUBER, *The Prophetic Faith*, pp. 9-10.
[3]) Compare *inter alia* Ps. cxxx.
[4]) H. L. GINSBERG, "The Rebellion and Death of Ba'lu", *Orientalia* V (1936), pp. 161-198; W. F. ALBRIGHT, "The Psalm of Habakkuk", *Studies in Old Testament Prophecy*, edited by H. H. ROWLEY (Edinburgh, 1950), pp. 1-18; JOHN HASTINGS PATTON, *Canaanite Parallels in the Book of Psalms* (Baltimore, 1944), pp. 5-11.

more extensive and diverse. The profuse employment of this literary device and its great variety mark it as a major stylistic feature of biblical poetry. The following patterns are illustrative:

a b / a c	Exod. xv 3
a b c d / a b e f	xv 6
a b c / a b d	xv 6cd, cf. Ps. lxvii 3 (Heb. 4); lxvii 5 (Heb. 6)
	Ps. lxxvii 17; xcii 10; xiv 1
a b a / a c a	Ps. xlvii 6 (Heb. 7)
a b c / d e f	Ps. ciii 1. Cf. also Ps. cxxiv 1bc, 2ab.
a b c / g h i	
a b c	Ps. ciii 20a
a b d	21a
a b e	22a
a f b	22c
a b c d / a b e f	Ps. xcvi 1-2
a b c d / a b e f / a b e g	Ps. xcvi 7-8. Cf. xxix.
a b c d / a f c d / a g c d	Ps. cxxxv 19-20.

Of the many stylistic comments that emerge from a scrutiny of these and other examples, we confine ourselves to these two: (1) the members of the series tend to focus upon the final member, (2) often the member which follows the series and breaks the repetitive sequence gives point and force to the whole series. The most obvious example, of course, is the last psalm, where the effect is almost overwhelming in its climax, "Let everything that has breath praise Yahweh!"

We turn now to the place of repetition in the strophic structure of Hebrew poetry. There are a number of examples where successive strophes begin with the same emphatic construction such as the imperative in Ps. xxxvii 1, 3, 5, 7, 8: *fret, trust, commit, betill, refrain* or the same key-word is repeated:

> Thy steadfast love, O Yahweh, extends to the heavens   xxxvi 5a
> How precious is thy steadfast love, O God   7a
> O continue thy steadfast love to those who know thee   10a

Or strophes may end in similar fashion as we have seen in the refrains, but it must also be recognized that the same key-words sometimes appear at the close of successive strophes. Again, beginning and end sometimes show correspondence [1]). Very interesting are the

---

[1]) E.g. Gen. xlix 22a and 26d; Pss. lxvi 2 and 4bc; cxxxiv 1a, 2b; Amos v 18 and 20; viii 9a and 10 f.; ix 5 and 6.

108   J. MUILENBURG

numerous instances where a new strophe takes up the major key-word
of the previous strophe, as, for example, when the first line repeats
the key-word of the last line before. Note the following [1]):

> Our feet have been standing
>   within your gates, O Jerusalem!
> Jerusalem, built as a city ...   Ps. cxxii 2b and 3a
> Blessed are those who dwell in thy house
> Blessed are the men whose strength is in thee.   Ps. lxxxiv 4a, 5a.

We have a number of cases where strophes are connected with the
presence of a single key-word or expression in successive or nearly
successive strophes: *ḥesed* "steadfast love" (xxxvi 5-6, 7-9, 10-12) or
rash'a or *r'sha'im* "the wicked" (xxxvii 10-11, 12-13, 14-15, 16-17, 20,
21-22, 32-33, 35-36, 39-40). But the most impressive and interesting
of all is the repetition of single words or phrases within the strophe,
usually three times in which the third member characteristically
receives the stress, thus preserving the emphasis and intensity so
characteristic of repetition in its primitive forms [2]). The most familiar
example is Ps. cxxi 7-8:

> Yahweh will keep you from all evil;
>   he will keep your life.
> Yahweh will keep your going out and your coming in
>   from now and forevermore.

A stylistically superior example is Ps. cxxxix 11-12:

> If I say, "Let only darkness cover me
>   and light about me be night,"
> Even darkness is not too dark to thee,
>   the night is light like the day,
>   as the darkness, so the light.

One more example notable for its rhetorical felicity:

> O mighty mountain (lit. "mountain of God"), O mount Bashan!
>   O many-peaked mountain, O mount of Bashan!
> Why, O many-peaked mountain, do you envy
>   the mountain God desired for his abode,
>   yea, where Yahweh will dwell forever?   Ps. lxviii 15-16,
>   Heb. 16-17)

---

[1]) See also Pss. cxxviii 4, 5; cxxxii 10, 11; Isa. xliv 28d and xlv 1a.

[2]) Gen xlix 22-26 (the blessing of Joseph, a model of Hebrew repetitive style);
Is. xli 41-43; xlii 1-4 (note the strong emphasis on *mishpat*); lx 1-3 (three-fold
repetition of "dawn" and "light" noun and verb forms); 4-5, 19-20 ("your light,
your everlasting light, your everlasting light" cf. lx 1-3); Zeph. i 7, 14-16 (*yom*
repeated ten times); Pss. lxviii 1-3 (Heb. 2-4), 19-21 (Heb. 20-22); lxxxii 1-4;
cxxiii 1-2; cxxxiv; cxxxv 19-21.

Perhaps a more convincing approach to an examination and evaluation of the repetitive style in ancient Hebrew rhetoric would be to subject the individual poems to analysis. Such an undertaking would reveal the importance of this literary method not only for an evaluation of the Hebrew temperament and literary manner but also for hermeneutics. The words must be allowed to have their own way with the reader. The supreme exemplar of the Hebrew repetitive style is Second Isaiah, and nowhere is the sheer artistry of this style exhibited more happily and impressively than in his great poems. The first two poems (xl 1-11 and xl 12-31) are masterpieces of iterative utterance [1]). The third poem, too, achieves the same high level, but in a somewhat different fashion. The finale of the poem reads: למשפט נקרבה יחדו. Then Yahweh presents the content of his *rib* with the nations (vss. 2-4). The nations *fear* and *tremble*; each man *helps* his neighbor in making an image, and says to his neighbor, "Be strong" (חֲזַק) or, as usually rendered, "take courage". So the crattsman *encourages* (וַיְחַזֵּק) the goldsmith, and they *fasten* (וַיְחַזְּקֵהוּ) it with nails so that it cannot be moved. Thus the three verbs which are given great stress are ירא, חזק, עזר. Then comes the finale to the first triad of strophes, and it is precisely these three verbs which receive the burden of the poet's thought:

> But thou, Israel, my servant,
>> Jacob, whom I have chosen,
>> offspring of Abraham, my friend;
> whom I took (הֶחֱזַקְתִּיךָ) from the ends of the earth,
>> and called from its remote regions;
>> to whom I said, "You are my servant,

---

[1]) SIGMUND MOWINCKEL ("*Die Komposition des deuterojesanischen Buches*", *ZAW* 49 [1931], pp. 87-112, 242-260) views the present ordering of the book as the work of the compiler of the poems. The *Stichworte* are understood by him to provide the clue for the ordering. "Der Sammler kann selbstverständlich nach einem gewissen Plan gearbeitet und gewisse Gesichtspunkte für die Ordnung der Einzelstücke gehabt haben. — Es soll daher der Versuch gemacht werden, das Sammlungs- oder vielleicht besser: Anreihungsprinzip des Sammlers aufzuzeigen." The difficulty with this view of an external ordering is that it does not recognize the genuine lines of continuity which persist from poem to poem nor the ordered structure of the whole. Moreover, the reduction of the poems to a collection of small pieces or fragments ignores the strophic structure of the poems and the relation of key-words to the literary structure. To be sure, these key-words sometimes pass beyond the limits of the individual poems, but in each case it is apparent that they are employed as a transitional device explicable only on the assumption that it is the work of the original writer and not the compiler.

110   J. MUILENBURG

> I have chosen you and not cast you off";
> fear not (אַל תִּירָא), for I am with you,
>
> be not dismayed, for I am your God;
> I will strengthen you, I will help you (עֲזַרְתִּיךָ),
>
> I will uphold you with my victorious right hand.   xli 8-10.

The second triad of strophes (vss. 11-13, 14-16, 17-20) develops these three verbs, by repetition, by solemn and climactic divine self-asseveration[1]), by a lyrical song (vss. 17-20), vivid imagery (e.g. the threshing sledge), and by various emphatic particles. But then, quite remarkably, the trial scene is repeated, repeated with greater urgency and intensity, but the issue is, of course, precisely the same, i.e., the nations' response to Yahweh's historical *rib*, and the outcome is the same. It is to be noted that the sequence of the first two triads is exactly the same, and this is also true of the third except that the chapter ends with the judgment of the nations in the second member of the third division of the poem. But is this likely? If we assume this to be the case, the structure is destroyed, for we naturally expect a third strophe to compare with the other triads (and there are other poems in the Old Testament of three triads of three strophes each!). Moreover, content also demands a reference to the Servant of the Lord as in the climax of vss. 8-11.

Again, a purely literary examination of xlii 1-4 reveals that it has essentially the same style as xli 8-10, but more important it brings the whole motif of judgment, perfectly stated in the opening strophe, to a triumphant culmination. It opens with the climactic *hen* (cf. 24a and 29a), then continues, line upon inevitable line, to describe the judgment in language which is now recognized as coming from the court of law[2]). Observe how every climax of the strophe falls on *mishpat*, thus the end links with the beginning to make of the poem the magnificently ordered composition that it is:

---

[1]) Cf. e.g. vs. 13.   כי אני יהוה אלהיך מחזיק ימינך
האמר לך אל־תירא אני עזרתיך

[2]) JOACHIM BEGRICH, *Studien zu Deuterojesaja*, pp. 134-137; SIDNEY SMITH, *Isaiah Chapters XL-LV*, pp. 54-57, 164 and note 25-32; JOH. LINDBLOM, *The Servant Songs in Deutero-Isaiah* (Lund, 1951), pp. 14-18. See also LUDWIG KÖHLER, *Die hebräische Rechtsgemeinde*. Jahresbericht der Universität Zurich, 1930/1931. Compare also DUHM's words in his commentary (1922), p. 312 where he points out that *mishpat* like the Arabic *din* is the judicial authority and exercise of justice of the people of God, the sum of the beneficent institutions of the people of Yahweh. *Mishpat*, he says, is related to the *mishpatim* of Deut. xxi as *ha-torah* is to *torah*.

HEBREW RHETORIC: REPETITION AND STYLE 111

Behold, my servant, whom I uphold,
  my chosen, in whom I delight,
I have put my spirit upon him,
  he will bring forth *mishpat* to the nations.
He will not cry or lift his voice,
  or make it heard in the street;
A bruised reed he will not break,
  and a dimly burning wick he will not quench;
  he will faithfully bring forth *mishpat*.
He will not fail or be discouraged
  till he has established *mishpat* in the earth;
  and the coastlands wait for his law.

The significance and function of xlii 1-4 thus become crucial. They become even more crucial when it is understood, as it usually is not, that by every canon of literary form xlii 5 must begin a new poem. The usual arguments for the excision of the so-called Servant song are familiar and well worn, but recent scholarly inquiry has made it more and more likely that all the Servant songs are related to their contexts. Excision raises more difficulties than it solves as the history of Second Isaiah study makes eloquently clear. The only plausible solution, then, on the basis of literary form, in which the repetitive style has been of major service, is that xlii 1-4 belongs inextricably with the whole of chapter xli. It need only be added that when this is done, the major continuity of the poems begins to appear in fresh light and the prophet achieves a stature commensurate with his stature as Israel's profoundest theologian and supreme master in the art of literary composition.

THE LINGUISTIC AND RHETORICAL USAGES OF THE PARTICLE כי IN THE OLD TESTAMENT

JAMES MUILENBURG

Union Theological Seminary, New York, N. Y.

AMONG the Hebrew particles there is one group that plays a distinctive lexical and rhetorical role.[1] They are the signals and sign-posts of language, markers on the way of the sentence or poem or narrative, guides to the progress of words, arrows directing what is being spoken to its destination. They serve to indicate how words are disposed into the fabric or texture of speech, how the literary types are fashioned into connected wholes. They confirm or establish or stress what is being said, or underline and give notice to what is about to be said, or mark the goal or climax of what has been said. They are by no means static linguistic entities, morphemes to be scrutinized independently of their contexts, but are rather agents of movement. The intended meaning becomes alive and dynamic in the ways that the particles are employed. Whether negations, affirmations, interrogatives, interjections, or instruments of connection, they perform their work in many different ways and wear many guises. Their meaning is often contingent upon the particular function they seek to serve, so that the same word may be rendered quite differently in the same context. Without an understanding of their precise function not only are the nuances of a text often obscured, but the articulation and accents of the thought are also lost to view. If we are to appreciate this group of particles, then, it is essential that we discern their function in living speech; we must be sensitive to their sounds in oral discourse, think of them at times as "vocal gestures," and recognize what they are designed to do. It is possible that they were originally ejaculations or cries or exclamations, calling the hearer to attention, bidding him heed, giving him notice or warning, or stirring him to action.[2] Their phonetic quality suggests as much, and their position

---

[1] We are thinking here of such words as the following: אהה, אוי, אז, אח, איכה, אך,
.אכן, הוי, הלא, הנה, הנם, כה, כי, כן, לכן, על־כן

[2] See N. H. Tur-Sinai, "The Origin of Language" in *Language: an Enquiry into its Meaning and Function*, edited by Ruth Nanda Anshen (1957), p. 44:

> Language arose as an exclamation, an emotional cry, at first not voluntary, but reflex, a reaction to external influence. But this reflex cry is not language

in many different kinds of predications would seem to confirm some such view. Be that as it may, it is clear that a comprehension of their various usages is necessary if we are to appreciate the nature of Hebrew rhetoric in the many different forms which we encounter in the Old Testament.

Perhaps the most notable illustration of the importance of the Hebrew particle is the morpheme כִּי. It is not only one of the words most frequently employed in the Old Testament, but also one with the widest and most varied range of nuance and meaning. Pedersen calls it the most comprehensive of all Hebrew particles.[3] All the lexicons point to its original demonstrative character. It is designed to give emphasis, to give force to a statement.[4] Brockelmann speaks of its original usage as a demonstrative interjection,[5] and Pedersen similarly.[6] This is confirmed by the fact that it frequently falls outside the pattern of Hebrew meter; it is thus given special stress by standing metrically isolated while still giving force to the colon which follows.[7] But כִּי is more than a demonstrative; it is also a deictic word; that is, it points or shows the way forward. "It may mean that something is now coming to which we must pay attention."[8] Since it is the destiny of words to lose their original dynamic associations and connotations — *libelli sua fata habent!* — it is not surprising that כִּי should be diluted to the more colorless אֲשֶׁר or completely omitted from contexts which would originally have made much of it (e. g., in introducing direct

---

and is not sufficient to explain linguistic expression except in a small proportion of language phenomena, viz., interjections such as "oh, ah, ha" and onomatopoea, as "crow, cuckoo, to buzz, twitter," and the like. There is no recognizable way from it to the other facts of language. And this is just the problem facing us: "How did the emotional cry engender a fully developed idiom, capable of expressing the most varied concrete and abstract ideas?"

Compare especially p. 50: "Prior to names and to any concrete term, language thus had short demonstrative words serving to point out and refer to the simplest relations: here and there, above and below, flat, pointed, and the like."

[3] Johannes Pedersen, *Israel: Its Life and Culture I–II* (1926), p. 118. A rough estimate of the number of times the word appears in the Old Testament is about 4.500.

[4] Gesenius-Buhl (17th ed.), Brown-Driver-Briggs, Köhler-Baumgartner *inter alia*.

[5] *Grundriss der vergleichenden Grammatik der semitischen Sprache*, II Band *Syntax* (1913), p. 111: "Im Hebr. können einzelne Wörter im Sätze auch durch die demonstrative Interjection כִּי hervorgehoben werden …"

[6] *Israel: Its Life and Culture I–II*, p. 118.

[7] T. H. Robinson, "Anacrusis in Hebrew Poetry," *Werden und Wesen des alten Testaments*, edited by Paul Volz, Friedrich Stummer, and Johannes Hempel (1936), pp. 37–40.

[8] Pedersen, *ibid.*, p. 118.

discourse or in the divine self-asseverations). We need not enter at this point into its usages in the cognate tongues; it is sufficient to mention its presence in Akkadian, Ugaritic, Moabite, Egyptian Aramaic, and its relation to כ, כה and the Aramaic דך. That the word has a long pre-history is suggested by the fact that in our earliest Hebrew poems it already conforms to a fixed style, as in the Song of Lamech:

עדה וצלה   שמען קולי
נשי למך   האזנה אמרתי
כי איש הרגתי לפצעי   וילד לחברתי
כי שבעתים יקם־קין   ולמך שבעים ושבעה

(Gen. 4:23–24)

Our intent in the following discussion is (1) to summarize the elemental usages of כי in emphatic word-contexts, (2) to examine its function in predications of greater extent (cola and sentences), (3) to explore the areas where it introduces motivations of various kinds, and, above all, (4) to indicate how the originally *demonstrative* or *emphatic* meaning of the word combines with its *deictic* character to influence the style and composition of various literary types and forms.

1. כי with על כן to express emphatic cause or result:[9]

   ... and Gideon said, Alas, O Lord Yahweh, כי על כן I have seen the angel of Yahweh face to face.   (Judg. 6:22)

   ... while I fetch a morsel of bread, that you may refresh yourselves, and after that you may pass on, כי על כן you have come to your servant.   (Gen. 18:5). So similarly in formulae of courtesy.

2. כי with הנה to give dramatic and climactic force to the oracle:[10]

   כי־הנה, Yahweh commands,
   And the great house shall be smitten into fragments,
   And the little house into bits   (Amos 6:11)

   כי הנני, will raise up against you a nation,
   O house of Israel, says Yahweh.   (Amos 6:14)

   כי הנה the Lord, Yahweh of hosts,
   Is taking away from Jerusalem and from Judah
   Stay and staff ...   (Isa. 3:1)

---

[9] Here and in the citations *infra* no attempt is made at completeness; the passages may be said to be representative. Gen. 19:8; 33:10; 38:26; Num. 10:31; Jer. 29:28. In all of these the demonstrative and deictic features of כי are plain.
[10] Isa. 3:1; 26:21; 65:17; 66:15; Ps. 11:2; Amos 4:13; Jer. 1:15; Mic. 1:3; Hab. 1:6.

3. כי with עתה, again introducing a climactic affirmation or giving force to the predication, as the following superbly illustrates:[11]

כי לולא התמהמהנו כי־עתה שבנו זה פעמים   (Gen. 43:10)

כי־עתה I shall lie in the earth;
Thou wilt seek me, but I shall not be.   (Job 7:21)

4. אמנם כי. The asseverative force of כי is accentuated by the emphasis of the adverb from the root אמן.[12] Note the association of other particles in the same context:

אמנם ידעתי כי־כן
But how can a man be just before God?   (Job 9:2)

אמנם כי you are the people
And wisdom will die with you.   (Job 12:2)

ועתה כי אמנם כי אם גאל אנכי
וגם יש a kinsman nearer than I.   (Ruth 3:12)

5. יען כי may introduce the invective followed by the threat with its characteristic emphatic לכן[13]

יען כי this people draw near with their mouth
And honor me with their lips . . .
Therefore, behold, I will again do marvelous things with this people . . .   (Isa. 29:13, 14)

6. עקב כי[14]

And now the sword shall never depart from your house;
עקב כי you have despised me . . .   (II Sam. 12:10)

7. על כי־[15]

הלא על כי־אין אלהי בקרבי מצאוני הרעות האלה   (Deut. 31:17b)

[11] Gen. 22:12; 26:22; 29:32c; 31:42; 43:10; Exod. 9:15; Num. 22:13; Isa. 49:19cd; Job 3:13; 4:5; 8:6; 13:19. Further stylistic usages are encountered in the words of the covenant mediator or of the cult prophet, such as "For now I know," and especially in the priestly oracles of salvation.
[12] Job 36:4; also I Kings 8:27; II Chron. 6:18.
[13] Isa. 3:16; 7:5; 8:6. More frequently of course with אשר.
[14] Amos 4:12. With אשר in Gen. 22:19; 26:5, etc.
[15] Compare the use of על without the כי in the invectives of Amos 1:3–2:16, also Ps. 139:14.

8. כי גם[16]

כי גם I walk in the valley of deep gloom,
    I will fear no evil.   (Ps. 23:4)

9. כי אף[17]

כי אף God say you must not eat of any tree of the garden?
                                            (Gen. 3:1)

10. כי אך. The opening particle, the imperative, the infinitive absolute, and the whole tenor and context suggests the emphasis, and the כי אך re-enforces it.

Now then, hearken to their voice; כי אך, you shall solemnly warn them, and show them the ways of the king who shall reign over them.   (I Sam. 8:9; cf. II Kings 5:7)

11. The word is often used adversatively to denote a striking contrast:[18]

כי my eyes are toward thee, O Yahweh God.   (Ps. 141:8a)

12. כי לולי[19]

ואולם as Yahweh, the God of Israel lives, who has restrained me from hurting you כי לולי | you had made haste and come to meet me truly (כי אם) by morning there had not been left to Nabal as much as one male.   (I Sam. 25:34)

13. כי־אז[20]

כי | ידעתי היום כי לא Absalom were alive and all of us were dead today, כי־אז you would be pleased.   (II Sam. 19:7)

An excellent example of the diverse use of כי in the same verse is II Sam. 2:27

And Joab said, "As God lives כי לולא you had not spoken, כי אז the men would have given up the pursuit of their brethren in the morning."

---

[16] Isa. 1:15; Hos. 9:16. כי גם appears more frequently: Num. 22:23; I Sam. 22:17; Isa. 7:13; 26:12; 66:8; Jer. 6:11; 14:5, 18; 23:11; 46:21, etc.

[17] I Kings 8:27; Prov. 15:11.

[18] I Chron. 29:14; Isa. 8:23; 28:28. Most frequently after the negative. See 14 infra.

[19] כי לולא: Cf. Gen. 31:42; 43:10; II Sam. 2:27; also II Sam. 19:7; Num. 22:29.

[20] Job 11:14 f.; 22:23–26.

14. Emphatic negative, where the כי accentuates the negative, לא כי No, but:[21]

> And he said, "כי לא as the commander of the army of Yahweh I have now come." (Josh. 5:14)

Compare Lam. 3:22 for similar use of כי לא־, meaning *never*:

> The steadfast love of Yahweh כי לא ceases (with emendation. Cf. RSV).

> כי לא his mercies come to an end.

15. כי אם | performs various functions according to the context. Note how the כי fortifies the conditional in I Sam. 20:9. Its deictic function is equally notable:

> כי | אם I knew that it was determined by my father כי evil should come upon you, would I not tell you. (Cf. also Josh. 23:12)

Or the כי may accentuate the concessive as in Lam. 3:31 f.

> כי the Lord will not cast off for ever,
> כי אם he cause grief, he will have compassion.

The nuance of כי אם in Exod. 22:22, succeeding the initial אם, and the three infinitive absolutes point to the emphatic character of the casuistic law:

> אם־ענה תענה אתו כי אם־צעק יצעק אלי שמע אשמע צעקתו

More interesting is the way in which it introduces the covenant formulation:[22]

> כי אם־ you listen attentively to my voice and do all that I say, then I will be an enemy to your adversaries. (Exod. 23:22)

Observe the impressive context which precedes vv. 20 f.

---

[21] Gen. 17:15; 18:15; 42:12; 45:8; Deut. 13:9 f.; II Sam. 16:18; I Kings 2:20; 3:22 f.; Isa. 36:19; Job 39:27. Cf. also the causal כי after negatives: Gen. 3:4-5; 24:34; Isa. 7:7 f.

[22] Cf. J. Muilenburg, "The Form and Structure of the Covenantal Formulations," *Vetus Testamentum*, IX (1959), pp. 347-65. That we are dealing here with fixed stylistic forms is confirmed not only by the presence of the conditionals in covenantal context (Exod. 19:3b-8; Josh. 24; I Sam. 12; Jer. 7:1-15, etc.), but also by the place in which they appear at the close of the treaties of ancient Near Eastern Texts and at the conclusion of the great legal collections.

An excellent example of the function of כי אם is seen in Prov. 2:1–6. The particle relates itself to the preceding predication by accentuating the conditional אם (3a) and then presses the conditional forward to the אם- which follows (4a). All of the protases, dominated by the three-fold conditional כי or כי אם, are designed to focus upon the emphatic particle אז (5a), which reaches its culmination in the characteristic motivation, introduced by the causal כי- (6a):

> My son, אם- you received my words
>> And treasure up my commandments with you,
> Making your ear attentive to wisdom
>> And inclining your heart to understanding;
>
> כי אם you cry out for insight
>> And raise your voice for understanding,
> אם- you seek it like silver
>> And search for it as for hidden treasures;
>
> אז you will understand the fear of Yahweh
>> And find the knowledge of God.
> כי- Yahweh gives wisdom;
>> And from his mouth come wisdom and understanding.
>
> . . . .
>
> Then (אז) you will understand righteousness and justice
>> And equity and every good path;
> כי- wisdom will come into your heart,
>> And knowledge will be pleasant to your soul.
>
>> (Prov. 2:1–10)

Observe also those contexts where כי אם appears after negative clauses with the meaning of *except* or *unless* in emphatic contexts:[23]

> כי as the rain and the snow come down from heaven,
>> And return not thither כי אם- water the earth,
> Making it bring forth and sprout,
>> Giving seed to the sower and bread to the eater,

---

[23] Gen. 32:27; Ruth 3:18. Compare also those passages where it follows a noun in the sense of *nothing but* (Gen. 28:17; Isa. 42:19; Mic. 6:8), also where it is a sharp antithesis to a prohibition or negative clause, as in I Sam. 8:19: "Nay, but!"; Ps. 1:2. For the usage of אפס כי, see Num. 13:28; Deut. 15:4; Judg. 4:9; Amos 9:8. See Arno Kropat, "Die Syntax des Autors der Chronik verglichen mit der seiner Quellen." *Beihefte zur Zeitschrift für die alttestamentliche Wissenschaft*, XVI (1909), p. 31. Also T. J. Meek, "I Kings 20:1–10," *JBL*, LXXVIII (1929), pp. 73–75, where it is demonstrated that כי אם cannot be rendered adversatively in vs. 6 (contra RSV), but simply "for if."

So shall my word be that goes forth from my mouth;
  It shall not return to me empty,
כי אם‎ it shall accomplish that which I purpose,
  And prosper in the thing for which I sent it.
                                        (Isa. 55:10–11)

Finally, כי אם‎ appears as an emphatic and climactic contrast
to a preceding affirmation with the meaning of *nevertheless*:

כי אם‎ Kain shall be wasted.   (Num. 24:22)

The foregoing discussion has amply demonstrated the intimate
association of the particle כי‎ with other emphatic particles, has confirmed our estimate of the diversity of its function in a vast variety
of rhetorical and literary contexts, has established its importance as
an instrument of stress or emphasis, and has illuminated the ways in
which it relates itself to its rhetorical contexts, whether by bringing
the predication to a focus or by directing it forward to its goal or by
indicating the movement of the particular literary unit. We shall now
turn to some of its stylistic usages in relation, not to individual
particles but clauses, cola, or complete literary forms.

1. First of all we may consider instances where the כי‎ clause is
equivalent to the demonstrative pronoun, where the clause "covers"
the demonstrative or is synonymous with it:[24]

By this I know כי‎ thou art pleased with me,
  כי‎ my enemy has not triumphed over me.   (Ps. 41:12)

These things I remember
  As I pour out my soul:
כי‎ I went with the throng,
  And led them in procession to the house of God,
With glad shouts and songs of thanksgiving,
  A multitude keeping festival.   (Ps. 42:5)

2. Similarly the instances where the כי‎ clause is equal to the
interrogative pronoun, *what, who*, etc.:[25]

What is my strength, כי‎ I should wait?
  And what is my end, כי‎ I should be patient?   (Job 6:11)

---

[24] Ps. 56:10: "This I know כי‎ God is for me." Job 13:16. Cf. Exod. 3:12.
[25] For the כי‎ clause with מה‎, Gen. 20:9 f.; 31:36; I Sam. 20:1; 29:8; I Kings 11:22;
Job 21:15; Isa. 22:1, 16; Mal. 3:14. Cf. Job 3:12; 6:11; 7:12, 17; 15:12–14. For its
association with מי‎, Judg. 9:28; I Chron. 29:14; Isa. 36:5; II Sam. 7:18, etc.

What is man כי־ thou art mindful of him,
And the son of man כי thou dost care for him.   (Ps. 8:5)

Who am I כי I should go to Pharaoh, and כי bring the sons of Israel out of Egypt.   (Exod. 3:11)

Who am I, O Yahweh God, and what is my house, כי Thou hast brought me thus far.   (I Chron. 17:16)

3. Notable are the instances where the כי is used emphatically at the end of a clause, illustrated also in the Akkadian and Ugaritic texts. Here it often has the meaning of *how*.[26] The original demonstrative meaning is especially clear.

And God saw כי־ good it was.   (Gen. 1:12b, 18b, 25b)

. . . the sons of God saw the daughters of men כי fair they were . . .   (Gen. 6:2)

All nations surrounded me;
In the name of Yahweh כי I cut them off.   (Ps. 118:10)

4. The particle is not infrequently employed with ה interrogative הכי:[27]

And David said "(יש־עוד) הכי any one left of the house of Saul, that I may show him kindness for Jonathan's sake?"
                (II Sam. 9:1)

And Esau said, "הכי (RSV "is he not rightly") called Jacob?"
                (Gen. 27:36)

The rhetorical effect of הכי is best illustrated by Job 6:22 f. where it introduces a whole series of emphatic questions:

[26] Gen. 12:14; 18:20; Job 22:12 ("how lofty they are"); Deut. 31:29; Jer. 2:19; Lam. 3:22. H. L. Ginsberg, "Notes on 'The Birth of the Gracious and Beautiful Gods,'" *JRAS* (1935), p. 56: "In *kypt*, *k* represents the כי i. 1 of the Hebrew lexica, i. e., a particle with purely demonstrative or emphatic force; cf. *k(tsh)*, II, AB 2, 29, *ktl'akn*, *ibid.*, 4–5, 104; *kysh*, *ibid.*, 7, 53. Note that as a rule a verb which is strengthened by this sort of *k* generally stands at the end of its clause in the language of Ugarit; and this is always the case in the O. T.: Gen. 18, 20; Ps. 49:16; 118:10 f. (Thr. 3:22)." Robert Gordis, "The Asseverative Kaph in Ugaritic and Hebrew," *JAOS* 63 (1943), pp. 176–78; W. F. Albright, "The Refrain 'And God Saw KI TOBH' in Genesis," *Mélanges bibliques redigés en l'honneur de André Robert*, pp. 22–26. See especially Gesenius-Buhl's lexicon, *ad loc.* for an excellent statement of the demonstrative force of the כי in such contexts.
[27] Gen. 29:15; II Sam. 23:19; Job 6:22. For negative הלוא כי־ cf. I Sam. 10:1. Cf. I Sam. 24:20; Isa. 36:19.

הכי־אמרתי, "Make me a gift?"
   Or, "From your wealth offer a bribe for me?"
Or, "Deliver me from the adversary's hand?"
   Or, "Ransom me from the hand of oppressors?"

5. Frequently, too, it introduces a direct quotation, tantamount to *thus* or *this* or *here* or *as follows*:[28]

> And he said כי I will be with you. . . .   (Exod. 3:12)

> He said כי these seven ewe lambs you will take from my hand, that you may be witness for me כי I have dug this well.
>   (Gen. 21:30)

6. Not dissimilar are the numerous cases where כי introduces the object clause, notably, of course, after verbs of seeing, hearing, believing, remembering, forgetting, but *especially* after *knowing* where the rhetorical context is noteworthy, as in the cultic asseverations of the priest or cultic prophet or the king in the liturgies of the Psalter.[29]

> But Yahweh said to Moses, "Put out your hand, and take it by the tail, . . . כי־ they may believe that Yahweh, the God of their fathers, the God of Abraham, the God of Isaac, and the God of Jacob, has appeared to you."   (Exod. 4:4 f.)

> Now I know כי Yahweh will help his anointed.   (Ps. 20:7)

7. It is only to be expected that the particle should precede the oracular formula כה אמר יהוה, and, of course, in climactic contexts.[30]

> כי thus says the Lord Yahweh.   (Amos 5:3a)

> כי thus says Yahweh to the house of Israel.   (Amos 5:4a)

---

[28] It is not without significance that כי is often translated asseveratively as *surely* or *truly* in such contexts. See, e. g., Gen. 29:33; Exod. 4:25; Josh. 2:24; Judg. 6:16; I Sam. 2:16; 10:19. In many cases the particle is related with other emphatic particles or introduces a solemn affirmation or negation.

[29] Gen. 1:10c; 6:6; Isa. 14:29 and especially Exod. 6:7; 7:5, 17; 8:11, 22; 9:14, 29. 30; 10:2; Deut. 4:35, 39; 7:9; 31:21, 27, 29; Pss. 4:4; 41:12; 46:11; 51:5; 56:10; 59:14; 83:19; 119:75; Isa. 49:25; 52:3; Ezek. 2:5; 5:13; 6:7, 10, 13, 14; 7:4, 9, 27; 11:10, 12; 12:15, 16, 20. An examination of these and many similar contexts substantiates the view that we are dealing with conventional cultic speech. A survey of the verb זכר with כי would prove fruitful.

[30] Isa. 18:4; 21:16; 57:15; Jer. 4:3, 27; 10:18; 16:3, 5; 20:4; 22:6, 11 etc. etc. The oracular introduction with כי is frequent in Jeremiah, but the shorter text represented by the LXX sometimes omits it. In Second Isaiah the particle is given special force because of the prophet's tendency to expand it with impressive theologoumena.

8. Consistent with the foregoing is the presence of the particle before emphatic statements of many kinds. Illustrative are II Sam. 14:14 and Num. 23:23. Often these are rendered by the asseverative *surely*, etc., but by no means always. See the discussion of motivations below.

9. We have observed some of the usages of כי אם, but often כי is used alone as a conditional, as we shall have occasion to see in the casuistic laws. Here again we witness the emphatic or demonstrative and the deictic functions of the word. It can be employed as an introduction to the protasis or to the apodosis.[31]

> כי־גם you make many prayers,
>   I will not listen.   (Isa. 1:15b)

> כי־ you pass through the waters, I will be with you;
>   כי you walk through fire, you shall not be burned.
>
>   (Isa. 43:2)

ופרשת אליו כפיך:	אם־אתה הכינות לבך
ואל־תשכן באהליך עולה:	אם־און בידך הרחיקהו
והיית מצק ולא תירא:	כי־אז ‖ תשא פניך ממום
כמים עברו תזכר:	כי־אתה עמל תשכח

                                       (Job 11:13–16)

10. Very characteristic, of course is the causal כי, which is particularly noteworthy for the role it plays in the many kinds of motivations of various literary forms.[32]

> כי God knows כי in the day you eat of it your eyes will be opened, and you will be like God, knowing good and evil.
>
>   (Gen. 3:5)

> כי you have done this, cursed are you among all animals.
>
>   (Gen. 3:14)

---

[31] Exod. 21:2; Deut. 6:25; II Sam. 2:27; Job 22:23 ff.; Prov. 2:3 ff. For a detailed and comprehensive treatment of conditional clauses in the Old Testament, see Paul Friedrich, *Die hebräischen Conditionalsätze*, (Königsberg, 1884), which is particularly illuminating for its examination of related particles and other parts of speech and larger predications.

[32] II Sam. 12:10; I Kings 13:21b; 21:29; Isa. 7:5; 15:1, etc. See the discussion of motivations below. For some interesting comments upon causal כי, see Therese Frankfort, "Le-כִּי de Joel 1:12," *Vetus Testamentum* X (1960), pp. 445–48 and compare A. S. Kapelrud, *Joel Studies* (1948), pp. 23–44. The frequency of the causal particle in Joel is worth observing.

11. Related to the conditional and causal usages is the temporal כי at the beginning of a clause or sentence:[33]

> כי Israel was a child, I loved him,
>   And out of Egypt I called my son.   (Hos. 11:1)

> כי you till the ground, it shall no longer yield to you its strength;
> you shall be a fugitive and a wanderer on the earth.
>
>   (Gen. 4:12)

12. A vivid comparison or similitude is sometimes introduced by כי:[34]

> כי־ as the heavens are higher than the earth,
>   So are My ways than your ways
>   And My thoughts than your thoughts.
> כי as the rain and the snow come down from heaven,
>   And return not thither but water the earth,
> Making it bring forth and sprout,
>   Giving seed to the sower and bread to the eater,
> So shall My word be that goes forth from my mouth.
>
>   (Isa. 55:9–11a)

13. More impressive is the way the particle concludes a parable and interprets its meaning:[35]

> כי the vineyard of Yahweh of hosts
>   Is the house of Israel,
> And the men of Judah
>   Are his pleasant planting.   (Isa. 5:7–a–d)

14. Not infrequent is the use of כי as an introduction to a dramatic scene:[36]

> כי הנה, he who forms the mountains, and creates the wind,
>   And declares to man what is his thought;
> Who makes the morning darkness,
>   And treads on the heights of the earth —
> Yahweh, the God of hosts, is His name!   (Amos 4:13)

---

[33] Gen. 6:1; Num. 33:51; Job 7:13; Ps. 32:3; Isa. 1:12; 8:19. Cf. Job 11:14 f.

[34] Isa. 11:9cd; 24:13; 25:4 f.; 61:11; 62:5; 65:22cd; 66:22; Jer. 5:26 f.; Hos. 5:14; Obad. 16.

[35] Isa. 51:3; 52:2 f.; 54:3; 55:9.

[36] Isa. 3:1 ff.; 9:4, 5, 6; 16:8; 24:13; 25:4; 34:5 f.; Jer. 4:15, 19ef; Joel 1:6 ff.; 2:11; Amos 6:11, 14; Mic. 1:3; Obad. 16.

15. Most characteristic and moving is the introduction to climactic divine self-asseverations:[37]

> כי I Yahweh your God am a jealous God . . .   (Exod. 20:5b)

> כי I am Yahweh your God,
>> The Holy One of Israel, your Savior.   (Isa. 43:3ab)

16. Concessive clauses are introduced by כי:[37a]

> כי they fast, I will not hear their cry וכי they offer burnt offering and cereal offering, I will not accept them; כי (*adversative*), I will consume them by the sword, by famine, and by pestilence.   (Jer. 14:12)

17. Nothing is more common than the appearance of the particle after an urgent imperative[38] in numerous literary contexts: judgment, warning, expostulation, exhortation, prayer, lament, hymn, promise, invitation, thanksgiving, the herald's call or message (*Botenspruch*), etc., etc. For the assurance or promise see 21 *infra*.

> Arise, O Yahweh!
>> Deliver me, O my God!
> כי־ thou dost smite all my enemies on the cheek.   (Ps. 3:8)

18. Similarly the particle occurs after an urgent question:[39]

מבטן יצאתי ואגוע:	למה לא מרחם אמות
ומה־שדים כי אינק:	מדוע קדמוני ברכים
ישנתי אז | ינוח לי:	כי־עתה שכבתי ואשקוט

                                              (Job 3:11–13)

19. In the same category is the employment of כי after exclamations, most notably after the cry of "Woe!"[40]

[37] Isa. 41:13; 43:10; 45:22cd; 46:9cd; 52:6. Compare also Isa. 22:25d; 24:3b; 25:8d; 34:16de; 40:5c; 58:14d.

[37a] Eccles. 4:14; Ps. 21:12; Prov. 6:35; Isa. 54:10; Jer. 14:12; 49:16ef; Ezek. 11:16; Mic. 7:8. See the perceptive discussion by Th. C. Vriezen, "Einige Notizen zur Übersetzung des Bindeswortes KI," *Von Ugarit nach Qumran*, *BZAW* 77 (1958). *Eissfeldt Festschrift*, pp. 266–73. Note especially the discussion of Num. 23:23; Ruth 1:12 f.; and Ps. 37:24.

[38] Ps.. 6:5 f.; 12:2 (*bis*); 25:16; 16:1, 2 f.; 31:10 f. (*bis*), 18; 38:2 f., 4 f., 16, 18 f. (*bis*); 39:13; 41:5; 44:23–25; 51:3–5; 54:1–5; 69:18, etc., etc.

[39] Job 3:20–25; 7:21; 22:2; Ps. 44:21–23; Isa. 7:13; 28:9; 36:5; Jer. 4:22; Mic. 6:4. Cf. Gen. 31:15 f. Compare also Gen. 20:9; Judg. 14:3; I Sam. 20:1; Isa. 22:1; 52:5; Mic. 4:9.

[40] אוי I Sam. 4:7c; Isa. 3:11; 6:5 (*ter*); Jer. 6:4; 15:10; 48:16; Ezek. 24:6 f.; הוי Hab. 2:6–19, etc.

> Wail, Alas for the day!
>> כי the day is near.   (Ezek. 30:2)
>
> Woe to them!
>> כי they have brought evil upon themselves.   (Isa. 3:9de)
>
> Woe to us, כי we are ruined!   (Jer. 4:13d)

20. The rhetorical function of כי is illustrated nowhere so clearly as in its tendency to appear in successive lines or sentences, both in prose and in poetry:[41]

> And I said, "Woe is me! כי־ I am lost; כי I am a man of unclean lips, and I dwell among a people of unclean lips; כי my eyes have seen the King, Yahweh of hosts."   (Isa. 6:5)

> Comfort, O comfort my people,
>> Says your God.
> Speak kindly to Jerusalem,
>> And proclaim to her —
> כי her warfare is ended,
> כי her iniquity is pardoned,
> כי she has received from Yahweh's hand
>> Double for all her sins.   (Isa. 40:1–2)

Among the numerous literary contexts where כי plays an emphatic rhetorical role, see the call of Jeremiah (Jer. 1:4–10).

21. The motivation (*Begründung*) for the oracle of assurance is commonly introduced by כי:[42]

> Then you shall see and be radiant,
>> Your heart shall thrill and rejoice (with emendation);
> כי־ the abundance of the sea shall be turned to you,
>> The wealth of nations shall come to you.   (Isa. 60:5)

22. The strophes are often introduced by כי:[43]

> כי Yahweh is enraged against all the nations   (Isa. 34:2a)

> כי my sword has drunk its fill in the heavens   (Isa. 34:5a)

---

[41] Gen. 3:19; Isa. 9:3–5; 10:20–23; 15:1, 5–6; 25:1cd, 2, 4; 26:3–5; 28:18–22; 43:2 ff.; 57:14–16; 65:8–10; Job 3:24 f.; I Chron. 29:14–18; Ps. 118:1–4, 10–12.

[42] Isa. 60:9, 10, 12, 16, 20; 65:20; Jer. 3:12.

[43] Pss. 5:5; 18:32; Isa. 22:5; 16:8; 17:10; 60:10; 61:8; Amos 5:12; Obad. 15. J. Muilenburg, "The Literary Character of Isaiah 34," *JBL* LIX (1940), pp. 339–65; "A Study in Hebrew Rhetoric: Repetition and Style," *Vetus Testamentum Congress Volume* I (1953), pp. 97–111.

כִּי Yahweh has a sacrifice in Bozrah   (Isa. 34:6e)

כִּי for Yahweh has a day of vengeance.   (Isa. 34:8a)

22a. The conclusion of the strophe is often introduced with כִּי:[43a]

כי־יודע יהוה דרך צדיקים   ודרך רשעים תאבד:
(Ps. 1:6)

23. At other times both the introduction and conclusion of the body of the poem are marked by כִּי:[44]

כִּי Yahweh, Most High, is terrible.   (Ps. 47:3)

כִּי the shields of the earth belong to God;
He is highly exalted.   (Ps. 47:10)

24. The body (*Hauptstück*) of the poem is frequently introduced by כִּי:[45]

כִּי thou hast rejected thy people, the house of Jacob.
(Isa. 2:6)

25. It also marks the conclusion of the poem or oracle:[46]

כִּי thou hast delivered my soul from death,
My feet from falling (see BH *appar. crit.*),
That I may walk before God
In the light of life.   (Ps. 56:14)

26. Or it may be the means of interpreting the meaning of a preceding dramatic utterance, as in the two oracular proclamations introduced by כִּי after the moving dirge of Amos 5:2. Cf. also Isa. 2:2-4, 5 f., 7-11 = 12-19; 28:7-13 (note v. 11); 63:15 f.; Amos 6:9-11.

*   *

*

[43a] Ps. 6:6; 9:5, 11b, 13, 19; 16:8b; Isa. 28:8, 20; 52:15cf; 60:5, 9, 16, 20; 62:5; Amos 6:14.

[44] J. Muilenburg, "Psalm 47," *JBL* LXIII (1944), pp. 235-256. Compare Ps. 109:2 and 31; Isa. 30:9 and 18.

[65] Isa. 1:2c, 3:1, 16; 8:6, 11; 14:29c. So frequently in hymns, laments, exhortations, invectives, threats, etc. See our discussion of motivations below.

[46] Pss. 1:6; 4:9b; 5:13; 11:7; 21:13; 37:40c; 47:10; 99:9c; 100:5; Isa. 1:20c; 5:7; 7:9; Jer. 2:13; 4:3 f.; 4:8cd, 22, 27; 31:34e.

We may now inquire more precisely into the function which the particle כי performs in Hebrew speech in the contexts of various types or genres. We have seen that the word is employed in many linguistic and rhetorical settings, that it is characteristically associated with emphatic words or clauses, that it frequently appears in a strategic position in the poem or narrative, whether at the beginning or at the end, and that it often confirms or underlines what has been said, or, at times, undergirds the whole of the utterance and gives point to it. Now if this morpheme was originally a demonstrative interjection, as Brockelmann and others have contended, it is interesting to observe that this emphatic character is almost always present. Within the Old Testament it is of course impossible to trace the history or development of the particle because its usage has already been established in the earliest records, although it is clear that it is employed much more profusely in certain strata than in others, and that certain usages prevail in some books or sources, while others prevail in others. We can learn much, however, by noting where the word most characteristically appears in a given *Gattung*, the degree to which it reflects an oral provenance, and what the precise nuance or meaning is in the place that it occupies in the *Gattung*. Now when one attempts to survey the types or genres of Old Testament literature in the light of the usage of כי, it soon becomes apparent that it is most frequently employed as a word of motivation. This, of course, has already become clear in the way it is related to exclamations, imperatives, asseverations, promises and assurances, questions, conditionals, etc. We may turn, then, to a brief examination of some representative genres of Hebrew speech in order to clarify this motivating function.

1. First of all the forms of legal teaching in the Old Testament, most notably the casuistic and apodictic laws.[47] The formulation of the casuistic law is not native to Israel, but is encountered in the other legal collections of the ancient Near East.[48] But not infrequently there is added to the casuistic law "grammatically subordinate sentences in which the motivation for the commandment is given." These motivations are found in the different codes of Old Testament law, and it

---

[47] Albrecht Alt, *Die Ursprünge des israelitischen Rechts*, published originally in the Berichten über die Verhandlungen der Sächsischen Akademie der Wissenschaften (Leipzig, 1934), and reprinted in *Kleine Schriften zur Geschichte des Volkes Israel*, Band I, pp. 278–332.

[48] As in the Urnammu, Lipit Ishtar, Eshnunna, Hammurabi, Hittite, and Assyrian laws.

seems probable that they are distinctively Israelite, since nowhere
in the other collections do we meet them.[49] It must be borne in mind
that the words of motivation are of many kinds, but it is the particle
כִּי above all others which is employed most characteristically. In
Israel the casuistic law is expanded by motivations, though it is
probable that these represent for the most part later accretions to
the original:[50]

> If ever you take your neighbor's garment in pledge, you shall
> restore it to him before the sun goes down; כִּי that is his only
> covering, it is his mantle for his body; in what else shall he
> sleep? And כִּי he cries to me, I will hear כִּי־חָנּוּן אָנִי.
>
> (Exod. 22:25 f.)

> If there is among you a poor man, one of your brethren, in
> any of your towns within your land which Yahweh your God
> gives you, you shall not harden your heart or shut your hand
> against your brother . . . You shall give to him freely, and
> your heart shall not be grudging when you give to him; כִּי for
> this Yahweh your God will bless you in all your work and in
> all you undertake. כִּי the poor shall never cease out of the
> land; therefore I command you, You shall open wide your
> hand to your brother . . .   (Deut. 15:7–11)

Interestingly, it is the apodictic law which most frequently receives
the motive clause, as in the different decalogues:[51]

> You shall have no other gods before me . . . You shall not bow
> down to them or serve them כִּי I Yahweh your God am a
> jealous God, visiting the iniquity of the fathers upon the
> children to the third and the fourth generation of those who

---

[49] B. Gemser, "The Importance of the Motive Clause in Old Testament Law."
Supplements to Vetus Testamentum Congress Volume I, pp. 50–66. Note Gemser's
comment on p. 52: "In absolutely none of these lawbooks or-codes or-collections
(*sic!*) can one single instance of motive clauses be discovered. The motive clause is
clearly and definitely a peculiarity of Israel's or Old Testament law. The famous and
fortunate distinction by A. Alt of casuistic and apodictic laws does not explain this
conspicuous difference between the legal forms of the Ancient Near East and Israel."
Gemser gives a useful survey of the motive clauses in the various Old Testament
legal codes, describes the terminology of motivation, and classifies the kinds of
motivation to which appeal is made.

[50] Exod. 20:25 f.; 22:20–23; 23:9; Lev. 25:47–55; Deut. 15:7–11, 12–18; 21:1, 10,
14, 15–17, 22–23.

[51] See W. Zimmerli, "Das zweite Gebot" in *Festschrift für Alfred Bertholet* (1950),
pp. 550–53.

hate me, but showing steadfast love to thousands of those who love me and keep my commandments.   (Exod. 20:3, 5–6)[52]

No man shall take a mill or an upper mill-stone in pledge, כי he would be taking a life in pledge.   (Deut. 24:6)

Consecrate yourselves therefore, and be holy; כי I am Yahweh your God.   (Lev. 20:7)

2. Motive clauses introduced by כי are also present in many blessings:[53]

Happy is the man who finds wisdom,
    And the man who gets understanding,
כי the gain from it is better than gain from silver
    And its profit better than gold.   (Prov. 3:13 f.)

3. Similarly, the curse:[54]

Cursed be their anger, כי it is fierce;
    And their wrath, כי it is cruel!   (Gen. 49:7ab)

4. Conspicuous are the motivations for the naming of a child, which sometimes assume the form of nativity oracles:[55]

And Adam knew his wife again, and she bore a son and called his name Seth, כי God has appointed for me another child instead of Abel, for Cain slew him.   (Gen. 4:25)

And Yahweh said to him, Call his name Jezreel; כי yet a little while, and I will punish the house of Jehu for the blood of Jezreel, and I will put an end to the kingdom of the house of Israel.   (Hos. 1:4)

---

[52] Exod. 20:7, 8–11; Deut. 5:9, 11, 14 f., 16; Exod. 34:14, 18, 24. The motivation of the holiness of Yahweh is of course frequent in the Holiness Code: Lev. 20:26; 21:8, 15, 23; 24:22; 25:17; 26:1, 44. For the theological significance of these motivations, see Gemser and also von Rad, *Theologie des Alten Testaments*, Band I, pp. 199 ff. For the use of the particle in the rituals see R. Rendtorff, *Die Gesetze in der Priesterschrift* (1954) and especially K. Koch, *Die Priesterschrift von Exodus 25 bis Leviticus 16* (1959).

[53] Pss. 28:6; 31:22; 89:16–19; 112:1–6; Prov. 8:34 f. Cf. Deut. 33:8 f.; Ps. 1:6. For discussion of this *Gattung* and of the curse, see Gunkel-Begrich, *Einleitung in die Psalmen* (1933), pp. 293 ff.

[54] Gen. 3:14 f., 17–19; Isa. 3:11, Mal. 2:2.

[55] Gen. 17:5; 29:32, 33, 34 (cf. 35); 30:19 f.; Isa. 8:3 f.; Hos. 1:6, 8 f.; Matt. 1:20 f. Compare Isa. 62:4.

5. Israel's Wisdom literature is rich in the use of the particle, as is illustrated in the exhortations of the sage:[56]

> Hear, my son, your father's instruction,
>   And reject not your mother's teaching;
> כי they are a fair garland for your head,
>   And pendants for your neck.   (Prov. 1:8 f.)

6. Closely akin to the exhortations of the sage are the admonitions, warnings, and prohibitions with their characteristic nuances:[57]

> Be not envious of evil men,
>   Nor desire to be with them;
> כי their minds are full of violence,
>   And their lips talk of mischief.   (Prov. 24:1 f.)

7. The particle finds a characteristic place in the oracle of assurance (*Erhörungsorakel*) as it is spoken in the cult or in the divine assurance to an individual:[58]

> Be not afraid of them,
>   כי I am with you to deliver you, says Yahweh.
>
>   (Jer. 1:8)

8. The summons to lamentation is characteristically followed by the reason for the summons:[59]

> Wail, O ships of Tarshish,
>   כי your stronghold is laid waste.   (Isa. 23:14)

9. Similarly the summons to praise and singing is frequently followed by the causal כי:[60]

> O sing to Yahweh a new song;
>   Sing to Yahweh, all the earth!
> Sing to Yahweh, bless His name;
>   Tell of His salvation from day to day.

[56] Prov. 4:13, 15 f., 20 ff., 23; 5:20 f.; 22:17 f.; 23:26–28.

[57] Prov. 1:15 f.; 3:11 f., 25 f.; 4:15 f.; 5:20 f.; 6:1–3, 25 f.; 22:22 f.; 23:17 f., 19–21.

[58] Jer. 1:14–19; 11:21–23; 15:19–20; Pss. 21:8–12; 22:23–25; 57:10 f.; 86:12 f.; 109:30 f.

[59] Isa. 23:1; Joel 1:5–7, 8, 11, 13; Jer. 4:8; 9:9, 16–19, 20 f.; Mic. 1:10–12, 16; Jer. 49:3. Cf. Jer. 14:2–4; 16:5.

[60] Pss. 33:1–4; 100; 117; 135:1–7; 136; 147:1; 148; 149:1–4. Cf. also the hymns of the divine enthronement: 47; 96 (supra); 99.

Declare His glory among the nations,
His marvelous works among all the peoples.
כי great is Yahweh, and greatly to be praised;
He is to be feared above all gods.
כי all the gods of the peoples are idols;
But Yahweh made the heavens.   (Ps. 96:1-5)

10. The petitions of the prayers of Israel are naturally developed
by the causal כי:[61]

Be merciful to me, O God, be merciful to me,
כי in Thee my soul takes refuge.   (Ps. 57:2)

11. Oracles of judgment are often grounded in the same way,
particularly the announcement of the imminent Day of the Lord:[62]

כי Yahweh of hosts has a day
Against all that is proud and lofty,
Against all that is lifted up and high.   (Isa. 2:12)

*   *

*

It is clear that the many motive clauses throughout the literature
of ancient Israel, in all their literary guises and patterns, in all their
rich diversity of occasion and circumstance, in all their varying contexts and settings, constitute a major feature, not merely of a manner
of speaking or of the formal structures in which thoughts are ordered
and articulated, but also of the faith of Israel. In the motivations we
have a vivid reflection of the pedagogical and educational methods of
the wisemen, of their concern to make clear and to explain to their
hearers what life is like, the rewards for right conduct and the consequences of evil, why it is that men must think well of good and think
ill of wrong and act accordingly. They are intent upon showing the
ways of God with men. They know that *es bildet sich ein Charakter in
Strom der Welt,* and they witness in many ways to the divine intention
behind the course of a man's life. They are telling their auditors that
their decisions are fateful for their happiness and contentment, for

---

[61] Pss. 56:1; 59:2-5; 61:2-4, 5 f.; 63:2-4; 69:2-10; 71:4-5; 83:2 ff.; 86:1-5; 88:2-4.
[62] Isa. 13:6; 31:7; 34:8; 63:4; Jer. 46:21ef; 50:27cd, 31cd; Joel 2:1, 11; 4:14;
Zeph. 1:7. Cf. Jer. 34:5; Ezek. 30:2 f.; Joel 1:15.

their peace and well-being. The motive clauses frequently have a
pastoral purpose. They seek to provide an impetus and inspiration for
obedience. They are meant to restore men to what they were intended
by God to be when they were created. They expose to them the
resources that are at their disposal, to warn them against the disregard
and flouting of the grace of the Torah, which is given them as a light
upon their way, indeed their very life. Priest and prophet are one in
their memories of the sacred past, of the Exodus event which evoked
both thanksgiving and the motive for obedience, and of the Sinai
event which reminded them of their belonging to the transcendent
Lord and King. It is these events which undergird many of the motivations, whether they are expressed or implied. In the motivations
Yahweh is establishing his point of contact with his people. In them
he is telling Israel why he has done as he has done, that he has not
acted without cause (Ezek. 14:22). In them he is calling Israel to its
responsibility. In them Israel is made to confirm from within that he
is justified in his acts and words. He does not act capriciously; he has
a reason for his course of action, he has a plan and a purpose and a
design behind his divine rule in the world. But more than that, in the
motivations Israel can confirm voluntarily that the ways of God are
right, that his ways should be their ways also, and that his intentions
should be the source of their illumination, the guide of their actions,
and the motives for their desire to do what they ought to do.[63]

Finally, the particle כִּי is important for its function in many of the
literary types. This has already been demonstrated in the foregoing
discussion, especially in our scrutiny of the motivations. Here we shall
do no more than list some of the major literary genres in which it
plays a distinctive rhetorical, literary, and above all a "theological"
role. That the word does not appear in many of the exemplars of a
particular *Gattung* is by no means a refutation of our contention; the
Hebrew poet or narrator, while deeply influenced by custom and
convention, is never a slave to form, and he resists a literary stereotype. It is the versatility in which forms are employed that accounts to
a degree at least for the literary supremacy of the Old Testament.
Moreover, we must remember that particles other than כִּי were at the
disposal of the Old Testament poets and lawgivers and narrators.

---

[63] B. Gemser, von Rad (Vol. I, note 49). Also Hans Walter Wolff, "Die Begrün-
dungen der prophetischen Heils- und Unheilssprüche," *ZAW* 52 (1934), pp. 1–21.
Wolff analyzes the different patterns of the various forms and types together with
the particles of motivation. On the a–b type he comments: "Aber mit grosser
Regelmässigkeit leitet die Konjunktion כִּי den Begründungssatz ein."

1. *The oath.* The oath is not only a formal but also an emphatic way of speaking; it is only to be expected that the contexts in which it is employed should be emphatic and that emphatic particles and phrases should accompany it. Its essentially oral character calls attention to the vitality of the particular particle in its context. Most characteristic is its appearance after the oath "As Yahweh lives," but it is not restricted to this formulation. To be noted also is its employment after verbs of swearing. Our first example illustrates the gravity and solemnity of the context:[64]

> . . . and David called to the army, and to Abner the son of Ner, saying, "Will you not answer, Abner?" Then Abner answered, "Who are you that calls to the king?" And David said to Abner, "Are you not a man? Who is like you in Israel? Why then have you not kept watch over your lord the king? כי one of the people came in to destroy the king your lord. This thing that you have done is not good. As Yahweh lives כי בן־מות אתם אשר you have not kept watch over your lord Yahweh's anointed. And now see (ועתה | ראה) where the king's spear is, and the jar of water that was at his head."
>
> (I Sam. 26:14–16)

> Lift up your eyes round about and see;
>   They all gather, they come to you.
> As I live, the oracle of Yahweh, כי you shall put them all on
>   as an ornament,
>   And you shall bind them on as a bride does.   (Isa. 49:18)

> And Saul said, "God do so to me and more also; כי you shall surely die (with inf. abs.), Jonathan."   (I Sam. 14:44)

> כי as I swore to you by Yahweh, the God of Israel, saying "כי Solomon your son shall reign after me, and he shall sit upon my throne in my stead"; כי כן will I do this day.
>
> (I Kings 1:30)

---

[64] After verbs of swearing, see Gen. 22:16; Isa. 45:23; Jer. 22:5. After oath clauses like חי יהוה, I Sam. 14:29, 44; 20:3; 25:34; 29:6; Jer. 22:24. Cf. Gen. 42:16. In Job's oath of clearance, note 31:11, 12, 18, 23, 34. Cf. J. Hempel, *Die althebräische Literatur und ihr hellenistisch-jüdisches Nachleben*, pp. 60, 79 f., 140, for an illuminating discussion of the oath. For discerning linguistic comment, see S. R. Driver, *Notes on the Hebrew Text and the Topography of the Books of Samuel* (1913), pp. 117, 118, 247, and 229. Here the significance of successive כי particles in the oath formulations is discussed.

2. The invective (*Scheltrede*) provides the motivation for the usually following threat (*Drohrede*), and the terminology of motivation is particularly abundant and diverse.[65] The oracles against the nations in Amos 1:3–2:16 use על, which is doubtless an abbreviation for the original כי על. We have already seen how the original *Woe* is characteristically followed by the particle.[66]

עשה הרתוק כי הארץ מלאה משפט דמים והעיר מלאה חמס: והבאתי רעי
גוים וירשו את בתיהם והשבתי גאון עזים ונחלו מקדשיהם: (Ezek. 7:23 f.)

3. Exhortation (*Mahnrede*) is constantly amplified by the reason or basis which prompts it:[67]

For thus says Yahweh to the house of Israel:

Seek Me and live;
    But do not seek Bethel,
And do not enter into Gilgal
    Or cross over to Beersheba;
כי Gilgal shall surely go into exile,
    And Bethel shall come to naught.   (Amos 5:4 f.)

4. The hymn is an excellent example of how the כי appears at certain strategic points in the composition, notably as the introduction to the body of the poem and frequently, too, to the conclusion.[68]

5. What is true of the hymn is also true of the lament, especially the lament of the individual:[69]

O that my vexation were weighed,
    And all my calamity laid in the balances!
כי then it would be heavier than the sand of the sea;
    Therefore my words have been rash.
כי the arrows of the Almighty are in me;
    My spirit drinks their poison   (Job 6:2–4a)

[65] See Hans Walter Wolff, *ibid.*, p. 2 and *passim*.
[66] Gen. 3:14, Isa. 3:16 f.; 29:13 f.; Jer. 30:15 f. See oracles of judgment above. Cf. Amos 4:12.
[67] Deut. 4:6, 7, 24, 31, 32, 39 and often in Deuteronomy; cf. also Zeph. 2:3 f.
[68] Gunkel-Begrich, *Einleitung in die Psalmen*, pp. 42 f. Exod. 15:21; Pss. 30:2; 47:3; 89:3; 95:3; 96:4; 98:1; 106:1; 107:1; 116:1 f.; 147:1; 148:5. See also 13:6; 47:8; Isa. 12:6.
[69] Job 9:25–35; 13:23–28; 14:7, 16; Pss. 5:2–7; 26:1; 28:1–5; 35:1–8; 38:2 f.; 51:3–8.

6. The priestly oracle of salvation (*der priesterliche Heilsorakel*) employs the particle most impressively since it provides the basis for the divine assurance in the language of the first person asseverations of theophanic speech:[70, 71]

> Fear not, כי I am with thee;
> Be not dismayed, כי I am thy God.   (Isa. 41:10)

> Then fear not, O Jacob, my servant, says Yahweh,
> Nor be dismayed, O Israel;
> כי הנני I will save you from afar,
> and your offspring from the land of their captivity.

> . . .

> כי־ I am with you to save you, says Yahweh.   (Jer. 30:10 f.)

7. The lawsuit or judicial speech (*Gerichtsrede*) which belongs to the whole realm of Israel's legal existence, is naturally influenced by the force of the particle.[72] It introduces the reason for the judicial summons:

> Hear, O heavens, and give ear, O earth;
> כי Yahweh has spoken:
> Sons have I reared and brought up.
> But they have rebelled against me.   (Isa. 1:2)

[70] J. Begrich, "Der priesterliche Heilsorakel," *ZAW* 52 (1934) Neue Folge. Band 11, pp. 81–92. See also L. Köhler, "Die Offenbarungsformel 'Fürchte dich nicht!' im Alten Testament," *Schweizerische Theologische Zeitschrift* XXXVI (1919), pp. 33–39. For other examples in theophanic contexts see Gen. 21:17; 26:24; Deut. 20:1; 31:6. See also Köhler, *Deuterojesaja stilkritisch untersucht* especially for the discussion of theophanic style.

[71] The writer is happy to record his indebtedness to Professor Morgenstern for his earliest interest in biblical theophanies. His articles in the *Zeitschrift für Assyriologie* written many years ago (XXV [1911]; XXVIII [1913] still deserve careful reading and pondering. It is now clear that theophanic terminology is present in numerous cultic and liturgical contexts. Second Isaiah has been deeply influenced by them as the following passages *inter alia* demonstrate: 41:8–13; 43:1–5; 44:2–5; 51:7 f.; 54:4–8. Jer. 30:10 ff. is probably influenced by Second Isaiah. See Ps. 50:7–11 and Deut. 31:28 f.

[72] Deut. 31:28 f.; Ps. 50:7–11; Mic. 6:1–8. J. Begrich, *Studien zu Deuterojesaja.* Beiträge zur Wissenschaft von Alten und Neuen Testament, (1938); Herbert B. Huffmon, "The Covenant Lawsuit in the Prophets," *JBL* LXXVIII (1959), pp. 385–95; J. Muilenburg, *Interpreter's Bible* V (1956), *passim*.

8. It is not surprising that the Torah liturgy should also have it. The composition of Isa. 56:1–8 rewards close inspection; observe how the Torah of 1b is motivated by the כי clauses of 1cd, the admonitions of vs. 3 by the divine oracle of vv. 4–7 introduced by כי כה אמר יהוה and culminating in the motivation of 7ef. The Torah liturgy in Isaiah 33 culminates appropriately in the magnificent climax:[73]

> כִּי Yahweh is our judge, Yahweh is our ruler,
> Yahweh is our king; he will save us.   (v. 22)

9. The announcement of the herald or messenger (*Botenspruch*) proclaims the urgency of the report or news by the motive clause introduced by כי or by other motivating particles, above all למען, especially in Second Isaiah.[74]

> Flee for safety, O people of Benjamin,
> From the midst of Jerusalem!
> Blow the trumpet in Tekoa,
> And raise a signal on Bethhaccerem;
> כִּי evil looms out of the north,
> And great destruction.   (Jer. 6:1)

10. A study of the employment of the particle in prose contexts would prove fruitful because it would reveal many other nuances of usage, show how it helps to articulate the predication, and demonstrate the frequency with which it is used to direct the narrative to its conclusion. Among the many passages which illustrate its function are the following: Gen. 3:1–20; 12:10–15; Deut. 4:1–7, 15–40; Josh. 24:16–27; II Sam. 19:6–8; Ruth 1.[75]

---

[73] Gunkel-Begrich, *ibid.*, 408 f.; Aubrey Johnson, "The Psalms," *Old Testament and Modern Study* (edited by H. H. Rowley), 1951, p. 178. See also H. Gunkel, "Jesaja 33, ein prophetische Liturgie," *ZAW* XLII (1924), pp. 177–208; *ibid.*, "Der Micha-Schluss," *Zeitschrift für Semitistik und verwandte Gebiete* II (1924), pp. 145–78, translated into English in *What Remains of the Old Testament*, pp. 115–49. Gunkel regards the Torah liturgies in the prophets as imitations; it is more probable that they bore some relation to the cult. Cf. Aubrey Johnson, *The Cultic Prophet in Ancient Israel*, 1944.

[74] L. Köhler, *Deuterojesaja stilkritisch untersucht* (1923), pp. 102 ff.; Martin Noth, "History and the Word of God in the Old Testament," *Bulletin of the John Rylands Library* 32 (1950), pp. 194–206; Adolphe Lods, in *Studies of Old Testament Prophecy* (edited by H. H. Rowley), pp. 103–10. It is interesting to observe that in the ancient Near Eastern parallels I have examined the motivations are absent (as in the laws). See Isa. 40:1–2; 41:11–13, 17–20; 44:1–5, 21 f.; 45:18–23; 51:1–8, 12–16.

[75] J. Pedersen, *ibid.*, I–II, pp. 119 f.

It goes without saying that no attempt has been made at completeness in the foregoing discussion. Nor has account been taken of
other particles which belong to the same general class as כי. But it is
hoped that enough has been said to suggest something of the importance that our word has for a grasp of Hebrew rhetorical expression,
and with that of course our understanding of the mentality of Israel
as it is reflected in its use of words. For from an original exclamatory
interjection or cry it has developed into a vast variety of nuances and
meanings, yet always preserving in one fashion or another its original
emphatic connotations, and, far from standing isolatedly in its contexts, it presses speech onward *from* one remembered point *to* another
anticipated end. It would be an error to suppose that such a study has
only aesthetic or literary value. On the contrary, it may often aid us
in our interpretation and appreciation of the precise meaning of the
ancient text. At a deeper level and one that is as difficult to penetrate
as it is important to assess is the relation between the use of the
particles, in the present case the particle כי, and Israel's understanding
of time as it is reflected in terminology, syntax, literary forms and
structures, and the movement of words.

The Terminology of Adversity in Jeremiah

JAMES MUILENBURG

Among the scholars who have directed their attention to a study of the book of Jeremiah and have helped us to come to an understanding not only of the character of the book as a whole, but also of the nature of the composition of its several strata or streams of tradition, the name of Herbert May holds a place of distinction.[1] It is no little satisfaction to do honor to one whom the writer is proud to count among his most treasured friends, a colleague on the Revised Standard Version committee, and a teacher whose influence has extended far beyond the confines of the classroom and, indeed, of his own land.

Whenever one undertakes to read through the book of Jeremiah and to gain a synoptic view of its contents, he cannot but be impressed by the vast scope of the materials associated with his name,[2] by the diversity of the literary genres and the stylistic versatility of their formulations, by the many personal crises which evoked the prophet's poignant response, by the momentous historical events of a distraught and turbulent international age, and by the large number of symbols and images whereby Jeremiah seeks to body forth his prophetic message.

It is the purpose of this modest offering to Professor May to call attention first of all to the presence of semantic or lexical motifs which persist throughout the prophet's *ipsissima verba* and to the

---

[1] H. G. May, "Towards an Objective Approach to the Book of Jeremiah: The Biographer," *JBL* LXI (1942), 139-56; "Jeremiah's Biographer," *JBR* X (1942), 195-201; "The Chronology of Jeremiah's Oracles," *JNES* IV (1945), 217-27; "Individual Responsibility and Retribution," *HUCA* XXXII (1961), 107-20.

[2] Of the 1434 pp. in Kittel's *Biblia Hebraica*, 108 pp. are given to the book of Jeremiah.

The Terminology of Adversity in Jeremiah

imagery which accompanies them, but, more particularly, to focus upon one field of speech and symbol which appears to the writer to have received less attention than it deserves. Among these motifs one recognizes, for example, the constant tensions between the language of *mendacity* and the language of *veracity*, between what is spurious and what is authentic, between truth and falsehood.[3] Nowhere is this language employed more profusely than with Jeremiah,[4] and what makes it so impressive is that it enters into every literary genre, whether one thinks of the lawsuits with their indictments, or of the laments and confessions, or of the castigations of the false prophets, or of the exhortations and sermons. More significantly, it penetrates Jeremiah's own self-awareness, his interior conflicts, the authenticity of his credentials as Yahweh's appointed and commissioned covenant mediator, which he is called upon to defend against his detractors, and supremely his dialogical encounters with Yahweh (cf. 15:18; 20:7). Closely related to the semantic field of mendacity and veracity is the speech of fidelity and infidelity, of commitment and trust, on the one hand, and of faithlessness and disloyalty on the other, where the familial symbol of father-son and the nuptial symbol of husband-bride are frequently invoked, and in varying contexts. Also closely related are the tensions between apostasy and repentance, the two ways of turning. The verb *šûb* is one of the most frequently employed, and with great versatility and in a great variety of syntactical constructions, connotative nuances, and stylistic forms.[5]

Accompanying these and other persisting semantic motifs and frequently illuminating them are numerous figures of speech. The book of Jeremiah fairly teems with images and symbols of many different kinds. Simile and metaphor, apostrophe and personification, metonymy and synecdoche, parable and vision, and not a few symbolic ac-

---

[3] Martin A. Klopfenstein, *Die Lüge nach dem Alten Testament* (Zürich and Frankfort, 1964).

[4] While Jeremiah employs a considerable number of words to express different kinds of mendacity, such as מרמה (5:27; 9:5, 7), תרמית (8:5; 14:14 [Q]; 23:26), and שוא (2:30; 4:30; 6:29), we confine ourselves to the one word which appears more frequently than any other, the word שקר. It will be observed that it pervades all his prophecies, and, what is more, it is preserved in the prose narratives of Baruch, which, as we shall see, is in many ways surprising since this is by no means always the case: 3:10, 23; 5:2, 31; 6:13–8:10; 9:2, 4 (E.T. 3, 5); 13:25; 14:14; 16:19; 20:6; 23:14, 25, 26, 32; 27:10, 14, 15, 16; 28:15; 29:9, 21, 23, 31. The little poem of 9:1-7 (E.T. 9:2-8) is a superb example of the motif. Here the terminology of truth and falsehood is exceptionally rich and the imagery especially striking.

[5] William L. Holladay, *The Root Sûbh in the Old Testament* (Leiden, 1958), pp. 128-39.

Translating and Understanding the Old Testament

tions[6] punctuate and interpret the prophecy from beginning to end. In this respect Jeremiah is not unlike his spiritual predecessor, the prophet Hosea, with whom he shows himself akin in other ways.[7] Notable among these spheres of imagery is the motif of *water* or *rain*.[8] This is not at all surprising because throughout his prophetic career Jeremiah wages unwearying battle against the cults of fertility. Already in one of his earliest poems we encounter a striking instance of the motif, precisely where the pericope reaches its impressive climax:

> For two evils my people have committed:
>> they have abandoned me,
>> the fountain of living water,
> to hew for themselves cisterns,
>> broken cisterns,
>> that can hold no water.   2:13; cf. 3:3; 5:22, 24; 6:7; 18:23 (E.T. 9:1); 13:1 ff.; 14:3 ff.; 15:18; 17:8; 18:14; 31:35.

Of quite a different order, but in many ways equally revealing, are the repeated references to birds.[9] Sometimes these are general and rather stereotyped (7:33; 9:10; 12:4; 15:3; 16:4; 19:7; 34:20) and may have their prototypes in the curses and maledictions of other texts from the ancient Near East. At other times, however, they are very moving and impressive formulations. When Jeremiah thinks of the passing away of the world, he characteristically mentions the birds. The most telling of these passages appears in the heart of a poem describing the return of the created universe to primeval chaos:

> I looked on the earth, and lo, it was chaos and waste,
>> and to the heavens, and they had no light.
> I looked on the mountains, and lo, they were quaking,
>> and all the hills moved to and fro.
> I looked, and lo, there was no man,
>> and all the birds of the sky had fled. 4:23-25; cf. 9:9 (E.T. 10).

[6] H. W. Robinson, "Prophetic Symbolism" in *Old Testament Essays* (Papers read before the Society for Old Testament Study), (1927), pp. 1-17; G. Fohrer, *Die symbolischen Handlungen der Propheten, AThANT* XXV (Zürich, 1953).

[7] Karl Gross, "Die literarische Verwandtschaft Jeremias mit Hosea," Dissertation Berlin, 1930; *idem*, "Hoseas Einfluss auf Jeremias Anschauungen," *NKZ* XLII (1931), 327-43.

[8] H. Kaupel, *Das Wasser in der Bildersprache der Propheten, BK*, 1949; Philippe Reymond, *L'Eau, sa Vie, et sa Signification dans l'Ancient Testament,* Supplements to Vetus Testamentum VI (1958); Otto Kaiser, *Die mythische Bedeutung des Meeres in Ägypten, Ugarit, und Israel, BZAW* LXXVIII (1962); L. Alonso Schökel, *Estudios de Poetica Hebrea* (1963), pp. 269-307.

[9] G. R. Driver, "Birds in the Old Testament," *PEQ* LXXXVII (1955), 129-40.

The Terminology of Adversity in Jeremiah

In a text of quite another kind Jeremiah contrasts poignantly the homing instinct of the birds with the conduct of the people:

> Even the stork in the heavens
>   knows her times;
> and the turtledove, swallow, and swift
>   keep the time of their coming;
> but my people know not
>   the ordinance of Yahweh.   8:7; cf. 5:27.

Much more extensive is the frequent reference to animals. While the beasts of the field are sometimes mentioned in the same stereotyped fashion as the birds, it is much more characteristic of the prophet to give us their names and to speak of them with discernment, i.e. with features which characterize each.[10]

We turn now to the area of our central interest, the semantic field of adversity and affliction in Jeremiah. Especially within recent years attention has been focused upon Baruch's passion narrative,[11] but, as we shall have occasion to observe, the vocabulary of suffering and pain and grief is actually more abundant in Jeremiah's own words. The richness of the prophet's terminology is all the more noteworthy because so often the relevant terms are concentrated within the narrow compass of a single strophe or literary genre (note, e.g., 8:18-23 [E.T. 8:18–9:1]). The survey which follows does not profess to be in any way complete. We omit, for example, the extensive lexical field of wrath and anger, which is as revealing for a grasp of the prophet's theology as for an insight into the interior conflicts and tensions which the oracles portray.[12]

1. *Sickness and wounds.*

The two words are not infrequently associated in the Old Testament, and for good reason since to the ancient Hebrew the wounded

---

[10] Note, e.g., the *lion* (2:15, 30; 4:7; 5:6; 12:8; cf. 25:38), the *leopard* (5:6; 13:23), *horse* or *stallion* (4:13; 5:8; 8:6, 16; 12:5); the restive young *camel* (2:23), *ass* (14:6; 22:19), the *calf* (14:5; 31:18), *jackal* (9:11; 10:22; 14:6); *snakes* (8:17). For ancient Near Eastern parallels to ravening animals as instruments of punishment, see D. R. Hillers, *Treaty-Curses and the Old Testament Prophets. Biblica et Orientalia.* No. 16 (1964), pp. 54-6. See also F. S. Bodenheimer, *Animal and Man in Bible Lands.* Collection des Travaux de l'Académie Internationale d'Histoire des Sciences, 1960.

[11] Heinz Kremers, "Leidensgemeinschaft mit Gott im Alten Testament," *EvTh* XIII (1953), 122-40.

[12] Abraham Heschel, *The Prophets* (New York, 1955), pp. 106-7, 115-17.

Translating and Understanding the Old Testament

person is understood to be sick (cf. 6:7; 10:19) .[13] Chief among the
words used for *wound* is the noun שבר, which appears frequently and
always in strategic collocations. The verb form is one of the most
commonly employed in the Old Testament, most often with the meaning of *break* or *shatter*. Jeremiah employs it in this sense too (2:13;
19:10-11; cf. 28:12-13) . The noun may be rendered *fracture, breach,
shattering, crash, blow,* and so, in a more extended sense, *disaster* or
destruction. It is used graphically in military contexts, as in the poems
on the northern foe:

> For I bring evil from the north,
>   and great destruction (ושבר גדול) . 4:6*b*.

> Disaster follows hard upon disaster (שבר על־שבר) ,
>   the whole land is laid waste.   4:20; cf. 6:1.

But it is most characteristically and frequently used with the meaning
of *wound* [14]:

> They have healed the wound (שבר) of my people but lightly,
>   saying, "Peace, peace,"
>   when there is no peace.   6:14–8:11.

> Because of the wound (שבר) of the daughter, my people,
>   am I wounded (השברתי) ,
>   I mourn, and dismay has seized me.   8:21; cf. 14:17.

Only the original Hebrew is able to reveal the passion and poignancy
of some of the formulations. We content ourselves with two examples:

> אוי לי על־שברי נחלה מכתי
> ואני אמרתי אך זה חלי ואשאנו   10:19.

Here in this remarkably condensed and pregnant outcry we encounter
several characteristics of Jeremiah's style: the pervasive assonance reflecting the prophet's grief, the citation of his own words, "Woe is
me! This is my affliction" (RSV. lit. "my sickness"), and the concentration of key words of suffering and pain. It will be noted that

---

[13] Josef Scharbert, *Der Schmerz im Alten Testament*, Bonner Biblische Beiträge,
herausgegeben von F. Nötscher und Th. Schäfer (Bonn, 1955) , pp. 98, 108. Cf. Ludwig Köhler, *Hebrew Man* (London, 1956) , p. 18: "We must, however, point out
here that the Old Testament contains no expression of opinion at all as to what
is healthy and what is sick. . . . Furthermore the language of illness is very little
developed."

[14] Johannes Pedersen, *Israel: Its Life and Culture, I-II* (London, 1926) , p. 313:
"Evil is in its strongest form a breach, *shebher*, an infringement upon the whole,
which is peace. Breaches are most frequently mentioned in the prophets, in particular Jeremiah. His whole soul is scarred with breaches (10:19) because his
people are broken." Cf. 8:21; 14:17; 30:12.

46

The Terminology of Adversity in Jeremiah

the word שבר is parallel with מכה, which appears frequently in Jeremiah in similar contexts (6:7; 14:17; 15:18; 19:8; 30:12, 14, 17). A second example, likewise autobiographical and burdened with the weight of sorrow, is given in the laconic lament concerning the prophets:

> My heart is broken (נשבר) within me.[15]
>   all my bones are shaking;
> I am like a drunken man,
>   like a man overcome by wine,
> because of Yahweh
>   and because of his holy words.   23:9.

Again the assonance of grief is heard, but now accompanied, as so often in Jeremiah, by a vivid figure.

As we have observed, the motif is characteristically employed in rhetorically significant contexts, as in the concluding imprecation of the confessional lament of 17:14-18:

> Bring upon them the day of evil;
>   destroy them with a double destruction (שברון שברם).   17:18b.

Our final passage is so rich in the terminology of affliction that it might be taken as an expression *in nuce* of the general theme to which we are addressing ourselves:

> For thus Yahweh is saying[16]:
> "Your hurt is incurable (אנוש לשברך),
>   your wound is grievous (נחלה מכתך).
> There is no[17] medicine for your wound (מזור),
>   no healing for you.
> All your lovers have forgotten you;
>   they care nothing for you;
> for I have dealt you the blow (מכת) of an enemy,
>   the punishment of a merciless foe,
> because your guilt is great,
>   your sins flagrant.
> Why do you cry out over your hurt (שברך),
>   your pain (מכאבך) is incurable."   30:12-15a.

---

[15] For the psychical functions of physical organs, see J. Pedersen, *op. cit.*, pp. 150 ff. and *passim*; H. W. Robinson, "Hebrew Psychology," in A. S. Peake (ed.), *The People and the Book* (Oxford, 1925), pp. 262-64; A. R. Johnson, *The Vitality of the Individual in the Thought of Ancient Israel*, 2nd ed. (Cardiff, 1964), pp. 75-87; J. Scharbert, *op. cit.*, pp. 93-97.

[16] Johannes Hempel, *Heilung als Symbol und Wirklichkeit im biblischen Schrifttum* (Göttingen, 1965), p. 311: "Die Heilkunde des AT gehört in den

Translating and Understanding the Old Testament

The lexical data for wounding and healing here are ample and diverse. One half of the words concern these motifs. The key words appear in crucial contexts. The two most important, with which we have already become familiar, שבר and מכה, appear in the opening bicola and are then repeated climactically and chiastically, the second in the motivating clause of 14a, the first in the outcry of lament in 15a. But to these two words for "wound" Jeremiah now adds a third, מזור. It should properly be rendered "ulcer" or "boil" (so KB *ad loc.*) [18]. The final colon introduces still another term of affliction, employed in this form only once elsewhere in Jeremiah, but there illuminatingly in the description of Baruch's adversities (45:3) : incurable *your pain* (מכאבך; cf. 15:18). [19]

2. *Travail and anguish.*

A lexical field, more limited in extent than the foregoing, but equally revealing, is the terminology associated with anguish and anxiety. It is here that we encounter one of the most striking features of Jeremiah's speech and thought, his constant preoccupation with the mystery and perplexity of his birth. Already in the opening words of his call we listen to the solemn words of appointment and the prophet's anguished expostulation:

> Before I fashioned you in the body I knew you,
>> before you came forth from the womb I set you apart,
>> a prophet to the nations I have appointed you.
> Ah, Lord Yahweh!
>> Behold, I cannot speak,
> for I am only a boy.   1:5-6.

The words were remembered and on many an occasion conditioned the cast of Jeremiah's mind and the texture of his reflections. His

---

Zusammenhang mit der altorientalischen Volksmedizin, aber gerade auf deren Hintergrund zeigt sich ihre religionsgeschichtliche Sonderstellung. Sie konzentriert Krankmachen und Heilen auf ihren Gott, seinen Willen und seine (prophetischen) Werkzeuge, die sich im Töten und Heilen als solche legitimieren und seine souveräne Macht repräsentieren." See also G. von Rad, *Old Testament Theology*, I (New York, 1962) , 274. For parallels in the treaty curses, see D. R. Hillers, *op. cit.*, p. 65.

[17] Deleting "to uphold your cause," which intrudes upon the metaphor and may be a marginal gloss.

[18] See Mitchell J. Dahood, "Philological Notes on Jer. 18:14-15," *ZAW* LXXIV (1962) , 208. Cf. Hos. 5:13.

[19] Scharbert, *op. cit.*, pp. 45-47. Cf. 51:8; Isa. 53:3-4; Pss. 32:10; 38:18 (E.T. 17) ; Job 33:19. For Near Eastern parallels in the treaty curses, see D. R. Hillers, *op. cit.*, p. 65.

The Terminology of Adversity in Jeremiah

anguish is concentrated in his being born, born to be the kind of man he was. It comes to its most poignant expression in the confessional laments, which are for all the world personal commentaries on his birth. Thus, in one of the most impassioned of these personal disclosures he cries out:

> Woe is me, my mother, that you gave me birth,
>   a man of strife and a man of contention with the whole land.　　15:10.

Surely this is one of the most inward of Jeremiah's woes, and its force is enhanced, as in similar contexts, by the assonance of sorrow. In another confession he utters his desperation even more outspokenly and daringly:

> Cursed be the day
>   on which I was born!
> The day my mother gave me birth,
>   let it not be blessed!
> Cursed be the man
>   who brought the news to my father,
> "A son is born to you,"
>   making him very glad. . . .
> Why did I come forth from the womb
>   to see toil and sorrow,
>   and spend my days in shame?　　20:14-15, 18.

The same motif comes to expression in contexts of quite a different kind, notably in the poems about the northern foe. In the final lines of a succession of poems where the prophet's lyrical gifts reach their culmination we are given a picture that is almost ghastly in its effects, where the assonance again reenforces the wording:

> For I heard a cry as of a woman in travail (חולה),
>   anguish (צרה) as of one bringing forth her firstborn child.
> The cry of the daughter Zion gasping for breath,
>   stretching out her hands,
>   "Woe is me! I am fainting before murderers."　　4:31.

But nowhere are the anguish and torment and distraughtness of the prophet portrayed more passionately than in the lament of 4:19 ff.[20]

> O my bowels, my bowels! I writhe! (read אוחילה),
>   O walls of my heart!
> My heart is beating wildly,

---

[20] See D. R. Hillers, "A Convention in Hebrew Literature: The Reaction to Bad News," *ZAW* LXXVII (1965), 86-90.

Translating and Understanding the Old Testament

> I cannot keep silent,
>> for you have heard, O my soul, the sound of the trumpet,
>>> the alarm of war.   4:19.

The language penetrates other formulations too:

> What will you say when they set as head over you
>> those whom you yourselves have taught
>>> to be friends to you?
> Will not pangs (חבלים) take hold of you,
>> like those of a woman in travail (אשת לדה) ?
>>>   13:21 [21]; cf. 6:24; 22:23.

The word *distress* or *trouble* (צרה) often appears in related contexts (4:31; 6:24; 15:11). It may be well to remind ourselves that this terminology is all but absent in the Baruch prose narratives.

3. *Horror, terror, and desolation.*

The motifs are already anticipated in the prophet's call:

> Do not be dismayed (אל־תחת) by them,
>> lest I dismay you (אחתך) before them.   1:17*b*.

On more than one occasion the lines are echoed, and in similarly personal contexts:

> Let those be put to shame who persecute me,
>> but let not me be put to shame.
> Let them be dismayed (יחתו),
>> but let not me be dismayed (אחתה).
>>>   17:18*ab;* cf. 14:4, 8; 16:19; 30:10.

In the great lament we have already cited the thought is very much the same, although a different word is used:

> On account of the wound of the daughter, my people, am I wounded,
>> I mourn, and dismay (שמה) has seized me.   8:21.

Jeremiah was destined to be a messenger of judgment, so much so that his enemies taunt him with the name "Terror on every side" (מגור מסביב), a sentence he himself employed in his poems on the foe from the north (6:25) and in the title he gave to Pashhur when he was imprisoned in the upper Benjamin Gate of the Temple (20:1-4). It is revealing that he should refer to the nickname in his confessional disclosures:

[21] So RSV. The rendering is conjectural.

50

The Terminology of Adversity in Jeremiah

> For I hear many whispering,
>   "Terror on every side!"
> "Denounce him! Let us denounce him!"
>   say all my familiar friends,
>   watching for my fall.   20:10.

Our motifs are amply illustrated in numerous passages. Singularly, they appear in the climax of the indictment in the opening poem:

> Be appalled (שׁמּו), O heavens, at this,
>   bristle with horror (שׂערו), be utterly desolate (חרבו מאד). 2:12.

Such terminology appears elsewhere:

> An appalling and horrible thing (שׁמה ושׁערורה)
>   has happened in the land:
> the prophets prophesy falsely,
>   and the priests rule at their direction.   5:30-31a; cf. 23:14.

One of the words most frequently employed by Jeremiah, nearly always in referring to the destruction of the land, is שׁמם and its congeners, above all the noun שׁממה.

> Hark! a rumor! it comes!
>   a great commotion out of the north country
> to make the cities of Judah a desolation (שׁממה),
>   a lair of jackals.   10:22.

An even more eloquent instance of the motif appears in the heart of one of the most piercing of the divine self-disclosures:

> Many shepherds have destroyed my vineyard,
>   they have trampled down my portion,
> they have made my pleasant portion
>   a desolate wilderness (למדבר שׁממה).
> They have made it (Syr., Targ., Vulg.) a desolation (שׁממה),
>   desolate (שׁממה), it mourns to me.
> The whole land is made desolate (נשׁמה),
>   but no man lays it to heart.   12:10-11; cf. also 4:27; 6:8.

The noun שׁמה, always employed in contexts of judgment, is used similarly:

> The lions have roared against him,
>   they have roared loudly.
> They have made his land a waste (שׁמה),
>   his cities are in ruins, without inhabitant.   2:15; cf. 4:7.

But the word can also denote a dreadful and terrifying event. One example must suffice:

51

Translating and Understanding the Old Testament

> . . . making their land a terror (שׁמה),
>   a hissing for ever.
> Every one who passes by it is horrified (ישׁם)
>   and shakes his head.   18:16; cf. 19:8.

Jeremiah also knows the language of fear and trembling, of dread and anxiety. In a passage whose precise meaning is much controverted he portrays these sensations vividly, not only by the key words of affliction and pain, but also by the imagery with which he accompanies them:

> We hear a cry of panic (חרדה),
>   of terror (פחד) and no peace.
> Ask now and see,
>   can a man bear a child?
> Why then do I see every man
>   his hands on his loins, like a woman in labor?
> Why has every face turned pale?   30:5-6.

4. *Abandonment, rejection, and alienation.*

Among the most characteristic literary genres in the book of Jeremiah are the lawsuits with their indictments and verdicts. In these the charge launched against Judah is that she has *abandoned* or *forsaken* Yahweh. The verbal key word עזב is more frequently used than any other, for it is the antonym par excellence of the election. It is also a covenant word since it signifies the cancellation of the covenant bond. In a climactic context associated with the prophet's call, the word appears in a bicolon which summarizes all the indictments which are to follow:

> So I will pronounce my judgments against them
>   on account of all their evil in abandoning me (עזבוני).   1:16.

The lawsuits which follow (2:1–4:4) perpetuate the charge. In the climax of the first (2:1-13) it is formulated even more dramatically and succinctly: *me have they abandoned* (2:13ab). In precisely the same rhetorical collocation, the two strophes of the following poem stress the indictment with great effectiveness:

> Is it not this you have brought upon yourself,
>   your abandoning (עזבך) Yahweh your God?   2:17.

> Realize how evil and bitter is
>   your abandoning (עזבך) Yahweh your god.   2:19b.

The Terminology of Adversity in Jeremiah

The poems included in the lyrical sequence on the foe from the north preserve the crucial function of the motif in similar fashion:

> How can I forgive you?
> Your children have abandoned me   (עֲזָבוּנִי)
> and have sworn by no-gods.   5:7a

Again and again the people ask Jeremiah why it is that Yahweh has sent his terrible judgment upon them, why the land has been devastated and the city destroyed, and his reply is always the same: *they have abandoned their God.* It is true that some of these formulations bear the imprint of deuteronomic recasting, but the thought is certainly central to Jeremiah himself. The following text is illustrative:

> And when you tell this people all these words, and they say to you, "Why has Yahweh pronounced all this great evil against us? What is our iniquity? What is the sin we have committed against Yahweh our God?" then you shall say to them: "Because your fathers have abandoned (עָזְבוּ) me and not kept my law.
> 16:10-11; cf. 9:11-13 (E.T. 9:12-14) ; 19:3-4; 22:8-9.

When we turn to the second verb which Jeremiah uses to describe Judah's defection from Yahweh, we observe that the relevant texts have the same cumulative and decisive character. The verb מאס performs the same function as the word עזב and is present in similar contexts. It is usually rendered "refuse" or "reject."

> Hear, O earth!
> Behold, I am bringing disaster upon this people,
>   the fruit of their devices,
> because they have not given heed to my words;
>   and as for my law, they have rejected it (וַיִּמְאָסוּ).   6:19.

In the final pericope of the poems on the northern foe (6:27-30) and in the climactic conclusion, Jeremiah plays upon the word in dramatic fashion. He had been appointed an assayer and tester among his people. The imagery of refining is vividly described. The prophet's efforts are all to no avail, so the judgment is pronounced:

> Refuse silver (כֶּסֶף נִמְאָס) they shall be called,
>   because Yahweh has refused (מָאַס) them.
> 6:30; cf. the judgment upon the wise in 8:8-9.

The verb נתש, to "pluck up" or "uproot," belongs to the terminology of rejection. It is already sounded in the series of parallel verbs in the prophet's call (1:10) and is echoed in related series over and over again as a leitmotif (18:7; 24:6; 31:28; 42:10; 45:4). In a prose pas-

Translating and Understanding the Old Testament

sage which does not belong to Jeremiah but is consonant with his thought elsewhere, Yahweh addresses his people in the first person:

> Behold, *I will pluck them up* (נתשם) from their land, and *I will pluck up* the house of Judah from among them. And after *I have plucked them up*, I will again have compassion on them, and I will bring them again each to his heritage and each to his land. . . . But if any nation will not listen, then *I will utterly pluck it up* and destroy it, says Yahweh.
>
> 12:14b-17.

We observe here one of the most common literary features of Old Testament rhetoric, the propensity to employ the same or similar semantic terms in clusters. We may cite one example where it is not difficult to hear the authentic accents of the prophet:

> Hast thou utterly rejected (המאס) Judah?
>   Does thy soul loathe (געלה) Zion?
> Why hast thou smitten us
>   so that there is no healing for us?
> Do not spurn us (תנאץ), for thy name's sake;
>   do not dishonor (תנבל) thy glorious throne;
> remember and do not break thy covenant with us.   14:19, 21.

Judah's rejection of Yahweh has left him no alternative but to reject her. Interestingly, his pronouncements of judgment are formulated stylistically much as in the deuteronomically colored passages cited above (e.g. 23:33, 39). In an interior divine self-disclosure, throbbing with *pathos* and with the conflict between covenant love and covenant judgment, Yahweh speaks:

> I have abandoned (עזבתי) my house,
>   I have forsaken (נטשתי) my heritage;
> I have given the beloved of my soul
>   into the hands of her enemies.   12:7; cf. 7:29.

Much in the same spirit Yahweh admonishes Jerusalem in a climactic context:

> Be warned, O Jerusalem,
>   lest I be alienated (תקע) from you;
> lest I make you a desolation,
>   an uninhabited land.   6:8.

Only here among the prophets does the verb יקע occur. RSV renders "be alienated," which doubtless gives the nuance required, but Köhler-Baumgartner define it "turn one's back in disgust" (so Bright, *ad loc.*).

The Terminology of Adversity in Jeremiah

5. *Grief and mourning.*

In the foregoing survey of some of the major areas of affliction and adversity, we have not infrequently come upon passages where Jeremiah gives voice to his sorrow and pain. It is often said that Jeremiah is the most subjective of the prophets, and it is true that he speaks more of himself and more intimately and inwardly than the other messengers of Yahweh. Our closest parallels to his way of speaking, to the literary genres in which he records his grief, and to many of the most characteristic key words are to be found in the book of Psalms, upon which, it is sometimes averred, he exerted his influence. The task before us now is to scrutinize the lexical deposit of suffering, to record how and where the words appear, and to call attention once more to the interior continuities of the prophet's utterances.

We shall speak first of all of a series of elemental words, exclamations, and shouts and assonant sounds, which Jeremiah uses in situations that evoke his astonishment and revulsion. To the first of these we have already referred, the expostulation of protest on the occasion of his call to be a prophet:

> Ah (אהה), Lord Yahweh!
> Behold (הנה), I cannot speak,
> for (כי) I am only a boy.   1:6.

Each of the introductory particles appears elsewhere in similar contexts. The first belongs to the class of words described many years ago by Rudolf Otto as *numinose Urlaute,* numinous elemental sounds. When Yahweh reveals the appalling disaster that is to befall the leaders of Judah at the coming of the foe from the north, Jeremiah cries out in the same way: "Ah (אהה), Lord Yahweh, you have surely deceived this people" (4:10). When he is denied the office of intercessor and the prophets deceive the people by their optimistic assurances, he registers his protest in identical manner (14:13). It is interesting to observe that Baruch preserves the expression (32:17).

The second particle is the outcry of אוי, "Woe!" We listen to it in the poems on the foe from the north. In our first example, it is accompanied by other ejaculatory words:

> Behold (הנה), he comes up like clouds,
>   his chariots like whirlwind;
> His horses are swifter than eagles—
>   Woe to us (אוי לנו) for (כי) we are ruined!
> Wash your heart from evil, O Jerusalem,
>   that you may be saved.

55

Translating and Understanding the Old Testament

How long (עד־מתי) shall evil thoughts
lodge within you?   4:13-14; cf. 13:27.

The second example is drawn from the same historical situation, but here it appears in a series of shouts before the relentless advance of the foe:

Woe to us (אוי לנו), for the day declines,
for the shadows of evening lengthen.   6:4*b.*

We hear the words again in the dying shriek of the prostitute:

Woe is me (אוי־נא לי)! I am fainting before my murderers!   4:31*c.*

Finally, Jeremiah opens one of his most stirring confessions with the cry,

"Woe is me (אוי־לי), my mother."   15:10*a;* cf. also 4:13 and 45:3.

The word הוי, "alas," is used with the same frequency. The one instance we shall cite is notable not only for its impressive repetition, but also for the extraordinary economy of the cola:

They shall not lament for him,
  "Alas, my brother," or "Alas, sister!"
They shall not lament for him,
  "Alas, lord," or "Alas, his majesty!"   22:18*bc;* cf. 23:1; 30:7; 34:5.

The cry, עד מתי, "How long," which appears in the laments of the Psalter and in other texts from the ancient Near East, is present in Jeremiah too. In the final words of a shattering lament Jeremiah cries out:

How long must I see the standard,
  and hear the sound of the trumpet?   4:21; cf. 4:14 cited above.

In more plaintive mood he bewails the drought:

How long will the land mourn,
  and the grass of the field wither?   12:4*a.*

Poignantly he speaks to his people:

How long will you waver,
  O faithless daughter?   31:22*a;* cf. 13:27; 23:26.

The word קול is sometimes used as an interjection, "hark," and introduces the messages of destruction and woe, as in 3:21; 8:19; 10:22; 25:36. At other times it is used in the familiar sense of "voice," but mostly in contexts of indictment and affliction (4:15-16; 9:21 [E.T.

The Terminology of Adversity in Jeremiah

19]) . The word הנה, "behold," similarly often introduces messages of judgment and doom (1:15; 2:35; 4:13; 5:15; 6:10*b*; 8:15; 9:14 [E.T. 15]; 10:18, etc.) .

The prophecies of Jeremiah present us with a veritable thesaurus of terms designating sorrow, mourning, and wailing. They not only contain laments and dirges, but also employ the *termini technici* for the literary genre. The prophet calls upon the people to cut off their hair and to raise a קינה on the bare heights (7:29*a*) , or to take up a בכי and נהי for the mountains, a קינה for the pastures of the wilderness (9:9 [E.T. 9:10]) . Yahweh instructs him to call for the professional mourning women מקוננות to come that they may lift up a נהי over the people, and Jeremiah addresses the women with solemn summons:

> Hear, O women, the word of Yahweh,
>> let your ear receive the word of his mouth;
> teach your daughters a lament (נהי)
>> and each to her neighbor a dirge (קינה) .   9:19 (E.T. 9:20) .

Among the terms denoting grief or sorrow, the noun יגון, which appears relatively seldom, is found in crucial contexts and expresses in a word the motif which is elsewhere amplified and elaborated. The opening colon of the great lament of 8:18-23 (E.T. 8:18–9:1) is corrupt and requires emendation (see BH *ad loc.*) , but does not involve the alteration of our word:

> My grief (יגון עלי) is beyond healing,
>> my heart is sick (דוי) within me.   8:18.

In a final outburst of anguish and grief in a confessional lament Jeremiah cries out:

> Why, O why did I come forth from the womb
>> to see toil (עמל) and sorrow (יגון) !   20:18.

In the closing pericope of what was doubtless at one time the conclusion to the original form of the book, Yahweh significantly quotes Baruch's tale of travail and agony:

> Woe is me! for Yahweh has added sorrow (יגון) to my pain (מכאבי) ;
> I am weary with my groaning (אנחתי) , and I find no rest.   45:3.

We observe once more that the language of suffering is concentrated, that the cry of "Woe!" is motivated by a chronicle of affliction, and, above all, that God himself endures a grief incalculably greater than Baruch's.

Translating and Understanding the Old Testament

An examination of the nomenclature of mourning reveals the
diversity of the linguistic data. Translations seldom do sufficient
justice to the nuances and connotations of the words or to their precise
function in a particular context. Thus the same word is often employed where the Hebrew has several different words with a variety
of meanings or shades of meaning. One should always be on the look-
out for *le mot juste*, especially in parallel lines, but also where the
same word is employed within a single literary unit or literary genre.
We now cite several instances of the motif of mourning. The first is
drawn from a graphic description of the foe from the north and constitutes its climax:

> For this gird you with sackcloth,
>   lament (ספדו) and wail (הילילו) .   4:8; cf. 8:21.

The final verb gains its force by the assonance of the onomatopoeia,
but also by the fact that it underlines and accentuates the preceding
parallel verb. Our second example is also taken from the poetic
sequence of the northern foe and brings the poem to its finale:

> O Daughter, my people, gird on sackcloth,
>   and roll (התפלשי) in ashes;
> make mourning (אבל עשי) as for an only son,
>   most bitter lamentation (מספד תמרורים) ,
> for suddenly the destroyer
>   will come upon us.   6:26; cf. 12:11; 14:2.

Each of the first four cola contains a predication of mourning and
is brought to a dramatic focus by the concluding motivation. Our
third exemplar (16:1-9) is of a quite different order. The pericope is
a prose narrative. The formulation is to be ascribed to the deuteronomic or scribal editor, but there is no reason to question its authenticity. Jeremiah is forbidden to enter the house of mourning (בית
מרזח). He is not to lament (לספוד) or bemoan (תנד) his fellow
countrymen. The dead are not to be buried or lamented (יספדו) . No
one shall lament for the people or lacerate himself (יתגדד) or make
himself bald (יקרח) for them. The verb *mourn* (אבל) is sometimes
paralleled with the verb לדר, to put on black, as in 4:28 (cf. also 8:21;
14:2) . At other times it is linked with the verb נוד, to move to and
fro in the manner of those who mourn:

> Who will have pity (יחמל) on you, O Jerusalem,
>   or who will bemoan (ינוד) you?   15:5a; cf. 16:5.

Even more impressively:

The Terminology of Adversity in Jeremiah

Weep not (אל־תבכו) for the dead,
   and do not bemoan him (אל־תנדו) ;
but weep bitterly (בכו בכו) for him who goes away,
   for he shall return no more
      to see his native land.   22:10; cf. 31:18.

The sound of weeping is heard elsewhere, especially in the confessional lament of the long liturgy of 3:1–4:8:

A voice is heard on the bare heights,
   the weeping (בכי) and pleading (תחנוני) of Israel's sons,
because they have perverted their way,
   they have forgotten Yahweh their God.   3:21.

And again in the lament to which we have had occasion to refer before:

O that my head were waters,
   and my eyes a fountain of tears,
that I might weep (אבכה) day and night
   for the slain of my daughter, my people.   8:23 (E.T. 9:1).

And finally in the pathetic lines from the Little Book of Comfort:

A voice is heard in Ramah,
   lamentation (נהי) and bitter weeping (בכי תמרורים) ,
Rachel is weeping (מבכה) for her chidlren:
   she refuses to be comforted because they are not.
               31:15; cf. 9:9 (E.T. 9:10; 31:9) .

If we are to release our study from exclusively semantic confinement, then it becomes imperative that we take account of the style, rhetoric, and literary types of the materials that have come under our inspection. Now the most obvious reflection to make is that they are clothed in the rhythms, parallelisms, and structures of ancient Hebrew poetry. The terminology of adversity is woven into the patterns of the rhetorical forms. Its key words often determine the articulation and movement of the literary unit. The other prophets, to be sure, also employ poetry for their proclamations, but in Jeremiah the lyrical impulse is more native, more inward, more existential. In not a few contexts, as in the poems on the foe from the north and sometimes in the laments, he is more poet than prophet.[22] The prophet's

---

[22] G. von Rad, *Old Testament Theology*, II (Edinburgh, 1965) , 201: "This again shows us that Jeremiah is much more keenly inflamed, and in an entirely novel way, by a poetic impulse which exists quite independently from prophecy. It also raises the question of how we are to evaluate this remarkably large increase of the element of pure poetry."

Translating and Understanding the Old Testament

feelings and reflections are transmuted into free lyrical verse, in striking contrast to the so-called deuteronomic sections and the biographical narratives of Baruch.[23] Nowhere is this more clear than in the speech of adversity and affliction. There is nothing contrived or studied about it. It records itself variously: in exclamations and interjections, in emphatic particles, in passionate shouts and urgent expostulations and warnings, and, above all, in extraordinarily striking assonances. Yet all these are couched in the forms and patterns characteristic of Hebrew poetry.

We have called attention from time to time to the affinities of Jeremiah's speech and literary types with the language, forms, and images encountered in the literatures of the other peoples of the ancient Near East. These relationships cannot of course be denied. It is very clear that Jeremiah has been influenced by such predications. But it is important to point out that while he does indeed make use of conventional forms and conventional semantic property, he is by no means dominated by them. He is not simply a borrower; it is even doubtful whether he was aware of appropriating "foreign" modes of speech. Rather, he subordinates them to his own unique manner of speaking, to his own experiences, and to his own literary propensities. We are to think here, then, as in the case of his employment of the conventional literary types among his own people, not so much of conscious literary borrowing, but rather of spiritual and cultural affinity. It has been pointed out by G. von Rad that in the so-called confessions of the prophet the formulation and style vary considerably. While they are indeed related to the *Gattung* of the individual lament, "Jeremiah interpenetrated the conventional usage of the old cultic form with his own concern as a prophet, and transformed it."[24] But more than that, the dialogical and conversational manner of the prophet emerge more strikingly than anywhere else in the Old Testament. His capacity for empathy, both social and cosmic, his profound sympathy with his own people, despite their waywardness and infidelity, his ability to identify himself interiorly with their afflictions

[23] Ernst Cassirer, *Language and Myth* (New York, 1946), pp. 34-35: "The modern science of language, in its efforts to elucidate the 'origin' of language, has indeed gone back to Hamann's dictum, that poetry is 'the mother tongue of humanity'; its scholars have emphasized that speech is rooted not in the prosaic, but in the poetic aspect of life, so that its ultimate basis must be sought not in the preoccupation with the objective view of things and their classification according to certain attributes, but in the primitive power of subjective feeling."

[24] G. von Rad, *op. cit.*, p. 201.

The Terminology of Adversity in Jeremiah

are after all more significant than all the many parallels, impressive as they often are, that may be adduced to his utterances.[25]

Closely related to the terminology of sickness, pain, and indeed every manner of affliction is the pervasive motif of healing and of Yahweh as Israel's Physician.[26] Here again the prophet is strongly under the influence of his spiritual predecessor Hosea (5:13; 6:1; 7:1; 11:3; 14:4). The motif is an ancient one and has its roots in the traditions associated with Moses. In the diminutive pericope immediately following the Song of Miriam which is formulated in deuteronomic style, the finale is given as a divine first-person self-asseveration, "For I am Yahweh, your Healer" (Exod. 15:26). As we should expect, the pleas for healing are heard in the prayers and laments, and thanksgivings are raised for restoration to health and well-being. Given the psycho-physical character of Israel's mentality, it is not surprising that the terminology is frequently employed for forgiveness. As in Hosea, apostasy is understood as sickness. In the very heart of the great liturgy of 3:1–4:4, Yahweh pleads with his recreant sons:

> Return, O faithless sons,
> I will heal your faithlessness.   3:22.

The false prophets heal the wound of the people only lightly, promising health and restoration when there is none (6:14–8:11). Poignantly the people cry out that Yahweh has smitten them so that there is no healing for them (14:19). In one of his confessions Jeremiah cries out that his wound is incurable, refusing to be healed (15:18), and in another he pleads passionately for healing:

> Heal me, O Yahweh, and I shall be healed,
> save me, and I shall be saved;
> for Thou art my praise.   17:14.

Similarly in a moving lament he gives vent to his grief:

> Is there no balm in Gilead?
> Is there no physician there?
> Why then has the health of the daughter, my people,
> not been restored?   8:22; cf. 30:13, 17.

[25] The list of parallels could be greatly extended beyond those we have cited. See *inter alia* Geo. Widengren, *The Accadian and Hebrew Psalms of Lamentation as Religious Documents; a Comparative Study* (Stockholm, 1937), p. x; Adam Falkenstein and Wolfram von Soden, *Sumerische und Akkadische Hymnen und Gebete* (Zürich, 1953).

[26] J. J. Stamm, *Erlösen und Vergeben im Alten Testament* (Bern, 1940), pp. 78-84; Johannes Hempel, "Ich bin der Herr, dein Arzt," *TLZ* (1957), cols. 809-26; *Heilung als Symbol und Wirklichkeit im biblischen Schrifttum.*

Translating and Understanding the Old Testament

Theologically, all the outcries and fervent pleas and poignant plaints have their *raison d'être,* their setting or context, and their presuppositions in the faith that there is One who hears the words of his servants. He is their healer who knows their afflictions and adversities, and knows them more deeply than they do.

The profuse terminology of adversity and affliction in Jeremiah is to be explained, at least in part, by the interior conflicts within the prophet himself. From the very beginning he was fashioned and set apart (1:5 הִקְדַּשְׁתִּיךָ) to be the prophet of Yahweh to an apostate age, to be separated from normal human relationships, and to stand over against the leaders of Judah. Yet the radical paradox which underlies his prophetic activity and ministry is that he feels himself deeply drawn to those upon whom he is called to pronounce judgment. His mission as Yahweh's prophet conflicts with his mission as intercessor for the people, an office which was obviously congenial to him, but one which he is denied again and again. There were many prophets in Jeremiah's time, but he finds himself pitted over against them. He denies that they have been called and sent by Yahweh. His ministry is closely connected with the Temple and its precincts, but he is excluded from them and on one occasion is placed in the stocks. During the Babylonian siege he urges the king to capitulate and is even suspected of going over to the enemy. His familiar friends reject him and cry out in denunciation and derision against him. He laments that it is his cruel fate to sit alone, filled with the divine indignation and unsupported by any solace from man or God (15:17). His foes are those of his own household (12:6). He is unsustained and uncomforted by wife and children. But, above all, he is torn and shattered by the sense of the apparent absence and neutrality of God. All the forces that make for solidarity and community for which he so deeply longed are withdrawn from him. It is his destiny to walk alone. His afflictions are the afflictions of an isolated soul, and they are doubtless accountable for the language he employs to body forth his message.

Finally, the terminology of adversity has its explanation in the character of Jeremiah's mission and calling. Like the prophets before and after him he is under the compulsion of the divine imperative to speak all that is commanded him. And like them he is to suffer the pain of rejection and obloquy and persecution. Isaiah of Jerusalem too was warned that all his prophetic preaching would be of no avail, that throughout his long career he would encounter naught but stubborn resistance and deafness, but that he must nevertheless persist in proclaiming the divine word of judgment against his own people.

The Terminology of Adversity in Jeremiah

Ezekiel is also sent to a stubborn and rebellious people, and in his call receives from God's hand a scroll inscribed on both sides "with mourning, lamentations, and woe," which he devours at Yahweh's command, thus taking to himself the words that he is to utter. But the autobiographical accounts are relatively limited. With Jeremiah it is otherwise. He is sent to speak all that he is commanded to speak, but is admonished not to fear, for Yahweh will be with him to deliver him from his foes. Yahweh will make him "a fortified city, an iron pillar, and bronze walls against the whole land" (1:18; cf. 15:19-20). He is to live his prophetic life under the abiding assurance that he is speaking for God, and that the divine will and purpose will prevail. God's strength will be sufficient to meet Jeremiah's weakness. None of the prophets was so little "a man of iron" as Jeremiah. It is revealing that he so often employs the verb יכל, "to be able." Over against Jeremiah's inability and frailty stand the ultimate power and sovereignty of God. Over against his "failures" stand the vindication and "success" of the divine Victor. Yet, despite the frequent assurances of divine help and support, these are shrouded and concealed from him. Upon occasion he could rejoice in Yahweh's nearness (15:16) and that the only legitimate source of human pride and glorying was to know and understand Yahweh "who practices covenant love, justice, and righteousness in the earth" (9:23-24). The apostle Paul knows these words (II Cor. 10:17), but despite all his "boastings," all the adversities and afflictions he had suffered, he is left with nothing but his weakness. Of these he dares to boast, and in his darkest hour he is solaced by the words which came to him, "My grace is sufficient for you, for my power is made perfect in weakness" (II Cor. 12:9)

Part Three

*OLD TESTAMENT HISTORY
AND THEOLOGY*

11

Baruch the Scribe

James Muilenburg

THE historical period extending from the reign of Ashurbanipal, the last of the great Assyrian monarchs (663–627 BC), to the accession of Cyrus as ruler over the Persian Empire in the year 538 BC is one of the most amply documented as it is one of the most culturally significant in the history of the ancient Near East. It is also one of the most literate and articulate. Thanks chiefly to the discovery of the library of Ashurbanipal by Hormuzd Rassam in 1853, we have at our disposal today a wealth and variety of literary works and inscriptional remains to which it would be difficult to adduce a parallel. The long period of Assyrian hegemony over Western Asia was slowly drawing to a close, and forces of great vitality were challenging not only the structures of Assyrian imperial organization, but also the mentalities and interior dispositions of the peoples of the Near East. New ideas were beginning to stir in that world, and everywhere men were animated by historical forces and psychological drives more potent than anything that had been known since the period of 'the first internationalism' seven centuries earlier.[1] The perplexities and dishevelments of the age, its fears and forebodings,

---

[1] The phrase is Breasted's. Compare S. A. Cook, 'The Fall and Rise of Judah', *The Cambridge Ancient History*, eds. J. B. Bury, S. A. Cook and F. E. Adcock (Cambridge: at the University Press, 1929), vol. III, p. 394: 'There was an interconnection of peoples, for a parallel to which we must go back to the Amarna Age.'

The Former Prophets and the Latter Prophets

its malaise and nostalgia for tradition are reflected in one fashion
or another in the literature of the times, not only in Assyria, but
also throughout the vaster ranges of its empire.[2] Ashurbanipal
was a scholar and a scribe, and boasts of his proficiency as copyist
and decipherer of the ancient Sumerian and Akkadian records.[3]
His reign marks the zenith of Assyrian art and literature,
and it is to him more than to any other that we owe our knowledge of the age.[4] He dispatched royal scribes throughout
Assyria and Babylonia in order that they might assemble
the ancient texts, copy and translate them, and prepare them
for deposit in the library. Business texts and letters appear in
profusion, but also omen texts, reflecting the distraughtness
and insecurity of the men of that age,[5] lengthy chronicles or

[2] W. F. Albright, *From the Stone Age to Christianity* (Baltimore: The
Johns Hopkins Press, 1940), pp. 240–55. 'It is not surprising that this
age of growing insecurity, when the very foundations of life were
trembling, should give rise to an earnest effort to find a cure for the
increasing *malaise* of the social organism' (pp. 240f.). 'The question of
theodicy always comes to the fore during prolonged times of crisis, when
human emotions are winnowed and purified by a sustained catharsis'
(p. 252).

[3] Jack Finegan, *Light from the Ancient Past* (Princeton: Princeton
University Press, 1946). Note the following words of Ashurbanipal: 'I
received the revelation of the wise Adapa, the hidden treasure of the
art of writing . . . I read the beautiful clay tablets from Sumer and the
obscure Akkadian writing which is hard to master. I had my joy in the
reading of inscriptions on stone from the time before the flood' (p. 181).
See also E. Speiser, 'Mesopotamia Up to the Assyrian Period: Scribal
Concepts of Education', in *City Invincible*, eds. Carl H. Kraeling and
Robert M. Adams (Chicago: The University of Chicago Press, 1960),
p. 107 and B. Landsberger, *ibid.*, pp. 110f., for an estimate of Ashurbanipal's claims.

[4] A. T. Olmstead, *History of Assyria* (New York: Charles Scribner's
Sons, 1923), pp. 489ff.

[5] *The Reports of the Magicians and Astrologers of Nineveh and Babylon
in the British Museum*, ed. R. Campbell Thompson (London: Luzac &
Co., 1900), vol. II; François Thureau-Dangin, *Rituels accadiens* (Paris:
Ernest Leroux, 1921); *ANET*, 2nd ed. (Princeton: Princeton University
Press, 1955), pp. 334–8, 349–52. Note the comment of Campbell
Thompson, *op. cit.*, p. xv: 'The astrologer or the prophet who could

Baruch the Scribe

annals,[6] administrative documents of different kinds, treaties and rituals and much else. It was a period of *Sturm und Drang* in which men sought to overcome the incoherence and uncertainty of the times by appealing to astrologists and magicians to discern the signs of the times, or by recourse to the ancient texts, whether cosmological or mythological, to encounter the end of one age and the beginning of another, or by reflecting upon the great cultural deposits of the remote past to discover resources for the present. It was a scribal age, an age of many scribes, in which the monarch himself played a central role and provided an impetus to learning and education which extended far and wide throughout his realm.

It should occasion no surprise that the corrosive forces at work throughout Western Asia during this period should exact their toll from the kingdom of Judah, the last buffer state between Assyria and Egypt, the ultimate goal of Assyrian imperialist aggression, not only politically and economically, but also psychologically and culturally. From an early period Israel's faith was governed by the conviction that the sequences of history were embraced by an all-controlling purpose and an ultimate sovereignty. It is significant, therefore, that a substantial part of the Old Testament was composed during this period of the decline and fall of one empire and

---

foretell fair things for the nation, or disasters and calamities for their enemies, was a man whose words were regarded with reverence and awe ... The soothsayer was as much a politician as the statesman, and he was not slow in using the indications of political changes to point the moral of his astrological observations.'

[6] D. D. Luckenbill, *Ancient Records of Assyria and Babylonia* (Chicago: University of Chicago Press, 1927), vol. II, pp. 290ff.; D. J. Wiseman, *Chronicles of Chaldean Kings, 626–556 BC* (London: Trustees of the British Museum, 1956). Note Luckenbill's comment, *op. cit.*, p. 290: 'In the reign of Ashurbanipal (668–626 BC) we reach the high-water mark of Assyrian historical writing – as regards quantity and literary merit ... Furthermore, the great literary activity of Ashurbanipal seems to have come in the second part of his reign, after the overthrow of Shamash-shum-ukîn in 648 BC, and even when our documents are dated by eponyms we are in doubt as to their sequence, since the order of the eponymous years from 648 on is in doubt.' See also Olmstead, *loc. cit.*

The Former Prophets and the Latter Prophets

the emergence and rise of another.[7] Even if we make full allowance for later accretions and supplementations, the amount of the literary precipitate is very impressive.[8] There was, first of all, the so-called great Deuteronomic work, extending from Deuteronomy through II Kings, a work which sought to explain why it was that the two kingdoms of Israel and Judah were destroyed, why the Lord of history had decreed his judgment upon the historical people κατ' ἐξοχὴν.[9] The great prophetic books of Jeremiah, Ezekiel, and Second Isaiah also come from this time, as do the smaller prophetic works of Zephaniah, Nahum, Habakkuk and Malachi.[10] The book of Lamentations too must be assigned to the period shortly after the downfall of Judah and the end of the monarchy.[11] If the book of Job belongs to this time, as some scholars hold, the situation becomes even more impressive.[12] Just

[7] Compare Hermann Gunkel, in 'Kultur der Gegenwart', *Die orientalischen Literaturen*, herausgegeben von Paul Hinneberg (Leipzig and Berlin, 1925), Teil I, Abteilung vii, p. 96: *'Die Literatur hatte vor den grossen Katastrophen ihre klassische Zeit erlebt. Das geistige Leben stand demals fast auf allen Gebieten, die Israel überhaupt gepflegt hat, in höchster Blüte.'* See also John L. McKenzie, s.j., 'Reflections on Wisdom', *JBL* 86 (March, 1967), p. 8: 'The scribes of Israel who were also the sages of Israel were not the first to collect in writing the memories of their people. The libraries of Nippur and of Ashurbanipal were obviously deliberate efforts to collect entire literary traditions. It is not without interest that both collections were made shortly before political collapse; and one wonders how much scribal activity was instigated by Josiah, who attempted a revival of the Davidic monarchy.' For an authoritative account of the latter, see *inter alia* R. de Vaux, 'Titres et fonctionnaires egyptiens a la cour de David et de Salomon', *RB* 48 (1939), pp. 394–405.

[8] If one undertakes to count the pages in Kittel's edition of the Masoretic Text, it will be recognized that almost four hundred pages out of the 1,434 may well come from our period.

[9] Gerhard von Rad, *Studies in Deuteronomy*, SBT 9, trans. David Stalker (London: SCM Press, 1953), pp. 74–91.

[10] Bruce T. Dahlberg, 'Studies in the Book of Malachi' (Dissertation, Union Theological Seminary, New York, 1963).

[11] Norman K. Gottwald, *Studies in the Book of Lamentations*, SBT 14 (London: SCM Press, 1954).

[12] R. H. Pfeiffer, *Introduction to the Old Testament* (New York: Harper & Brothers, 1941), p. 677; S. L. Terrien, 'Introduction to Job',

Baruch the Scribe

as Ashurbanipal and later Nabonidus sought to find in the past some threshold into the inchoate future, some ποῦ στῶ from which to withstand the agitation of stormy political seasons, so the composers of Deuteronomy had sought to comprehend the turbulence of the present within the context of the age of Moses and the words attributed to him. It has too long been our practice to speak of Deuteronomists, traditionists, and redactors. But such terms are nondescript. In all probability it is in not a few instances with scribes with whom we have to do, scribes who were not only copyists, but also and more particularly composers who gave to their works their form and structure, and determined to a considerable degree their wording and terminology.[13] In Judah as in Assyria we are living in a scribal age, an age of scribes who occupied a strategic position in the royal house of David and were entrusted with the archives of both palace and Temple.[14] The names of most of the scribes during the history of the monarchy are unknown to us, but it is not without significance that they appear more conspicuously and frequently in the latter part of the seventh century and the beginning of the sixth than they do

---

IB 3, pp. 884–91; 'Quelques remarques sur les affinités de Job avec le Deutéro-Isaïe', *SVT* 15, Congrès de Genève (Leiden: E. J. Brill, 1966), pp. 295–310.

[13] McKenzie, *loc. cit.*: 'The Israelite wise men who were the scribes of Deuteronomy knew that the past is not meaningful unless it is continuous with the present . . .' Moshe Weinfeld, 'Deuteronomy – the Present State of Inquiry', *JBL* 86 (Sept., 1967), pp. 249–62, especially p. 254, where Weinfeld attributes the crystallization of Deuteronomy to the scribes of Hezekiah and Josiah. See also his article on 'The Origin of the Humanism in Deuteronomy', *JBL* 80 (Sept., 1961), pp. 241–7.

[14] Salo W. Baron, *A Social and Religious History of the Jews*, vol. I, 2nd rev. ed. (New York: Columbia University Press, 1952), p. 153: 'We would know few priests or scribes by name were it not for their accidental appearance in the political arena, but their anonymous contributions, however slow and imperceptible, were as vital and lasting as the more spectacular contributions of the others. There is no means of measuring human greatness. Would one venture to decide who was greater, the anonymous author of Deuteronomy, or Jeremiah, the prophet, the tragic grandeur of whose life has been so rich a source of inspiration? As it happened, both these men were priests.'

The Former Prophets and the Latter Prophets

either during the United Monarchy of David and Solomon, or, for that matter, at any other time in the history of the monarchy. It seems probable that Josiah's policy of reviving the United Monarchy also involved the restoration of the officials of the royal court.[15]

If we leave the book of Job out of account, since its date is still much controverted, there are two books which occupy a position of pre-eminence above all others. Ever since the publication of Duhm's commentary on Jeremiah in 1901, it has been recognized that Jeremiah contains not a few passages which are closely related in style, terminology, and representation to Deuteronomy.[16] The affinities are not limited to these passages, however, but are to be recognized in other prose narratives as well. The best explanation for these affinities is that we are dealing in both works with a conventional mode of composition.[17] We encounter much the same style in the Deuteronomic history as we do in Deuteronomy, though there are differences in representation and theology. It has been suggested by more than one scholar that it is to the scribal family of Shaphan that we are to turn for the authorship of the Deuteronomistic history,[18] and while this can be little more than

---

[15] See *inter alia* de Vaux, *loc. cit.*; Joachim Begrich, 'Sōfēr und Mazkir; ein Beitrag zur inneren Geschichte des davidischalomonischen Grossreiches und des Königreiches Juda', *ZAW* 58 (1940–41), pp. 1–29.

[16] See above all Sigmund Mowinckel, *Zur Komposition des Buches Jeremia*, Videnskapsselskapets Skrifter II. Hist.-Filos, Klasse, 1913, No. 5, Kristiania, 1914 and *Prophecy and Tradition*, Avhandlinger Utgitt av Det Norske Videnskaps-Akademi in Oslo, II. Hist.-Filos. Klasse, 1946, No. 3.

[17] John Bright, 'The Date of the Prose Sermons of Jeremiah', *JBL* 70 (March, 1951), pp. 15–35.

[18] A. Jepsen, *Die Quellen des Königsbuches* (Halle: Max Niemeyer Verlag, 1956), pp. 94f.; Weinfeld, 'Deuteronomy – the Present State of Inquiry', *JBL* 86 (Sept., 1967), p. 255, n. 35. Weinfeld rightly points out that a distinction should be made between Deuteronomy and the historiography of the Deuteronomic history and the 'editorial part of Jeremiah. But these three literary strands have a common theological outlook and identical stylistic features and therefore must be considered as a product of a continuous scribal school. In my opinion this school is to be connected with the family of Shaphan the scribe who took an active part in the discovery of the book in the time of Josiah'.

Baruch the Scribe

a conjecture it has much to commend it. That is to say, in both instances we are dealing with scribal style and with a scribal *modus scribendi*. What is more, it has been frequently pointed out that Jeremiah is to be understood as a second Moses or that he performs the functions of the Mosaic office (compare Deut. 18.15ff. and Jer. 1.4–10).[19]

The importance of Jeremiah in the history of Israel's religion and more especially of Israel's prophecy is generally recognized. It is often pointed out that we know Jeremiah more intimately than any other of the prophets. But this has often led to the mistaken conclusion that it is his interior self disclosures that mark his uniqueness. On the other hand, we are frequently informed today that he is only following conventional and traditional literary forms derived from the cult.[20] That Jeremiah was indeed an important person in his age cannot be legitimately questioned, indeed far more important than we are wont to think. Once we have recognized wherein his true importance lies we are on our way to solving some of the most contended and controversial issues which the man and his book pose for us. We must view the prophet first of all and above all as a major figure in the political, cultural, religious, and indeed international life of the period. His call to be a prophet does not overstate matters. He is appointed to be a prophet over the nations, and this was how he was meant to be understood. If we may trust our text, as I think we may, then

---

[19] H. J. Kraus, *Die prophetische Verkündigung des Rechts in Israel*, ThSt 51 (Zurich: Evangelischer Verlag AG, 1957); P. B. Broughton, 'The Call of Jeremiah: the Relation of Deut. 18.9–22 to the Call of Jeremiah', *ABR* 6 (1958), pp. 37–46; James Muilenburg, 'The "Office" of the Prophet in Ancient Israel', *The Bible in Modern Scholarship*, ed. J. Philip Hyatt (Nashville: Abingdon Press, 1965), pp. 74–97; Norman Habel, 'The Form and Significance of the Call Narratives', *ZAW* 77 (1965), pp. 297–323; W. L. Holladay, 'The Background of Jeremiah's Self-Understanding', *JBL* 83 (June, 1964), pp. 154ff. See also W. Zimmerli, *Ezechiel*, BKAT XIII (Neukirchen-Vluyn: Verlag der Buchhandlung des Erziehungsvereins, 1955), pp. 13–37.

[20] Henning Graf Reventlow, *Liturgie und prophetisches Ich bei Jeremia* (Gütersloh: Gütersloher Verlagshaus Gerd Mohn, 1963).

The Former Prophets and the Latter Prophets

Jeremiah was summoned to be Yahweh's covenant mediator, the royal emissary from the heavenly court, the divinely accredited spokesman to an age in radical ferment.[21] He is to address his nation and other nations with the word that has been committed to him to proclaim. He is endowed with the charismatic gift and is given authority and power over kingdoms and nations to pluck up and tear down, to build and to plant. The awareness of this great commission animates the prophet's mind throughout his career. Precisely because he was ordained for such a destiny he incurred the wrath of all those in high places he dared to oppose. Precisely because he is representative of the divine sovereignty or government he ventures to attack the corruption of all the venerable institutions by which his contemporaries sought to order their lives.

The cultural milieu of Jeremiah's ministry is international. The confusion and chaos within the kingdom of Judah have their source in remote lands, and Jeremiah finds himself destined to speak to that situation. The threat or actual presence of war persists throughout the ancient Near East during the period of his ministry. The book throughout bears witness to the precariousness of the international crisis, most notably in the year of the Battle of

---

[21] G. Ernest Wright, 'The Fruit of a Lifetime', *Interpretation* 18 (July, 1964), p. 362: 'The prophet was an officer of the heavenly government whose function, comparable to that of the royal herald in both Egypt and Israel, was to be the line of direct communication between the divine Suzerain and his vassal, Israel ... In other words, it is most important in our attempt to understand the office to stress not simply the psychology of ecstasy but the Israelite understanding of God's government of Israel and the manner in which the human phenomenon of ecstasy was taken up and transformed in that government.' Compare Georg Fohrer, 'Remarks on Modern Interpretation of the Prophets', *JBL* 80 (Dec., 1961), p. 310: 'The herald's message is originally not prophetic but typical for the royal messenger. Prophecy did not create it, but borrowed it from that source – probably by way of the prophets of the royal court, as we know them from Mari and Byblos ... The basic form of the prophetic oracles was certainly not exclusively bound to the cult or to the law, but could be sought and given everywhere and in all contexts.'

Baruch the Scribe

Carchemish in 605 BC (25.1–13; 36; 45; 46) and during the long period between the two deportations of 597 and 587. Jeremiah appears in the Temple at the beginning of Jehoiakim's reign and delivers his great sermon (7.1–15; 26.1–24); he confronts the envoys as they leave a plenary session of the emissaries of the nations surrounding Judah at the beginning of Zedekiah's reign (so the true text of 27.1); again and again he excoriates the delinquencies of Jehoiakim, and engages in bitter polemic against the leaders of the nation and Temple. He contends with other prophets and denies their accreditation since they have not stood in the heavenly council (23.18). Most significantly he is recognized by Nebuchadnezzar and the Chaldean commander after the fall of Jerusalem, is shown extraordinary preferential treatment, and is given the choice of determining his own future either by accompanying Nebuzaradan, the captain of the guard, personally (note *with me* in 40.4) to Chaldea, or by joining his fellow-countrymen at Mizpeh (39.11ff.; 40.1ff.; 42.1ff.). Nothing could illustrate better the importance of Jeremiah in the politics of his age or the dominating position that he held, whether in the royal councils or in the affairs of state. Unfortunately, the prestige of the prophet's office is obscured for us in the *ipsissima verba* of chs. 1–25, for here chronological and biographical data are all but wanting, and we are left in the dark as to the occasions when his words were spoken, as, for example, in connection with the oracles on the foe from the north or the lawsuits or the self-disclosures. It is when we pass from these chapters to those that follow that the situation changes strikingly, for here the mode of reporting is of quite a different order. We turn, therefore, to ch. 36, the single chapter in the book which casts light upon the history of its composition.

The thirty-sixth chapter of the book of Jeremiah brings to a culmination the sequence of prose narratives beginning with ch. 26.[22] That the two accounts are designed to form the beginning

[22] Martin Kessler, 'Form-Critical Suggestions on Jer. 36', *CBQ* 28 (Oct., 1966), pp. 389–401.

The Former Prophets and the Latter Prophets

and ending of the literary complex is demonstrated by the many stylistic and linguistic features they share in common. Both chapters begin with a superscription, the occasion of both is a popular assembly in a time of great national crisis, in both we listen to the prophet's solemn and public indictments, and the motivation of repentance and forgiveness is common to both. In both the prophet's life is imperilled, in both the princes are favourably disposed to Jeremiah, in both the members of the house of Shaphan play a significant role, and throughout both the stress is constantly upon speaking and hearing.

In the fourth year of Jehoiakim Jeremiah receives a command from Yahweh to take a scroll and to write upon it all the words he had spoken to him from the time of his call in the reign of Josiah, presumably 627 BC (25.3) to the present. It was in that year that the armies of Chaldea under Nebuchadnezzar had delivered a decisive defeat to the Egyptian foe under Pharaoh Neco. The turning-point in the history of the Near East thus coincides with what was doubtless a turning-point in the prophet's career. It is not too much to suppose that the two events were closely related. If so, it is a remarkable witness to the fatefulness of the issues which were involved for Judah and for the other peoples of the Near East.

Jeremiah summons Baruch, the son of Neriah, and he writes at the prophet's dictation. Thereupon Jeremiah informs Baruch that he has been debarred from the Temple, but that he is to go and read there all the words he had written. Baruch complies with the prophet's demand. In December of the following year a fast is proclaimed. Precisely what it was that motivated the event we are not told, but it may well be that it was related to the victory of Chaldea at Carchemish and to the prophet's conviction that his oracles on the foe from the north had at long last been fulfilled. In the hearing of all the people and then the princes, Baruch reads from the scroll in the לִשְׁכָּה or cabinet room of Gemariah, the son of Shaphan, the secretary of state, perhaps in exactly the same

Baruch the Scribe

place where Jeremiah had delivered the Temple speech some years previous (26.10, cf. 7.2).[23] The presence of all these princes more than suggests that they were quite aware of the impending crisis. The atmosphere was doubtless electric. When Micaiah, the grandson of Shaphan, heard all the words of Jeremiah from the mouth of Baruch, he goes to the cabinet room of the secretary in the royal palace to report to the princes who were gathered there. The latter order a certain Jehudi whose genealogy is traced back to the third generation to command Baruch to come to them. The words here are ironically much the same as those which Yahweh has employed in his command to Jeremiah (cf. v. 2). So Baruch comes, scroll in hand. The narrative at this point is dramatic. The princes say to Baruch, 'Sit down and read it' (*sic!*). Baruch accedes to their demands, and the princes turn to each other in fear and tell Baruch that they will have to report what has happened to the king. Significantly they enquire, 'Was it at his dictation?' and Baruch acknowledges that it was he! The princes then counsel Baruch that he and Jeremiah should go into hiding so that no one may know where they are. It is obvious that Baruch has fallen into friendly hands and it may be assumed that they were friendly to Jeremiah too. But what is more they recognize the validity of their credentials.

We are informed that the scroll was placed in the cabinet room of Elishama the secretary. It is not improbable that it was the repository of other documents. The princes report to the king, who orders Jehudi to procure the scroll, and the latter brings it to the king. Again the narrative is graphic and extraordinarily compressed, without any show of emotion. It is winter, and the king is seated before the open hearth. As Jehudi reads, the king cuts with a pen knife every three or four columns and consigns them to the flames. There is no terror or show of grief, in striking contrast to the time when Josiah had listened to the Book of the Covenant (II Kings 22). The supporters of Jeremiah of whom we

[23] Kurt Galling, 'Die Halle des Schreibers', *Palästinajahrbuch des Deutschen evangelischen Instituts* 27 (1931), pp. 51–58.

The Former Prophets and the Latter Prophets

have heard previously – Elnathan and Delaiah and Gemariah – urge the king not to burn the scroll, but to no avail. Jehoiakim gives orders that Baruch the secretary and Jeremiah the prophet be seized, but his designs are thwarted because 'Yahweh had hid them' (cf. 26.24).

The account is notable for several reasons. Nowhere else in the Old Testament do we have a comparable report of a prophet dictating all his prophecies over a period of many years, nowhere else do we hear of a prophet employing an amanuensis for the purpose of transcription, nowhere else do we have a narrative so rich in graphic and circumstantial detail. The book is addressed to Israel, Judah, and all the nations. Since several manuscripts of the Greek (see *BH ad loc.*) read *Jerusalem* for Israel, many scholars emend the text accordingly, but the procedure is unwise since the whole phrase is meant to mark the momentousness of the event – an event, as we have seen, which is commensurate to the solemnity and gravity of the national and international crisis. We are informed that the book was read three times in the course of a single day, so it cannot have been very long (compare the similar case in II Kings 22). It may have been a summary or condensation of the prophet's utterances. The question naturally arises why such a document needed to be put to writing at all. Why could not a single utterance or speech have sufficed for the particular purpose in view? The fact that the words were addressed to Israel, Judah, and all the nations when Assyrian power had come to an end and Chaldea was now in ascendant – a circumstance of which the prophet could not but be aware – may offer some explanation. But there is a deeper reason. The words of Yahweh are for the particular hour, to be sure, but they are more. They are at once a witness to the fulfilment of past predictions, notably the oracles on the foe from the north,[24] and a witness

[24] Douglas Jones, 'The Traditio of the Oracles of Isaiah of Jerusalem', *ZAW* 67 (1955), p. 229: 'There can be little doubt that the motive which led Jeremiah to dictate the oracles of his life's ministry was to demonstrate how old predictions were on the point of fulfilment. The foe from the North could now be identified.'

Baruch the Scribe

for the future, the time that is still to come (Isa. 30.8; 55.10f.; Jer. 32.14).[25]

The momentousness of the event is further demonstrated by another consideration of the first importance. Jeremiah summons to his service a scribe or secretary by the name of Baruch, the son of Neriah. Speculations are numerous as to why the prophet needed someone to whom he could dictate his prophecies. Was it that he could not write, as some have supposed, or that his handwriting was poor, as has been suggested by others? We are not informed how it was that Jeremiah came to know Baruch, how long and in what capacity he had known him previously, or anything about his past history. But we are plainly told that Baruch was a scribe or secretary. On the face of it, of course, the designation could indicate that he was only an amanuensis or private secretary. But a careful inspection of our narrative and the fact that Baruch appears in other notable contexts of the prose narratives suggest that he was a man of some importance and was well known and highly regarded by his confreres and peers. The most plausible explanation for Jeremiah's summoning of Baruch is precisely that the occasion called for one who could represent him in the Temple, one who would have ready access to the chamber of

[25] Johannes Pedersen, *Israel: Its Life and Culture* I–II, trans. Aslaug Møller (London: Oxford University Press, 1926), pp. 167f.; H. Wheeler Robinson, *Inspiration and Revelation in the Old Testament* (Oxford: Clarendon Press, 1946), pp. 170f.; Aubrey R. Johnson, *The One and the Many in the Israelite Conception of God*, 2nd ed. (Cardiff: University of Wales Press, 1961), pp. 1ff.; *The Vitality of the Individual in the Thought of Ancient Israel*, 2nd ed. (Cardiff: University of Wales Press, 1964), pp. 87f.; Isaac Rabbinowitz, 'Towards a Valid Theory of Biblical Hebrew Literature', *The Classical Tradition: Literary and Historical Studies in Honor of Harry Caplan*, ed. Luitpold Wallach (Ithaca: Cornell University Press, 1966). Note p. 324: 'The utterance of prophetic words, in fine, is for the purpose of getting them into the world so that they may act upon that world; as such they are conceived as transcending the limits of communication, and do not necessarily require an audience.' In the present context, the words of Jeremiah do indeed have an audience, but their range of meaning extends far beyond it into the history of the time.

The Former Prophets and the Latter Prophets

Gemariah, son of Shaphan,[26] to whom Jeremiah was bound by many years of friendship, esteem, and mutuality of respect. That is to say, Baruch was more than a private secretary. He was a person of some eminence, one who was favourably known to his professional colleagues. The cabinet room would be an advantageous locale from which he could address the assembled throng in the outer court.

We are singularly fortunate in having the twofold reference to the cabinet room of the scribe, in the first instance in the Jerusalem Temple (36.10) and in the second in the royal palace (36.21). The two were closely connected, and we may be confident, quite intentionally.[27] The men who are gathered in the chambers are in both cases שָׂרִים or royal officials. To be sure we hear elsewhere

[26] G. G. Findlay, 'Baruch', *Dictionary of the Bible*, ed. James Hastings, rev. ed. Frederick C. Grant and H. H. Rowley, eds. (London: Thomas Nelson and Sons and New York: Charles Scribner's Sons, 1963), p. 91: 'He belonged to the order of "princes", among whom Jeremiah had influential friends (26.16; 36.25); Baruch's rank probably secured for Jeremiah's objectionable "roll" (ch. 36) the hearing that was refused to his spoken words.'

[27] Galling, *op. cit.*, pp. 51–56. See especially the excellent chart on p. 53. Cf. Adolf Erman, *The Literature of the Ancient Egyptians*, trans. M. Blackman (London: Methuen & Co., 1927), p. 185: 'It [the scribal school] was attached to the temple which Ramesses II built for Amūn on the west bank of Thebes, the so-called Ramesseum.' See also C. F. A. Schaeffer, *The Cuneiform Texts of Ras Shamra-Ugarit*. The Schweich Lectures of the British Academy, 1936 (London: Oxford University Press, 1939), pp. 34–35: 'The library was housed in a building situated between the two great temples of Ugarit, one dedicated to Baal and the other to Dagon. . . . As was usual at this time, a school of scribes was attached to the library. Here the young priests were set to copy documents and were instructed in liturgical and sacred literature.' For its royal connections, see p. 34. Cf. S. Mowinckel, 'Psalms and Wisdom', *Wisdom in Israel and in the Ancient Near East*, H. H. Rowley Festschrift, eds. M. Noth and D. W. Thomas, *SVT* 3 (Leiden: E. J. Brill, 1955), p. 207: 'There is every reason to believe that the school for scribes in Jerusalem, as elsewhere in the Orient, was closely connected with the temple; this is apparent from the very fact that the "wisdom literature" of Israel was considered to belong to the canonical writings.' Aage Bentzen, *Introduction to the Old Testament* (Copenhagen: G. E. C. Gad, 1948), vol. I, p. 171, refers also to a temple school at Mari.

Baruch the Scribe

of chambers or rooms belonging to private persons or eminent families (35.4), and they are also referred to later in Ezekiel, Ezra, Nehemiah, and I–II Chronicles. But the לִשְׁכָּה of the scribe referred to in 36.10 is certainly to be distinguished from these, in the first place because it was immediately connected with the royal palace and in the second because it bore the title of a distinctive office.[28] Among the other peoples of the Near East from ancient times the training of the scribe was connected with the Temple and his service associated with the royal house. We hear frequently of scribal schools and of the training that was received there.[29] Such training was closely related to what falls under the general category of wisdom, at least as it was understood in Egypt and Mesopotamia.[30] That is, the scribes were wise men

[28] Galling, *op. cit.*, p. 54.

[29] In addition to the foregoing, see Lorenz Dürr, *Das Erziehungswesen im Alten Testament und im Antiken Orient.* Mitteilungen der Vorder-asiatischen-Aegyptischen Gesellschaft (E.F.) 36 Band, 2 Heft (Leipzig, 1932); de Vaux, *op. cit.*, pp. 394–405; Millar Burrows, *What Mean These Stones?* (New Haven: American Schools of Oriental Research, 1941), p. 183; R. de Langhe, *Les textes de Ras Shamra-Ugarit et leurs rapports avec le milieu biblique de l'Ancien Testament* (Paris: Desclée de Brouwer, 1945), vol. I, pp. 332ff.; Samuel N. Kramer, *The Sumerians; Their History, Culture, and Character* (Chicago: University of Chicago Press, 1963), pp. 230f.; A. Leo Oppenheim, 'A Note on the Scribes in Mesopotamia', *Studies in Honor of Benno Landsberger on his Seventieth Birthday*, Assyriological Studies No. 16 (Chicago: The Oriental Institute of the University of Chicago, 1965), pp. 253–6; William McKane, *Prophets and Wise Men*, SBT 44 (London: SCM Press, 1965), pp. 36f.; John Gray, *Archaeology and the Old Testament World* (London and New York: Thomas Nelson and Sons, 1962), pp. 8off. See also W. G. Lambert, *Babylonian Wisdom Literature* (Oxford: Clarendon Press, 1960), p. 8: 'One point of organization on which we are regrettably ill-informed is the relation of the scribes to the temple. General considerations would lead us to suppose that the scribal schools were attached to a temple, but we are in no position either to affirm or to deny if all scribes were *ipso facto* priests.'

[30] McKenzie, *op. cit.*, p. 4: 'We know that wisdom literature is associated with scribal schools in Egypt and Mesopotamia, and we can assume that the same association existed in Israel.' Cf. G. Fohrer, *Introduction to the Old Testament*. Initiated by E. Sellin, trans. D. E. Green (New York: Abingdon Press, 1968), p. 315: 'Baruch, Jeremiah's scribe and biographer, was at least educated in the wisdom school.'

The Former Prophets and the Latter Prophets

because they had been reared in the wisdom school and had mastered its curriculum, not only in calligraphy, though this was to be sure of the first importance, but in other disciplines associated with governmental administration and finance as well. That the United Monarchy under David and Solomon was profoundly influenced by the organization of the Egyptian court is now well known,[31] and there is every reason to believe that the same is true of the period with which we are concerned. Egyptian influence is doubtless primary, but it is probable that Mesopotamian influence also made itself felt, particularly in the period of Assyrian domination. It could scarcely have been otherwise when one takes into account the international character of the age and, indeed, the international character of wisdom. In any event, it is clear that the office of the scribe was one of distinction. He was the most eminent and influential of the royal officials and was charged with governmental affairs as well as many other functions.

It is not exceeding the limits of evidence to contend that both the northern and southern kingdoms had scribal schools similar to those among the other peoples of the Near East,[32] and one may venture to assert with some confidence that they were associated with the royal house and the national sanctuaries.[33] Sigmund Mowinckel maintains that Solomon founded a school for scribes in Jerusalem and there introduced the international poetry of wisdom of the Orient.[34] I am inclined to support this contention as a real possibility, but would go somewhat farther perhaps by contending that wisdom in this case should be construed as broadly as it was among other Near Eastern peoples, to include such works as the Yahwist and the court history which teems with wisdom motifs. The training in the scribal schools was of a diversified kind. There were doubtless, too, many different kinds of

---

[31] de Vaux, *loc. cit.*; Begrich, *loc. cit.*

[32] So de Vaux, Mowinckel, and others.

[33] Cf. *inter alia* R. B. Y. Scott, 'Priesthood, Prophecy, Wisdom, and the Knowledge of God', *JBL* 80 (March, 1961), p. 10.

[34] Mowinckel, 'Psalms and Wisdom', *Wisdom in Israel and in the Ancient Near East*, p. 206.

Baruch the Scribe

scribes as there were different kinds of priests and prophets in Israel.

As we have already had occasion to observe, it was with the scribal family of Shaphan that Jeremiah was on intimate terms. The former were among the central figures associated with the Reform of Josiah,[35] and it is likely that in the early period of his ministry Jeremiah was favourably disposed to the movement.[36] Both Shaphan and his son Ahikam are members of the delegation sent to Huldah (II Kings 22.11–13), and Elasah, another son of Shaphan, serves as an agent in connection with the letter to the exiles (29.3). Finally, it was a grandson of Shaphan with whom Jeremiah was on friendly terms during the trying period after the fall of Jerusalem (43.1–7). What relationship Baruch may have had to Shaphan and his family we do not know, but it is not unlikely that it was similarly intimate. Baruch could enter the cabinet room of the scribe because he had a rightful place there and was himself a member of the royal officials who had come together on the crucial occasion of the public reading of the scroll. He was among colleagues.

Many attempts have been made to reconstruct the scroll which Jeremiah dictated to Baruch.[37] We are not left without some clues as to its probable content. It must have contained the oracles of judgment preserved in 1.1–25.13 from the thirteenth year of

[35] H. J. Katzenstein, 'The "'Asher 'al ha-bayith" from the Days of the United Kingdom to the Downfall of Samaria', *Memorial Volume to Eliezer Shamir, Sdeh Elijahu*, 1957, pp. 120–8; 'The Royal Steward Asher 'al ha-Bayith', *IEJ* 10 (1960), pp. 149–54; 'The House of Eliakim, a Family of Royal Stewards', *Eretz Israel* 5 (Jerusalem: Israel Exploration Society and the Hebrew University, 1958), pp. 108–10 (in Hebrew). Katzenstein maintains that the position was hereditary in one family and that there was a direct line of succession from Hilkiah (Isa. 22.20–24; II Kings 18.18; 19.2) to Gedaliah.

[36] H. H. Rowley, 'The Early Prophecies of Jeremiah in their Setting', *BJRL* 45 (1962–63), pp. 225ff. or *Men of God: Studies in Old Testament History and Prophecy* (London and New York: Thomas Nelson and Sons Ltd., 1963), pp. 158ff.

[37] Note, for example, Otto Eissfeldt, *The Old Testament: an Introduction*, trans. Peter R. Ackroyd (New York: Harper and Row and Oxford: Basil Blackwell, 1965), p. 351.

The Former Prophets and the Latter Prophets

Josiah to the year 604 when the scroll was dictated. But what
are we to say of the prose narratives? While absolute certainty is in
the nature of the case excluded, the probabilities strongly favour
the assumption that they are the work of Baruch.[38] It is certain
that Baruch continued to be the companion of Jeremiah until
after the fall of the nation in 587. It is in these narratives, if anywhere, that we have an authentic exhibit of the scribal mode of
composition. They open with the accession of Jehoiakim to the
throne of Judah in 608, the occasion for the Temple speech (26.1).
The account merits careful inspection because we can compare it
with the report given in 7.1–15. The scribe gives the speech in his
own way, abridging it by omitting details, but adding others such
as the exact temporal locus, transforming the probably poetic
form of the original into prose, and above all by recounting the
sequence of episodes which followed upon its delivery. There is
every reason to believe that he composed the other speeches or
proclamations of Jeremiah in the same way. We move from the
prophet's poetic formulations to the scribe's prose. It is noteworthy that all the speeches reported by Baruch, whether
Jeremiah's or those of others, have the same style and terminology.[39] Following the practice of ancient historians, he reports
what was spoken in his own style and language. We are fortunately
not at a loss to learn whence he derives this manner of speaking.
We encounter the same style elsewhere in Deuteronomistic
contexts; the manner of Baruch is the manner of the scribes, not
only of his own time, but long before.[40]

[38] For reconstructions of Baruch's work, see T. H. Robinson, 'Baruch's
Roll', *ZAW*, Neue Folge Erster Band, 1924, pp. 209–21; Pfeiffer,
op. cit., p. 502; Mowinckel, *Prophecy and Tradition*, pp. 61f.; Norman K.
Gottwald, *A Light to the Nations: an Introduction to the Old Testament*
(New York: Harper and Brothers, 1959), p. 353; Fohrer, *Introduction to
the Old Testament*, p. 436.

[39] Leonhard Rost, 'Zur Problematik der Jeremiabiographie Baruchs',
Viva Vox Evangelii, Festschrift für Landesbischof D. Hans Meiser (Munich:
Claudius-Verlag, Oskar Koch and Co., 1951), pp. 241–5.

[40] Mowinckel, *Prophecy and Tradition*, p. 63: 'Baruch was a "scribe"
and belonged to "the learned": that the "Deuteronomists" are also

Baruch the Scribe

It is probable that Baruch and his professional confreres have been influenced by the official state or temple archives. The numerous superscriptions (26.1; 27.1; 28.1; 29.1–3; 32.1; 34.1; 36.1; 39.2; 40.1; 41.1, etc.) suggest as much.[41] They are to be compared with the formal openings of the reigns of the kings of Judah and Israel reported in the books of Kings. While different literary types are to be recognized in the complex of Jer. 26–45, it is the biographical narrative that predominates.[42] These should not be confused with the legends that are reported concerning Elijah and Elisha.[43] Complaints that are often registered against Baruch that his style is monotonous or ponderous are quite beside the point as are the characterizations which speak of his 'popular narrative art'.[44] To be sure there is considerable diversity in the style of the narration, but nowhere is it alien to the scribal manner of reporting. Notable among its features is the proclivity to cite words of the participants in the events (26.2–6, 13–15; 27.5b–11,

associated with the learned circles of the scribes, is obvious; already Jeremiah offers us a piece of evidence that "the law", the *tora*-tradition, and the pursuit of it, belongs to the "scribes" (Jer. 8.8).'

[41] Hans Schmidt, *Die grossen Propheten übersetzt und erklärt* in Die Schriften des Alten Testaments, Zweite Abteilung, Zweiter Band (Göttingen: Vandenhoeck & Ruprecht, 1915), p. 377: '*Als Vorbild für sein biographisches Werk haben dem Baruch wahrscheinlich offizielle Staats – oder Tempelchroniken gedient. Die Art, wie er jedes Ereignis mit einem Datum versieht, die in solchen öffentlichen Urkundenführung zu Hause ist, legt diese Vermutung nahe.*'

[42] For a form-critical study of the narratives, see Martin Kessler, 'A Prophetic Biography: A Form-critical Study of Jeremiah: chs. 26–29, 32–45' (Dissertation, Brandeis University, Boston, 1965), ch. II.

[43] *Contra* Klaus Koch, *Was ist Formgeschichte?* (Neukirchen: Neukirchener Verlag des Erziehungsvereins, 1964), pp. 224ff.

[44] So Johannes Hempel, *Die Althebräische Literatur und ihr hellenistisch-jüdisches Nachleben* (Wildpark-Potsdam: Akademische Verlagsgesellschaft Athenaion M.B.H., 1930), p. 155: '*Stilistische Vorzüge weist dies Buch nur in beschränktem Masse auf. Seine Darstellung ist oft reichlich schwerfällig.*' But note Hempel's comment on the same page: '*Überragend in ihrer Wahrhaftigkeit, einzigartig in ihrer Verbindung tiefster-menschlich-persönlicher Anteilnahme mit einer sicheren Erfassung sachlich entscheidender Züge am Werk des dargestellten Meisters, stehen die Erzählungen Baruchs von Leben und Leiden des Jeremia in der altorientalischen Literatur . . .*'

233

The Former Prophets and the Latter Prophets

12b–15, 16b–22; 28.2–4; 29.4–23, 24b–28; 32.17–25, 27–44; 33.2–17, etc.). Even more striking and more central to the narrator's interest is his profound interest in the person of Jeremiah. Nevertheless, despite his intimate association with the prophet and his affection for him, he nowhere indulges in subjective words of sympathy. Jeremiah does not appear as a hero or saint. The events that are recorded tell their own story. It was a long career of suffering and apparent defeat.[45] Dramatic elements are not wanting. Note the finales of 26.6, 24; 27.22c; 28.9, 16c, 17; 29.9b, 23d; 32.5b, 8d, 15b, 25; 35.19b; 36.19, 26b, 31d, etc.). The canvas upon which the scribe portrays the events of the prophet's career is crowded with many *dramatis personae*. Kings, princes, priests, prophets, scribes, and others appear upon the stage, and Jeremiah moves in the midst of them, a solitary and often tragic figure. From our modern point of view, it is amazing that Baruch makes his appearance so seldom in the narratives, though where he does appear, it is clear that he must have played a not insignificant role.[46]

But there are other features in Baruch's prose narratives that demand our attention. While we have insisted that he writes in the characteristic manner of the scribe, there are a number of indications that he is deeply immersed in the ancient traditions and formulations of the covenant. He is a faithful reporter of his master's covenant-faith. He employs the classical messenger's formula כֹּה אָמַר יהוה with very great frequency as he does the formula for the reception of the divine word, *The Word of Yahweh came to me saying*. He follows the schemata of the revelatory forms with consistency, and employs the characteristic phrase נְאֻם יהוה

---

[45] Heinz Kremers, 'Leidensgemeinschaft mit Gott im Alten Testament: Eine Untersuchung der "biographischen" Berichte im Jeremiabuch', *EvTh* 13 (Aug., 1953), pp. 122–40.

[46] Note the central role that Baruch plays in the account of the purchase of the field in 32.6–25 and in the crisis after the city's fall in 43.1–7 where he is censored for having influenced Jeremiah in his counsel to the people. On the former passage see Jones, *op. cit.*, pp. 227–9.

Baruch the Scribe

and more especially the strategic and characteristic transitional phrase וְעַתָּה precisely in the manner of Jeremiah's *ipsissima verba*.

His profuse use of the terminology of hearing is very striking. But dominating all else are the frequent conditionals, so crucial and central to the covenantal and legal formulation, most notably in the book of Deuteronomy. Nowhere are the affinities of Baruch with the latter more in evidence than here (compare *inter alia* Jer. 33.20f., 25f.; 37.10; 38.6, 17f.; 40.4bc, 5; 42.5, 6, 9f., 15f.).[47]

The sequence of prose narratives comes to a dramatic and moving finale in ch. 45.[48] It is probable that the Greek text has preserved the right order in placing it at 51.31–35. It is surely quite singular that an oracle should be addressed to an individual (cf., however, the divine word addressed to Ebed-melech in 39.15–18). The precise date and occasion are carefully given, the fourth year of Jehoiakim, at the time that Jeremiah dictated the scroll to Baruch. A number of scholars, offended by the sharp break in chronology here, have deleted the entire temporal reference, but there is no legitimate support for the procedure (1) because it is dominated by western views of compilation and editing and (2) because the passage as we have it makes very tolerable sense. For one thing, it may have been purposely designed as part of the framework with ch. 36. It is very probable that it was meant to be the divine word which illuminated all the foregoing narratives, the single divine disclosure to Baruch which had guided and directed him through all the travailing years, ever since the time, now many years ago, when the word of Yahweh had come to him. As he had written the terrible words of judgment upon the royal house and the people of Judah, line after line, he must have been torn with anxiety and sorrow. If he was closely related to the

[47] James Muilenburg, 'The Form and Structure of the Covenant Formulations', *VT* 9 (Oct., 1959), pp. 354–7.

[48] Kremers, *op. cit.*, pp. 128–40; Artur Weiser, 'Das Gotteswort für Baruch und die sogenannte Baruchbiographie', *Theologie als Glaubenswagnis*. Karl Heim *Festschrift* (Hamburg: Furche-Verlag, 1954), pp. 35–46.

The Former Prophets and the Latter Prophets

inner circle of royal officials, as we have contended, we can readily grasp the depth of his feelings.

Those who were closest to Baruch would be the first to bear the brunt of Chaldean hostility, and he would surely himself be among them. The oracle opens with unusual solemnity: 'Thus says Yahweh, the God of Israel, to you, O Baruch.' Interestingly, Yahweh cites Baruch's own words of lamentation. The oracle is at once a rebuke and a word of comfort. In a supremely moving divine self-disclosure Yahweh tells Baruch what he is doing in the earth, breaking down what he has planted and plucking up the whole land. It is highly revealing that the last words to which we are to listen echo the words of Jeremiah's call (1.10, cf. 31.28). The sorrows and griefs of Baruch are here mastered by the sorrows of God.[49] It was not a time in Judah for one to expect the realization of his ambitions and aspirations. Baruch was not to seek vindication for himself; he is to rest only in the assurance that there was an agony deeper than his own and that his life would be spared. The words accompanied him from the hour that he had read the scroll aloud before the members of the royal cabinet and the gathered crowd of Judeans. Throughout all the vicissitudes of the years he had been upheld by the momentous word from God.[50] It is surely clear why he placed the chapter at the close. It belonged with ch. 36 certainly, but it belonged even more profoundly at the point where he had completed the record of Jeremiah's trials and rejections, the end of the *via dolorosa* he had been fated to walk with the prophet. It tells us much about Baruch. In the rest of the narratives we hear of him but seldom; here a flash of unexpected light illumines the page.

It has been the purpose of the foregoing account to call attention

[49] Cf. G. von Rad, *Old Testament Theology*, vol. II, trans. D. M. G. Stalker (Edinburgh: Oliver and Boyd and New York: Harper and Row, 1965), p. 208: '. . . here a human being has in a unique fashion borne a part in the divine suffering.' See also Abraham J. Heschel, *The Prophets* (New York: Harper and Row, 1962), pp. 256ff.

[50] W. Rudolph, *Jeremia*, HAT (Tübingen: J. C. B. Mohr [Paul Siebeck], 1958), p. 245.

Baruch the Scribe

to the importance of Baruch in the prophetic activity of Jeremiah and more particularly to set forth some of the characteristic features of scribal composition. It is very possible, indeed probable, that Baruch had a major hand in the compilation and editing of the original work extending from 1.1 to 45.5. If so, it is probably to him that we are to look for such prose additions as we find in 1.15–19, 3.6–12a, and elsewhere. It has been our contention that the so-called 'Deuteronomic additions' by no means represent a separate source, but conform to conventional scribal composition and are therefore to be assigned to Baruch. The ambitions of Baruch to which reference is made in ch. 45 suggest that he may well have been a person of some eminence, corresponding to the prestige of his master. This is confirmed by the fact that his brother Seraiah served as the royal quartermaster (51.59). But it is also confirmed, in my opinion, by a circumstance of even greater significance. The traditions associated with Baruch, brief as they are, did not end with his deportation to Egypt after the fall of the nation. It has sometimes been averred that he was Jeremiah's literary executor, and if our contentions concerning his part in the composition of the book have any force in them, then this is probably true. But Baruch was to outlive his own career. He was remembered and became the inspirer of elaborate traditions and legends. The literature connected with his name is surprisingly large.[51] He moves into the future as few others in the history of Israel's traditions. It is surprising that he should find so eminent a place in the Jewish apocalypses. It is easy to understand why such protological figures as Enoch, Noah, Abraham, and Moses should play a central role in these compositions. Not so with

---

[51] R. H. Charles and W. O. E. Oesterley, *The Apocalypse of Baruch* (London: SPCK, 1917), pp. vii–viii: 'It may be wondered why there was such a considerable Baruch-literature, for we can hardly suppose that the books mentioned represent more than a part of those written under the pseudonym of Baruch; but the fact is that, whatever may have been the reason, a good deal of legend clustered round the name of Baruch in ancient times among the Jews, and it was one which evidently enjoyed much popularity.'

The Former Prophets and the Latter Prophets

Baruch. It is indeed true that he had survived the destruction of the Temple, the end of the Davidic monarchy, and the fall of the nation, but this can hardly suffice as an explanation of his continuing importance in the history of tradition. Rather, if I am not mistaken, we are to see in these ancient compositions an authentic witness to the importance of Baruch during his own lifetime. His distinction, all but suppressed in the biblical records, is recovered in legend and apocalypse and wisdom. This is not to credit these narratives with historical authenticity, though there are indeed many authentic echoes which derive from historical memory. The perplexities which seared his heart, the griefs which laid him low, the search for a wisdom that could withstand the threat and torment of inchoate times, the wrestlings with the demands of the *Torah* upon his people's life, all these have their source in Baruch's own life, a life that was lived courageously and often agonizingly in company with the prophet Jeremiah.

BIBLICAL THEOLOGY | *Take the sword of the Spirit, which is the word of God . . . (Eph. 6:17)*

FATHER AND SON

JAMES MUILENBURG

God is a Father. How shall we understand this, especially in a culture where the meaning of fatherhood has been so greatly altered, yet where tragically the problem of the father has become so acute, not only in America, but throughout the world? For ancient Israel *the family* is the basic and elemental unit of solidarity. It is a *psychic whole,* i.e., the same life and vitality pervades it. At its head is the father, and all others are related to him in a unique way, for, profoundly, the self or *nephesh* of the father is perpetuated in the selves of his sons. The father *lives on in the life of the son;* and the son knows deeply that his life is lived in the life of his father. The father is in the son and the son in the father. It belongs to the deepest level of man's existence that he become a father.

This is a central issue in the Bible. It was a tragic state to be a FATHERLESS man or a barren wife! Poor Sarah, for the fate of history is involved in her bearing the child. Poor Rebekah and Rachel, for Yahweh had closed their wombs from bearing. Who is Abram but *exalted father* (that is the meaning of the name), and Israel came to know that "we are Abraham's sons." Indeed the whole human race is descended from one father; herein is its unity. We belong to a family, and in mature theological thinking we are all involved in Adam and Adam's life. In Adam's fall we sinned all.

The radical significance of the family (*mushpahah*) in the Bible is superbly illustrated by the composition of the Book of Genesis. Here we have a great variety of traditions which originally had little or nothing to do with each other. The Abraham stories had no original connection with the Jacob stories, and the twelve sons of Jacob are aetiological accounts to explain the origin of the twelve tribes. The traditions of the *Urgeschichte* (Gen. 1-11) from the first man to Abraham are drawn from many sources. Yet all these materials, utterly diverse and drawn from the flotsam and jetsam of oral legendry, have been fashioned into a family narrative, from first man to first Hebrew, from first Hebrew (according to the

178   THEOLOGY AND LIFE

Yahwist) to first Hebrew (according to the Elohist) and then to Israel the people of God. It is a work for which we vainly seek any parallel in the history of world literature.

The many genealogies of Scripture are the successions of fathers and sons, of sons who become fathers and perpetuate the lives and vitalities of their fathers. It is the genealogies which bind history together. Yahweh calls the generations from the beginning. In the tenth chapter of Genesis we have a genealogy in which the peoples of the world are persons, but they all belong to a single family. Have we not all one father? Now one might object that this is placing unity upon a purely physical basis, but for the ancient Hebrew the physical and psychical are intimately related. The physical is the bearer of the psychical reality. The New Testament opens with an extended genealogy, and the *Gospel According to Luke* presses it back to Adam, the first father. Thus the Christ is related to the father-son reality of the whole Old Testament.

The father-son relation runs throughout the whole Bible, from beginning to end, and in the New Testament it bears its abundant fruition. The word *father* is, of course, a primitive and elemental word, an *Urwort* or *Urlaut*. It knows no derivative, for it has none. It probably comes from the child's earliest prattle: *ba, ba, ba*, hence our word babble, i.e., saying *ba, ba*. In Hebrew it is *ab*, in Aramaic *abba*, in Arabic *AB*, in Accadian *AB*, in Greek *pappas*, in Latin and French *papa*, in English *papa*, cf. *pope, pape*. Man's earliest sounds are transformed into words for *mamma* and *papa*, words of elemental association. It is characteristically Semitic that the father plays the primary role in the Bible, but certainly the mother is not ignored, cf. *emunah, hanan, rahmim*. Into this question we cannot enter here, the relation, e.g., of motherhood to the unmotivated grace and of fatherhood to covenant (as a psychiatrist recently suggested to me!).

One of the remarkable characteristics of modern psychiatry is the large place it makes for this elemental bond between parent and child. Modern fiction has dealt with the theme profoundly, as has modern drama. Where can one find a more moving illustration than in Alan Paton's two books, *Cry the Beloved Country* and *Too Late the Phalarope*. The

THEOLOGY AND LIFE   179

former is a deeply moving story of two fathers, Stephen Kumalo and James Jarvis, both of whom suffer the loss of their sons. And the last thoughts of Absalom Kumalo as he lies in his prison cell waiting death are of the son to be born after his going. In *Too Late the Phalarope,* when Pieter Van Vlaanderen's adultery with a black girl has been discovered in that harsh climate where racial discrimination is sanctified by religion, the old family Bible is taken down where the names of fathers and sons of the Van Vlaanderens have been inscribed for 150 years. Then Pieter "took the pen and ink, and he crossed out the name of Pieter Van Vlaanderen from the Book, not once but many times, not with any anger or grief that could be seen, nor with any words." Eight days later the father is dead bowing deep over the Book of Job. These scenes are not unfamiliar to us. That haunted soul, Thomas Wolfe, confessed towards the end of his harried life that from the beginning there was only one idea that he ever wanted to express:

> . . . the deepest search in life, it seemed to me, the thing that in one way or another was central to all living was man's search to find a father, not merely the lost father of his flesh, not merely the lost father of his youth, but the image of a strength and wisdom external to his need and superior to his hunger, to which the belief and power of his own life could be united.

The Father-Son Relation in The Old Testament

We were saying that the father-son symbol runs through the Bible from beginning to end. Let us examine, then, some of the decisive moments, the segments of time where it emerges, the *kairoi,* to use Professor Tillich's word, in the on-going stream of Israel's time (*chronos*). Yahweh appears to Moses for the first time. Moses resists the urgency of Yahweh's command to go to Egypt, raising all the *alibis* and excuses he can conjure up. What, after all, is he to say to Pharaoh, king of Egypt. And Yahweh said:

> You shall say to Pharaoh, Thus says Yahweh,
> 'Israel is my firstborn son, and I say to
> you, Let my son go that he may serve me.'

Here a new and specifically Old Testament element comes to light: the father-son relation is not directed to an individual

180   THEOLOGY AND LIFE

person but to a people. The relationship is not of blood but
of God's free and unmotivated grace, the adoption of a people. No other sons are mentioned, only one son, Israel.

The centuries pass, and the northern kingdom is on the
brink of destruction, and in the depths of the crisis Hosea, the
prophet, arises to speak of the covenant between God and
Israel, which is portrayed as marriage. In the dark hours of
infidelity and waywardness Yahweh brings back the memories
of Israel's earliest days:

> When Israel was a child, I loved him, and out of Egypt I called my son.
> The more I called them, the more they went from me.
> Yet it was I who taught Ephraim to walk, I took them in my arms;
> But they did not know that I healed them.
> I led them with cords of compassion, with the bonds of love,
> And I became to them as one who eases the yoke on their jaws,
> And I bent down to them and fed them.
> . . . . . .
> How can I give you up, O Ephraim!
> How can I hand you over, O Israel!

That Yahweh cannot do, for he is God and not man. Love
is the mark of fatherhood. Over and over again the note
sounds. The processes of generation are never primary,
though Israel knows much about these profound relationships, for Israel understands the psychical forces which must
be associated with any true meeting of self with self. What
motivates Yahweh in his relations with his son is his everlasting love, love that abides beyond all the breaking and
violating of the bonds. But there is more here. God suffers
for his son. There is weeping in the lines quoted above, Yahweh's weeping for his lost son. Like David, and if I may
say so, like Stephen Kumalo and the elder Van Vlaanderen,
he is crying, "My son, my son!" It is not surprising, therefore, that Wheeler Robinson can write a book on *The Cross
in Hosea*. It is clear that Hosea is here continuing a tradition that is rooted in earliest historical times, yet a relation
that is viewed as adoption in an historical event: *the Exodus
from Egypt is the birth of God's son*. We can now turn back
to the Book of Genesis and understand better why the birth of
a son is so fateful a matter to Sarah, Rebekah, and Rachel.

In the southern tradition, too, the sonship of Israel becomes
a major motif. The Book of Isaiah opens impressively in a

THEOLOGY AND LIFE   181

universal context in which all nature is called upon to witness to what Yahweh is saying·

> Hear, O heavens, and give ear, O earth, for Yahweh has spoken:
> Sons have I reared and brought up, but they rebelled against me.
> The ox knows its owner, and the ass his master's crib,
> Israel does not know, my people has no understanding.

These are the words that even the heavens and the earth must
hear, and the first word, contrary to the normal Hebrew
order, is *sons*. That surely is the first word of God to his
people. But more than this, there were two things that Yahweh had done: he had reared them up (*giddalti*) and brought
them up (*romanti*). Yahweh had cared for his sons, had
nurtured them and trained them to be sons. Then the tragic
reversal: they rebelled against the father, like all sons perhaps. The ox and the ass know their dependence upon their
provider; the bonds of nature assert themselves. But Israel
does not know, i.e., she has not entered into the filial relationship (Cf. also 30:1, 9).

Jeremiah perpetuates the tradition of the Elohist historian
and Hosea. He describes a poignant reflection of Yahweh.
Yahweh is speaking:

> I thought
>   how I would set you among sons, and give you
>   a pleasant land,
>   the most beautiful heritage of the nations,
> And I thought you would call me "My Father"
>   and would not return from following me.

In another context we hear Israel's plaintive cry in the midst
of her affliction:

> Have you not just now called to me,
>   My Father, thou art the intimate one of my youth—
>   will he be angry for ever,
>   will he be indignant to the end?
> Behold, you have spoken,
>   but you have done all the evil that you could.

Here we get a poignant expression of the intimate relationships between Father and Son, and this is one of the primary
characteristics in the Old Testament. The nature cults too
were aware of this intimate relationship, but there the bonds
are primarily physical. I am not discounting the importance

182   THEOLOGY AND LIFE

of these connections in the nature cults; on the contrary, it is possible that Israel herself was influenced by them. But what is central in the relation with Israel is moral responsibility and obligation. Hosea and Jeremiah do not leave us in any doubt on this matter: the bonds are justice, faithfulness, obedience, goodness. In Jeremiah the motif is so rich that one is tempted to quote at length. Let me confine myself to two more passages. The first is drawn from the *Little Book of Comfort* (chaps. 30-31):

> With weeping they shall come, and with consolations
>   I will turn them back,
> I will make them walk by streams of water,
>   in a straight path in which they will not stumble;
> For I am a father to Israel,
>   and Ephraim is my first-born.

We have no trouble recognizing the origins of words such as these. They go deep into Israel's past and her self-awareness.

The words continue:

> I have heard Ephraim:
> "Thou hast disciplined me, and I was disciplined,
>   like an untrained calf;
> Restore me, that I may be restored;
> For after I had turned away I repented;
>   and after I was instructed I smote upon my thigh."

Then Yahweh:

> Is Ephraim my dear son, is he my darling child?
> For as often as I speak against him, I do remember
>   him still.
> Therefore my heart yearns for him;
> I will surely have mercy upon him, says Yahweh.

Here, surely, is the language of a Father; every father longs for the son's return. The gospel's imperishable story of the prodigal and his more deeply prodigal brother is anticipated in such Old Testament contexts.

There are other great prophetic passages which would reward our study, not least of all in Second Isaiah, who usually brings the major Old Testament motifs to their fulfillment and culmination. But we had better turn for a moment to another area: specifically, to that of the royal psalms, which in our generation have come to assume a place of central impor-

THEOLOGY AND LIFE   183

tance in connection with the royal theology of Israel. It was out of the fabric of this royal ideology that the conception of the Christ was understood in the New Testament. I confine myself to one or two notable passages. The first of these is the second psalm. Yahweh is addressing the nations who are in tumult and rebellion:

> Then he will speak to them in his wrath,
>   and terrify them in his fury, saying,
> 'I have set my king
>   on Zion, my holy hill.'

And the reply of the Davidic king follows:

> I will tell of the decree of Yahweh
> He said to me, "You are my son,
>   today I have begotten you."

Here again the relation is one of adoption, not of generation. The King is adopted to be Yahweh's royal son.

Psalm 89 is one of the most impressive liturgies preserved for us from the royal archives of the temple cult. Again Yahweh is the speaker, and he is speaking of the king of the line of David:

> He shall cry to me, 'Thou art my Father,
>   my God and the Rock of my help (salvation),
> And I will make him the first born,
>   the highest of the kings of the earth.
> My steadfast love I will keep forever;
>   and my covenant will stand firm for him.
> I will establish his line forever;
>   and his throne as in the days of the heavens.

The royal theology is the true background for an understanding of the Kingship of God in the New Testament. Here Fatherhood and Kingship are related, for in both authority is deeply involved.

The Father-Son Relation in the New Testament

We turn now to the New Testament. When one consults the concordance on the father-son relationship as expressing the relation between God and man, he is struck by the relatively few contexts in the Old Testament where they appear together whereas in the New Testament there are literally

184   THEOLOGY AND LIFE

hundreds of such contexts. But this is by no means the end
of the matter. What fatherhood really means and what it involves we come to understand from the Old Testament.
There we know deeply what it means to be a father and what
it means to be a son. There is no indication anywhere, so far
as I have been able to discover, that this understanding is
altered in the New Testament. It is radically deepened, to be
sure, but the categories are not different.

Of the many words used to describe the relation between
Jesus and God there is none, perhaps, so familiar to us as
Father and Son. Again and again the Synoptic gospels repre-
sent Jesus as addressing God as 'My Father':

> Not everyone who says to me 'Lord, Lord,' shall enter the kingdom of
> heaven, but he who does the will of my Father who is in heaven.
> (Matt. 7:21)
> For whoever does the will of my Father who is in heaven is my brother
> and sister and mother. (Matt. 12:50)
> Come, ye blessed of my Father, inherit the kingdom prepared for you.
> (Matt. 25:34)
> My Father, if it be possible, let this cup pass from me. (Matt. 26:39)

When we speak together the Lord's Prayer, we speak but one
word, 'Father,' and all else is expansion, and if we substitute
the word Father every time the pronoun 'thy' appears, we
shall see not only how central the word of address is, but
much more: we shall see that all that is asked for from the
Father is represented in the Old Testament passages where
fatherhood is made illuminating for us. This is even true of
the closing words, whether they be original or not: For Thine,
O Father, is the *kingdom,* Thine, O Father, is the *power,* and
Thine, O Father, is the *glory* (*doxa* and *kabod*: *honor,* and
dignity or *prestige*). This is also true of the momentous
words:

> 'I thank Thee, Father, Lord of heaven and earth, that thou hast hidden
> these things from the wise and understanding and revealed them to
> babes; yea, Father, for such was Thy gracious will; and no one knows
> the Son except the Father, and no one knows the Father except the
> Son and anyone to whom the Son chooses to reveal him.'

Then, precisely the immortal words:

> 'Come to me, all who labor and are heavy laden, and I will give you
> rest.'

THEOLOGY AND LIFE   185

In the Garden of Gethsemane he travailed in agony, even to death, and cried:

> 'Abba, Father, all things are possible to thee; remove this cup from me; yet not my will but Thy will be done.'

The son is obedient to the Father. And on the cross he cried:

> 'Father, forgive them, for they know not what they do.'

The son asks forgiveness, not for himself, but for those who slew him.

In the eighth chapter of Romans the Father-Son relation rises to unprecedented heights. The whole chapter should be read to grasp the dimensions of Paul's thought. These words must suffice:

> For you did not receive the spirit of slavery to fall back into fear, but you have received the spirit of sonship (*huiothesia*). When we cry, 'Abba, Father' it is the spirit itself which beareth witness with our spirit that we are children of God, and if children, then heirs, heirs of God and fellow-heirs with Christ, provided we suffer with him in order that we may also be glorified with him.

Here, too, in Paul the whole creation is involved in the supreme work accomplished by Christ in which we all enter into the ultimate heritage of sonship. In our ordination to the ministry we turn to the great finale of Ephesians:

> For this reason I bow my knees before the Father, from whom every family in heaven and earth is named, that according to the riches of his glory he may grant you to be strengthened with might through his Spirit in the inner man. . . . There is one body, and one Spirit . . . one Lord, one faith, one baptism, one God and Father of us all, who is above all and through all and in all.

In the Fourth Gospel we move even beyond Paul and Ephesians, at least in certain respects. What is even more interesting is that here the relationships with the Old Testament are particularly close and illuminating, another evidence, as it has long seemed to me, that its nearest affinities are with sectarian Judaism and not with Greek thought, as should now be clear to all who have studied the Dead Sea Scrolls. Observe, for example:

> The Son does only what he sees the father doing: whatever the father does that the son does also.

186   THEOLOGY AND LIFE

How Semitic and biblical that is!

> For the Father loves the Son. He does not conceal what he does but reveals himself to him.

How Semitic and biblical!

> The Father gives life; so the son gives life to whom he will.

That is good Old Testament thought.

> The Father passes on his judgment to the son.

In the Old Testament the Father is judge.

> The glory of the father and the son.

This also is in the Old Testament.

> To know the Father is to know the son.
> Like Father, so son.

Let us rest there. It must be clear to us all that if we are to listen to the words of the New Testament we must undersand what fatherhood and sonship really mean, and for this we must turn to the Old Testament. We all know how much this relationship has been sentimentalized and distorted in many modern churches, how the biblical understanding has been completely corrupted by modern versions of the relation. And we have often paid dearly for our sentimental piety. Modern psychiatry is eloquently confirming the biblical understanding of the relationship. In our counselling the Bible will prove to be an inexhaustible store of help and comfort. We all have the experience of men coming to us who want us to be their father. But there is another respect in which we shall learn much from Scripture: although the physical basis for fatherhood is not to be ignored or discounted, the relationship in the Old Testament is always one of adoption. This raises the question of the adequacy and value of the Virgin birth Christology. The problem is not so simple as we might think on the surface, in view of the psycho-physical character of Biblical mentality. Yet the question does pose itself, and the issue is important, not least of all because we have other Christologies (adoptionist, resurrection, *etc.*).

Finally, what our study has shown is that Jesus Christ as Son of God is profoundly related to Israel as God's son. All that we have learned about *corporate personality* in recent

THEOLOGY AND LIFE   187

years, i.e., Israel as a person (and from the beginning!), should open up avenues of Christological understanding of which we have heretofore taken too little account. To confess Jesus as the Son of God is to affirm a faith upon which the whole Bible casts an abundant light. Saint Ambrose, writing in the fourth century, has voiced a familiar hymn to Christ:

> O, Splendor of God's glory bright,
> From light eternal bringing light,
> Thou Light of light, light's living Spring,
> True Day, all days illumining.

> Dawn's glory gilds the earth and skies,
> Let Him our perfect Morn, arise,
> The Word in God the Father One,
> The Father imaged in the Son.

The Beginning of the Gospels

and the

Qumran Manual of Discipline

James Muilenburg

In the desert prepare the way of the LORD;
Make straight in the wilderness a highway for our God.

In one fashion or another, all four of our evangelists begin their accounts of the life and ministry of Jesus with these words. They are drawn from the prologue in heaven with which the great prophet of the Exile introduces his remarkable sequence of eschatological poems. This epic—I use the word with some latitude—ranges through the whole of the great tradition from the creation of the world to the period when the old Semitic empires were dying and the Semitic "time of troubles" was drawing to its close with the conquests of Cyrus the Persian. The prophet sees the denouement of the drama of God's action in history in his coming again in a final act of new creation and new redemption. The vistas which open before him are as vast in their cosmic scope as they are universal in their historic sweep. It is against that background that the evangelists tell their story.

Within the past few years these words have acquired a fresh significance and perhaps, indeed, an immediacy of context through the discovery of the scrolls near Khirbet Qumran, on the northwest shore of the Dead Sea. You have doubtless heard of these remarkable documents, and perhaps, too, of the discovery of literally thousands of fragments from other scrolls by the Ta'amire bedu who inhabit that region. I propose to address myself this afternoon to one of the most interesting of the complete scrolls, the so-called *Manual of Dicipline,* or the *Manual of the New Covenant,* first discovered in 1947.

James Muilenburg is Davenport Professor of Hebrew and Cognate Languages. This article is a shorter version of his address at the Opening Exercises in James Chapel on September 22, 1954.

23

The daily concerns, preoccupations, and aspirations of this little community of men—probably the Essenes—in the period immediately prior to and during the beginnings of the Christian movement, are in many ways those which animate us in our life here at Union.

In this ancient writing from Qumran we meet an eschatological orientation which sets the stage in a remarkable way for our reading of the New Testament. And it is precisely in this connection that the words of Second Isaiah appear in our manual.[1]

> Now when these things come to pass in Israel ... they will separate themselves from the midst of the session of perverse men to go into the wilderness to prepare there the way of the LORD, as it is written.
> In the wilderness prepare the way of [the LORD],
> Make straight in the desert a highway for our God. (VIII.12b.14)

For the community the passage is interpreted as requiring assiduous study of Scripture: "This means studying the Torah which He commanded through Moses, so as to do according to all that was revealed time after time, and according to that which the prophets revealed through His Holy Spirit." (VIII.15—16) There is much legalism in the manual; in season and out, the members of the community are admonished to observe every jot and tittle of the law. But the prophets are quoted again and again—if anything, more frequently than Moses. As a matter of fact, the Qumran community made much use of the apocalypses, as is shown by the substantial extracts from Aramaic Enoch, the Book of Daniel, and by the apocalypse of Lamech. It is abundantly attested by our Discipline Scroll that a major part of the daily life of the community was devoted to scriptural study, interpretation, and meditation. Thus they sought to make straight the way of the Lord in the wilderness, to prepare for the coming of God.

Yet the creation of a sacred library and the study of the sacred books were but one expression of the life of the covenant community at Qumran. The scroll, as we now have it, opens with what appears to be a ritual for the annual renewal of the covenant and for receiving new members into the order. In that sense the ritual may represent a ceremony of initiation as well as one of rededication on the part of the others. Together they pledge themselves (*offer themselves willingly*) to live a life of absolute obedience to the will of God, a life of *obedience* and *holiness* and *purity* and *perfection* and

---

I am indebted throughout this account to the translation of W. H. Brownlee, "The Dead Sea Manual of Discipline," which I have followed closely though not slavishly. This translation appeared in *Bulletin of the American Schools of Oriental Research*, Supplementary Studies 10-12 (New Haven, 1951).

24

truth and *devotion* (hesed), and *brotherhood* (the N.T. *koinonia*). These words occur again and again, and, though they are used in a variety of meanings, nothing is clearer than that they were more than catchwords and ideals. The ordinances which govern the whole assembly are:

> to seek God...to do what is good and upright before him, as he commanded by Moses and by all his servants the prophets, to love everything which he has chosen and to hate everything which he has rejected, to keep far from every evil and to cling to every good deed; to practice truth and righteousness and justice in the land, and to walk no more in the stubbornness of a guilty heart and lustful eyes...And let all those dedicated to this truth bring all their knowledge (intelligence) and their strength and their wealth into the community of God. (1.2-6,11)

Through this common act of commitment they are brought into the covenant of grace—they are united into one holy community, they clarify their minds by the divine commands, and they direct their strength according to the perfection of God's ways and their wealth according to His just purpose.

Another section of the manual contains a teacher's vademecum: "For the wise man (*lam-maskil*) that he may teach and instruct all the sons of light in [succeeding] generations of mankind with regard to their works in their respective societies." (III.13-14) Then follows a general statement of the community's world view, which seems on the face of it to represent absolute determinism: "From the God of knowledge exists all that is and all that will be. Before they came into existence he established the design of them, and after they come into existence in accordance with his glorious purpose they fulfill their task, and nothing can be changed." (III.15-16) All men are divided into two classes, the children of light and the children of darkness. To each God has assigned a spirit by which they walk: to the one, the prince of lights who directs the sons of light in their paths and helps them in times of temptation and danger; to the other, the angel of darkness, and all their transgressions and guilt are under his dominion. (III.22) At this point the manual adds one of its characteristic and most illuminating phrases, "according to God's mysteries until the end of time" (*eschaton*). (III.23) It is this sense of an infinite mystery transcending all human attempts to define the structures of life that lifts the veil of legalism, in order that the light of grace may enter to perform its effectual work.

But before we turn to this other aspect of the community's theology, I should like to say a word about its daily life. The recent excavations have added their witness to the accounts in the manual

25

of some of the rites which were a part of the life of the community. Ritual ablutions, which many scholars describe outright as baptism, were a practice of the community; some, at least, of the cisterns with their elaborate steps which have been unearthed at Khirmet Qumran *may* have been used for such purposes. Another rite was a common sacred meal, recalling our Christian Eucharist; here the excavations have aided us in visualizing the rite, for they have brought to light a large assembly room, with a podium upon which the lector stood to read to the gathered assembly. Next to this room were found more than eleven hundred earthenware dishes, six hundred of them in perfect condition, so I think there is little doubt that we have come upon the refectory where the sacred meals were celebrated. We have also found the scriptorium of the scribes, so the excavations have proved to be a most illuminating commentary on the scrolls themselves. In future interpretation, it is essential that we read them not only in the light of what Josephus and Philo have to tell us and the witness of other scrolls which I have not mentioned, but also in the light of the evidence which the spade has revealed.

The discipline of the community covered far more than its ritual life. Let me list some of the more interesting of the precepts by which the communal life is to be governed:

1. If there be found among them a man who lies in the matter of wealth, and it become known, they shall exclude him from the purity of the Many for one year, and he shall be fined one fourth of his food allowance. (VI.25)

2. He who answers his neighbor (or *fellow*) with a stiff neck, or speaks with a quick temper so as to reject the instruction of his comrade, by disobeying his fellow who is enrolled before him or has taken the law into his own hands, he shall be fined for one year and be excluded. (VI.26-27.)

3. And the man who vilifies his fellow unjustly, when it is known, shall be fined for one year and be excluded. (VII.4)

4. Whoever bears a grudge against his fellow who has not been convicted shall be fined for a year (and/or) six months, and the same applies to anyone who takes vengeance for himself. (VII.8-9)

5. Whoever laughs foolishly with audible voice shall be fined for thirty days; but he who puts forth his hand to muffle it (?) shall be fined for ten days. (VII.14-15)

6. The man who slanders his neighbor shall be excluded for one year from the purity of the Many. (VII.16)

In striking contrast to these regulations and laws which govern the Essene community, we have toward the close of the scroll a poetic section of great beauty. In the midst of it we hear the words of a kind of *apologia pro vita sua:*

I will repay no man with evil's due;
Only with good will I pursue a man;
For with God is the judgment of every living thing;
And He will reward a man with his due.

26

> I will not be envious of an evil person;
> The wealth of violence my soul shall not covet. (X.18-19b)

Significantly, immediately following these words which recall the highest levels of Old Testament ethical insight (e.g., Micah 6:1-8 or Job 31), the devotee delivers himself into the hands of God, aware that his efforts and achievements will not suffice in the final reckoning of life:

> For as for me, my justification belongs to God;
> And in His hand is the perfection of my way,
> Together with the uprightness of my heart.
> Through His righteousness my transgressions shall be blotted out;
> For from the fountain of His knowledge He has opened my light,
> And my eye has beheld the wonders He has done,
> And my heart is illuminated with the mystery to come.
>
> Eternal Being [He who is eternal] is the support of my right hand;
> Upon the rock of strength is the way of my treading;
> It shall not tremble for aught,
> For God's faithfulness [or truth] is itself the rock I tread.
> And His might is the support of my right hand.
> And from the fountain of His righteousness [flows] my justification.
> (XI.2c-5c)

The writer continues thus for some moments, and then lapses once more into thought concerning himself:

> But I belong to wicked humanity
> And to the assembly of perverse flesh,
> My iniquities, my transgression, my sin,
> (Together with the perversities of my heart)
> Belong to the assembly of worms and of things that move in darkness.
> (XI.9b-10a)

There is deep brooding in these lines and in others like them; he alternates again and again between thoughts of law and responsibility and thoughts of a divine mercy beyond all neat calculations of less and more, an ultimate compassion which comprehends all our failure and futility and evil in the embrace of the infinite mystery. These personal contemplations stand in sharp contrast to all that the manual has to say of obligation to the law.

> And I, if I totter,
> God's dependable mercy is my salvation forever;
> And if I stumble in the guilt of flesh,
> My justification through God's righteousness will stand everlastingly.
> And if He begin my affliction,
> Even from the Pit He will draw out my soul,
> And He will direct my steps in the way....
> In His steadfast righteousness He has justified me
> And in His great goodness He will pardon (or *atone for*) all my iniquities;
> And in His righteousness He will cleanse me from man's impurity,
> And from the sin of the children of men.

27

For without Thee a way cannot be perfect,
And apart from Thy will naught can be accomplished.
Thou hast taught all knowledge;
And everything that has come to pass [has been] by Thy will. (XI.12-18b)

Today, as two thousand years ago, Khirbet Qumran lies solitary
and barren, far from the old Roman road leading from Jerusalem
to Jericho. It is a lonely region, wakened only by the occasional cry
of shepherds leading their flocks along the tortuous paths of the
cliffs which tower to the west. Here the light works its ancient miracle.
At night the country sleeps in the cold of the desert, illuminated
by the white fire of the moon and the incandescence of the myriad
stars, disturbed only now and then by the eerie call of the hyena and
the jackal. But when the first light begins to break in the east, the
land yields itself to the blessed ministration of the rising sun. It
welcomes God's greater luminary by taking to itself its warmth and
light, flushing first in varying colors—then it casts all its reticence
aside, gleaming in the white light until the earth is tense with the
illumination, too great to bear. As the day wears on and evening
comes, the plateaux of Moab to the east respond to the setting sun
in colors granted by the vanishing light; as darkness begins to fall
the land grows deeper red until finally all is still. Immediately below
the Khirbet lie the heavy waters of the Dead Sea; behind it rise
the towering cliffs where the holy men of long ago hid their precious
scrolls from the ruthless hands of the Roman invader. And now
after two thousand years of silence we turn to them in wonderment
and, I trust, with that meed of gratitude which is their due.

It was here that these men whom I cannot but call the true Israel
contemplated the eternal problems of human destiny—of man's in-
effaceable and inexpugnable awareness of absolute obligation to the
Unconditioned Ought, and his terrible sense that after he has done
his best he is yet but an unprofitable servant. Only after all man's
urgent longing to do what is right, to love his neighbor, to obey God's
will, to live a life of purity and holiness, to achieve that perfection
for which he dimly discerns that he was born, does he arrive at the
ranges beyond, where all is but faith and all is but grace, *sola fides,
sola gratia.*

It is not surprising, therefore, that as the manual comes to a close
we breathe a pure air where all is gift and no gain, where lips are
touched to music and to song. The writer, for here is surely the
composition of an individual, has experienced release from bondage
to the Law; he has felt the wonder of forgiveness and God's atonement, and so he rises to heights of praise and adoration:

28

I will sing with knowledge
And all my music is for glory of God;
And the strings of my harp are for the measuring of His holiness;
While the flute of my lips I will raise
As the measure of His justice.

I will bless Him expressing marvelous thanks;
And I will meditate upon His might;
And upon His mercies I will lean all the day.
I know that in His hand is the judgment of every living thing
And all His deeds are truth.
And when trouble is unleashed (   ) I will praise Him;
And for His salvation I will sing praise as well.

The problems surrounding the life and thought of the Qumran community are many, and we shall be occupied with them for many years to come. But in the manual of the community's discipline we are not far from that frontier where law and grace, responsibility and justification, meet and encounter one another. This encounter is set throughout in the matrix of expectation of the coming of the New, of atonement and forgiveness. It was here that John the Baptist came proclaiming in the wilderness that the time had come— like his near contemporaries, he sought to prepare the way of the Lord and to make His paths straight.

Part Four

SCHOLARSHIP AND INTERPRETATION

Introduction

UPON the roster of those who have contributed most significantly and illuminatingly to our understanding of the records of the Old and New Testaments, the name of Hermann Gunkel is inscribed indelibly. Were this *Who's Who* to be ordered according to importance of contribution or subsequent influence, there can be little doubt that he, like Abou ben Adhem, would lead all the rest. His approach to the biblical materials and his methodology in delineating their character and purpose have been appropriated, in one fashion or another, by all who move in the mainstream of contemporary biblical studies. He gave new direction to biblical scholarship, instilled vitality into research and rescued it from mere craftsmanship, opened fresh vistas for our grasp and interpretation of the individual literary units, and, more than any other, before or after, inspired in his students and successors an appreciation of the true character of the many and diverse literary forms or genres represented in the biblical records. No scholar excelled him in describing and illuminating the biblical modes of speech in all their nuances; none equaled him in ability to transmit to his students the fascination and excitement of biblical study.

In his early years as a student and then later as a professor at the Universities of Halle (1889-94) and Berlin (1894-1907) Gunkel came under the influence of some of the towering scholars of his day: men like Heinrich Zimmern, the Orientalist; Paul de Lagarde, under whom he studied Arabic; Eduard Meyer and Leopold von Ranke, the historians; Adolf Erman, the Egyptologist; Paul Wendland and Eduard Norden, the classical philologists; and Adolf von Harnack, the theologian and New Testament scholar. He was well-schooled in the methodol-

iii

Introduction

ogy of historical criticism, exemplified classically by Julius Wellhausen, notably in his monumental work *Prolegomena to the History of Ancient Israel* (1878). This approach sought to understand the books of the Bible by a critical analysis of their composition, their authorship, date, provenience, purpose, and sources.

While Gunkel recognized the validity of historical criticism as a legitimate, even necessary, discipline, he was convinced that it failed to answer many of the most natural and insistent questions raised not only by the modern reader, but by the biblical records themselves. He responded enthusiastically to the great work by J. G. Herder, *The Spirit of Hebrew Poetry* (1782-83), which followed the trail blazed by Bishop Richard Lowth's famous lectures at Oxford, *De sacra poesi Hebraeorum praelectiones academicae* (1753). In Herder he met one with a temper and cast of mind not unlike his own. Imagination and insight into the manners and nuances of speech, appreciation and literary sensitivity, openness to the whole world of Near Eastern culture as it found expression in the great literary monuments, and withal a rare ability to identify oneself in spirit and empathy with the mind and mood of the biblical writers in all their manifold ways of speaking, made it possible for him, as for Herder, to press scholarly inquiry beyond the confines of source analysis and phenomenological scrutiny. He knew how to *listen* to a text, and always insisted that it be read aloud in order that the reader might the better discern its movement and direction, its rhythm and assonance, its key words and accents. Research for him was as much an art as a science. He was insistent upon permitting the biblical speakers to have their say in their own fashion. He was aware they were *human* beings, like ourselves, and was not embarrassed in drawing upon contemporary history and everyday experience for the illumination of the ancient text. He recognized that in the pages of the Old and New Testament we have to do, not with literature in our modern understanding of *belles lettres*, but rather with extracts drawn from the daily life of persons and communities. This is not to say that he did not discern the aesthetic qualities of the biblical compositions; on the contrary he was rarely gifted in his ability to illuminate the many different genres of biblical speaking and the interior forces within the life of the people which gave them birth.

Gunkel was interested in writing a history of Israel's literature, and was convinced that historical criticism was insufficient for such a task. The isolation of the oldest traditions from their secondary accretions failed to penetrate the text itself, and did less than justice to the long period of oral transmission that often lay behind them. It was unable

iv

to provide any trustworthy chronological ordering of the materials since our knowledge of the dates of substantial sections of the Old Testament is too insecure. Moreover, large parts of the Old Testament are anonymous, and even where we do know the names of the writers, the biographical data are, with rare exceptions, almost completely wanting. What is more, Gunkel averred, the prevailing methodology of his time isolated Israel's literature and culture too completely from the wider environment of the other peoples of the ancient Near East, and consequently limited its horizons, obscured the function that the words were designed to serve, and failed to profit from the light that the cognate texts shed upon many biblical passages.

Since it is impossible, then, to write a history of Israel's literature in the conventional sense as a chronologically ordered and biographically oriented narrative, Gunkel proposed another way of viewing the materials, an approach that was at once more consonant with the Hebrew manner of speaking and more characteristic of Hebrew cultural mentality, where the typical and formal dominate over the individual and personal, especially in the earlier periods of Israel's history. The task of the literary historian is first of all to isolate the individual literary unit by determining its beginning and ending; he must then seek to identify its type or genre (*Gattung*) by observing its formal characteristics, style, mode of composition, terminology, and rhetorical features. Once the literary genre has been recognized and described, then its origin must be traced back to its provenience in the pre-literary stage of formulation. Since convention and custom determine to a considerable degree the fashioning and terminology of the literary types, Gunkel was intent upon collecting as many specimens or examples of each type as possible, not only within the Old Testament, but also in the related literary remains of the other peoples of the ancient Near East and even in Western culture. He perceived that much of the "literature" of the Old Testament was originally spoken, that its provenience was oral rather than written, and, like Martin Luther and Bishop Lowth and Herder, he sought to do justice to the speaking manner and oral style of each literary type and to release it from bondage to the printed page.

But the identification of the literary forms was only the first step in composing a literary history. One must inquire at one and the same time into the situation in personal or communal life in which the particular form or genre served its function, that is, the occasion in which this kind of speech was employed. Songs of victory were sung for the conquering hero upon his return from battle, dirges intoned over the bier of the dead, hymns chanted in the temple precincts, lawsuits carried

Introduction

on at the city's gates, prophetic oracles proclaimed in the marketplace, priestly rituals and liturgies recited in the sanctuary. There are scores of *Gattungen*, or literary forms, in the Old Testament and New Testament, each with its own *Sitz im Leben*, or life situation, and each performing its particular function. To many of these Gunkel was again able to adduce many striking parallels in the literatures of the other peoples with whose history and culture Israel and the early Christian community were closely related.

Gunkel's first major work, *Schöpfung und Chaos in Urzeit und Endzeit* (1895), was a religio-historical study of Genesis 1:1-2:4a and Revelation 12. The myth of the chaos dragon, present in both texts, was traced throughout the literatures of the ancient Near East and the Old and New Testament. The nature of myth was carefully described, and its transformation in the biblical records clearly set forth. A relatively short time later, in 1901, his great commentary on the Book of Genesis appeared in the "Göttinger Handkommentar zum Alten Testament." Here the scholar's interpretative and exegetical powers came to fruition. He not only demonstrated the validity of his methodology, but also made the ancient legends and traditions speak again in their original accents. In some respects the commentary has never been superseded. The introduction, *Die Sagen der Genesis*, was published separately and translated into English, and has appeared most recently in paperback with an introduction by W. F. Albright. While it shows a complete mastery of the critical problems of the book, it is primarily concerned with elucidating the features which mark the legend as a genre, the progress of the successive narratives, and the motifs which persist throughout.

Not long after the publication of the Genesis commentary, Gunkel was offered an opportunity to present an examplar of the literary history of Israel. In the volume on *Die orientalischen Literaturen* (1906) in Hinneberg's series *Die Kultur der Gegenwart*, he prepared a programmatic sketch of what he considered to be a proper literary history. It is a fascinating report, illuminated by acute insight into the types and forms of Israel's speech, by analysis and characterization of each *Gattung*, and by a revealing description of the concrete situation in daily life in which the *Gattung* had its place. A series of essays, *Reden und Aufsätze* (1913), some of which were drawn from previous publications, included a number of articles related to form criticism. Among them were "Fundamental Problems of Hebrew Literary History," (reprinted in *What Remains of the Old Testament* [1928]), "Egyptian Parallels to the Old Testament," and "The Close of Micah." A smaller

vi

Introduction

work, *Das Märchen im Alten Testament* (1917), while not so well known as other works, traces the genre of the folktale and its prevailing motifs throughout the Old Testament, and again adduces many parallels drawn from the literatures of other peoples.

But perhaps the most impressive monument to Gunkel's contributions to biblical learning is the German encyclopedia bearing the title *Die Religion in Geschichte und Gegenwart* (1st ed., 1909-13). In 1910 he became one of its editors, and the second edition (1927-31) bears on its title page the names of Hermann Gunkel and Leopold Zscharnack. More than a hundred articles come from Gunkel, and the work as a whole bears the stamp of his religio-historical point of view. In both editions Gunkel contributed the article on the Psalms. Already in 1917 he had written a little book on selected Psalms, *Ausgewählte Psalmen*, and from that time on his attention centered more and more on the Psalter. In the period between the first and second editions of *RGG* he prepared a monumental commentary on the book (1926), and the companion introductory volume, *Einleitung in die Psalmen*, appeared the year after his death in 1932. Joachim Begrich, his devoted and accomplished pupil, saw the work to completion. It is in every way a masterly performance. In more than 450 large and closely-packed pages the literary features of each literary type are described in exhaustive detail. More than sixty pages are devoted to the Hymn alone, and every representative of the type, in other parts of the Old Testament and in the cognate literatures as well as in the Psalter itself, is cited.

The article on the Psalms given below is drawn from the second edition of *RGG* and provides a succinct and admirable synopsis of Gunkel's larger monumental work. *Multum in parvo!* For the reader who wishes to understand the nature of Hebrew poetic composition, its rhetoric and composition, its different literary genres and the style and structure which characterize each, this essay should prove rewarding. He will come to recognize and appreciate the distinctive qualities which mark each type, whether Hymn or song of Yahweh's enthronement, Community or Individual Lament, Thanksgiving Psalm or Royal Psalm, Liturgy or Torah, Blessing, or the fusion of several poetic types. But he will gain more because he will be able to enter into the devotional life of ancient Israel in a new way; he will sense the spirit which animates the worshiper as he enters into the divine presence on various occasions of celebration and festival; he will be listening to Israel's response to the divine revelation recorded in the other books of the Old Testament, and find himself perhaps participating in the ecstatic shouts of joy and praise, in petitions for forgiveness and healing, in

vii

Introduction

prayers of contrition and confession, in historical recitals and rehearsals, in full-throated adorations and triumphant paeans. He will hear Israel singing, Israel in her most authentic moods, and will come to discern something of that which lay deepest in the soul of the pious suppliant and worshiper.

Gunkel recognized that the earliest psalms were all cultic in character, but he believed that many of them were later liberated from their cultic setting into spiritual songs and prayers. His student, Sigmund Mowinckel, took issue with him here. Mowinckel was convinced that all the psalms were cultic, and in six important monographs, entitled *Psalmenstudien* (1921-24), he sought not only to define their cultic provenience and *Sitz im Leben*, their cultic terminology and imagery, but also the occasions of celebration and festival, of mourning and lamentation, and their relation to other contexts in the life of ancient Israel. The second monograph of the Psalmenstudien, *Das Thronbesteigungsfest Jahwäs und der Ursprung der Eschatologie* (1920), a work of more than three hundred large pages, is one of the most influential and important contributions to our understanding of the Psalter. Like Gunkel's works, it is composed in an engaging and eminently readable style. Mowinckel followed Gunkel in his isolation of the *Gattung* of the psalm of the divine enthronement, but whereas Gunkel recognized only six specimens of this type (Pss. 47, 93, 96-99), Mowinckel found many more, in whole or in part, altogether about forty. He associated them with the annual celebration of the enthronement of Yahweh on the occasion of the New Year's festival and found in the Babylonian *akitu* celebrations the source of their composition and content. Thus the association of the chaos dragon conflict in the primeval abyss with the coronation of the king could be explained, Mowinckel contended, only by a common setting. While scholars today believe that he has overstated his case, many of them recognize the importance of his view and hold to it in a more or less modified form. It should be noted, too, that Mowinckel discussed in these hymns the origins of Israel's eschatology.

Other scholars too have departed from Gunkel in his classification of the literary types and have suggested alternative forms, such as the prayer of the falsely accused, emphasized by Hans Schmidt, in his *Das Gebet der Angeklagten in den Psalmen* (1928), or the hymns associated with the annual celebration of a royal festival on Mount Zion in which the election of David and the election of Jerusalem were celebrated, described by Hans-Joachim Kraus in his work *Die Königsherrschaft Gottes im Alten Testament* (1951) and his *Worship in Israel*

viii

Introduction

(1966). Kraus has also written a full-length commentary on the Psalms in the "Biblischer Kommentar" (1960), and while one is constantly aware of the presence of Hermann Gunkel, Kraus has taken account of the many contributions since Gunkel's day which have profited from archeological discoveries, new methodological procedures, and reinterpretations of the cultic life of ancient Israel. Type or form criticism is proving a great stimulus for our understanding of the theology of the Old and New Testaments; indeed, it is not too much to say that it has transformed our approach to the biblical records and has provided us with a deeper grasp of the nature of Israelite and early Christian mentality and faith, as we can see, *inter alia*, in the contributions of Gerhard von Rad and Rudolf Bultmann and their disciples.

JAMES MUILENBURG

San Francisco Theological Seminary
San Anselmo, California
April, 1967

PROLEGOMENON

The second half of the nineteenth century was a period of widespread intellectual and cultural ferment. It found expression not only in the fields of philosophy and the natural sciences, but also in the social and historical disciplines and in the study of religion in its diverse phenomenological and confessional manifestations. The thinking of the time was not infrequently dominated by the philosophy of Hegel (1770-1831), particularly by his delineation of the structures and patterns of history; by the positivism of August Comte (1798-1857), and by the evolutionary theories of Charles Darwin (1809-1882) and Herbert Spencer (1820-1903). It was during this period that cultural anthropology achieved the status of a major academic discipline, thanks to the labors, above all, of Edward B. Tylor, whose two volumes on *Primitive Culture* (1871) marked an epoch in the history of the study of primitive folkways and religion. Not unrelated to Tylor's work were the sociological and ethnological researches of Sir James Frazer (1854-1941), whose monumental work on *The Golden Bough* extended the study of primitive religion to the whole of antiquity, of the French School, whose most eminent representatives were Émile Durkheim (1858-1917) and Lévy-Bruhl (1857-1939), and, not least of all, Max Weber (1864-1920) in Germany. The comparative methodology reflected

1

PROLEGOMENON

in all these works had been anticipated to a degree by the
monograph of John Spencer, Master of Corpus Christi College in Cambridge, on *De legibus Hebraeorum ritualibus
et earum rationibus* (1695) and Johann Gottfried von
Herder's *Vom Geist der Ebräischen Poesie* (1782-83), but
received fresh impetus in the investigations of Adolf Bas-
tian (1826-1905), who has sometimes been called the
founder of social anthropology, and of Albert Eichhorn
(1856-1926), whose influence was later reflected in the
writings of Hermann Gunkel, Hugo Gressmann, and others.
The comparative study of religion came to a head in the
two volumes of Wolf Wilhelm Baudissin (1847-1926), *Studien zur semitischen Religionsgeschichte* (1876-78).

Of particular importance for our present purpose was
the rise and development of historical criticism of the Old
Testament, most notably in the work of Julius Wellhausen
(1844-1918) whose great book *Prolegomena zur Geschichte Israels* (1878; English translation, *Prolegomena to the
History of Israel* 1885) has remained a classic to this day,[1]
and of the brilliant Dutch scholar, Abraham Kuenen
(1828-91).[2] Wellhausen had his predecessors in Karl H.
Graf (1815-69) and Eduard Reuss (1804-09) and others,
but his influence has always been primary. His work represented a radical departure from the traditional view of
the composition of the biblical materials and consequently
resulted in a radically different construction of the origin
and history of Israel's religion. He was ably supported by
many of his contemporaries—in Germany by such eminent
scholars as Bernhard Duhm, Bernhard Stade, Karl Budde,
Alfred Bertholet, and Karl Steuernagel; in England, by S.
R. Driver, John Skinner, T. K. Cheyne, G. Buchanan Gray,
A. B. Davidson, George Adam Smith, C. F. Burney, and
not least of all by W. Robertson Smith, who wrote the pref-

[1] Hans-Joachim Kraus, *Geschichte der historisch-kritischen Erforshung
des Alten Testaments von der Reformation bis zur Gegenwart*, Neukirchen, 1956, pp. 222-49.

[2] Simon J. De Vries, *Bible and Theology in the Netherlands*, Wageningen, 1968.

ace to the English edition of the *Prolegomena* (1885).
During the period from 1835 to 1885 the records of the
major peoples of the ancient Near East, notably those from
Egypt and Mesopotamia, were recovered and subjected to
intensive scrutiny. Adolf Erman composed his *Neuägyp-
tische Grammatik* in 1880, and Sir Flinders Petrie laid the
foundations for excavating technique on the basis of his
excavations at Naucratis (1884-85). A long succession of
scholars contributed to the field of cuneiform studies,
among them Friedrich Delitzsch, Heinrich Zimmern, and
Paul Haupt.[3]

It is within this cultural context that we are to understand and assess the academic career and scientific contributions of one of the most gifted, versatile, and creative
scholars of the period—William Robertson Smith. The
learning of the age exerted a cumulative effect upon his
fertile and many-faceted mind. Heir to the achievements
of his predecessors and early contemporaries, he was destined, in turn, to influence the course of biblical and Semitic studies in the generations succeeding his own. He could
count among his friends some of the foremost scholars of
his age, most notably Julius Wellhausen, Sir James Frazer,
and A. B. Davidson. But there were forces of another kind
that were to exert a fateful, even tragic influence upon
Robertson Smith—the theological situation in Scotland
during his lifetime.[4] The Church of Scotland was torn by
internal dissensions, and in 1843 the Free Church, the dis-
senting party, came into existence by ascribing to the Act
of Separation. Among the 396 ministers who broke with the
Church was William Pirie Smith, the father of William
Robertson, who had been for some time headmaster of a
prominent school in Aberdeen, but now accepted a call
from the two small parishes of Keig and Tough in Aber-

---

[3] W. F. Albright, *History, Archaeology, and Christian Humanism*, New
York, 1964, pp. 106-07, 130 ff.

[4] John Sutherland Black and George Chrystal, *The Life of William
Robertson Smith*, London, 1912; James B. Pritchard, "W. Robertson
Smith, Heretic," *Crozer Quarterly*, (1947), pp. 146-160.

4   PROLEGOMENON

deenshire. On November 8, 1846 William Robertson Smith
was born. He was a frail child, but precocious. He did not
attend school, but received instruction from his father until
the time that he was to leave home for the university. It is
reported of him that he mastered the Hebrew alphabet and
was able to read the Hebrew words before the age of six.[5]
His father was a rigid disciplinarian and taught the boy
Latin and Greek, mathematics, and "rational conversation."
At the unprecedented age of fifteen years (1861), he entered the University of Aberdeen, having won the Bursary
Competition with a stipend of thirty pounds. In 1865 he
was awarded the degree of Master of Arts and the Town
Council Medal. In 1866 he entered New College, Edinburgh, where he studied under A. B. Davidson, Professor of
Hebrew and Old Testament exegesis, who had published
his great commentary on the Book of Job in 1862. He took
young Robertson Smith under his wing and made a profound impression upon him, as he was to do in later years
upon George Adam Smith and John Skinner. At the end
of his first year at New College (1867) Robertson Smith
went to Germany to study under Kamphausen, Köhler, and
Lange at the University of Bonn. During this period he was
deeply interested in physics.

His first teaching experience came in 1868-69 when he
served as assistant to P. G. Tait, Professor of Physics at the
University of Edinburgh. He wrote a number of articles on
physics, but also on philosophy, theology, and biblical studies.[6] In the spring of 1869 he returned to Germany, this
time to Göttingen, where he responded to the stimulating

[5] Black and Chrystal, pp. 11-12.

[6] Note *inter alia* his letters on "Newton and Hegel" in the *Edinburgh
Courant*, December 29, 1869; January 18 and 21, 1870; his paper "On
the Flow of Electricity in Conducting Surfaces," in *Proceedings of
R.S.E.*, vol. II, 1870; "The Question of Prophecy in the Critical Schools
of the Continent," *British Quarterly Review*, April, 1870. His lectures
on the Nazirites, Habakkuk, and on the prophets were given in the
same year.

influence of Albrecht Ritschl[7] but also pursued his interests in physics and mathematics. The year following his return to Scotland marked a turning point in his career. Professor Sachs, the occupant of the chair of Hebrew at the
Free Church College at Aberdeen, died, and A. B. Davidson persuaded him to apply for the position and pressed
his candidature. On May 25, 1870 he was elected to the
chair of Oriental Languages and Old Testament exegesis.
In the summer of 1872 he returned to Germany at the University of Göttingen where he studied Arabic poetry under
the aegis of Paul de Lagarde. Here he was exposed again to
higher criticism, as he had been before at Bonn and Edinburgh, and acquired many friends among his German colleagues.[8]

After teaching at Aberdeen for some six years (1870-
76) the question of his orthodoxy was raised in the Free
Church. He had contributed several articles to the ninth
edition of the *Encyclopaedia Britannica,* among them one
on "Bible," which scandalized the orthodox leaders of the
church.[9] He was accused of heresy, and he asked for a formal trial when the General Assembly of the Church gave
an adverse report on him. While the indictment was
dropped at the time, he was harassed by charges of heresy
for years, until in 1881 he was formally removed from his
chair.[10] Shortly thereafter he became editor-in-chief of the

---

[7] Black and Crystal, *op. cit.,* p. 111: "His [Ritschl's] lectures were indeed the most important experience of the summer, and the beginning
of a friendship to which they led is a landmark in the history of Smith's
theological views even more important than the first impressions of the
German school which he had received at Bonn in 1867."

[8] Black and Chrystal, pp. 146-153. Heinrich Ewald had already retired
and was succeeded by de Lagarde. Robertson Smith visited other university centers such as Halle, Leipzig, and Dresden.

[9] For the numerous contributions to the ninth edition of the *Encyclopaedia Britannica,* during the years 1875-1888, see Black and Chrystal,
op. cit., pp. 620-24. The article on "Bible" was written in 1875.

[10] For a detailed report of the heresy trials, see Black and Chrystal,
Chapters VI-X. See also J. B. Pritchard, *op. cit.,* pp. 150-58.

Encyclopaedia Britannica. He served in this capacity until the completion of the work in 1888.

While Robertson Smith had defended himself eloquently and courageously, and at times caustically, throughout the long years of the heresy trials, the experience exacted great physical and mental strain and no little inward grief from a man of frail constitution and sensitive temper. But he was sustained and buoyed up by the support he received not only from the greatest scholars of his day, from men like Wellhausen and Kuenen and others of similar stature, but also from many of his own countrymen with whom he always felt himself on terms of interior rapport and, what is more, by many of the best minds of the Church.[11] Mass meetings were held in his support, and he was invited to give a series of popular lectures at Edinburgh and Glasgow. These were attended by large and enthusiastic audiences and were published under the title *The Old Testament in the Jewish Church* (first edition, 1881; second edition, 1892). A second series followed in the next winter, this time on the prophets of Israel, and again with the same enthusiastic response. The lectures were published under the title *The Prophets of Israel and Their Place in History to the Close of the Eighth Century* B. C. (first edition, 1882; second edition, 1885).[12] When President Eliot of Harvard University learned of the verdict against Robertson Smith, he inquired through Lord Bryce whether he would accept appointment to his institution.[13]

We have referred to Robertson Smith's studies in Arabic under Lagarde at Göttingen (1872). Three years later he himself offered a course in the subject to a small class of

---

[11] Black and Chrystal, 404 ff.

[12] Smith's work was a great classic for his time and belongs in the great succession of those who have contributed most fruitfully to our understanding of the prophets: in Scotland scholars like A. B. Davidson, George Adam Smith, John Skinner, and Adam Welch; in Germany, Bernhard Duhm, *Theologie der Propheten* (1875) and his successors: C. H. Cornill, Gustav Hölscher, Hermann Gunkel, and others.

[13] Black and Chrystal, pp. 340 ff., 406; J. B. Pritchard, pp. 155 f.

advanced students. But he was determined to gain a thorough mastery of the language. In the winter of 1878-79, during a lull in the heresy trial, he spent an enforced leave from his teaching by going to Cairo. Here he made rapid progress, and had time to visit some of the famous archaeological ruins in the neighborhood of the city. He also spent some time in visiting Palestine where he made friends among the people. The following year he returned to Egypt, and traveled extensively throughout the Middle East, spending some two months at Jeddah and visiting Palestine, Syria, Tunis, and southern Spain. He acquired an intimate knowledge of the literature of the Near East, but more especially a first-hand acquaintance with the manners and customs and daily life of the people. This experience was to stand him in good stead for his future work, both for his knowledge of the language and for his anthropological studies.

Throughout these years Robertson Smith continued to cultivate his intimate friendship with John Ferguson M'Lennan (1827-1881), who had contributed an article on "Law" to the eighth edition of the *Encyclopaedia Britannica* and had composed a monograph on *Inquiry into the Origin of Capture in Marriage Ceremonies,* better known as *Primitive Marriage* (1865) and *Studies in Ancient History* (1867). He had also contributed an essay on "The Worship of Plants and Animals" to *The Fortnightly Review* (1866) in which he supported the thesis that from earliest times and among widely separated races, animals were worshipped by tribes who were named after them and which were believed to belong to the same stock or breed as themselves.[14] M'Lennan's studies exerted a strong influence upon him. He had written a long letter to M'Lennan on totem warfare in Coptos and Tentyra, and on sorcery in the Old Testament.[15] But his first important contribution to

[14] Black and Chrystal, p. 369.
[15] *Ibid.,* pp. 143-45.

this field was his article on "Animal Worship and Animal Tribes among the Arabs and in the Old Testament," which was published in *Journal of Philology,* No. 17, June, 1880. Robertson Smith's interests had become increasingly directed to the comparative study of primitive customs and their meaning, which were to find expression first of all in his article on "Sacrifice" in the *Encyclopaedia Britannica,* but then later in the two major classical works on *Kinship and Marriage in Early Arabia* (1885) and *The Religion of the Semites* (first edition, 1889; second edition, 1894).

In view of his expulsion from his academic chair at Aberdeen and of his mastery of Arabic during the years of the long drawn out trials, it was Robertson Smith's good fortune to receive an appointment in 1883 as Lord Summoner's Professor of Arabic at the University of Cambridge. In 1885 he was elected to a professorial fellowship at Christ's College, and in 1886 he became university librarian. In 1889 he was appointed to the chair of Professor of Arabic. In 1888-91 he delivered the Burnett lectures on *The Religion of the Semites* at Aberdeen. His health was very precarious at the time. His last years were full of suffering, yet to the end he continued his labors and was particularly active in laying the groundwork for the *Encyclopaedia Biblica,* which he had hoped to edit. This was unfortunately denied him, but when the work appeared under the aegis of John Sutherland Black, his intimate friend and biographer, and T. K. Cheyne, it was appropriately dedicated to him. He died at Cambridge at the age of forty-eight on March 31, 1894 and was buried at his birthplace at Keig.

William Robertson Smith lived on in the life of his pupils, among whom he could count such eminent scholars as A. A. Bevan, F. C. Burkitt, R. H. Kennett, Norman McLean, and S. A. Cook. Without question he was one of the foremost scholars of his generation. He vindicated the right of free and untrammeled critical historical inquiry of the Old Testament scriptures. He was a man of great

originality with an almost encyclopaedic range of knowledge and astonishing brilliance. The General Assembly
of the Church, which had pronounced him a heretic during
his lifetime, adopted a formal resolution at his death:[16]

> His brilliant career as a student, distinguished alike in
> classics, in science, and in philosophy, and the rapid
> steps by which he advanced to a foremost place among
> the Biblical scholars of Europe, are still fresh in the
> memory of the Church and of the community. His in-
> tellectual energy and industry, his quick apprehension,
> his singular command of his varied knowledge, along
> with a rare power of clear and felicitous expression,
> combined to rank him among the most remarkable men
> of his time.

His numerous contributions to the ninth edition of the
Encyclopaedia Britannica reveal not only the range of his
intelligence, but also his precision and competence along
a wider frontier. His study of the prophets continued for
many years to be a classic. But surely not least of his
achievements was his research into what we may appropriately style cultural anthropology, to which he made a
singularly illuminating contribution, above all in his Burnett lectures on *The Religion of the Semites*. Its limitations
have often been pointed out by later scholars, but he would
have been among the first to recognize the defects in his
work. In the context of his own time, he loomed large as
a commanding figure. Moreover, it is not impossible that
in certain respects his work may serve as a corrective to
some of the excesses of our time.

In April, 1887 the Burnett Trustees of the University of
Aberdeen issued an invitation to Robertson Smith to deliver three courses of lectures on "the primitive religions
of the Semitic peoples, viewed in relation to other ancient
religions, and to the spiritual religion of the Old Testament

---

[16] Black and Chrystal, p. 560.

and Christianity." The subject was congenial to him because it provided him the opportunity to bring together in
orderly and coherent fashion the results of many years of
study and research and, more particularly, to bring his anthropological studies to bear upon the literature and religion of the Old Testament. Indeed, all of his previous
investigations seemed somehow to converge upon this
momentous task. Without any understanding of the development and growth of the Old Testament records and a
proper recognition of their temporal sequence such an undertaking would have been impossible. More than any other
scholar of his time he had made the achievements of the
Wellhausen school familiar in Great Britain, most notably
by his appreciative preface to the *Prolegomena to the History of Israel*,[17] and by his early work on *The Old Testament in the Jewish Church*. In the former work Wellhausen
had studied the religious institutions of Israel in a thorough
and penetrating manner from the data provided only by
the Old Testament; Robertson Smith was to center his interest upon Israel's institutions also, but in the context of
Semitic religion in general. In another way his work bore
affinities with Wellhausen's. In the third volume of his
Skizzen und Vorarbeiten, on *Reste arabischen Heidentumes*
(1887), Wellhausen had made a detailed study of the
religious conceptions of the Arabs, gathering together for
the first time all the remains of primitive beliefs in the sur-
viving Arabic literature. Robertson Smith was similarly
interested in primitive Arabian religion and worship,
though his stress was quite different from Wellhausen's. For
him "religion was a part of the organized social life into
which a man was born and to which he conformed through
life in the same unconscious way in which men fall into

[17] Cf. pp. ix-x: "The reader will find that every part of the *Prolegomena*
is instinct with historical interest, and contributes something to a vivid
realization of what Old Israel really was, and why it has so great a
part in the history of spiritual faith . . . Here the reader will learn how
close are the bonds that connect the critical study of the Old Testament
with the deepest and unchanging problems of living faith."

any habitual practice of the society in which they live."[18] Wellhausen laid greater emphasis upon the individual and upon spontaneity.

Robertson Smith's previous work on "Animal Worship and Animal Tribes among the Arabs and in the Old Testament" (see above), his important study on *Kinship and Marriage in Early Arabia* (1885), and his article on "Sacrifice" in the *Encyclopaedia Britannica* equipped him to an exceptional degree for his fresh undertaking. He was indebted to others besides Wellhausen. He paid tribute to John Spencer's work, to which we have already made reference, and especially to his contemporary, M'Lennan, whose monograph on marriage had stimulated his own work on *Kinship and Marriage in Early Arabia*. He was indebted also to E. B. Tylor, the social anthropologist, whose interests coincided much with his own, and, above all others in this area, to Sir James Frazer, who was quick to recognize his own indebtedness to Robertson Smith. He had profited from Lagarde in his Arabic studies. His travels in the Near East had given him such a mastery of spoken Arabic that he could speak it fluently, and, what is more, an unusually intimate contact with the life of the people. All of these influences played a role in the preparation for the *Lectures on the Religion of the Semites*. But there was another force which made itself felt in the lectures, *viz.*, Robertson Smith's personality. He was open and receptive to all that he saw about him in his journeys in Arabia. He came to know the common people intimately. He not only mastered their language, but was also a keen observer of their customs, practices, and religious rites. One of the most impressive features of his work is the extraordinary detail of his discussion, teeming, as it does, with innumerable concrete first-hand observations. This is quite consistent with the burden of his thought: "it is of the first importance to realize clearly from the outset that ritual and practical

---

[18] *Lectures on the Religion of the Semites: the Fundamental Institutions.* Third edition, 1927, p. 21.

usage were, strictly speaking, the sum-total of ancient religions" (p. 20). While Robertson Smith from his earliest years had a keen interest in theology,[19] it is as an anthropologist and a student of comparative religion that he speaks. It is probable that his third series of lectures were devoted to theological concerns, but the first two series have quite another character. He was the first to apply the anthropological approach to the study of the Old Testament, and it was his design to view the Old Testament in the context of the ancient Semitic religion that he believed to lie behind it and to accompany its early stages.

Robertson Smith sets out at once to delineate the purpose and design of his lectures. He is not concerned to give an account of the religions that have a Semitic origin, but rather of "Semitic religion as a whole in its common features and general type" (p. 1). He seeks to gain an insight into that sphere of Semitic culture which will cast maximum light upon the religion of ancient Israel. Originally the Semites represented a clearly defined linguistic and ethnic unity, a cultural homogeneity, and a geographical region determined by the limits of the Arabian Peninsula, which Smith assumed to be the original home of all the Semitic peoples. The origins of the religions of these peoples he finds in the Arabs. It is among them that we encounter the most primitive forms of religion; in their records we see a reflection of nomadic mentality and the unchanging character of nomadic life. So he availed himself of the pre-Islamic literary records and the references to Semitic life and practice in the classical literature. The criticism that has been most frequently launched against *The Religion of the Semites,* present already in the first reviews of his work, is its neglect of the Babylonian and Assyrian sources. It is probable that he anticipated the objection, but he avers that the latter represent a relatively late stage of cultural and religious development. They reflect an established monarchical form of govern-

---

[19] James D. Smart, *The Interpretation of Scripture,* Philadelphia, 1961, pp. 39, 242.

ment, an organized pantheon, and an elaborate mythology. Mythology takes the place of dogma and belief. It was not an essential part of ancient religion and had no binding force upon the worshippers. It was only later that it acquired great importance. The ancient religions of the Babylonians and Assyrians presuppose a long period of social and religious growth. The Arabian sources, on the contrary, while admittedly late, preserve the primitive culture emanating from a much earlier age. We must not confuse *ancient* and *primitive*. Moreover, the Babylonians and Assyrians were not pure Semites; there was a strong infusion of early, non-Semitic culture in their veins, and their literature reflects cultural borrowing. In the light of our contemporary knowledge of the ancient Near Eastern peoples, much of this will sound precarious and alien, but it must be remembered that Near Eastern scholarship in the nineteenth century was poles removed from what it is today. Nevertheless, even in the time of Robertson Smith, voices were raised in protest against this neglect of the cuneiform monuments from Babylonia and Assyria. Be that as it may, the criticism does not invalidate all that Robertson Smith has to say; on the contrary, his work is a monument of scholarship, a great work for its own day and not without importance for our own. It is a vast storehouse of phenomenology of Arabian folkways and religion, and much of it is relevant to many Old Testament contexts, though, perhaps not to the degree assumed in a previous generation.

For a proper understanding of *The Religion of the Semites,* it is essential that we not only recognize its purpose or intention, but also that we take note of its methodology. The writer employs a vast canvas upon which to sketch or portray what he considers to be the primitive religion of the Semites, and he draws his materials from a vast variety of sources, both within the Semitic quadrilateral and outside it. He is at pains to stress again and again the unity which persists beyond all the diversities of the practices and rituals of the Semitic tribes. Like his contemporary, Tylor, he writes as an anthropologist and, like him and like Renan, Baudissin, Wellhausen, Sayce, M. J. Lagrange, and others before and after him, he is intent upon comparing the cultural and social phenomena that are common to all the Semitic tribes and even to the communities lying outside the orbit of the Arabian Peninsula. But more than that, after all has been said, it is a more specific and basic comparison that comes within his range of vision: the relation of primitive Semitic religion with the religion of the ancient Hebrews. The significance of Robertson Smith in the history of scholarship is that he belongs at one and the same time to the students of anthropology, to the pioneers of comparative religion, and to the company of those Old Testament scholars who, like B. Duhm, B. Stade, Karl Budde, and others, were among the first to compose a history of Israel's faith on the basis of historico-critical presuppositions.

We may press our inquiry into the methodology of the book more concretely and succinctly, especially since it emerges as the major topic of the opening lecture. When we undertake to gain a synoptic view of the entire work with its spacious panorama, is it possible to subsume the long and detailed discussion under a single rubric? The author is very clear and emphatic in his reply to our query. As we have had occasion to observe before, it is not with mythology that we are here first of all concerned, for, as the writer contends, mythology represents a developed stage in the history of religion. Nor is it with beliefs or doctrines that we have in the first instance to do, for they, too, are derivative. Primitive religion is not a system of beliefs with practical applications; rather it is a body of traditional practices which were the common possession of early society. What is essential in primitive religion is the proper observance of rites and customs, of rituals and cultic activities, obedience to which is regarded as piety and is believed to secure the favor of the gods. Rules of conduct antecede general principles formulated in words. "Religious institutions are older than religious theories" (p. 20). In the popular religions of antiquity, all religious relationships are inextricably bound to fixed institutions, such as cult, sacrifice, and precedent. In a word, the methodology of the book is to sketch the life history of early religious institutions, to engage in an inquiry into "the religious institutions which governed the lives of men of Semitic race" (p. 22).

It may be observed that this stress on institutions is not remote from our contemporary study of the Old Testament, as is illustrated, on the one hand, by such works as those of Johannes Pedersen[20] and Roland de Vaux, O.P.,[21] and, on the other, by the many studies of the religion and theology of ancient Israel.

The fundamental principle and basic presupposition of Semitic religion is the solidarity of the community. It is not the family but the clan or tribe which is the elemental social unit. The primary religious fact is the relationship of the god and his worshippers. Together they form an organic society, a single community of kinship. It is blood relationship that determines the bond, not only between members of the clan, but also between the members of the clan and its god. Every clan has its own god, who is understood as its progenitor. The only bond which has binding force, which unites men into a single social and cohesive whole, is the community of blood. The ancient conception of kinship is participation in one blood, which flows through the veins of parent and child and through every member of the clan or tribe. The relationship is therefore viewed as physical, and this holds too for the relationship between men and gods.

The god, as we have said, is the progenitor of the tribe who lives on friendly and human terms with his descendants. He is their protector against a common enemy and the participant in all their fortunes. As their ancestor, he is con-

[20] *Israel: Its Life and Culture* I-II, Copenhagen, 1926; III-IV, 1940.
[21] *Ancient Israel: its Life and Institutions,* Translated by John McHugh. New York, 1961.

cerned for their welfare and survival. According to the social organization of the particular clan, he is originally viewed as mother under the primitive matriarchate, later as father, as is illustrated in the *'ab* preformatives of proper names, such as Abiel, "el is my father," or Abibaal, "Baal is my father." The relationship of the father to his descendants is moral as well as physical, and it is here that we may discern the origin of ethics. It is not fear that motivates the minds of the worshippers of the clan, but rather reverence and loyalty. Robertson Smith, therefore, rejects the ancient dictum of Statius, *primus in orbe deos fecit timor,* commonly supported by the anthropologists of his day. In the religion of the Hebrews and in Christianity, the divine fatherhood is quite central, but it is completely dissociated from a physical relationship (cf. Hos. 11:1; Deut. 32:6). "Man was created in the image of God, but he was not begotten; God sonship is not a thing of nature, but a thing of grace" (p. 41). With the breaking of the old tribal system among the northern Semites, the idea of the divine descent was necessarily altered. The bonds which united them were not political, and the god was now no longer father but king. Yet the father-son kinship survived among the more eminent and influential families, who traced their origin to a common ancestor. But as king, he was addressed as lord, and his worshippers were his servants. Here too, we find the proper names illuminating: 'Abd-Eshmun, "servant of Eshmun," 'Abd Baal, 'Abd Osir, etc. This usage survives in not a few Old Testament contexts. Yahweh's worshippers are his servants, and Israel is his servant too. The idea is not so much one of authority or of slavery, but of allegiance and loyalty.

It is not surprising that in his discussion of Semitic religion Robertson Smith should give priority to the conception of *holiness.* More than any other term, holiness expresses the nature of what is uniquely divine. It is a *sui generis* word and manifests itself wherever and whenever men sense themselves to be in the presence of divinity. It is at once the most important and most comprehensive conception for the sacred. The writer is acutely aware of the difficulties of definition, especially in relation to the primitive materials that are at his disposal. He has little to say of the sense of the numinous, so much stressed by Rudolf Otto in his study on *The Idea of the Holy*, although he does speak repeatedly of the sense of awe, reverence, and dread of the worshippers. He takes as his starting point the connection of the gods with certain places or areas. In ancient religion, gods, like men, have a physical environment in and through which they act and manifest themselves. The god has a natural life and a natural habitation which must not be violated or infringed upon. Originally holiness is entirely without ethical significance; it has nothing to do with morality or purity of life. The activity and dominion of the gods are conceived as being bound by certain physical limits; they have their abodes in certain "holy places" or sanctuaries. Holy persons, things, and times presuppose the existence of sacred areas where men minister or celebrate. The basic conception underlying the conception of holiness is restriction or prohibition. A holy place is one which is prohibited to common use. The contrast between what is *common* and what is *holy* is present in all primitive religion. The Hebrew root *herem* is an expression of this prohibition; it is that which is reserved or devoted to the god. The same idea is found in the root חמי, which denotes a sacred enclosure protected from encroachment (p. 150). Sanctuaries come into existence and altars are erected where the divinity makes himself known, as in the numerous theophanies preserved in the Old Testament, especially in the patriarchal traditions. The system of restrictions and the rules of holiness are expressed by the Polynesian word *tabu*. To this subject Robertson Smith devotes an extended discussion (pp. 153 ff., and the two "additional notes" on "holiness, uncleanness and taboo" and "taboos on the intercourse of the sexes," pp. 446-56). In his discussion of various holy areas or regions the writer has been strongly influenced by the animistic theories of E. B. Tylor. All nature is alive and animated, but there are certain spots which are the favorite haunts of animate life, to which reverence was attached. The fifth chapter is devoted to a discussion of holy waters (pp. 165-184), sacred trees (pp. 185-197), sacred caves and pits, (pp. 197-200), and sacred stones or altars (pp. 200-212). Altars, shrines, or sanctuaries were subsequently often erected at or near these sites, and the persons associated with them become holy."

In the context of his discussion of the primitive religion of the clans, Robertson Smith enters into a long discussion of baalism and the land of the Baal. The worship of the Baal is the religion of the Semitic culture lands; it has as its presuppositions the pursuit of agriculture and private property. The title *baal* "possessor" already points to changed economic and legal relationships. Agriculture which is carried on by individuals leads to private possession. The baal is the possessor of a particular district; every district has its baal. So we hear of Melcarth, the Baal of Tyre, of Astarte, the Baalath of Byblus, of the Baal of Lebanon, of Mount Hermon, of Mount Peor; etc. The baals are associated with the soil that requires no irrigation; they are its fertilizers, the owners of its produce, and are entitled to its natural gifts. According to the author, baal worship was never known to the pastoral bedouins except in so far as they came under the influence of the inhabitants of the agricultural oases, who had borrowed from neighboring culture lands. Through his character as lord of the ground the baal is spatially bound. Yahweh in the Old Testament is the baal of the land of Palestine, and the title was employed in the proper names, such as those of Saul's son Ishbaal and his grandson Meribaal. Hosea thinks of Yahweh as Israel's Baal, the giver of grain, wine, and oil (Hosea 2). He becomes the creator and embodiment not only of all plant life, but of all fertility, both animal and human. The author refers to the influence which the conception of the baals as the productive and reproductive powers exercised in the development of a highly sensuous mythology, where the gods are divided into sexes and the Baal is conceived as the male principle of reproduction, but he does not elaborate since it falls outside the scope of his immediate interest and concern.

The solidarity of the clan or tribe in the kinship of its members and the holiness of certain restricted places or areas form the prolegomena to the major theme of *The Religion of the Semites,* viz., the ritual of sacrifice among the early Semites and the Hebrews. To this subject more than half of the book is devoted. Sacrifice is the oldest and most essential of all primitive religious rites and is antecedent to every other form of religion. All religion is the activity of the community and finds its most concrete embodiment and expression in sacrifice. It is our best key to an understanding of the interior character of the primitive nomadic religion.

The primary significance of sacrifice is that it is a communal meal in which the god and his worshippers participate. Together they eat the flesh and drink of the blood of the sacred animal. In their eating and drinking they are bound in a mystic communion. The form that the sacrifice takes then is that of a sacramental meal of the tribe. Its purpose is to renew and celebrate the "natural" community of blood within the tribe and its father god. The sacrificial offering is the totem animal of the tribe, which may be slaughtered only on the occasion of the sacramental meal.[22] In Semitic antiquity there is no sharp distinction between the nature of gods, of men, and of beasts. "The kinship between gods and their worshippers, on the one hand, and

---

[22] The stress on totemism and of its importance in the origins of early Semitic religion and in its survivals in the Old Testament pervades a large part of the book, including its appendices. Perhaps no single feature has received greater discussion, both favorable, especially from the anthrolopogists, and unfavorable. For an extended comment, see the *Introduction* to the third edition by Stanley A. Cook.

kinship between the gods and certain kinds of animals, on the other, are deep-seated principles of Semitic religion" (p. 289). In the sacramental meal the god and his worshippers are *commensals,* and every aspect of their mutual relationship is included in what this involves. They who eat and drink together are united for all social relationships. Hospitality is one of the basic institutions of the primitive nomadic Semite. Covenants are sealed by partaking of the same food, the deity probably to be understood as the third party.

Closely related to the view of sacrifice as a ritual of communion between the god and his worshippers is the conception of atonement. From very early times the two were intimately connected. Atonement is the act of communion which is meant or designed to wipe out all previous estrangement. In it the community is restored to its former relationship of harmony and peace with the deity. To the author communion and atonement are the two basic realities of early Semitic religion. The ceremonies attendant upon the celebration of the sacrifice are intended "to establish a life-bond between the worshipper and his god, but are dissociated with the death of the victim and from every idea of penal satisfaction" (p. 336). In the sin-offerings which date from the time of national distress of the seventh century B. C. the victim is slain "before Yahweh," and only the priests may eat of its flesh. On this circumstance, the author comments (p. 350):

> I am not aware that anything quite parallel to the ordinary Hebrew sin-offering occurs among the other Semites; and indeed no other Semitic religion appears to have developed to the same extent the doctrine of the consuming holiness of God, and the consequent need for priestly intervention between the laity and the most holy things.

The historical movement of Israel's religion is intimately associated with the development of piacular or expiatory offerings, a subject to which the author devotes an exten-

ded discussion with the intention of discerning their origin
and religious significance. He regards these as going back
to a very early period, but as attaining great significance
in the period of national decline and stress of the seventh
century B. C. During this period the old sense of friendly
rapport with the deity gave way to a feeling of malaise and
a need to conciliate the favor of Yahweh, who had hidden
his face from the house of Israel. The ancient piaculum
to our author was not a means of gaining forgiveness for
sins; rather it was founded on a myth expressed in the
ritual. Thus, among the Cathaginians and the Arabs of
Dumaetha the sacrifice was often a human victim. The
piaculum, in short, was a communion of blood, that is, of
life, between man and his god, and is derived from the old
conception of kinship and of nature between the deity and
his worshippers.

To evaluate or assess the importance of the contribution
of Robertson Smith to our understanding of ancient Semitic religion, it is essential that we distinguish between its
significance in the context of his own time and its relevance
in the context of contemporary Semitic and biblical scholarship. The publication of the *Lectures* received a mixed
response. To those who could not accept its historical-
critical presuppositions concerning the composition of the
Old Testament, especially of the Pentateuch, the work
carried little or no weight and was, indeed, roundly con-
demned. The reaction of many of the leading Churchmen
was much the same and resulted in years of heresy trials.
Yet everywhere, in conservative as well as radical quarters,
it was recognized that it was indeed a *magnum opus,* an
achievement of great learning and monumental range. The
evolutionary presuppositions which underlay the exposition
were, of course, rejected by not a few. On the other hand,
the book was enthusiastically received by others throughout Britain and in Germany. It was translated into German,
and edited by Professor R. Stübe, who placed it in the

very first rank of religious scientific presentations and considered it epoch-making in the history of the study of Semitic religion. Karl Budde wrote a long critical review in the *Theologische Literaturzeitung* (1890, No. 22, pp. 528-44). In general the most enthusiastic reviews came from anthropologists like Sir James Frazer, E. B. Tylor, F. B. Jevons, and others. Smith's work has left its impression upon all subsequent literature, even when the name of the original author had ceased to be mentioned. He was one of the founders, if not preeminently *the* founder of the modern study of Semitic and other religions, according to one of his most distinguished reviewers. Similar encomia were composed by many others in literary and scientific journals.

The third edition of the *Lectures* was published in 1927 and edited by Stanley A. Cook. Professor Cook provides an appreciative, illuminating, and perceptive introduction in which he undertakes to assess and interpret the importance and value of the work in the context of the scholarship of his time. He devotes a substantial section to a criticism of the totemic theory, but his sympathies with that view are stronger than that of any scholar today. More important are the detailed and exhaustive notes of more than two hundred finely printed pages appended at the end of the book. Whatever judgments one may register concerning the judgments that are there expressed, they offer us an encyclopaedic body of anthropological data, cultural phenomenology, and primitive religon to which it would be difficult to find a parallel.

It is not quite so easy to assess the significance of *The Religion of the Semites* for contemporary scholarship. The whole direction of our approach to the Semitic world has altered radically. For it is not to the desert of Arabia that we now look, but rather to the great Semitic and non-Semitic cultures of the ancient Near East. We have already called attention to the major defect of Robertson Smith's work, viz., its total neglect of these cultures. There are not a few who take quite a different view of the value and relevance of the Arab tribes and their religion and folkways for an understanding of the religion of Ancient Israel. Exception has often been taken, too, to the evolutionary doctrine which doubtless influences the exposition of the development of Semitic religion. It has been averred that there is an implicit positivism in the interpretation of the sources, both written and unwritten, from the desert clans. It is certain that Robertson Smith was deeply influenced by the animistic theories of E. B. Tylor; there is no scholar today who would attempt to write the early history of Israel's religion from this point of view, though it must be added that Robertson Smith had his successors as, for example, in the work on *Hebrew Religion* (1930) by W. O. E. Oesterley and T. H. Robinson. Similarly, the view that Israel's religion, like that of the Arab clansmen, was in its origin *totemic* is rejected by all scholars today. Yet, despite all these caveats *The Religion of the Semites* is not only a monument in the history of Semitic studies, but also a vast storehouse of anthropological data of great interest, an extraordinary gathering together of cultural and religious phenomena, a work of colossal learning from a mind that was fertile, perceptive, creative, and open. The emphasis upon the importance of institutions in the study of religions would receive widespread acceptance today. It is a salutary, even necessary approach to an understanding of religion. Finally, we have often been too exclusive in our stress upon the great Near Eastern cultures in their relation to the Old Testament records. We may be confident that powerful nomadic influences continued to exert themselves upon Israel's religion throughout its history.

We initiated our discussion with a general account of the intellectual and cultural environment of the second half of the nineteenth century, the period of Robertson Smith's scholarly activity and the background against which he pursued his researches into Semitic and biblical religion.

It is our intention now to discern, as best we can, some of the major trends since his day in the area of his greatest interest and concern. First of all we may mention a substantial number of works devoted to nomadism and "the nomadic ideal."[23] Chief among these are A. Musil's, *The Manners and Customs of the Rwala Bedouins* (1928), M. von Oppenheim's, *Die Beduinen* (1939-1952; three volumes thus far), and J. R. Kupper's *Les nomades en Mésopotamie au temps des rois de Mari* (1957).[24] Related to these works are the studies on tribal organization by A. Causse, *Du groupe ethnique à la communauté religieuse* (1937) and S. Nyström, *Beduinentum und Jahwismus* (1946). We have remarked repeatedly that the most serious defect of Robertson Smith's *magnum opus* was its neglect of the inscriptional materials from the peoples of the ancient Near East. Although archaeology was still a budding science in his day, the Egyptian hieroglyphic and Mesopotamian cuneiform had been deciphered and numerous inscriptions translated. It is not surprising, therefore, that practically all subsequent research has to one degree or another taken account of the revelations from the mounds and of the literary remains or archives of the Near Eastern peoples. For example, Rudolf Kittel in his monumental work, *Geschichte des Volkes Israel* (I. seventh edition, 1932; II. 1925; III. Second edition, 1927-29), utilized the ancient records in his discussion of the institutions of Israel as did many others, among whom were I. Benzinger, *Hebräische Archäologie* (1894; third edition, 1927); later A. G. Barrois,, *Manuel d'Archéologie Biblique* (vol. I, 1939; vol. II, 1953), and most recently, R. de Vaux in his excellent work on *Les Institutions de l'Ancien Testament* (vol. I, 1958; vol. II, 1960.) Translated by John

[23] Karl Budde, "Das nomadische Ideal im Alten Testament," *Preussische Jahrbücher*, v. 85, 1896, pp. 57-79; A. Causse, *Les "pauvres" d'Israël*, 1922, Chap. V; J. W. Flight, "The Nomadic Idea and Ideal in the Old Testament," *JBL*, XLII (1923), pp. 158-226.

[24] For detailed bibliography, see R. de Vaux, *Ancient Israel: Its Life and Institutions*, 1961, pp. 519-20.

McHugh under the title *Ancient Israel: Its Life and Institutions,* 1961) and in his important article on "Les Patriarches hébreux et les découvertes modernes" *RB,* LVI (1949), 5-36; preceded by LIII (1946), 321-48; LV (1948), 321-47).[25] W. F. Albright from the beginning of his career to the present has taken account of the ancient Near Eastern records; for the period under our inspection, and see now his *Yahweh and the Gods of Canaan* (1968).[26] The life and culture of Israel are discussed by A. Bertholet, *Kulturgeschichte Israels* (1919; English translation, by A. K. Dallas, *A History of Hebrew Civilization* 1926), with more than occasional references to the great cultures of the Near East. A work which addresses itself to the same subject, but more expansive in its range and more perceptive in its grasp of Semitic and biblical mentality, is Johannes Pedersen's *Israel: Its Life and Culture* (Vol. I, 1926; Vol. II, 1940), which is replete with anthropological data. Like Robertson Smith, Pedersen makes use of the nomadic materials and understands Israel's cultural history largely in their setting. The clan or tribal organization of Israel has been carefully studied by Causse, Nyström, and de Vaux in the works already mentioned, and by Ed. Meyer (and B. Luther) in *Die Israeliten und ihre Nachbarstämme* (1906) and by Martin Noth's influential work on *Das System der Zwölf Stämme Israels* (1930).

The ancient Semitic sanctuaries and the rites associated with them have been subjected to scrutiny in several substantial works by Robertson Smith's contemporaries, such as W. W. von Baudissin, *Studien zur semitischen Religionsgeschichte* (vol. II, 1878), Friedrich Baethgen, *Beiträge zur semitischen Religionsgeschichte* (1888), and M. J.

---

[25] For the best compilation of texts from the ancient Near East, including *inter alia* the laws, myths, rituals, incantations, hymns, and prayers, see James B. Pritchard, *Ancient Near Eastern Texts Relating to the Old Testament*, Princeton, 1950.

[26] Note also his three earlier works: *From the Stone Age to Christianity: Monotheism and the Historical Process*, Baltimore, 1940; *Archaeology and the Religion of Israel*, Baltimore, 1942; *History, Archaeology, and Christian Humanism*, New York, 1964.

Lagrange, *Études sur les Religions sémitiques* (1903; second edition, 1905), and a smaller work by T. Canaan, *Mohammedan Saints and Sanctuaries in Palestine* (1927). Among the most recent studies of the sanctuary is the series of essays on "The Significance of the Temple in the Ancient Near East" in *The Biblical Archaeologist Reader* (vol. I, edited by D. N. Freedman and G. Ernest Wright, Anchor Books, 1961, pp. 145-200): Part I, "The Egyptian Temple," by Harold H. Nelson; Part II, The Mesopotamian Temple," by A. Leo Oppenheim; Part III, "The Temple in Palestine-Syria," by G. Ernest Wright; Part IV, "Temple Synagogue, and Church," by Floyd V. Filson. Note also the essay which follows by Frank M. Cross, Jr. on "The Priestly Tabernacle." The rites of sacrifice among the Assyrians and Babylonians have been treated *inter alios* by E. Dhorme, "Le sacrifice accadien à propos d'un ouvrage récent" in *Revue de l'histoire des Religions,* CVII, no. 2-3, 1933 pp. 107-25 and in his "Les religions de Babylonie et d'Assyrie," in *Mana: Introduction à l'Histoire des Religions,* (1945, pp. 220-233). Sacrificial rituals among the Arabs were described by J. Wellhausen in his *Reste arabischen Heidentumes* (1887; second edition, 1897), and later by J. Henninger, "Das Opfer in den altsüdarabischen Hochkulturen" in *Anthropos,* XXXVII-XL, 1942-45, pp. 779-810 and "Le sacrifice chez les Arabes" in *Ethnos* (Stockholm), XIII (1948), pp. 1-16. Henninger also has treated the Nilus evidence in "Ist der sogenannte Nilus-Bericht eine brauchbare religionsgeschichtliche Quelle?" in *Anthropos,* I, 1955, pp. 81-148. Canaanite sacrifice has also received much attention. Among the contributions to this important area of Semitic and biblical study are the works of Theodor Gaster, "The Service of the Sanctuary: a Study in Hebrew Survivals," in *Mélanges Syriens offerts à R. Dussaud,* II, 1939, pp. 577-82; R. Dussaud, *Les origines cananéennes du sacrifice israélite*[2] (1941) and *Les découvertes de Ras Shamra (Ugarit) et l'Ancien Testament* (1937; 2nd ed. 1941) John Gray, *The*

Legacy of Canaan (Supplements to *VT*, V, 1957); and R. de Vaux, *Studies in Old Testament Sacrifice*, Cardiff, 1964.

What directions our future study of the Old Testament and the literatures of the other peoples of the ancient Near East will take is not easy to say. It is probable, however, that we shall continue to find numerous affinities between the culture of Israel and that of her Semitic and non-Semitic neighbors. The materials from Ugarit and Mari and the other mounds will continue to reveal disclosures of different kinds which bear either directly or indirectly upon the Old Testament, whether one thinks of the linguistic and philological data, or of the literary styles and genres, or of the social practices and institutions, or of the historical information provided by references and records, or of religious phenomenology. We shall probably come to see ever more clearly that much of the Old Testament goes back to a very early period, that its literary expression has many parallels to that of other peoples, that its social institutions are related to those of her neighbors, and that its religion was much less "primitive" than has sometimes been supposed. Our knowledge of the history of the transmission of the Old Testament text will continue to produce fruitful results in the light of the records from Qumran. Finally, the sociology of religion will come to assume an ampler place in our future study and will serve as a corrective to some of the views now widely held in this field of inquiry. The influences from the Arabian desert and from the great empires and peoples will be more properly assessed, and a better understanding of the uniqueness of Israel in the ancient world will be achieved.

James Muilenburg
Seminary Professor
San Francisco Theological
Seminary and Graduate
May 1969   Theological Union

17

James Muilenburg

BUBER AS AN INTERPRETER OF THE BIBLE

THE DISTINCTIVE position which Martin Buber occupies in the contemporary study of the Bible is to be explained by something more than his independence as a critical scholar or by his wide-ranging interests in fields which lie beyond the immediate biblical horizon. For more than a generation he has devoted himself to a careful scrutiny of the Biblical text and has entered into a living and interior encounter with the ancient Hebrew words as no other scholar of our time. He has a profound grasp of the Biblical way of speaking: he discerns the accents, stresses, and culminations of words, their nuances and connotations; the ways in which they stand in relation to each other and the way of their ordering; their re-occurrence in fresh contexts where they are remembered, appropriated, re-fashioned, and actualized, yet continue to stand in relation to the context in which they first appeared and then press on into the con-temporaneity of the new situation, where they are again actualized into the present (*vergegenwärtigt*) and are there given new depth and dimension. Buber's extraordinary recognition of the power and vitality of words is rooted in his sense of the nature of human life in speaking and listening, in his understanding of man as a hearing-speaking being and of the *sui generis* nature of that engagement, of its implications and dynamic.

Martin Buber's independence is further shown by his approach to the Jewish Scriptures. While he has schooled himself in the methods and techniques of historical criticism and the criticism of literary types (*Gattungsforschung*) his own methodology represents a radical departure and, indeed, a protest against their adequacy as a means of arriving at the heart of the Biblical message. Not infrequently he raises the same questions as the modern critic, but his means of answering them is different. One of the most striking features of Buber's study of the Bible is the way in which he employs the ancient Near Eastern materials for an understanding, either by way of comparison or by way of contrast, of the uniqueness of Israel's faith. Arabic, Accadian, Egyptian, and Canaanite (Ugaritic) literary traditions and practices are constantly drawn upon for the elucidation of particular passages. The sociological interest is often marked, thanks in part to the influence of Max Weber, with whom he was associated in his early years at Frankfurt. In comparison with other modern Biblical scholars, his interest in historical background is relatively slight, despite his frequent emphasis upon the historical character of Biblical revelation. His primary concern is the existential appropriation by the individual of the Biblical event in the present moment. The existential encounter is for him always central and is not subject to historical conditioning.

Buber is not only the greatest Jewish thinker of our generation, not only a profoundly authentic exponent and representative of the Hebrew way of thinking, speaking, and acting, not only a celebrated teacher 'both to Jew and to Greek,' but also the foremost Jewish speaker to the Christian community. He, more than any other Jew in our time, tells the Christian what is to be heard in the Old Testament, what the Old Testament is really saying and what it certainly is not saying, what the direction is in which the words are moving on their way through history. He, more than any other Jewish writer, tells the Christian what he ought to know and what he ought to see, what the road on which he walks is like, whence the journey begins and whither it leads. Whatever else may be said of him, Buber is the great Jewish teacher of Christians. What is more, he has a deep interest in and sure grasp of much of the New Testament, a warm appreciation of the historical Jesus, and a recognition of the place where Jew and Christian go different ways. More than any other Jewish thinker of our time, he stands at the frontier which separates Christianity from Judaism.[1] He is the best contemporary corrective to the persistent Marcionism of large segments of the Christian Church. He gives Jewish answers to Christian questions, the kind of answers Christians must have if they are to understand themselves. Interestingly, the parts of the Old Testament which most engage his attention are those which are most cherished by Christians. Considering the profound influence of the theology and eschatology of Ezekiel upon the development of Judaism, it is significant that Buber has so little to say concerning him. On the contrary, Hosea and Jeremiah and, above all, Second Isaiah play a central role in his un-

---

[1] *Two Types of Faith; Between Man and Man*, pp. 5–6.

derstanding of the *Heilsgeschichte*. With this all Christians, but perhaps not all Jews, will heartily agree.

General Categories of Biblical Interpretation

Let us examine, first of all, several of the points of view which dominate Buber's understanding of the nature of the Old Testament. The Bible for him is essentially one book, united by several great themes and by its pervasive existential character. He is impressed by the continuity of its various parts, even when on the surface it may not be apparent to the modern Western reader. As we shall see, the presence of persistently recurring key words and key sentences provide for him a way of understanding this continuity. Everywhere man is called to meeting and encounter (*Begegnung*). Whatever the historical situation and whatever the literary guise—whether narrative, song, lament, or prophetic proclamation, Israel is called upon to meet her God, Yahweh, in encounter, a live and lived dialogue in which the eternal first person I addresses the second person Thou. Revelation, Buber is saying, comes in community, through the immediacy of word and event. Israel can address her God with the intimacy of *Thou* because He has first addressed her with His divine *I* and has accompanied His unique words with the eventful words of His activity. The Word of God is never, therefore, a generalization or abstraction, but always a living, concrete, historical *here and now* in which Yahweh and His people engage. The word of God is the symbol *kat' exochen* for the dialogical encounter. "Everything in Scripture is genuine spokenness" (*Gesprochenheit*).[2] We must not seek to distil from it a moral or a 'truth'; to do so would separate the hearer from his involvement and meeting; it would make of him a spectator rather than a hearer. Again, the Bible is unified by its constant proclamation of a message (*Botschaft*); everywhere the reality of the messenger's proclamation is present or assumed.[3]

The three central themes which control the dialogue 'between heaven and earth' are creation, revelation, and redemption. The demand with which the Bible meets the generations, says Buber, is to

---

[2] *Die Schrift und ihre Verdeutschung*, p. 56.

[3] *Ibid.*, pp. 55f. "Die hebräische Bibel is wesentlich durch die Sprache der Botschaft geprägt und gefügt . . . Gleichviel wie es sich mit irgendwelchen Stücken der Bibel verhielt ehe sie in die Bibel eingingen: in jedem Gliede ihres Leibes ist die Bibel Botschaft."

384   JAMES MUILENBURG

become recognized as the record of the authentic history of the world; namely, that the world has an origin (*Ursprung*) and a goal (*Ziel*). It demands of the individual that he surround his life with this true history, that in its origin he may find his origin and in its goal his goal. Between origin and goal is revelation, but not as something I can appropriate to myself or possess but as something which is ever moving according to concrete time and circumstance, the concrete moment in which the hearer listens to the voice speaking of origin and goal. "Creation is the origin, redemption the goal. But revelation is not a fixed, dated point poised between the two."[4] Buber is in accord with Oscar Cullmann that Judaism knows no midpoint of the *Heilsgeschichte;* even the revelation at Sinai is not such a midpoint, but rather an ever-recurring hearing and becoming aware in the present moment of its actualization (*Vergegenwärtigung*). One must admit that all of this is exceedingly interesting and suggestive and that it is an adequate statement of many great contexts of Old Testament faith. It is a question, however, whether they hold true for all of the Bible.[5]

Buber's discussion of creation, redemption, and revelation should be understood and pondered in the light of what he has to say about mythology and eschatology in the introduction to his *Königtum Gottes*. Whether or not one agrees with his definitions, the reality to which he points is one of the first importance for a grasp of many great prophetic and liturgical contexts (e.g., Second Isaiah and Psalms), and more especially for a true understanding of Biblical eschatology:[6]

The myth is the spontaneous and proper speech of the expecting as of the remembering faith. But it is not its substance. Out of mythical plasticity (*Bildsamkeit*) the figures of eschatology, though not its impetus and power, are to be understood. The true eschatological life of faith—in the great woes of historical experiences—is born out of the genuine historical life of faith; every other attempt to discern its derivation mistakes its nature.

The Biblical Text

Basic to an understanding of Buber's interpretation of the Bible is his view of the original Hebrew text and, more particularly, of the

[4] *Israel and the World*, p. 94.

[5] *Prophetic Faith*, pp. 194, 197, 213–217. For a discussion of creation, redemption, and revelation, see Maurice Friedman, *Martin Buber*, and Will Herberg, *The Writings of Martin Buber*, pp. 29–32.

[6] *Königtum Gottes* (2nd ed.), p. IX.

ways in which the ancient Semitic original may be transmitted to the modern Western mind in modern Western speech. It is highly significant, therefore, that his first great undertaking, in cooperation with Franz Rozenzweig, was a translation of a large part of the Old Testament into German, in which he sought to reproduce as faithfully and closely as possible the original words into their modern equivalent. The volume by Buber and Rozenzweig on *Die Schrift und ihre Verdeutschung* (Berlin, 1936) gives us an excellent account of their views concerning Hebrew literary composition, the nature of the Hebrew language, and the methods by which the genius of one speech may be transmitted into the genius of another.[7] All previous translations, they aver, are like a palimpsest which obscures the underlying text, reflecting the literary modes and theological terminology of the times in which they were composed. It is the design of Buber and Rozenzweig to remove the palimpsest, to recover the original speech with all its manifold features, and to employ only such words, alien as they may sometimes seem to modern ears, as will express the Hebrew original. Not only must the symbols and images of the Hebrew be preserved, but also the subterranean stream of ancient Hebrew sensuousness, its sentence structure and 'architecture,' its repetition of key words and sentences in varying contexts, and above all its rhythm and speaking quality. Such literary features as assonance, alliteration, and rhythm provide the clue for discerning the intent of the speaker and are an indispensable tool for sound exegesis. Here Buber is calling attention to matters which are indeed of the first importance for a grasp of the text, for to arrive at its true meaning one must be able to articulate the major motifs as they are bodied forth in form and sound. All too often scholars have dealt cavalierly with the text and have deleted passages which are absolutely essential to their true understanding. Yet one may question whether Buber's attempt to preserve the rhythmical units (*Atemzüge*) has not sometimes involved some loss, for the parallelism of lines, to which Bishop Lowth originally called attention in 1753, is in reality sometimes obscured. Rhythm is present, however, not only in poetry,

---

[7] This work is basic to an understanding not only of the translation but also to the methodology involved in the interpretation of the text. Among the more relevant discussions are "Über die Wortwahl in einer Verdeutschung der Schrift," "Zur Verdeutschung der Preisungen," "Leitwortstil in der Erzählung des Pentateuchs," "Das Leitwort und das Formtypus der Rede," all by Buber, and "Die Schrift und das Wort," "Das Formgeheimnis der biblischen Erzählungen," by Rozenzweig.

but, according to Buber, throughout the Old Testament, and the
translation presents it effectively. Scores of illustrations might be
drawn from the translation to show how the form and sound is
presented. I limit myself to but one illustration taken at random: [8]

> Darum
> will ich so dir tun, Jisrael!
> Deswegen,
> dass ich dir dieses tun will,
> bereite dich,
> deinen Gott gegenüberzustehn,
> Jisrael!
> Ja denn, wohlan,
> der die Berge bildet,
> der den Geistbraus schafft,
> der dem Menschen ansagt
> was sein Sinnen ist,
> macht nun aus Morgenrot Trübnis
> und tritt einher auf den Kuppen der Erde,
> sein Name:
> ER IST DA, der Umscharte Gott.   Amos 4:13.

The form clearly demonstrates where the accents lie; the emphatic
words *Darum* and *Deswegen* and the repetition of the lines which
follow them, the repetition of *Israel*, the succession of participial
phrases (the threefold *der*), the single word *prepare* (*bereite dich*),
and the superb climaxes *to meet your God* and *his name, Yahweh
of hosts (sein Name:* ER IST DA, *der Umscharte Gott)*, and much
else aid us in entering into the interior nature of prophetic speech.
This example is by no means exceptional: indeed it may be said to
be characteristic of the whole Old Testament. It can be readily seen
how important these formal devices are for Biblical hermeneutics.
Buber has made use of these stylistic devices again and again in his
interpretation; e.g. the Song of Deborah, the Tower of Babel story,
the covenant narratives, and the Psalms.

Much attention is given to linguistic matters. Many cultic *termini
technici*, such words as *mishpat, ṣedakhah, ḥesed, emunah, ruaḥ,
kabod*, and the divine appellations *Yahweh* and *El* are treated at
considerable length.[9] It is doubtful, however, whether Buber has
taken into sufficient account the diversity of their usages. For example, *ḥesed* seldom means lovingkindness or grace in the Old Testa-

---

[8] *Das Buch der Zwölf*, pp. 70–71.

[9] *Die Schrift und ihre Verdeutschung*, pp. 144–167.

ment; *covenant love* or the RSV *steadfast love* expresses the covenant connotation better. It is even more doubtful that the pronominal words ER, DU, SEIN are an adequate rendering for the divine name Yahweh. The assumption that throughout the Old Testament the original meaning of the word, *he who is present* (as Buber assumes it to be), was recognized by Israel is, to this writer, extremely unlikely. Even if Buber's interpretation of the tetragrammaton were correct, which is doubtful, the persistence of the original denotation in the minds of succeeding generations is highly questionable. For Buber to render *Yahweh* in the Amos quotation given above as ER IST DA goes against all that we know of the history of words. Moreover, this is by no means an isolated example of Buber's linguistic understanding. In his effort to preserve the primitive, dynamic connotations of words he goes too far, and sometimes allows what he conceives to be their etymology to determine their subsequent meanings.

Hermeneutical Methodology

A major issue in Buber's interpretation of the Biblical text is his methodology. We have given hearty approval to his stress upon the presence of key words, upon the interior structure of compositions, and to his appeal to the rhythm of a passage. But he would be the first to admit that this method does not answer many important critical questions, the questions with which historical and literary criticism are concerned. Yet he finds this approach to the text not only inadequate but mistaken. In the introduction to the first edition of *Königtum Gottes,* he says he can give to the symbols J and E, the strata which historical critics find in the Hexateuch, only very limited validity. Modern scholars, he says elsewhere,[10] have not proved the existence of such independent documents. He would speak rather of types of traditions, which, to be sure, have passed through a long period of transmission and have there received supplements and expansions. He is intent upon discerning the substance of the tradition in its original form and to note its tendencies and directions in the later development of the tradition. Of the Abraham stories, for example, he says that "the whole work serves a single intention: to stretch a line . . . every single point of which has its precise place and value."[11] The most thorough and detailed illustration of Bu-

---

[10] *Prophetic Faith,* p. 4.

[11] *Ibid.,* p. 88.

ber's methodology is to be found in a long article on the narrative
of Saul's election as king.12 In sharp disagreement with prevalent
historicocritical views, such as is represented in Otto Eissfeldt's *Einleitung in das Alte Testament* (1934), he rejects the presence of two
or three major sources and finds instead four major sections of material: (a) the narrative, (b) a very slightly edited battle history,
(c) annalistic notes, and (d) insertions within the sections of the
narrative. His analysis is thorough and painstaking and one with
which scholars will have to come to terms.

Our task is to begin with "the first stage at which we find evidence,
the stage which no literary evidence can shake," and we must inquire
of the text what the faith of Israel was at that particular stage. Then
we must go back to earlier stages where the same faith is clearly
reflected and so on until we arrive at the place where it first finds expression. Having established this point we are prepared to move forward and to trace the development of the faith in the light of the
major affirmations of the original 'event.' In his *Königtum Gottes*
Buber begins with Gideon's famous rejection of the kingship (Judg.
8:23) where he finds such a stage, but in his *Prophetic Faith* he begins
more appropriately with the Song of Deborah, and then proceeds
to the Shechem assembly in Josh. 24, the Sinaitic covenant (Exod.
19-24), and the narratives of the Fathers in Genesis.

Buber's reflections on the nature of saga and legend are of considerable importance, for he properly calls attention to the historical nucleus preserved in them.13 But once the legend has been
crystallized, there can be no additions or changes. He can appeal
here to primitive Semitic mentality in such matters. The only question here is the extent of the nucleus, and here Buber obviously
would go much farther than most scholars. He then sets himself to
separating the 'historical content' of a text, a question of the first
importance to the modern student. He mentions first of all the
social-historical background, then 'the point of view of the history
of the Spirit and especially the history of religion.' Here it is not a
matter of the authenticity of the external event, but of the religious
act or position of the period under discussion. Again, he appeals to
the *uniqueness of the fact*, which only 'the intuitively scientific meth-

12 *Vetus Testamentum*, 6, No. 2, pp. 113–173.
13 *Prophetic Faith*, pp. 5–6; *Moses*, pp. 13ff.

BUBER AS INTERPRETER OF THE BIBLE   389

od,' which seeks for the *concreteness* at the basis of an evidence, can recover.[14]

There can be no question that Buber has raised issues of the very first importance for an understanding of the Biblical text. One can only applaud his appreciation of the creative forces that go to the making of Hebrew literary composition and his constant concern to relate critical questions to the crucial and central matter of faith. In his studies of Abraham he has rescued the patriarch from a mere figure of the *Urgeschichte,* and the traditions from a collection of more or less inchoate fragments. "His work," Buber says finely, "became the basis of a narrative system of faith." One might wish, however, that he had taken the motifs of Gen. 12:1ff. and worked them out more concretely in terms of their fulfilment in the birth of the child. What he has to say of the traditions here are, as a matter of fact, best illustrated by a recognition of the Yahwist source, against the existence of which, however, he protests.[15] Again, in his analytical treatment of the Samuel-Saul narratives (I Sam. 7-13), he argues much in the fashion of any modern historical critic. With his rejection of the usual formulation of the Wellhausen hypothesis and the minute dissections of the critics he will find widespread agreement today, not least of all among the Scandinavian scholars, who apply their own methods of traditio-historical criticism to the Biblical texts, although it must be added that Buber would diverge sharply from them in their tendency at times to subordinate the historical revelation of the Old Testament to the patterns of Near Eastern mythology.

To begin with the Song of Deborah as the starting point of investigation into the history of Israel's faith is entirely appropriate; the same is not true, of course, of the Gideon utterance, which has no such claim to historicity among many critics. In his attempt to isolate the historical content of a passage, his appeal to the social-cultural background is certainly valid, and he has employed it in several contexts, notably in the Elijah narratives, with telling effect.[16] When he calls upon the *uniqueness of the fact* (italics are Buber's), he is dealing with a much more difficult matter, however, and the

14 *Prophetic Faith, idem.*

15 *Prophetic Faith,* p. 87; *Moses,* p. 6: *Königtum Gottes,* pp. XIV-XV. In the last-named work, however, he makes a considerable concession to the usual critical view, and his characterization of the 'tradition' (XV) both of J and E is one with which many scholars would agree.

16 *Ibid.,* pp. 70–80.

invocation of 'the intuitively scientific method' as a way of approach
to the text, as over against what he styles 'speculative theory,' only
makes difficult matters more difficult. Perhaps this may account for the
charge of subjectivity which is often levelled at him. The results of
this attitude may explain such categorical and unsupported expressions as 'this undoubtedly ancient verse' (I Sam. 3:1), 'which is also
unmistakably early' (3:11), 'this is not a late source' (I Sam. 8), 'the
antiquity of which cannot be doubted' (2 Sam. 23:1-7),[17] 'which
I regard as inimitably Isaianic' (Isa. 19:23-25).[18] In many of these
judgments, as a matter of fact, the writer concurs, but for very
definite reasons which he believes will stand the test of scholarly inspection. Finally, it must be said that only a detailed discussion can
deal fairly with Buber's critical views. There is one sentence, however in the *Prophetic Faith* (p. 4) which is of such importance for a
study of the Bible that it must be given in its completeness.

But even if we were allowed to speak of "sources" and if it were even
possible to fix their dates (and also the dates of the additions and redactions),
we would thereby only be able to establish layers of the *literary*, not the *religious* development, and these two need not in any way parallel one another,
as it is very possible that a primitive religious element is only found in a late
literary form.

If these wise words had been heeded in the past, the course of
Biblical criticism would have been quite different from what it has
been. Fortunately, the force of Buber's comment is today widely
recognized, above all in our understanding of the priestly traditions.

The Application of the Methodology

We turn now to several major examples of Buber's interpretations. In all of them he employs the methodology of key words to
great advantage. A wonderful example is his treatment of the Song
of Deborah (Judg. 5). This early poem of ancient Israel has received
much attention in the history of Old Testament research, but Buber's
approach illuminates the text in an entirely fresh way by his calling
attention to the literary stresses of the poem, above all upon Yahweh
and Israel. It is thus out of his recognition of recurring key words in
crucial contexts that he is able to discern the central disclosures of

[17] *Ibid.*, pp. 61f., 68.
[18] *Ibid.*, p. 150.

the poem and the nature of the faith which inspires it.[19] In *König-tum Gottes* Buber discusses another very early poem, the 'Song of Moses' (Exod. 15:1b-18), where he is inclined to isolate vv. 1b-11, 18 as the original poem, and vv. 12-17 as a later supplement. But if one is to employ the clue of key words, which proved so fruitful in the Song of Deborah, then it is clear that the poem is a literary unit, for here we have the same fundamental relationship of Yahweh and His people Israel. The motif of the people is clearly dominant in vv. 12-17 (cf. especially vv. 13 and 16cd); Yahweh's activity in this section (12-13) connects well with v. 10; the motif of the enemy is present in both (10-11 and 14-16). V. 18 does not follow well upon 11b but comes excellently after v. 17 as the tenses *inter alia* plainly show.[20]

In his diminutive book, *Right and Wrong*, Buber sets himself to an interpretation of five of the Psalms of the Psalter (12, 14, 82, 73, 1). In his translation of this book he speaks of all the poems as *Preisungen*, but as a matter of fact the number of laments exceeds the hymns and are, indeed, an authentic expression of Israel's life in relation to 'the God of the sufferers' (*Prophetic Faith*, pp. 155-235). All of the psalms studied are interpreted in the light of their key words. The study of Psalm 1 is especially rewarding because of the low estimate in which it is held by many commentators. The motif of *the way*, so central a motif of Biblical faith, is properly emphasized, and due recognition is given to the Law, which elsewhere in Buber's writings seems to receive less than its due. The one criticism I would have with the study is its distinction between *sinners* and *wicked*. I doubt whether a close analysis of the form and key words justifies such a conclusion.[21]

One of the best expositions of the prophets of Israel is to be found in *Prophetic Faith*, particularly the chapter on "The Great Tensions," in which Buber gives us a profound interpretation of the prophetic activity of Elijah, Amos, Hosea, and Isaiah. It is not only filled with keen insight and warm appreciation, to which few parallels can be found in contemporary treatment of the prophets, but also with a deep understanding of the fateful issues involved in the ministry of these prophets. Relatively little is said of the historical situa-

---

[19] *Prophetic Faith*, pp. 8–12.

[20] *Königtum Gottes*, pp. 129–131. See the valuable study by F. M. Cross and D. N. Freedman in *Journal of Near Eastern Studies*, 14 (1955), pp. 237–250.

[21] *Right and Wrong*, pp. 52–62. (Included in *Good and Evil: Two Interpretations* —Ed.)

tion, national and international, of their times, but what is given is
penetrating and succinctly stated. For example, very little is said of
the great international movements of the ninth century B.C., of
the rise of Assyria under Assur-nazir-pal and Shalmanezer III, of the
inner politics and mercantile interests of Phoenicia, or of the com-
plexity of Israel's international problems during this period. These
are by no means minor considerations. Yet one may agree that what
Buber has to say about the nature of Baal worship is of great consequence. Nowhere, so far as the writer is aware, has anyone succeeded in portraying the inner mysteries of nature worship and of
the sexual drives associated with them with such power, lucidity
and interior grasp.[22] Only through such an appreciation of the hold
which nature religion exerts on its devotees is one able to sense the
momentousness of the conflict between Yahweh and Baal or its significance in the history of world religion.

The Origins of Israel's Faith

On more than one occasion Buber has addressed himself to the
crucial questions associated with the beginnings of Israel's faith in
Yahweh as her God.[23] He rejects emphatically the widely current
view among scholars that Israel first came to know Yahweh at Mount
Sinai and argues forcefully that the traditions which represent him
as the God of the Fathers have a secure historical foundation. When
it is pointed out that the prophets constantly place the origins of
Israel's religion in the time of Moses, he replies that with one exception (Hos. 12:9; 13:4. cf. 11:1) this is nowhere stated, and that
Hosea's words are to be understood only as referring to the adoption
of Israel as the people of Yahweh (cf. Exod. 4:22). The relevant
passages in Exodus make it indisputably clear that the God who revealed himself to Moses at the Burning Bush was the God of the
Fathers (Exod. 3:3, 13-16). When Moses inquires about the name of the
God who speaks to him (Exod. 3:13), the true meaning of his words
is "what finds expression in or lies concealed behind the name."
"Moses expects the people to ask the meaning and character of a
name of which they have been aware since the days of their fathers."[24]

22 *Prophetic Faith*, pp. 74–76, 78f.

23 *Königtum Gottes* (2nd ed.), pp. XXIII-XLIV, 73–86; *Prophetic Faith*, pp. 13–59;
Moses, pp. 39–55, 94–100, 100–118.

24 *Moses*, pp. 48-9.

Again, when the Priestly historian (the designation is mine!) reports Yahweh as saying, "I am Yahweh. I appeared to Abraham, to Isaac, and to Jacob as El Shaddai, but by my name Yahweh I did not make myself known to them" (Exod. 6:2-3), the meaning is that the Fathers "did not know him in the quality characterized by his name; and that this had now been discovered."[25] Further, Buber asserts that in the period of religious laxity in Egypt "the name itself degenerated into a sound simultaneously empty and half-forgotten." In such an hour as that in which Moses proclaimed the holy event which he had experienced, the people were saying, "What is this God really like?"[26] Yahweh's reply to Moses' question is *'Ehyeh 'asher 'ehyeh*, which is explained as meaning "I shall be present as I shall be present," somewhat in the manner of Exod. 33:19: "I will be gracious to whom I will be gracious, and will show mercy on whom I will show mercy."

Now it must be admitted that there is force in much of what Buber has to say. His discussion exhibits learning as well as insight. On the other hand, his explication of the question about the name leaves this writer unpersuaded. The whole tenor of the passage seems to him to indicate that what is happening here is something really and decisively *new*; that Yahweh should say that He was the same God who had revealed Himself to the Fathers is perfectly natural and precisely what one would expect. Religious founders find support in their appeal to an antecedent past. Yahweh is saying substantially, "I am the God you have been worshipping all the time, the God of your fathers." Moreover, the very striking statement of the Priestly historian in Exod. 6:2f. can only mean what it clearly says, that He was known to the Fathers as El Shaddai and not as Yahweh.[27] The comment about Israel's failure to remember the name and its vital significance is neither persuasive nor likely. Into the vexing question of the meaning of the tetragrammaton we cannot enter here, but, again, Buber's explanation, which in this case is in some ways attractive, does not seem convincing. Surely the meaning 'to be present' is not the usual interpretation of the Hebrew verb *hayah*, as refer-

---

[25] *Ibid.*, p. 49.

[26] *Ibid.*, p. 51.

[27] Observe that in Genesis Yahweh employs the same revelatory or theophanic words, "I am Yahweh" (Gen. 15:7; 28:13). Are they to be understood in the same way as in Exodus?

ence to the standard lexicons will show.[28] Rather the primary meaning *is to come to pass, to happen,* i.e., '*I cause to come to pass what I cause to come to pass.*' Yahweh is the God of event, of eventfulness, and He will bring about that which He assures Moses and his people He will bring about. This suits the context admirably and strikes at the center of the Bible's understanding of the nature of divine revelation. It was the supreme event in the life of Israel when Yahweh made Himself known in the great theophany with his *hieros logos, I am Yahweh,* and then, significantly, "who brought you out of the land of Egypt, out of the house of bondage." He had caused to come to pass what actually did come to pass; this is the demonstration that He is Lord of history and the Sovereign of Israel's historical destiny.

In the light of the foregoing discussion, it is clear that Buber rejects the Kenite theory of the origins of Israel's faith in Yahweh. Now it must be recognized that the arguments in support of this theory are by no means coercive and that there is much that is wrapped in obscurity. In the second edition of his *Königtum Gottes* he seeks to meet the objections to his view and to his rejection of the Kenite hypothesis, and in *Moses* he enters into the subject again.[29] He is surely correct in stressing the family character of the narrative, but to say that Jethro did not come to Israel as priest of Midian runs counter to the very opening words of the narrative in Exodus 18: *Jethro, the priest of Midian.* The position of the narrative in its present context is said to be the work of the Redactor, for which no explanation is offered or defence given. The fact that Sinai is specifically called 'the mountain of God' (Exod. 3:1, 4:27) is not given any weight. Buber finds it incredible that Jethro should speak such momentous words as his "Now I know that Yahweh is greater than all gods" to a community which was not his own. But this does not take into account that Moses had married into the priest's family with all that that implies, and that on the 'mountain of God' he had received his revelation of Yahweh. Later in the discussion we are informed that the true meaning of Jethro's words is as follows: "I have now come to know that your god is the greatest, but have also recognized in him the true form and the true name of my god, the

---

[28] Little if any support will be found in Brown-Driver-Briggs Hebrew lexicon, or in Köhler-Baumgartner, or in Gesenius-Buhl (17th ed.). *See also* Thorleif Boman, *Das hebräische Denken im Vergleich mit dem griechischen* (Göttingen, 1954), pp. 27–39.

[29] Pp. 42ff.

fiery gleam of the middle whose rays have illumined me." Entirely aside from the unwarranted interpretation in the final phrase of this sentence, Jethro's admission here is scarcely less astonishing than the interpretation of the Kenite theory which Buber finds so incredible. Moreover his assertion that it was after all Moses who offered the communal sacrifice 'without the need for making any special mention of the fact' (!) is hard to credit in view not only of the words of v. 12, but also of the whole movement and structure of the passage: the *berachah* (v. 10), the solemn and momentous "Now I know," and the culminating sacrifice. The three events follow one another in almost inevitable sequence. Buber holds that it was Jethro who was won over to Yahweh and was convinced by the demonstrations of his power that his God and Moses' God were one and the same. The whole movement of the narrative seems to suggest quite the reverse.

The god of Midian is a mountain and fire god (p. 97), which is in all probability true. Now it has often been pointed out that the character of Yahweh in Genesis and Exodus is quite different in this respect. With the exception of the Sodom story, which is in many ways unique in Genesis, Yahweh nowhere reveals Himself in the imagery of fire, whereas in the period following Moses the associations of fire with Yahweh are characteristic and frequent. Further, it is said that Jethro may have recognized the name *Yahweh* as the correct one as the result of the mighty wonders of the Exodus. It is just as likely that he came to a fresh recognition of the *new character* which Yahweh his god had revealed in the events of the Exodus. It is Yahweh's *mighty works* in deliverance, leading, and providing which make all the difference. Other objections might be raised; we shall confine ourselves, however, to the episode of the adjudication of disputes in Exod. 18: 13-23. Such an undertaking is religious: the people 'inquire of God' and Jethro delivers a highly significant speech beginning with "Listen to my voice." It is Jethro, priest of Midian, who instructs Moses, and in language which leaves little doubt as to his expertness in such matters (cf. 18:19-23!). It must be admitted again that the Kenite theory has not been demonstrated, but the arguments in its favor are somewhat more impressive than is suggested by Buber's analysis of the narrative.

We must deal more briefly with another event, but one of great importance not only for an understanding of Israel's origins, but also of the whole Old Testament. I refer to the 'Eagle Speech' in Exod.

396   JAMES MUILENBURG

19:3-8. Buber rightly calls it 'the hour of the Covenant.' He calls
attention to the rhythmic character of the utterance, "almost every
word of which stands in the place fixed for it by sound and sense;"
indeed one should say 'every word' without qualification. But then we
are told to our amazement that the words "when ye hearken, hearken
unto my voice and keep my Covenant" do not find a place within
the firm rhythm. The truth is that the rhythm demands these words,[30]
the grammatical construction requires them,[30] without them the
excellent literary structure is destroyed, and, most serious of all, the
very heart of the Covenant reality is obscured. The issue here is neither
speculative nor academic; it raises the question of the nature of the
Covenant itself. First a word about the rhythm: the deletion of the
words in question actually destroys the parallelism of lines, so marked
a feature of the passage, a consideration to which Buber so often and
properly appeals. The structure of the narrative is plain for all to
see, and this applies more particularly to the words of the three sub-
sections, each introduced by a key word ('atem, 'atah, 'atem 4, 5, 6.)
More important is the weighty word *And now*; hereupon follows
the great sentence, composed of a *protasis* (*If you will truly listen to
my voice and heed my Covenant*) and *apodosis* (*then you shall become my precious possession*, etc.). The omission robs the utterance of the great contingency, strikes out the underlying imperative of obedience, and opens the floodgates of anti-Semitism, which
misunderstands the uniqueness of Israel's election and the uniqueness of its accountability and responsibility. This protasis-apodosis
construction continues in the tradition from beginning to end, and
many of the most exalted passages of the Bible preserve the authentic memory of its deep-lying origins. It is highly significant that the
Deuteronomists and the prophets who preserve the authentic Mosaic
covenantal tradition perpetuate it, and in contexts of great importance.

That the excision of the crucial covenantal words of Exod. 19:5
is well pondered is shown by the discussion of the decalog. As usual,
there is much here that is illuminating and suggestive, but there are
also a number of questions of interpretation which raise doubts. The

---

[30] It is very doubtful whether Buber has done justice to the grammar and syntax
of the passage. Note his unusual rendering of the particle *'im* as *when* and of the
infinitive absolute of the verb to hear, and observe the awkwardness which results
from the deletion of the crucial word.

most important of these is that the decalog was not the basis upon which the covenant was made.[31]

The concept of the document in the making of the Covenant appears to me secondary, and to have derived from the fact that the Covenant was misunderstood at a late time as the conclusion of a contract.[32]

That contractual relationships do not adequately express the meaning of the covenant is surely true. The great introductory words spoken in theophany (Exod. 20:2), the genuine *hieroi logoi* of the revelation, are words of grace corresponding to the New Testament *kerugma*, but the words which follow are the Torah belonging with the *kerugma* of grace, the *didache* of the early Christians. The omission of the decalog from its present context or from the theophany is not only contrary to what we know of all other Old Testament theophanies, where the theophany *always* issues into words and living speech, but also a cancellation of Israel as the people of the Torah in its covenantal origins, Torah as understood as direction, guidance, and teaching. The matter raised here is of special consequence since Buber so staunchly and rightly upholds the historicity of the event. It must be made clear that he does not reject the decalog as Mosaic; he simply detaches it from its present theophanic, covenant context, but this is precisely the issue both here and in the Eagle Speech.

The God of the Sufferers

The final chapter of *Prophetic Faith* is devoted to 'the God of the Sufferers.' Jeremiah, Job, Ezekiel, Psalm 73, and Second Isaiah are discussed in the light chiefly of the perplexing problems of theodicy. The chapter is so rich in insight that it is impossible to do justice to it; the Biblical figures are grasped in all their profundity, and their relationship to the major motifs of the *Heilsgeschichte* is clearly and vividly discerned. As we have had occasion to observe, Ezekiel does not figure large in the on-going drama of faith, and the treatment of the prophet is brief and perhaps not as illuminating or sympathetic as one might wish. The Book of Job 'in its basic kernel' cannot, according to Buber, be assigned to a time later (or earlier) than the beginning of the exile, a position which has the weighty

[31] *Moses*, p. 137.

[32] *Ibid., idem.* It is to be noted again that Buber gives no defence for this judgment.

support of R.H. Pfeiffer (*Introduction to the Old Testament,* p. 677).

Buber has a most interesting interpretation of Jeremiah's 'obituary notice' on King Josiah (Jer. 22:15-16); actually, however, the passage is part of the invective against Jehoiakim. The words referring to Josiah read as follows:

> Did not your father eat and drink
>   and do justice and righteousness:
> Then it was well with him.
>   He judged the poor and needy;
>   then it was well.
> Is not this to know me?

The reference to 'eating and drinking' is a famous *crux interpretum* which has received many different explanations. But Buber proposes a solution which has much to commend it.

Josiah's 'eating and drinking' here belong [he says], to the *covenant making* as much as the 'eating and drinking' of the elders of Sinai (Ex. 24,11), and henceforth fulfils it by himself practicing justice and righteousness, and as regards men by vindicating the cause of the poor and needy. 'This is to know me,' YHVH says to Jeremiah—that is that knowledge which Hosea declared to be the innermost essence of the relationship of faith; whosoever helps the suffering creature, comes into close contact with the Creator, and this is here called 'knowing YHVH'.

More might have been given us concerning Jeremiah's attitude to institutions, especially in comparison with his contemporary Ezekiel.

The most detailed and perceptive discussion of *Prophetic Faith* is the treatment of Second Isaiah. Buber rightly recognizes the close relation between Isaiah of Jerusalem and Second Isaiah and also the latter's familiarity with the so-called Priestly tradition, as we have it, for example in the first chapter of Genesis. Interestingly, considering Buber's general critical conservatism, several passages are denied the prophet's authorship (e.g. chap. 47; 49:14-16; 50:1-3) .[33] I should assign all these passages to the prophet, but there are scholars who would defend Buber's position here. The section on the Suffering Servant is an original contribution to a subject which has engrossed the attention of Biblical scholars perhaps more than any other in the Old Testament. Buber seems to support the view that the so-called 'songs' come "from another period in the life of the prophet than the rest of the book, and apparently a later period."[34] This view is still

---

[33] *Prophetic Faith,* p. 205.
[34] *Ibid.,* pp. 218–9.

BUBER AS INTERPRETER OF THE BIBLE   399

championed by many scholars, though the present direction of research supports their originality. The writer is quite confident that the literary structure of the poems demands that we accept them in their present contexts.

Outside the 'songs' the Servant is clearly Israel, as is explicitly stated again and again. Buber recognizes that the reference to Israel in the heart of one of the servant songs (49:3) is original, but he interprets it as referring to an individual: "*Thou* are the Israel in whom I will glorify myself."[35] The Suffering Servant cannot cover the life span of a single man. The three stages of the Servant's activity are rather to be understood as the way of one servant.

passing through all the different likenesses and life cycles. We do not know how many of them the prophet himself saw in his vision. . . . Neither can we presume what historical figures he included in the servant's way; it was laid upon the anonymous prophet to announce the mystery, not to interpret it.[36]

There is much to be said for this view; it is more than an interesting proposal and must be reckoned with as a genuine possibility. Yet the critical foundations are questionable; *viz.* the separation of the poems from their contexts, the notorious *Irrweg* followed by many scholars since the publication of Duhm's commentary in 1892. Moreover, Buber does not do full justice to the reality of corporate personality in biblical faith. Nowhere in the Old Testament is this mentality more clearly present than in Second Isaiah, and it is through an understanding of its meaning and significance that Israel as a community and Israel as a person are joined into one. Precisely for this reason the Servant of the Lord, both the 'songs' and the rest of the prophecy, were susceptible to christological formulation.

Yahweh as Melekh

We come finally, to what is the most significant and fruitful of all of Buber's contributions to Biblical study: the kingship of God and the role he plays as Leader. While the imprint on the title page of the first edition of *Königtum Gottes* bears the date of 1932, Buber had been lecturing for some twenty years on the origins of messianism and its later development. The messianic faith of Israel

---

[35] *Ibid.,* p. 223. The Masoretic text hardly supports this rendering, and it must therefore be considered highly precarious.

[36] *Ibid.,* p. 230.

400   JAMES MUILENBURG

is for him its central content. From its early beginnings it presses forward toward the fulfilment of the relation between God and the world in the complete kingly rule of God. *Königtum Gottes* deals with the early period of Israel's faith, and it is already there that we encounter the representation of Israel's faith in a divine kingship as actually historical. The second stage in Buber's study is concerned with the sacral character of the Israelite king as the Anointed of Yahweh, while the third stage brings the two foregoing motifs together in attempting to show how both conceptions—already in the period of the kings—move out of history into eschatology.

For the eschatological hope—in Israel the historical people in an absolute sense (Tillich), but not in Israel alone—is first of all an historical hope; it is 'eschatologized' first through the growing disappointment of history.[37]

This representation of Yahweh as *Melekh* is naturally shrouded in all sorts of mythological imagery, and is influenced by the great Near Eastern myths of the divine king. But what is unique in Israel is its experience *in history* of a divine call to recognize Yahweh as their only king. Nowhere is the myth central; it is merely the guise in which historical memory is preserved in all its dimensions. We have witnessed the important place which the Gideon utterance (Judg. 8:23) has in Buber's thought and how he finds the expression of this same faith in earlier periods. Indeed, it goes back to the Sinaitic covenant and before that event to the call of Abraham. We are left in no doubt as to the central meaning of Yahweh's role as *Melekh*. Buber traces the development of the faith through the anti-monarchical period of the 'judges' (*shophetim*), then turns, in extraordinarily well-documented discussions, to the divine kingship in the ancient Near East, the West Semitic tribal god, Yahweh as *Melekh,* the royal covenant, and the theocracy. All of these chapters in *Königtum Gottes* are of the first importance, not least of all because of the detailed and excellent notes which accompany them.

The divine *Melekh* is first of all and always the Leader. He is the leading God of Abram, he is Israel's leader from Goshen to Sinai and from Sinai to the Land of Promise, and so on throughout Israel's history. He is the God of the way, *der Wegegott* (Eichrodt); he leads Israel on its 'way' through history. Buber supports his interpretation of Yahweh as Leader with ample documentation, so that there can be little doubt of the correctness of his position. In-

---

[37] *Königtum Gottes,* p. X.

deed, one would have no difficulty in showing how this faith in a leading God moves throughout the whole of the Bible, from its earliest
strata and throughout the New Testament also. The theological importance of this understanding of the faith of Israel is very great.

A vast literature has gathered about the subject, both of Yahweh
as King and of the sacral kingship, in recent decades, but it is not always borne in mind that Buber has been a pioneer in this field.
The myth and ritual school in England; the Scandinavian school
of the divine kingship, especially represented in the work of Engnell
and his followers; and the American school of W. F. Albright have all
given strong support to many of Buber's views, though in different
ways. Sigmund Mowinckel's *He That Cometh* discusses at great length
the same theme of messianism to which Buber has devoted so much
attention. Aubrey Johnson has written a careful and restrained study
of the *Sacral Kingship.* To be sure, Buber would part company
with many of the views expressed in some of this literature; he
certainly would not accept Mowinckel's interpretations throughout,
nor would he go to the extremes of some of the members of the
Swedish school of Engnell or of the English myth and ritual school.
But all of these movements in modern scholarly research are in one
way or another dealing with matters to which Buber has devoted a
lifetime of painstaking study. Moreover, it is doubtful whether anyone
has presented with greater vividness and lucidity the reality of the
divine kingship and the sacral king than Martin Buber, and it is
certain that no one has discerned or set forth their theological implications with equal profundity.

Today scholars recognize that the ark was the throne upon which
Yahweh was seated as King, though invisibly. The celebrations of the
divine enthronement in the New Year's festival, which have become
generally known through Mowinckel's famous work in the second
volume of his *Psalmenstudien,* corroborate many of Buber's views,
although he is hesitant in giving assent to Mowinckel's admittedly
exaggerated position. G. Ernest Wright has demonstrated the presence of royal terminology in the accounts of the covenant relation,[38]
and George E. Mendenhall has rendered probable the influence of
Hittite covenant treaties between king and vassals upon their form

[38] "The Terminology of Old Testament Religion and Its Significance," *Journal
of Near Eastern Studies,* 1 (1942), 404–14; "The Faith of Israel," *Interpreter's Bible,*
1, 355–6.

402   JAMES MUILENBURG

and structure.[39] Martin Noth has called attention to the similarities between the prophetic commissions and the words of the messenger from the king in the Mari inscriptions.[40] Many passages in the Old Testament, hitherto considered late, but now recognized as early, are precipitates of the royal ideology of the court, and the Psalter bears clear testimony to the importance of the sacral king in Israelite thought.

In all these ways and, indeed, in many others, Buber's views are receiving striking confirmation. While we have not dealt in any detail with his existential interpretation of the Bible, this, too, has left a deep impression upon contemporary scholarship, not least of all in the current stress upon the actualization into the present moment (*Vergegenwärtigung*) of the *heilsgeschichtliche* events in the cultic celebrations. Even his classical treatment in *I and Thou* has influenced contemporary Biblical hermeneutics. One has only to examine the Hebrew of many psalms or of Second Isaiah to see how fruitful this category of understanding may be for the elucidation of the text. Yet it is still true that Buber's many studies on the origins and history of messianism are his most important contribution to an understanding both of the Old and New Testament. He, more than any other Jewish scholar of our time, has opened the Scriptures of the Old Covenant for the Christian community. Without an understanding and appreciation of the Old Covenant, the Scriptures of the New Covenant must remain forever closed.

[39] *Law and Covenant in Israel and the Ancient Near East* (Pittsburgh, 1955).

[40] "History and the Word of God in the Old Testament," *Bulletin of the John Rylands Library*, 32 (1950).

JAMES MUILENBURG

DEPARTMENT OF OLD TESTAMENT
UNION THEOLOGICAL SEMINARY

VIII. *On the Interpretation of the Bible*

Questions have been raised concerning my interpretation of biblical texts and teachings, the clarification of which seems to be requisite. Here, too, much has been understood otherwise than meant and I must attend to a more exact understanding.

1. Muilenburg ascribes to me the view[75] that revelation "comes in community." That is not my view at all. Even when the community as such, whether merely passive, whether also with an active movement, seems to take part in an event of revelation transmitted in historical form, even when the report includes a divine address directed to a "You" (plural), I can understand as the core of the happening discernible by me only a central human person's coming into contact with transcendence.

2. It is in some measure inexact to say, as he does[76] that I am in accord with the Protestant theologian Oscar Cullmann "that Judaism knows no midpoint of the *Heilsgeschichte*." That I have pointed long before Cullmann to "absence of caesuras" of the Jewish view of history would not be worth mentioning if what were involved therein were simply a question of individual priority; but what is involved is that the insight that for the Jew there is no fixed center of history was expressed from out of Judaism itself.

3. Muilenburg doubts[77] that I have taken sufficiently into account the different usages of words. The word *hesed* is adduced as an example, in regard to which it is said that it signifies only seldom loving kindness or grace: "covenant love" better expresses "the covenant connotation." Muilenburg, however, has not at all taken into consideration what I myself at one time have written on this subject in the essay, "On the Translation of the 'Psalms' " attached to the Psalm volume of my translation of the Bible. I quote myself:

75 Muilenburg, p. 383.

76 *Ibid.*, pp. 384f.

77 *Ibid.*, p. 386.

Hesed is a trustworthiness between the beings, *and, to be sure, essentially that of the covenant relationship* between the liege lord and his vassals, nearly always the faithfulness to the covenant of the Lord, who preserves and protects his vassals, but also that of the subjects, who devote themselves faithfully to their lord. The German word stem corresponding to this concept of reciprocity is '*hold*' (gracious, pleasing, gentle) . . . '*Holde*' means in middle high German the vassal . . . In the psalms God's 'Hasidim' are his vassals, his 'faithful followers.'

I have many times pointed to the fact that the etymology, often even the etymology within the people, of a word recurring in the Bible must be important for the translator because the repetition in the Biblical text frequently serves to allow one passage to be illuminated by another. Thus in the translation the significant transformation of words was borne in mind as much as possible.

4. Muilenburg's placing together[78] of Exodus 15:12-17 with the Song of Deborah seems to me not to withstand a more exact examination. The specific "*Leitwortstil*" (the clue of the key words) which in the Song of Deborah has taken the character of a primitive refrain is only rudimentarily still to be found in these verses.

5. Muilenberg asks why I have rendered *tehillim* by "praisings" instead of by "Psalms." Now, simply because *tehilla* signifies just praise; that is: because the redactor responsible for the title of the book evidently wanted to make clear through the choice of this word that all these songs, even the complaining one and the begging for salvation, are ultimately to be understood as songs of praise, as praisings, and thereby as the poetic expression of a great *trust*.

6. Neither in the original nor in my translation of Psalm 1 does "the Law" appear.[79] *Torah* is spoken of, the "instruction," namely the instruction of the right "way" by God. In distinction to "the Law" (*nomos*) Torah is first of all a *dynamic* concept, i.e., the verbal origin and character cleaves to the name and is repeatedly emphasized ("the Instruction that one will instruct you," Deuteronomy 17:11), and second, the tie between the divine instructor, the "*moreh*" (Isaiah 30-20), and his instruction is given in the word itself. Thus the objectification of the concept contradicts its essence.

7. My conjecture concerning Exodus 19:5 cannot be refuted through a reference to the *Leitwortstil*,[80] for a personal pronoun is in

78 Muilenburg, pp. 388f.

79 Cf. *ibid.*, p. 391.

80 *Ibid.*, pp. 396f.

728   MARTIN BUBER

general, even when it is emphatically used, not important enough to be understood as a key-word; even so little can one derive a counter-proof from "and now" since this too, indeed, was for a reworker the word bidden here. (Parenthetically: I have only spoken of a "reworking": the words "or an interpolation" stem from a misunderstanding of the translator of which I have only now become aware.) Since I hold the reworking of the original course of words to be Deuteronomic, the reference of my critic to "the Deuteronomists" does not prove anything. What is meant, by the way, by Muilenburg's comment[81] about our translation of the particle *im* in this passage being "unusual," is incomprehensible to me; the particle has not been translated differently by us here than elsewhere.

8. To refute the criticisms advanced against my interpretation of the Tetragrammaton (and against my attitude toward the "Kenite hypothesis" that is linked up with it) would require a special chapter; but I believe that I have already answered them in the essentials in my books on the subject, namely in *The Kingship of God* (*Königtum Gottes*) and in *Moses*.

9. In the question of the Decalogue the difference in opinions does not seem to me to be so great as Muilenburg[82] assumes. I do not, to be sure, hold it to be a *document* on which the conclusion of the Covenant is established, but I hold it to be the text of a proclamation whose origin is to be traced back to a revelation. I do not hold it to be an objectifiable "law," but I recognize myself in the Thou that is addressed by the commanding of this command, and I recognize my fellowmen whom I meet on the roads of my life in this same Thou.

10. Glatzer has[83] contrasted with my interpretation of the Biblical "law" my exegetical attitude: if I had followed this, he says, then I would have had to recognize and acknowledge that "*within the context* of the Old Testament the laws do appear as an absolutum." That they appear so in the context, however, is indeed incontestable; what concerns me is the question whether taken altogether they *rightly* appear so, in other words: whether, for example, the details of the sacrifice stand in the same relationship to happening revelation as the Decalogue. We do not know which "Torah"—texts Jeremiah had in mind when he says (8:8), "the lying pen of the scribes" has been

---

81 *Ibid.*, p. 396, note 30.
82 *Ibid.*, pp. 397f.
83 Glatzer, pp. 378f.

Part Five

ARCHAEOLOGY

REPORT OF THE DIRECTOR OF THE SCHOOL IN JERUSALEM

To the President and Trustees of the
  American Schools of Oriental Research:

I have the honor to submit the following report of the activities of the American School in Jerusalem for the academic year 1953-1954.

Because of the lack of a trained field archaeologist on our staff, we did not engage in any major excavations and were unable to co-operate with the British School of Archaeology in their operations at Tell es-Sultan. Yet two members of our group, Professor Boone Bowen of Emory University and Ivan Kaufmann, a student at Union Theological Seminary, participated in the 1954 campaign for the entire season, and the other members visited the excavations from time to time under the expert guidance of Miss Kathleen Kenyon. In the late spring Professor and Mrs. James A. Kelso of Pittsburgh-Xenia Theological Seminary arrived to continue the excavations at Beitin, undertaken by Professors Albright and Kelso in 1934. While the excavations at Khirbet Qumran were in progress the members of the School had ample opportunity to observe the important work going on there under the direction of Father R. de Vaux of the École Biblique and Mr. G. Lankester Harding, director of the Department of Antiquities.

4

But more important than the excavations, so far as our activities this year are concerned, was the opportunity of studying the scroll fragments from the Qumran caves. Professor Frank M. Cross, Jr. of McCormick Theological Seminary, Annual Professor for the year, served as representative of the American School on the scroll project. In the autumn the fragments from Cave IV, representing some three hundred or more manuscripts, were brought to the Palestine Museum where they were prepared for identification and subsequent classification into individual manuscripts. This painstaking process consumed many months, but by spring it was possible for Professor Cross, who was responsible for the biblical texts in the square (Aramaic) character, to engage in detailed study of several texts. The results of his work are very important for the history of the text. He also found time to undertake a number of paleographical studies.

Our annual Fellow, Mr. Oleg Grabar, now a member of the faculty of the University of Michigan, brought to completion the large assignment of putting together, describing, and analyzing the painted fragments from Khirbet el-Mefjir for the final publication of the palace, to be edited by R. W. Hamilton. His study of the chief Umayyad sites and the Umayyad remains in the museums in Jerusalem and Damascus helped him to reach conclusions concerning the life of the Umayyad rulers and their art which should reflect themselves in all subsequent treatments of the subject. James Ross, a graduate Fellow from Union Theological Seminary, engaged in a detailed study of the text of Isaiah 40-66 in the light of the Dead Sea Scrolls (DSIa). Throughout the year the library was in constant use. Fortunately we were able to secure the efficient services of Mrs. Grabar, who was not only in charge of circulation but also checked the shelves and prepared hundreds of new index cards.

The director had the opportunity to make two paleographical studies of the scrolls, one of them a manuscript of Isaiah, the other an important text of Qoheleth [both published in BULLETIN, No. 135]. Because of recent discussion of the topographical problems associated with Tell en-Naṣbeh, he reviewed *de novo* the entire range of the question of its identification. Late in the spring he made a small sounding near Khirbet el-Mefjir and uncovered conclusive evidence of Iron Age occupation in that region.

Precisely because the School was not engaged in any major archaeological operation, it was possible to take special advantage of the opportunities for seeing the land, making topographical studies, and studying as best we could the sites which had been exposed by excavations. Our major trip in the fall covered many of the most famous Near Eastern sites in Syria and Lebanon, among which the visits to Palmyra, Ras esh-Shamra, and Byblos were the most memorable. There were at least three trips to Petra. The more frequent of the shorter trips included Jericho, Khirbet Qumran, Bethel, Dothan, and Tuleilat Ghassul. Indeed there were relatively few weeks throughout the year when there was not some pilgrimage to ancient sites. Mr. Grabar made a special tour of famous Umayyad remains. A number of the members of the School spent a fortnight in Egypt; others visited museums and sites in Turkey.

Most of the members of the School found so much to occupy their time in research that there was little need or demand for scheduled lectures. Professor Cross directed Mr. Ross's work on the text of Isaiah while the director read some of the North-Semitic inscriptions, the Manual of Discipline, and other texts with a small group.

If the year proved to be a singularly happy and fruitful one for the members of the School, as I believe it was generally agreed to be, then the major reason was our good fortune in having a personnel which was devoted to the interests of scholarship and research. By and large the most profitable hours were the long discussions at tea and at dinner on many subjects of intense interest to us all, and it was a happy circumstance that we represented not only different academic backgrounds but also rather varied scholastic interests within the area of Near Eastern life and culture. This pleasant social situation was greatly fructified by the steady stream of scholars from all over the world who converged upon the School. When we arrived at the School Professor Kurt Galling, representing the German archaeological institute, was there with his party. Later Professor E. Hammershaimb of the University of Aarhus spent several months with us, and he was followed by his New Testament colleague, Johannes Munck, who spent a similar period at the School. The distinguished Cambridge prehistorian, Miss Dorothy Garrod, made her home with us for an extended period while she installed the famous Carmel man in an impressive domicile in the museum. Gerald FitzGerald, veteran of many campaigns in Palestine, also joined our ranks for a short period. During the spring Professor T. Vriezen of the University of Groningen became one of us. Among our distinguished American guests were Professor and Mrs. Jeffery, whose return to the School was greeted by all our members and our staff with great *éclat*, Dr. Florence Day of the Metropolitan Museum, Professor Charles Fritsch of Princeton Seminary, visiting lecturer, Professor Willis Fisher of the University of Southern California, Professor Siegfried H. Horn of Washington, D. C., Professor and Mrs. David Wieand of Bethany Biblical Seminary, and Professor S. A. Cartledge of Columbia Theological Seminary. The year began with a most welcome visit from Professor A. H. Detweiler, and ended with another equally welcome from Professor and Mrs. Carl Kraeling.

It is a pleasure to report that the buildings and grounds are in excellent condition. This is in no small measure due to the devoted services and efficiency of the members of our staff. Mahmud holds the grounds as his special province. The hedges are well trimmed; the flowers were in bloom throughout the year, even in the coldest weather, and in the spring they came out in great luxuriance. Imran not only served as our chauffeur but proved an expert mechanic in every area of our plant. Omar continued as the faithful and indispensable *major domo* of the School while the *Haj* kept vigilant watch throughout the hours of the night. Wadi'a kept the rooms tidy and spotless while Miryam assisted in the kitchen with characteristic loyalty. As everyone knows who has been at the School in recent years, it is these people who make the School a real home. One major change has taken place in the School's property. The fence bordering the south has at long last been removed and has been re-set three meters to the north.

I wish finally to express my gratitude to the Trustees for making it possible for me and my family to spend the year at the School and to profit from the many advantages it has to offer. My cordial thanks are also due President Kraeling and Professors Detweiler and Albright for their constant interest in our activities, for their generous encouragement, and for their wise counsel. The School is indebted again to Mrs. Kraeling for her assiduous and devoted efforts in behalf of the physical comfort and improved appearance of our plant. But above all, I wish to record my appreciation to my wife, who not only fulfilled the many duties connected with the operation of the hostel and the comfort of its guests but also was in almost complete charge of the business of the School. If there was a steady hand at the helm, it was hers.

JAMES MUILENBURG

7

A Letter From Palestine

By James Muilenburg

Although the season of the winter rains is upon us, many days are clear and cold. When the sun makes its appearance, the whole land seems transformed. The hills have a mysterious way of taking to themselves its light and heat, and the atmosphere has a crisp, vibrant quality which reminds one of early morning in New York. These are the times when the members of the School long to go on pilgrimages. But when the rains come, we stay inside pursuing our various researches and struggling meanwhile to keep warm. This year the rain descended suddenly and in fury. For more than three days it came down in torrents, and the winds blew a biting unrelenting gale. The refugees in their frail shelters and black goat hair tents did all they could to maintain themselves against the icy blasts, but the downpour was too violent, and many hundreds were housed in public buildings. Yet whenever any of us sought to commiserate with them, they would reply, "Nushkur Allah" (let us thank Allah), "for he has at long last sent his gift of rain to the thirsty land."

I was just saying that the land responds quickly to the ministrations of the sun; it answers just as quickly to the rain. In a few days the hills and valleys, which lie brooding for months in the heat and light of the sun, change their garb to every imaginable shade of green. It is a good time to go down from Jerusalem to Jericho, perhaps the most ancient city in the world now that we have reached below the neolithic levels in our excavations there and the city where the rich and privileged throughout the millenia have gone to escape the cold and to luxuriate in the sun. Herod built his winter palace there, and Hisham, the Umayyad king, constructed his palace nearby at Khirbet 'al Mafjar with an artistic lavishness and ornateness that must have outdone even Herod. Many of the remains of this famous Umayyad palace are now housed in the Palestine Museum of Antiquities, and large portions of it are being restored, to the astonishment of all who see the meticulous work of restoration in progress. One of our students, Oleg Grabar, the School Fellow this year, is preparing a special treatment on the antiquities of Khirbet 'al Mafjar, Hisham's winter residence.

Since leaving New York on the second of July we have met Union people wherever we have gone. As we were entering the House of Commons one of the students from the music school came running to us.

James Muilenburg, Davenport Professor of Hebrew and the Cognate Languages, is on leave for the entire academic year, serving as director of the American School for Oriental Research in Jerusalem.

In the American Church in Paris we met other students from the music school. In Holland we saw something of Pieter de Jong, Paul Aalders, and Tina Harsvelt. On the streets of Copenhagen a Union student introduced himself and told us of his first studies on Soren Kierkegaard. During the meetings there of the International Congress of Old Testament Scholars Paul and Betty Rice Achtemeier, who had been on an extensive bicycling tour through Scandinavia, arrived for a day's visit and joined us in the deliberations and festivities of the Congress. Here at the American School of Oriental Research Jim Ross and Ivan Kaufman are carrying on their studies. Jim is making a detailed study of the text of the Book of Isaiah in the light of the Dead Sea Scroll evidence and the relationship of the masoretic text to both the Scroll and the Septuagint. He is also reading a number of the North-Semitic inscriptions under my direction. Ivan is reading through the Book of Joshua with special reference to its topography, and has done something on the important but difficult problem of ceramics. He has a good eye, an indispensable instrument for the archaeologist, and his small but select collection of antiquities has aroused the envy of other members of the School. Gus Jeeninga, who had his first year at Union, stayed at the School for over six weeks. He not only accompanied us on our various field trips but spent much time in the library working on the geography of this holy land. Now the good news has reached us that Dr. and Mrs. Jeffery are to visit Palestine, and we are looking forward to their visit the latter part of January. Dr. Jeffery is giving a series of lectures on Islam at Amman and Jerusalem. Just last week we learned of the possibility that Mrs. Harrison Elliott and her daughter Jean might be with us for the Christmas holidays, a prospect which has filled us with delight.

The American School will do no excavating this year in the absence of a field archaeologist. But several of us are planning to stay at Tell es Sultan (Jericho) for several weeks while the "dig" of the British School of Archaeology under Miss Kathleen Kenyon is going on. It is probable that Jericho is as important an archaeological enterprise as was ever undertaken in Palestine. You may have seen reports of it in one of the spring issues of *Life* or in the current issue of the *National Geographic*. We have not yet, alas, found any traces of the Jericho of the time of Joshua, despite the extensive trenches that have been sunk into the mound. My own theory is that it is located on an immediately neighboring mound, but Albright and De Vaux think the remains of the period (Late Bronze) may have disappeared through some natural disturbance. Father de Vaux and Lankester Harding, the Director of the Jordan Department of Antiquities, are planning their final campaign at Khirbet Qumran, in the immediate vicinity of which the famous scrolls were discovered in 1947 and the hundreds of priceless scroll fragments since then.

23

But since we are doing little actual digging, we are making the most of field trips both throughout Jordan, Palestine and the Near East. I have written a good deal about these trips in the monthly newsletters of the School and in personal letters to President Van Dusen and Dr. Terrien, so I will try not to repeat myself too much here. We have visited a number of the great caravan cities of the Roman period including Palmyra, Dura Europos, Jerash, Baalbek, and Petra. Although most of us had been well schooled in Roman history and culture, not one of us had the remotest notion of the profound influence of Rome upon the whole of the Near East. Not only are its roads everywhere in evidence but its ancient temples, baths, palaces, walls, forums, tombs, and other monuments suddenly break upon one's vision as he travels the vast expanses of desert waste. If you want to receive an impression of the grandeur of these old cities and the thrilling story of their past, read Rostovtseff's beautifully written *Caravan Cities.*

As all those of you who have studied Old Testament in recent years would expect, we made a special point of visiting Mari (Tell Hariri) and Ugarit (Ras esh-Shamra). Mari flourished during the time of Abraham. It is not far from Harran whence the patriarch migrated, and we now know that the cultural and linguistic characteristics of the people of Mari closely approximate the representations of the Book of Genesis. But unhappily Andrè Parrot and Dossin had not yet begun their ninth campaign, so we had to make the best of things. We visited the famous treasury where more than 20,000 inscriptions were unearthed just a few years ago, studied the elaborate drainage system and the hot and cold water baths, but our attempts to find the massive red ziqqurat ended in futility. The scores of rooms in Zimri Lim's famous palace can be easily traced, though their present state can never give a notion of what they looked like almost four thousand years ago.

Ras esh-Shamra was the culmination of our trip through Syria and Lebanon. Professor Claude Schaeffer was carrying on his excavation there. The view one receives as he approaches the ancient mound is awe-inspiring. There in the distance lies Mont Casios, where Baal Zaphon, the god Baal Hadad, dwelt. The mountain was luminous in the light of an Oriental morning. But at the crest clouds hovered as if to shroud the sacred dwelling of the gods. As we drew near the tell the clouds grew dark, and Baal Hadad emerged in fury, hurling his lightning and roaring his thunder and pouring down his rain in torrents. But Professor Schaeffer was not deterred and generously showed us the recent excavations, including the vast palace of the Ugaritic kings. Ras esh-Shamra is a chapter by itself, but I can divulge a piece of news of some importance for the history of the Near East. Only recently a series of Hittite tablets have been discovered, all of them beautifully incised and as clear as if they had just issued from the hand of the scribe. We can now hope to learn something more about this important center in one

24

of the most significant periods of the past, the great international age when peoples were everywhere on the move and Israel stepped on the stage of world history.

I had hoped to say a good deal about our interests in ceramics. It is a vast field, and a peculiarly tricky one, but one for which Jerusalem now offers exceptional opportunities of study and research. This, too, I shall have to reserve for another time. But I do want to say something about what is after all our major investigation this year. I refer, of course, to the scroll fragments. These are now deposited by hundreds in the Palestine Museum of Antiquities. The Qumran materials have been assigned to Dr. Frank Cross of McCormick, Pere Milik of the Dominican School, and John Allegro, one of G. R. Driver's and H. H. Rowley's students. But I have been granted the privilege of doing my own special work on some selected pieces. I have now spent a month on two small fragments from Isaiah trying to master their paleographic features and studying the text. It has been enormously rewarding and has opened up a field of interest in which Old Testament scholars will all have to labor in the next fifty years. To handle these scroll fragments — more than two thousand years old, small leather pieces encrusted with calcium and very dim, — then to see them gradually emerge into intelligibility as they are carefully cleaned, and finally to identify the particular fragment, whether biblical or extra-biblical, this is enough to excite the most stolid of spirits and the most unromantic soul. It requires a vast amount of time, but whoever has any concern for the biblical text and realizes that these little pieces represent a text a thousand years earlier than our earliest Hebrew manuscripts will sense something of the fateful significance of what we are doing. The time has come when all theological institutions of standing will have courses in paleography, and it is my hope that Union will be among the first to respond to the significance of what is now going on in Palestine where the scrolls keep coming month by month from the members of the Ta'amireh bedu inhabiting the northwest shores of the Dead Sea. It is no secret that literally hundreds of fragments are still in their hands. I have had nothing to say about the Wadi Muraba'at finds, although we have already discovered two original letters here from Simon ben Kocheba, the bar Cochbar of the Second Revolt, a number of other secular documents, and many early biblical texts corresponding word for word with the masoretic tradition.

I realize that I have but touched upon several aspects of our life here in Jerusalem, and I certainly have told extremely little about what is going on in our investigation of the scrolls. But that story will gradually be unfolded in the next few decades. If any of you have gathered from what I have written that it has been an exciting year far beyond all our expectations, I must confess that something like that is the literal truth.

25

Bulletin of the American Schools of Oriental Research

A HYKSOS SCARAB JAR HANDLE FROM BETHEL

JAMES MUILENBURG

Scarab-impressed jar handles are by no means unique, and the one shown in the accompanying photograph can hardly be classified as an *objet d'art*. But it has several features which are quite singular and perhaps warrant this brief note.

Scarab impressed on jar handle from Bethel.

The jar handle was found at Beitin by Imran Abdo, the School's driver, in the huge pile of sherds at the northwest corner of the field of Abdul Mahid Mohammed, the site of the camp of the 1934 excavations and the place where the present excavations are going on under Professor James L. Kelso. The impression measures 2.6 by 1.6 cm. The pattern is a model of symmetry. Two *nefers* appear on each side of the horizontal dividing lines, the crosses of the *nefers* opposite each other. Between the *nefers* is another symbol, which is hard to make out. Conceivably it is a crudely formed *re'*, but more likely a *neb*, though neither is certain. What distinguishes this particular stamp from others is the " ladder " which divides the symbols and accentuates the symmetry of the whole. The rungs stand out very clearly, and at the upper and lower ends forks emerge from each side. Examination of the standard works of Newberry, Petrie, and Alan Rowe produced no good parallel.[1] "Ladder" legs are well known from the thirteenth to the sixteenth dynasties and even in the eighteenth,[2] and the cross patterns with bars between the intersecting horizontal and vertical lines are familiar enough, but nowhere has the writer been able to find anything which approximates this "ladder" motif at Beitin. There can be no doubt as to the date of the scarab impression. Its style conforms closely to that of the late Hyksos period.[3] The design as a whole is a characteristic conventionalization of Egyptian signs, and has no particular meaning other than the word *nefer*, the symbol of excellence, fineness, or beauty. The owner, prompted by a belief in the efficacy of similars, may have felt that the scarab-impression would bring him good luck or at least ward off ill. In any event, to find a "ladder" at Bethel is unusual!

---

[1] The cross patterns in Flinders Petrie, *Hyksos and Israelite Cities* (London, 1906), Plate IX, Nos. 140, 188, 189, all Yehudiyeh scarabs, may be compared; see also his *Buttons and Design Scarabs* (London, 1925), Plate IX, Nos. 372, 374, and the Yehudiyeh scarabs 1527, 1528. But these all conform much more closely to the ribbed patterns. Among the inscribed jar handles, the double lines are common, but the only ones in the Palestine Museum of Antiquities which seem to have anything suggesting "rungs" are the Shebna seal from Tell en-Nasbeh, the Bakyah seal from Ain Shems, and possibly the Shaban seal from Tell ed Duweir. But even in these the "ladder" motif is by no means clear.

[2] Petrie, *Buttons and Design Scarabs*, p. 18.

[3] Mr. Lankester Harding, Père de Vaux, Père Couroyer, and Père Vincent all reached the same conclusion independently upon examination of the impression.

Bulletin of the American Schools of Oriental Research

A QOHELETH SCROLL FROM QUMRAN

James Muilenburg

While in some ways the Book of Qoheleth stands alone in the Old Testament, there is perhaps none which is so closely related in literary form and content to the literatures of other peoples, both ancient and modern. Commentators have had little difficulty in citing parallels from the literary works of the peoples of the ancient Near East.[1] Striking affinities have been found in Egyptian,[2] Accadian,[3] Ugaritic,[4] Persian,[5] Aramaic,[6] and, above all, Greek[7] literary remains. The thought of the book, too, has been interpreted in a variety of ways.[8] Its Hebraic character has been both challenged and supported by different writers.[9] Its literary character baffled the older generation of scholars, and the book was consequently subjected to a radical rearrangement.[10] A Solomonic origin has been given up by all modern scholars, and it has subsequently

---

[1] Note the relatively large number of parallels given in Pritchard, *Ancient Near Eastern Texts*, pp. 506-7. These could easily be multiplied many fold.

[2] See the commentaries of H. W. Hertzberg, *Der Prediger (Qohelet) übersetzt und crklärt*, Leipzig, 1932; Kurt Galling, *Prediger Salomo (Handbuch zum Alten Testament* series), Tübingen, 1940; and P. Humbert, *Récherches sur les sources égyptiennes de la littérature sapientiale d'Israel*, Neuchatel, 1921.

[3] G. A. Barton, *A Critical and Exegetical Commentary on the Book of Ecclesiastes*, ICC series, New York, 1908.

[4] Such affinities as have been pointed out thus far are chiefly linguistic, as in the studies of Albright, Dahood, and others, but there are relationships in thought and style with Qoheleth in *Aqhat* and perhaps in the other epics also.

[5] The Rubaiyat of Oman Khayyam is most frequently mentioned.

[6] Notably in "The Words of Aḥiqar" to which H. L. Ginsberg has called attention more than once, e. g. in *Studies in Koheleth* and in his translation of Aḥiqar in Pritchard's ANET.

[7] Barton, Hertzberg, Galling, Albright (*From the Stone Age to Christianity*, pp. 270-71), H. Ranston (*Ecclesiastes and Early Greek Wisdom Literature*), as well as many older commentators like Margoliouth, Plumptre, and P. Menzel.

[8] A fair sampling would include the discussions of W. A. Irwin, D. B. Macdonald, (*The Hebrew Literary Genius* and *The Hebrew Philosophical Genius*), Robert Gordis, H. L. Ginsberg, Hertzberg, Galling, Gottfried Kuhn (*Erklärung des Buches Koheleth*), and Paul Humbert.

[9] Foreign influences certainly cannot be denied, but ultimately Qoheleth must be read as a product of the Hebrew mind in the Greek period. The sage's reflections gain force and poignancy in relation to the characteristic affirmations of classical Hebrew thought. Note his attitude toward time, which is certainly not Hebraic, but is nevertheless occupied with a major Hebraic concern.

[10] As in Paul Haupt's *Polychrome Bible* edition of the book.

been dated as early as the fourth century B. C. and as late as the time of Herod.

Linguistically, the book is unique.[11] There is no question that its language has many striking peculiarities; these have been explained by some to be late Hebrew,[12] for which the language of the Mishna is said to offer more than adequate support.[13] The Aramaic cast of the language has long been recognized,[14] but only within recent years has its Aramaic provenance been claimed and supported in any detail.[15] Recently, Mitchell J. Dahood, in two articles of the first importance, has written on "Canaanite-Phoenician Influence in Qoheleth," defending the thesis that the Book of Ecclesiastes was originally composed by an author who wrote in Hebrew but was influenced by Phoenician spelling, grammar, and vocabulary, and who shows heavy Canaanite-Phoenician literary influence.[16]

It is at this point that the scroll fragments of Qoheleth, recently discovered in Cave IV near Khirbet Qumran, enter the scene to make their contribution to current discussion. They are few in number and the extent of the text is not very great, but in many ways they cast welcome light on script, orthography, date, literary arrangement, language, and text, of which account will have to be taken in all future studies.

Of the four fragments belonging to our group, two are of considerable size, two diminutive. The largest measures 174 mm. at the top margin by 58 mm. (maximum height). The text covers one main column and portions of two others at each side. The first column contains a few words from 5: 13-17, the second substantial portions of 6: 3-8, the third five words from 7: 7-9. The second piece is smaller in size, measuring 98 mm. by ± 4 cm. Since it contains the bottom margin of the main column of the previous fragment, it is possible to estimate the number of lines in each column and to determine the approximate size of the scroll. The complete line is ± 11 cm. in length, the average number of letter-spaces 35. Each column contains about twenty lines. The width of the top margin is 15 mm., of the lower, 10 mm. From top to bottom the scroll would measure 15 cm. Of the two miniature pieces, one (4 cm. by 3 cm.) belongs immediately before the second of the fragments de-

---

[11] This has been almost universally recognized since the time of Grotius. For recent statements, cf. Frank Zimmermann, "The Aramaic Provenance of Koheleth," JQR (1946-47): "The Book of Qoheleth is quite peculiar linguistically" (p. 17); C. C. Torrey, "The Original Language of Qoheleth," JQR 39 (1948-49), where the uniqueness of the language is explained by the fact that the Aramaic idioms do not seem to have been assimilated (p. 153); Mitchell J. Dahood, "Canaanite-Phoenician Influence in Qoheleth," *Biblica* 1933 (1952): "Linguistically, the Book of Ecclesiastes, Hebrew Qoheleth, has always been an enigma" (p. 31); F. C. Burkitt, "Is Ecclesiastes a Translation?" JTS 23 (1922), p. 22.

[12] Margoliouth in *Jewish Encyclopedia* V, p. 33; Robert Gordis, JQR 37 (1946-47), p. 83.

[13] Effectively answered by Margoliouth, *idem*, where he points out the linguistic affinities of Qoh. with the Phoenician inscriptions (e. g. Eshmunazar, Tabnith).

[14] Certainly as early as the time of Grotius, who listed a hundred words and phrases as Aramaisms.

[15] Frank Zimmermann, C. C. Torrey, H. L. Ginsberg.

[16] *Biblica* 33 (1952), pp. 30-52, 191-221.

scribed above (7: 1-2), the other (22 mm. by 20 mm.) to the bottom
of the third column of the first piece (7: 19-20).

The text is inscribed on bright tan leather in an excellent state of
preservation. The leather is soft, pliable, and smooth. It shows no

signs of cracking or scaling; what may appear to be cracks in the accompanying photograph are in actuality only folds. The black of the ink stands out clearly, and the obscurities, while important in their way, are relatively few.

The writing is a beautiful specimen of Essene scribal art. The letters are large and spacious, superbly wrought both in their prevailing uniformity and in the artistic flourishes of which the scribe appears to be especially fond. The writing is never crowded or crabbed; each letter stands out sharply and clearly. Ligatures appear, though not in great number. An impression of the size of the letters may be gained by the following measurements: the diagonal of the *aleph* 4 mm., the crest of the *daleth* 2.5 mm., of the *he* 4 mm., of the *heth* 3 mm., the distance between the tips of the *'ayin* 2 mm., of the *shin* 5 mm. While the crest of the *qoph* measures 4 mm., the downward shaft seldom exceeds 2 mm. The second of the larger pieces contains a fair-sized erasure in the third line from the bottom, and the first line of the third column of the first piece possibly contains another.

No attempt is made here to enter into any detail concerning the paleographical features of the Qoh. fragments. It became apparent almost at once that the affinities of the script lie with DSIa and the Manual of Discipline. There are exceptions, to be sure, as in the case of final *pe*, which is identical with that of the Habakkuk commentary. Allowing for the special characteristics of the scribe's handwriting, not a few letters are similar to both DSIa and the Manual. Noteworthy examples are *beth*, *waw*, *resh*, and *shin*. On the other hand, a number of the letters are similar to those in the Edfu papyri, dating from the latter part of the third century B. C.[17] The left leg of the *aleph* of both Qoh. and Edfu is short and projects outward to the left; the diagonal spine is correspondingly long. The *gimel* is much alike in both, the arm to the left emerging high from the main line. The projection to the right of the left fork of the *he* is very much the same. The bending of certain medial consonants is particularly noticeable, as, for example, in *kaph*, *mem*, *nun*, and *pe*.[18] Some specimens of final *nun* are almost identical, the tail forming an elaborate curve. Most striking of all, however, are *qoph* and *'ayin*. The former has an exceptionally short vertical line, while the tail of the *'ayin* is even more diminutive and is written immediately below the head.

The upshot of our comparison with 4Q, DSIa and the Manual, on the one hand, and the Edfu papyri, on the other, makes it clear that 4Q lies between the former and the latter. From a paleographic standpoint, therefore, one must date our fragments about the middle of the second century B C. This gives the *coup de grâce* to earlier views of the

[17] The paleographical observations are based upon the ostraca published by Lidzbarski in *Ephemeris für semitische Epigraphik* II (1908), pp. 246-7; III, Tables I-III between p. 36 and p. 37. For detailed bibliographical references, see Albright JBL (1937), pp. 154-55, notes 23-26. On the date of the Edfu materials there is now quite general agreement.
[18] Albright, *idem*, p. 154.

date of composition, such as those of Graetz,[19] Renan,[20] Leimdörfer,[21] König,[22] and others, and makes unlikely a dating in the second century. A temporal locus some time in the third or late fourth century seems most probable.[23] But if this is correct, then we are in possession of a scroll which comes within some two centuries at most of the time of composition. It is interesting to speculate whether Qoh. had already achieved an approach to canonical status in the Essene community. That the text is inscribed on leather is in itself not decisive, but Ben Sira's borrowings may suggest something concerning its status in his time.[24]

In view of the profuse employment of *matres lectionis* in several of the Qumran scrolls, notably DSIa [25] and the preservation of Phoenician spelling,[26] which was completely without them, the witness of our scroll is not without importance. We do not, of course, have the *editio princeps* of Qoh. here, but it is only a relatively short time removed from the time of its original composition and centuries older than MT. The orthographical situation can be stated briefly: 4Q uses the *scriptio plena* less frequently than DSIa, to which it is paleographically kin, but more often than MT. The orthographical variants of 4Q with MT are as follows:

1. 5:14 *ky'*. This is the only use of what Burrows calls the metathetic *aleph* with this word.[27] Elsewhere (6:4, 7:6) the shorter form is used. See further under our discussion of the text below.

2. 5:17 *bkwl*   MT *bkl*.

3. 6:4 *bh*   MT *b'*. Burrows cites several examples of similar usage. "These suggest rather writing from dictation or memory by a scribe who used *he* or *aleph* indifferently as a

---

[19] From the time of Herod.

[20] Around 100 B.C. Compare Haupt's view that the author lived between ca. 175 B.C. and the first decade of the reign of Alexander Jannaeus (104-78 B.C.).

[21] Leimdörfer ascribed the work to Simon ben Shetach.

[22] 125-100 B.C.

[23] So Robert Gordis. Ginsberg accepts a date in the third century for his Aramaic original and a Maccabean dating for the translation into Hebrew, a view which 4Q now makes extremely unlikely or impossible. Cf. R. H. Pfeiffer, *Introduction to the Old Testament*, p. 731, who thinks that the period 170-160 B.C. is "most in harmony with the characteristics of thought and language."

[24] H. W. Hertzberg (*Der Prediger (Qohelet) übersetzt und erklärt*, Leipzig, 1932, pp. 23-25) lists a number of verbal agreements between Ben Sirach and Qoh. and reaches the conclusion that the former knew and employed the latter. Compare also his observation, "Auch die Erwägung, dass Qoh schliesslich trotz seiner auffallenden Haltung ein kanonisches Buch geworden ist, macht es fast unmöglich, noch weiter hinunterzugehen (Ed. Meyer, *Ursprung und Anfänge des Christentums*, II, 1921, S. 39). Denn der wesentlich einwandfreie JSir ist nicht mehr kanonisch geworden, von Makk und Sap ganz zu schweigen." On the whole problem of canonicity, see Barton, pp. 2-7.

[25] Millar Burrows, BASOR 111, pp. 16-24 and 113, pp. 24-32; also JBL 58 (1949), pp. 195-211, especially p. 196: "The most conspicuous but least surprising feature of the orthography is the extravagant use of the *scriptio plena*."

[26] Dahood, *ibid.*, 35-43.

[27] JBL 58 (1949), pp. 201-2.

vowel-letter." So also in 4Q. In 5:14 the word appears with
an *aleph* (*bsb'*).[28]

4. 6:4 *wbḥwšk*　　MT (bis) MT *wbḥšk*
5. 6:5 *lw'*　　　　MT *l'*
　　wlw'　　　　MT *wl'*
　　nwḥt　　　　MT *nḥt*. Delitzsch and others after him
have interpreted the meaning of this much discussed word
in the light of Mishnaic and Talmudic usage, "better than";
Hertzberg (p. 151) accepts it as a possibility, and Gordis
(*Koheleth—the Man and his World*, p. 249) supports the
rendering without qualification: "There is greater satisfaction for this one (the still-born) than for the other." So also
Ludwig Levy, *Das Buch Qoheleth* (Leipzig, 1912, p. 101):
ihr ist wohler als jenem. To be compared are the Peshitta,
the Targum, Symmachus, διαφοράς, and Vulg. *distantiam boni
et mali*. But in the light of usage elsewhere, both in the Bible
and in the inscriptions, the meaning "rest" is more probable. In the Bible (e. g. Qoh. 4:6; 6:5; 4:17) it appears in
seven texts (Dahood, p. 46), and the same number of times
in the Phoenician inscriptions (Dahood, *idem*). Perhaps the
most famous among the latter is the celebrated phrase in the
Aḥiram inscription: *wnḥt tbrḥ 'l gbl*. See the discussions
of Lidzbarski,[29] Albright,[30] and Dahood.[31]

6. 6:6 *lw'*. See discussion under text.
　　hlw'　　　MT *hl'*
　　hkwl　　　MT *hkl*
7. 6:7 *kwl*　　MT *kl*
　　lw'　　　MT *l'*
8. 6:8 *kmh*　　MT *ky mh*. It seems likely that here we have
a preservation of Phoenician spelling in the omission of the
mater lectionis, especially significant since the scribe usually
employs the fuller form elsewhere (*ky* or *ky'*). Cf. Dahood, p.
46 on *kqwl* (7:6).

[28] Millar Burrows, *ibid.*, p. 203; also Herbert H. Powell, *The Supposed Hebraisms
in the Grammar of the Biblical Aramaic*, Berkeley, 1907, p. 9 ff.; Frank Zimmermann, "The Aramaic Provenance of Qohelet," JQR 36 (1945-46), p. 46 and note 4;
Edward P. Arbez, CBQ 12 (1950), pp. 176-79.

[29] OLZ XXX (1927), pp. 455-56: "Die Bedeutung von *nḥt* im Phönizischen ist
durch mehrere Beispiele gesichert, *brḥ* hat im Hebräischen gewöhnlich den Sinn
"fortlaufen, fliehen . . . Daher liegt es am nächsten, auch in der Wendung *wnḥt
tbrḥ* diesen Sinn anzunehmen."

[30] JAOS 67 (1947), p. 156, nt. 26: Albright's comment here is especially apposite
for our passage: "The word *nḥt* (i. e. nôḥat < nauḥatu), "peace," corresponds to
Heb. *menûḥah*, which has just this meaning, e. g., I Kings 8: 56); it occurs as *nḥt*
also in Ugaritic (V AB, D: 47 — Keret II, vi: 24) where *l-nḥt l-kḥt drkt* should be
rendered "on the peaceful throne of authority," resolving the characteristic
hendiadys."

[31] Dahood, *ibid.*, pp. 46-47: "From the root *nwḥ* one would expect some such
formation as *nûḥah* or *nôḥah*, as is illustrated by the noun *šûḥah* from the root
šwḥ. Morphologically, *nḥt* is a Phoenicianism." Dahood also calls attention to the
appearance of the word *nḥt* three times in the Azitawadd inscription.

9. 7:5 *lšmw'*   MT *lšm'*
     g'rwt   MT *g'rt*
10. 7:6 *šhwq*   MT *šhq*
11. 7:8 *mršytw*   MT *mr'šytw*. Both DSIa and the Habakkuk
commentary contain many instances of the omission of the
aleph. For the former see 40:11 *tlym* for MT *tl'ym*; 40:15
mznym for MT *m'znym*; 65:1 *nmṣyty* for MT *nmṣ'ty*; 65:9
whwṣyty for MT *whwṣ'ti*. Of the many examples in the latter
cf. col. v, l. 14 *wysphw* for *MT wy'sphw*.[32] Similarly the
Manual of Discipline.

The text of 4Q witnesses to a number of variants. But besides these
there are several phenomena which deserve some attention. Let us consider these first of all. In 6:4 the scribe has allowed his eye to skip from
the first *wbhwšk* to the second, but after writing *šmw* he noticed his
blunder and inserted the omitted words above the line to the left, including the *šmw*, which he erased at the beginning of the second line.

The second passage where some question might be raised appears at
the very end of the second large fragment, the last word of 7:6. The
familiar clause of the author of Qoh. *kgm zh hbl* has been called into
question by a number of scholars and deleted by several as out of place;[33]
4Q certainly contains the words, but there is substantial space before the
last word of the last line as the number of letter spaces for each line
clearly shows, about ten spaces, one might estimate. Perhaps the safest
assumption is that there was an erasure here; it is not likely that the
text diverged in any way from MT.

It will be observed in the accompanying photograph that an open
space indicating a paragraph appears at the close of the foregoing passage (7:6). The next line, the first of the third column, would normally
contain about 35 letter spaces. But the first word of the second line of
this column, *hkm*, is only 15 letter spaces from the last word of 7:6 in
MT. Now 7:7 has always been a crux, and the majority of comentators
have sought to remedy what they believe to be a textual disturbance
either by emendation or by inserting Prov. 16:8, *ṭwb m'ṭ bṣdqh mrb*
tbw'wt bl' mšpṭ, after Delitzsch.[34] This would suit the demands of space
admirably, and the sequence of thought would be improved. It is possible
that some such line appeared here (note e. g. the *mem* in precisely the
correct position). Unfortunately the reading here is extremely obscure.
For a time the writer thought he could discern a *ṭeth* impressed in the
leather, but this is by no means certain. An alternative would be to
accept a substantial erasure of over 15 letter-spaces, which would be followed by the first three words of 7:7 in MT. But one thing can be
claimed as certain: the letters in the first line (7:7) do not correspond

---

[32] O. H. Lehmann, PEQ (1951), pp. 49-50, sees the loss of the phonetic value of
the *aleph* as supporting a late date for the Qumran scrolls because of Rabbinic
parallels. See Burrows' discussion, *ibid.*, p. 202; also Arbez, *ibid.*, p. 176, 179.
[33] So D. C. Siegfried (*Prediger und Hoheslied*), McNiele (*Introduction to Ecclesiastes*), Haupt, Barton, Galling, and others.
[34] Delitzsch, McNiele, Galling; others like Siegfried, Haupt, and Barton regard
the vs. as a gloss. See also F. Horst in Kittel, BH [3-7] for a somewhat similar solution.

to MT at all. They may be a scribal blunder and were therefore erased, but since the text is notoriously difficult one must consider other possibilities.

The textual variants between 4Q and MT are as follows:

1. 5:14 *ky'*   MT *k'šr*
2. 5:15 *gm* (cf. 7:6). So Jacob ben Chayyim. MT *wgm*
3. 6:3 *hnpl mmnw*   MT *mmnw hnpl*
4. 6:4 *hlk*   MT *ylk*
5. 6:6 *w'm lw'*   MT *w'lw*. Twelve MSS of Ken.-deRossi read *w'ylw*. MT *'lw* is usually taken as an Aramaic loanword.[35] It is probable that we have the word represented in the Aḥiram inscription, however, as Dussaud and others have suggested.[36] Our text seems to support Vincent's view that the word is a combination of *'m lw'*, or it may simply be the Hebrew equivalent for the Aramaic or Phoenician word. The text of Ezek. 3:6b is admittedly difficult, but Ewald's proposed reading many years ago of *'m l'* as the equivalent of *'lw* finds some support here. In any event the meaning is certainly conditional.
6. 7:2 *š]mḥh*. Cf. vs. 4, Esth. 7:4 and Kenn. 107. MT *mśth*
7. 7:4 *byt*   MT *bbyt*. The omission of the *beth* before the construct state of *byt* can be paralleled by other instances in the Old Testament as also in Ugaritic.[37]
8. 7:6 *gm*. So Jacob ben Chayyim.   MT *wgm*
9. 7:7 *wy'wh*   MT *wy'bd*. The leather is torn, but the *'ayin* is clear on the leather, and the other letters can be made out without difficulty. Compare Prov. 12:8; Job 33:27; Jer. 3:21, Manual of Discipline I. 25.
10. 7:19 *t'zr*. So 14 MSS of Kenn. and LXX.   MT *t'z*.

We may summarize our findings briefly as follows:

1. The scroll is a superb exemplar of Hebrew writing, a calligraphic work of high order. It is one of the most beautifully written of all the scrolls which have yet appeared.

2. Paleographically the scroll can be dated about the middle of the second century B. C. both by its relationship to DSIa and the Manual of Discipline, which represent a later development, and by its affinity with the Egyptian papyri and ostraca of the third century.

3. It goes without saying that the *Hebrew* Book of Qoh. must now be dated before c. 150 B. C., and how much earlier we cannot yet say on the basis of the evidence afforded by the fragments. In any event we must reckon with the possibility that Qoh. had attained canonical status, or something approaching it, in the Essene community by the middle of the second century B. C.

[35] Barton, p. 135; Brockelmann, *Grundriss der vergl. Grammatik der semitischen Sprachen* II, p. 644; H. L. Ginsberg, *Studies in Koheleth, ad loc.*
[36] See Albright's discussion in JPOS VI (1926), pp. 80-81.
[37] C. H. Gordon, *Ugaritic Handbook* I (Rome, 1947), p. 83.

4. The orthography mediates between the extremes of DSIa and MT. Such a statement is not designed as a chronological datum, however, for the presence or absence of the *matres lectionis* does not follow a unilinear development.

5. The scroll gives no support whatsoever for the numerous shifts in order which have been proposed, unless, of course, we assume that the shifts took place before c. 150.

6. The transition between 7:6 and 7:7 is obscure, but such evidence as the text provides, lends some force to the view that Qoh. may have had another text before him.

7. The text contains a number of interesting variants. Each of these must be considered by itself, but several are strong enough to suggest that they preserve the original reading.

8. Does the scroll cast any light on the problem of the language of Qoheleth? In at least one instance (*kmh*) the view of Dahood concerning the Phoenician affinities of the book is confirmed. On the other hand, the evidence does not strengthen the view of the proponents of an Aramaic original, but seems rather to support a Hebrew *Vorlage*. The only matter on which it is possible to reach a degree of assurance is that by about the middle of the second century B. C. a Hebrew Qoheleth was current among the inhabitants of the community at Khirbet Qumran.

Bulletin of the American Schools of Oriental Research

FRAGMENTS OF ANOTHER QUMRAN ISAIAH SCROLL

JAMES MUILENBURG

We are now beginning to get a general impression of the scribal activity of the community inhabiting Khirbet Qumran on the northwest shore of the Dead Sea. The size of the scriptorium (40 x 13 ft.) with its benches and desks speaks for itself, and suggests that the transcription of sacred and other writings constituted no small part of the religious activity of the group. More than that, we are in a position to study and evaluate the quality and diversity of the handwriting during the period of the community's *floruit*. But certainly not the least interesting of the features which mark the inscriptional material from Qumran is the range and extent of the library. Among the scriptural writings, the prophets hold a prominent place, above all the prophecies of Isaiah. Of these we possess not only the two major manuscripts from Cave 1, the St. Mark's Isaiah (1QIs^a) and the Hebrew University Isaiah manuscript (1QIs^b), but also many fragments representing between eight and ten separate scripts or scrolls and at least two commentaries, one written on papyrus, the other on leather. So far only Deuteronomy and Psalms rival Isaiah in the number of scrolls represented.

The examination of the present scroll fragments was undertaken chiefly as a paleographical exercise. In themselves they do not have the interest of many other pieces, but they offer an exceptional opportunity for paleographic study, since the affinities with other scrolls are marked and reveal a development beyond that of DSIa and the Manual of Discipline.

At the same time, if we possessed only these fragments and no others
from the Dead Sea caves, they would have exceptional interest for the
biblical scholar because of their antiquity and their relationship to the
Masoretic text.

The fragments were found in Cave 4, topographically the most impressive of all the Qumran caves, by members of the Ta'amireh tribe

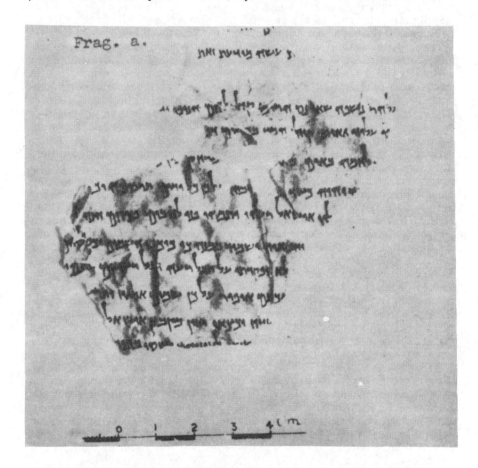

inhabiting the region along the northwest shore of the Dead Sea. Two
of them were found to fit perfectly into each other so that the upper
half of the letters of the one was met point for point by the lower half
of the letters of the other. Together they constitute the smaller of the
scroll fragments (Frag. a). It is badly torn on all sides and has suffered considerable mutilation, as is apparent both from the cracks in
the leather and from a hole measuring 2 x 1.5 cm. Its maximum dimensions are 83 mm. x 74 mm. The text is drawn from Isa. 12:5-13:16. The

second piece (Frag. b) fortunately preserves the left-hand margin, and two or three lines (ll. 14-16) extend almost to the limit at the right. Thus it is possible to determine the width of the column. The lines vary from 59 to 70 letter spaces (including spaces between words). Like Frag. a it is badly torn except at the left-hand margin and presents an extremely ragged and broken appearance. It contains a number of small perforations and a large hole measuring 58 mm. x 25 mm. The maximum dimensions of the piece are 123 mm. (the width of the column) x 121 mm. The words are drawn from Isa. 22:13d-23:6a.

The biblical text is on the whole carefully and legibly transcribed. Signs of uncertainty or confusion are rare. In Frag. a (l. 3) the scribe has written a *lamedh* over a *ḥeth*, but since he wrote the original letter with a somewhat heavy hand, it is more prominent than the *lamedh*. In Frag. b (l. 15) the *'ayin* is badly smudged. In l. 12 the final letter of M. T. *ytd* is clearly represented, but is difficult to make out. It does not look like a *daleth*. In the next to the last line of the same fragment there is a curious crowding of letters so that the words *lmw dmw*, although they are the end of one sentence and the beginning of another, appear as one. The writing is small. The average height of the letters is not over 2 mm. The somewhat elaborate terminal letters are by contrast all the more conspicuous. Final *nun* is 6 mm. long, final *kaph*, *mem*, and *pe* 5, final *qoph* 4. The crest of the *kaph* measures about 1 mm. and that of the *aleph*, *he*, and *shin* about 2 mm. Yet, despite the diminutive size of the letters, the scribe employs a skilled and practiced hand. He writes with ease, somewhat rapidly, and in a somewhat cursive style. He has a persistent tendency throughout to slant his letters to the right, a characteristic to be taken into account when weighing paleographic evidence. While the letters are small and the writing flowing and free, it is evident that either the point of the scribe's pen was blunt or, more likely, that he wrote with a firm hand. The result is that the inking not infrequently produces heavy. This is particularly apparent in the top bar of the *he* and *ḥeth*, the spine of the *aleph*, the crest of the *lamedh*, and the foot of the *qoph*.

With but one absolutely clear exception the orthography of 4Q corresponds to that of M. T. In Frag. b, l. 10 (Isa. 22:22) the *plena* reading *swgr* appears instead of the M. T. *defectiva*. It is probable that the *plena* also appears in l. 14 for the verb *yšbw*, since the tips of the *yodh* and the *waw* can be traced on the leather. In another instance the scribe originally gave the *defectiva* for the participle *yšb* (l. 8), but later corrected it by inserting the *waw* above the line, the *plena* of M. T. (Isa. 22:21).

After a detailed study of the script and an examination of the numerous obscurities on the leather, the following documents were subjected to scrutiny in order to determine their paleographic and temporal affinities with the fragments: DSIa, DSIb, the Manual of Discipline, the Habakkuk commentary, the Hodayoth (*aleph* and *beth*), the War of the Sons of Light and the Sons of Darkness, the Nash Papyrus, and the ossuaries. The general picture which emerged from our study was clear. With few exceptions 4Q belongs with Habakkuk and War, possibly a little later, but before the ossuaries, though not long before. A general estimate of the date would be the latter half of the first century B. C.

The text of 4Q conforms closely to that of M. T. Divergences are few

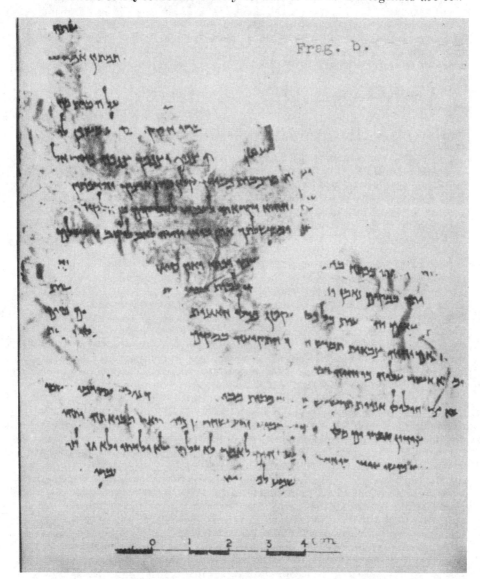

as we have already noted in connection with the discussion of orthography. In this respect it contrasts with DSIa, which is very much more *plene*. Perhaps the most interesting textual feature appears at the beginning of the first fragment. A space designating the end of a paragraph appears between Isa. 12:5 and 13:2, about 85 letter spaces, more than two verses of biblical text. Now it is obvious that there is insufficent space in the missing portion for a passage of this extent. Indeed, it could not have contained more than a maximum of 30 letter spaces. The only conclusion one can reach is that Isa. 12:6-13:1 was missing from Frag. a. The most likely explanation for the omission is the similarity of the final words of 12:5 (*h'rṣ*) and 13:1 (*'mwṣ*), a notable *homoioteleuton*.

In Frag. a, l. 5. (Isa. 13:7) 4Q reads *trpynyh* against M. T. and DSIa *trpynh*.

In line 8 of the same fragment (Isa. 13:11) 4Q has *l' wpqdty*, M. T. simply *wpqdty*. The reading is absolutely clear, but it is difficult to explain.

In Frag. b, the first line, the letters *šth* are clear. They can only represent *wštw* of M. T. The latter preserves the older orthography for the infinitive absolute (Ges.-Kautzsch; Bauer-Leander, 57).

In line 7 of the same piece (Isa. 22:20) 4Q and M. T. agree over against DSIa in two instances: 4Q and M. T. have *wqr'ty*, DSIa omits the *aleph* as it does not infrequently (so also the Manual of Discipline). In the same line M. T. and probably 4Q read *Ḥlqyhw* as against DSIa *Ḥlqyh*.

In l. 14 (Isa. 23:1) 4Q and M. T. read *hylylw*, DSIa *'ylylw*.

In line 15 (Isa. 23:2), on the other hand, 4Q and DSIa agree in reading *'brw*. M. T. *'br*. In the same line 4Q has *yy'r* or *yw'r*, M. T. and DSIa *y'wr*, a type of orthographic practice familiar in the scrolls.

It will be observed that 4Q nowhere diverges in favor of the LXX. This is by no means a unique situation, for many other texts follow the Masoretic tradition. On the other hand, we meet a number of fragments which are closely related to what may have been the Hebrew *Vorlage* of the LXX, as has been shown by the article on the Samuel fragments by Professor Frank M. Cross in an earlier number (132) of the BULLETIN. This will be confirmed when all the biblical materials from Cave 4 are presented in the official publication. For not only are there many more fragments from Samuel which support Professor Cross's conclusions, but fragments from other biblical books also seem to follow the same Septuagintal, or rather, pre-Septuagintal tradition. Thus we are confronted with an interesting problem for the history of the text: on the one hand, we have evidence which pushes the sources of the Masoretic tradition back to a much earlier date than heretofore supposed, while on the other hand, we have strong support for a very early Septuagintal tradition, which in recent years has been increasingly out of favor. Scholars may range themselves on one side or the other, but the total evidence of the Qumrân scrolls cannot be disregarded. We cannot return to the days of Bernhard Duhm and his contemporaries in their somewhat cavalier use of the LXX; on the other hand we cannot absolutize the Masoretic text by refusal to recognize a tradition which runs counter to it.

THE SITE OF ANCIENT GILGAL

JAMES MUILENBURG

The location of ancient Gilgal has long remained one of the unsolved problems of Palestinian topography. Of the sites of such other early sanctuaries as Shechem and Shiloh, we have considerable knowledge. These have been excavated, and the results have served to illuminate both the history and religion of ancient Israel. But the situation with Gilgal is quite otherwise. Even its name raises difficulties. Was it originally a *gilgal*, a circle of stones such as is found not infrequently in eastern Palestine? Or does the tradition reflect the existence of a Canaanite sanctuary, later appropriated by the Israelites after their crossing of the Jordan? Or did Gilgal first receive its name from the twelve stones which tradition credits the Israelites with having brought up from the bed of the Jordan and with having set up at this place as a memorial to Yahweh's deed in their behalf? The answers to such questions are by no means simple; yet it may be pointed out that nineteenth-century discussion has been dominated all too frequently by views of Israel's religion, such as worship of stones *etc.*, which contemporary scholarship has all but repudiated.

The importance of Gilgal in the history of Israel and its significance in her cultic life have in recent years been placed in a clearer perspective by the form-critical studies of Albrecht Alt,[1] Martin Noth,[2] Gerhard von

---

[11] Which is not to suggest that this actually occurred.

[1] "Josua" in *Werden und Wesen des alten Testaments* (Berlin, 1935), pp. 13-29. Reprinted in *Kleine Schriften*, I (München, 1953), pp. 176-192. Other relevant studies reprinted in *Kleine Schriften* are as follows: "Die Wallfahrt von Sichem nach Bethel" (I. pp. 79-88), "Die Landnahme der Israeliten in Palästina" (I. pp. 89-125), "Erwägungen über die Landnahme der Israeliten in Palästina" (I. pp. 126-175), "Das System der Stammesgrenzen im Buche Josua" (I. pp. 193-202), and scattered references in Vol. II.

[2] *Das Buch Josua* in the *Handbuch zum alten Testament* series, Tübingen, 1953. See also *passim* in his *Überlieferungsgeschichtliche Studien*, Erster Band (1943).

11

Bulletin of the American Schools of Oriental Research

Rad[3] and by the cultic interpretations of these scholars and Hans Joachim Kraus.[4] It is not to be expected that their conclusions will receive universal assent, but we are certainly nearer a solution of the vexing problems associated with Israel's history, above all of the Conquest, than a quarter of a century ago.[5] In this reconstruction Gilgal occupies a position of considerable significance. It is not our design, however, to enter into these interesting matters at this point, but rather to turn in a very summary fashion to the results of a general scrutiny of the biblical passages involving Gilgal. Let us state them as succinctly as possible:

1. The probable *termini* of Gilgal's *floruit* are ca. 14th (13th?) century B. C. to the Reforms of Josiah in 621 B. C. or possibly to the fall of the southern kingdom in 586 B. C.[6]

2. The three major periods of Gilgal's history are (1) the Conquest, (2) the early monarchy, and (3) the prophetic period of the eighth and early seventh centuries.[7]

3. The narratives in Joshua 1-9 and Judg. 2: 1-5 are Benjamite: in its earliest phase Gilgal was the first foothold on Palestinian soil, the base for military operations and the military and religious center of the tribe of Benjamin.[8]

4. In the early period, therefore, Gilgal was a camp and probably continued as a military center of mobilization long afterward, as seems to be indicated by the narratives of I Samuel.[9]

5. The Conquest as reported in the early strata of Joshua 1-9 and Judg. 2: 1-5 has its center and rallying point at Gilgal. The aetiological stories begin and end there, and the Saul traditions connect with them satisfactorily.

6. These stories are in the main sanctuary reports. They have their origin in the sanctuary, and the influence of the sanctuary is discernible throughout. The cultic character of Josh. 3-4 is plain for all to read.[10] And if there remains any lingering doubt, Josh. 5 will dispel it completely, for there we have in the most pregnant and solemn style the accounts of the (1) circumcision of the people, (2) the celebration of the passover and the end of the manna, and (3) the theophany which gives validation to the existence of the sanctuary.[11]

---

[3] *Das formgeschichtliche Problem des Hexateuchs*, 1938.

[4] "Gilgal: ein Beitrag zur Kultusgeschichte Israels," *Vetus Testamentum*, I. pp. 181-191. Kurt Möhlenbrink, "Die Landnahmesagen des Buches Josua" (ZAW 56, 1938, pp. 238-268) has analyzed the Conquest narratives from a cultic-historical point of view, and has dealt with the relations of Gilgal to the Shechem and Bethel traditions. Kurt Galling has also written at length on the sanctuary traditions of Bethel and Gilgal (ZDPV 66, 1943, pp. 140-155; 67, 1945, pp. 21-43).

[5] Not merely the aetiological character of the narratives but the thoroughgoing accommodation to Mosaic traditions make the historical problems of *Joshua* almost insurmountable. Chronicles contain no reference to Gilgal.

[6] Only two references appear after Micah 6: 5: Neh. 12: 29 (Beth ha-Gilgal) and I Macc. 9: 2. The former passage is certainly not our Gilgal, and the identification of the latter "is extremely difficult if not impossible" (W. O. E. Oesterley in Charles' *Apocrypha and Pseudepigrapha ad loc.*). On the Nehemiah passage see also Alt, PJB 28 (1932), p. 10, and Galling ZDPV 67 (1945), p. 21.

[7] The references to Gilgal in the Elijah-Elisha narratives may conceivably apply to our site, but for the present it must be regarded as uncertain.

[8] So Alt, Noth, Von Rad, and others. A thorough study of the Benjamite traditions in the Old Testament is one of the desiderata for an understanding of the history of Israel.

[9] I Sam. 13: 4, 7, 8, 12, 15; 15: 12, 21, 23. Perhaps there is more than meets the eye in II Sam. 19: 15.

[10] See especially Kraus's stimulating study. Kraus confines his attention chiefly to Josh. 3-4, but the cultic interests persist beyond this point.

[11] Observe the form and style of Josh. 4: 1-7 and 19-24. The common literary

7. Gilgal, as represented in the present form of *Joshua*, is clearly the amphictyonic center for the twelve tribes of Israel.[12]

8. The tradition of the *twelve* stones dates from a time when the twelve tribes were felt to possess some unity or solidarity. It seems likely that this tradition had its origin in the time of Saul and David.[13]

9. In all probability Gilgal was the seat of an annual festival, a pilgrimage center, as is suggested by more than one passage. Von Rad thinks of the Feast of Weeks, Kraus of the Passover.

10. During the early monarchy, particularly under Saul, Gilgal holds a place of great distinction. It is not only the place of his coronation but also the center of mobilization of his troops. The Book of Hosea clearly points to the importance of Gilgal during this period.

11. From an early period Gilgal is bitterly castigated, but more especially by the eighth-century prophets, Hosea and Amos.[14]

12. The constant association of Bethel with Gilgal has a two-fold explanation: (1) the two sanctuaries were connected by an important road, so that intercourse between the two was close and (2) they both go back to traditions connected with the earliest phases of Israel's history and therefore achieved a role in *Heilsgeschichte*.

THE MODERN SEARCH FOR GILGAL

On May 14, 1838 Edward Robinson wrote in his journal of travels:

> If we had not yet satisfied ourselves as to the site of the former Jericho, we had nevertheless been able to ascertain definitely in respect to her ancient neighbour Gilgal, that no trace either of its name or site remains. . . . Neither Sheikh Mustafa, nor the Sheikh of the village, nor any of the Arabs, had ever heard of such a name in the valley of the Jordan. At Taiyibeh indeed, the priest who had been delving a little in scriptural topography, told us that the name Jiljilia still existed in this vicinity; but when we met him here, he could only point to the ruined convent of St. John on the bank of the Jordan as the supposed site.[15]

Some years later, in 1864, Zschokke, in surveying the same region, inquired " in various forms " from the inhabitants of modern Jericho after the location of Gilgal. He was finally directed to a low mound in the plains of Jericho to the southeast of the town, which, it was reported, was known as ' Dschildschul.' [16] The spot was obviously Shejeret en-Nitleh, about two and one-third miles from modern Jericho. In 1873 Lieut. Conder reported hearing the same name applied to Birket Jiljulieh in the same region from three Bedu.[17] On April 25th of the following year

features of the stories in chap. 5, the strong accommodation to Mosaic traditions, their climactic ordering and their themes bespeak their cultic provenance. It is generally agreed that the last pericope (vss. 13-15) belongs to Gilgal.

[12] So Alt, Noth, Von Rad, and Kraus.

[13] So Alt and Noth. In connection with the difficult problem of the relationship existing between the major sanctuaries (Shechem, Shiloh, and Gilgal) one must allow not only for the overlapping of traditions but also for the rise and fall of the prestige of these centers.

[14] Galling, ZDPV 36 (1945), pp. 34-43.

[15] *Biblical Researches*, (11th ed., 1874), I. p. 557.

[16] *Beiträge zur Topographie der westlichen Jordansaue* (1866), pp. 26-27. Since so much of the structure of the En-Nitleh case is founded on Zschokke, it is well to cite his exact words: " Schon früher hatte ich in Riha nach Galgala gefragt und dieses Wort in verschiedenen Formen ausgesprochen, welche nach meiner Meinung, die arabische Ableitung zuliessen, endlich bemerkte unser Scheich Achsein, dass er einen kleinen Hügel kenne, der Dscheldschul heisse."

[17] *The Survey of Western Palestine* (London, 1883), III. p. 173.

Clermont-Ganneau made fresh inquiries as to Gilgal and was told by the people of Jericho that the name " was only used by the Franks." [18] Shortly before, the Archimandrite of the Russian Establishment at Jerusalem " asked to be shown Jiljulieh, and the peasants took him to Tell el-Mufjir, to which they gave the name required." [19] Captain Warren had a very similar experience, Khirbet el-Mefjir being pointed out to him as the true location of Gilgal. Gustav Dalman says that the name is not known among the Arabs today; apparently only Europeans know of the tradition, and their information is drawn from their persistent questioning of the natives who evidently do not agree in their answers.[20] It is significant that when the question was rightly put, as by Clermont-Ganneau, who was especially competent in such matters, and by the Archimandrite of the Russian establishment, not the slightest reference was made to en-Nitleh but rather to Khirbet el-Mefjir. Be that as it may, the tradition is obviously a very fluid and floating one. The name *Jiljûlieh* is indeed known, but it may be a reminiscence of a famous *gilgal* in the region where *gilgals* are well known or, as seems more likely, it is a reminiscence of the Byzantine Galgala and behind it, possibly the biblical Gilgal somewhere in the region. The distance from Khirbet el-Mefjir to en-Nitleh is only 5,000 yards.[21]

The search for Gilgal took a new turn in 1931 when A. M. Schneider wrote an article on the location of the Byzantine Galgala. He was impressed by the ruins at Khirbet el-Mefjir and supposed them to represent the remains of the Byzantine church often mentioned in the pilgrim travel accounts. In this, of course, he was completely mistaken since we know now, as the result of the excavations carried on by Baramki in 1936, that the ruins actually represent the eighth-century palace of the Umayyad ruler Hisham (724-743 A. D.).[22] For some scholars this seemed to put an end to the matter since no remains earlier than Hisham were to be found.[23] But Schneider's examination of the pilgrim records proves to be particularly important since they seem to point consistently to Khirbet el-Mefjir as over against en-Nitleh. To be sure, Schneider made no claims for biblical Gilgal here, and one must always reckon with the possibility that Byzantine Galgala was not located at the same site

---

[18] *Archaeological Researches in Palestine* (London, 1896), p. 37. Clermont-Ganneau adds his comment that this " distinctly lessens the value of this identification."
[19] Clermont-Ganneau, *ibid.*, p. 37.
[20] PJB. Siebenter Jahrgang (Berlin, 1911), p. 31. Dalman rejects Zschokke's precise identification outright, " Dass an einem einzelnen dieser völlig gleichartigen Hügelchen der Name *dschildschûl* gehaftet haben sollte, ist unglaublich." He goes so far as to say that Zschokke was simply deceived by his guides. In the whole region, he adds, there is nothing visible of an ancient Gilgal. This is perhaps an overstatement, because the Byzantine remains on many of these little hills certainly suggests the possibility that it may have been Galgala. Dalman himself prefers to identify the ancient site with 'en el-Gharaba near the Wadi Kelt in the neighborhood. We shall not undertake to discuss this view except to say that whatever arguments there are against Khirbet en-Nitleh apply *a fortiore* to '*ên- el-Gharaba*.
[21] It is less than an hour's walk. The tamarisk tree can be seen from a considerable distance.
[22] " Das byzantinische Gilgal (*chirbet mefjir*)," ZDPV, 54 (1931), pp. 50-59.
[23] Noth, *Josua*, p. 25.

as Old Testament Gilgal. Ancient names have a way of shifting from place to place.

Yet in the same year Albrecht Alt took up the cudgels in behalf of Khirbet el-Mefjir as the location of ancient Gilgal and seconded Schneider's observations.[24] He fortified Schneider's arguments by a re-examination of the pilgrim records and by his own intimate familiarity with the region. To be sure Khirbet el-Mefjir lies to the northeast, possibly more north than east of Tell es-Sulṭân, but it is notorious that the biblical records give only general directions. Moreover, one might add to Alt's observations that the Israelites were approaching Jericho from the east, and the eastern direction would therefore be primary in the mind of the writer of the account. As to the requirements for water, Alt mentions the Wâdi en-Nuwei'me, which is as a matter of fact dry most of the year. Josh. 3:15 reports, however, that the Jordan was overflowing its banks at this time, and if this should preserve an authentic memory, then the *wâdi* would contain a sufficient supply. But we need not appeal for support to this evidence since it is possible that this is a later tradition designed to aggrandize the miracle of the crossing. It will be noted on our map (Fig. II) that a *wâdi* is indicated along the southern border of the *tells*, but it is in reality what the Arabs of the region call a *khôr* (not *ghôr*!), a "lowland" between two elevations. Not more than two kilometers to the east of our sounding there is a spring called Khôr Maṣâyid, i. e. "the *khôr* of the hunting ground," which flows throughout the year, in the rainy season abundantly, at other times more sparingly. Moreover the Bedu of the region informed me that there were a number of water-holes in the region east of Tell 2 toward the Jordan River. Finally, when once the invaders had conquered their foes and established themselves, there would be no difficulty at all about water, since there was an abundant supply within easy range at the Fountain of Elisha and elsewhere.[25]

We turn now to the topographical evidence to be gleaned from the literary records, which must assume a central role in any discussion of Gilgal's location. For convenience the following table gives the measurements of all the places involved in the problem. It is not to be expected that absolute accuracy can be attained, but the data given here have been checked and re-checked several times by different persons and may be regarded as substantially correct:

> Khirbet el-Mefjir to Tell es-Sultan: 2200 yds., 1.35 Roman miles, 1.25 modern miles, 10.87 Roman stadia.
> Khirbet en-Nitleh to Tell es-Sultan: 5200 yds., 3.27 Roman miles, 3.01 modern miles, 26.19 stadia.
> Khirbet el-Mefjir to Tulul Abu el-'Alayiq: 3700 yds., 2.2 Roman miles, 2.1 modern miles, 18.28 stadia.
> Khirbet en-Nitleh to Tulul Abu el-'Alayiq: 5675 yds., 3.5 Roman miles, 3.2 modern miles, 28.03 stadia.
> Khirbet el-Mefjir to modern Jericho: 2.18 Roman miles, 3½ km., 2 + miles, 17.4 stadia.

---

[24] PJB 27 (1931), pp. 47 ff.

[25] Moreover, it is well known that inhabitants of ancient villages sometimes travelled considerable distances for their water supply.

15

Khirbet en-Nitleh to modern Jericho: 2.53 Roman miles, 3.73 km., 2.33 modern miles.
Khirbet el-Mefjir to el-Maghtas: 10,300 yds., 6.35 Roman miles, 5.8 modern miles, 50.09 stadia.
Khirbet en-Nitleh to el-Maghtas: 6,200 yds., 3.82 Roman miles, 3.52 modern miles, 30.63 stadia.
Khirbet el-Mefjir to the Jordan (nearest point) ca. 4¼ miles.
Khirbet en-Nitleh to the Jordan (nearest point) ca. 3 miles, ca. 5 km.
Khirbet en-Nitleh to Khirbet el-Mefjir: 5000 yds., 2.85 miles.

Our first topographical datum concerns Gilgal only indirectly. In Josh. 2:1, 3:1, and Mic. 6:5 the Israelites leave Shittim for the Jordan. We are not given any precise details, but Josh. 3:1 suggests that the distance was not great: "Early in the morning Joshua rose and set out from Shittim with all the people of Israel; and they came to the Jordan and lodged there before they passed over" (RSV). Abel-shittim has been identified with Kefrein and with Tell el-Ḥammâm, but Nelson Glueck has made a strong case for the latter.[26] Now the nearest ford to Tell el-Ḥammâm (and to Kefrein also, for that matter) lies at El-Maghtas, a distance of a little more than six miles (Fig. I). Tradition has long held this place to be the site both of the Crossing and of the baptism of Jesus, and today there are many monasteries near the spot commemorating the two events.[27] Examination of the accompanying map (Fig. I) will indicate how favorable a place this is for the crossing.[28] The second reference is Josh. 4:19, the most precise of all topographical references in the Old Testament involving Gilgal. Here it is said that the Israelites "encamped in Gilgal on the east border of Jericho." To be sure en-Nitleh lies more directly east of Jericho than does Khirbet el-Mefjir, but, as we have seen, from the point of view of the writer the latter could be described as east of Tell es-Sultan. Moreover, despite the fact that the reference to Jericho might apply to a considerable area, the inference is clear enough that Gilgal must lie in immediate proximity to ancient Jericho.[29]

In Josh. 15:7 we are provided with what would seem at first to be a fruitful clue, since the language is definite. In the description of the boundary of the tribe of Judah we read: "and the boundary goes up to Debir from the valley of Achor, and so northward turning at Gilgal, which is opposite the ascent of Adummim, which is on the south side of the valley." Adummim is usually identified with Ṭal'at ed-Dam on the

[26] *Explorations in Eastern Palestine, IV.* Part I: Text (New Haven, 1951), pp. 378-382.
[27] It is not our task here to account for alternative traditions except to say that they seriously complicate the topographical requirements. Why, for example, the Israelites should move from Abel-shittim to ed-Damiyeh is hard to explain in view of the topographical elements involved.
[28] One might comment that Khirbet en-Nitleh lay on the direct line of march from el-Maghtas to Tell es-Sultan, which is true, but this view encounters strategic objections which we shall consider below.
[29] Since Khirbet el-Mefjir is nearer Tell es-Sultan than is Khirbet en-Nitleh, the balance of probability favors the former. Moreover, as Alt has pointed out (*ibid.*, 47 f.), nowhere in our traditions is Gilgal brought into relation with places near Khirbet en-Nitleh, like Beth-hoglah and Beth ha-Arabah, as we should expect in such boundary descriptions as Josh. 15: 6 and 18: 12.

Number 140 December, 1955

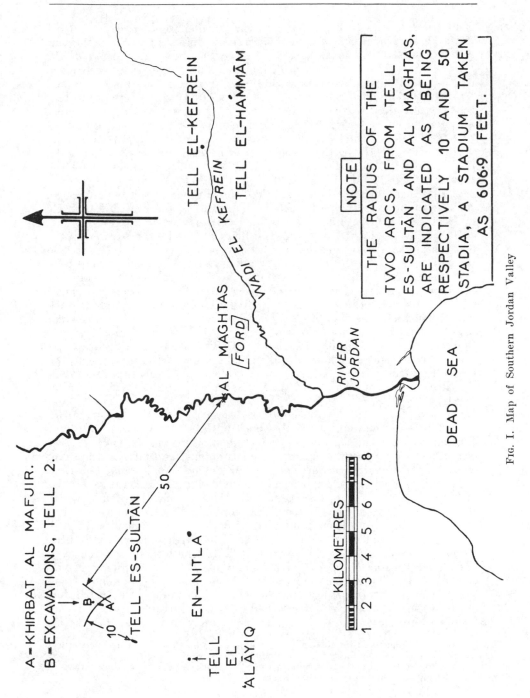

Fig. I. Map of Southern Jordan Valley

17

road from Jericho to Jerusalem. In the parallel passage of Josh. 18:7, however, we read *Geliloth,* and this receives some support from the versions (B Γαλιαωθ; A Αγαλλιλωθ; Syr. *Geliloth*). Judg. 2:1 speaks of the angel of Yahweh going up from Gilgal to Bochim (generally recognized as Bethel). This association with Bethel is one of the most common features of the Gilgal references in the Old Testament. Now the important road leading from modern Beitin to Khirbet el-Mefjir is probably an ancient one, but we have no evidence that it ever proceeded beyond to Khirbet en-Nitleh.[30] In other words, if we identify Gilgal near Jericho with Khirbet el-Mefjir the association is natural and easily explicable, but this is not the case with en-Nitleh. We shall not consider here the journey of Elijah and Elisha from Gilgal to Bethel, since it is possible that the Gilgal here mentioned refers to the Jiljulieh of the central range, some seven miles to the north of Bethel, nor the Gilgal of Elisha's miracle in II Kings 4:38-41, though this is by no means certain.[31]

Rather let us turn to Josephus and his witness. In the Antiquities V, 6, 4 Josephus, in recording the events of Josh. 3-4, writes as follows: " So the Hebrews went on further fifty stadia, and pitched their camp at a distance of ten stadia from Jericho." Now a glance at the table of distances given above will show at once that the only data which agree with Josephus are those which refer to the crossing at el-Maghtas with Khirbet el-Mefjir as the destination, the latter being 10.87 stadia from Jericho and 50.09 stadia from en-Maghtas. This involves two assumptions, to be sure: (1) that Josephus was aware that Tell es-Sultan was the site of ancient Jericho and (2) that he knew el-Maghtas to be the place of crossing. But no other localities, including Tulûl Abu al-'Alâyiq, the Roman Jericho, which we should naturally expect, fit the requirements.

Our next authority is Eusebius of Caesarea. In the Onomasticon (Klostermann's edition, p. 65) Jerome translates the relevant words of Eusebius as follows: *Galgala, haec est quam supra posuimus Golgel, ad orientalem plagam antiquae Ierichus cis Iordanem* and later in the same context, *et ostenditur usque hodie locus desertus in secundo Ierichus miliario.*[32] It is obvious that Eusebius is following the account in *Joshua* in his first passage, but the second tells us that Gilgal is situated " at the second milestone from Jericho " or, to render Eusebius more exactly, " at about the second Roman milestone from Jericho." This fits Khirbet el-Mefjir and Tulûl Abu al-'Alayiq best. En-Nitleh is more than three Roman miles both from Old Testament and from Roman Jericho.

In his famous account of the Holy Land (*de Situ Terrae Sanctae,* xvi, ca. 530 A.D.) Theodosius locates Gilgal one mile from Jericho. If he had either 'Alâyiq or modern Jericho (*Erîḥa*) in mind, neither Khirbet el-Mefjir nor Khirbet en-Nitleh would satisfy the requirements, but the former comes closer to them. Again, surprisingly, if he knew of a tradi-

---

[30] It is possible, too, that there was a road running north and south which either passed through or came near Khirbet el-Mefjir as there is today.

[31] Galling refers all Old Testament passages to Khirbet el-Mefjir as does Kraus.

[32] Eusebius has ὡς ἀπὸ δύο σημείων Ἱεριχοῦς.

tion which places ancient Jericho at Tell es-Sultan, Khirbet el-Mefjir comes very near to his distance, being 1.25 modern miles and 1.35 Roman miles away whereas en-Nitleh is more than twice the distance involved.

The famous pilgrim Willibald (726-723 A.D.) places Galgala about five miles from the Jordan River and two miles from Jericho, which is fairly satisfactory for Khirbet el-Mefjir but impossible for en-Nitleh.[33] In the year 1106 the Russian Abbot Daniel visited the famous church at Galgala, and his description clearly suits Khirbet el-Mefjir. Travelling north from modern Jericho he arrives at the fountain of Elisha, then proceeds " ein Werst " (ca. 16.068 km.) further toward the east to Gilgal; to the west lies Mount Qarantal.[34] Finally, we are fortunate in having the account of Brocardus, who was more than usually careful in his topographical directions. In the year 1283 he describes his journey in this region. He is travelling from Phasaelus toward the south, on the road to Jericho, veers slightly to the east, and arrives at Galgala. As he advances he sees Qarantal on the right of the road and visits it, and from there he proceeds to the fountain of Elisha, which is described as being south of Galgala.[35]

The foregoing discussion has produced two results of the very first importance for the identification of Gilgal near Jericho. The first of these concerns the name Jiljulieh (or the many alternative forms in which the name is transmitted). The proponents of the Khirbet en-Nitleh theory have made much of this, but upon closer inspection the force of the arguments simply vanishes. Considering the reporters involved, Khirbet el-Mefjir really has a better case than Khirbet en-Nitleh, but the appeal to the name is in the very nature of the case suspect. All we can say with confidence is that the name is known in the region of the plain east of Jericho, nothing more. The second argument, which rests upon the topographical evidence drawn from the literary records, definitely supports Khirbet el-Mefjir rather than Khirbet en-Nitleh. As one reads through the literature on the subject of Gilgal's identification, he is struck again and again by two features of the discussions which support en-Nitleh as the site of the ancient sanctuary: (1) the vague generalizations which are given to support this view and (2) both the discrepancies in the distances involved and the downright inaccuracies.

But we are still confronted with a problem of great importance. What

---

[33] Cited by Abel, *Géographie de la Palestine* (Paris, 1938), II, p. 337. How Abel can write that this puts us in the region of the tamarisk of en-Nitleh is hard to understand. The distance is three miles from the Jordan whereas Khirbet el-Mefjir is more than four; en-Nitleh is 2.33 miles from Jericho, which is satisfactory enough, but Khirbet el-Mefjir is very slightly over two miles.

[34] Schneider, *op. cit.*, pp. 57-58. The text is given in Venevitinov, *Pravoslavnavo palestinskovo obstschestvo* (St. Petersburg, 1833), p. 51. See also Albrecht Alt, *op. cit.*, pp. 47 ff.

[35] J. O. M. Laurent. *Peregrinatores medii aevi quatuor* (Leipzig, 1864), p. 57. His words are worth noting: De Phesech fere contra austrum; sed tamen declinando, parum ad orientem ad quinque leucas est locus Galgale . . . De Galgalis ad dimidiam leucam eundo in Iericho ad dextram ultra uiam est mons Quarantena dictus . . . Subter quarantenam fere quantum bis potest iacere arcus oritur fons Helisei . . . Hic fluit iuxta locum Galgale a parte australi.

evidence do we have in either of the two places of any settlement during
the biblical period? To such a question only excavation can give an
answer. First, then, Khirbet en-Nitleh. As early as 1874 Clermont-
Ganneau made a small sounding in the area, and found a quantity of
potsherds, mosaic cubes, and bits of glass. " It is certain that a building
of some importance existed on the former spot [evidently the little mound
immediately to the east of the tamarisk tree, Shejeret en-Nitleh] to
judge by the abundance of the mosaics, but there is nothing in that to
testify for or against its identity with Gilgal, and the matter still seems
to me extremely doubtful." [36] In the spring of 1950 James L. Kelso excavated at least four of the little *tells* near Shejeret en-Nitleh, the most
impressive of which lies immediately east of the famous tamarisk tree.
Clermont-Ganneau's observations are quite correct. It must have been
a building of some importance. But Kelso, despite the fact that he dug
to virgin soil, found no evidence anywhere of anything earlier than the
fourth century A.D. It must always be borne in mind in dealing with
sites in the Jericho plain that this region was the seat of literally scores
of monasteries and convents, many of which still exist today. But it
was recently suggested to the writer that perhaps Kelso had not gone
down far enough. Since this was a distinct possibility and all efforts had
to be exhausted to do justice to the en-Nitleh view, the writer conducted
a small operation in the two major areas of Kelso's excavations. We
purposely picked out what appeared to us to be the most favorable spot
for inserting a small trench. Our two workmen, both veterans of Miss
Kenyon's excavations at Jericho, penetrated more than a meter below the
lowest point of the 1950 " dig," but we found nothing. Despite the fact
that the area is still strewn with Byzantine sherds, bits of irridescent
glass, and innumerable tesserae, we recovered in the upper level of one
of our pits only one tiny piece of glass and one Byzantine sherd. We took
the opportunity to make another survey of the many small *tells* in the
area, as, indeed, we had done on at least two previous occasions, but
nowhere did we discover anything but Byzantine remains. Now the
possibility will doubtless have occurred to the reader that the impressive
structure near Shejeret en-Nitleh may well have been the site of Galgala,
a possibility that was constantly in the writer's mind throughout the
winter of our explorations. The presence of a substantial structure would
seem to encourage such a possibility. Yet one must then reckon with
the records of the pilgrim texts of later times, which do not seem to
yield much encouragement to that view. In this connection it is well to
point out that fine pillars with beautiful crosses carved in them were
found in Hisham's palace at Khirbet el-Mefjir, and the possibility is at
least open that these may have come from the Byzantine edifice.

No single argument has been launched more frequently against the
identification of Khirbet el-Mefjir with biblical Gilgal near Jericho than
the absence of archaeological confirmation. It is said, and quite rightly,
that Baramki and those who worked with him found no evidence of
anything earlier than the Umayyad period. Now it must be remem-

[36] *Op. cit.*, p. 37.

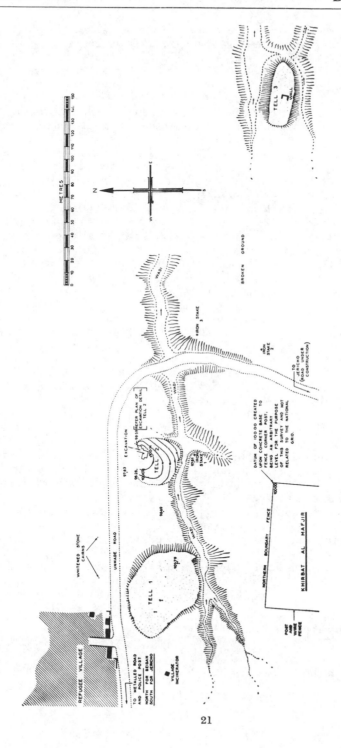

Fig. II. Environs of site believed to be Gilgal.

bered that Khirbet el-Mefjir is a mound of considerable size and that
while the Hisham palace area is spacious, it nevertheless occupies a
relatively small portion of the area.[37] All have agreed, both opponents
and proponents of the Khirbet el-Mefjir view, that the place urgently
requires excavation. Moreover, in our various reconnoiterings throughout the winter the writer became convinced that there were a number
of places in the immediate proximity of the mound which held considerable possibilities. Into these explorations we need not enter here.[38] But
the upshot of our search of several months was to apply to G. Lankester
Harding, Director of Antiquities for the Kingdom of Jordan, for permission to make soundings on or near Khirbet el-Mefjir. He generously
granted our request, being himself deeply interested in the problem and
disposed to favor the Khirbet el-Mefjir identification. That very day,
in wandering about the *tell* in connection with his not infrequent visits
to the famous Umayyad palace, he came upon an Iron-Age jar handle.
Certainly this was sufficient to whet our archaeological appetite, and
after receiving the enthusiastic approval of W. F. Albright, acting president of the ASOR in the absence of Carl H. Kraeling, we began our
preparations.

As one proceeds north from Tell es-Sultan on the old Jericho-Beisan
motor road one turns directly east at the refugees' camp for about a
kilometre. On its right is a small *tell*, known as Deir el-Ghannâm (see
PEF 1894). Here one meets the north-south road, which is being paved
for service between Jericho and Khirbet el-Mefjir. Turning to the left,
one crosses the Wadi Nuwe'ime, and gradually ascends the *tell*, which
is about 7½ meters high.[39] Immediately on the right is a mound with
rich Ghassulian remains, and about a hundred yards or so farther on the
left one reaches the winter home of Awni Dajani, Inspector of Antiquities for West Jordan. Contiguous with Mr. Dajani's property lie the
famous ruins of Hisham's palace, which form a large isosceles triangle
with a base of about 200 meters and a perpendicular to the apex of about
500 meters. Beyond this, i. e. beyond the bath area which contains the
famous mosaics, there is a substantial area of several hundred yards.
Immediately northeast of the eastern line of the palace area we come
upon a number of small hillocks, all of them *tells* (Fig. II). One of them
has a large cemetery, and in our examination of two other *tells* we found
other burials. It was to these *tells* that we directed our attention.

After completing our preparation and assembling the necessary equip-
ment at the School our party set out very early in the morning of May
15. Professor J. L. Kelso of Pittsburgh-Xenia Theological Seminary, the
colleague of W. F. Albright at Tell Beit-Mirsim and Beitin, graciously
accepted our invitation to join the party for the day. Awni Dajani, who

---

[37] Several hundred yards extend to the north beyond the area of Hisham's palace.
The surface is strewn with sherds of the Byzantine period.

[38] Among the *tells* which were more carefully examined were Tell Abu Ghannâm
immediately to the south of Khirbet el-Mefjir (cf. PEF. 1894, p. 177), and Tell
el-Muṭlab, a Roman ruin recently excavated by the Department of Antiquities.

[39] According to the Jordan Bureau of Land Registry Deir al-Ghannâm, immediately
to the south of the *tell*, has a height of — 248 meters, while the *tell* itself has an
elevation of — 240.5 meters.

was in a real sense the Maecenas of our venture, was the second member of the party. Mr. Peter Parr, veteran of several archaeological campaigns, two of them with Miss Kenyon at Tell es-Sultan, proved an indispensable colleague, and if the expedition achieved significant results, it is largely due to his interest and co-operation. Finally, Imran Abdo, the School's driver, participated in one way or another throughout our

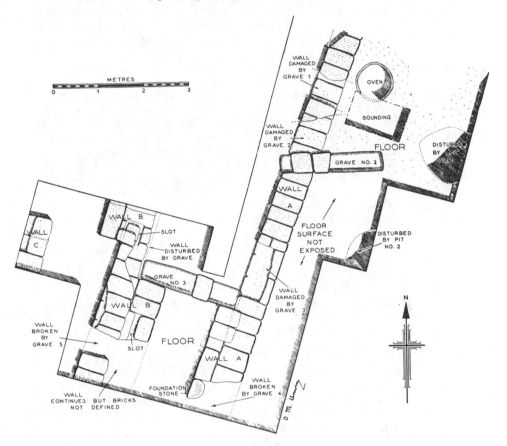

FIG. III. Plan of Excavation at Khirbet el-Mefjir.

operations. We began with about ten workmen, most of them members of Miss Kenyon's excavations nearby, two pickmen, two hoemen, and the rest basket boys.

Our first project was to make a survey of the various *tells* in the area. Within an hour we had accumulated a respectable number of indisputably Iron Age sherds from *tells* 1, 2, and 3 (Fig. II). Then came the problem of where to dig. That decision was up to the director of the sounding. Now in our study of the *tells* I had been impressed by one elevation (Tell 2) which clearly showed the presence of mud bricks, together with a number of Iron Age sherds. It is not a particularly striking ruin. It is roughly circular in form with a diameter of about thirty feet. It rises to a height of only 13.2 feet from the " *wadi* " to the south and 9.5 feet from the floor of the plain at the north. The pickmen began work at the base of the northeastern part of Tell 2, at the spot to which the line points in Fig. II. The trench was about 1½ meters in width. Immediately we encountered mud brick and more sherds, many of them, to be sure, nondescript, but some with characteristic forms. Before the end of the morning we had come upon a fair-sized oven of excellent construction with a maximum diameter of 82 cm. Immediately to the north there was a large deposit of grey ash. Continued digging revealed a hard floor which was disturbed by a large pit at the southeast. In this area most of the remains were fallen mud brick. But soon we struck a wall, the width of which at this point was 63-65 cm. During the afternoon the character of the wall became clearer, and we saw a construction of large and beautifully made bricks, with an average length of 38 cm. and an average width of 17 cm. (Fig. III). Its orientation was SSW by NNE. More sherds were recovered, none of them later than Iron II.

This ended our first day's operations. We had achieved at least one result, one of major importance it seemed to us in the history of the problem of the location of Gilgal. We certainly made no pretentions of having discovered the site. What we did demonstrate was the presence of an Iron Age settlement at Khirbet el-Mefjir or, at least, a few hundred yards to the north. Since this was our first interest, we considered terminating our operations then and there. But as we began to reflect upon our findings, it seemed obvious to us that we should seek to determine something concerning the structure of which the mud brick walls were a part. We therefore set out again some days later, this time with Peter Parr and our driver. We had set a guard day and night over the *tell* so that it was exactly as we left it some days before. We more than doubled the number of workmen, and it was our good fortune that they proved to be an unusually energetic and happy lot. Many of them we had come to know from the excavations at Tell es-Sultan. Mr. Dajani offered us his summer home for the period of our operations and looked to our comfort in a score of ways.

The next three days were spent in following the wall. Again and again our progress was hampered by the presence of burials, none of them containing any noteworthy remains. When we had gone some nineteen feet we came upon what promised to be a significant grave; it was very narrow, but its length was more than seven feet. The clearing of the grave revealed Wall B, and in the course of uncovering the wall we came across a long beam employed as an anti-earthquake device. This area was broken and badly disturbed, but we succeeded in exposing another floor between Wall A and Wall B. It looked like a corridor or court, some 3.6 feet in width and over 8 feet in length (i. e. of the area cleared). Farther to the east we came upon the remains of another wall, Wall C.

Then we returned to Wall A again, but were not able to uncover its entire length because of the intense heat. In the course of the excavations a number of sherds appeared, and especially in the area of the corridor or court we found a substantial number of well burnished red sherds. The total length of the portion of Wall A uncovered by the excavation was some thirty feet, and it extended beyond this, how far we were unable to determine. The distance between the outer walls (A and C) was about 18.3 feet. Nowhere did we encounter any indication of stratification. At the close of our operations we made a sounding in the northern area near the oven of well over a meter, but came upon nothing, not even a single sherd.

All the sherds of any consequence were transported to the American School, and there they were washed and prepared for further study. We had made a preliminary study of them at the *tell* and were aided by the volumes on Tell Beit Mirsim, Tell en-Nasbeh, and other excavations. Of particular interest was a large jar-handle (Fig. IV, No. 11), which Père de Vaux and Professor Kelso independently dated to Early Iron, conceivably even to Late Bronze. This confirmed the judgment of Peter Parr, and it has now received the weighty support of Professor Albright. Unhappily the highly burnished red sherds were lost in transit to America.

A brief description of the more important sherds follows (see Fig. IV):

Kh. M. II. 1-4, 18, 23 (Fig. IV, 1-5).	Collared jar rims. Pinkish ware, grey core, gritty. Hard fired. Creamy slip.	TN. II. 303, 304, 306, 308 (700-586). Megiddo I. Jars 70, 76, 124. Strata V-VII. (1100-600). Lachish III. Type 481 (700-586) Tell Far'ah (RB. 1947. p. 583, No. 8). Iron 2.
Kh. M. II. 7.	Storage jar handle. Oval section. Wall carinated at upper attachment. Grey core, fired pink outside. Creamy slip.	Far'ah (RB. 1947, p. 583, No. 8). Iron 2.
Kh. M. II. 8.	Foot of chalice or potstand. Grey ware, fired pink on outside. Fine grits. Ring burnish on outside. Fired hard.	
Kh. M. II. 9. 12 (Fig. IV, 15).	Bowl rims. Finely burnished ware, fired red on outside and inside. White grits. Wheel burnished. No slip.	Lachish III. Type 639. Level III (800-586) TBM I. pl. 63, No. 4. 9-7th cents.
Kh. M. II. 11 (Fig. IV, 18).	Rim frag. of large bowl. Grey ware, fired red on outside and inside.	Cf. Ain Shems IV. No. 21. Level 6. 950-875.
Kh. M. II. 13.	Neck of jug. Pinkish buff ware. Creamy slip outside.	Lachish III. Type 267. Tomb 1002. 800-700. Type 269. Tomb 106. 7-6th cents.

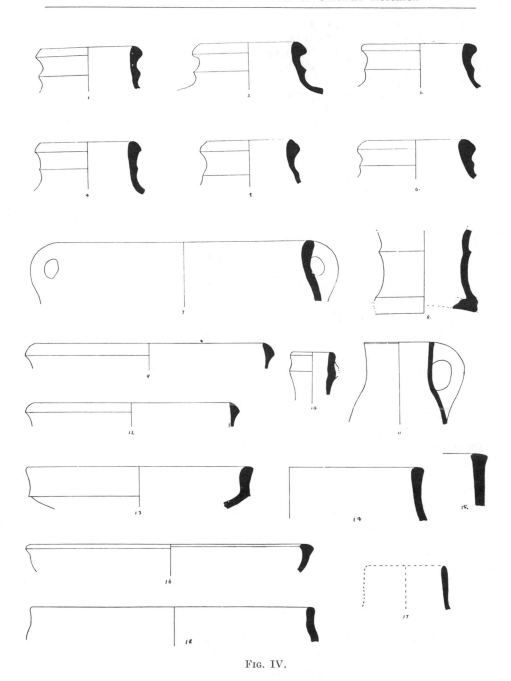

FIG. IV.

Kh. II. 16. (Fig. IV, 13).	Rim of bowl. Curved sides, rim thickened, projecting in and out. Buff ware, fairly soft.	TBM III. P. 26a. No. 5. Level A. 9-7th cents. TN Pottery. 5. 1398. Level I. 750-350. Megiddo I. Pl. 24. No. 36. Strata III-II. 750-600.
Kh. M. II. 15. (Fig. IV, 9).	Bowl rim, vertical, slightly projecting inside and out. Coarse ware, not too well fired. Perhaps traces of ring burnishing on top of rim.	TN Pottery. S. 1466. Level II. 1000-700. Cf. Megiddo I. Bowl No. 60. Stratum III. 750-650.
Kh. II. 26 (Fig. IV, 7).	Rim handle of cooking pot. Hard pinkish ware, traves of burning.	TBM I. Pl. 56. No. 10. Level A. 9-7th cents. TN. S. 1042. Level I. 700-350. Tell el-Fûl. AASOR. IV. Pl. 246. No. 1. 1100-1000.
Kh. II. 27 (Fig. IV, 11).	Neck and handle of jug. Red ware. Probably oval mouth.	TBM. I. Pl. 57. Mo. 10. Stratum A. 9-8th cents. Lachish III. Type 219. Tomb 1002. 800-700.

Tell 2 represents an ancient settlement. The evidence of the sherds points to the Early and Middle Iron periods (1200-600 B. C.). The neighboring *tells* also yielded sherds from this period, and Mr. Dajani assures me that there are others in the region immediately to the north, and to the east of Khirbet el-Mefjir where he has found Iron Age sherds. The *tells* are all very small, but the results of our sounding of Tell 2 should encourage excavation. Finally, the structure on Tell 2 was obviously one of substantial proportions. It was impossible to press the excavation to the point where its main outlines were discernible, but it is more than likely that it covered the entire *tell*. Considering the weight of the evidence adduced in the first part of our discussion it is hardly too much to say that Gilgal was located in this region.

Part Six

HOMILETICS AND MEDITATIONS

A Confession of Jeremiah
By James Muilenburg

Woe is me, my mother! that you bore me
As a man of strife and a man of contention to all the earth!
I have neither lent nor borrowed,
Yet all of them curse me.
So be it, O LORD, if I have failed to entreat thee,
Or to plead with thee for the good of my enemies,
In their time of trouble and trial!

Have I an arm of iron,
Or a brow of bronze?
Thou knowest, O LORD!
Think of me, and visit me;
Avenge me on my persecutors,
Through thy forbearance put me not off.
Know that for thy sake I have borne reproach
From those who despise thy words.

As for me, thy word is my joy and delight;
For I bear thy name, O Lord, God of hosts!
I sat not in the company of the sportive,
Nor made merry with them;
Under thy mighty power I sat alone,
For thou dids't fill me with indignation.
Why is my pain unceasing, my wound incurable,
Refusing to be healed?
Wilt thou really be to me like a treacherous brook,
Like waters that are not sure?

Therefore thus says the LORD:
"If you turn, I will restore you,
And you shall stand in my presence;
And if you bring forth what is precious, without anything base,
You shall be my mouthpiece.
They may turn to you,
But you shall not turn to them.
And I will make you toward this people
A fortified wall of bronze;
They may fight against you,
But they shall not overcome you;
For I am with you to help you,

15

And to deliver you," is the oracle of the LORD.
"I will deliver you from the hand of the wicked,
And will redeem you from the clutch of the cruel."

JER. 15: 10-12, 15-21

I T HARDLY seems possible that such a confession was meant for other eyes than Jeremiah's. It is not often that men expose themselves so completely, though the literature of confession has grown steadily throughout the centuries. One is tempted to ask what it is within us that draws us so strongly to such expressions as these, and why millions of people feed each year on the vulgar pulp literature of the news-stands which abounds in so-called intimate "confessions". In confession Jeremiah reveals the innermost depths of his soul; in conversation and dialogue he breaks through the egoistic boundary of his existence; in prayer he opens the soul's east window of divine surprise. These words find few close parallels in all literature. Within the Christian tradition we think at once of Paul and Augustine and Luther and Kierkegaard who stand in the same line with Jeremiah. And if we were to venture outside, we should think at once of some of the terrible conflicts in Dostoevski's novels (men, e.g. like Rashkolnikoff or Ivan Karamazov), or we should think even of Hamlet. Jeremiah has a religious dimension and a profundity that Hamlet does not have, and of course Jeremiah is Scripture and Hamlet is not. But the two have much in common. They both know that the times they live in are out of joint and that they have a peculiar responsibility to their times; they both are torn by baffling contradictions; both are men of great solitariness and yet of very keen and healthy social instincts. Of all the solitary figures in religion, few are so alone, so utterly isolated and forlorn and lonely as Jeremiah, and yet one feels all the time, as Jeremiah obviously does, that he is really not that kind of person. He should have married a wife, but this was forbidden him. He should have had children, he if anyone, but this great resource was denied him too. The temple community should have been his great refuge, but he was at odds again and again with its official representatives and even with his prophetic colleagues. He really had no one but God. We must remember this when we listen to the broken cries of this confession. I remember hearing Margaret Webster say one time that people never discuss the play *Hamlet* without discussing Hamlet the man and only Hamlet. Everyone, actor and spectator alike, wants to talk about Hamlet. That is one reason, I suppose, that it has now been playing more or less regularly for 300 years. I mention this because that is precisely what we always do with Jeremiah. We are interested in him as a man; we never discuss the book without discussing him. And I suspect we all know why this is so.

But let us turn to the confession itself. Jeremiah launches forth with a terrible woe: *Woe is me, my mother, that you bore me a man of strife and contention.* The prophet was much troubled about his birth, and, there are indications that he brooded much over it. One is reminded of Hamlet's terrible,

16

merciless castigation of his mother Gertrude, for Shakespeare understands this too. Perhaps all of us cry out like this at some time or another although we may not express it in Jeremiah's words. We understand deep within us this ultimate protest against being born as we were born, born to be the kind of persons we are, with all our peculiar moods and drives and dispositions and tempers. *Alas, my mother!* says Jeremiah, and in that cry he echoes every man's final cry. I wonder whether this is the reason that this cry is so often the last one to burst from the lips of dying men. But then Jeremiah turns immediately, almost shockingly, to defending himself. *I am neither a borrower nor a lender.* In other words, I have never got myself into trouble. "Yet I am cursed! But perhaps I deserve to be cursed." He admits that possibility, perhaps he has some deep premonition of his corruption here. "But that cannot be, for I have prayed for those who did the wrong, those who cursed me, in their time of troubles and trial." For a man who needed companionship and love his deepest reality was the opposition of his foes:

> *Have I an arm of iron,*
> *Or a brow of brass?*

This excessive outburst produced its own revulsion in Jeremiah. He now turns to God in a quiet mood where we see him most like himself:

> *Thou knowest, O LORD!*
> *Think of me, visit me;*
> *Know that for thy sake I have borne reproach*
> *From those who despise thy words.*
> *As for me thy word is my joy and my delight;*
> *For I bear thy name, O LORD God of hosts.*

In these words, and the rest of the passage we have the very essence of piety. Jeremiah's words sound like words of perfect serenity. But if anything is clear he is very disturbed and troubled. And the reason is obvious, I think. This piety is utterly self-centered and exclusive. It is full of self-righteousness. And as so often in this kind of piety, the mailed fist is exposed beneath. *Avenge me of my persecutors!* He then turns, much more healthily, to longing for friends, but note how he expresses it.

I sat not in the company of the sportive, says Jeremiah, *nor made merry with them*—but he certainly would have liked to. This is why the next line is so terribly poignant: *under thy mighty power I sat alone.* Again he seems to have divined where his difficulty lies, for he cries out over his incurable wound, his unceasing pain which refuses to be healed.

Jeremiah's cries have been wild and incoherent; he passes from mood to mood in almost reckless abandon. Now finally he stands on the abyss of *the everlasting nay.* He has focussed his fierce emotion upon himself with such intensity that finally God is called to the board and is accused of treachery and deception. "Art thou like a spring torrent, like a wadi which gushes with water in the springtime and then becomes a dry river bed the rest of the year?

17

Art thou only a fantastic vision which comes now and then, a deceitful mirage?"

But then finally comes the amazing shift. Therefore, thus saith the LORD.

If you turn, I will restore you,
And you will stand in my presence.

Throughout his ministry Jeremiah had called upon Judah ever and again to turn to repent; *turn, O backsliding Israel.* But now it is he who is called upon to turn, he first of all and above all. Precisely because he is so intensely religious, so intensely near to God, he is most in need of repenting. His intensely religious mood has actually separated him from the men to whom he ministered, and, more astonishing, it has actually separated him from God. For Jeremiah is too self-centered ever to see himself as he is. "Every egocentric human being deceives himself. Complete insight and egocentricity cannot exist side by side, which is why insight is lessened by egocentricity."

This is what Jeremiah finally comes to see, and the Hebrew brings this out perfectly. *If you return, then I will cause you* (make you) *return.* That is what the word literally says, Jeremiah's turning from himself will be recognized as God's work, not his own, for the resources of his piety are not great enough for that.

I sought the LORD and afterward I knew,
He sought my soul to seek him seeking me;
It was not I that found, O Saviour true,
No, I was found by thee.

If you bring forth what is precious without anything common, then you will be as my mouth. Let the fierce bellows of your spirit roar, but make sure that they are stirring the fires to purge the dross which is actually separating you from God. And when you see how recreant you yourself are, how much of an apostate you really are, how much you have made yourself and your own experience your God, then you will know the sources of men's waywardness and infidelity. You will know why you are destined from your birth to be a prophet; then you will know that I, the Lord, am not a treacherous stream or a desert phantom where men wail mirage, but that I am your deliverer and your redeemer. Jeremiah now stands on the verge of *the everlasting yea.* For through his terrible suffering and conflict he was writing a living commentary to the word of the gospel: *For whosoever seeks to gain his life will lose it, and whosoever loses his life will preserve it.*

Contributors

Charles W. Iglehart is Professor of Missions at Union Seminary . . . *James Muilenburg* is Professor of Old Testament at Union Seminary . . . *Robert B. Lee* is a graduate of the School of Sacred Music and is now a candidate for the B.D. degree.

A Meditation On Divine Fatherhood

By James Muilenburg

WHEN YOU PRAY, SAY "FATHER". With this first word of the Lord's Prayer belongs a second, *Hallowed be Thy Name*. These two words belong together, and they must not be separated. In them is expressed the piety of the Bible. And yet we shall speak only of the first word, the beginning of the beginning. But what does that word mean?

The language of the Bible is the language of the *family*, of a people who knows what it means to live within the family relationship: *husband* and *wife*, *brother* and *brother*, *father* and *child*, *mother* and *child*. At the very beginning the relation between husband and wife is grasped: therefore a man leaves his father and mother and cleaves to his wife, and they become one flesh. Then follows the story of two brothers, of the brother who lost his brother. In her earliest epic Israel lives by the faith that Abraham is the father, the father who will become the father of many nations. *In thee shall all the families of the world be blessed.* When Israel languished in exile and was blind to the meaning of her existence (Isaiah 40:27), the prophet of the exile who grasped the meaning of Israel's life in the world calls his people back to the ancient roots:

> Look to the rock whence ye were hewn,
> To the pit of the well whence ye were digged;
> Look to Abraham your father,
> And to Sarah who bore you.

This is the source of Israel's security and peace and hope.

Jacob, who is Israel, becomes the father of the twelve sons of Israel. When Israel moves into the center of her history, among the nations of the world, David the King, the historical person who knows how to deal with the forces of coercion in history, solves the political problem. David had many sons, but he never knew what it was to be a father. Tamar and Amnon and Absalom, and Adonipah and Solomon are children who needed a father and never had one. So the ultimate cry breaks from the lips of the King at the very point when his kingdom suffers its maximum threat from his dearest son, "Absalom, my son, my son."

The literature of the world reflects this existential relation between father and son. Whenever we remember the Iliad at all, we recall Priam weeping for his son Hector as seven times he is dragged behind the chariot wheels of the victorious foe around the walls of fair Ilion. And what is Hamlet but the cry of a son for his father, and the outraged protest against a false substitute.

The frustration and bewilderment which afflicts the soul of contemporary man is expressed in the brokenness of the family relationship. For the family is the primal human unit by which we are all bound in an indissoluble bundle of life. Here body and soul become one. The meaning of our conception and

3

generation is perpetuated in a continuing loving relation. In this mysterious matrix we become men, and if we are denied the relation to which we are legitimate heirs we live distraught and troubled, until somewhere, somehow we find our father and mother and brother. The memory of our fathers blesses or haunts us all our days. Those who know this secret best are the psychiatrist, the poet, the artist, and the playwright.

Only dimly do we divine the depths of the tragedy of the rifts in family life in our generation. Our people stand in David's place, not least of all the man of power and prestige, the professional man, the business man, and the politician, who have not time to be fathers to their sons. We have torn the fabric to which we belong: the relation between husband and wife, and father and child. One of the plays now showing on Broadway, *The Death of a Salesman,* is the story of a father who has lost his sons. No one who has seen it can ever forget the terrible experience. It is terrible because we who see it know that we are all involved in that story. When Biff stands over the grave of his father, he pronounces the final verdict and inscribes the epitaph: *He never knew who he was.* The father ate the sour grapes, and the teeth of the children were set on terrible edge. Or take *Cry the Beloved Country,* the story of two fathers, the Reverend Stephen Kumalo and Mr. Jarvis, who lose their sons. They both cry with David, "My son, my son," and in their common cry of fatherhood the barriers between race and class and economic status are broken down. They both come to plumb the depths of their fatherhood; i.e. they know what it means to be born into the world, and by the strange metamorphosis of pain and travail the world becomes a family (cf. Mark 3:31-34).

But what does father really mean? What does it mean to be a father, and what does it mean to be a son? One must *have* a father, and one must *be* a father. The modern Oriental understands this better than we do. For the East knows that the father lives in his son, and the son knows he lives on the life of his father. His father is in him. The father has a "blessing" in him which he bestows upon his son, and the son, whether he know it or not, lives in the well-being and peace (shālōm) of the blessing. There is a living, organic, elemental relation here which man must not defy. Otherwise the blessing becomes a curse. It is Israel who knows that its life is fashioned in the relation of father-son, son of Abraham, but more than that, son of God (Exodus 4:22-23; Hos. 11:1; Isa. 63:16; 64:8).

The Bible knows that this relation is not described solely in terms of physical kinship; yet it knows that the physical and the spiritual are dynamically inter-related. But it is not of nature alone: *Woe to him who says to his father, "What are you begetting?"* The bond is of nature, of course, but infinitely more than nature. Whoever lives the life of a father is a father. So Elisha, the pastor and shepherd of souls, seeing his master carried off in a chariot of fire cries, as he sees Elijah disappearing into the heavens, "My father my father, the chariots of Israel and the horsemen thereof!" David never

4

understood that, or understood it too late. Again the father is the lord of his household. He recognizes that he is responsible to it and for it, and he does not relegate his responsibility to another, neither to school nor the state nor any other institution. For a mother cannot take the place of a father. The son knows he is his father's servant, and we must not be offended by this. The child who is not yet on the way to becoming a father will understand this. As soon as he grows to manhood he is made aware that he must become a father, and at the marriage ceremony this is made very clear to him. Next year at this time may you be blessed with a son!

Israel knows that she is a son, but a disobedient son, apostate and re-bellious: *Sons have I reared and brought up, but they have rebelled against me.* Israel, called to be a first-born son, knows she has corrupted her heritage. *I am no more worthy to be called thy son.* She stands in a genealogical relationship all her life. This is what she believes by faith, but she cannot live up to this ultimate relation, the finale of the complete genealogy in Luke's gospel. So the new Adam is born to be a son, the first-born of many brothers. And when the true son is born of the true Father, there in the final moment on the cross, we can hear the cry of God: "My son, my son." And so we discern our ulti-mate relation in the father-son. *For we have not received the spirit of bondage to fall back into fear* — including the harassing fears which afflict our genera-tion — *but we receive the spirit of sonship.* When we cry our first and only cry, "*Abba, Father,*" it is the Spirit himself which bears witness with our spirit that we are children of God, heirs of God and fellow heirs with Christ, provid-ed we suffer with him in order that we may also be glorified with him.

"I believe in God the Father Almighty and in Jesus Christ his only son, our Lord." We are not isolated, insecure, alienated, and forlorn. We have one Father, One Lord and Father of us all, and we are brothers in the Son. This is our home and this our family. When we live by the faith that here we belong together, our frictions and misunderstanding and want of charitableness seem very unreal. We do not surrender our human relationships at all, but all our human relationships are transfigured by the new recognition; we are bound in the embrace of an ultimate and perfect and sovereign and redeeming love. So when we pray our Lord's Prayer, sometimes amidst groanings which cannot be uttered, sometimes when all seems dust and ashes, sometimes amidst frettings and whimpers and distraughtness, then we still lift our voices together and we say, "Father". And to this ultimate cry we add the maximum petition of holiness: *hallowed be Thy Name.*

Part Seven

EARLY WRITINGS AND REPORTAGE

Chapter I.

Introduction: History of the Problem

Before the history of Christian origins can be written and the development of primitive Church doctrine traced, higher criticism must provide the data which it alone, as a true science, can provide. Documents of early Christian history are few, and even these are of little value to the student of historical theology so long as their date or temporal order remains unknown. But criteria for determining the time of composition of writings vary, and application of different criteria may yield widely different results. Moreover, there are always factors and contingencies present which may account for phenomena in a way different from that of the criterion applied. For example, the test of the stage of doctrinal development reflected in a writing has frequently determined its temporal and local situation. Yet, it is very conceivable that there were communities far from the great highways of commercial intercourse which clung for long to forms and systems obsolescent in the cities. Again, even in a metropolis, there may well have been teachers and preachers who retained what the dominant theology had already discarded as unnecessary and even harmful. The test of linguistic characteristics may be no less deceptive. For words may continue long in the vocabularies of certain groups when they have grown archaic in others. Moreover, words undergo strange vicissitudes, so that their meanings may vary in different places. Criteria must be applied with care, then, and always with the recognition that other factors may enter in which will modify one's conclusions.

Cases in point are the two extra-canonical writings of the Epistle of Barnabas and the Teaching of the Twelve Apostles. Outside of the New Testament, there are no two documents of more importance for the reconstruction of the early history of Christian dogma than these two monuments of primitive Christianity. Yet, results have varied widely in the investigations of their date, their theological position,

1

— 2 —

their literary character. Both writings have been attributed numerous, and often conflicting, shades of theological interest. Both have been declared polemical and both irenic. Both have been described as colored by later interpolations. As respects the date, the divergence has been no less great. The Epistle of Barnabas has been staunchly assigned, and with much zeal, to the reigns of Vespasian, Domitian, Nerva, and Hadrian. Among the foremost defenders of the Vespasian hypothesis were Weizäcker,[1] Lightfoot,[2] and Bartlet.[3] Wieseler,[4] Riggenbach,[5] and Luthardt[6] argued for a date under Domitian. Hilgenfeld,[7] Funk,[8] and Bardenhewer[9] upheld the view that the letter belonged to the reign of Nerva. Finally, Harnack,[10] Volkmar,[11] Loman,[12] and Keim[13] assigned the writing to the reign of Hadrian. Critical questions relating to the Teaching of the Twelve Apostles have received even more numerous and more divergent solutions. At one extreme, Sabatier insisted that the document presented such vivid marks of primitiveness and genuineness, especially in the eschatological character of its piety, that it was to be dated before the gospels, as early, he declared, as 50 A. D. At the other extreme, Bigg pointed to a late doctrinal development,[14] placed the compilation in the fourth century, and inquired only whether it was pure romance or a fiction containing but a substratum of reality. J. A. Robinson, independently

---

1. Zur Kritik des Barnabasbriefes aus dem Codex Sinaiticus.
2. S. Clement of Rome, ii, 503—512.
3. The N. T. in the Apostolic Fathers, in loc.
4. Jahrb. für deutsche Theol., iv., 1870, 603 f.
5. Der sogenannte Brief des Barnabas.
6. Der johannische Ursprung des 4. Evangeliums, 1874, 75 f.
7. Nov. Test extra canonem receptum, ii, 1877.
8. Theol. Quart., lxvi, 1884, 3—33; lxxix, 1897, 618—636.
9. Geschichte der altkirchlichen Literatur, i, 86 ff.
10. Geschichte der altchristlichen Literatur, i, 1893, 56—62; ii, 1897, 410—418.
11. Monumentum vetustatis christianae ineditum.
12. Theologisch Tijdschrift, 1884, 182—226.
13. Jesu von Nazara, i.
14. Certain linguistic arguments are also put forward by Bigg, but his emphasis is placed on such considerations as baptism by affusion, absence of interest in Christ's humanity, absence of chiliasm, employment of the Lord's prayer in such a compilation as the Didache, Alexandrine thought in the prayers, persecution of Christian by Christians (16 : 4), etc.

— 3 —

of Bigg, came to the conclusion that the compiler's manual was to be taken not "as representing the Church of his own time or place, but rather as an imaginative picture of the primitive Church, as it was planted by the Apostles in Gentile lands". Such a view of the work, he admits, "deprives it indeed of most of its historical value; but it explains the fact that the picture of the Church which is there drawn remains, after nearly forty years of eager investigation, isolated and unique: history has found no time and no locality to which such a representation can be reasonably assigned". But the great majority of scholars have sided neither with Sabatier nor with Bigg. One group would place the Teaching at the close of the first century; another group date it betwen 130 and 160 A. D.

From the very beginning it was seen that the central problem of the Teaching of the Twelve Apostles was its relation to the Epistle of Barnabas. The two writtings had in common a long passage known as the Two Ways, and several other passages more or less similar. Yet there were so many differences between the writings in doctrinal point of view, literary character, and purpose that it became fundamentally important to determine which was the original and which the dependent. If historians were to make use at all of these extremely valuable sources, they could do so only by ascertaining their date, locality, character, and purpose. As a matter of fact, no single question of early Christian literature outside of the New Testament has been more discussed and more controverted than that of the bearing of the one writing upon the other. Almost immediately upon the publication of the editio princeps of the Teaching by Bishop Bryennius in 1883, there arose a storm of debate over the Bishop's dictum that the Teaching of the Twelve Apostles was dependent for at least its early chapters upon the Epistle of Barnabas. Harnack and Hilgenfeld rose to the defence of Bryennius, but Zahn and a host of others stoutly maintained that the Teaching was the true and admirable source, and the Epistle of Barnabas the sad result of a rather unintelligent and incoherent copyist. Critic vied with critic in extolling the originality of the Teaching and criticizing the inferiority of the Epistle. "Hätte dem Verfasser der Doctr. der Barnabas vorgelegen, so hätte er den Inhalt von dessen c. 18—20 in unvergleichlich künstlicher Weise verarbeitet. . . . Gerade ihm ist zuzutrauen, was für den Verfasser der Doctr. eine Unmöglichkeit gewesen wäre"

1*

— 4 —

(Zahn).[1] "Il est impossible d'admettre que l'auteur de la Didachè, pour réaliser quelques parties de son plan si régulier, ait glané cà est là dans ces chapitres de Barnabas quelques phrases ou parties de phrases si étrangement disposées" (Massebieau).[2] "It is hardly conceivable that so energetic and forcible a writer as the author of the Teaching should have culled his materials from the confused, ill-ordered mass of Barnabas, and subjected himself to the tedious process of extracting and re-arranging" (Hitchcock and Brown).[3]

Already in March, 1884, the hypothesis of a common source as the basis of the Two Ways was proposed.[4] Dr. Wordsworth described this source as a "catechism founded on the Sermon on the Mount, and an expansion, indeed, of our Lord's teaching about the broad and narrow way." Canon Spence[5] and others acquiesced in this, or a very similar, view. In the 1886 edition of Harnack and Von Gebhardt's great work, there appeared a Latin fragment of the Teaching which Von Gebhardt himself had discovered. It was without the Christian passage 1 : 3 b—2 : 1, just exactly as the Apostolic Church Order and the Syntagmae Doctrinae were without it. Here, then, according to the opinion of many scholars, was the source of the great passage common to Barnabas and the Teaching. Krawutzcky's reconstruction of the primitive manual in 1882 had anticipated with marvellous accuracy the discovery of the MS. Holtzmann[6] advanced the view that the Teaching and the Epistle were two co-ordinate recensions, "jenes als die ältere, aber sorgloser und willkürlicher gefertigte, dieses als die wohl spätere, jedenfalls aber viel treuere Recension der Allegorie˙ von den zwei Wegen". This "allegory of the two ways" he identified with the lost I u d i c i u m P e t r o u. Bratke,[7] on the basis of Holtzmann's article, supported the view of a common Grundlage, and contended that this source emanated "aus einer alten Quellenschrift über die zwei Wege" and represented a later addition to the Didache. With the publication in 1886 of

---

1. Forsch. zur Gesch. des N. T. Kanons, III, 1884, 312 f.
2. L'enseignement des douze apôtres, 1884, 35.
3. Teaching of the Twelve Apostles, 1885, xxxvii.
4. The Guardian, March 19, 1884, "The Teaching of the Twelve Apostles".
5. The Teaching of the Twelve Apostles, 1885, 113.
6. "Die Didache und ihre Nebenformen", J P T, 1885, 154 ff.
7. "Ueber die Einheitlichkeit der Didache", J P T, 1886, 302 ff.

— 5 —

Charles Taylor's The Teaching of the Twelve Apostles, the view of a common source received further support. In these two lectures Taylor produced a large number of striking parallels from the Talmud and other Jewish literature, and proved beyond the possibility of question the strongly Jewish character of the contents of the Teaching. Taylor's investigations received almost immediate recognition everywhere. Within a year, the conviction of a primitive Jewish manual, a catechism for Jewish proselytes, had become almost general. Dissenters were few, and objections concerned matters of lesser importance. There were those, like Dr. Warfield,[1] who insisted that the manual was from the beginning a Christian catechism. "Its essence seems to me to be Christian", he writes, "it appears to be still based on Matthew's gospel in a real sense, and to be throughout the free composition of a hand that was at once Jewish and Christian". Other disagreements dealt with the textual history of the documents.

In the same year, Harnack published his Die Apostellehre und die jüdischen beiden Wege.[2] In this famous article he gave up his former view of the direct dependence of the Teaching upon the Epistle of Barnabas. After tracing the history of the Teaching in the church, he concludes that it is almost certain that an older recension of the Two Ways lies at the basis of our writing. This likewise bore the name of Didache. In the post-apostolic age the writer of Barnabas incorporated this instruction into writing, probably without knowing it as the Teaching of the Apostles. He quotes it from memory, and thus the order in which he has reproduced the sentences is probably explained. In the original Two Ways, 1 : 3b—2 : 1 was wanting, and 3 : 1—6 was perhaps absent from many copies of it. The present form of the Didache is the work of some unknown Christian who edited the original manual and added to it chapters 7—16. But the original Teaching was probably the Greek behind the Latin version. In Die Chronologie (1897) Harnack sees the hypothesis of a common source as the only way out; indeed, he says, it has long ceased to be a hypothesis, for the history of the Two Ways or the composition of the Didache shows

---

1. "Notes on the Didache", JBL, 1886, 86 ff.
2. An expansion of his article "Apostellehre" in Herzog's Realencyclopedae, vol. xvii, 656 ff. Von Gebhardt and Harnack's edition of the Teaching (TuU, II, 5) also appeared in 1886.

— 6 —

that there was a shorter form of the Two Ways, which is older than our Didache. Finally, in the New Schaff-Herzog Encyclopedia, Harnack finds it an "extremely probable conjecture that the 'Two Ways' is a Jewish production, intended for proselytes, derived from the decalogue and an amplification of its commands, which along with the O. T. has come over into the Christian Church". In all of his discussions, however, Harnack insists on the priority of the Epistle of Barnabas over the completed Teaching.

Only here and there have protesting voices been raised. In 1898, Bigg came out in support of a late date for the Teaching. With the discovery of the complete Latin 'version' by Schlecht in 1900, the true nature of this witness became known. The fact that it appeared in a collection of homilies, the Epistle lessons for a part of the year, combined with a number of other facts, tended to raise doubts as to its value. In 1908, Gustav Hoennicke in his Das Judenchristentum im ersten und zweiten Jahrhundert perceived with unusual insight the literary character and Jewish tone of both documents. Much to my regret, it was not until six months after the presentation of my thesis that Hoennicke's work came into my hands.[1] In 1920, J. A. Robinson published three lectures on Barnabas, Hermas and the Didache. In this volume he upheld the priority of Barnabas over the Teaching and the dependence of the Teaching upon both the Epistle and the Shepherd. In 1923, R. H. Connolly adduced the evidence of the Didascalia,[2] which had become better known through the recent discoveries of large sections of the Latin version, for a Teaching which included not only the latter chapters of the work, but the so-called 'Christian interpolation' as well. The next year he published with comment the two small fragments of the Teaching which had come to light in the Oxyrhyncus Papyri.[3] One of these contained 1 : 3—1 : 4, and thus furnished another witness to the presence of the 'Christian interpolation' in the Teaching. In the same year, Horner published another fragment of the Teaching

---

1. In revision I have attempted to do him justice, but almost invariably my own conclusions had reproduced his own before I had learned of his position.

2. JTS, 1923, 147 ff.

3. Edited originally by Grenfell and Hunt. See art. by R. H. Connolly in JTS, 1924, 151 ff.

— 7 —

in Coptic,[1] which contained parts of chapters 10 and 12 and all of chapter 11. The textual evidence for the 'common source' theory has received other reverses too. The proponents of this view have had their difficulties in accounting for parallels outside the Two Ways sections, and there is little or no agreement as to the material to be included in the 'common source'.

The present state of the question cannot by any means be regarded as settled. So diverse have been the judgments and opinions of investigators that a renewed attack upon the problem is not only permissible but imperative if criticism is to perform its appointed task. That the problem needs solution there will be few to deny. It is not merely a question of the character as such of these two 'apostolic' writings. Our problem concerns such vital interests as the origin and growth of the N. T. canon, the development of early Christian doctrine, the character of liturgical forms, the relation of Christian documents to their Palestinian or Hellenistic background, the reason for their subsequent influence, and the reflection of environment in early Christian writings. Strange as it may seem, in view of its universally recognized importance, a thoroughgoing and detailed examination into the literary relations of the Teaching of the Twelve Apostles and the Epistle of Barnabas has never been undertaken. Even the work of Robinson undertakes to comment on comparatively few parallel passages, and these briefly perforce, because of the semi-popular nature of his addresses.

To enter upon such a study may seem venturesome, to say the least, when so many scholars have already rendered their own decisions on the matter. One must indeed be reluctant to tread paths of investigation already trod by such eminent scholars as Harnack and Zahn and J. Rendel Harris and Bartlet. But the present state of the problem is surely such that no one would welcome more than these very scholars a research into the evidence for and against the literary dependence of one of these writings upon the other. Moreover, the presence of new materials, which throw some light on a problem, always invites further study and investigation. This, then, is the purpose of the dissertation: to study the Epistle of Barnabas and the Teaching of the Twelve Apostles with a view towards determining their literary relationships.

---

1. J T S, 1924, 225 ff.

— 8 —

The evidence concerns itself only with the literary aspect of the question. Doctrinal considerations have been mentioned only incidentally. Whatever may be the evidence contributed by the criterion of doctrinal development, the testimony of literary relations is the concern of the present research. Such knotty problems as the organization of the Church, clinic baptism, and asceticism are here dismissed as secondary to the purpose in view. The question of the kind of genuineness represented by the Church manual, important as it is for the historian of the beginnings of Christianity, receives no answer. Whether the Teaching is a work of the imagination, compiled irrespective of existing conditions, or whether it is a source of the first rank for reproducing the ecclesiastical life of a community, is not the question this dissertation undertakes to answer. It is only the literary aspect of the problem that the following chapters treat. This has inevitably called forth many corollary questions. As we have seen, it was clear from almost the beginning that the textual history of the two documents had an important witness to give. But the decisive moment came in my study of the literary character of the two writings. The more I read them and the more closely I examined them, the more convinced I became that here was the open way to the solution of the whole problem. This study afforded me the first revelation as to the true relationship of the two writings. Almost as revealing was the examination into the Jewish character of both documents. Anyone who will spend a few hours reading the Talmud and then go to the Epistle of Barnabas will be struck by their similarity in literary method and style. Before the parallel passages of the Epistle and the Teaching could be treated in any detail, the whole question of their literary integrity had to be studied. So intimately are Chapters VII and VIII of this thesis related that over-lapping here and there was inevitable. Moreover, the evidence of Ch. 8 can be fairly appreciated only by constant and repeated reference to the corresponding passages in Ch. 7, where the Greek passages must be compared in order to feel the unity of the whole. The evidence presented in the following pages is, of course, cumulative. It is only by a consideration of the various kinds of testimony, whether of text or literary genre or rabbinic character or of comparison of parallel passages, that the decision has been made.

— 9 —

The results to which my investigation have led are somewhat remote, I confess, from the original purpose of the dissertation. It was contemplated at the beginning to ascertain the date of the Epistle of Barnabas by showing its connection and relationship with some of the N. T. books, the writings of Justin Martyr, Pseudo-Aristeas, and the Teaching of the Twelve Apostles. General reading had convinced me of the approximate accuracy of Harnack's date for the Epistle in 131 A. D. But so complicated has been the relationship between the Epistle and the Teaching, and so fundamentally important, that I have chosen to restrict the present study to but one aspect of the more general problem.

The results may be stated in one short sentence: The Two Ways chapters of the Epistle of Barnabas are authentic. They are the original work of the writer of the remaining chapters of the Epistle. The author of the twenty-one chapters is one and the same. On the other hand, the Teaching, much as it bears the stamp and impress of the compiler's genius, is a compilation throughout and is the work of many authors. The theory of a common source is only a theory, and has no basis in actuality. Both the Teaching and the Epistle came into being in substantially the same form as we have them today. The elaborate textual histories of Warfield and Harnack disappear as soon as the true relation of Barnabas 18—20 to the rest of the Epistle is perceived. The Teaching of the Twelve Apostles is dependent upon the Epistle of Barnabas for the common materials.

Luther and Zwingli Quartercentenary

A Protestant Conference at Marburg

By James Muilenburg

Associate Professor of History and Literature of Religion,
Mount Holyoke College

The Religious Conference of Marburg, on September 12–14, did not profess to be of the proportions of Lausanne, Stockholm, or even of the recent meeting at Copenhagen. It was far from being an œcumenical council, or even a representation of Protestant Christendom; but in response to invitation the sons of the Reformation came from the North and the South, from the East and the West, to pay homage to a great historical event, striking historical personalities, and a common cause. From Britain came, among others, Professor Garvie, Prof. H. R. Mackintosh, and Professor Niven; from Denmark, Bishop von Roskilde; from Switzerland, Bishop Nuelsen and Professor Brunner, whom so many American theological students have come to know and love; and from America, Professors Porter of Yale, W. A. Brown and Rockwell of Union Theological Seminary. France and Italy, and even far-off Iceland, were represented. The one conspicuous absence was Archbishop Söderblom, who was to have played a conspicuous part in the discussions, but was prevented by illness from lending his able hand to the work of harmony and mutual understanding.

The Marburg conference was avowedly a gathering for the purpose of achieving some measure of church unity, to heal up old wounds, if possible, and to allow the present somehow to make partial atonement for the failings of the past. But its immediate purpose was to celebrate the 400th anniversary of the famous conference between Luther and Zwingli on the subject of the Lord's Supper. The name of Luther is still very dear to German Protestants. Their ties to him are not only religious; they are racial as well, and that means much, especially in Germany. For the past decade, other Reformation events have been commemorated with warmth and zeal, and one may safely venture the prophecy that the coming years have many more in store.

Of course, the question that inevitably raised itself at the conference is the question that must raise itself to the casual student of history and religion: Why celebrate Marburg? Why celebrate a tragedy, a dark spot on the escutcheon of Protestant history? Why drag forth, consciously and willfully, a skeleton out of the closet of Reformation history when there are so many brilliant and significant treasures to exhibit? The answer, of course, is to be found in more than an instinctive love for festivity and display. It may be questioned from a profounder point of view whether the Marburg meeting of 1529 was such a tragedy after all. Certainly, it has a real place in the history of the Reformation, as well as in the life of Luther, and it has a great place even in the present if history is to be allotted any weight at all.

A Notable Conflict

The choice of Prof. Walter Köhler of Heidelberg as the opening speaker was a most happy one. Because of his notable researches on the relations between Luther and Zwingli, he was pre-eminently qualified to speak on "The Motive, Progress and Results of the Religious Parley of 1529." In an incisive and brilliant historical sketch, he laid the setting and groundwork for the succeeding sessions. To understand the Marburg conference, he said, one must understand the backgrounds of its chief participants, the religious and political development of the preceding decade, and above all, the nature of the problem which was essentially at stake. The tradition of freedom flowed strong in the veins of Zwingli. His childhood had been peaceful and his career smooth, without any inner spiritual upheaval or conflict. Luther's, on the other hand, was a fiery and strenuous youth. He experienced sudden conversion and made a swift and determined decision. He was one who could cry out in Pauline mood, as the torments of hell wracked his tempestuous soul, "Oh, my sins, my sins!" He was a man of no compromise. In the character of the two men one may already read the outcome of the Marburg parley.

It must be realized that only a few years before 1529 Luther and Zwingli were at one regarding their beliefs, not merely as children of Catholic heritage, but as Reformers. At the beginning Zwingli did not advocate a symbolic signification of the Lord's Supper; no more than Luther, at the beginning, laid stress only on the corporeal presence of Christ. Both believed in the presence of Christ in the sacrament, and both believed that the true significance of the sacrament lay in the forgiveness of sins through the sacrifice of Christ on the cross which was there communicated. It was only later, after the issue was raised by Honius in Holland as to the meaning of "This is my body," that a tense relationship arose. Here it was interpreted as, "This *represents* my body." As a gold ring testifies to the bride of the love of the bridegroom, so in the breaking of the bread and the offering of the cup Christ places before our eyes the act of redemption. The Lord's Supper recalls this act, and is thus a supper of remembrance.

It was on this point that the breach between Luther and Zwingli became pronounced. To Luther forgiveness of sins was guaranteed only if Christ was himself corporeally present. He stressed the objectivity of the presence. To Zwingli, with a strong humanistic interest upon him, religion was a matter of the Spirit. "An object of faith," said Zwingli to Luther, "is that whereon belief can rely; to eat a body is not something upon which salvation can depend. God, and God alone, must be worshiped—not flesh and blood. We believe in our heart in Christ's death for us; who trusts Christ has Christ present in the Spirit." His stress was on subjectivity.

Luther judged aright when he burst forth, "You have another spirit than we." For Luther the *Word* was centrally important; for Zwingli, the remembrance (Gedächtnis). It was essentially a struggle of *religion* against *religion*. These are the contrasts that are still alive today: emphasis upon mystical experience and emphasis upon the Word. There is "another spirit" on this side and the other.

Neither Zwingli's tears nor Luther's words settled the dispute. But the Marburg conference of 1529 offers no occasion for mockery or ridicule. On both sides it was a struggle for truth. Moreover, Marburg has a lesson to teach, for the present brings the past into fulfillment. And this is the purpose of the Marburg conference of 1929.

The address of Professor Hermelink, Dean of the Theological Faculty of Marburg University, on "The Essential Nature of Protestantism and Its Expression in the Various Denominations," was characterized by a plea for the witness and judgment of history. Again and again, he repeated his desire not only to allow history to cast its full light upon the religious judgments of the present, but also to recognize that the outcome of the historical process was essentially just and desirable. "Who has not wished," he asked, "that Luther and Zwingli might have come to an agreement at Marburg, and thus furthered the cause of church unity?" But let us think the historical situation through: as things stood then, it would have meant a unified, closed system of belief and ecclesiastical life parallel to the Roman Catholic system of force. Who would venture to accuse Luther of sectarianism, or Zwingli of stubbornness? Who would undertake to condemn as heretics all those in the history of Protestantism who took their own holy way and thus became leaders of new groups and denominations? We do not venture to act as corrector of the past. We wish it as it is and as it was.

Yet, Protestantism is compelled today, more than ever before, to be conscious of its inner strength and its essential nature. But what constitutes the unity of Protestantism? What is the basis upon which churches can unite? What are the central contentions that must be maintained if the Church is to remain truly Protestant? These principles of unity Professor Hermelink enumerated as follows:

1. Protestantism is a unity in its protest against Roman Catholicism, a *positive* protest which must be ever asserted and proclaimed anew against all forms of holy canon law or any mechanical meeting with God.

2. Protestantism is a unity in its return to the *gospel* as the final guide for faith and life.

3. Protestantism is a unity in its recognition of the congregation as the germ of religious and ecclesiastical life.

4. Protestantism is a unity in its principle of the priesthood of all believers, the independent moral decision of its believers and confessors.

5. Protestantism is a unity, most profoundly and inclusively, in its belief in the gospel which alone justifies the sinner and assures him of the gracious mercy of his God through Christ and his work. Grace only through faith in Christ, who assures us of salvation, through faith which permits good works to grow as fruit on a healthy tree—it is here that Protestant experience begins.

Protestantism's Common Tasks

It was only to be expected that the address of Rudolf Otto on "The Common Tasks of Protestantism and the Method of Their Fulfillment" should be keenly anticipated on every hand by members of the conference. Professor Otto speaks with an authority that few in the religious world today possess. Long before he spoke the hall was crowded, and as he ascended the stairs, quietly and impressively, one felt a deep sense of suspense, as though here would sound a trumpet call to a united Protestant Church. The following is but an inadequate outline of his thought: We have come here to witness before the world that we are one as children of the Reformation, to vow that we are united in a common cause, and to call to remembrance the tasks that confront us as Protestants. "I mean the tasks which confront Protestantism as a great spiritual *Communion*, and which it as a Communion has to accomplish, if it is to remain true to its calling." These tasks are primarily twofold. The first is the recognition that up to the present Protestantism is without any organ for collective action. The result is that when it is attacked or assaulted, or when a question is put to it as a whole, there is no instrument which can function for all its bodies. Catholicism has gained much of its strength by its solidarity and ability to act as a unit when questions affecting its interests, its nature, and its position toward current questions arise. Professor Otto was not proposing the hasty establishment of an external Church Union. "We will not attempt by elastic generalizations to establish a common 'faith' by taking a common denominator of dogmatic formularies." Nor did he favor "the formation of a universally accepted outward constitution," nor "an all-inclusive superorganization of Protestant Church organizations." "But it appears to us, that in the wholly undogmatic form of a *Union for common practical Purposes*, somewhat in the shape of a 'Universal Protestant Senate for the Protection of Common Protestant Interests' there is offered a modern means by which important common Protestant tasks may be fulfilled, which without it would fail of fulfillment."

The second great task of Protestantism in the present is to form some sort of institution or organ which will undertake the study of common problems, and thus prepare the way for fruitful interrelations, for the interchange of ideas, and for common intercourse. Such subjects as present themselves most seriously are, first of all, great moral questions. The shrinking of the world-arena has made it imperative that if the church is "to fulfill its office of condemning sin and of urging men to righteousness and to godly obedience," it cannot do so without "defining its attitude to the great collective sins of society in their manifold forms." In preaching, teaching, and discipline, it must be willing to face the intricate problems with respect to family and marriage, to training and popular education, to relationships of various classes, and to race relations. Again, there are questions of general culture which the shrinking of the world-arena makes inevitable. Further, there is the great problem presented by the presence of Protestant minorities. And finally, there is the subject of the "Œcumenical" movement. "But according to our opinion, the over-arching 'œcumenical' roof can only be firmly built, if it rests on *three* firm pillars, which carry it, and of these that of Protestantism as a whole, alongside those of the Eastern and Anglican Communions, is like a clearly distinct and self-inclusive part in the whole. And it would appear to us a lack if, alongside the two definite unities of Anglicanism and the Eastern Church, Protestantism should co-operate only in *separated* groups, and not on its side, too, as a Protestant *working-unity*."

History Re-enacted

Perhaps the most impressive feature of the Marburg "Religionsgespräch" was the afternoon gathering in the Hall of Knights in the old Schloss of Landgrave Philip, where a group of Marburg students re-enacted the debate between Luther and Zwingli. The men were well selected. Their faces were strong and wholesome, their voices clear and pleasant. Dressed in the characteristic costume of Luther and his theological contemporaries, they seated themselves about a long table, each with a large and hoary volume before him. The debate was based on old Hessian and Swiss records. Chancellor Feige opened the session. As the discussion wore on, the light of the candles became brighter, and as it flickered, the play of light and shadow upon the faces of these staunch theologians, the sound of their clear voices throughout the hall, with their splendid German stress and emphasis, the constantly recurring reference to Scriptural passages, brought historical memories which crowded down upon that group from all over Europe, and from America.

A Note of Disappointment

It may be seriously questioned whether the Marburg meetings advanced the cause of church unity in any degree at all. It may be even questioned whether the ambitions of the leaders were realized. So far as I was able to observe, the speakers seldom or never came to grips with the problems that were really at stake. Yet exchange of views and candor are always helpful in groups striving for harmony, and it must be admitted that there was occasionally some plain talk. Moreover, the experience of common worship and common religious sentiment is a tie that binds even closer than agreement in matters relating to theological statement and conviction. Creedal animosities vanish when hearts beat together in united aspiration.

But if the cause of church unity was not materially advanced at Marburg, certainly one did not leave without certain vivid impressions. For one thing, one felt that the history of the time of Luther and Zwingli and Calvin had not yet lost its glow. One experienced inevitably something of the thrill and adventure of those stirring theological times. When one contemplated that Luther and Zwingli were but young men at the time of the controversy—but thirty-five years old—the pulse beat even higher. Another impression was that theology was something which did really matter; it was more than interesting speculation upon questions that aroused the curiosity of the eclectic few. Moreover, one felt that here, at least, many of the leaders *knew* their theology, and knew it well. They not only had a vivid historical sense; they had an appreciation of the meaning and significance of the philosophical and theological contributions of the past.

But moved as one might be by the lure of history and the force of earlier theological thought, one could not help but feel that these carried with them a serious danger. The pronounced sixteenth-century cast of expression was always marked. One could not help but wonder how much this vocabulary meant to men and women who were living in a twentieth-century civilization, to whom the whole controversy between Luther and Zwingli might seem utterly divorced from the sphere wherein their lives were moving. Yet, wanting as these ancient formulations might seem to our contemporaries, the emphasis upon sin and salvation, upon redemption and the centrality of Jesus, however foreign their classic statements may appear to those ungrounded in the history and theology of the past, is the emphasis which a living religion must ever and again reassert.

Part Eight

BIBLIOGRAPHY

A Bibliography of James Muilenburg's Writings

R. LANSING HICKS

BOOKS AND MONOGRAPHS

"The Embassy of Everaard van Weede, Lord of Dykvelt, to England in 1687," Lincoln, Nebraska, 1920 (Published as Vol. XX, Nos. 3, 4, of Nebraska *University Studies.*)

Specimens of Biblical Literature. New York: Thomas Y. Crowell, 1923.

The Literary Relations of the Epistle of Barnabas and the Teaching of the Twelve Apostles. Marburg, 1929. (Ph.D. thesis, Yale University, 1926.)

The Way of Israel. New York: Harper, 1961.

CONTRIBUTIONS TO BOOKS

"The Return to Old Testament Theology," in *Christianity and the Contemporary Scene.* Edited by R. C. Miller and H. H. Shires. New York: Morehouse-Gorham, 1943, pp. 30-44.

"The Faith of Ancient Israel," in *The Vitality of the Christian Tradition.* Edited by G. F. Thomas. New York: Harper, 1945, pp. 1-35.

"Survey of the Literature on Tell en-Naṣbeh," "The Literary Sources Bearing on the Question of Identification," and "The History of Mizpah of Benjamin," in *Tell en-Naṣbeh,* Vol. I. Edited by C. C. McCown. The Palestine Institute of the Pacific School of Religion, Berkeley, California, and the American Schools of Oriental Research, New Haven, Connecticut, 1947, pp. 13-49.

234   ISRAEL'S PROPHETIC HERITAGE

"The Interpretation of the Bible," in *Biblical Authority for Today*. Edited by A. Richardson and W. Schweitzer. Philadelphia: Westminster, 1951, pp. 198-218.

"Ethics of the Prophet," in *Moral Principles of Action: Man's Ethical Imperative*. Edited by Ruth Anshen. New York: Harper, 1952, pp. 527-542.

"The History of the Religion of Israel," in *The Interpreter's Bible*, Vol. I. Edited by G. A. Buttrick. Nashville: Abingdon-Cokesbury, 1952, pp. 292-348.

"The Poetry of the Old Testament," in *An Introduction to the Revised Standard Version of the Old Testament*. Edited by L. A. Weigle. New York: Thomas Nelson, 1952, pp. 62-70.

"Introduction and Exegesis to Isaiah, Chapters 40-66," in *The Interpreter's Bible*, Vol. V. Edited by G. A. Buttrick. Nashville: Abingdon-Cokesbury, 1956, pp. 381-773.

"The King Came Riding," in *Sermons from an Ecumenical Pulpit*. Edited by M. F. Daskam. Boston: Starr King, 1956, pp. 119-128.

"Adam and Second Adam," in *A Handbook of Christian Theology*. Edited by M. Halverson and A. A. Cohen. New York: Meridian, 1958, pp. 11-13.

Also announced for publication: article on "Isaiah" (book and prophet) in the new edition of the *Encyclopedia Americana*; articles on "Isaiah," "Jeremiah," "Poetry," and other subjects in the revised edition of *Hastings' Dictionary of the Bible* (one-vol. edition); articles on "Ataroth," "Gilgal," "Holiness," "Jeremiah," "Mizpah," "Obadiah," and numerous other subjects in the forthcoming *Interpreter's Dictionary of the Bible*; and articles on "Hebrew Prophecy" and "Ezekiel" in the new edition of *Peake's Commentary on the Bible*.

ARTICLES IN PERIODICALS

1924   "Teaching the Bible from the Literary Angle," in *Christian Education*, December.

1929   "Luther and Zwingli Quartercentenary," in *The Congregationalist*, December 26, pp. 854-856.

1931   "The German High Church Movement and Its Outstanding Leader—Friedrich Heiler," in *Crozer Quarterly*, VIII, pp. 162-176.

BIBLIOGRAPHY   235

1932   "Literary Form in the Fourth Gospel," JBL, LI, pp. 40-53.

1933   "The Literary Approach—The Old Testament as Hebrew Literature," in JNABI, I, Part II, pp. 14-22.

1934   "Finding the Real Gospels" (a review article on C. C. Torrey's *The Four Gospels*), in *The Congregationalist*, February 22, pp. 130-131.
       "The Legacy of Israel and Our Heritage in a Time of Crisis" (presidential address), in JNABI, II, pp. 1-12.
       "The Old Testament in the Church School," in *The Christian Register*, September 6, pp. 525-527.

1940   "The Literary Character of Isaiah 34," in JBL, LIX, pp. 339-365.
       "What Is Essential in the Christian Religion?" in RL, IX, pp. 352-362.

1942   "Imago Dei," in RR, VI, pp. 392-406.

1944   "Psalm 47," in JBL, LXIII, pp. 235-256.

1945   "The Old Testament and the Christian Minister," in USQR, I, No. 1, pp. 10-18.

1946   "An Evaluation of the Methods and Assumptions of the Historical Study of the Bible," in mimeographed material circulated in November, 1946, by the Study Department of the World Council of Churches.

1952   "The Importance of Archaeology for the Minister," in USQR, VII, No. 3, pp. 15-19.
       "The Literary Values of the Revised Standard Version," in *Religious Education*, XLVII, pp. 260-264.

1953   "A Study in Hebrew Rhetoric," in *Suppl.* VT, I (Congress Volume: Copenhagen), pp. 97-111.

1954   "Fragments of Another Qumran Isaiah Scroll," in BASOR, 135, pp. 28-32.
       "A Hyksos Scarab Jar Handle from Bethel," in BASOR, 136, pp. 20-21.
       "A Qoheleth Scroll from Qumran," in BASOR, 135, pp. 20-28.

1955   "The Beginning of the Gospels and the Qumran Manual of Discipline," in USQR, X, No. 2, pp. 23-29.
       "Mizpah of Benjamin," in ST, VIII, pp. 25-42.
       "The Site of Ancient Gilgal," in BASOR, 140, pp. 11-27.

1956   "The Birth of Benjamin," in JBL, LXXV, pp. 194-201.
       "The Dead Sea Scrolls—A Symposium," in *The New Republic*, April 6, pp. 24-25.

236   ISRAEL'S PROPHETIC HERITAGE

"The Significance of the Scrolls," in USQR, XI, No. 3,
pp. 3-12.
"The Theology of the Dead Sea Scrolls," in *Andover-
Newton Theological School Bulletin*, XLIX, No. 1, pp.
3-14.

1957   "Is There a Biblical Theology?" in USQR, XII, No. 4,
pp. 29-37.

1958   "Preface to Hermeneutics," in JBL, LXXVII, pp. 18-26.

1959   "The Form and Structure of the Covenantal Formulations," in VT, IX, pp. 347-365.

1960   "The Biblical Understanding of What God Requires,"
in *The Alumni Bulletin* of Bangor Theological Seminary, XXXV, No. 2, pp. 6-11.
"Father and Son," in *Theology and Life* (Lancaster Theological Seminary), III, pp. 177-187.
"Modern Issues in Biblical Studies: The Gains of Form
Criticism in Old Testament Studies," in ET, LXXI, pp.
229-233.
"Old Testament Scholarship: Fifty Years in Retrospect,"
in JBR, XVIII, pp. 173-181.
"The Story of Israel: A Review Article," in *The Alumni
Bulletin* of Bangor Theological Seminary, XXXV, No.
3, pp. 14-15.

1961   "The Linguistic and Rhetorical Usages of the Particle
ki in the Old Testament," in HUCA, XXXII, pp.
135-160.
"The Biblical View of Time," in HTR, XIV, No. 4,
pp. 225-252.

                          BOOK REVIEWS

1935   W. O. E. Oesterley and T. H. Robinson, *Introduction
to the Books of the Old Testament* (JNABI, III, p. 54).

1938   J. Baillie and H. Martin, editors, *Revelation* (JBR, VI,
pp. 214-216).
G. A. Cooke, *The Book of Ezekiel*, 2 vols. (CC, February 2, p. 145).
M. Crook and others, *The Bible and Its Literary Associations* (JBR, VI, pp. 98-99).

BIBLIOGRAPHY　　　　　　　237

A. Lods, *The Prophets and the Rise of Judaism* (JBR, VI, pp. 50-51).

W. O. E. Oesterley, *A Fresh Approach to the Psalms* (RR, II, p. 486).

1939　M. Buttenwieser, *The Psalms* (RR, IV, pp. 55-60).

E. G. Kraeling, *The Book of the Ways of God* (JBR, VII, pp. 92-93; RR, IV, pp. 342, 347).

W. O. E. Oesterley, *Sacrifices in Ancient Israel* (RR, III, pp. 184-189).

1940　W. A. Wordsworth, *En-Roeh* (JBR, VIII, pp. 116-117).

1941　W. F. Albright, *From the Stone Age to Christianity* (JBR, IX, pp. 41-43).

J. J. Stamm, *Erlösen und Vergeben im Alten Testament* (JBL, LX, pp. 430-433).

1942　B. Heller, *The Odyssey of a Faith* (CC, November 4, pp. 1353-1354).

D. Jacobsen, *The Social Background of the Old Testament* (CC, December 2, p. 1492).

J. Morgenstern, *Amos Studies* (JBL, LXI, pp. 294-299).

R. H. Pfeiffer, *Introduction to the Old Testament* (JBR, X, pp. 39-41).

1943　G. E. Phillips, *The Old Testament in the World Church* (RL, XII, pp. 314-315).

H. W. Robinson, *Redemption and Revelation* (JBR, XI, pp. 176-178).

1944　W. A. Irwin, *The Problem of Ezekiel* (JBR, XII, pp. 203-205).

W. J. Pythian-Adams, *The People and the Presence* (JBR, XII, pp. 254-255).

1945　S. A. Cartledge, *A Conservative Introduction to the Old Testament* (JBL, LXIV, p. 273).

J. D. Davis, *The Westminster Dictionary of the Bible,* revised by H. S. Gehman (RL, XIV, pp. 607-608).

R. B. Y. Scott, *The Relevance of the Prophets* (JBR, XIII, pp. 51-52).

R. E. Wolfe, *Meet Amos and Hosea* (CC, May 2, pp. 552-553).

1946　J. Finegan, *Light from the Ancient Past* (USQR, I, No. 4, pp. 33-34).

H. Fredriksson, *Jahwe als Krieger* (RR, XI, pp. 50-56).

N. Glueck, *The River Jordan* (RL, XVI, pp. 154-155).

238   ISRAEL'S PROPHETIC HERITAGE

1947   G. A. Danell, *Studies in the Name Israel in the Old Testament* (JBL, LXVI, pp. 234-237).
H. H. Rowley, *The Rediscovery of the Old Testament* (JBL, LXVI, pp. 225-226).

1948   M. Burrows, *An Outline of Biblical Theology* (*Theology Today*, IV, pp. 421-422).
J. Coppens, *La Connaissance du Bien et du Mal et le Péché du Paradis* (JBL, LXVII, pp. 396-399).

1949   E. A. Leslie, *The Psalms* (RL, XIX, pp. 143-145).

1950   W. A. L. Elmslie, *How Came Our Faith?* (JBR, XVIII, p. 69).
A. R. Johnson, *The Vitality of the Individual in the Thought of Ancient Israel* (JBL, LXIX, pp. 404-405).
G. Knight, *From Jesus to Paul* (*Theology Today*, VI, pp. 565-567).
R. H. Pfeiffer, *A History of New Testament Times, with an Introduction to the Apocrypha* (*Interpretation*, IV, pp. 93-95).

1951   A. Haldar, *The Notion of the Desert in Sumero-Accadian and West-Semitic Religions* (JBL, LXX, pp. 340-341).
T. J. Meek, *Hebrew Origins*, rev. ed. (USQR, VI, No. 2, p. 47).
H. H. Rowley, editor, *Studies in Old Testament Prophecy* (USQR, VI, No. 2, p. 46).

1952   W. Eichrodt, *Man in the Old Testament* (USQR, VII, No. 3, p. 56).
J. Lindblom, *The Servant-Songs in Deutero-Isaiah* (JBL, LXXI, pp. 259-261).
J. B. Pritchard, editor, *Ancient Near Eastern Texts relating to the Old Testament* (USQR, VIII, No. 2, pp. 55-56).
J. C. C. Van Dorssen, *De Derivata van de Stam '-m-n in het Hebreewsch van het Oude Testament* (JBL, LXXI, pp. 127-129).

1953   *The Revised Standard Version of the Old Testament* (USQR, VIII, No. 2, pp. 40-43).

1955   J. Klausner, *The Messianic Idea in Israel* (USQR, XI, No. 1, pp. 63-65).
J. B. Pritchard, *The Ancient Near East in Pictures Relating to the Old Testament* (USQR, X, No. 3, pp. 58-59).

BIBLIOGRAPHY   **239**

1956 M. Burrows, *The Dead Sea Scrolls* (JBL, LXXV, pp. 146-148).
R. C. Dentan, editor, *The Idea of History in the Ancient Near East* (USQR, XI, No. 3, pp. 53-54).
B. D. Napier, *From Faith to Faith* (CC, January 4, p. 15).
M. Noth, *Geschichte Israels*, 2nd ed. (*Bibliotheca Orientalis*, XIII, pp. 43-44).
E. Würthwein, *Der Text des Alten Testaments* (*Bibliotheca Orientalis*, XIII, p. 48).

1957 K. Barth, *Church Dogmatics*, Vol. I, *The Doctrine of the Word of God* (USQR, XII, No. 3, pp. 83-86).
J. Bright, *Early Israel in Recent History Writing* (*Interpretation*, XI, pp. 461-462).
G. Davies, A. Richardson, and C. Wallis, editors, *The Twentieth Century Bible Commentary* (JBR, XXV, pp. 60-61).
S. Mowinckel, *He That Cometh* (CC, August 7, 942-943; JBL, LXXVI, pp. 243-246).
G. Östborn, *Yahweh and Baal* (RR, XXI, pp. 177-180).
H. Ringgren, *The Messiah in the Old Testament* (CC, August 14, p. 967).
B. J. Van der Merwe, *Pentateuchtradisies in die Prediking van Deuterojesaja* (JBL, LXXVI, pp. 77-78).
G. E. Wright, *Biblical Archaeology* (USQR, XIII, No. 1, pp. 53-55).

1958 S. H. Blank, *Prophetic Faith in Isaiah* (JBR, XXVI, p. 329).
M. Burrows, *More Light on the Dead Sea Scrolls* (*Saturday Review*, June 7, pp. 21-33).
O. Eissfeldt, *Einleitung in das Alte Testament*, 2nd. ed. (JBL, LXXVII, pp. 258-259).
T. H. Gaster, *The Dead Sea Scriptures in English Translation* (RR, XXII, pp. 73-76).
L. Köhler, *Der Hebräische Mensch* (*Bibliotheca Orientalis*, XV, p. 121).
V. de Leeuw, *De Ebed Jahweh-Profetieen* (JBL, LXXVII, pp. 261-263).
A. Van Selms, *De Rol der Lofprijzingen. Een der Dode Zee-Rollen vertaald en toegelicht* (JBL, LXXVII, pp. 266-268).
D. Howlett, *The Essenes and Christianity;* R. E. Murphy,

240   ISRAEL'S PROPHETIC HERITAGE

The Dead Sea Scrolls and the Bible; K. Stendahl, editor, *The Scrolls and the New Testament* (USQR, XIII, No. 3, pp. 57-59).

1959   M. Burrows, *More Light on the Dead Sea Scrolls* (JBL, LXXVIII, pp. 362-365).

P. J. Cools and others, *De Wereld van de Bijbel* (JSS, IV, pp. 272-274).

F. M. Cross, *The Ancient Library of Qumran and Modern Biblical Studies* (USQR, XIV, No. 3, pp. 54-56).

H. Gese, *Der Verfassungsentwurf des Ezechiel, Kap. 40-8* (JSS, IV, pp. 74-76).

S. H. Hooke, editor, *Myth, Ritual, and Kingship* (USQR, XIV, No. 2, pp. 67-69).

L. Köhler, *Old Testament Theology* (USQR, XIV, No. 2, pp. 66-67).

S. Mowinckel, *He That Cometh* (USQR, XIV, No. 4, pp. 70-71).

M. Noth, *Gesammelte Studien zum Alten Testament* (*Bibliotheca Orientalis*, XVI, p. 242).

J. Van Der Ploeg, *The Excavations at Qumran* (USQR, XIV, No. 3, pp. 53-54).

1960   J. M. Allegro, *The Treasure of the Copper Scroll* (*Saturday Review*, August 6, p. 20).

J. Bright, *A History of Israel* (USQR, XV, No. 4, pp. 327-329).

B. S. Childs, *Myth and Reality in the Old Testament* (JBL, LXXIX, pp. 379-380).

J. Doresse, *The Secret Books of the Egyptian Gnostics* (*Saturday Review*, August 6, p. 20).

C. Rabin and Y. Yadin, *Aspects of the Dead Sea Scrolls* (JSS, V, pp. 92-98).

SERMONS, MEDITATIONS, BIBLIOGRAPHIES, AND REPORTS

1946   "A Survey of Recent Theological Literature: The Old Testament," in USQR, II, No. 1, pp. 23-25.

1949   "A Confession of Jeremiah," in USQR, IV, No. 2, pp. 15-18.

"Report on the Activities of the American Schools of Oriental Research," in JBL, LXVIII, pp. xxxiii-xxxv.

BIBLIOGRAPHY   241

1950 "A Bibliography for Ministers—II" (annotated), in USQR, V, No. 3, pp. 21-27.
"A Meditation on Divine Fatherhood," in USQR, VI, No. 1, pp. 3-5.
"Report on the Activities of the American Schools of Oriental Research," in JBL, LXIX, pp. xxxix-xli.

1951 "Report on the Activities of the American Schools of Oriental Research," in JBL, LXX, pp. xxix-xxxi.

1954 "A Letter from Palestine," in USQR, IX, No. 2, pp. 22-25.
"Report of the Director of the School in Jerusalem," in BASOR, 136, pp. 4-7.

1959 "A Bibliography for Ministers: Old Testament" (with G. Landes, annotated), in USQR, XIV, No. 2, pp. 41-51.
"Faith Comes by Preaching," in USQR, XV, No. 1, pp. 13-18.

1960 "Psalm 96: A Chapel Meditation," in *The Union Voice* (Union Theological Seminary in Manila), XVI, No. 2, pp. 4-5.

THE REVISED STANDARD VERSION
OF THE OLD TESTAMENT

Dr. Muilenburg became a member of the Standard Bible Committee in May, 1945, and rendered active and significant service through twenty extended sessions of the Committee until the completion of the Old Testament revision in June, 1951. To him was assigned the work of making the first drafts of Isaiah, chs. 1-30, and of Obadiah, as well as a special commission to review the first draft of Isaiah, chs. 40-53. Also he did editorial work, with Dean Luther Weigle and Executive Secretary Fleming James, on the final drafts of Deuteronomy and the Psalms.

Because of his keen perception of literary style and his careful analyses of the forms of Biblical literature, Dr. Muilenburg brought to the Committee expert knowledge of the strophic structure of Old Testament poetry. He undertook special studies in this field for the Committee, and most of his recommendations were adopted.

The chairman of the Committee, Dean Weigle, has characterized Dr. Muilenburg as "a man whose judgment and competence commanded the respect of all his colleagues" and as "a good team worker—a man who can engage in debate with his fellows in a genuine spirit of cooperation in the desire to find the truth and the best way of expressing it."

ADDITIONS TO A BIBLIOGRAPHY OF JAMES MUILENBURG'S WRITINGS

Ivan Jay Ball, Jr.

San Francisco Theological Seminary

Works published prior to 1962 are for the most part given in "A Bibliography of James Muilenburg's Writings" by R. Lansing Hicks in Israel's Prophetic Heritage: Essays in honor of James Muilenburg, Edited by Bernhard W. Anderson and Walter Harrelson, New York: Harper & Brothers, Publishers, 1962, pp. 233-242.

CONTRIBUTIONS TO BOOKS

"The 'Office' of the Prophet in Ancient Israel," in The Bible in Modern Scholarship: Papers read at the 100th meeting of the Society of Biblical Literature, December 28-30, 1964. Edited by J. Philip Hyatt. Nashville: Abingdon, 1965, pp. 74-97.

"A Liturgy on the Triumphs of Yahweh," in Studia Biblica et Semitica: Theodoro Christiano Vriezen Dedicata. Edited by W. C. van Unnik and A. S. van der Woude. Wageningen: H. Veenman en Zonen, 1966, pp. 233-251.

The Psalms: A Form-Critical Introduction by Hermann Gunkel with an Introduction by James Muilenburg. Facet Books. Biblical Series--19. Philadelphia: Fortress Press, 1967, pp. iii-ix.

"The Intercession of the Covenant Mediator (Exodus 33:1a, 12-17)," in Words and Meanings: Essays Presented to David Winton Thomas on his retirement from Regius Professorship of Hebrew in the University of Cambridge, 1968. Edited by Peter R. Ackroyd and Barnabas Lindars. Cambridge: At the University Press, 1968, pp. 159-181.

Lectures on the Religion of the Semites: The Fundamental Institutions[3] by W. Robertson Smith with an Introduction and Additional Notes by S. A. Cook [ed. 1927], Prolegomenon by James Muilenburg [pp. 1-27]. Library of Biblical Studies. New York: Ktav, 1969.

"The Terminology of Adversity in Jeremiah," in Translating & Understanding the Old Testament: Essays in Honor of Herbert Gordon May. Edited by Harry Thomas Frank and William L. Reed. Nashville: Abingdon, 1970, pp. 42-63.

"Baruch the Scribe," in Proclamation and Presence: Old Testament Essays in Honour of Gwynne Henton Davies. Edited by John I. Durham and J. R. Porter. Richmond: John Knox Press, 1970, pp. 215-238.

286

CONTRIBUTIONS TO COMMENTARIES, DICTIONARIES AND ENCYCLOPEDIAS

"Old Testament Prophecy" and "Ezechiel," in Peake's Commentary on the
    Bible, Edited by Matthew Black & H. H. Rowley. New York: Thomas
    Nelson and Sons, Ltd., 1962, pp. 475-83, 568-90.

Consultant and Contributor to The Interpreter's Dictionary of the Bible.
    An Illustrated Encyclopedia in four volumes. New York: Abingdon,
    1962. Vol. A-D, "Ataroth" p. 305; "Ataroth-Addar" pp. 305-06.
    Vol. E-J, "Gilgal" pp. 398-99; "Holiness" pp. 616-25; "Jeremiah the
    Prophet" pp. 823-35. Vol. K-Q, "Magor-Missabib" p. 226; "Merathaim"
    p. 351; "Mizpah" pp. 407-09; "Nehelam" pp. 532-33; "Obadiah, Book
    of" pp. 578-79.

Contributor to Dictionary of the Bible. Edited by James Hastings.
    Revised Edition by Frederick C. Grant & H. H. Rowley. New York:
    Charles Scribner's Sons, 1963. "Glory (in OT)" pp. 331-32;
    "Isaiah" pp. 423-24; "Isaiah, Book of" pp. 424-27; "Jeremiah"
    pp. 465-70; "Poetry" pp. 778-80; "Sabbath" pp. 866-67; "Selah"
    p. 894.

Contributor to Encyclopedia Americana, 1966, Vol. 15, "Isaiah" and
    "Isaiah, Book of" pp. 407-09; International edition, 1973, pp.
    484-86.

Contributor to Encyclopaedia Judaica. Jerusalem: Macmillan & Co.,
    1972. E.g. "Budde, Karl Ferdinand Reinhard," Vol. 4, col. 1455.

ARTICLES IN PERIODICALS

"The Son of Man in Daniel and The Ethiopic Apocalypse of Enoch," in
    JBL 79 (1960) 197-209.

"The Biblical Understanding of the Future," in Journal of Religious
    Thought 19 (1962-63) 99-108.

"What I believe it means to be saved," in USQR 17 (1961-62) 291-93.

"The Speech of Theophany," in Harvard Divinity Bulletin 28 (1963-64)
    35-47. The Dudleian Lecture delivered on January 31, 1963.

"Abraham and the Nations. Blessing and World History," in Int 19
    (1965) 387-98.

"Form Criticism and Beyond," in JBL 88 (1969) 1-18. The Presidential
    Address delivered at the annual meeting of the Society of Biblical
    Literature on December 18, 1968, at the University of California,
    Berkeley, California.

287

BOOK REVIEWS

1961 Johannes Hendrik Scheepens, Die Gees van God en die Gees van
         die Mens in die Ou Testament (JBL 80 [1961] 396).

      Walter Beyerlin, Herkunft und Geschichte der ältesten Sinai-
         traditionen (JBL 80 [1961] 383-384).

      H. N. Bream, J. M. Myers and O. Reimherr, eds., Biblical Studies
         in Memory of H. C. Alleman (USQR 17 [1961] 78-79).

      Gerhard von Rad, Genesis: A Commentary (Religion in Life 31
         [1961/62] 145-146).

1962 G. Ernest Wright, ed., The Bible and the Ancient Near East (Int
         16 [1962] 104-106) and (USQR 17 [1962] 243-244).

1963 Curt Kuhl, The Old Testament: Its Origins and Composition (USQR
         19 [1963] 156-157).

      Harvey H. Guthrie, God and History in the Old Testament (USQR 19
         [1963] 55-57).

      Walter Eichrodt, Theology of the Old Testament, Vol. I (USQR 19
         [1963] 49-50).

      Roland de Vaux, Ancient Israel: Its Life and Institutions (USQR
         18 [1963] 159-160).

1964 Klaus-Dietrick Schunck, Benjamin: Untersuchungen zur Entstehung
         und Geschichte eines israelitischen Stammes (JBL 83 [1964]
         207-208).

      Claus Westermann, ed., Essays on Old Testament Hermeneutics (TT
         21 [1964] 228-230).

1965 C. R. North, The Second Isaiah (Int 19 [1965] 360-364).

1966 Th. C. Vriezen, De godsdienst van Israël (JBL 85 [1966] 110-112).

      G. A. F. Knight, Deutero-Isaiah. A Theological Commentary on
         Is 40-55 (JBR 34 [1966] 253-257).

      J. D. Smart, History and Theology in Second Isaiah (JBR 34 [1966]
         253-257).

1967 Hans-Joachim Kraus, Worship in Israel: A Cultic History of the Old
         Testament (USQR 22 [1967] 276-279).

1971 Gabriel H. Cohn, Das Buch Jona im Lichte der biblischer Erzählkunst
         (Bib 52 [1971] 141-145).

      Otto Kaiser, Einleitung in das Alte Testament (BO 28 [1971] 213-215).

Additions to the Bibliography of
James Muilenburg's Writings

Thomas F. Best

"The Book of the Twelve," Review of Raymond Calkins, *The Modern Message of the Minor Prophets* (*Christendom* 12 [1947] 525–26).

Review of Ben Zion Bosker, *The Wisdom of the Talmud* (*Journal of Religious Thought* 9 [1951] 70–71).

"Buber als Bibel-Interpret," in the German edition of *The Philosophy of Martin Buber*. Edited by Paul Arthur Schilpp and Maurice Friedman, translated by Curt Meyer-Clason. Die Philosophen des 20. Jahrhunderts. Stuttgart: W. Kohlhammer Verlag, 1963, pp. 364–83.

"Biblical Images of the City," in *The Church and the Exploding Metropolis*. Edited by Robert Lee. Richmond, Virginia: John Knox Press, 1965, pp. 45–59.

Contributor to *Encyclopedia Americana*, International Edition, 1968, Vol. 24, "Scrolls, The Dead Sea," p. 456.